Chaucer in the Eighteenth Century

Chaucer in the Eighteenth Century

The Father of English Poetry

DAVID HOPKINS
TOM MASON

OXFORD
UNIVERSITY PRESS

Great Clarendon Street, Oxford, OX2 6DP,
United Kingdom

Oxford University Press is a department of the University of Oxford.
It furthers the University's objective of excellence in research, scholarship,
and education by publishing worldwide. Oxford is a registered trade mark of
Oxford University Press in the UK and in certain other countries

Impression: 1

Published in the United States of America by Oxford University Press
198 Madison Avenue, New York, NY 10016, United States of America

British Library Cataloguing in Publication Data
Data available

Library of Congress Control Number: 2021952587

ISBN 978–0–19–286262–4

DOI: 10.1093/oso/9780192862624.001.0001

Printed and bound by
CPI Group (UK) Ltd, Croydon, CR0 4YY

In Memoriam John Burrow
(1932–2017)

Preface

How and why do some old poems survive to be read by succeeding generations, particularly by generations who are well pleased by new poems of their own? This book is an enquiry into the means by which the body of verse associated with the fourteenth-century poet Geoffrey Chaucer continued to give pleasure throughout the eighteenth century, despite the changes in language, prosody, sensibility, religious sentiment, political assumption, and literary expectation that had occurred since Chaucer's day. Most of the evidence for our enquiry comes from printed books: mentions of Chaucer and Chaucerian verses in biographies, editions, versions, and imitations of his work; in critical accounts, dictionaries, anthologies, and selected 'beauties'; and in poems or literary histories tracing the larger course of English poetry. Some attention is also paid to the appearance of Chaucerian characters in plays, ballads, and illustrations, as well to critical commentary on authors other than Chaucer. We pay most detailed attention to works that claim, in one way or another, Chaucerian *paternity* and that manifest the necessary combination of continuity and difference which that relationship implies.

In order to sustain attention to the principal concerns of our enquiry, we have made no consistent attempt to compare eighteenth-century responses to Chaucer with those of later centuries—though modern Chaucer scholarship has occasionally been referred to for supportive or illustrative purposes. We hope that our book will appeal to three main types of reader. Since eighteenth-century responses to Chaucer often, we argue, offer insights into the poet's work that are of intrinsic rather than merely historical interest, we hope that our discussions will interest those whose main concern is with Chaucer's poetry itself. Students whose principal interest is in eighteenth-century literature will, we hope, be glad to have their attention drawn to an unfairly neglected area of the century's writing. And, though our argument involves much detail that is specifically focused on one particular body of material, we hope that the book will be of interest to anyone concerned with the processes by which poetry of one author or period is subsequently received, interpreted, and recreated by other authors.

Extensive quotation has been made from both Chaucerian and eighteenth-century texts to provide the necessary support for the critical contentions included in our study. Quotations from translations and adaptations of Chaucer are presented in parallel with their originals, with underlining sometimes employed to draw attention to key similarities of phrasing. Italicization (unless indicated otherwise) is that of the original texts. Quotations have generally been taken from standard modern scholarly editions, where those are available. But some works are quoted, when the occasion demands or where there is no modern edition, from earlier editions. This is particularly the case with quotations from the works of Chaucer himself, which are taken from the texts of his work available to the various eighteenth-century poets and critics under discussion. These texts—which we present in an unmodernized form—vary considerably from those in modern editions. For reasons of space, no attempt has been made to correlate the early Chaucerian texts with those of modern editions or to gloss the quotations from the early editions. Line numberings, however, are provided, keyed to the *Riverside Chaucer* (or, in the case of the 'Chaucer Apocrypha', to the supplementary Vol. 7 to W. W. Skeat's edition of Chaucer, or, in one instance omitted by Skeat, the edition of John Urry), which will enable readers to locate the quotations in the poems from which they are taken, to compare early and modern texts, and to make use of the glossing and annotation provided by modern editors.

Chaucer's works are cited by abbreviated titles given in the List of Short Titles. Abbreviations (see also below) are used for a number of other works which are cited frequently throughout the book. Other references are provided in full on first appearance, but in short-title form thereafter. All works referred to are listed in the Bibliography.

We would like to express our thanks to Sandra Hopkins, Charles Martindale, and Myra Stokes, who read the entire book in manuscript and made many invaluable suggestions for improvements. We owe debts of various kinds to several generations of research students at the University of Bristol. We are also grateful to the anonymous readers for Oxford University Press for some small corrections and additions, and for their general enthusiasm for our project.

David Hopkins
Tom Mason

Contents

List of Short Titles

Dryden, *Works*   John Dryden, *Works*, ed. H. T. Swedenberg et al., 20 vols (Berkeley, CA, 1956–2000)

Johnson, *Works*   *The Yale Edition of the Works of Samuel Johnson*, ed. E. L. McAdam Jnr et al., 23 vols. (New Haven, CT, 1958–)

Lipscomb   *The Canterbury Tales of Chaucer Completed in a Modern Version,* ed. William Lipscomb, 3 vols (Oxford, 1795)

Morell   *The Canterbury Tales of Chaucer, in the Original, from the Most Authentic Manuscripts, and as They Turn'd into Modern Language,* ed. Thomas Morell (London, 1737)

Ogle   *The Canterbury Tales of Chaucer: Modernis'd by Several Hands,* ed. George Ogle, 3 vols (London, 1741)

Pope, *Poems*   *The Twickenham Edition of the Poems of Alexander Pope,* ed. John Butt et al., 11 vols (London, 1939–69)

Speght 1598   *The Workes of Our Antient and Learned English Poet, Geffrey Chaucer,* ed. Thomas Speght (London, 1598)

Speght 1602   *The Workes of Our Antient and Learned English Poet, Geffrey Chaucer, Newly Printed,* ed. Thomas Speght (London, 1602)

Speght 1687   *The Works of Our Ancient, Learned, and Excellent English Poet, Jeffrey* Chaucer, ed. Thomas Speght (London, 1687)

Tyrwhitt 1775–78   *The Canterbury Tales of Chaucer,* ed. Thomas Tyrwhitt, 5 vols (London, 1775–78)

Tyrwhitt 1798   *The Canterbury Tales of Chaucer,* ed. Thomas Tyrwhitt, 2 vols (2nd edn, Oxford, 1798)

Urry   *The Works of Geoffrey Chaucer: Compared with the Former Editions, and Many Valuable MSS,* ed. John Urry (London, 1721)

Warton, *History*   Thomas Warton, *The History of English Poetry,* 4 vols (London, 1774–81)

Abbreviations of Chaucer's Works
Used in Reference

ClT	*The Clerk's Tale*
Complaint	*The Complaint of the Black Knight*
Court	*The Court of Love*
Cuckoo	*Of the Cuckoo and the Nightingale*
FL	*The Flower and the Leaf*
FranT	*The Franklin's Tale*
GP	*General Prologue*
HF	*The House of Fame*
KnT	*The Knight's Tale*
Lamentation	*The Lamentation of Mary Magdalene*
Letter	*The Letter of Cupid*
LGW	*The Legend of Good Women*
ManT	*The Manciple's Tale*
MerT	*The Merchant's Tale*
MilT	*The Miller's Tale*
NPT	*The Nun's Priest's Tale*
PardT	*The Pardoner's Tale*
PrT	*The Prioress's Tale*
RvT	*The Reeve's Tale*
SqT	*The Squire's Tale*
TC	*Troilus and Criseyde*
WBP	*The Wife of Bath's Prologue*
WBT	*The Wife of Bath's Tale*

List of Illustrations

Introduction

Posthumous literary reputation, 'that second Life in others' Breath, / Th' Estate which Wits inherit after Death', is an acquisition almost as capricious, as mutable, and as unfixed in Alexander Pope's *The Temple of Fame* as it had been in Chaucer's poem from which his 'Vision' took its 'Hint' (see Fig. 0.1).[1] Pope's poem is rich in reasons why fame might be denied, or be awarded unjustifiably, and how, if given, it may be afflicted by envy and decay. Immediate popularity, Pope finds, is no guarantee of lasting reputation. Some names that are 'fresh ingrav'd' on the 'Rock of Ice' on which stands the edifice of Fame vanish as soon as they are discerned. There is no certainty that even long-established fame will last. 'Hostile time' has defaced the inscribed names of many of those whose fame was 'wide' in 'ages past', including the names of some to whom 'Poets once had promis'd' longevity.

And yet, despite these depredations, Pope, like Chaucer, discovers some few names that do not, nor ever will decay, and whose fame has even increased with time. In Pope's edition of 1736 (and many subsequent printings), readers of *The Temple of Fame* were faced on the same page with an account of these unmelting names in the poem of Pope's youth and in its ancient source:[2]

For on that other side I sey	Yet part no injuries of heav'n could feel,
Of that hill which northward ley,	Like crystal faithful to the graving steel:
How it was written full of names	The rock's high summit, in the temple's shade,
Of folke, that had afore great fames,	Nor heat could melt, nor beating storm invade.
Of old time, and yet they were	There names inscrib'd unnumber'd ages past
As fresh, as men had written hem there	From time's first birth, with time itself shall last;
The self day, or that houre	These ever new, nor subject to decays,
That I on hem gan to poure:	Spread, and grow brighter with the length of days.
But well I wiste what it made;	
It was conserved with the shade	
(All the writing that I sye)	
Of the castle that stoode on high,	
And stood eke in so cold a place,	
That heate might it not deface.	

(*HF*, 3. 1151–64)

(Alexander Pope, *The Temple of Fame*,
(London, 1715), 45–52)

[1] *The Temple of Fame, A Vision* was printed twice in 1715. In both editions, the poem is followed by extensive annotation.

[2] See *The Works of Alexander Pope, Esq.; with Explanatory Notes and Additions*, 4 vols (London, 1736), 3. 6–7, from which quotations below are taken. The text of Chaucer's poem that is printed at the foot of the page in this edition (as here, in italics) is substantially that of Speght 1598, with Pope's punctuation and parentheses.

Chaucer in the Eighteenth Century. David Hopkins and Tom Mason, Oxford University Press.
© David Hopkins and Tom Mason (2022). DOI: 10.1093/oso/9780192862624.003.0001

Fig. 0.1 Suitors for fame. An illustration to *The Temple of Fame* from *The Works of Alexander Pope Esq.* (London, 1751).

The Ice of Nova Zembla

Pope regarded this perpetual endurance of ice-inscribed names as an idea in need of support. Having described the mountain, he departed from Chaucer to paint an extended simile consisting of a description of the ice-mountains of Nova Zembla off the coast of northern Russia. In early editions of *The Temple of Fame*, Pope insisted that 'Tho' a strict Verisimilitude be not requir'd in the Descriptions of this visionary and allegorical kind of Poetry, which admits of every wild Object that Fancy may present in a Dream, and where it is sufficient if the moral Meaning atone for the Improbability', *his* simile was grounded upon fact:

> Men are naturally so desirous of Truth, that a Reader is generally pleas'd, in such a Case, with some Excuse or Allusion that seems to reconcile the Description to Probability and Nature. The Simile here is of that sort, and renders it not wholly unlikely that a *Rock* of *Ice* should remain for ever, by mentioning something like it in the Northern Regions, agreeing with the Accounts of our modern Travellers.[3]

The principal modern traveller in this case was the explorer Friedrich Martens, whose translator had described ice-mountains 'that stand firm on the shoar, and never melt at the bottom, but increase every year higher and higher, by reason of the Snow that falls on them, and then Rains that freezes [*sic*] and then Snow again alternately'. Martens's account (along with that of some other travellers) informs Pope's description:[4]

> So *Zembla*'s Rocks (the beauteous Work of Frost)
> Rise white in Air, and glitter o'er the Coast;
> Pale Suns, unfelt, at distance roll away,
> And on th'impassive Ice the Lightnings play;
> Eternal Snows the growing Mass supply,
> Till the bright Mountains prop th'incumbent Sky:
> As *Atlas* fix'd, each hoary Pile appears,
> The gather'd winter of a thousand Years.
>
> (Pope, *The Temple of Fame*, 53–60)

Pope's simile achieved considerable, and lasting, fame of its own as an example of his descriptive powers.[5] Joseph Warton maintained that 'A real lover of painting, will not be contented with a single view and examination of this beautiful winter piece, but will return to it again and again, with fresh delight. The images are distinct, and the epithets lively and appropriated, especially the words, *pale, unfelt, impassive, incumbent, gathered.*'[6]

It is not clear, however, if, in using the term 'appropriated', Warton was thinking of the passage as a pure description or as a kind of allegory of lasting fame, for it is not easy to determine whether this is a simile intended to illustrate or to ennoble the subject—to use the terms employed by Johnson to describe Pope's simile of the Alps in *An Essay on Criticism*—to 'shew it to the understanding in a clearer

---

[3] Alexander Pope, *The Temple of Fame, A Vision* (London, 1715), p. 47, italics and roman reversed.

[4] See Geoffrey Tillotson in Pope, *Poems,* 2. 222, 410–11.

[5] Byron, in the course of a discussion of Keats's 'Sleep and Poetry', quoted this passage to demonstrate that 'in descriptive poetry' Pope, even when a young poet, 'will be found, on a fair examination, to surpass any living writer'. See Lord Byron, *The Complete Miscellaneous Prose,* ed. Andrew Nicholson (Oxford, 1991), p. 116.

[6] Joseph Warton, *An Essay on the Genius and Writings of Pope,* 2 vols (London, 1782), 1. 360.

view' or to 'display it to the fancy with greater dignity'.[7] How ice might, at extreme latitudes, *not* melt is clear; how fame might endure, less so. Several of the epithets admired by Warton emphasize the difference between the ice of Nova Zembla and that found in warmer climes. The suns that shine on Pope's ice-mountains are 'pale', 'unfelt', and 'at distance roll away'. The ice is 'impassive', a word which Johnson in his *Dictionary*, citing this passage, glossed as 'exempt from the agency of external causes'. It is as if the ice-mountains of Nova Zembla represent a different world from that in which modern poets militant have to suffer: the world of envy, of linguistic decay, of things silently gone out of mind and things violently destroyed.

In his introductory note to the first editions of *The Temple of Fame*, Pope suggested that 'We find an uncommon Charm in Truth when it is convey'd by this Side-way to our Understanding.' It seems to be the case, however, that, for Pope, while composing this poem, eternal literary fame existed somewhere between a 'Truth' and a supposition, a supposition that is in accord with 'Probability and Nature' only to the degree that—as he put it on his note on Nova Zembla—it is 'not wholly unlikely that a Rock of Ice should remain for ever.'[8]

But Fame, when Pope finally beholds her, is an arbitrary and unpredictable goddess, hardly distinguishable from 'her blind sister, fickle *Fortune*' and apparently dependent on the spinning edifice of Rumour. Where Chaucer had commented on multiplicity of testimony in the house of Rumour, Pope emphasized the confusion, desperation, and temporality:

... such a grete Congregation	Above, below, without, within, around,
Of folke as I saw rome about,	Confus'd, unnumber'd multitudes are found,
Some within, and some without,	Who pass, repass, advance, and glide away;
Was never seen, ne shall be eft—	Hosts rais'd by fear, and phantoms of a day ....
And every wight that I saw there	Each talk'd aloud, or in some secret place,
Rowned everich in others ear	And wild impatience star'd in ev'ry face.
A new tyding privily	
Or else he told it openly.	
(*HF*, 3. 2034–46)	(Pope, *The Temple of Fame*, 458–61, 466–7)

It is probably to some degree necessary, when considering the lasting reputations of many bodies of poetical work, to entertain such a double and paradoxical view of literary fame as Pope's: that it is fixed and mutable, clear and unchangeable at one level, unstable and almost invisible (or incomprehensible) at another. Such a double view is an absolute imperative when considering the reputation or reputations of Chaucer's poems in the eighteenth century.

---

[7] See Johnson, 'Life of Pope'; *Works*, 23. 1200.
[8] Pope, *The Temple of Fame, A Vision*, p. 45.

Chaucer's Fame

It was sometimes assumed that Chaucer's fame resembled the ice-rocks of Nova Zembla: that his name was placed firmly in 'Fames eternall beadroll' (as Spenser put it)[9] soon after his death, remained in general estimation, and increased in honour with the passage of years. Derek Brewer has observed that Chaucer 'from his own day onwards, has been accepted as a major English poet' and that his work 'has been present as a general, much-enjoyed, if often little understood, possession of the English literary mind, solidly "there", since his own lifetime'.[10] In a similar vein, Helen Cooper has argued that Chaucer 'is the only English writer who has been read without a break for longer than printing has existed'.[11] And David Crystal has written that 'Chaucer's status as "the father of English poetry" has put at least some of *The Canterbury Tales* in front of every generation of schoolchildren since the fifteenth century'.[12]

These writers are certainly correct in suggesting that Chaucer's *name* was continuously remembered and invoked from the fifteenth century onwards. But Crystal's description of the specific terms in which Chaucer's fame has endured is more questionable. If Alexander Pope read Chaucer as a boy, he was highly unusual in doing so. There are a great many writers in the eighteenth century, as in earlier and later periods, whose works reveal no trace of their having ever looked into Chaucer, as adults or as children. And even when some experience of Chaucer's work is evident, Chaucer's fame was apparently not quite the same for any two readers at the same time, or, in some cases, even for some individual readers at different times in their lives.

One reason for this was that his poems were thought to be subject to a mutability that did not affect those written in ancient (and dead) languages. It may be significant that in his Temple, Pope confines fame to those ancient writers whose works could be seen indisputably to have pleased very many and pleased very long—particularly Homer, Virgil, and Horace. Chaucer's language and sentiments were deemed by several of Pope's contemporaries to be irredeemably 'antiquated'. Where eighteenth-century commentators occasionally suggested that some modern poets had provided an unchangeable permanent linguistic standard, Pope, like Dryden before him, was certain that the language would continue to change rapidly and change inexorably, and despaired of the possibility of lasting fame for a writer in English:

---

[9] Edmund Spenser, *The Faerie Queene,* IV. xxxii, 292.
[10] Derek Brewer, ed., *Chaucer: The Critical Heritage,* 2 vols (London, 1978), 1. 3.
[11] Helen Cooper, 'Welcome to the House of Fame: 600 Years Dead: Chaucer's Deserved Reputation as "the Father of English Poetry"' *Times Literary Supplement,* 27 October 2000, pp. 3–4.
[12] David Crystal, *The Stories of English* (London, 2005), p. 106.

No longer now that Golden Age appears,
When *Patriarch*-Wits surviv'd a *thousand Years*;
Now Length of *Fame* (our second Life) is lost,
And bare Threescore is all ev'n That can boast:
Our Sons their Father's *failing Language* see,
And such as *Chaucer* is, shall *Dryden* be.[13]

(*An Essay on Criticism*, 178–83; Pope, *Poems*, 1. 293)

There would seem to be an inherent paradox in presenting Chaucer's image of unchanging fame (as Pope did in 1736), while at the same time subjecting it to substantial alteration.

Chaucer's Eighteenth-Century Eclipse?

Against the notion that Chaucer's poems were continuously read and continuously esteemed may be set the common belief that in the seventeenth and eighteenth centuries the medieval poet was of little importance. A striking lack of interest in the presence of Chaucer is evident in the writings by several historians of eighteenth-century literature, who have tended to assume that, in this period, it is the entirely new work that is alone significant, and that translation and critical comments on the works of the past are necessarily to be relegated to the margins.[14] Similarly, some students of the medieval period have confined Chaucer's significant afterlife to the fifteenth century. For some nineteenth-century scholars, editors, critics, commentators, and general readers, Chaucer's eighteenth-century admirers were the proper objects of pure derision: their appreciation of Chaucer was based on ignorance and characterized by insensibility. The history of Chaucer scholarship was frequently told as a teleological narrative that began with pygmies and culminated in the gigantic triumphs of a glorious present. It was sometimes assumed *a priori* that no two things could be more incompatible than Chaucer's poetry and 'Neo-classicism'. Eighteenth century-readers not only did not understand Chaucer's poems, they *could not* have understood them. An appetite for the conceits of Cowley, the insipidities of Waller, the acerbities of Dryden, the polish of Pope, or the orotundities of Johnson, it was often assumed, must *perforce* have precluded a taste for the apparent simplicity and very different

---

[13] Alexander Pope, *An Essay on Criticism* (London, 1711), p. 28. Dryden (*Works*, 6. 40) had given permission for his own poems to be rewritten, as he had rewritten Chaucer's.

[14] Little or no mention of Chaucer is included in Steven N. Zwicker, ed., *The Cambridge Companion to English Literature, 1650–1740* (Cambridge, 1998) and Thomas Keymer and Jon Mee, eds, *The Cambridge Companion to English Literature, 1740–1830* (Cambridge, 2004). Similar volumes in the Palgrave Macmillan 'Transitions' series, Moyra Haslett, *Pope to Burney, 1714–79: Scriblerians to Bluestockings* (London, 2003) and Kay Gilliland Stevenson, *Milton to Pope: 1650–1720* (London, 2000), are extremely sparse in their references to Chaucer, and he is mentioned in only one of the forty-one chapters of the Wiley-Blackwell *A Companion to Eighteenth-Century Poetry*, ed. Christine Gerrard (Oxford, 2006).

sophistication of Chaucer. While more-or-less respectable Chaucerian scholarship was often reckoned to have begun with the work of Thomas Tyrwhitt, full critical understanding was confined to the nineteenth century—and the late nineteenth century at that. Eighteenth-century compositions, therefore, that declare themselves to derive, in one way or another, from Chaucer's works were largely ignored.

Such assumptions have proved to be remarkably enduring. A casual, or unlucky, reader of some twentieth-century and twenty-first century academic writing might easily gather that Chaucer was of no importance to eighteenth-century literature, and that eighteenth-century writers contributed nothing to Chaucer's afterlife. The first chapter, for example, of one *Companion to Chaucer*, entitled 'Afterlife', devotes a page-and-a-half to 'The Fifteenth-Century Chaucer' and two pages to 'The Renaissance Chaucer'. Then follows a white space, a new heading, and a paragraph which begins: 'After a period of comparative neglect in the seventeenth and early eighteenth centuries, Chaucer's reputation flowered once more in the nineteenth century.'[15] Equally (or more) significantly, Chaucer does not appear at all in the index of the volume of *The Cambridge History of English Literature* devoted to the years 1660–1780 and his works are mentioned only in passing in the text.[16] Most strikingly of all, Michael Alexander, in a book specifically devoted to the afterlife of medieval culture, maintained that 'Pope shows knowledge of no early writer in English. In his time, the recovery of writings in Middle English lay in the future.'[17]

Allusion, Criticism, and Versions

There is no justification for such silences. Eighteenth-century editions and biographies of Chaucer had been meticulously documented in Eleanor Prescott Hammond's *Chaucer: A Bibliographical Manual* (1908)—together with accounts of modernizations and translations, including, of course, Alexander Pope's *Temple of Fame*. Hammond's work was supplemented in 1925 by the three volumes of Caroline Spurgeon's *Five Hundred Years of Chaucer Criticism and Allusion, 1357–1900*, which devoted over 200 pages to recording, and sometimes reproducing, eighteenth-century Chaucerian references of every kind— making clear that it is almost impossible to identify specific groups, types, or communities among the poet's readers: Chaucer left traces in the writings of lexicographers, booksellers, lords, ladies, gentlemen and commoners, bishops and politicians, scholars and poets, the young and the old, the rich and the poor.

[15] Peter Brown, ed., *A Companion to Chaucer* (Oxford, 2002), p. 13.
[16] John Richetti, ed., *The Cambridge History of English Literature, 1660–1780* (Cambridge, 2005).
[17] Michael Alexander, *Medievalism* (New Haven, CT, 2007), p. 10.

The most pertinent critical remarks on Chaucer by eighteenth-century writers were collected by Derek Brewer in 1978 in Volume 1 of *Chaucer: The Critical Heritage*. Brewer's volumes confined themselves to a strict definition of the word 'criticism', and therefore excluded poetical responses to Chaucer on the grounds that the 'various critical views' implicit within them are to be found explicitly stated elsewhere, and that inclusion would have 'required impractically vast volumes for relatively small critical return'.[18] That assumption was questioned by Betsy Bowden, who published a collection of *Eighteenth-Century Modernizations from 'The Canterbury Tales'* in 1991. The critical case for paying attention to some of these pieces was made by Bowden in several books and articles—as well as by Brewer himself in 1997.[19] Bowden's collection was confined to versions of *The Canterbury Tales*, and excluded those of other Chaucerian works, and of the many apocryphal poems which were much admired in the eighteenth century. A full account of these was given in 2001 by Kathleen Forni.[20]

Over the past twenty-five years or so, there has been considerable interest from students of eighteenth-century poetry in Chaucer's part in the formation or construction of the 'English Literary Canon'.[21] At the same time, there have been a number of discussions of Chaucer's afterlife that have touched on aspects of the poet's eighteenth-century fame.[22] While helpful in a great many ways, none of these works, individually or together, provide an account of Chaucer's eighteenth-century afterlife that addresses the extraordinary variety of the pertinent phenomena. Nor do they do much to counter the late-nineteenth-century animadversions on Chaucer's eighteenth-century afterlife—the most full and most

---

[18] Brewer, *Chaucer: The Critical Heritage*, 1. 1.

[19] Betsy Bowden, *Chaucer Aloud: The Varieties of Textual Interpretation* (Philadelphia, PA, 1987); Betsy Bowden, 'Four Eighteenth-Century Modernizations of The Shipman's Tale as Audiovisual Performance', *Translation and Literature*, 3, 30–46; Betsy Bowden, 'Tales Told and Tellers of Tales: Illustrations of the Canterbury Tales in the Course of the Eighteenth Century', in *Chaucer Illustrated*, ed. William Finley and Joseph Rosenblum (Newcastle, DE and London, 2003), pp. 121–90; Betsy Bowden, *The Wife of Bath in Afterlife: Ballads to Blake* (Bethlehem, PA, 2017); Derek Brewer, 'Modernizing the Medieval: Eighteenth-Century Translations from Chaucer', in *The Middle Ages after the Middle Ages in the English-Speaking World*, ed. Marie-Françoise Alamichel and Derek Brewer (Martlesham, 1997), 103–20.

[20] Kathleen Forni, *The Chaucerian Apocrypha, A Counterfeit Canon* (Gainesville, FL, 2001).

[21] See especially, e.g. Howard D. Weinbrot, *Britannia's Issue: The Rise of British Literature from Dryden to Ossian* (Cambridge, 1991); David Fairer, *English Poetry of the Eighteenth Century* (Harlow, 2003); Kevin Pask, *The Emergence of the English Author* (Cambridge, 1996)); Jonathan Brody Kramnick, *The Making of the English Canon* (Cambridge, 1998); Trevor Ross, *The Making of the English Literary Canon* (London,1998); Richard Terry, *Poetry and the Making of the English Literary Past, 1660–1781* (Oxford, 2001). Many of these works are economically epitomized, along with much new material, in a single chapter, Barrett Kalter, 'Chaucer Ancient and Modern', in *Modern Antiques: The Material Past in England, 1660–1780* (Lewisburg, PA, 2012), 69–108.

[22] See, e.g. Joseph A. Dane, *Who is Buried in Chaucer's Tomb? Studies in the Reception of Chaucer's Book* (East Lansing, MI, 1998); Stephanie Trigg, *Congenial Souls: Reading Chaucer from Medieval to Post Modern* (Minneapolis, MN, 2002); Thomas A. Prendergast, *Chaucer's Dead Body: From Corpse to Corpus* (London, 2004).

devastating account of which is represented by the chapter on 'Chaucer in Literary History' in Volume 3 of *Studies in Chaucer, his Life and Writings* (1892) by the Yale professor of English language and literature, Thomas Raynesford Lounsbury. Lounsbury's is perhaps the most wittily acerbic of all accounts of eighteenth-century responses to Chaucer. Were it not for his occasional appreciation of some eighteenth-century verse, it might be tempting to apply to him lines from Alexander Pope's *An Essay on Criticism*: 'All Books he reads, and all he reads assails, / From *Dryden's Fables* down to *Durfey's Tales*.'[23] It was on the basis of extensive reading of various kinds that Lounsbury maintained that it was 'in the seventeenth century, especially in the middle and latter half of it, that the reputation of Chaucer touched the lowest point to which it ever fell', and that the eighteenth century was 'largely ignorant of' Chaucer, and 'indifferent about him'.[24] For Lounsbury, there were great similarities between the diction and sensibilities of the late nineteenth and fourteenth centuries, the eighteenth representing an unfortunate intervening miasma. For example, Lounsbury suggested, with unanswerable confidence, that 'No one at this day, who has carefully studied' both Chaucer's and Pope's poems on Fame 'would think for a moment of placing the modern work on a level with the ancient'.[25]

The Fame of Pope's Temple

The question of whether or not Pope's *Temple of Fame* could be placed 'on a level with the ancient' was, in fact, far from uncontentious, even in the eighteenth century. Indeed, Pope's own attitude towards the suggestions made in his poem about Fame—and their possible application both to Chaucer's original and to *The Temple of Fame* itself—were shifting and ambivalent rather than fixed and constant, and such ambivalence is reflected in some readers' responses to the poem. Pope insisted that *The Temple of Fame* had been 'Written in the year 1711', when he was, as he put it in the poem, very much 'a Candidate for Praise'. In his first editions of 1715, Pope's 'Advertisement' presents the poem as one in which the 'Hint' has been 'taken from *Chaucer's House of Fame*', but in which the 'Descriptions and most of the particular Thoughts' are his own. It is not clear at this date how many of Pope's readers were expected to be familiar with Chaucer. On the one hand, Pope provided directions for readers 'who would compare' his poem with Chaucer's, assuming that some will have a copy to hand. At the same time, he suggested that the

---

[23] Pope, *An Essay on Criticism*, 616–17; Pope, *Poems*, 1. 309. Thomas D'Urfey published *Tales, Tragical and Comical* (London, 1704) and *Stories, Moral and Comical* (London, 1707), the first avowedly modelled on Dryden's *Fables*, according to the opening of the volume's 'Preface'; hence, Pope's pointed contrast between high and low forms of literature.

[24] See Thomas R. Lounsbury, *Studies in Chaucer, His Life and Writings*, 3 vols (London, 1892), 3. 73.

[25] Ibid. 3. 184.

fame of Chaucer's poem was in need of refreshment. In the first note on the poem, *The House of Fame* is numbered among the 'Masterpieces' of the kind of allegorical writing that Pope regards as in need of critical defence and deems worthy of revival.

In his *Works* of 1717, Pope printed *The Temple of Fame* in pride of place amongst his own poems.[26] The discussion of Chaucer, however, was reduced and the extensive annotation removed. In the edition of 1736, as we have seen, Pope, now the recipient of the most extraordinary contemporary fame, printed large parts of Chaucer's text. This suggests that by this date Pope was supposing that some of his readers at least would have little difficulty with Chaucer's vocabulary, and would enjoy—as in his *Imitations of Horace*—savouring the complex relation between the ancient and modern work.

Pope's shifting assumptions about Chaucer's status are echoed in the responses of his readers. Samuel Johnson considered that the 'learning' that was so remarkably exhibited in *The Temple of Fame* was demonstrated more in Pope's alterations to, than in his reproduction of, his original:

> The *Temple of Fame* has, as Steele warmly declared, *a thousand beauties*. Every part is splendid; there is great luxuriance of ornaments; the original vision of Chaucer was never denied to be much improved; the allegory is very skilfully continued, the imagery is properly selected, and learnedly displayed.[27]

As we will see in Chapter 8, Johnson may have regarded Pope's attempt to revive allegorical poetry as mistaken in principle. As he saw it, since the 'scene is laid in remote ages' and the 'sentiments' 'have little relation to general manners or common life', the poem could not hope for popular fame: 'it seems never to have obtained much notice, but is turned silently over, and seldom quoted or mentioned with either praise or blame'.[28] But in giving such an account, Johnson had clearly forgotten that he had himself quoted the poem in his *Dictionary*, and in the Preface to his edition of the plays of Shakespeare. And he presumably did not know that his friend Joseph Warton had commented upon the poem extensively and minutely in printed (but unpublished) pages of his *Essay on the Genius and Writings of Pope*.[29]

While the drift of Joseph Warton's commentary does indeed suggest that Chaucer's original had been 'much improved', Joseph's brother Thomas, the literary historian, had offered the opposite view in 1774:

> Pope has imitated this piece, with his usual elegance of diction and harmony of versification. But in the mean time, he has not only misrepresented the story, but marred the character of the poem. He has endeavoured to correct its extravagancies, by new

[26] See James McLaverty, *Pope, Print and Meaning* (Oxford, 2001), p. 74.
[27] Johnson, 'Life of Pope'; *Works*, 23. 1196.
[28] Ibid. 23. 1196.
[29] In the Advertisement to the first edition of the second volume of his *Essay*, Joseph Warton thought it 'necessary and respectful to inform the reader, that this volume was printed, as far as the 201st page [the part of the book that contains the discussion of *The Temple of Fame*], above twenty years ago'.

refinements and additions of another cast: but he did not consider, that extravagancies are essential to a poem of such a structure, and even constitute it's beauties. An attempt to unite order and exactness of imagery with a subject formed on principles so professedly romantic and anomalous is like giving Corinthian pillars to a Gothic palace. When I read Pope's elegant imitation of this piece, I think I am walking among the modern monuments unsuitably placed in Westminster-abbey.[30]

Thomas Warton's comments, however, do not seem to have represented the general view of Pope's poem, which continued to find appreciative readers, both in its own right and as a representation of Chaucer's poem, into the nineteenth century. Warton's comments on the Gothic palace, indeed, were met with resistance. The biographer and poet William Roscoe was to remark in the first volume of his edition of Pope's *Works* (1824) that *The Temple of Fame* was 'one of the noblest, although one of the earliest' of Pope's 'productions'. Where other commentators had argued the case for and against Pope's extensive alterations, Roscoe presented the relation between the eighteenth-century and the fourteenth-century poems as paradoxical. On the one hand, Pope had changed everything; on the other, the effect of reading the more recent poem was to lose any sense of clear distinction between the old and the new:

> That the hint of this piece is taken from Chaucer's House of Fame, is sufficiently obvious, yet the design is greatly altered, and the descriptions, and many of the particular thoughts, are his own; notwithstanding which, such is the coincidence and happy union of the work with its prototype, that it is almost impossible to distinguish those portions which are originally Pope's, from those for which he has been indebted to Chaucer.[31]

The variable fortunes of Pope's *Temple of Fame* and its perceived relation to the poem on which it was founded are not untypical of eighteenth-century responses to Chaucer more generally, and it is this variety of response and opinion that makes the tracing of Chaucer's fame and generalizations about its nature and character in the period so difficult.

Eighteenth-Century Editions of Chaucer's Works

The most obvious evidence of Chaucer's continuing 'presence' in eighteenth-century English culture would seem to be found in, or to be constituted by, representations of the texts of the whole or part of Chaucer's works, with their

---

[30] Warton, *History*, 1. 396.
[31] *The Works of Alexander Pope, Esq.: with Notes and Illustrations by Himself and Others*, ed. William Roscoe, 10 vols (London, 1824), 1. xi. As will be observed in Chapter 11, Roscoe remarked that 'In the establishment of the English language, Chaucer may be said to have laid the foundation of a building which it was the good fortune of Pope to complete' (p. xi).

attendant annotation. The eighteenth-century editions of Chaucer, however, are few, and it is far from clear what story, or what kind of story, they tell—or if they tell a consistent or coherent story at all.

Some of Chaucer's poems were attractively printed at the back of Dryden's *Fables Ancient and Modern* in 1700—significantly their first appearance in roman type, as opposed to the black letter used in seventeenth-century printings. The *Fables* text had been taken from Thomas Speght's edition of *The Workes of Our Antient and Learned English Poet, Geffrey Chaucer* (1598). It was unemended but lightly repunctuated in accordance with late-seventeenth-century conventions.

A complete edition of *The Works of Geoffrey Chaucer: Compared with the Former Editions, and Many Valuable MSS* was advertised in both the 1715 printings of Pope's *Temple of Fame*. It is described there as 'Begun by *John Urry* late student of *Christ-Church*' and 'compleated by the Care of the Students of *Christ-Church*'. It eventually appeared in 1721. This was the only complete eighteenth-century edition of *The Canterbury Tales* until 1775 and remained the only modern text of the rest of Chaucer's works until late into the nineteenth century. The editorial methods of John Urry were—and continue to be—condemned by most subsequent editors. Convinced that all Chaucer's lines consisted of ten syllables, Urry consulted a series of manuscripts in search of missing words, or spellings—including final and medial *-és*. He spelled the endings of words in a form that would alert eighteenth-century readers to what he thought was the correct pronunciation. The problem (as we will see in Chapters 2 and 5 below) was that Urry inserted some words without manuscript support, spelled some words in a way that was entirely foreign to fourteenth-century grammar and orthography, and sometimes produced ten-syllable lines where any iambic pattern was almost entirely obscured. Urry's volume was accompanied by an attractive, though inaccurate, 'Life of Chaucer' by John Dart, and, most importantly, an extensive glossary by Timothy Thomas.[32] The book did much to help Chaucer make sense, and despite condemnation by subsequent editors, was extensively used—not least by Thomas Warton.

One of the most vehement condemners of Urry's text (but an admirer of Thomas's glossary) was the classical scholar, translator, theologian, and librettist of four of Handel's oratorios, Thomas Morell. In 1737, Morell published, probably at his own expense, *The Canterbury Tales of Chaucer, in the Original, From the Most Authentic Manuscripts; and as They Are Turn'd Into Modern Language by Mr. Dryden, Mr. Pope, and Other Eminent Hands*. This was the first volume of what would have been an arduous and highly original project. In preparing an entirely

---

[32] Urry's and the other eighteenth-century editions are discussed in detail in William L. Alderson and Arnold C. Henderson, *Chaucer and Augustan Scholarship* (Berkeley, CA, 1970) and in Paul G. Ruggiers, ed., *Editing Chaucer: The Great Tradition* (Norman, OK, 1984). As will be observed in Chapter 5, Urry's younger associates were not entirely convinced by the principles which had guided Urry himself in preparing the text, and inclined rather to Dryden's view of Chaucer's metrical aims and achievements.

new text, Morell, like Urry, consulted a range of manuscripts, but, unlike Urry, included nothing without authority. The title page proclaims that the edition is accompanied with 'References *to* Authors, Ancient *and* Modern, Various Readings *and* Explanatory Notes'. Glosses and simple explanations are provided at the foot of the page, further reflections towards the back of the volume. The Chaucerian text is followed by modern versions by Betterton, Dryden, and Morell himself.

Morell's project was not extended beyond *The Knight's Tale*.[33] The complete *Canterbury Tales* were almost entirely re-edited by Thomas Tyrwhitt in 1775, and republished in 1798. Tyrwhitt's was also an extraordinary undertaking. Tyrwhitt treats Morell and Morell's methods with great respect, while working with a slightly different selection of manuscripts. His explanatory notes are fuller and more useful than any that had appeared before, and he is frank in confessing that there are some passages he does not understand. The glossary that followed in an additional volume in 1778 drew on the whole extent of Chaucer's works and is more complete than that of Timothy Thomas, on which it draws. Chaucer's works were then included in the first volumes of several publications offering themselves as complete collections of English poetry: those edited by John Bell (1777–82), Robert Anderson (1792–1807), and Alexander Chalmers (1810).

It is sometimes assumed that readers at any date will use the latest edition of any author that they are reading. But that assumption is frequently mistaken. Many readers in the eighteenth and early nineteenth centuries appear to have read Chaucer's poems as they were prepared and presented in the seventeenth, or even sixteenth, centuries. Dryden, when writing his Preface to *Fables* in 1699, consulted Speght's edition of 1602 (or 1687), but, as we have seen, reprinted the originals from which he made his versions (contained in the same volume) from Speght's 1598 edition. Similarly, Pope owned copies of both the 1598 and 1602 editions but appears to have worked from the older copy he had been given as a child.[34] Urry's edition of 1721 was superseded by Tyrwhitt's text only for *The Canterbury Tales*, and his text of *Troilus* and other poems was reproduced in many

---

[33] A letter from Morell of 1771 preserved in the British Library (BL Add. MS 34728) suggests that he had continued with his work on the edition (perhaps even completed it) but that his financial situation had prevented further publication beyond Volume 1. See Ruth Smith, 'Thomas Morell and His Letter about Handel', *Journal of the Royal Musical Association*, 127 (2002), 191–225 (p. 212).

[34] Pope's copy of Speght 1598, with his marginal annotations, is preserved in the Hurd library at Hartlebury Castle, Worcestershire. See Maynard Mack, *Collected in Himself: Essays Critical, Biographical, and Bibliographical on Pope and Some of His Contemporaries* (Newark, DE, 1982), 179–94. There are a few marks in the margins of this copy (e.g. on *The Squire's Tale* on p. 188) not noted by Mack. Michael Hunter describes a copy of Speght 1602 (without marginal marks) signed 'A. Pope'. See Michael Hunter, 'Alexander Pope and Geoffrey Chaucer', in *The Warden's Meeting: A Tribute to John Sparrow*, ed. Anthony Davis (Oxford, 1977), 9–32. Speght's most significant addition in 1602 was perhaps that of small, pointing hands or manicules to mark lines and passages of particular interest: often sententiae but also remarkable expressions of other kinds. As will be discussed in Chapter 11, as late as 1730 Pope (aged forty-two) told Joseph Spence, 'I read Chaucer still with as much pleasure as almost any of our poets. He is a master of manners and of description, and the first tale-teller in the true enlivened natural way.' See Joseph Spence, *Observations, Anecdotes and Characters of Books and Men*, ed. James M. Osborn, 2 vols (Oxford, 1966), 1. 179.

late-eighteenth-century and nineteenth-century editions. Bell printed Tyrwhitt's *Canterbury Tales*, but used Urry for the rest of the Chaucerian *oeuvre*, a pattern followed by Anderson. Chalmers also used Tyrwhitt's *Canterbury Tales*, but went back to Speght's editions of 1598 and 1602 (or 1687) for the remainder.

The paucity of editions of Chaucer might seem to suggest a difference in the relative standing of Chaucer and that of Spenser, Shakespeare, and Milton. There were new editions of *The Fairie Queene* in the eighteenth century by John Hughes, John Upton, and Ralph Church. These were supplemented by the extensive commentaries of (among others) Thomas Warton. Shakespeare's plays were edited by Rowe, Pope, Theobald, Hanmer, Warburton, Johnson, Steevens, and Malone. *Paradise Lost* received extensive explanatory commentary from Patrick Hume, the Jonathan Richardsons (father and son), and editions from Richard Bentley and Thomas Newton. This would seem to suggest that there was a market for these poets, and a demand for explication and explanation—not merely the result of changes in language—far exceeding that for the works of Chaucer.

The lack of a proper scholarly edition for much of the eighteenth century certainly made for difficulties in the basic comprehension and understanding of his work. All the texts of Chaucer's works (with the partial exception of Tyrwhitt's) mingled vocabulary, orthography, and grammar from different centuries and different localities so completely that it was difficult for even the most assiduous reader to establish a coherent sense of Chaucer's language. The texts of several poems contained interpolations, presumably of scribal origin, in which obscenity was sometimes accentuated: Chanticleer in *The Nun's Priest's Tale* is an even more vigorous treader of hens in Speght's and Urry's texts than in modern editions, and Damian's attributes, in *The Merchant's Tale*, are more graphically obvious. Both Urry and Morell marked the final syllables that they thought should be sounded. Tyrwhitt provided no such help. His rules of scansion, while consistent, may not, therefore, have been easy to apply to the text he presents.

The limitations and uncertainties of the available editions do not, however, seem to have prevented the enjoyment of Chaucer as a poet to the degree that one might suppose. Tyrwhitt encouraged the world to decry and dismiss Urry's edition, principally on the grounds that Urry had interpolated syllables to make Chaucer's text conform to eighteenth-century metrical expectations. But there is evidence to suggest that Urry's volume, which is handsomely and spaciously printed, offered readers a pleasurable experience, and that the glossary which it contained was found useful both by general readers and enthusiasts—including Tyrwhitt.

Apocryphal Works and Biographies

The uncertainties attaching to Chaucer's texts were most consequential—detrimentally so—as they concerned the canon, for the confusions here profoundly affected the biographies of Chaucer written in the period. Although Urry's assistants and Tyrwhitt had raised doubts about some of the inclusions in the canon, all editions of Chaucer's works after 1532 included many apocryphal works. All eighteenth-century and most nineteenth-century biographies of Chaucer depended upon deductions from the collected works, deductions which were elaborated rather than retrenched in successive editions.[35] They therefore mingle Chaucer's life with parts of the lives of others—the politically messy life of Thomas Usk, for example, or that of Sir John Clanvowe. They assume that Chaucer at the age of eighteen wrote a poem now sometimes ascribed to the early sixteenth century. They describe his education at both Oxford and Cambridge, retail verbatim conversations with Petrarch and Boccaccio, get Chaucer in and out of prison, and grant him extensive lands and glorious castles. The process was circular and apparently inescapable: poems that fitted the emerging biography and chronology (young men write unguarded poems about sexual love) were thereby confirmed in their apparent authenticity, which in turn contributed more details to the biography. These works did not think of themselves as fanciful. The 'Life of Chaucer' in *Biographia Britannica* (1747–63), for example, has extensive notes and makes a sustained effort to compare and reconcile testimonies from a variety of sources, and to peruse the poems carefully, on the assumption that 'the most certain accounts we have of Chaucer are those taken from his own writings'.[36]

As well as providing sources for deductions about his life, Chaucer's 'apocryphal' works were admired, even loved. *Biographia Britannica* regards *The Court of Love*—a poem supposedly composed when Chaucer was about eighteen and attending Cambridge University—as evidence of both of his 'great strength of genius' and precocious and already practiced metrical mastery (p. 1294). In *The Testament of Love*, the same source claims, 'one plainly sees a great Philosopher broken by misfortunes, deserted by companions, and exposed to the censures of an evil world, delivering himself in prison with freedom and spirit, though in a melancholy mood, and in the language of sorrow' (p. 1301). Even Thomas Tyrwhitt, who attempted to confine his biographical account to incontestable fact, and provided 'An Abstract of the Historical Passages of the Life of Chaucer' rather than a Life, depended fundamentally on inferences drawn from the spurious *Testament of Love* for his account of 'Chaucer's' middle years.[37] This general tendency

---

[35] Some doubts about the authenticity of some of the works attributed to Chaucer, however, had been voiced before Tyrwhitt. Speght himself had ascribed *The Testament of Cresseid* to Henryson and *The Letter of Cupid* to 'Occleve'. That attribution was endorsed in Urry's edition by John Dart, who also cast doubts on the authorship of some other poems.

[36] See *Biographia Britannica, or, The Lives of the Most Eminent Persons Who Have Flourished in Great Britain and Ireland, from the Earliest Ages, Down to the Present Times*, 7 vols (London, 1747–63), 2. 1294. The Life of Chaucer in this collection (which is discussed further in Chapters 4, 5, and 12) was probably the work of the historian Dr John Campbell (1708–75).

[37] Tyrwhitt warned against 'arguing from pieces which [Chaucer] never wrote, as if they were his' (Tyrrwhitt 1775–78, 1. xxv), and pointed out that, faced by conflicting suggestions as to whether Chaucer was educated at Oxford or Cambridge, 'Biographers ... instead of weighing one against the

reached an extraordinary culmination in William Godwin's *The Life of Geoffrey Chaucer* published in two large volumes in 1803 (a work which will be examined further in Chapters 5 and 12).

As the eighteenth-century lives of Chaucer build and elaborate upon their predecessors, so most eighteenth-century portraits were based on that included in Thomas Hoccleve's *The Regiment of Princes,* but add details suggestive of sensitivity and education. Where the portrait in Speght's edition Chaucer is surrounded by his 'progenie', as if this were the basis of his fame (see Fig. 0.2), in the related engravings by George Vertue and Jacobus Houbraaken Chaucer appears wiser, more contemplative, at once perhaps very slightly amused and with eyes suggestive of long and painful experience (see Figs 0.3 and 0.4).

When text, biography and glossing were taken together it was easy for nineteenth-century commentators to claim that all eighteenth-century 'Chaucers' were, in important respects, *imaginary*: the name 'Chaucer' referred to a substantially fictional figure, some of whose supposed works were quite different from those of the true Chaucer now so elaborately rescued from heaps of rubbish, forgery, and misrepresentation.

Modernizations, Imitations, and Paraphrases

Late nineteenth-century contempt was directed against versions of Chaucerian poems described variously as 'paraphrase', 'retelling', 'imitation', 'modernization', 'translation', '*refacimento*', or 'done into English as it is now refined'. These were common in the eighteenth century. The number of writings from Dryden to Wordsworth, by both professional and amateur poets, that reworked Chaucer's poems is remarkable. Most of these were considered by nineteenth-century commentators to be travesties. Walter Skeat in 1878, for example, described Dryden's versions as 'very elaborate paraphrases, in which the idiomatic forms and colours of the old writer vanish in the process of adaptation' and as poems which 'bear no closer resemblance, in spirit or expression, to Chaucer than Pope's translation bears to Homer'. Interestingly, Skeat assumes that the '*Fables* of Dryden are as well known to the mass of the public as any poems in the language', but doubts whether 'they have increased the desire for a more intimate acquaintance with Chaucer, or contributed to the extension of his fame'.[38]

Not only did Chaucer father a great many retellings of his poems, but his works seem to have been turned to by many self-consciously modern poets wishing to

---

other, have adopted both; and tell us very gravely, that he was first at Cambridge, and afterwards removed from thence to compleat his studies at Oxford' (Tyrwhitt 1775–8, 1. xxv), but he did not question one of these testimonies: that provided by the spurious *Court of Love.*

[38] *Poetical Works of Geoffrey Chaucer,* ed. Robert Bell, revised with a preliminary essay by Walter W. Skeat, 4 vols (London, 1878–80), 1. 62–3.

Fig. 0.2 Detail of portrait of Chaucer from frontispiece to Thomas Speght's edition (London, 1602 edition), engraved by John Speed for Speght's first edition of 1598.

take poetry, and occasionally prose fiction, in new directions, to widen its scope, or to return it to a more 'natural' or (as in Pope's *Temple*) a more fanciful path. There is considerable testimony suggesting that some of these versions were highly valued in their own right. Roscoe's contention that *The Temple of Fame* was among the 'noblest' of Pope's poems has already been mentioned. And, as will be observed in Chapter 3, Dryden's version of *The Knight's Tale* was considered 'the most animated

Fig. 0.3 A portrait of Chaucer by George Vertue, explicitly based on that provided
by Thomas Hoccleve. From Vertue's *Twelve Celebrated English Poets* (London, 1730).

and harmonious piece of versification in the English language' by many readers
throughout the eighteenth century, including Thomas Warton.[39]

While the initial approach of every translator was appreciative, many of them
writing, perhaps, more for love than money, in practice most appear to have
found particular parts of Chaucer's work (or work attributed to Chaucer) more

---

[39] Warton, *History*, 1. 367.

Fig. 0.4   Portrait of Chaucer from *The Heads of Illustrious Persons of Great Britain Engraven by Mr. Houbraken and Mr. Vertue. With Their Lives and Characters by Thomas Birch* (London, 1747).

congenial than others. Some passages proved unintelligible or irreproducible, others prompted wide divergence from the original, or the addition of extraneous material, often borrowed from other poets of other times. Such additions need not necessarily represent a failure of Chaucer's poems to recreate themselves in the mind of the later poet. For the poets, as for prose critics, and some editors, appreciating and understanding Chaucer often involved a process both of recognition and of discrimination. It was partly a wide literary experience that enabled some eighteenth-century writers to understand, enjoy, and reproduce Chaucer's poems, however partially. A particular phrase, action, event, or *sententia* in a poem by Chaucer has recalled a parallel phrase, action, event, or *sententia* in the work of another author, ancient or modern. The history of Chaucer's reception by a single mind or by many minds, therefore, necessarily demands some consideration of the other poems and critical principles that were active in that single mind or were generally known to the receiving audience. Chaucer's case is neither entirely separate nor separable from the general course of poetry or from those fluctuations, variations, reversals, and revivals that seem to mark the history of poetry more widely.

Modernizations and rewritings of Spenser and Milton such as Edward Howard's *Spenser Redivivus* (1687) and John Hopkins's *Milton's Paradise Lost Imitated in Rhyme, in the Fourth, Sixth, and Ninth Books* (1699) do not seem to have made much impression, or to have affected the reputations of either poet. There is, however, considerable evidence to suggest that at least some of the versions of Chaucer's poems made a lasting contribution to keeping Chaucer's name fresh and drew many readers to his poems, partly, perhaps, because of the abilities and standing of those composing such works: Dryden, Pope, and Wordsworth. For such reasons, the present study attempts to place discussions of some of the eighteenth-century poems most obviously 'fathered' by Chaucer alongside other examples of eighteenth-century poetical and critical thought and activity, including historical, biographical, and philological Chaucer scholarship, as exhibited in biographies, editorial annotation, and literary histories. The working hypothesis is that, as far as Chaucer is concerned, the history of scholarship, the history of critical opinion, and the history of poetry did and do not constitute separate or separable narratives. The present study attempts to demonstrate that an interest in the poetical present or classical past on the one hand, and an interest in the history of poetry, language, and manners of the fourteenth century on the other, often went hand in hand and were mutually enlightening. Editors and antiquaries were invigorated by the work of poets; poets were assisted and directed by the interests of scholars. Accordingly, this book provides an account of the fortunes of Chaucer's poems in the eighteenth century both in general terms and by way of minute analysis of particular editorial and poetical responses. General accounts, consisting of short descriptions of editions published, references made, encomia offered, and comparisons drawn, are followed by extended reconstructions of interior compositional, critical, and editorial processes by particular writers at particular times.

Chronologies

The present study focuses mainly on the eighteenth century as strictly defined. But its starting and finishing points are inevitably somewhat blurred. The first book to be studied in depth was published in May 1700, but was the work of a poet then in his sixty-eighth year. The last work to be considered in any detail was published in 1841, though several of its contributors had been active long before that, and no attempt has been made to 'cover' early nineteenth-century responses to Chaucer in the depth that is afforded to those of the eighteenth century. Twelve chapters are divided into three groups, concentrating loosely in turn upon the opening, the middle, and the closing decades of the century. The discussion is in places minutely particular; at other moments (since 'Chaucer' as perceived by one writer in 1700 was a partial reflection of 'Chaucer' as perceived by another in 1598, and 'Chaucer' as perceived in 1803 is not independent of the 'Chaucer' of 1700), the opinions of commentators widely separated in time are addressed and compared.

The first four chapters consist of a discussion of the critical inheritance, as it were, bequeathed to eighteenth-century writers by earlier commentators, and of various accounts of Chaucer published in the closing years of the seventeenth century, and examines some of the contradictions apparently contained therein. Chaucer's literary reputation looks, on the face of things, to have been continuous, but that apparent continuity may obscure enormous variations of engagement and esteem that override or complicate the conventional divisions of literary history.

There then follows a discussion of the difficulties presented by the historical, biographical, metrical, editorial, and critical remarks on Chaucer in the Preface to Dryden's *Fables Ancient and Modern* (1700). Dryden's observations on Chaucer are compared with those of a range of predecessors from Thomas Speght to the passing remarks of Dryden's contemporaries: Charles Gildon, Thomas Rymer, Joseph Addison, and the team associated with John Urry. It is suggested that Dryden cast old thoughts in an entirely new light, thus providing a considerable and lasting impetus for the more general appreciation and understanding of Chaucer's works.

The third chapter attempts to explain the surprising critical success of Dryden's proposition—and illustration in his *Palamon and Arcite*—that *The Knight's Tale* was of the 'epique kind' and not much inferior to the *Iliad* and the *Æneid*, its diction 'as harmonious' as that of Virgil and its story 'more pleasing' than either classical heroic poem, particularly in its treatment of love. For many readers, from Thomas Morell to Walter Scott, Dryden had, it seems, *demonstrated* that Chaucer's poem could stand beside and give equal pleasure to those of Virgil and Homer, with which it shared some leading notions. Such a verdict, we suggest, should not be lightly dismissed.

The fourth chapter attempts to follow the vestigial traces of Dryden's widely ranging processes of thought as he read and recomposed *The Nun's Priest's Tale*. It is suggested that Dryden's poem is an extreme exemplification of, and provided a model for, the reading process of many in the eighteenth century: Chaucer's lines and Chaucer's narratives connected themselves with an extraordinary *variety* of books and events, ancient and modern.

The second part of the book considers the early eighteenth-century revival of poetical, critical, and editorial interest in *The Canterbury Tales* in general, and in the characters of the *General Prologue* and of the comic tales in particular— an interest expressed in the composition of a series of poems exhibiting various relationships with their originals. Chapter 5 examines some of these versions in general, and in particular a translation of the *General Prologue* attributed to Thomas Betterton and published by Alexander Pope. Various versions of the *Merchant's*, *Shipman's*, *Miller's*, and *Reeve's Tales* are discussed in Chapter 6, and of the *Wife of Bath's Prologue* and *Tale* in Chapter 7. Chapter 8 contains a discussion of the traces of Chaucer's works and of Chaucer's reception in Johnson's *Dictionary*. The Chaucer whose traces were strongest in the first half of the eighteenth century, it is suggested, was the poet who was felt, as Johnson put it, to have 'shewed life in its native colours'.

If the attention of many poets, readers, and editors was devoted to the comic or naturalistic *Canterbury Tales*, secondary but nearly equal attention was given to some poems considered to be 'romances' and to a number of poems not now included in the Chaucerian canon. Various responses to, and representations of, these works are examined in Part III. Chapter 9 discusses versions of Chaucerian or pseudo-Chaucerian dream visions, complaints, and poems depicting *Courts of Love* by John Dryden, Arthur Maynwaring, John Dart, and William Wordsworth. Chapter 10 considers various responses to *The Squire's Tale* and to the *Tale of Sir Thopas* in the context of more general discussions of the virtues and inanities of 'romance'. Chapter 11 is devoted to the versions by Pope and Jane Brereton of *The House of Fame*. Various models of the process by which 'fame' might endure are tested against the evidence so far provided.

Chapter 12, the final chapter, offers a glance at the afterlives of the eighteenth-century afterlives. It attempts to survey the various accounts of Chaucer current and interacting in the minds of readers in the closing years of the eighteenth century and the early years of the nineteenth century, particularly those of Thomas Tyrwhitt, William Lipscomb, George Ellis, William Wordsworth, William Godwin, Charles Cowden Clarke, and Leigh Hunt.

The discussion of the 'Multitudes ... Who pass, repass, advance, and glide away' sometimes takes a meandering path, descending to self-proclaimed ephemera, and in one place to the erotic publications of the unrelievedly disreputable Edmund Curll. But the general direction follows Pope's remarks to his friend Joseph Spence—'It is easy to mark out the general course of our poetry, Chaucer, Spenser, Milton, and Dryden, are the great landmarks for it'—together with Spence's suggestion that Pope's 'own name added to the four he mentioned would complete the series of our great poets in general'.[40] The eighteenth-century response to Chaucer, both scholarly and creative, as we have seen in this Introduction, has been regularly

---

[40] Spence, *Observations, Anecdotes, and Characters*, 1. 178.

dismissed, by-passed, or travestied. It is, indeed, as we have seen, full of paradoxes, oddities, imperfections, and contradictions. But at its best it manifests an engagement with Chaucer's work that is profoundly rich in insight, both into Chaucer's poetry itself, and into the larger processes by which, at any time, the poetry of the past is given new life in the present.

PART I
CHAUCER IN 1700

1

Chaucer and the Progress of Poetry

The Seventeenth-Century Bequest

The 'Testimonies of Learned Men concerning Chaucer and his Works' which occupy eleven double-column folio pages in John Urry's edition of *The Works of Geoffrey Chaucer* give every appearance of having been compiled with care.[1] Where Thomas Speght's editions (1598, 1602, 1687) had summarized the 'Judgements and Reports of some learned men of this worthy and famous Poet' almost as an addendum—in 1598 under the heading 'His Death'—and had ended with those of Sidney and Spenser, the 'Testimonies' in Urry's volume are presented as a series of quotations, scrupulously referenced, and range from John Gower, John Lydgate, and Thomas Hoccleve to Thomas Rymer and John Dryden. The eighteenth-century compiler selected several testimonies from the seventeenth century, but also provided a fuller account of the sixteenth-century record.

If there is a common assumption governing the 'Testimonies', it would seem to be that represented by George Puttenham's calling Chaucer the 'father of our English Poets', a term which was regularly used from Hoccleve, in the Prologue to his Book 'De *Regimine* Princeps', who writes of 'mayster *Chaucer*' as his 'fadir reverent', to Dryden in the Preface to his *Fables*, who expresses veneration for Chaucer as 'the Father of *English* Poetry'. The term 'father' is, however, used by the different authors quoted in different senses and with different applications. Chaucer is, in the various accounts, the father of various things—sometimes of Protestantism, sometimes of learning and expressiveness generally, sometimes of the English language itself. Even those writers who call him 'the Father of *English* Poetry' present him sometimes as the father of *all* English poetry, and sometimes as one of several founding figures. Hoccleve's *fadir* forms part of a respectful address to a revered and well-known teacher. In the 'Anonymous Verses taken by Mr. *Speght* out of a Book of Mr. *Stow*'s', Chaucer is numbered, with Gower, among the 'Fathers and

---

[1] It is not certain who made the compilation. William Thomas, who revised the 'Life of Geoffrey Chaucer' and assisted his brother Thomas with the 'Glossary', is the most likely candidate. In the closing sentence of the 'Life' the 'Reader is refer'd' to 'the following Testimonies for a fuller account of the Judgement of Learned Men both in *Chaucer*'s time and since, concerning Him and his Works' (Urry, Fol. f1ᵛ).

Chaucer in the Eighteenth Century. David Hopkins and Tom Mason, Oxford University Press.
© David Hopkins and Tom Mason (2022). DOI: 10.1093/oso/9780192862624.003.0002

founders of enornat eloquence, / That enlumined have our grete Britaine'.[2] Here, linguistic and poetical fatherhood run together. Sir Richard Baker is cited, in one place, as calling Chaucer 'the *Homer* of our Nation', but in another Chaucer is linked with Gower, as by the anonymous writer recorded by Stow, as one of the 'two famous Poets in this time [of Henry IV] and the Fathers of English Poets in all the times after'.[3] The nature of Chaucer's 'fatherhood' in the various testimonies is neither obvious nor particularized.

Edmund Spenser's Chaucerian Paternity

In Speght's first two editions (1598 and 1602), Chaucer's principal 'fatherhood' had been related to poets of Speght's own time, and the effects of Chaucer's 'fatherhood' in one particular case—that of Edmund Spenser—had been clear and indisputable.[4] Such a situation perhaps became even clearer to Speght between 1598 and 1602. In the introductory letter 'F. B. to his very loving friend, T. S.' included in Speght's 1598 edition, it had been said that

> Maister *Spencer*, following the counsaile of *Tullie in de Oratore*, for reuiuing of antient words, hath adorned his owne stile with that beauty and grauitie, which Tully speakes of: and his much frequenting of *Chaucers* antient speeches causeth many to allow farre better of him, then otherwise they would.[5]

The last phrases here perhaps imply that Spenser had been overvalued on account of his borrowing of old words from Chaucer. Such a possibility, however, is clearly dismissed in 1602, where the influence of Chaucer on Spenser is presented in unequivocally positive terms:

> … his much frequenting of *Chaucers* auncient words, with his excellent imitation of diverse places in him, is not the least helpe that hath made him reach so hie, as many learned men doe thinke, that no Poet either French or Italian deserues a second place under him.[6]

The alteration (presumably Speght's own)[7] does not go into further detail, but describes Spenser both as having absorbed Chaucer's vocabulary and as having imitated Chaucer's poetry to profitable effect in larger ways. Chaucer's 'fathering'

---

[2] Urry, Sig. g[v].
[3] Ibid. Sig. i[r].
[4] For a general account of the relations between Chaucer and Spenser, see John Burrow, 'Chaucer', in *The Spenser Encyclopedia*, ed. A. C. Hamilton et al. (London, 1996), pp. 144–8.
[5] Speght 1598, sig. aii[v].
[6] Speght 1602, Sig. aiii[r].
[7] The alteration was noticed by Eleanore Prescott Hammond in *Chaucer: A Bibliographical Manual* (New York, 1933), p. 126 and is discussed by Alice S. Miskimin in *The Renaissance Chaucer* (New Haven, CT, 1975), p. 255.

of Spenser, Speght clearly thought, was one of the main factors that had given Spenser an advantage over his chief European poetic rivals.

In Urry's 'Testimonies', the number of quotations from Spenser was extended, almost filling a page. But Spenser's is no longer the deciding testimony, and Spenser's authority and Chaucer's reflected excellence are no longer assumed to be unquestionable. In Speght's editions, almost all the testimonia on Chaucer were offered as unqualified encomia. But the fuller 'Testimonies' presented by Urry give more scope for the various 'Learned Men' to speak in their own voices and to disagree with one another. Speght's 'Life' of Chaucer had ended with a quotation from Sidney:

> Sir *Philip Sidney*, in his Apology for Poetry, saith thus of him; Chaucer undoubtedly did excellently in his *Troilus* and *Creseid*; of whom truly I know not whether to marvel more, either that he in that misty time could see so clearly, or that we in this clear Age, walk so stumblingly after him.[8]

In 1721, Sidney's words stand on their own, and the quotation is continued for one significant sentence: 'Yet had he great wants, fit to be forgiven in so reverent an Antiquitie'.[9] There are similar implications in other instances where Spenser is differently presented by Speght and Urry. Speght had reported Spenser's response to Chaucer thus:

> Dan Chaucer, Well of English, undefiled
> On Fames eternal beadrole worthy to be filed.
> I follow here the footing of thy feet,
> That with thy meaning so I may the rather meet.
>
> (Speght 1598, Sig. ciii^v)

But his Spenserian passage had been constructed by combining the final couplets from stanzas xxx and xxxiii of Canto 2 of Book IV of *The Fairy Queen*. Urry also printed in full the intervening lament of stanza xxxii:

> But wicked Time that all good thoughts doth waste,
> And works of noblest Wits to nought out-weare,
> That famous Monument hath quite defac'd,
> And robb'd the world of treasure endless dear,
> The which might have enriched all us here.
> O cursed Eld! the Canker-worm of Wits,
> How may these Rhymes (so rude as doth appear)
> Hope to endure, sith works of heavenly Wits
> Are quite devour'd, and brought to nought by little bits?
>
> (Urry, Sig. h2^r)

---

[8] Speght 1687, Sig. B2^v.
[9] Urry, Sig. H^r.

Urry's quotation highlights the ways in which the effects of Chaucer's poetic 'fatherhood', particularly in the sphere of vocabulary and diction, had been seen, even by his poetic 'son' Spenser, as more potentially problematic than Speght had been willing to allow. This can be partly attributed to a number of literary developments that had occurred between Spenser and the early eighteenth century, to which we should now turn.

Purity of Language, Depredations of Time, and the Animadversions of Thomas Rymer

It was clear from many of the 'Testimonies' included in Urry's edition that Chaucer's poems, like all sublunary things, had been subject to depredations of all-destroying time more extensive than Spenser's immediate subject of lament, the loss of the continuation of *The Squire's Tale*. The 'Canker-worme of Wits' had, they showed, eaten away at several parts of Chaucer's fame. Even Spenser's proposition that Chaucer's English constituted a well of English undefiled had been questioned. At the foot of the right-hand column of the page devoted to quotations from Spenser is a quotation from the Anglo-Dutch antiquary, Richard Verstegan (*c*. 1550–1640), who observes that Chaucer has been 'of some called the first illuminator to the English tongue', but begs to dissent:

> Of their opinion I am not, though I reverence *Chaucer*, as an excellent Poet for his time. He was indeed a great mingler of English with French.[10]

Verstegen's remarks presented readers of Urry's volume with two propositions limiting the case for Chaucer's fatherhood. One is that poetical excellence is historically contingent: Chaucer was excellent 'for his time'. Chaucer's effect on the language is not doubted, but he is seen as having corrupted rather than adorned or refined the tongue. Verstegen's opinion was endorsed in the 'Testimonies' by a quotation from the etymologist and lexicographer Stephen Skinner (1623–67):

> By his very example Chaucer the poet almost ruined the native grace and elegance of our language—it had much earlier been adulterated by the Norman conquest—when he brought in whole wagonloads of words from that same French.[11]

It was presumably as a contribution to the debate about Chaucer's language that Urry's 'Testimonies' included two passages from Thomas Rymer's *Short View of Tragedy* (1693):

---

[10] Urry, Sig. h2^r.
[11] Ibid. Sig. i^r. Urry quotes Skinner in Latin. The translation above is taken from Johnson, *Works*, 18. 183.

Chaucer found an Herculanean labour on his hands; and did perform to admiration. He seizes all Provencal, French or Latin that came in his way, gives them a new garb and livery, and mingles them amongst our English: turns out English gowty, or super-annuated, to place in their room the foreigners, fit for service, train'd and accustomed to Poetical Discipline.

    Chaucer threw in Latin, French, Provencal, and other Languages, like new Stum to raise a Fermentation: In Queen *Elizabeth*'s time it grew fine, but came not to an Head and Spirit, did not shine and sparkle till Mr. *Waller* set it a running.[12]

The mention of 'Poetical Discipline' in the first extract, and of 'Mr. Waller' in the second, suggest that Rymer's concern was, in large part, *metrical,* and was significantly related to recent thinking about that subject. The compiler of Urry's 'Testimonies' had, in fact, been selective in his quotations from Rymer, and, as Thomas Pope Blount recorded, Rymer had also observed that 'Our Language retain'd something of the Churl; something of the *Stiff* and *Gothish* did stick upon it, till long after *Chaucer*', and, indeed, did *not* 'Shine and Sparkle, till Mr. *Waller* set it a *running*'.[13] For Rymer, as for several of his contemporaries, Chaucer's apparent metrical stiffness, lumbering rusticity ('something of the Churl'), and near-barbarism ('*Gothish*') had had severely limiting consequences. Where Spenser had said that Chaucer was a 'Heroical Poet', Rymer dissented. In his Preface to his translation of René Rapin's *Reflexions on Aristotle's Treatise of Poesie* (1674), Rymer had been at pains to justify the potential, 'the weight, the fullness, the vigour, force, gravity, and the fitness of the *English* for *Heroick Poesie*', and to justify the claims of the English Language against those of other modern European languages, but had been unable to include examples of any forbears older than Spenser, 'the first of our *Heroick Poets*':

> Nor shall I speak of *Chaucer*, in whose time our Language, I presume, was not capable of any Heroick Character.[14]

That versification was again uppermost in Rymer's thoughts is clear from his remarks here on French alexandrines, which, he says, 'are too faint and languishing, and attain not the *numerosity*, which the dignity of Heroick Verse requires, and which is ordinary in an *English* Verse of *ten syllables*'.[15]

---

[12] Urry, Sig. iv.

[13] Sir Thomas Pope Blount, *De Re Poetica: Or, Remarks upon Poetry, with Characters and Censures of the Most Considerable Poets, Whether Ancient or Modern, Extracted Out of the Best and Choicest Criticks* (London, 1694), p. 247.

[14] René Rapin, *Reflections on Aristotle's Treatise of Poesie*, trans. Thomas Rymer (London, 1694), Sigs A6ᵛ–A7ʳ. Spenser, though, Rymer thought, 'wanted a true *Idea*' with the result that 'All is fanciful and chimerical, without any uniformity, without any foundation in truth, his Poem is perfect *Fairy-land*.'

[15] Ibid. Sig. A6ʳ.

Edmund Waller, Francis Atterbury, and Thomas Pope Blount

The key term in this discussion appears to be *numerosity*.[16] There were many seventeenth-century accounts of the course of poetry and of the development of the language which suggested, with Rymer, that if Chaucer had been the *first* refiner, or fermenter, of metrical English, the process of refinement, or fermentation, had continued. Chaucer had started a process that had culminated in the language, and particularly the verse, of the immediate present—the exemplary representative of which had formerly been Edmund Spenser, but was now Edmund Waller. Thomas Rymer and Thomas Pope Blount were not alone in pointing most directly to the poems of Waller when describing the point at which the English language first became 'capable of any Heroick character'. Blount writes with greater warmth of Waller than of any other poet, ancient or modern. Waller's 'Name', he says, 'will ever be dear to all Lovers of *Poetry*' because his mere name 'carries every thing in it, that's either Great or Graceful in *Poetry*'. Most importantly for the present argument Waller, rather than any predecessor, is seen by several seventeenth-century commentators as the effective *inventor* of these qualities: 'He was indeed the Parent of *English* Verse, and the First that shew'd us our Tongue had Beauty and Numbers in it.'[17] John Dryden had suggested in 1664 that 'the excellence and dignity' of rhyme were 'never fully known till Mr, Waller taught it'.[18] In 1691, he had gone further in proclaiming Waller '*the Father of our* English *Numbers*'.[19]

One poem, although composed in tetrameters rather than in the more heroic ten syllables desiderated by Rymer, was sometimes pointed to both as exemplary of the new versification and as describing its *necessity*. Waller's poem 'Of English Verse', first published in Sir John Denham's *Poems, &c. Written upon Several Occasions* (1668), was cited by several writers as an authoritative statement of the inevitability and concomitant debilitations of linguistic change. In his edition of *The Works of Mr. Edmund Spenser* (1715), John Hughes prefixed some remarks on Spenser's language and the destructive passage of time with a paraphrase of Waller's poem:

> It is a Misfortune, as Mr *Waller* observes, which attends the Writers of *English* Poetry, that they can hardly expect their Works shou'd last long in a Tongue which is daily changing; that whilst they are new, Envy is apt to prevail against them; and as that wears off, our Language it self fails. Our Poets therefore, he says, shou'd imitate

---

[16] The term was taken up by Thomas Morell, trans. and ed., *Poems on Divine Subjects. Original and Translated from the Latin of M. Hl. Vida and M. A. Flaminio* (London, 1732), p. xxv: 'An exact Numerosity … was not Chaucer's main Care; but that he had sometimes a greater Regard for the Sense, than the Metre.'

[17] Blount, *De Re Poetica*, p. 243.

[18] 'To Roger, Earl of Orrery', prefixed to *The Rival Ladies*, 1664 (Dryden, *Works*, 1. 100).

[19] Preface to Walsh's *Dialogue Concerning Women*, 1691 (Dryden, *Works*, 20. 3).

judicious Staturies, that chuse the most durable Materials, and shou'd carve in *Latin* or *Greek*, if they wou'd have their Labour preserv'd for ever.[20]

This account, and similar ones, of Waller's poem is odd in that it describes, as if it were a solemn treatise, a poem which proclaims its own slightness, lightness, and apparent ephemerality. For, alongside his reflections on the changeability of language, Waller may have been thinking of *The Court of Love* (see Chapter 9), where the poet—believed by all to be by the supposed Cambridge undergraduate Chaucer—wins from Rosalinda an acceptance of his love by means of a demonstration of poetic excellence:[21]

> *Of English Verse.*
>
> Poets may boast [as safely vain]
> Their work shall with the world remain
> Both bound together, live or dye,
> The Verses and the Prophecy.
>   But who can hope his lines should long
> Last in a daily changing Tongue?
> While they are new, envy prevails,
> And as that dies, our Language fails;
>   When Architects have done their part
> The Matter may betray their Art,
> Time, if we use ill-chosen stone,
> Soon brings a well-built Palace down.
>   Poets that lasting Marble seek,
> Must carve in *Latine*, or in *Greek*
> We write in Sand, our Language grows,
> And like the Tide our work o'er flows.
>   *Chaucer* his Sense can only boast,
> The glory of his numbers lost,
> Years have defac'd his matchless strain,
> And yet he did not sing in vain,
>   The Beauties which adorn'd that age
> The shining Subjects of his rage,
> Hoping they should immortal prove
> Rewarded with success his love,
>   This was the generous Poets scope
> And all an *English* Pen can hope,
> To make the fair approve his Flame
> That can so far extend their Fame
>   Verse thus design'd has no ill fate
> If it arrive but at the Date

---

[20] R. M. Cummings, ed., *Edmund Spenser: The Critical Heritage* (London, 1971), p. 248.
[21] Waller's poem is given here in the arbitrarily punctuated text of the first printing.

> Of fading Beauty, if it prove
> But as long liv'd as present love.
>
> (pp. 234–5)

Waller's suggestion is not that particular words have become unintelligible. The 'sense' that the 'Beauties' of Chaucer's age so admired remains. It is *numerosity* that has been lost. The mention of 'a daily changing Tongue' may imply that Waller was thinking partly of the sound and pronunciation of words. He has guessed that Chaucer's verse was once thought beautiful but is not so now. Where Spenser had lamented—with the loss of *The Squire's Tale* particularly in mind—that the 'famous Monument' of Chaucer's Work had been 'quite defac'd' by Time, for Waller 'Years have defac'd' Chaucer's matchless strain'. The 'glory of his numbers' has been entirely lost.

Discussions of seventeenth-century and eighteenth-century comments on Chaucer's versification sometimes imply that the difficulties which writers of that period found chiefly turned on the question of sounding or not sounding a final -*e*, a problem that, it is said, vanished with the publication of Thomas Tyrwhitt's edition of *The Canterbury Tales* in 1775. This assumption will be questioned in later chapters of the present study. For the moment, the crucial point is that for Waller, the governing metaphors concern the power of the *new*. Where the ill-chosen stone of the architect crumbles on account of its own fragility, the sand in which an English poet writes is drowned or washed away by a sea of new words. Chaucer's old versification has been replaced by a new versification—one which Waller himself has brought into being and is exemplifying in this very poem.

Because admiration for Waller, and comparisons in which his versification is favoured over Chaucer's have seemed ridiculous and inexplicable to many readers in later generations, it should be noted that much more was required by admirers of Waller than equality of syllables: five—or in this case, four—clearly iambic feet. The new versification was not merely mechanical. If it avoided the '*Gothish*', it was the opposite of the '*Stiff*'. While the language does not perhaps, in Rymer's and Blount's terms, 'Shine and Sparkle', it is clearly set 'a *running*'. Waller's assumption is that if his words are pronounced exactly as in speech, the metre will both establish itself and guide the voice—and the mind. Elision, and contraction are allowed ('the gen'rous Poet's scope'), as well as the substitution of initial trochaic for iambic feet.

Francis Atterbury, in his Preface to *The Second Part of Mr. Waller's Poems* (1690), pointed to several ways in which Waller had shown how verse could be made easier to read—and read aloud—and easier to follow: 'the new turn of verse which he brought in, and the improvement he made in our numbers'. Waller's improvements were that he

> brought in more polysyllables, and smoother measures, bound up his thoughts better, and in a cadence more agreeable to the nature of the Verse he wrote in; so that wherever the natural stops of that were, he contrived the little breakings of his sense so as to fall in with 'em.[22]

Particularly appropriate to Waller's lines on Chaucer perhaps are Atterbury's and Sir Thomas Pope Blount's comments on Waller's alignment of the 'Natural Stops' of verse and the 'little breakings of his sense':

> Since the stress of *Our* Verse lyes commonly upon the last Syllable, you'll hardly ever find him using a Word of no Force there. I would say, if I were not afraid the Reader would think me too nice, that he commonly closes with *Verbs*, in which we know the life of Language consists.[23]

In Waller's 'Of English Verse', it may be noted, the following verbs are rhyme-words: *remain, die, prevails, fails, seek, grows, flows, boast,* and *prove.* And polysyllabic words appear in sufficient numbers to sustain the iambic pattern amongst unruly monosyllables and teach them 'Poetical Discipline'. Of the three purely monosyllabic lines, two are unremarkable ('And, like the Tide, our work o'er flows', 'And yet he did not sing in vain'), but one appears to withhold its own metrical completion: 'But who can hope his lines should long / Last'. Another run-on line is used to almost exactly opposite effect, making it as impossible to rest on the line ending than on the moment signifying the terminus of female loveliness: 'Verse, thus design'd, has no ill fate / If it arrive but at the Date / Of fading Beauty'. This may serve as a reminder that when Dryden had suggested in 1664 that Waller 'first made Writing easily an Art: First shew'd us to conclude the Sense, most commonly, in Distichs', the qualification 'most commonly' is important.[24] Waller offered as many permissions as prescriptions. The appearance of ease is artfully preserved. No two lines in this poem have identical metrical patterns. Pauses are varied. Even when a medial pause divides two successive lines into equal, four-syllable hemistichs, the iambic pattern is severely disrupted:

> While they are new | envy prevails,
> And as thát díes| our Language fails.

In the light of such observations, it is perhaps not clear why Waller would have regarded Chaucer's 'matchless strain' as having been essentially different in kind from his own.

---

[22] Francis Atterbury, ed., *The Second Part of Mr. Waller's Poems* (London, 1694), Sig. A6ʳ.
[23] Blount, *De Re Poetica*, p. 247.
[24] 'To Roger, Earl of Orrery', prefixed to *The Rival Ladies*, 1664 (Dryden, *Works*, 1. 100).

Waller's poem was, however, self-defeating, in that it struck its readers, for more than a hundred years, as having defied the laws it invoked. Waller's chosen vocabulary, and therefore his chosen metre, did not seem to have dated. The 'beauties' of *his* 'numbers' were not 'lost'. New words had not 'overflowed' his vocabulary. Atterbury's Preface, again, represents a common impression that Waller had made permanent discoveries *within* the English language:

> 'tis a surprizing Reflection, that between what *Spencer* wrote last, and *Waller* first, there should not be much above twenty years distance: and yet the one's Language, like the Money of that time, is as currant now as ever; whilst the other's words are like old Coyns, one must go to an Antiquary to understand their true meaning and value … He complains indeed of a Tyde of words that comes in upon the *English* Poet, o'reflows whate're he builds: but this was less his case than any mans, that ever wrote; and the mischief on't is, this very complaint will last long enough to confute it self. For though *English* be mouldring Stone, as he tells us there; yet he has certainly pick'd the best out of a bad Quarry.[25]

Thomas Pope Blount repeated Atterbury's comments, considering that Waller 'undoubtedly stands first in the List of Refiners, and for ought I know, last too', on the grounds that '*English*' may have come to 'full Perfection' in Waller's hands 'in *Charles* the *Second*'s Reign'.[26]

But John Hughes maintained in 1715 that Chaucer and Spenser were exceptions to the claims of Waller's 'Of English Verse'. The intrinsic value, the 'native Strength' of these writers had defied and would continue to defy the injury of Time:

> Notwithstanding the Disadvantage he has mention'd, we have two Antient *English* Poets, *Chaucer* and *Spenser*, who may perhaps be reckon'd as Exceptions to this Remark. These seem to have taken deep Root, like old *British* Oaks, and to flourish in defiance of all Injuries of Time and Weather. The former is indeed much more obsolete in his Stile than the latter; but it is owing to an extraordinary native Strength in both, that they have been able thus far to survive amidst the Changes of our Tongue, and seem rather likely, among the Curious at least, to preserve the Knowledg of our Antient Language, than to be in danger of being destroy'd with it, and bury'd under its Ruins.[27]

Chaucer's language would not die because the 'Curious' would learn his words and pass on their understanding to others. Many other writers were less sure. For some, the claims of the present were paramount and irresistible. In several poems describing the progress or course of English poetry, Chaucer's poetical 'fatherhood' is pushed ever further into misty antiquity.

---

[25] *The Second Part of Mr. Waller's Poems*, Sig. A4ᵛ–A5ʳ.
[26] Blount, *De Re Poetica*, p. 244.
[27] Cummings, *Edmund Spenser: The Critical Heritage*, p. 248.

Michael Drayton on Chaucer and Spenser

A continuous account of English poetry can be found in Michael Drayton's 'To my most Dearely-loved friend Henery Reynolds Esquire, Of Poets and Poesie', included in *The Battaile of Agincourt* (1627), where Drayton reports the account that his tutor gave him (then 'a proper goodly page, / Much like a Pigmy, scarce ten yeares of age') of the poets he will need to study in order to become a poet himself. Though these include 'Princely *Surrey*' and '*Wyat* with reuerence, whom we still do name / Amongst our Poets', it was, as Drayton saw it, Chaucer who was the first English poet to discover the poetic possibilities of the English language:

> That noble *Chaucer*, in those former times,
> The first inrich'd our *English* with his rimes,
> And was the first of ours, that ever brake,
> Into the *Muses* treasure, and first spake
> In weighty numbers, delving in the Mine
> Of perfect knowledge, which he could refine,
> And coyne for currant, and as much as then
> The *English* language could expresse to men,
> He made it doe; and by his wondrous skill,
> Gave us much light from his abundant quill.
>
> (Michael Drayton, *The Battaile of Agincourt*
> [London, 1627], p. 205)

Drayton discriminates carefully between Chaucer and his contemporary John Gower, who, he says, 'fell far short of the others store'. There is, however, some slight reservation even in the account of Chaucer. Chaucer had made the language do 'as much as then / The *English* language could expresse'—the implication being that *since then* the 'English language' had been able to 'expresse' *more*. Spenser, as Drayton sees it, was second only to Homer:

> Grave morrall *Spencer* after these came on
> Then whom I am perswaded there was none
> Since the blind Bard his *Iliads* up did make,
> Fitter a taske like that to undertake,
> To set downe boldly, bravely to invent,
> In all high knowledge, surely excellent.
>
> (Drayton, *The Battaile of Agincourt*, pp. 205–6)

George Daniel: 'Nor Let Vs Call Him Father Anie More'

The difficulties of comparing the history of classical poetry with the history of verse in the English language and of allowing any ancient *English* author to be the father of present poets were perhaps most fully admitted by only one writer, George Daniel.[28] In one poem (composed c. 1646), 'An Essay; Endeavouring to

---

[28] Daniel's poems are preserved in a folio volume now in the British Library (Add. MS 19255), which was edited in four privately printed volumes by A. B. Grosart in 1878.

Ennoble our English Poesie by Evidence of Latter Qvills; and reiecting the former', Daniel addressed the problem directly:

> Shall wee derive
> Our English fflame, our Glories Primitive
> From antique Chaucer? Blesse me witt, if right
> Were onlie right, I feare a present night
> Would cover all his Credit.

Chaucer, Daniel suggests, is merely antique; his merits are obscured by the present. In contrast, the very earliest writers of 'antique Greece' had been 'Verdant and glorious' and 'not lesse flourishing' at the 'first rise then after'. The works of Homer

> Shine
> Even to these Times of ours, with Light Devine?
> ffull in exalted Rapture, Poesie
> Appeares in them almost a Prodigie.

The same can be said of 'the Catalogue of Splendent Rome' whose poets 'we iustlie Call / The learned Fathers of Apolloe's Hall'. It appears that, for Daniel, Chaucer's disqualifications as a true father of English poetry include a failure to rise to an elevated notion of the function of poetry:

> Where doth he rouse
> The fresh prun'd ffeathers of an Active Muse?

Daniel concedes that 'our Grandsires Laugh'd once at his Baud'rie / Laid out in Rime; (forsooth rare Poetrie!)', but contends that Chaucer

> doth not rise
> Like ancient Poets, in huge Extasies
> Of vncontrolléd ffancie, to Survay
> Inestimable Nature.

As Daniel saw it, a number of more recent English poets had risen to this position; English poetry, properly so called, began with Sidney, entered into full glory with Spenser, and reached perfection with Ben Jonson, a perfection continued in the work of Waller and Denham: 'these iustly wee may call / Fathers; high-placed in Apolloe's Hall'.[29] These poets are the inheritors of the 'Light Devine' of the Latin and Greek poets. It is in comparison with these that Chaucer is declared 'in-authenticke':

> Chaucer's furnishment
> Adds nothing to our Poesie, in his Store;
> Nor let vs call him Father anie more.

---

[29] See Cummings, *Edmund Spenser: The Critical Heritage*, p. 83.

George Daniel seems to have been the only writer to deny Chaucer's 'fatherhood' of English poetry outright. Some other poets may have entertained similar sentiments but kept them quiet. Chaucer's name continues to appear in the list of chosen poets in most poems describing the progress of poetry. Some lines from one of these poets, Sir John Denham—whose verse, as we have seen, represented for Daniel the culmination of the English verse tradition—were included in the 'Testimonies' in Urry's edition of Chaucer:

> Old *Chaucer*, like the Morning Star,
> To us discovers Day from far,
> His Light those Mists and Clouds dissolv'd,
> Which our dark Nation long involv'd;
> But he descending to the shades,
> Darkness again the Age invades.
> Next (like *Aurora*) *Spencer* rose,
> Whose purple Blush the Day foreshews.[30]
>
> (Urry, Sig. h2ᵛ)

Denham, presumably recording the experience of his own generation, sees the progress of poetry as one where the fifteenth century and most of the sixteenth were a second Dark Age. Although Jonson and Shakespeare are praised alongside Spenser, Denham's poem sees Abraham Cowley (a self-declared poetical son of Spenser) as the culmination of all.

Addison's Contempt

What seems to have happened at the end of the seventeenth century, however, was that Spenser's verse-music was felt by many to have been an improvement upon all that had gone before, but to have itself become antiquated. Chaucer's eloquence appeared clumsy beside Spenser's, and Spenser's appeared clumsy beside the work of modern poets. Spenser's poetry, rather than resisting the depredations of time, had contributed to making Chaucer appear as unreachably ancient as he did to Joseph Addison in *An Account of the Greatest English Poets* (1694). Addison's addressee, Henry Sacheverell, had asked for a 'short Account' of all those who have 'spent their Noble Rage in British Rhimes' from 'Chaucer's days to Dryden's Times'. Addison accepted the general consensus that English poetry began with Chaucer:

> Long had our dull Fore-Fathers slept Supine,
> Nor felt the Raptures of the Tuneful Nine;

---

[30] The lines are from Denham's *On Mr Abraham Cowley, His Death and Burial amongst the Ancient Poets*, first printed in 1667.

> Till *Chaucer* first, a merry *Bard*, arose;
> And many a Story told in Rhime and Prose.

He found, however, little to enjoy in Chaucer's works:

> ... Age has Rusted what the *Poet* writ,
> Worn out his Language, and obscur'd his Wit:
> In vain he jests in his unpolish'd strain,
> And tries to make his Readers laugh in vain.

For Addison, Chaucer resembled an ageing, perhaps rustic, comedian whose timing and delivery had gone, and was at several removes of antiquity from the glorious achievements of Addison's poetic present. Spenser had not fared much better than Chaucer in Addison's mind:

> Old *Spencer* next, warm'd with Poetick Rage,
> In Antick Tales amus'd a Barb'rous Age;
> An Age that yet uncultivate and Rude,
> Where-e're the Poet's Fancy led, pursu'd
> Through pathless Fields, and unfrequented Floods,
> To Dens of Dragons, and Enchanted Woods.

The telling phrase here is, perhaps, 'Barb'rous Age'. Addison regards himself and his friend as altogether too sophisticated, too adult, to be pleased by the fancies of any age except the present:

> But now the Mystick Tale, that pleas'd of Yore,
> Can Charm an understanding Age no more
> The long-spun Allegories fulsom grow,
> While the dull Moral lies too plain below.
>
> (*The Annual Miscellany: For the Year 1694*
> [London, 1694], pp. 318–19)

Addison shows in *An Account of the Greatest English Poets* that he had read Cowley and Milton with great attention. But Pope thought that similar care had not been lavished by Addison on either Chaucer or Spenser. He told Joseph Spence that Addison had written this poem

when he was very young; and as such, gave the characters of some of our best poets in it, only by hearsay. Thus his character of Chaucer is diametrically opposite to the truth; he blames him for want of humour. The character of Spenser is false too; and I have heard him say, that he never read Spenser till fifteen years after he wrote it.[31]

---

[31] Joseph Spence, *Observations, Anecdotes and Characters of Books and Men*, ed. James Osborn, 2 vols (Oxford, 1966), 1. 58.

Samuel Cobb and Ennius

There were young men besides Addison in the last decades of the seventeenth century for whom Spenser had begun to appear merely antiquated. Samuel Cobb, looking back, in his poem *Poetæ Britannici* (1700), at the course of English poetry, gave a version of what became the conventional literary history—deriving from a story about Virgil who, asked why he was reading the antiquated Roman poet Ennius, responded that he was 'gathering of gold out of Ennius's dunghill':

> … *Chaucer* rose, and pointed out the Day.
> A Joking Bard, whose Antiquated Muse
> In mouldy Words could Solid sense produce.
> Our *English Ennius* He, who claim'd his part
> In wealthy Nature, tho' unskill'd in Art.
> The sparkling Diamond on his Dung-hill shines,
> And Golden Fragments glitter in his Lines.
> Which *Spencer* gather'd, for his Learning known,
> And by successful Gleanings made his own.

For Cobb, however, Spenser's veneration of Chaucer was a doubtful blessing. Spenser's Chaucer-derived lexicon had been properly rejected and corrected by Ben Jonson:

> He cull'd and pick'd, and thought it greater praise,
> T'adore his Master, than improve his Phrase.
> 'Twas counted Sin to deviate from his Page;
> So Sacred was th' Authority of Age!
> The Coin must sure for currant Sterling pass,
> Stamp'd with old *Chaucer's* Venerable Face.
> But *Johnson* found it of a gross Allay,
> Melted it down, and flung the Scum away.
> He dug pure Silver from a *Roman* Mine,
> And prest his Sacred Image on the Coin.
> We all rejoic'd to see the pillag'd Ore;
> Our Tongue inrich'd, which was so poor before.
>
> (Samuel Cobb, *Poetæ Britannici*
> [London, 1700], pp. 10–11)

In the closing years of the seventeenth century, Chaucer's standing was equivocal, and his fatherhood doubtful. For many readers, his position resembled that of Ennius to the Romans rather than Homer to all succeeding poets. The odd line, phrase, plot, or thought might be borrowed, but he could no longer serve as a model of any kind. There were others, like Sir Aston Cokain and Thomas Fuller, who invoked Ennius more positively.[32] But for many, Chaucer was a precursor rather than actively a father of modern English poetry. For some poets, it was not clear whether the difficulties presented by Chaucer's verse were to be attributed to changes in language or to sheer *ineptitude*. This was the suggestion of Samuel Wesley in *An Epistle to a Friend concerning Poetry* (1700):

> Of CHAUCER's Verse we scarce the *Measures* know,
> So *rough* the *Lines*, and so *unequal* flow;
> Whether by Injury of *Time* defac'd,
> Or *careless* at the *first*, and writ in *haste*;
> Or *coursly*, like old *Ennius*, he *design*'d
> What After-days have *polish'd* and *refin'd*.
>
> (p. 12)

If the accounts offered by Samuel Cobb and Samuel Wesley are taken together, they might seem to suggest that by 1700 Chaucer's critical standing had, after years of continuous decline, reached a nadir. That there was no new edition of Chaucer's works for over a hundred years from 1602 would seem to tell its own story. The black-letter reprint in 1687 of Speght's edition was presumably published in response to *some* kind of demand, but that demand may have been of an antiquarian bibliophilic kind, for a handsome, old-looking, near-facsimile volume.[33] The new poets of the seventeenth century—Ben Jonson, Edmund Waller, John Denham, Abraham Cowley, John Milton, John Dryden—had, for many, offered pleasures that could no longer be found in medieval work, or even in Spenser.

Edward Bysshe and Charles Gildon: Chaucer's 'Nature' and 'Antiquated Phrase'

But the case can be exaggerated. If many direct and formal accounts of the progress of poetry present Chaucer's case as increasingly fragile, there are several indirect, incidental and occasional passing references that suggest the opposite: that Chaucer's poems were well known by some, were not found difficult to read, and were thought to offer the immediate pleasures of recognized human truths. In Charles Gildon's, *The Post-Boy Rob'd of his Mail* (1692), each supposedly intercepted letter in the collection is followed by the comments of an imaginary club of Wits. Among the comments on Letter 10 (a lament of a lover) is the following:

---

[32] See Sir Aston Cokain, 'A Remedy for Love', in *Small Poems of Divers Sorts* (London, 1658), p. 8; Thomas Fuller, *The History of the Worthies of England* (London, 1662), p. 65.

[33] Speght 1598 survives in three issues, Speght 1602 in two, but Speght 1687 in only one. The margins and font sizes, from title page to glossary, are far more generously arranged in 1687. For discussion, see Tim William Machan, 'Speght's "Works" and the Invention of Chaucer', *Text*, 8 (1995), 145–70. The text of 1602, however, was not altered in 1687.

as the incomparable Mr. *Dryden* says, *All Objects lose by too familiar view*, certainly ... Absence to him that truly loves must be the greatest of Torments, as Love is the most violent of Passions. As 'tis excellently describ'd by old *Chaucer* ... in his *Knights Tale*:

> His Sleep, his Meat, his Drink is him bereft,
> That lean he waxeth, and dry, as a Shaft;
> His Eyes hollow, and grisly to behold;
> His Hew pale, and Ashen to unfold.
> And solitary he was, ever alone,
> And waking all the night, making moan.

Here indeed ... are all the effects of a desperate Passion, natural, and beautiful, tho' drest in so antiquated a phrase.[34]

The excellence of Chaucer's description, the letter suggests, overrides the antiquity of his language. The description of the physical effects of passion are assumed to be 'natural', and, because natural, beautiful. The quotation from Chaucer is followed by a general truth from Spenser:

> Nought under Heav'n so strongly doth allure
> The Sense of Man, and all his Mind possess,
> As Beautys loveliest Bait, that doth procure
> Great Warriours Rest, their Rigor to suppress,
> And mighty Hands forget their Manliness.

which elicits the comment:

> These Poets ... drew their Picture from Nature; since 'tis evident Love triumphs over our other passions, Ambition it self being forc'd to submit, when once Love opposes it.[35]

Gildon's remarks would seem to imply that he and his readers, like the members of his imaginary club, are familiar with *The Knight's Tale* and well able to perceive the strength of Chaucer's thought and the accuracy of his descriptions despite, or through, the antiquated phrase. It is, however, here as so often, difficult to determine the realities behind the implication. Gildon himself did not often refer to Chaucer; Chaucer's poems do not seem to have come to the forefront of his mind when discussing any pressing critical question, or when composing poetry himself.[36]

---

[34] Charles Gildon, *The Post-Boy Rob'd of His Mail: or, the Pacquet Broke Open* (London, 1692), p. 267 (with italics and roman reversed). The quotation from *KnT* is in black-letter, suggesting that Gildon was using one of the Speght editions.

[35] Ibid. p. 268.

[36] However, in Gildon's poem *Libertas Triumphans* (London, 1708), the 'Harmonious Genius of this Isle, / That on our Ancient Bards were wont to smile' is invoked. The bards in question 'By Nature made capacious' of inspiration are '*Chaucer, Spenser, Milton*'.

Chaucer's name does appear among the poets listed in 'Authors cited in this Book' from whom Gildon was to draw examples of the finest poetry for the second volume of his *Complete Art of Poetry* (1718), but Chaucer's poems are represented only in the versions composed by more recent poets. The mention of Chaucer's name and the exclusion of his verse may seem particularly odd in that Gildon prided himself on having extended his anthology further back in time that those of his predecessor and rival, Edward Bysshe, who had informed readers of his *Art of English Poetry* (1702) that he had omitted Chaucer and Spenser because 'the Garb in which they are Cloath'd, tho' then Alamode, is now become so out of Fashion, that the Readers of our Age have no Ear for them', and that, for similar reasons, even 'the Good *Shakespear* himself is not so frequently Cited' in Bysshe's collection 'as he would otherwise deserve to be'.[37] Gildon, in contrast, included many passages from Shakespeare and Spenser that Bysshe had deemed unsuitable.

The different aims of the two anthologies may explain the difference in emphasis. Bysshe's *Art* was offered as a handbook for aspiring writers of verse. His anthology, he hoped, would be trawled, like his list of rhymes, for epithets and similes that might be immediately incorporated into a modern composition. Gildon, however, was attempting to teach the Art of Poetry in a higher sense. It is, according to Gildon, not the language or the colouring which are the strength of a poem, but the boldness of the thoughts. Bysshe, as Gildon saw it

> aims only at giving Rules for the *Structure* of an *English* Verse, at Rime, and the like. And thus in his Collection, he aims at settling a sort of Dictionary of Epithets and Synonymous Words, which he tells us is the End of his Collection.

while the 'Design' of his own 'Collection'

> is to give the Reader the great *Images* that are to be found in those of our Poets, who are truly great, as well as their Topics and Moral Reflections. And for this Reason I have been pretty large in my Quotations from *Spenser*, whom he [Bysshe] has rejected, and have gone through *Shakespear*, whom he seems willing to exclude, being satisfy'd that the Charms of these two great Poets are too strong not to touch the Soul of any one who has a true Genius for Poetry, and by Consequence enlarge that Imagination which is so very necessary for all Poetical Performances.

Gildon's notion of the progress of poetry depends upon and is an example of this principle. '*Milton* and *Waller* were made Poets by *Spenser*' not only because they borrowed from and copied their predecessor, but because 'the true Ethereal Fire that they found in him, rous'd that Genius, which each of them had by Nature, into Act' (see Fig. 1.1).[38]

---

[37] Edward Bysshe, *The Art of English Poetry* (London, 1702), Sigs *2ᵛ–*3ʳ.
[38] Charles Gildon, *The Complete Art of Poetry*, 2 vols (London, 1718), 1. Sig. a6ᵛ.

Fig. 1.1 Chaucer at the centre of the leading seventeenth-century poets: Samuel Butler, John Milton, Edmund Waller, and Abraham Cowley. Engraving by George Vertue (1717).

The introduction of 'true Etheral Fire' represents a crucial intervention into the discussion. The notion enables Gildon to make a significant transformation of those narratives of the progress of poetry where there was no poetry between Chaucer and Spenser:

Chaucer, Gower, and *Lydgate,* were the first who made any tolerable Figure in that Dress; of whom *Chaucer* is the only one who may justly claim the Name of a Poet. After him, *English* Poetry was totally neglected.[39]

The dress of poetry—vocabulary and versification—that Gower and Lydgate wore was not sufficient to make them true poets. The 'great Images' and 'Moral Reflections' that can be found 'in those of our Poets, who are truly great' are to some degree independent of particular expression. Chaucer's name appears, alongside those of Virgil, Petrarch, Racine, and Boileau, as one of the authors included in the collection of extracts that make up the second volume of Gildon's *Complete Art of Poetry.* But (perhaps in partial contradiction of Gildon's principles) it is only the modern versions of Chaucer by Dryden that are included—many of which also appear in Bysshe.

Samuel Pepys and Chaucer

Despite his equivocal reputation, however, Chaucer was sometimes studied with loving care. One reader who was untroubled by critical dismissals of Chaucer was Samuel Pepys. On 8 July 1664, he collected his copy of Speght 1602 from the binders and 'thence to the clasp-makers to have it clasped and bossed.'[40] Pepys's entry for 9 August 1664 shows that he remembered the imprecation of Chaucer's Troilus to the rising sun to take its light away from Criseyde's bedroom and give it to those 'that smale seles graven.'[41] And on 21 November 1666, Pepys records that he went 'home to supper, and after supper' spent 'an hour reading' to his 'wife and brother something in Chaucer.'[42] Clearly for Pepys, as for his wife and brother, Chaucer's poems were neither obsolete nor repellently obscene.

The poems of Chaucer were, however, apparently popular with Pepys's male coterie. This is from his entry for 14 June 1663:

> So to Sir W. Penn to visit him ... By and by in comes Sir J. Mennes and Sir W. Batten, and so we sat talking: among other things, Sir J. Mennes brought many fine expressions of Chaucer, which he dotes on mightily, and without doubt is a very fine poet.

John Mennes's pleasure in Chaucer had issued into verse in *Musarum Deliciae* (1656). The volume included two poems written in a form that was to remain popular well into the eighteenth century—comic or satirical in purpose but composed

---

[39] Ibid. 1. 82.
[40] Samuel Pepys, *Diary,* ed. Robert Latham and William Matthews, 11 vols (London, 1970–83), 5. 199. Pepys also owned Caxton's edition of Chaucer's *The Canterbury Tales* (1483). His copies of Speght and Caxton are still preserved in the Pepys Library at Magdalene College, Cambridge, together with (as MS Pepys 2006) his small collection of Chaucerian MSS.
[41] *TC,* 3. 146–7.
[42] Pepys, *Diary,* 7. 1666.

in an imitation of Chaucerian English. It has been observed that Mennes's Chaucerian poems 'incorporate a number of reminiscences of 'The General Prologue'.[43] Mennes also remembered *The Merchant's Tale*:

> Lustfull he was, at Forty needs must wed,
> Old *Ianuary* will have *May* in Bed,
> And live in glee, for, as wise men have sayn,
> Old Fish, and young Flesh, would I have fayn,[44]
> And thus he swinketh; but, to end my story,
> Men sayn, he needs no other Purgatory.
>
> (Sir John Mennes, *Musarum Deliciae*
> [London, 1656], p. 75)

Mennes's quotation of a complete line from *The Merchant's Tale* may indicate traces of some enjoyment of the tale as a whole. Chaucer's 'unpolish'd strain' had not, as Mennes read it, 'obscur'd his Wit', but rather could be used as an antique spice for jokes, which, although from the past, are made to reflect upon the present.

Derek Brewer has observed that it was clearly 'the comic, bawdy, satirical elements in Chaucer' that 'mainly appealed to Mennes' and that Mennes 'probably represents quite well the sort of persons, courtiers, wits, men of affairs, to whom Chaucer's work continued to appeal'.[45] But, as this chapter has sought to establish, it is hard to determine *any* particular 'type' or 'sort' of person pleased by Chaucer in the later years of the seventeenth century—or of how far, in any given instance, an appreciation of Chaucer was felt to be compatible with a taste for the latest verse. It is significant that Francis Atterbury, Waller's warmest encomiast, was also the instigator of Urry's edition of Chaucer's *Works*. In his own copy of Waller's poems, against the lines 'Chaucer his Sense can only boast; / The glory of his numbers lost', Atterbury wrote:

> Not so, the beauty of his expression, and the variety and force of his numbers do this day appear in several parts of his poems, to those who read them with attentive skill.[46]

---

[43] *Chaucer: The Critical Heritage*, 1. 153.
[44] Compare *MerT*, 418–20: 'Old fish and yong flesh wolde I have ful fayn'.
[45] *Chaucer: The Critical Heritage*, 1. 153.
[46] Quoted in William L. Alderson and Arnold C. Henderson, *Chaucer and Augustan Scholarship* (Berkeley, CA, 1970), pp. 227–8.

2

The Father of Poetry and the Father of Criticism[1]

Chaucer Renewed?

In the interim between his hearing his friend Sir John Mennes (on 14 June 1663) recite 'many fine expressions of Chaucer', and his arranging (on 8 July 1664) to have Thomas Speght's second edition of the *Works* 'clasped and bossed', Samuel Pepys had met, or at least set eyes on, an old acquaintance from his University days:

> In Convent-garden tonight, going to fetch home my wife, I stopped at the great Coffee-house there, where I never was before—where Draydon the poet (I knew at Cambridge) and all the wits of the town … and had I had time then, or could at other times, it will be good coming thither, for there I perceive is very witty and pleasant discourse.[2]

Some time in 1698, thirty-four years after seeing Dryden in the 'great Coffee-house', Pepys entertained the poet for dinner. The discussion turned to Chaucer and to bad priests—or to bad priests and then to Chaucer. Pepys suggested to Dryden that he might compose a poem based on Chaucer's description of the Good Parson in the General Prologue to *The Canterbury Tales*. Dryden was happy to oblige, and, having completed the poem, wrote to Pepys on 14 July 1699:

> I remember last year, when I had the honour of dining with you, you were pleas'd to recommend to me, the character of Chaucer's Good Parson. Any desire of yours is a Command to me; and accordingly, I have put it into my English, with such additions and alterations as I thought fit … my Parson desires the favour of being known to you, and promises, if you find any fault in his character, he will reform it. Whenever you please, he shall wait on you, and for the safer Conveyance, I will carry him in my pocket.[3]

Pepys replied on the same day, offering his coach, an invitation to 'a cold chicken and salad, any noon after Sunday', and some remarks showing that he had a good

---

[1] Samuel Johnson considered that 'Dryden may be properly considered as the father of English Criticism, as the writer who first taught us to determine upon principles the merit of composition' (Johnson, *Works*, 21. 536).

[2] Samuel Pepys, *Diary*, ed. Robert Latham and William Matthews, 11 vols (London, 1797), 5. 27.

[3] John Dryden, *Letters*, ed. Charles E. Ward (Durham, NC, 1942), p. 115.

Chaucer in the Eighteenth Century. David Hopkins and Tom Mason, Oxford University Press.
© David Hopkins and Tom Mason (2022). DOI: 10.1093/oso/9780192862624.003.0003

notion of the form that Dryden's 'additions and alterations' to Chaucer's verses might have taken:

> You truly have oblig'd mee; and possibly in saying so, I am more in earnest then you can readily think; as verily hopeing, from this your copy of one good Parson, to fancy some amends made mee for the hourly offence I beare with from the sight of soe many lewd originals.[4]

In his letter, Dryden described the composition of his forthcoming volume in which 'The Good Parson' would appear: 'Having translated as many Fables from Ovid, and as many Novills from Boccace and Tales from Chaucer, as will make an indifferent large volume in folio, I intend them for the Press in Michaelmas Term next.'[5]

On Candlemas Day 1698, four months before writing to Pepys, Dryden had described in a letter to the poet Elizabeth Steward (the daughter of his cousin Elizabeth Creed) an earlier stage in the process of composition of his projected volume, before he turned to Boccaccio:

> ... betwixt my intervals of physique and other remedies which I am useing for my gravel, I am still drudging on; always a Poet, and never a good one. I pass my time sometimes with Ovid, and sometimes with our old English poet, Chaucer; translating such stories as best please my fancy.[6]

The precise order of composition of the poems that would eventually appear in 1700 as *Fables Ancient and Modern* is difficult to ascertain (for Dryden and his sources, see Fig. 2.1). Dryden's correspondence with Pepys and Elizabeth Steward might suggest that he passed from the Character of the Good Parson to other Chaucerian poems. But as he told the story in the Preface to *Fables*, he had started with Homer, turned to Ovid, and only then, as the verses accumulated, thought of Chaucer:

> 'Tis with a Poet, as with a Man who designs to build, and is very exact, as he supposes, in casting up the Cost beforehand: But, generally speaking, he is mistaken in his Account, and reckons short of the Expence he first intended: He alters his Mind as the Work proceeds, and will have this or that Convenience more, of which he had not thought when he began. So has it hapned to me; I have built a House, where I intended but a Lodge ... From translating the First of *Homer's Iliads*, (which I intended as an Essay to the whole Work) I proceeded to the Translation of the Twelfth Book of *Ovid's Metamorphoses* ... Having done with *Ovid* for this time, it came into my mind, that our old *English* Poet *Chaucer* in many Things resembled him, and that with no disadvantage on the Side of the Modern Author ... I soon resolv'd to put their Merits

---

[4] Ibid. p. 116.
[5] Ibid. p. 115.
[6] Ibid. p.109.

Fig. 2.1 The muse holding a copy of Dryden's *Fables*. Frontispiece to
John Dryden, *Fables, Ancient and Modern* (London, 1721 edition).

to the Trial, by turning some of the *Canterbury Tales* into our Language, as it is now
refin'd ... from *Chaucer* I was led to think on *Boccace*.[7]

Whatever the causation and whatever the stages of the process, it is hard to exag-
gerate the consequences of that arrival or return of Chaucer into Dryden's mind.[8]

---

[7] Dryden, *Works*, 7. 24–5.
[8] Dryden may have had some earlier acquaintance with Chaucer (see William L. Alderson and
Arnold C. Henderson, *Chaucer and Augustan Scholarship* (Berkeley, CA, 1970), pp. 59–60), but his
meeting with Pepys seems to have been the principal catalyst for his renewed engagement.

The last of Urry's 'Testimonies of Learned Men concerning Chaucer and his Works' is ascribed to 'Mr. Dryden in the Preface to his Fables', a passage where the focus moves from the speaker (Dryden) to the spoken of (Chaucer) and, in the present tense, to the way that Chaucer *speaks*:

> As he [*Chaucer*] is the Father of *English* Poetry, so I hold him in the same Degree of Veneration as the *Grecians* held *Homer,* or the *Romans Virgil:* He is a perpetual Fountain of good Sense; learn'd in all Sciences; and therefore speaks properly on all Subjects.[9]

Both in the 'Testimonies' and the critical part of the 'Life' in Urry's edition, Dryden's Preface is the dominating authority, standing towards the volume much as some of Spenser's remarks had stood towards Speght's edition of 1598. As, in 1602, the prime evidence of Chaucer's continuing power was his fathering of the best recent poet Edmund Spenser, so in 1721 that position is now occupied by John Dryden—in whose case Chaucer's fatherhood was equally proclaimed and even more evident. Almost every critical account of Chaucer in the eighteenth century and beyond quoted or paraphrased Dryden's critical remarks, his sentiments being endorsed or objected to by almost every commentator from John Dart and George Ogle to William Blake and Matthew Arnold.

The Harmony of Prose and the Refinement of Language

Dryden's Preface to *Fables Ancient and Modern* is an unusual piece of writing: chatty, impressionistic, personal, anecdotal, self-consciously unself-conscious. Dryden invokes 'the Practice of honest *Montaign*' when describing his own digressive procedures,[10] but insists that there is method in his meanderings. His principle of composition seems to consist in his method of making transitions and connections between poets and topics and his own sentences. He supports his method by citing Thomas Hobbes's argument that in 'the succession of one Thought after another' a man's '*Mentall Discourse*' is 'not altogether so casuall as it seems to be'.[11] But where Hobbes had described this kind of mental activity as essentially private and internal, pre-linguistic, and therefore *without* 'harmony', Dryden stressed the inseparability of his poetic and prosaic 'thoughts', and the consequent 'harmony' of the latter:

> Thoughts, such as they are, come crowding in so fast upon me, that my only Difficulty is to chuse or to reject, to run them into Verse, or give them the other Harmony of Prose.[12]

---

[9] Urry, Sig. I[v].
[10] Dryden, *Works*, 7. 31.
[11] Ibid. 7. 25, referring to the discussion 'Of the Consequence or Train of Imagination' in Hobbes, *Leviathan* I. iii.
[12] Dryden, *Works*, 7, 26–7.

Thoughts, Dryden says, crowd in upon him unordered, but because they are so intimately interconnected and 'so long studied and practis'd' they may be harmoniously presented. Although no thought is isolated or entirely without connection, each thought has a completeness of its own which is not necessarily negated by the apparent contradiction of the thought that follows or accompanies it.

Throughout his Preface, Dryden lays out paradoxes in a miscellaneous way, carelessly setting apparent contradictions side by side and leaving readers to reconcile them as best they can. Sir Thomas Pope Blount's summary of 'Characters and Censures' of Chaucer in his *De Re Poetica* had claimed to be a representative account of Chaucer's fame in the closing decade of the seventeenth century:

> … this is agreed upon by all hands, that he was counted the chief of the *English Poets*, not only of his own time, but continued to be so esteem'd till this age; and as much as we despise his old fashion'd Phrase, and Obsolete Words, *He* was one of the first Refiners of the *English* Language.[13]

But Blount's account, although it is presented as a simple statement of fact, is highly paradoxical. It is not clear, for instance, whether Blount's 'till this age' implies continuation or termination of Chaucer's fame. Chaucer, Blount says, was one of the first refiners of the English language, but that process of refinement has subsequently continued to the point where modern readers now despise his 'old fashion'd Phrase, and Obsolete Words'; and yet this somehow does not diminish Chaucer's continuing position as 'the chief of the *English Poets*'.

Dryden partly endorses the negative implications of this reaction. He knows that there are modernists among his readers who are 'offended' that he has 'turn'd these tales into modern English; because they think them unworthy of [his] pains, and look on Chaucer as a dry, old-fashion'd wit, not worth reviving'. Dryden, in a way that provoked the contempt of nineteenth-century medievalists, was prepared to concede much to his modern readers: '*Chaucer,* I confess, is a rough Diamond, and must first be polish'd e'er he shines.' Chaucer's phrasing is now obsolete; his words 'are given up as a Post not to be defended in our Poet, because he wanted the Modern Art of Fortifying'. The need for polish and for 'fortifying' has been caused by that general improvement in amplitude and selection of words, and development of accuracy in versification, that was, as Dryden sees it, observable in all literary traditions.

Of Chaucer's versification, says Dryden,

> We can only say, that he liv'd in the Infancy of our Poetry, and that nothing is brought to Perfection at the first. We must be Children before we grow Men. There was an *Ennius*, and in process of Time a *Lucilius*, and a *Lucretius*, before *Virgil* and *Horace*; even after

---

[13] Blount, *De Re Poetica*, p. 42.

Chaucer there was a *Spencer,* a *Harrington,* a *Fairfax,* before *Waller* and *Denham* were in being: And our Numbers were in their Nonage till these last appear'd.

In this respect, Chaucer was at a 'disadvantage' in comparison with Ovid: '*Ovid* liv'd when the *Roman* Tongue was in its Meridian; *Chaucer,* in the Dawning of our Language.' There is, as Dryden sees it, a similar difference and distance between 'the Diction of *Ennius* and *Ovid*' and between that 'of *Chaucer,* and our present *English*'. Chaucer and Boccaccio both 'refin'd their Mother-Tongues', but although many of Boccaccio's 'Phrases are become obsolete, as in process of Time it must needs happen', he is 'yet the Standard of Purity in the *Italian* Tongue' where Chaucer is not.[14]

At the same time, the opening of the Preface to *Fables* had offered an account of the course of English poetry very different from the common view of inevitable uninterrupted sophistication implied in the remarks quoted above. As we saw in Chapter 1, many writers had found a poetical desert between Chaucer and Spenser. Dryden describes a more recent lacuna: '*Spencer* and *Fairfax* both flourish'd in the Reign of Queen *Elizabeth*: Great Masters in our Language; and who saw much farther into the Beauties of our Numbers, than those who immediately followed them.'[15] The metrical secrets and potentialities of the English language are constant as things to be (partially) discovered in any 'age'.

At one place, Dryden invokes non-chronological and non-teleological historical sympathy for Chaucer:

> The Verse of *Chaucer,* I confess, is not Harmonious to us; but 'tis like the Eloquence of one whom *Tacitus* commends, it was *auribus istius temporis accommodata:* They who liv'd with him, and some time after him, thought it Musical; and it continues so even in our Judgment, if compar'd with the Numbers of *Lidgate* and *Gower* his Contemporaries.[16]

A similar assumption is made when Dryden maintains that, despite the differences in their relative positions in the development of their respective languages, both Ovid and Chaucer 'writ with wonderful Facility and Clearness'.[17]

But of all Dryden's remarks, the most surprising and puzzling is the apparent contradiction—to be discussed further later in this chapter and in Chapter 5— between the observation that 'Equality of Numbers in every Verse which we call Heroick, was either not known, or not always practis'd in Chaucer's Age' and the contention that in 'the Noble Poem of *Palamon* and *Arcite*' the '*Diction*'— which Dryden defined as including both 'the Choice of Words' and 'Harmony of Numbers'—is 'as poetical' as that to be found in 'the *Ilias* or the *Æneis*'.[18]

---

[14] Dryden, *Works,* 7. 26, 32, 34, 39–40.
[15] Ibid. 7. 25.
[16] Ibid. 7. 34.
[17] Ibid. 7. 31.
[18] Ibid. 7. 34, 44.

Dryden concludes his remarks on Chaucer with a protestation:

In sum, I seriously protest, that no Man ever had, or can have, a greater Veneration for *Chaucer*, than my self. I have translated some part of his Works, only that I might perpetuate his Memory, or at least refresh it, amongst my Countrymen.[19]

While some of Dryden's comments about Chaucer are addressed to his modernist readers, others are directed at antiquarians in his audience, those who 'suppose there is a certain Veneration due to [Chaucer's] old Language; and that it is little less than Profanation and Sacrilege to alter it', fearing that his 'good Sense will suffer in this Transfusion, and much of the Beauty of his Thoughts will infallibly be lost'. To these readers, too, Dryden is prepared to make concessions:

I grant, that something must be lost in all Transfusion, that is, in all Translations; but the Sense will remain, which would otherwise be lost, or at least be maim'd, when it is scarce intelligible; and that but to a few. How few are there who can read *Chaucer*, so as to understand him perfectly? And if imperfectly, then with less Profit, and no Pleasure.[20]

Dryden appeals over the heads of both modernists and antiquarians to those who care for sense and poetry irrespective of its provenance.

Textual Emendation: *Peneian Daphne*

Dryden's comments on Chaucer in his Preface are biographical, elucidatory, political, literary-historical, and critical, but also emendatory and editorial. Included in *Fables*, but nowhere mentioned in the Preface or on the title page, is a text of the Chaucer poems translated by Dryden, taken from Speght's edition but punctuated and printed in modern type. While it cannot be certain that Dryden himself had edited the text printed at the back of *Fables*,[21] it is clear that he had read at least parts of his text with a careful editorial eye. Unlike Sir Thomas Pope Blount, Dryden did not simply 'despise' Chaucer's 'Obsolete Words' or abandon them entirely as 'a Post not to be defended'. Some of Chaucer's words and phrases, he thought, were capable of recovery and correction. Dryden had discovered, while attempting to translate the medieval poet, that it was 'necessary sometimes to restore the Sense of *Chaucer*, which was lost or mangled in the Errors of the Press'.[22] His chosen example is a curious one, where Chaucer had been mistranscribed in the very act, as it were, of warning against mistranscription. The difficulty was presented

---

[19] Ibid. 7. 42.
[20] Ibid. 7, 41.
[21] Thomas Morell assumed that it had been edited by Dryden and therefore included it among his textual sources in his edition of 1737.
[22] Dryden, *Works*, 7. 40.

by three lines in *The Knight's Tale* which describe the pictures adorning the walls of the temple of the goddess of chastity:

> In the Story of *Palamon* and *Arcite,* where the Temple of *Diana* is describ'd, you find these Verses, in all the Editions of our Author:
>
> > *There saw I* Danè *turned unto a Tree,*
> > *I mean not the Goddess* Diane,
> > *But* Venus *Daughter, which that hight* Danè.[23]

Faced with these lines, Dryden appears to have thought that he might be able to discern what his predecessors had missed because he and Chaucer had been 'conversant in the same Studies'—in this instance the study of Ovid's *Metamorphoses,* on which Chaucer was drawing heavily at this point. Although most *Danas* in seventeenth-century texts are *Danæs,* seduced by Zeus in a shower of gold, Dryden had no difficulty in guessing that the '*Dane*' at this moment in Chaucer's tale was *Daphne.* The problem was that Dane/Daphne had been ascribed an odd parent: Venus, who has only *metaphorical* daughters elsewhere. Dryden recalled a phrase from Ovid's *Metamorphoses* ('Daphne Peneia') which he had himself rendered some seven years earlier: '*Daphne* her name, and *Peneus* was her Sire'.[24] He assumed that this identification had been also in Chaucer's mind, but not in the mind of Speght's compositor. So, Dryden judged, Speght's reading, 'after a little Consideration I knew was to be reform'd into this Sense, that *Daphne* the Daughter of *Peneus* was turn'd into a Tree'.[25] In his version of Chaucer's passage, Dryden adopted Ovid's epithet referring to Daphne's river-god parent, and made explicit reference to the pursuing deity:

> *Peneian Daphne* too was there to see
> *Apollo's* Love before, and now his Tree.
> (*Palamon and Arcite,* 2. 631–2; Dryden, *Works,* 7. 125)

The almost bathetic simplicity of that last line is probably a reflection of, and is perhaps intended to half-recall, Ovid's Latin, where Apollo almost comically opposes *conjunx* with *arbor*:

> ... 'at, quoniam conjunx mea non potes esse,
> arbor eris certe' dixit 'mea'.[26]

... which Dryden had rendered closely in his version of the story:

---

[23] Ibid, 7. 40.

[24] *The First Book of Ovid's Metamorphoses,* l. 609 (Dryden, *Works,* 4. 394).

[25] In the text of Chaucer's tale included in *Fables,* the name is emended to '*Diane* tourned vnto a tree' but the wrong parent remains: '*Venus* daughter, which that hight *Dane*'.

[26] Ovid, *Metamorphoses,* 1. 557–8. In the texts of Ovid used by Dryden, the words 'quoniam' and 'coniunx' are reversed.

'To whom the God, because thou can'st not be
My Mistress, I espouse thee for my Tree.'
(The First Book of Ovid's Metamorphoses, 754–5;
Dryden, *Works*, 4. 398)

Dryden considered himself here to be safely entering unoccupied new ground. He would not have taken similar liberties with a classical author. He would not, he owned, 'make thus bold with *Ovid*' for fear that learned critics would assume that 'I varied from my Author, because I understood him not'.[27] His confidence at this moment would seem to depend partly on the lack of competing scholarship and partly on his professional sense of which stories might most suitably adorn a temple of Diana. Dryden, interestingly, was considered to have been right in his assumptions, in his procedures, and in his resulting emendation. Thomas Morell, John Urry, and Thomas Tyrwhitt all accepted Dryden's correction—the first avowedly, the other two silently.

All these editors, however, while following Dryden in adopting Peneus as the father of 'Dane', altered the text in the interests of scansion. In his transcription, Dryden had marked the second syllable of Dane's name with a grave accent, guessing perhaps that a final *-e* was sounded—which, if *turned* were taken as a single syllable, would provide an iambic pentameter ('*There saw I* Danè *turned unto a Tree*'). Urry changed the name to *Daphne*, and indicated by his orthography that *turnid* also constituted two syllables, forcing him to cut the first syllable of *unto*. In the second line, he marked a final *-e* on *menè*, presumably assuming that *Diane* was trisyllabic. His text is metrically clear, but his emendation has made Chaucer's clarification redundant and inexplicable:

There saw I Daphne turnid to a tre,
I menè not the Goddess Diane,
But Peneus doughtir, which that hight Daphne.
(Urry, p. 16)

Thomas Morell ignored Urry, but in his textual appendix recorded that Daphne had been Venus's daughter in the printed editions of Chaucer. He noted that, the *Venus* reading '*being manifestly wrong, Mr.* Dryden *conjectured* Peneus, *and indeed* Pennyus *or* Penneus *is the Reading of all the* MSS'. He therefore printed the lines as on MS authority, but marking a final *-e* on four occasions:

There saw I *Dané* turned til a Tre,
I mené not the Goddess *Diané*
But *Pennyus* Doughtyr, which that hyght *Dané*.
(Morell, p. 147)

In his General Appendix (p. 408) Morell stressed the appropriateness of the patronymic: '*Daphne* is said to be the Daughter of *Peneus*, because the Banks of

---

[27] Dryden, *Works*, 7. 40.

that River abound with Laurel.' Tyrwhitt, who refused to deface his text with aids to scansion, put an initial *-y* on *yturned* and inserted a *hire* into the second line:

> There saw I Dane yturned til a tree,
> I mene not <u>hire</u> the Goddess Diane,
> But Pennyus Doughtyr, which that hyght Dane.
>
> (Tyrwhitt 1775–78, 1. 81)

Dryden's Prosody: On Chaucer's Versification

Dryden's detailed engagement with the question of *Penean Daphne* sheds some light on his larger thoughts about Chaucer's versification. In this area, Dryden's position seems at first sight to resemble that of those critics who had, like Waller, lamented that the glories of Chaucer's 'numbers' had been lost. Dryden's observations on this topic, however, were more limited in scope: Chaucer, as he read him, had not consistently observed a strict 'numerosity'. Dryden was therefore forced to dissent from Thomas Speght, who, in his preliminary remarks 'To the Readers', had implied that Chaucer's lines might, with more than a little phonetic allowance, be read in such a way as to accord with modern metrical expectations. Speght had not been confident that such scanning of Chaucer's lines could be consistently applied to the text he was providing, or to any that he had seen, and suggested that the imperfections of Chaucer's scansion might be attributed, as Chaucer himself had feared, to 'the negligence and rape of *Adam Scrivener*'.[28]

While Dryden had suspected that printers had caused the error over Daphne, he did not invoke scribal corruption as explaining *all* the metrical deficiencies in the texts of Chaucer and others that he read in Speght's editions of 1598, 1602, or 1687:

> [He] who publish'd the last Edition of him … would make us believe the Fault is in our Ears, and that there were really Ten Syllables in a Verse where we find but Nine: But this Opinion is not worth confuting; 'tis so gross and obvious an Errour, that common Sense (which is a Rule in every thing but Matters of Faith and Revelation) must convince the Reader, that Equality of Numbers in every Verse which we call *Heroick*, was either not known, or not always practis'd in *Chaucer*'s Age.[29]

Of all Dryden's remarks in the Preface, these on the relation of Chaucer's lines to late seventeenth-century practice were among the most discussed, and most frequently damned, and therefore require minute examination. As we shall see in Chapter 5, the debate continued throughout the eighteenth century and beyond, but many scholars in the nineteenth and twentieth centuries regarded these

---

[28] In support of his argument, Speght quoted the conclusion of Book 5 of *TC*.
[29] Dryden, *Works*, 7. 34.

remarks as an example of Dryden's culpable ignorance. Later scholars' better knowledge of the various manuscript sources in which Chaucer's works have been preserved and their consequent ability to piece out the imperfections of the early printed texts sometimes led them to be unsympathetic to, even contemptuous of, the conclusions drawn by Dryden in good faith from the texts that were available to him.[30] One common suggestion was that had Dryden deduced the use of the final -e (which was not consistently available in the texts available to him), all his troubles would have vanished in an instant and he would have discovered that Chaucer's lines do indeed consist uniformly and unvaryingly of ten iambic syllables.

Furthermore, if by *Heroic Verse* Dryden was thinking of his own and that of his most accomplished contemporaries, then the term might assume a large range of factors beyond the regular deployment of five iambic feet: varied placement of the pause(s), strong rhymes at the close of paragraphs, double rhymes only for (usually) comic effect, the shaping of half lines, allowable and invalid positions for trochaic and spondaic substitutions, subtle vowel and consonant patterns, variations in the degree of similarity between less-accented syllables and more-accented syllables, various relations between sense and versification ('natural pauses'), metrical similarity—or dissimilarity—between the first and second lines of a couplet, the necessary placement of elisions, the avoidance of open vowels and useless expletives, variation in the use of run-on lines, the elegant deployment of triplets, alexandrines and fourteeners, and much more.

These were arts, which, in the texts that Dryden knew, were certainly 'either not known, or not always practis'd in *Chaucer*'s Age'. Dryden hesitates between the two possibilities: theoretical ignorance or inconsistency of practice. '*Chaucer*'s Age' is indeterminately large, but presumably points to the poems printed in Speght's editions—which included items from the fifteenth century, some ascribed to named authors, many assumed to be composed by Chaucer himself.[31] Dryden suggested that Chaucer's verse is always 'Musical', 'even in our Judgement, if compar'd with the Numbers of *Lidgate* and *Gower* his Contemporaries'.[32] He was

---

[30] In one standard reference book, for instance, Eric Stanley quoted Dryden's remarks on Chaucer's versification at some length, and appended the following comments. Chaucer's verse, Stanley wrote

> would have been scanned by its earliest readers flexibly to some extent, but basically with each line consisting of ten (or, in four-stressed lines eight) syllables, five (or four) of them stressed; that is not how Dryden would have scanned Chaucer's verse, lame for want of half a foot or a foot in thousands of lines. Dryden's condescension in recognizing merits as one might in a Scotch Tune is insufficiently informed: but that must have been the perception of Chaucerian prosody from the 15th c. onwards. There is no justification for it.

See Douglas Gray, ed., *The Oxford Companion to Chaucer* (Oxford, 2003), p. 48.

[31] Contrariwise, a poem generally now ascribed to Chaucer is given the title 'Th. Occleue to his empty purse'.

[32] Dryden, *Works*, 7. 34.

probably thinking here of such poems as that included in Speght's edition as 'Iohn Gower vnto the noble *King Henrie the fourth*'. Lydgate is quoted in 'Chaucers Life': 'The Floure of Courtesie' is said to be '*made by John Lidgate*'.[33] Most of these poems included verses that were apparently of less than ten syllables, however those syllables were pronounced. In Lydgate's 'A ballade in the Praise and Commendation of Master Geffrey Chaucer of His Golden Eloquence', Dryden would have met with the following: 'Which first made to distil, and reine / The gold dew droppes ....'[34] 'The Storie of Thebes, Compiled by ION LIDGATE Monke of BVRIE' presents in the first columns of the Prologue, among prevailing pentameters, the following lines: 'Of estatis in the pilgrimage': 'Beseeching you, that ye will tell': 'Or let feed in a faint pasture'; 'If need be, spare not to blow'.

Dryden's statement that 'Equality of Numbers in every Verse which we call *Heroick,* was either not known, or not always practis'd in *Chaucer's* Age' was, as an inference, entirely just. No form of pronunciation or set of metrical principles could have made the verses included in Speght's edition scan *consistently* as iambic pentameters.

Some further appreciation of Dryden's position can be attained by a brief examination of the opening lines of *The Floure and the Leafe*. This poem was assumed by Dryden—as by all readers until well into the nineteenth century—to be a genuine work by Chaucer, but is now thought to date from the fifteenth century.[35] The only early source for this poem is Speght's edition of 1598 (there are no extant manuscripts), so it provides a useful means of appreciating Dryden's responses to a 'Chaucerian' text in which, so to speak, we are in much the same position as was Dryden.

Here is the opening of *The Floure and the Leafe*, with Speght's text of 1602 (in this case the copy text) printed on the left, and, on the right, the text prepared by Urry for his edition of 1721:[36]

When that Phebus his chaire of gold so hie	When that Phœbus his chair of gold so hie
Had whirled vp the sterrie sky aloft	Had whirl<u>id</u> up the sterrie Sky aloft,
And in the Boole was entred certainely,	And in the Bole was ent<u>rid</u> certain<u>ly</u>,
When shoures sweet of raine discended oft,	When shour<u>is</u> <u>sote</u> of rain descend<u>id</u> soft
Causing the ground, fele times and oft,	Causing the ground, fel<u>è</u> tim<u>is</u> and oft
Up for to giue many an wholesome aire,	Up for to give many an wholesome ai<u>r,</u>
And euery plaine was clothed faire	And ev<u>èry</u> plai<u>n</u> was <u>y</u>cloth<u>id</u> faire
With new green, and maketh small floures	With new<u>è</u> grene, and mak<u>ith</u> smal<u>è</u> flours
To springen here and there in field & in mede,	To spring<u>in</u> here and there in field <u>and</u> mede,

---

[33] Lydgate's *Complaint of the Black Knight*, on the other hand, is ascribed (by default) to Chaucer.
[34] Speght 1602, Fol. 321ʳ.
[35] The enormous and long popularity of this poem is outlined in Chapter 9.
[36] Speght's second (and third) editions of this poem differ slightly from the first. In line 2, *sterry* of 1598, for example, is replaced by *sterrie* in 1602—the spelling reproduced by Urry.

So very good and wholesome be the shoures,	So very gode and wholesome be the shours
That it reneueth that was old and dede,	That they renewin, that was old and dede,
In winter time and out of euery sede	In wintir time, and out of every sede
Springeth the hearbe, so that euery wight	Springith the herbè, so that every wight
Of this season wexeth glad and light.	Of this seson wexith richt glad and light.
(Speght 1602, Fol. 344ʳ)	(Urry, p. 473)

As will be seen immediately, few lines in this passage were left by Urry *exactly* as they had stood in 1600, or as in the transcription of Speght's 1598 text printed in Dryden's *Fables*. Urry's primary conviction—one maintained throughout his edition—is that Chaucer's verses 'originally consisted of an equal number of feet'. Missing feet must be found, and it must be clear to a modern reader where they are. Most of Urry's alterations are designed as aids towards pronunciation by an eighteenth-century reader. He therefore marks endings he thinks should be pronounced *id*, *is*, *ith*, *is,* regardless of how they are spelled in his source text. In the second line, for example, *whirled* is replaced by *worlid* to make clear that the word had two syllables—as it generally did not in the early eighteenth century, when it was frequently rhymed with *hurld*.

It is not clear how Urry hit on the possibility of sounding final *-ès* a few years after Dryden supposedly had not. Urry, like every other editor, was faced with the problem of guessing which *-ès* in his copy text were to be sounded and which not. Later editors complained that Urry often used a sounded *-è* with little care for grammar or etymology. His fondness for attaching them to adjectives seems prompted primarily by his desire to maintain iambic measure. In the first line of the passage quoted, an unsounded *-e* is removed from *chaire*. In the fifth line, *fele times* gains two syllables (*felè timis*), but the result is an ungainly line. Two syllables are added to the closing line of the first stanza ('And *everỳ* plain was *yclothid* faire'), and sounding *-ès* for the first line of the next ('With *newè* grene, and makith *smalè* flours'), so providing runs of ten easy syllables.

The fourth line is particularly interesting; *shoures sweet* are replaced by *shouris sote*; Urry perhaps thought that, as in eighteenth-century speech, *showers* could constitute one or two syllables, and that *sote* was the more Chaucerian spelling of *sweet*. At the end of the line, *descended oft* is replaced by *descendid soft*—to avoid the repetition with *oft* forming the rhyme in the following line. That would seem to be a rational emendation, attentive to the sense.[37] The last line ('Of this season

---

[37] This emendation was adopted by almost all subsequent editors. Henry Todd included in his *Illustrations of the Lives and Writings of Gower and Chaucer* (London, 1810, pp. 202–26) a version of this poem which he described as 'From the edition of Chaucer's Works in 1598, by Speght, in which the poem was first printed; compared with Speght's second edition in 1602, and with that of Urry.' He was prepared to include eight-syllable lines ('As I suppose, had more hearts ease' l. 20) where Urry had emended ('(As I suppose) had more of heartis ease'). Todd, however, accepted Urry's reading *soft* in line 4 with the comment '*Oft*, by an apparent errour of the press, in the old editions. Urry, *soft*'. While generally preferring Speght, Todd included some of Urry's additions, putting them in square brackets. The modern scholarly edition of the poem by Derek Pearsall, in which Speght's text (retained by Pearsall,

wexeth glad and light'), on the other hand, proved most difficult. It was short of a syllable—and *no pronunciation could make it otherwise*. So Urry adds a word: 'Of this season wexith _right_ glad and light). This is precisely the kind of addition, as we shall see in Chapter 5, that Morell disliked, and Tyrwhitt condemned.[38]

The purpose of this analysis is not to endorse the details of Urry's practice but to use his editorial interventions as a means of demonstrating the dilemmas facing thoughtful seventeenth-century or eighteenth-century readers of Chaucerian verse in Speght's edition, whether, like Dryden, they were led by Speght's texts to doubt whether it had ever scanned perfectly, or, like Urry, they were convinced that it had originally scanned, and could be made to do so again. Speght's texts, as they stand, simply *cannot* be made to scan as regular iambic pentameter verse. Since there are, in the case of *The Floure and the Leafe*, no other witnesses to the text of the poem, the only recourse for those wishing to endow it with perfect scansion is to make emendations, additions, or alterations in spelling—or all three.

Dryden on Chaucer's Intelligibility

In the Preface to *Fables*, Dryden offered a particular '*Specimen* of *Chaucer's* Language' which presented 'more than one Example of his unequal Numbers' as well as containing language 'which is so obsolete, that his Sense can scarce be understood'. Dryden's chosen example is a passage from the General Prologue to *The Canterbury Tales*, in which Chaucer 'excuses the Ribaldry, which is very gross, in many of his Novels'.[39] We will return to Dryden's problems with Chaucer's 'unequal Numbers' in this passage in Chapter 5, where the passage is quoted in full. Here, the discussion concentrates on Dryden's conviction that the language of the passage is obsolete, and thus incomprehensible.

Dryden's notion of what was and was not obsolete and obscure in Chaucer's language is in fact not as easy to determine as it may seem at first sight. Some notion of which words in the passage from the General Prologue might have been seen as 'obsolete' two centuries after Chaucer's death may be gathered from the glossary ('The old and obscure words in Chaucer explaned') in Speght's edition of 1602. Speght offers explanations of several words in the passage quoted by Dryden— 'arret' ('to charge'), 'nigh' ('neere'), and 'mote' ('must go')—but offers no other assistance. Timothy Thomas in Urry's edition was to be more helpful. He offers the following glosses: 'arett' ('to impute unto, accuse, charge one with; to account');

---

faute de mieux, as his copy text) is substantially emended, sometimes in ways that actually draw on the much-maligned Urry (see Derek A. Pearsall, ed., *The Floure and the Leafe and The Assembly of Ladies* (London, 1962)). Pearsall's textual notes to *The Floure* are on p. 127. Pearsall adopts Urry's readings *soft* for *oft* (l. 4); *bere* for *here* (l. 213); *nine* for *ninth* (l.293); and even the insertion of *how* (l. 354).

[38] Todd printed the line as it appeared in Speght 1602: 'Of this season wexeth glad and light', *Illustrations*, p. 204.

[39] *GP* 725–42; Dryden, *Works*, 7. 38–9.

'villany' ('a base, rude, dishonourable, or wicked word or action, such as none but a mean fellow, a villain, would be guilty of'); 'chere' ('behaviour; gesture'); 'Nye' ('nigh, near'); 'mote' ('must'); and 'everich' ('each; which is a contraction of it') (p. 26). The syntax of the passage, however, perhaps contributed more than the vocabulary to Dryden's difficulties—which may have been greater than Urry's. Dryden may, perhaps through oversight, have mistranscribed *of* for *if*, but his punctuation (the colon after *can* and following commas) suggests that he may have misunderstood the following passage. Here, the left-hand column presents the text as given in Speght 1598, and the right-hand column that quoted by Dryden in his Preface:

Who shall tellen a tale after a man	*Who shall tellen a tale after a man*
He mote rehearse as nye, as euer he can	*He mote rehearse as nye, as ever He can:*
Everich word <u>if it</u> been in his charge	*Everich word <u>of it</u> been in his charge,*
All speke he neuer so rudely ne large.	*All speke he, never so rudely, ne large.*

Dryden perhaps assumes that the sense was 'Each word of the tale (every word of it) is the responsibility of the re-teller, who reproduces them *all*, however uncouth or improper they are.'

Dryden's sense of what is and what is not obscure or difficult is perhaps further complicated by the lines from Chaucer which, in the remarks which immediately follow his quotation of the passage from the General Prologue, he presents as close to current phrasing and metrical practice. His example from *The Miller's Tale* demonstrates no peculiar or strikingly metaphorical arrangement of words. Dryden's point is only that it is intelligible both in meaning and metre to minds and to ears in 1700:

> Yet many of his Verses consist of Ten Syllables, and the Words not much behind our present *English:* As for Example, these two Lines, in the Description of the Carpenter's Young Wife:
>
> > *Wincing she was, as is a jolly Colt,*
> > *Long as a Mast, and upright as a Bolt.*[40]

Dryden here judged both the semantic and metrical expectations of his audience perfectly. Where he suggested that that the words of the couplet were 'not much behind our present *English*', many of his readers went a step further. The couplet was reproduced unchanged throughout the eighteenth century in versions of Chaucer's tale that were not otherwise archaic. The couplet became, in effect, part of current English. Even in the anonymous version of printed in 1791, the rhyme and some of the metrical shaping is preserved:

---

[40] Dryden, *Works*, 7. 39.

Ticklish and frisky as a mettled colt,
Tall as a spear and upright as a bolt,
Erect she walk'd.

('The Miller's Tale, from Chaucer', ll. 75–7, in Betsy

Bowden, ed., *Eighteenth-Century Modernizations from*

'The Canterbury Tales' [Woodbridge, 1991], p. 171)

But the alterations of Chaucer's original in the 1791 version suggest that most of the component parts were not in fact current English at that date, and perhaps had not been even in Dryden's day. Although many horses had been seen to 'wince' in earlier literature, the use of the word in its adjectival form appears to have died out—the description of an 'old wincing Mare' in *Musarum Deliciæ* (1656) being one of its last appearances.[41] There were no 'jolly colts' in eighteenth-century literature. And the phrase 'long as a mast' appeared only in versions of *The Miller's Tale*—where the couplet quoted by Dryden was reproduced exactly. Interestingly, both the Glossary in Urry's edition and Thomas Warton's *History of English Poetry* provided full explanations of the phrase, 'upright as a bolt', presumably because although 'bolt upright' was a very common expression, the metaphor was dead and there were in the eighteenth century a great many kinds of bolt, few of which might be described as 'upright'.[42] Again, the *exact* phrase appears only in reproductions of Chaucer's text.

But the prosodic shaping of the lines was nevertheless much praised, and emulated—though it is not easy to know exactly on what grounds. If Dryden read the lines something like this—

WIN-cing she WAS || as-is a-JOL ly-*COLT,* ||
LONG as a MAST || and UP right as a BOLT ||

—both lines would be read as having a marked medial pause, dividing sound and sense into clearly discernible units, and the ten syllables into groups of four and six. In the first hemistich, the pattern is similar in both half-lines. In the second hemistich, it is not—assuming that Dryden would have placed the accent on the first syllable of *wincing*. In the second line, the adjective–noun pattern is repeated while the metre is varied, the parallelism apparently helping the minds of seventeenth-century readers to choose rapidly between possibilities and so to receive the meaning. Dryden assumed—rightly as it turned out—that contemporary readers, having read 'Long as a mast', would, without difficulty, be able to determine the sense both of *upright* and of *bolt*. Chaucer's phraseology was at this moment, somehow, self-explaining and self-preserving. The analogy between Alison, colts, masts, and arrows is sharply directed and firmly confined, not least by the deviation from the word order common in speech.

[41] Sir John Mennes, *Musarum Deliciae* (London, 1656), p. 82.
[42] See Urry, Glossary, p. 12; Warton, *History,* 1. 427.

It may be significant that several of the (few) lines that Dryden was able to reproduce almost verbatim in his own versions of Chaucer employ a simple inversion,
and have a broadly similar metrical pattern to that of the Alison couplet, with a
strong pause after the second foot:

Black was his berd, and manly was his face

Black was his Beard, and manly was his Face
(*Palamon and Arcite*, 2. 40)

Great was theffect, and hie was his entente

Great was th'Effect, and high was his Intent
(*Palamon and Arcite*, 3. 1026)

One instance, describing the morning of the tournament in *The Knight's Tale*, was
noticed and particularly appreciated by one of Dryden's readers:

Vp rose the sunne, and up rose Emilye

Up rose the Sun, and up rose *Emily*
(*Palamon and Arcite*, 3. 190)

The success of this line was felt to depend on the cooperation of the reader's mind.
In his *Essay on Criticism*, John Oldmixon observed:

> Had Chaucer said, Up rose the Sun, and up rose Emily brighter than the Sun, Emily
> and the Reader would have been entertain'd with only a common Complement; but
> now the Reader fills up the Thought himself, and imagines that the Sun rose to prepare
> the Way for something brighter than himself: 'Up rose Emily'.[43]

On the evidence presented so far, Dryden seems quite happy to run two contradictory accounts of Chaucer's language and verse simultaneously. There is in Dryden's
remarks an entirely contrary movement within the conventional observations on
Chaucer's obsolescence. The saving notion seems to be that of linguistic 'purity'.
As Dryden saw it, 'From *Chaucer* the Purity of the *English* Tongue began.' So by
one account, Chaucer lacked 'the Modern Art of Fortifying', many of his words
have become obsolete, his lines are frequently 'lame for want of half a Foot, and
sometimes a whole one', and have only 'the rude Sweetness of a *Scotch* Tune …
natural and pleasing, though not perfect'.[44] But according to the other account,

---

[43] John Oldmixon, *An Essay on Criticism* (London, 1728), pp. 38–9.
[44] Dryden's comparison of Chaucer's verse to 'Scotch tunes' is not necessarily as denigratory as Eric
Stanley (see n 30) implies. Elizabeth Elstob, a passionate admirer of 'Northern Antiquities', quoted Dryden's remarks with evident and unqualified approval. See Elizabeth Elstob, *The Rudiments of Grammar
for the English-Saxon Tongue* (London, 1715), p. xxix. It is true that 'Scotch songs' were sometimes
regarded—particularly in their broadside form—as crudely primitive. In Thomas Otway's *Friendship
in Fashion* (London, 1678), for example, Valentine remarks: 'A *Scotch* Song! I hate it worse than *Scotch*
Bagpipe, which even the Bears have grown weary of, and have a better Musick' (p. 30). But careful
discriminations were made between more and less successful exercises in the 'Scotch' style. Charles
Burney, for example, singled out one of Henry Purcell's 'Scotch tunes' for special praise (see his *A General History of Music, from the Earliest Ages to the Present Period*, 4 vols (London, 1776–89), 3. 489). And
in his *A General History of the Science and Practice of Music*, 5 vols (London, 1776), Sir John Hawkins
looked back to the 'many fine Scots airs' that were included in Thomas D'Urfey's *Pills to Purge Melancholy* (London, 1720), praised the 'singularly sweet and pathetic melodies' and the 'melancholy and
plaintive kind of air' 'with which Scots music abounds' and which 'distinguishes the Scots melodies',
and described the way in which Scots music had 'enriched' that of the Italian tradition 'with some
peculiar graces' (see *General History*, 1. xvi; 2. 213; 3. 384; 4. 6).

Chaucer, like other 'Great Masters in our Language … saw much farther into the Beauties of our Numbers' than many contemporaries and many succeeding poets. 'Refinement' is sometimes a term associated with addition and adornment, but according to Samuel Johnson it may also be used to describe a 'mode of phraseology so consonant and congenial to the analogy and principles of its respective language as to remain settled and unaltered'.[45] A 'purified' language, according to such an account, will last like purified gold. It will retain its lustre across time.

This returns us to the most surprising and puzzling of Dryden's remarks on Chaucer's choice of words, which comes in this sentence:

> I prefer in our Countryman, far above all his other Stories, the Noble Poem of *Palamon* and *Arcite,* which is of the *Epique* kind, and perhaps not much inferiour to the *Ilias* or the *Æneis*: the Story is more pleasing than either of them, the Manners as perfect, the Diction as poetical, the Learning as deep and various; and the Disposition full as artful.[46]

Since in this very Preface, Dryden defined the word 'Diction' as including both 'the Choice of Words' and 'Harmony of Numbers', it is hard to envisage how stronger praise could be given in 1699 than to suggest that the 'Diction' of 'The Knight's Tale' was 'as poetical' as that of Virgil.

On the Imitation of Humane Life

In making that claim for Chaucer's diction, Dryden must have been using the term 'poetical' in a sense and with connotations different from the common usage: Chaucer's diction is 'poetical', perhaps, because it is appropriate for the trans-historical purposes of poetry—where ideally language *follows* thought. The notion had been intermittently present in some writings on Chaucer in the seventeenth century. Richard Brathwaite, for example, had ended his *Comment* on two of Chaucer's tales by offering an answer to a perhaps imaginary critic who had complained at the difficulty of Chaucer's language:

> Amidst this Discourse, a *Critick* stepping in, objected out of the Quickness of his Censure … that he could allow well of *Chaucer,* if his *Language* were *Better*. Whereto the *Author* of these Commentaries return'd him this Answer: 'Sir, It appears, you prefer *Speech* before the *Head-piece; Language* before *Invention;* whereas Weight of Judgment has ever given *Invention* Priority before *Language*. And not to leave you dissatisfied, As the Time wherein these *Tales* were writ, rendered him incapable of the one; So his Pregnancy of Fancy approv'd him incomparable for the other.' Which Answer

---

[45] Johnson, *Works*, 7. 70.
[46] Dryden, *Works*, 7.44.

still'd this Censor, and justified the Author; leaving … his *Works* to perpetuate his Honour.[47]

On the question of the relative importance of 'invention' and language, Dryden had disputed Thomas Hobbes's assertions that 'the first Beauty of an Epick Poem consists in Diction, that is, in the Choice of Words, and Harmony of Numbers' and that 'the Words are the Colouring of the Work, which in the Order of Nature is last to be consider'd'. Dryden's expression of disagreement with Hobbes was clear and emphatic:

> The Design, the Disposition, the Manners, and the Thoughts, are all before it: Where any of those are wanting or imperfect, so much wants or is imperfect in the Imitation of Humane Life; which is in the very Definition of a Poem. Words Indeed, like glaring Colours, are the first Beauties that arise, and strike the Sight; but if the Draught be false or lame, the Figures ill dispos'd, the Manners obscure or inconsistent, or the Thoughts unnatural, then the finest Colours are but Dawbing, and the Piece is a beautiful Monster at the best. Neither *Virgil* nor *Homer* were deficient in any of the former Beauties; but in this last, which is Expression, the *Roman* Poet is at least equal to the *Grecian*, as I have said elsewhere; supplying the Poverty of his Language, by his Musical Ear, and by his Diligence.[48]

Language, in Dryden's account, is not applied like paint over poor draftmanship, but constitutes the expression of 'Design', 'Disposition', and 'the Imitation of Humane Life', which is in the very Definition of a Poem'. Virgil's verse may be more polished than Homer's, but Virgil was dependent on Homer's 'invention'. Rymer had thought that Chaucer's language was incapable of 'the heroick'. Dryden thinks otherwise. By this new order of priorities, Chaucer can be seen to be as superior to several of the moderns as he is to Ovid. Dryden's very conception of *Fables, Ancient and Modern*, a volume the contents of which stretch from Homer to 1699, is a testimony to his faith in the existence of extra-chronological, trans-temporal, trans-linguistic, extra-cultural poetical merit.

'Our Fore-Fathers' and Chaucer's 'Comprehensive Soul'

Once the 'Imitation of Humane Life' is thought of as 'the very Definition of a Poem', then Chaucer's stature in *The Knight's Tale* and more generally might be deemed to be of the very highest, for it was in this that he excelled. Dryden's term 'Imitation' seems to be intended quite literally. When Chaucer describes some person or some thing, you *see* that person or thing. Again, Dryden is here joining the best current

---

[47] Richard Brathwaite, *A Comment upon the Two Tales of Our Ancient, Renowned, and Ever-Living Poet Sr Jeffray Chaucer, Knight …: The Miller's Tale and The Wife of Bath* (London, 1665), p. 199, italics reversed.
[48] Dryden, *Works*, 7. 29.

opinion, as when Sir Thomas Blount quoted William Winstanley's *Lives of the Most Famous English Poets* (1687):

> One gift [Chaucer] had above other Authors, says *Winstanley*, and that is, by the Excellencies of his Descriptions, to possess his Readers with a stronger Imagination of seeing that done before their eyes which they Read, than any other that ever Writ in any Tongue.[49]

Dryden followed such praise of Chaucer's powers of description, and asserted their superiority to those of other poets, even—despite the strong similarities between the two poets—Ovid. The details in Chaucer's descriptions, Dryden suggests, take us even closer to the essence of the persons they evoke than those of Chaucer's Roman predecessor:

> Both of them understood the Manners; under which Name I comprehend the Passions, and, in a larger Sense, the Descriptions of Persons, and their very Habits: For an Example, I see *Baucis* and *Philemon* as perfectly before me, as if some ancient Painter had drawn them; and all the Pilgrims in the *Canterbury* Tales, their Humours, their Features, and the very Dress, as distinctly as if I had supp'd with them at the *Tabard* in *Southwark*: Yet even there too the Figures of *Chaucer* are much more lively, and set in a better Light.[50]

Chaucer might be said to have imitated *Humane Life* not merely because of his portrayals of single personages but because he described so many persons and so many things, and thus captured the full variety of human passions and manners. Sir Thomas Blount had cited René Rapin's assertion

> That as the *Painter* draws Faces by their Features; so the *Poet* represents the *Minds* of Men by their *Manners*: and the most general Rule for Painting the Manners, is to exhibit every Person in his Proper *Character*.

'Chaucer', wrote Dryden, 'followed Nature everywhere'. In this respect, Dryden's remark can be seen as the development of a thought which Sir Thomas Pope Blount, again, borrowed from Rapin:

> The Soveraign Rule for treating of *Manners*, says *Rapin*, is to Copy them after *Nature*, and above all to study well the *Heart* of Man, to know how to distinguish all its *Motions*. 'Tis this which none are acquainted with: the Heart of Man is an *Abyss*, where none can sound the Bottom: it is a *Mystery*, which the most Quick-sighted cannot pierce into, and in which the most cunning are mistaken.[51]

The differences between Dryden's thinking and that of his predecessors, however, though slight, are large in their implications. Francis Beaumont and Thomas Speght had described Chaucer's purpose as to 'discover all Vices of [his] Age' and to describe 'all the People of the land, and the nature and disposition of them

---

[49] Blount, *De Re Poetica*, pp. 42–3.
[50] Dryden, *Works*, 7. 31–2.
[51] Blount, *De Re Poetica*, p. 23.

in those dayes'.[52] Dryden similarly emphasizes that Chaucer's descriptions are of the human world that is immediately in the poet's view: men and women with particular occupations, education, dress, and so on. But in Dryden's description, the 'manners' of Chaucer's personages are so carefully chosen and so profoundly evoked that a reader of his work sees those personages living at once not only in the medieval past but also in Dryden's present:

> He must have been a Man of a most wonderful comprehensive Nature, because, as it has been truly observ'd of him, he has taken into the Compass of his *Canterbury Tales* the various Manners and Humours (as we now call them) of the whole *English* Nation, in his Age. Not a single Character has escap'd him. All his Pilgrims are severally distinguish'd from each other, and not only in their Inclinations, but in their very Phisiognomies and Persons. *Baptista Porta*[53] could not have describ'd their Natures better, than by the Marks which the Poet gives them. The Matter and Manner of their Tales, and of their Telling, are so suited to their different Educations, Humours, and Callings, that each of them would be improper in any other Mouth. Even the grave and serious Characters are distinguish'd by their several sorts of Gravity: Their Discourses are such as belong to their Age, their Calling, and their Breeding; such as are becoming of them, and of them only. Some of his Persons are Vicious, and some Vertuous; some are unlearn'd, or (as *Chaucer* calls them) Lewd, and some are Learn'd. Even the Ribaldry of the Low Characters is different: The *Reeve,* the *Miller,* and the *Cook,* are several Men, and distinguish'd from each other, as much as the mincing Lady Prioress, and the broad-speaking gap-tooth'd Wife of *Bathe.* But enough of this: There is such a Variety of Game springing up before me, that I am distracted in my Choice, and know not which to follow. 'Tis sufficient to say according to the Proverb, that here is God's Plenty.

Dryden's impression of Chaucer's works was double and paradoxical: everything had altered since Chaucer's day; nothing had changed:

> We have our Fore-fathers and Great Grand-dames all before us, as they were in *Chaucer's* Days; their general Characters are still remaining in Mankind, and even in *England,* though they are call'd by other Names than those of *Moncks,* and *Fryars,* and *Chanons,* and *Lady Abbesses,* and *Nuns*: For Mankind is ever the same, and nothing lost out of Nature, though every thing is alter'd.[54]

Where Beaumont and Speght had confined Chaucer's powers to accurate description of his own time and of the vices of his own time, Dryden's slight alterations of emphasis have profound consequences: Chaucer brings his characters before us. The modern reader can see them—see them in their past-ness—but also recognize them as our ancestors and acknowledge a common genealogy. Dryden's profoundly paradoxical assumption that part of the experience of reading old

---

[52] Speght 1598, Sig. c.iiii[r].

[53] The Neapolitan physician Giambattista della Porta (1540–1615) had conducted a detailed examination of the influence of emotions on the human face in his *De Humana Physiognomia* (Vico Equense, 1586).

[54] Dryden, *Works*, 7. 37–8.

poems is to discover the coexistence of stasis with perpetual movement—to discover that nothing changes while everything changes—is expressed effortlessly and without embarrassment, and without weighting one proposition at the expense of another. On the one hand, everything is 'alter'd'. One result of reading a late-fourteenth-century work was to re-enforce Dryden's impression of an ever-changing language in an ever-changing world. *No thing* in the world is as it was when Chaucer wrote. The verb, however, is 'alter'd' not 'new-created'. Every thing is 'alter'd', but nothing has come out of nothing—and so, somehow, nothing has been lost.

On the Course of Poetry

Dryden places Chaucer in a literary history that moves in and out of chronology, that confuses and sometimes conflates past and present, describes the history of the art of poetry and development of that art sometimes sequentially and sometimes as a timeless co-existence of the past in the present—the present of Dryden's own mind and that of his readers.

Sometimes, Dryden presents himself as a self-confident modernist, maintaining, like others at the time, that the English language had only become adult during his own lifetime:

> We can only say, that [Chaucer] liv'd in the Infancy of our Poetry, and that nothing is brought to Perfection at first. We must be Children before we grow Men.... even after *Chaucer* there was a *Spenser*, a *Harrington*, a *Fairfax*, before *Waller* and *Denham* were in being; and our Numbers were in their Nonage till these last appeared.[55]

At other times, Dryden reminisces about the 1630s and 1660s rather as a poet in the 1990s might remember the 1930s and 1960s. His evidence is, characteristically, in part anecdotal:

> *Milton* has acknowledg'd to me, that *Spenser* was his Original; and many beside my self have heard our famous *Waller* own, that he deriv'd the Harmony of his Numbers from the *Godfrey of Bulloign*, which was turn'd into *English* by Mr. *Fairfax*.[56]

But there are also suggestions that Dryden's Preface includes some recent re-thinking of literary history. One piece of significant revaluation is evidenced in the change of mind that Dryden appears to have undergone regarding the work of George Sandys, the author of the translation of Ovid which he had described as almost beneath notice a few years earlier,[57] but which he now discusses in quite different terms, and draws on heavily in his own translations from the Roman poet.

---

[55] Ibid. 7. 34.
[56] Ibid. 7. 25.
[57] See the Dedication to *Examen Poeticum* (1693): Dryden, *Works*, 4. 370.

The poet who had come 'nearest' to copying the 'turn' of Ovid's verse, he now says, was

> the Ingenious and Learned *Sandys*, the best Versifier of the former Age; if I may prop-erly call it by that Name, which was the former Part of this concluding Century. For *Spencer* and *Fairfax* both flourish'd in the Reign of Queen *Elizabeth*: Great Masters in our Language; and who saw much farther into the Beauties of our Numbers, than those who immediately followed them. *Milton* was the Poetical Son of *Spencer*, and Mr. *Waller* of *Fairfax*; for we have our Lineal Descents and Clans, as well as other Families: *Spencer* more than once insinuates, that the Soul of *Chaucer* was trans-fus'd into his Body; and that he was begotten by him Two hundred years after his Decease.[58]

Not only is the refinement of language now not seen as uninterruptedly 'pro-gressive', but Dryden's view of his own place in literary history has also become complicated. David Fairer has argued that while Dryden 'venerated Chaucer and understood the family resemblance in the Chaucer-Spenser-Milton line' he nev-ertheless 'valued his own independence from it'.[59] Such a formulation seems to account for only part of Dryden's thinking. It is clear from his comparison of Chaucer with Boccaccio that Dryden did not think that the 'refinement' of the English poetical language began with Waller. Boccaccio and Chaucer, 'among other Things, had this in common, that they refin'd their Mother-Tongues'. It was because of 'Reasons of Time, and Resemblance of Genius, in *Chaucer* and *Boc-cace*', that he 'resolv'd to join them' in his own work.[60] Significantly in the present context, Dryden associates both writers' 'refinement' of their native languages with their metrical innovations. Boccaccio 'is said to have invented the Octave Rhyme, or Stanza of Eight Lines, which ever since has been maintain'd by the Practice of all *Italian* Writers, who are, or at least assume the Title of Heroick Poets', where the reader is presumably to see the correspondence with Chaucer's invention of the 'Heroic' couplet—the form in which Dryden is himself now writing.[61]

Such an account of the 'improvement of our numbers', however, is only one of the literary-historical stories that Dryden tells. The course of English poetry as Dryden sees it is complicated—partly because it is almost always more than merely English. Chaucer, the 'Father of English Poetry', resembles, in Dryden's account, not only Spenser but also Ovid—and in his *Knight's Tale*, Virgil and Homer—and, by implication, also resembles Dryden himself. In Dryden's sense of things, reading is never a solitary encounter of *one* reader with *one* writer.

---

[58] Ibid. 7. 25.
[59] David Fairer, 'Creating a National Poetry: The Tradition of Spenser and Milton', in *The Cambridge Companion to Eighteenth-Century Poetry*, ed. John Sitter (Cambridge, 2006), pp. 177–202 (pp. 179–80).
[60] 'Genius' here means something like 'cast of mind', rather than 'supreme intelligence'.
[61] Dryden, *Works*, 7. 26.

On Veneration and Fatherhood

Dryden's dominant image or idea of poetic connections is that of genealogy, of descent, of families: '*Milton* was the Poetical Son of *Spencer*, and Mr. *Waller* of *Fairfax*; for we have our Lineal Descents and Clans, as well as other Families.' In Dryden's Preface, family metaphors seem to be taken almost literally. Just as Chaucer's personages are our 'Fore-fathers and Great Grand-dames', so one poet 'fathers' another—who may, herself, of course, be a *female* poet.[62] Those poetical children may have children of their own and so produce a 'clan' of related poets. Chaucer was the father of Spenser, who was the father of Milton. Each clan has had its representatives in every 'age'. On occasions, one poetical and fictional personage may father—or in this case, mother—a fictional personage in a later poem: '*Dido* cannot be deny'd to be the Poetical Daughter of *Calypso*.'[63]

Dryden's most striking suggestion is that the resemblance between a poetical father and a poetical son may be stronger than that between a biological father and son in ordinary life. There is no observable irony, or only the merest flicker of a smile of detachment, when Dryden observes that '*Spencer* more than once insinuates, that the Soul of *Chaucer* was transfus'd into his Body; and that he was begotten by him Two hundred years after his Decease.'[64] Dryden claims to have found translating Homer 'a more pleasing Task than *Virgil*' because 'the *Grecian* is more according to my Genius than the *Latin* Poet'.[65] But his identification with Chaucer appears to be even stronger. He had been, he says, 'embolden'd' to go beyond literal translation in retelling some of Chaucer's stories and to have 'presum'd farther in some Places, and added somewhat' of his own by his discovery that he had a 'Soul congenial' to Chaucer's.[66] Such a congeniality of Soul, he realized, is as humbling as it is ennobling:

> I seriously protest, that no Man ever had, or can have, a greater Veneration for *Chaucer*, than my self. I have translated some part of his Works, only that I might perpetuate his Memory, or at least refresh it, amongst my Countrymen. If I have alter'd him any where for the better, I must at the same time acknowledge, that I could have done nothing without him: *Facile est inventis addere*, is no great Commendation; and I am not so vain to think I have deserv'd a greater.[67]

---

[62] Dryden told his publisher, Jacob Tonson, that the poem on his translation of Virgil by Lady Mary Chudleigh, later published in her *Poems on Several Occasions* (London, 1703), was 'better than any' of the poems (all by men) that were actually printed with the translation itself (see Dryden, *Letters*, p. 98). Female readers—and particularly female poets—seem to have been among Dryden's most fervent admirers. An entire elegiac volume, *The Nine Muses, Or Poems Written by Severall Ladies, Upon the Death of the Late Famous John Dryden, Esq.* (London, 1700) appeared in 1700. Elizabeth Thomas's *Miscellany Poems on Several Subjects* (London, 1722) contained seven poems addressed to or celebrating Dryden. The work of a notable 'daughter' of Chaucer, Jane Brereton, is discussed in Chapter 11 of this study.
[63] Dryden, *Works*, 7. 29.
[64] Ibid. 7. 25.
[65] Ibid. 7. 28.
[66] Ibid. 7. 40.
[67] Ibid. 7. 42.

Dryden's veneration of Chaucer is, at one and the same instant, historical and non-historical: 'As he [Chaucer] is the Father of *English* Poetry, so I hold him in the same Degree of Veneration as the *Grecians* held *Homer*, or the *Romans Virgil*: He is a perpetual Fountain of good Sense.'[68] Dryden's 'perpetual' seems to suggest that Chaucer was more than the 'father' of his immediate successors—Lydgate, say, Hoccleve, or Henryson. His good sense still flows. He can 'father' poems in the seventeenth century as he had in the fifteenth. The 'Grecians', Dryden suggests, looked to Homer as the inspirer and 'father' of all they wrote. The Romans looked back to Virgil as the 'father' of their poetry. Dryden's Chaucer resembles Homer rather than Ennius—the Homer whose *Iliad* Dryden was at this moment planning to turn into a living modern poem. In addition, and most importantly, where Dryden's predecessors had suggested that Chaucer resembled Homer in his *historical* relation to his successors, Dryden was the first to claim emphatically that Chaucer resembled Homer *in poetic merit*.

On Fame and Fate

In the Preface to *Fables*, Dryden sees himself as temporarily at the centre of a web connecting him in many and various ways to all the poets he has mentioned—and to poets in the future. He has retold Chaucer's stories. 'Another Poet, in another Age', he says, may retell his, 'if at least they live long enough.'[69] He is writing under the prompting of new, first-hand, intensely detailed experiences of particular poems—which have led, with apparent effortlessness, to large general theories of poetic interconnectedness and poetic interchange, synchronic, diachronic, and beyond the boundaries of time.

Dryden's new experiences, his sudden discovery of congeniality with Homer and with Chaucer, are presented as something to which his whole life as a reader and writer of poetry had been mysteriously tending. Dryden was under the (almost certainly mistaken) impression that Chaucer was being translated in France at the same time that he himself was translating him in England:

> [T]here is something in it like Fatality; that after certain Periods of Time, the Fame and Memory of Great Wits should be renew'd, as *Chaucer* is…. If this be wholly Chance, 'tis extraordinary; and I dare not call it more, for fear of being tax'd with Superstition.[70]

Dryden's language seems, again, not playful but almost religious, and suggests that the 'course' of poetry might be in some way predetermined by a more than human

---

[68] Ibid. 7. 33.
[69] Ibid. 7. 40.
[70] Ibid. 7. 42.

agency.[71] That such a notion was in his mind is suggested by the title page to the *Fables*, which contains a significant quotation from Virgil:

> nunc ultro ad cineres ipsius et ossa parentis
> (haud equidem sine mente, reor, sine numine divum)
> adsumus.
> ['But now, lo! by my sire's own dust and bones we stand—not I think,
> without the purpose and will of heaven.'][72]
>
> (Virgil, Aeneid, 5. 55–7, with Loeb translation)

These lines were spoken by Virgil's hero Aeneas, who, after many wanderings, has arrived once again on an island where he had buried his father, Anchises. The quotation is enigmatic. Was Dryden hinting that the course or development of English poetry, if not dictated by God himself, is nevertheless somehow divinely conducted? In turning to Chaucer, Homer, Ovid, and Boccaccio, his impression had not been one of alienation or otherness but one of profound recognition. He had found such a particular degree of congeniality between himself and Chaucer that he thought he could almost have written what Chaucer wrote. He regards the process of recognition with a 'veneration' approaching the religious.

In his own earlier translation of Virgil's lines, Dryden had stressed the happiness, in every sense, of Aeneas' landfall, and the joy with which Aeneas is to give honours to his father, Anchises:

> But since this happy Storm our Fleet has driv'n
> (Not, as I deem, without the Will of Heav'n,)
> Upon these friendly Shores, and flow'ry Plains,
> Which hide *Anchises*, and his blest Remains;
> Let us with Joy perform his Honours due;
> And pray for prosp'rous Winds our Voyage to renew.
> Pray, that in Towns and Temples of our own,
> The name of great Anchises may be known.
>
> (The Fifth Book of the Aeneis, 69–77; Dryden, Works, 5. 489)

If he was invoking his own impression of Virgil's lines when he came to cite them on the title page of *Fables*, Dryden's thought might have been that paying honours to an ancestor was a way of conjuring 'prosp'rous Winds' for himself. His own works would resemble the 'Towns and Temples' where the names of his great ancestors would become 'known', the means by which 'the Fame and Memory of Great Wits should be renew'd'. In Dryden's sense of things, literary time was a place in which everything was changing while remaining perpetually the same. Homer, Ovid, Boccaccio, and Chaucer might coexist in the present

---

[71] Samuel Johnson, in his *A Dictionary of the English Language*, 2 vols (London, 1755), glosses the word 'fatality' as 'predestination; predetermined order or series of things and events; preordination of inevitable causes acting invincibly in perpetual succession', or, more simply, 'Decree of Fate'.

[72] The wording is identical in the 'Delphin' edition of Virgil, which was the main edition used by Dryden when making his translation.

even though everything—kings, dynasties, denominations, and the very dress of thought itself—had altered.

Dryden's remarks on Chaucer continued to be cited with approval into the twentieth century. But during the eighteenth, they were felt to have been given crucial support and embodiment in the versions of Chaucerian poems which followed them in Dryden's *Fables*. It is to this topic that we turn in Chapters 3 and 4.

3

Palamon and Arcite

Archaism, Anachronism, Heroic Fortitude, and Uncaring Gods

The Fame of *Palamon and Arcite*

In his collection of versions from Chaucer published in 1741, George Ogle provided an interesting modification to the Prologue to *The Miller's Tale*, which, in the *Canterbury Tales* follows immediately after *The Knight's Tale*. Where Chaucer, in Urry's text, had reported that 'In all the Cump'ny n'as ther yong ne old' who did not consider the tale told by the Knight to be 'a nobill Story, / And worthy to be drawn in Memory',[1] Ogle transforms Chaucer's words into a set of remarks which apply equally to Chaucer's *The Knight's Tale* and Dryden's *Palamon and Arcite*. Ogle describes the tale told by the knight as 'A Tale so <u>nobly</u> plan'd, and sweetly told!' that it

> Pleas'd All of either Sex, both Young and Old;
> But most the Men of Sense, and Men of Taste:
> Stor'd with such Virtue! With such Beauty grac'd.
> They judg'd it, for the Stile, and for the Frame,
> Worthy to stand in the Records of *Fame*!
> (Ogle, p. 184)

Ogle here manages, simultaneously, to compliment Chaucer, the Knight, and Dryden. Ogle's 'Frame' is presumably what Dryden, in his Preface to *Fables*, had praised as the 'story' and 'disposition' of *The Knight's Tale*. For Chaucer, *The Knight's Tale* is 'a nobill Story' and was therefore particularly admired by 'the gentiles everochone'. For Dryden and for Ogle, it is 'noble' because its composition, structure, and scope invite comparisons with the heroic poems of Greece and Rome. Dryden had expressed a special preference for 'the Noble Poem of *Palamon* and *Arcite*', which, he had claimed, 'is of the *Epique* kind,

---

[1] Ogle, p. 24.

Chaucer in the Eighteenth Century. David Hopkins and Tom Mason, Oxford University Press.
© David Hopkins and Tom Mason (2022). DOI: 10.1093/oso/9780192862624.003.0004

Fig. 3.1 Theseus, Hippolyta, and the Theban women. From John Dryden, *The Fables ... Ornamented with Engravings from the Pencil of the Right Hon. Lady Diana Beauclerk* (London, 1797).

and perhaps not much inferiour to the *Ilias*, or the *Æneis*'. 'The Story', he had maintained, 'is more pleasing than either of them, the Manners as perfect, the Diction as poetical, the Learning as deep and various, and the Disposition full as artful'. In the opening poem to *Fables*, 'To Her Grace the Duchess of Ormond', Dryden had contended that Chaucer had 'tuned' an 'ancient song' to 'his British lyre' so successfully that the resulting poem was one 'Which

Fig. 3.2 A decorous disagreement between Palamon and Arcite. From From John Dryden, *The Fables … Ornamented with Engravings from the Pencil of the Right Hon. Lady Diana Beauclerk* (London, 1797).

Homer might without a blush rehearse, / And leaves a doubtful palm in *Virgil's* verse'.[2]

George Ogle was exaggerating only slightly in claiming that *Palamon and Arcite* had pleased and was likely to please 'All of either Sex, both Young and Old'.

[2] Dryden, *Works*, 7. 44, 48.

Palamon and Arcite appears to be one of those rare poems that met with immediate popularity and gained in esteem throughout the first, and a good way into the second century of its existence, meeting with equal admiration from young and elderly readers, from the amateur and the poetically sophisticated. Dryden's versions of Chaucer were praised in elegies on Dryden's death in 1700.[3] Many passages in *Palamon and Arcite* were anthologized in Edward Bysshe's *Art of English Poetry* only two years after the poem's publication. *Palamon and Arcite* was explicitly mentioned as the model for some poems and novels by men and by women.[4] It was frequently quoted in works with a wide readership.[5] The admiration of 'Men of Sense and Taste', as Ogle puts it, is displayed in annotations to scholarly editions of classical authors. The vocabulary of *Palamon and Arcite* provided citations for lexicographers, including, notably, Samuel Johnson.[6] Its phraseology was adopted by many poets. Its images appealed to painters and illustrators (see Figs. 1–3).[7] In his famous remarks about the language of English poetry, Thomas Gray drew many of his examples from *Palamon and Arcite*, arguing that they represented enrichments rather than archaisms, and that Chaucer's phrases had been revived and returned to living poetic currency by appearing in Dryden's poem. Dryden, Gray suggests, has not 'modernized' the language of Chaucer's poem, but has invented or selected a diction that stands outside time, combining intimate relations with the past with liveliness and intelligibility in the present.[8]

Esteem for Dryden's poem appears to have extended rapidly to Chaucer's original. In his edition of 1737, Thomas Morell printed Chaucer's poem first, following it with Dryden's version. Morell's annotations also suggest that he had studied Dryden's methods carefully and that he took Dryden's comparisons with Homer and Virgil with the utmost seriousness as constituting critical truth. The writings of John Dart, the antiquarian and part author of the 'Life' of Chaucer in Urry's edition, offer particularly interesting evidence of his having read Chaucer's original under strong impressions provided by Dryden's version. For Dart, as for Dryden,

---

[3] See, e.g. *Luctus Britannici, or, The Tears of the British Muses for the Death of John Dryden* (London, 1700), pp. 18, 55.

[4] See, e.g. Nathaniel Taubman, *Virtue in Distress, or, The History of Mindana* (London, 1706), Sig. A1[r]; Delarivier Manley, *The Power of Love: In Seven Novels* (London, 1720), pp. xv–xvi.

[5] See Eliza Haywood, The Female Spectator, 4 vols (London, 1745), 3. 55; 4. 68, 310; Samuel Richardson, *Clarissa* (London, 1748), 3. 284. References to *Palamon and Arcite* in these and several other works are discussed by Adam Rounce, in 'Eighteenth-Century Responses to Dryden's *Fables*', *Translation and Literature*, 16 (2007), 29–52.

[6] See s.v. *All-Seeing* in William Rider, *A New Universal English Dictionary* (London, 1759); Daniel Fenning, *The Royal English Dictionary* (London, 1763); Samuel Johnson, *A Dictionary of the English Language*, 2 vols (London, 1755). See, further, Amanda M. Leff, 'Johnson's Chaucer', *Age of Johnson*, 21 (2013), 1–20 (p. 10).

[7] See *Poets Gallery, ... Painted for Mr. Macklin, by the Artists of Britain, Illustrative of the British Poets* (London, 1789), pp. 10–11; John Dryden, *The Fables ... Ornamented with Engravings from the Pencil of the Right Hon. Lady Diana Beauclerk* (London, 1797).

[8] See Thomas Gray, *Correspondence*, ed. Paget Toynbee and Leonard Whibley, 3 vols (Oxford, 1935; rpt. 1971), 1. 192–3.

Fig. 3.3 Palamon and Arcite fighting (ferociously) by John Hamilton Mortimer. One of a series of illustrations (engraved in 1787) intended for an edition of Chaucer's work that never appeared. The series was sometimes bound up in copies of Urry's edition and the posthumous edition of Tyrwhitt's edition.

The Knight's Tale represents Chaucer's primary claim to equality of poetical esteem with the poets of Greece and Rome:

There is a wild Beauty in his Works, which comes nearer the Descriptions of *Homer*, than any other that followed him: And though his Pieces have not that regular disposition as those of the *Grecians*, yet the several Parts separately compared, bear an equal value with theirs; and Mr. *Dryden*, than whom there was no better Judge of the Beauties of *Homer* and *Virgil*, positively asserts that he exceeded the latter, and stands in competition with the former. Whoever reads the *Knight's Tale*, which is the best of his Performances, being a finished Epick Poem, and examines the Characters, the Sentiments, the Diction, Disposition and Time, will find that he was not unacquainted with the Rules of that way of Writing.[9]

A similar endorsement of Dryden's claims was included in Dart's *Westminster-Abbey: A Poem* (1721). Chaucer is there described as the 'Father of Verse' who 'First taught the Muse to speak the English Tongue'. Chaucer is presented as having transcended an illiterate age 'When Learning was with thick'ning Mists o'erspread' and 'rhyming Monks in barb'rous Numbers try / The Lives of Saints, and Feats of Errantry', and, as if 'through a Cloud of Night', to have 'fix'd his Sight' on the 'Beauties' of 'the fam'd Græcian Bard' and made Virgil's verse 'a Lanthorn to his Feet'. Where his predecessors had seen nature through 'the gaudy Prism and painted Glass' of contemporary literary styles and forms, Chaucer's understanding of Homer and Virgil had ensured that 'with a steddy View / And piercing Eye' he 'look'd all Nature thro', 'saw her plain, and drew her as she was'.

In Dart's poem, the supreme justification of these propositions is to be found in *The Knight's Tale*, where Chaucer's 'rough bold Strokes' are seen, in this tale of love and war, to surpass 'Art's curious Touch and nicest Care':

> The Warriour Tale, and *Arcite*'s Love survey,
> And let the *Greek* and *Roman* Bards give way.
> (John Dart, *Westminster-Abbey*.
> [London, 1721], pp. 57–8)

The phrasing of Dart's further account of *The Knight's Tale* in *A Poem on Chaucer and his Writings* (1722) suggests that his poem is as much an account of *Palamon and Arcite* as of Chaucer's tale. Dart describes the poem as one that recounts the 'daring Actions of <u>the Warrior train</u>'. '<u>Warrior train</u>' is Dryden's collective term for those who fight at the tournament.[10] Dart sees both poems as making a strong distinction between the characters and beliefs of Palamon and Arcite. Arcite is drawn 'like *Atrides*, <u>fiercely</u> Brave'. Dryden's Arcite speaks '<u>fiercely</u>' to his friend.[11] Dart describes Arcite as a 'Slave to <u>Desire</u>', perhaps recalling a finely contemptuous distinction that Dryden's Arcite makes between his feelings for Emily and those of Palamon:

> If Love be Passion, and that Passion nurst
> With strong <u>Desires</u>, I lov'd the Lady first.
> Canst thou pretend <u>Desire</u>, whom Zeal inflamed
> To worship, and a Pow'r Celestial nam'd?

---

[9] Urry, Sig. e4ᵛ.
[10] *Palamon and Arcite*, 3. 723–4; Dryden, *Works*, 7. 169.
[11] *Palamon and Arcite*, 2. 141–2; Dryden, *Works*, 7. 97.

>Thine was Devotion to the Blest above,
>I saw the Woman, and <u>desir'd</u> her Love.
>
>*(Palamon and Arcite*, 1. 315–20; Dryden, *Works*, 7. 73)

When Dart describes Palamon as attending to the 'Dues of <u>Honour</u>' he may be responding to the fact that '<u>honour</u>' is a word often in the mouth of Dryden's character,[12] and that, in the opinion of Dryden's Theseus, 'Force is of brutes, but <u>honour</u> is of man.'[13] At the end of the tale, Dryden's Arcite concedes that Palamon is a 'deserving Knight' for 'virtue, valour, and for noble blood, / Truth, honour, all that is comprised in good.'[14] Dart sees Palamon as balancing the 'Dues of <u>Honour</u>' and the '<u>Pow'r of Love</u>'—a phrase and a notion which Dryden had made central. In Book Two, Theseus declares that

>The <u>Pow'r of Love</u>,
>In Earth, and Seas, and Air, and Heav'n above,
>Rules, unresisted, with an awful Nod;
>By daily Miracles, declar'd a God.
>
>*(Palamon and Arcite*, 2. 350–3;
>Dryden *Works*, 7. 109)

The whole drift of Dart's poem, indeed, tends to suggest, with Dryden, that *The Knight's Tale*, in its parts and as a whole, is truly Homeric:

>Such Strength, such Vigour, glows in ev'ry Line,
>An *Iliad* rises through the great Design.[15]

Dryden's Heroic Claims: Pro and Con

In his Dedication to the *Aeneis*, Dryden followed René Rapin in asserting that 'A heroick Poem, truly such, is undoubtedly the greatest Work which the Soul of Man is capable to perform.'[16] And he had made his version of *The Knight's Tale* fresh from translating Virgil, and with an ever-deepening absorption in Milton's *Paradise Lost*. Dryden seems to have been unaware that the principal source of Chaucer's tale was Boccaccio's *Teseida*, a poem closely modelled on classical epics, particularly the *Aeneid*—a fact that, had it been known, would have made his claims for the epic stature of *The Knight's Tale* immediately plausible.[17] But as things stood, by maintaining that *The Knight's Tale* was 'perhaps not much inferiour' to the greatest epic poems known to him, Dryden was placing a little

---

[12] *Palamon and Arcite*, 1, 285–8, 299–301; Dryden, *Works*, 7. 71.

[13] *Palamon and Arcite*, 3, 741–2; Dryden, *Works*, 7. 171.

[14] *Palamon and Arcite*, 3, 820–7; Dryden, *Works*, 7. 175.

[15] John Dart, *A Poem on Chaucer and His Writings* (London, 1722), p. 2.

[16] Dryden, *Works*, 5. 267. René Rapin, *Reflections on Aristotle's Treatise of Poesie*, trans. Thomas Rymer (London, 1674), p. 72.

[17] See David Anderson, *Before the Knight's Tale: Imitation of Classical Epic in Boccaccio's 'Teseida'* (Philadelphia, PA, 1988).

known, little regarded poem—in which the battles are chivalric tournaments and love the principal motivation, and where description and speech predominate over action—near the very pinnacle of human achievement.

Not everyone agreed with Dryden's valuation. In his *Lectures on Poetry* (1742),[18] Joseph Trapp mentioned Dryden's praise for *The Knight's Tale* in the course of arguing, much as Rymer had done before him, that 'these latter Ages have scarce produc'd any Thing that deserves the Name of an Epic Poem'. Trapp assumed that Dryden's opinions on Chaucer's poem would be well known to his audience, but he regarded the opinions themselves as 'too monstrous to deserve a serious Refutation'.[19] Samuel Johnson objected with similar decisiveness that the story of Chaucer's poem, 'containing an action unsuitable to the times in which it is placed, can hardly be suffered to pass without censure of the hyperbolical commendation which Dryden has given it'.[20] And John Aikin judged that for most readers 'a love-adventure' like *The Knight's Tale* would not, *pace* Dryden's praise, 'stand in competition' with epic poems dealing with 'the destruction of one potent empire, or the foundation of another'.[21]

And yet, as we have seen, many readers of poetry were, like John Dart, entirely convinced by Dryden's claims. John Bancks, for example, could refer, as to an agreed matter of fact, to 'Heroic Tales, such as that of PALAMON and ARCITE, written by CHAUCER, and rendered into modern ENGLISH by Mr. DRYDEN; whose preface to his Fables may be consulted for the Character of this piece and its great Similitude to the true Epic'.[22] And Clara Reeve offered the opinion that Chaucer's

> Knight's tale is a complete Epic, and in *Dryden*'s opinion very little inferior to the Iliad or the Æneis.—'The story (says he) is more pleasing, the manners as perfect, the diction as poetical, the learning as deep and various, and the conduct as artful.' Permit me to remark that *Dryden*'s elegant, rich, and harmonious numbers, have preserved this, and many other of *Chaucer*'s works, from sinking into oblivion, and he has given the old Bard a share of his own immortality.[23]

Joseph Warton, Thomas Warton, and Sir Walter Scott: The Pleasures of Anachronism

As Trapp and Johnson had objected, *The Knight's Tale* appears, on the face of it, to bear only occasional resemblance to the *Iliad* or *Æneid*. The ideas at the core of the poem seem far removed from those of an 'heroic age'. Rather than a poem of the 'Epique kind', *The Knight's Tale* would seem to be a 'romance' of love, chivalry,

---

[18] Originally published in Latin in 1711–19; English translation, London, 1742.

[19] Joseph Trapp, *Lectures on Poetry* (London, 1742), p. 348.

[20] Johnson, *Works*, 21. 481.

[21] John Dryden, *Fables from Boccacio* [sic.] *and Chaucer*, ed. John Aikin (London, 1805), p. v.

[22] John Bancks, *Miscellaneous Works, in Verse and Prose*, 2 vols (London, 1738), 1. xiii.

[23] Clara Reeve, *The Progress of Romance through Times, Countries, and Manners*, 2 vols (Colchester, 1785) 1. 86.

and mercy, which culminates in a battle in which no one is killed. It is therefore remarkable that so many readers were prepared to accept Dryden's judgement and to rank his version of Chaucer's poem high in the total body of English poetry. Commenting on *The Knight's Tale* in his *History*, Thomas Warton, despite his local objections, observed:

> We are surprised to find, in a poet of such antiquity, numbers so nervous and flowing: a circumstance which greatly contributed to render Dryden's paraphrase of this poem the most animated and harmonious piece of versification in the English language.[24]

For Warton, the supreme animation and harmony of Dryden's poem is a direct reflection of that of his original. Although Warton does not liken *The Knight's Tale* to the *Iliad*, he appears to have found the 'frame', 'story', or 'disposition' of Chaucer's narrative profoundly pleasing:

> I cannot leave the KNIGHT'S TALE without remarking, that the inventor of this poem, appears to have possessed considerable talents for the artificial construction of a story. It exhibits unexpected and striking turns of fortune; and abounds in those incidents which are calculated to strike the fancy by opening resources to sublime description, or interest the heart by pathetic situations.[25]

Thomas Warton's intense, and apparently equal, pleasure in *Palamon and Arcite* and *The Knight's Tale* was shared with his brother Joseph. Where Thomas had commented on the 'sublime description' and the 'pathetic situations' that interested his 'heart' in *The Knight's Tale*, Joseph's mind was 'whirled away by a torrent of rapid imagery' in Dryden's *Palamon and Arcite*, and he predicted that it would be to his *Fables*, 'though wrote in his old age, that Dryden will owe his immortality, and among them particularly, to Palamon and Arcite'. The special merits of that poem were, he claimed, 'the blaze, the pomp, and the profusion' of 'animated poetry'.[26]

Most extensively and strikingly, Sir Walter Scott found Dryden's claims for the epic status of *The Knight's Tale* entirely persuasive. He suggested that the *Fables* provided the 'best examples' of Dryden's 'talents as a narrative poet; those powers of composition, description, and narration, which must have been called into exercise by the Epic Muse, had his fate allowed him to enlist among her votaries'. Scott, like Thomas Warton, was happy to endorse Dryden's claims for the 'design' of *The Knight's Tale*. Indeed, he argued that a poem which has 'excited' such 'interest … in its progress', and which 'when terminated, leaves no question to be asked, no person undisposed of, and no curiosity unsatisfied', might actually be thought 'more gratifying than the history of a few weeks of a ten years war, commencing long after the siege had begun, and ending long before the city was taken'. In *Palamon and Arcite*, Scott argued, Dryden selected 'for amplification and

---

[24] Warton, *History*, 1. 367.
[25] Ibid. 1. 367.
[26] Joseph Warton, *An Essay on the Genius and Writings of Pope*, 2 vols (London, 1782), 2. 12, 17.

ornament those passages most susceptible of poetical description'. Such passages constitute 'so spirited a transfusion of [Chaucer's] ideas into modern verse, as almost to claim the merit of originality'. There are some, indeed, in which 'the merit of invention [may be] added to that of imitation'.[27]

The Temple of Mars: Gothic and Classical; Sublimity and Comedy

Palamon and Arcite was seen by several readers in the century after Dryden's death as both profoundly 'gothic' and quintessentially classical. One passage that was thought to have combined the two elements with particular skill was Dryden's depiction of the Temple of Mars before which Arcite prays before his combat with Palamon in the tournament.[28] Scott, for example, pointed to Dryden's 'sublime description of the temple of Mars, painted around with all the misfortunes ascribed to the influence of his planet', while observing that 'it would be difficult to point out a single idea, which is not found in the older poem'.[29]

It may seem odd to call this a *pleasing* passage, since it consists of an attempt to visualize the self-inflicted evils that, under the influence of the planet, beset mankind:

There saw I first the darke imagining
Of felonie, and eke the compassing
The cruel ire, reede as any glede
The pickpurse, and eke the pale drede
The smiler, with the knife vnder the cloke
The shepen brenning with the blacke smoke
The treason of the murdring in the bedde
The open warre, with woundes al be bledde
Conteke with blody kniues, & sharpe manace
Al ful of chirking was that sory place.

There saw I how the secret Fellon wrought,
And Treason lab'ring in the Traytor's Thought;
And Midwife Time the ripen'd Plot to Murder brought.
There, the Red Anger dar'd the Pallid Fear;
Next stood Hippocrisie, with holy Lear:
Soft smiling, and demurely looking down,
But hid the Dagger underneath the Gown:
Th'assassinating Wife, the Houshold Fiend;
And far the blackest there, the Traytor-Friend.
On t'other Side, there stood Destruction bare;
Unpunish'd Rapine, and a Waste of War.
Contest, with sharpen'd Knives, in Cloisters drawn,
And all with Blood bespread the holy Lawn.
Loud Menaces were heard, and foul Disgrace,
And bawling Infamy, in Language base;
Till Sense was lost in Sound, and Silence fled the Place.

(*KnT*, 1995–2004; Speght 1598, Fol. 6ʳ)

(*Palamon and Arcite*, 2. 560–75; Dryden, *Works*, 7. 121–3)

---

[27] *The Works of John Dryden: Now First Collected Illustrated with Notes, Historical, Critical, and Explanatory, and a Life of the Author*, ed. Walter Scott, 18 vols (London, 1808), 1. 495–6.

[28] It was included in Bysshe's *The Art of English Poetry* as early as 1702, and in an edition of *Palamon and Arcite* published in Manchester in 1800, it is included in the 'Index to the Most pleasing and particular Passages' in the poem.

[29] Dryden, *Works*, ed. Scott, 1. 498.

Not everything in this passage was admired by all commentators. Thomas Warton, for example, objected to Dryden's phrases 'holy Lear', 'in Cloisters drawn', and 'the holy Lawn', seeing them as gratuitous attempts on Dryden's part to gratify 'his spleen against the clergy'.[30] But Warton had a much higher opinion of the lines immediately following, which describe a peculiarly grotesque suicide and a series of grim personifications. 'Dryden' he wrote, 'has finely paraphrased this passage':[31]

The slear of himselfe yet saw I there	The Slayer of Himself yet saw I there,
His hart blode hath bathed all his here	The Gore congeal'd was clotter'd in his Hair:
The naile ydriven in the shode on hight	With Eyes half clos'd, and gaping Mouth he lay,
With colde death, with mouth gaping vpright	And grim, as when he breath'd his sullen Soul away.
Amiddes of the temple sate Michaunce	In midst of all the Dome, Misfortune sat,
With Discomfort and sory Countenaunce	And gloomy Discontent, and fell Debate.
Yet saw I Wodnesse laghing in his rage	And Madness laughing in his ireful Mood;
Armed complaint on theft and fiers courage.	And arm'd Complaint on Theft; and Cries of Blood.
(KnT, 2004–12; Speght 1598, Fol. 6ʳ)[32]	(Palamon and Arcite, 2. 576–83; Dryden, Works, 7. 123)

In some ways, it is surprising that Warton should object to Dryden's introduction of satirical touches into his Temple, since he considered a 'rude' combination of apparent incongruities to be the characteristic mark of Chaucer's writing generally, and of this passage in particular:

> This group is the effort of a strong imagination, unacquainted with selection and arrangement of images. It is rudely thrown on the canvas without order or art. In the Italian poets, who describe every thing, and who cannot, even in the most serious representations, easily suppress their natural predilection for burlesque and familiar imagery, nothing is more common than this mixture of sublime and comic ideas.[33]

Dryden possibly, and Morell certainly—neither of them knowing of Chaucer's direct source—saw Chaucer's Temple as an imitation of Mercury's visit to the House of Mars in the Thebaid by the Roman poet Statius. In his Poems on Several Occasions (1727), Walter Harte included a translation of Book 6 of the Thebaid in which the passage in question occurs. In a note, Harte commented:

> Chaucer, who was perhaps the greatest poet among the moderns, has translated these verses almost word for word in his Knight's Tale ... scarce anything can exalt the reputation of Statius higher than the verbal imitations of our great countryman.[34]

---

[30] Warton, History, 1. 358 (footnote). Warton, though, was reading Urry's text, where Speght's 'smiler' is replaced with 'Smyter'. It may have been Speght's 'smiler' that prompted Dryden to suppose that Chaucer was thinking of hypocritical priests.

[31] Warton, History, 1. 359 (footnote).

[32] Speght 1598 glosses shode as 'the bush of hair head' and wodnesse as 'madness'.

[33] Warton, History, 1. 360.

[34] Walter Harte, Poems on Several Occasions (London, 1727), pp. 189–90. Compare annotations to Christopher Pitt's translation of Book 7 of the Aeneid in Joseph Warton, ed., The Works of Virgil in Latin and English, 4 vols (London, 1753), 3. 293. In his translation of Statius' Thebaid, William Lillington

The 'mixture of sublime and comic ideas', and of the medieval and classical in Dryden's passage was at its most potentially discordant when Chaucer began to include the various trades associated with Mars, god, and planet, in a passage where Warton found 'the impetuous dashes of a savage and spirited pencil':[35]

There were also of Martes deuision	The whole Division that to *Mars* pertains,
The Barbour, the Botcher, and the Smith	All Trades of Death, that deal in Steel for Gains,
That forgeth sharpe swordes on the stith.	Were there: The Butcher, Armourer, and Smith,
	Who forges sharpen'd Fauchions, or the Scythe.
(*KnT*, 2024–6; Speght 1598, Fol. 6ʳ)	(*Palamon and Arcite*, 2. 596–9; Dryden, *Works*,7. 123)

Thomas Tyrwhitt found the 'mixture of sublime and comic ideas' in this passage peculiarly uncomfortable. Although he does not mention Dryden, he seems to have been impressed—unconsciously, perhaps—by Dryden's inclusion of the Armourer as one of those who 'deal in Steel for gain', and even more by Dryden's removal from his list of Chaucer's 'Barbour'. In his edition, Tyrwhitt says, he was 'glad to avail' himself of the authority of two manuscripts which sanctioned his replacement of 'The barbour' with 'Th' armerer'.[36] This is perhaps an instance of Dryden's poetic intuition prompting Tyrwhitt's more scholarly research.[37]

Several conclusions can be drawn from a consideration of Dryden's Temple of Mars. In the first place, it is clear that the nineteenth-century scholars were quite wrong in suggesting that Dryden's versions prompted no one to turn to the Chaucerian originals. Sir Walter Scott, Thomas Warton, and perhaps Thomas Tyrwhitt, had clearly read the modern version alongside the ancient with considerable care, and had found them mutually illuminating. If not quite reading Chaucer *through* Dryden, they were reading the old poem in the light of the new. It is also clear that these writers were reading both Chaucer's *Knight's Tale* and Dryden's *Palamon and Arcite* as 'sublime' poems, and as 'imitations' of 'human life'—including its most terrible aspects—in which the classical and 'medieval' elements were felt to be inextricable.

Lewis noted that the description of '*Mars's* Temple and Palace' in *Palamon and Arcite* is 'not inferior' to that of Statius, and quoted Dryden's description at length to allow his reader to compare 'the Flowers of Genius and Fancy' in 'both Authors' (*The Thebaid of Statius, Translated into English Verse*, 2 vols (Oxford, 1767), 2. 303–5. Thomas Warton (who did know Boccaccio's *Teseida*) also believed that 'the ground-work of [Dryden's] whole description is in the Thebaid of Statius'. Warton points to several particulars, including Statius calling Mars *Armipotens* (see Warton, *History*, 1. 360–1).

[35] Warton, *History*, 1. 360.

[36] Tyrwhitt 1775–78, 4. 224–5.

[37] The two MSS lent to Tyrwhitt by Dr Askew have been identified as British Library Egerton 2864 and Add. 5140. See Paul G. Ruggiers, ed., *Editing Chaucer, The Great Tradition* (Norman, OK, 1984), p. 123. Tyrwhitt was also discountenanced by the inclusion of 'the pickepurse' on the walls of the Temple. Tyrwhitt's conjectural replacement of 'the botcher' with 'the bowyer' would seem, however, to be at odds with Dryden's sense that all the traders in death 'deal in *Steel*'.

Dryden's description of the funeral of Arcite was sometimes regarded as resembling passages in Homer and in Virgil. The laments of Palamon and Arcite, and the consolatory disquisitions of Egeus and of Theseus were seen as reflecting classical as well as Christian wisdom. At the same time, and often in the same minds, the 'wild' profusion of imagery in the description of the lists, the description of Emily, and the general importance given to love were peculiarly admired for their very difference from classical models. The actor, playwright, and novelist Samuel Jackson Pratt considered Chaucer's 'Knightes Tale, which Dryden has so nobly modernised, as the poem of Chivalry: the names, indeed, are classical; but the images, the sentiments, the characters, the very action of the poem itself, are all wild, and fanciful, and chivalrous'.[38] Many readers, however, recognized that both classical and 'chivalrous' elements in Dryden's version, and a combination of the two, had antecedents in poems that they admired, particularly those of Spenser, from the centuries between Chaucer's and Dryden's. It was, perhaps, the inextricable mixture of the two that gave them particular pleasure.

Dryden, Boileau, Palamon, and the Gods

Dryden's reflections on the nature of epic poetry were strongly influenced by contemporary French criticism. We have already witnessed his indebtedness to René Rapin in his larger conception of what constituted an heroic poem, 'truly such'. It is also clear from his Dedicatory 'Discourse Concerning the Original and Progress of Satire', prefixed to *The Satires of Juvenal and Persius* (1692; dated 1693), that Dryden's thinking on the subject was given considerable and particular impulse by Boileau's *L'Art poétique*, to a translation of which he had contributed ten years earlier. Boileau's account of the gods proper to poetry weighed particularly on Dryden's mind. In his 'Discourse', Dryden expressed his wish that he could 'remove' the 'difficulty' pointed out by Boileau ('a great *French* Critique, as well as an Admirable Poet') that 'the Machines of our Christian Religion, in Heroique Poetry, are much more feeble to Support that weight than those of Heathenism'.[39]

Boileau considered divine machinery essential to and omnipresent in an epic poem, and, like Rapin,[40] thought that machinery to be essentially fictional.[41] The gods are the 'Springs that move' men's 'hopes and fears' (615). An epic without

[38] See the footnote to Richard Mant's 'Verses to the Memory of Joseph Warton', in Samuel Jackson, *Harvest-Home*, 3 vols (London, 1805), 1. 63.
[39] Dryden, *Works*, 4. 17. Earlier in the 'Discourse', Dryden had called Boileau: 'a living *Horace* and a *Juvenal*' whose 'Numbers are Excellent, whose Expressions are Noble, whose Thoughts are Just, whose Language is Pure, whose Satire is pointed, and whose Sense is close' (Dryden, *Works*, 4. 12).
[40] *Reflections*, p. 193.
[41] Quotations are from *The Art of Poetry, Written in French by The Sieur de Boileau, Made English* (1683) in Dryden, *Works*, 2. 142–4, with line references given in text.

machinery is 'but a dull insipid Tale' (619). Mistaken modern authors, 'Thinking our God, and Prophets that he sent, / Might Act like those the Poets did invent', have tried 'in vain' 'These ancient Ornaments to lay aside' (620–3), while terrifying poor readers 'in each Line with Hell, / And talk of *Satan*, *Ashtaroth*, and *Bel*' (624–5). The 'Mysteries which Christians must believe', Boileau says, are incompatible with the 'shifting Pageants' of poetry (627–8). To confuse the two is to run a danger of inadvertent irreligion, and of making the 'true God' appear a 'God of Lies' (663).

In this context, one of Scott's remarks on *Palamon and Arcite* deserves particular notice. Scott observes that whenever astrological topics occur in Dryden's poetry, 'he dwells on them with a pleasure, which shows the command they maintained over his mind'. 'Much of the astrological knowledge displayed in the Knight's Tale', Scott points out, 'is introduced, or at least amplified, by Dryden.' There are several reasons for thinking that Chaucer's gods, created by combining classical elements with their influence as astrological planetary bodies, were particularly and profoundly attractive to Dryden, perhaps because this provided a solution to the problem defined by Boileau and other French theorists.

So much is this the case that it could be said that *Palamon and Arcite* demonstrates the epic status of *The Knight's Tale* by showing it to be a poem *about* the gods. So powerful is the resistless force of the deities in the poem that the mortals are allowed only the minimum of self-determinate action. Human beings' attempts to control their own destiny are crushed, even annihilated, by the will or influence of the divine agents. Though they are background figures in the early part of the poem, the gods invite increasing attention until, in the later stages, they come close to being the centre of interest. The human characters talk about them a good deal, blaming them for their misfortune or claiming their power as justification for human behaviour. The gods are depicted in all their many powers on the walls of their temples—powers that are developed and expanded upon when the three young people, by praying to them, show what they assume the gods capable of doing. The gods are then introduced in person, and the catastrophe in which the poem's action culminates is their work.

Of the human figures in the poem, Palamon is the one whose religious convictions appear most simple. Although he thinks he is freed from prison 'by Chance' (2. 137), he appears to believe in 'Eternal deities / Who rule the world with absolute Decrees, / And write whatever Time shall bring to pass, / With Pens of Adamant, on Plates of Brass' (1. 470–3). That belief, however, provides him with no comfort. He cannot see that the eternal deities care for 'the Race of Humankind' any more than for 'all his fellow-creatures'. Human beings are, if anything, in a worse condition than beasts, and bound by harder laws. Goodness, in particular goes unregarded. 'What worse', he asks 'could befall' to 'wretched Virtue' were 'Fate, or giddy Fortune' in ultimate control of all?

Here is Palamon's complaint in full:

O cruell goddes, that gouerne
This worlde with your word eterne
And written in the table of Athamant,
Your parliament and eterne graunt
What is mankind more unto you yholde
Than is the shepe, that rouketh in the folde?
For slain is man, right as another beest
And dwelleth eke in prison, and in arrest
And hath sicknesse, and great aduersite
And oft time giltlesse parde.
  What gouernance is in this prescience
That giltlesse turmenteth innocence?
And encreaseth thus all my penaunce
That man is bounden to his obseruance
For God's sake to leten of his will
There as a beest may all his lustes fulfill
And whan a beest is deed, he hath no payn
But after his death, man mote wepe & plain:
Though in this world he haue care and wo
Without doute it may stonden so.
  The answer of this lete I to diuines,
But well I wote, in this world great pine is
Alas I se a serpent or a thefe
That many a true man hath do mischiefe
Gon at his large, & where him list may turn
But I mote ben in prison through Saturn
And eke through Juno, ialous and eke wood
That hath stroied wel nigh al the blood
Of Thebes, with his wast walles wide;
And Venus sleeth me on that other side
For ielousie, and feare of him Arcite.

(KnT, 1303–33; Speght 1598, Fol. 3ʳ)

Eternal Deities,
Who rule the World with absolute Decrees,
And write whatever Time shall bring to pass,
With Pens of Adamant, on Plates of Brass;
What is the Race of Humane Kind your Care
Beyond what all his Fellow-Creatures are?
He with the rest is liable to Pain,
And like the Sheep, his Brother-Beast, is slain.
Cold, Hunger, Prisons, Ills without a Cure,
All these he must, and guiltless oft, endure:
Or does your Justice, Pow'r, or Prescience fail,
When the Good suffer, and the Bad prevail?
What worse to wretched Vertue could befall,
If Fate, or giddy Fortune govern'd all?
Nay, worse than other Beasts is our Estate;
Them, to pursue their Pleasures you create;
We, bound by harder Laws, must curb our Will,
And your Commands, not our Desires fulfil;
Then when the Creature is unjustly slain,
Yet after Death, at least, he feels no Pain.
But Man in Life surcharg'd with Woe before,
Not freed when dead, is doom'd to suffer more.
A Serpent shoots his Sting at unaware;
An ambush'd Thief forelays a Traveller;
The Man lies murder'd, while the Thief and Snake,
One gains the Thickets, and one thrids the Brake.
This let Divines decide; but well I know,
Just, or unjust, I have my Share of Woe,
Through *Saturn* seated in a luckless Place,
And *Juno*'s Wrath, that persecutes my Race;
Or *Mars* and *Venus* in a Quartil, move
My Pangs of Jealousy for *Arcite*'s Love.

(*Palamon and Arcite*, 1. 470–501;
Dryden, *Works*, Vol.17, 81–3)

For several readers, Palamon's words and the sentiments expressed here, both in Chaucer and in Dryden, were profoundly shocking. Thomas Morell, for example, disapproved of Palamon's irreligion, saying that it 'transgress[es] the Bound of Reason'. But he considered that Palamon's speech was essentially Homeric, and compared it to Philaetius's complaint against Jove in the *Odyssey*. Morell claimed, as had Pope in his edition of Homer's poem, and 'Philypsus', one of the interlocutors in Joseph Spence's *Essay on Pope's Odyssey*, that Palamon's words could be excused, since they were the expression of 'an Excess of Sorrow'. One should, moreover, Spence's 'Philysus' insisted, 'always take care not to attribute to the Poet, what he speaks under some other Person'. One cannot, for example, blame

Milton for making his Satan, in *Paradise Lost*, speak 'according to' his 'true Character'.[42]

But against this, it might be suggested that there is little indication in the verse of Chaucer or Dryden, or of Homer, to suggest any very great distance between the words of Palamon, or of Philaetius, and the mind of the composing poet—as there almost always is between Milton and Satan. Until the end of the passage, when Chaucer's Palamon points to the immediate cause of his pain ('ielousie, and feare of him Arcite'), Dryden seems to have given his Palamon words of a dignity that derives from their large generality. He has occasionally sharpened the charge against the 'absolute Decrees' of the 'Eternal ('What worse to wretched Vertue could befall, / If Fate, or giddy Fortune govern'd all?'), but was content to allow his Palamon, like Chaucer's, to 'let Divines decide' the appropriate theodicy.

Palamon, Spenser, and Lucretius in Praise of Venus

Palamon moves from the complete despair of his complaint to place his entire faith in Venus. His eloquent hymn to the goddess prompted Dryden to turn to the opening of Lucretius's *De Rerum Natura*—and above all to Spenser, Chaucer's poetic 'son', and also here an imitator of Lucretius.[43] Chaucer's Palamon prays to Venus by dwelling on her own love for Adonis, Lucretius by invoking her love for Mars. In both *The Knight's Tale* and *De Rerum Natura*, Venus is a star as well as a goddess. Chaucer's Palamon begins by mentioning the family of his goddess ('Fairest of faire: O lady mine Venus / Doughter of Jove, and spouse to Vulcanus') and ends his hymn with an appeal to the love she had for Adonis ('Thou glader of the mount of Citheron / For thilke love thou haddest to Adon / Have pite of my bitter teares smerte / And take my humble praier at thine herte').[44] These lines would not presumably have presented Dryden with metrical difficulties. And yet they have prompted him to deviate from strict heroic couplets, employing several alexandrines, and, towards the end of his version, triplets ending in twelve-syllable alexandrines—a line the management of which Dryden claimed he had learned from Spenser:[45]

---

[42] See Morell, p. 393; Pope, *Poems*, 10. 245; Joseph Spence, *An Essay on Pope's Odyssey*, 2 vols (London, 1726–27), 2. 63–4.

[43] In his edition of *The Faerie Queen*, John Upton noted Dryden's indebtedness to both Spenser and Lucretius, and pointed out that Spenser was responding precisely to details in Lucretius's Latin. He also insisted, however, that in one tiny particular Spenser was drawing on Chaucer: '*Pricked* is Chaucer's word, who perhaps had Lucretius too in view' (see Edmund Spenser, *The Faerie Queen, A New Edition*, ed. John Upton, 2 vols (London, 1715), 2. 603). Dryden's use of Lucretius in this passage is discussed by Paul Hammond, in 'The Interplay of Past and Present in Dryden's *Palamon and Arcite*', *The Seventeenth Century*, 23 (2008), 142–59.

[44] Speght 1598, Fol. C1ʳ.

[45] For Dryden's use of Spenserian alexandrines and triplets, see his Dedication to the *Aeneis*: Dryden, *Works*, 5. 322, 331.

Great Venus, Queene of beautie and of grace,
  The ioy of <u>Gods and men</u>, that vnder skie
<u>Doest fayrest shine</u>, and most adorne <u>thy place</u>,
That with thy smyling looke doest pacifie
The raging seas, and makst the stormes to flie;
<u>Thee, goddesse, thee</u> the winds, the clouds doe
                       feare,
And when thou spredst thy mantle forth on hie,
  The waters play and pleasant lands appeare,
And heavens <u>laugh</u>, and all the world shews
                 ioyous cheare.

Then doth the daedale earth throw forth to thee
  Out of her fruitfull lap aboundant <u>flowres</u>,
And spring breake forth out of his lusty bowres,
They all doe learne to play the Paramours;
First doe the merry <u>birds</u>, thy prety pages
Privily priked with thy lustful powres,

Chirpe loud to thee out of their leauy cages,
And thee their mother call to coole their kindly
                 rages.
Then doe the salvage beasts begin to play
  Their pleasant friskes, and loath their wonted
                 food;
<u>The Lyons rore</u>, the Tygres loudly bray,
The raging <u>Buls rebellow through</u> the wood,
<u>And</u> breaking forth, dare <u>tempt the</u> deepest flood,
To come where thou doest draw them with desire:
So all things else, that nourish vitall blood,
Soone as with fury thou doest them inspire,
In generation seeke to quench their inward fire.

So all <u>the world</u> by thee at first was made,
  And dayly yet thou doest the same <u>repayre</u> …
  Mother of laughter, and welspring of blisse,
O graunt that of my loue at last I may not misse.

(Spenser, *The Faerie Queene*, IV, x, 43–8)

Creator *Venus*, Genial Pow'r of Love,
The Bliss of <u>Men</u> below, and <u>Gods</u> above!
Beneath the sliding Sun thou runn'st thy Race,
<u>Dost fairest shine</u>, and best become <u>thy Place</u>.
For thee the Winds their Eastern Blasts forbear,
Thy Month reveals the Spring, and opens all the
                 Year.
<u>Thee, Goddess, thee</u> the Storms of Winter fly;
Earth smiles with <u>Flow'rs</u> renewing; <u>laughs</u> the
                 Sky,
And <u>Birds</u> to Lays of Love their tuneful Notes
                 apply.

For thee <u>the Lion</u> loaths the Taste of Blood,
And <u>roaring</u> hunts his Female through the Wood:
For thee <u>the Bulls rebellow through the</u> Groves,
<u>And tempt</u> the Stream, and snuff their absent
                 Loves.
'Tis thine, whate'er is pleasant, good, or fair:
All Nature is thy Province, Life thy Care;
Thou mad'st the World, and dost the World
                 <u>repair</u>.
<u>Thou Gladder of the Mount of</u> *Cytheron*,
Increase of *Jove*, Companion of the Sun;
If e'er *Adonis* touch'd thy tender Heart,
Have <u>pity</u>, Goddess, for thou know'st the <u>Smart</u>.

(*Palamon and Arcite*, 3. 129–48; Dryden,
Works, 7. 135–7)

Dryden is here not reproducing Chaucer's thoughts in servile imitation, but expressing the thoughts that Chaucer might have had, had he been living in 1700—having studied Lucretius and Spenser—in verse that combines precision and freedom in a way related to, but different from, that employed by either. As so often with Dryden, a response to one poet comes into inevitable and inexorable conjunction with memories of other, related, poets. If Dryden is rewriting Chaucer by adding from Spenser here, he is to some extent rewriting Spenser in couplets. Dryden's thought, perhaps, was that the Chaucerian soul which he and Spenser had inherited was highly innovative, always aspiring, always attempting something greater than it knows, never content merely to repeat its own sentiments or expressions.

Spenser's hymn to Venus is offered by an unnamed singer and comes from and leads nowhere. Palamon's prayer causes confusion and dissent among the gods. Palamon's wild enthusiasm seems to be voiced in complete ignorance of the goddess as we see her in person or in her temple—where we learn that 'The spreading snare for all mankind is laid, / And lovers all betray, or are betray'd'.

Arcite and the Gods; Arcite's Death

Dryden's Arcite, too, does and does not understand the theological system that governs his world—appears unsure, indeed, whether there *is* such a system. When he swears 'by the Gods, who govern Heav'n above' (2. 144), he does not know quite who or if they are. When, in prison, he assumes that Palamon is groaning in pain at the thought of his 'Captivity', Arcite reminds his friend that fortitude is necessary since he is suffering from the result of 'Fate' or 'Destiny' (1. 243–6). (See Fig. 3.4) Dryden's Arcite was here following Chaucer's in astrological thought, and, to some extent, in diction:

Fig. 3.4 The death of Arcite. Engraved by Francesco Bartolozzi from a design by William Hamilton, for No. 2 of *Macklin's British Poets* (London, 1790).

For goddes loue, take all in pacience	For Love of Heav'n, with Patience undergo
Our prison, for it maie none other be	A cureless Ill, since Fate will have it so:
Fortune hath yeven us this aduersite,	So stood our Horoscope in Chains to lie,
Some wicked aspect or disposicion	And Saturn in the Dungeon of the Sky,
Of Saturne, by some constellacion	Or other baleful Aspect, rul'd our Birth,
Hath yeven us this, altho we had it sworn	When all the friendly Stars were under Earth:
So stode the heven when that we were born	What'er betides, by Destiny 'tis done;
We mote endure this is short and playn.	And better bear like Men, than vainly seek to shun.
(KnT, 1084–91; Speght 1598, Fol. 2ʳ)	(Palamon and Arcite, 1. 243–8; Dryden, Works, 7. 69)

As Arcite sees it in the pressure of the moment, the workings of astrology, the 'Aspect' or 'Disposition' of Saturn, constitute 'Fate'. Later, however, he seems to fall under the influence, so to speak, of Juvenal's tenth satire, and to suppose the existence of an omniscient and ultimately beneficent god who may, or may not, be identical with 'Fortune, Fate, or Providence'—terms which themselves become for him near-synonyms:

Alas, why playnen men so in commune	But why, alas! do mortal Men in vain
Of purueyance of God, or of fortune	Of Fortune, Fate, or Providence complain?
That yeueth him full oft in many agise	God gives us what he knows our Wants require,
Well bette than hem self can deuise	And better Things than those which we desire:
Some man desireth to haue richesse	Some pray for Riches; Riches they obtain;
That cause is of her murdre or sicknesse	But watch'd by Robbers, for their Wealth are slain:
And some man wold out of his prison faine	Some pray from Prison to be freed; and come,
That in his house, is of his meyne slaine	When guilty of their Vows, to fall at home;
Infinite harmes bene in this mattere	Murder'd by those they trusted with their Life,
We wote not what thing we prayen here	A favour'd Servant, or a Bosom Wife.
We faren as he that dronke is as a mouse	Such dear-bought Blessings happen ev'ry Day,
A dronken man woten well, he hath an house	Because we know not for what Things to pray.
But he wot not, which the right way thider	Like drunken Sots, about the Street we roam;
And to a dronken man the way is slider	Well knows the Sot he has a certain Home;
And certes in this world so faren we	Yet knows not how to find th'uncertain Place,
We seken fast after felicite	And blunders on, and staggers ev'ry Pace.
But we go wrong full ofte truly	Thus all seek Happiness; but few can find,
Thus we may say all …	For far the greater Part of Men are blind.
(KnT, 1251–68; Speght 1598, Fol. 3ʳ)	(Palamon and Arcite, 1. 420–37; Dryden, Works, 7. 79)

This was a passage even more frequently excerpted by anthologists than Palamon's complaint.[46] Perhaps because Arcite's speech was directed more at human folly

---

[46] Bysshe prints the passage s.v. Fate (to which heading is added the note 'See Fortune, Predestination, and Free-Will'). Some of Dryden's lines are applied to the month of May in John Partridge's almanack Merlinus Liberatur: Being an Almanack for ... 1708 (London, [1708]). The passage is also included in Eliza Haywood's Female Spectator, 4. 374. It is subjected to moralistic interpretation in The Weekly Museum, 2 vols (London, 1774), 2. 104, and by Charles Theodore Middleton in A New and Complete System of Geography, 2 vols (London, 1777–78), 2. 74. Dryden's complex attitudes to the operations of Providence in this passage and throughout the poem are discussed by Abigail Williams

than against the dispensations of the deity, Thomas Morell confined his remarks to the first four lines of this passage as if they were the whole, and that the speech constituted a warning against making the gods, or God, responsible for human faults and human misfortunes.[47] But for Dryden, the main significance of the passage seems to have been that most of Arcite's complaint consists of an account of the manifold miseries of man. Later, overthrown by a sense of the hopelessness of his life and love, Arcite becomes openly hostile to hostile gods, and 'accusing Heav'n and Fate', blames 'angry *Juno*'s unrelenting Hate' for his sufferings (2. 88). He speaks of one 'side of heaven' as being his 'enemy': '*Mars* ruined *Thebes*; his Mother ruined me' (2. 104).

Both in Chaucer and Dryden, Arcite's death, following a pathetic speech, is almost scientifically brutal:

Swelleth the brest of Arcite, and the sore	Swoln is his Breast, his inward Pains increase,
Encreaseth at his hert more and more	All means are us'd, and all without Success.
The clotered blode, for any liche crafte	The clotted Blood lies heavy on his Heart,
Corrumped, and is in his body lafte	Corrupts, and there remains in spite of Art:
That neither veineblode, ne ventousing	Nor breathing Veins, nor Cupping will prevail;
Ne drinke of herbes, may be helping	All outward Remedies and inward fail:
By vertue expulsed, or anymall	The Mold of Natures Fabrick is destroy'd,
For thilke vertue cleaped naturall	Her Vessels discompose'd, her Vertue void:
Ne may the venim voide, ne expel	The Bellows of his Lungs begins to swell:
The pipes of his longes began to swell	All out of frame is ev'ry secret Cell,
And euery lacerte, in his brest adoun	Nor can the Good receive, nor Bad expel.
Is shent with venim and corrupcion	Those breathing Organs thus within opprest,
Him gaineth neither, for to get his life	With Venom soon distend the Sinews of his Breast.
Vomite upwarde, ne downward laxatife	Nought profits him to save abandon'd Life,
All is to brust thilke region	Nor Vomits upward aid, nor downward Laxatife.
Nature hath no dominacion	The midmost Region batter'd and destroy'd,
And certainly ther as nature wol not wirch	When Nature cannot work, th'Effect of Art is void.
Farewel phisike, go beare the corse to chirch.	
(*KnT*, 2743–60; Speght 1598, Fol. 9ᵛ)	(*Palamon and Arcite*, 3. 751–67; Dryden, *Works*, 7. 171–3)

Dryden's expansion of what follows in Chaucer offers a particularly striking example of his complicated responses to Chaucer's scepticism—or of his professions of inevitable and necessary ignorance:

His spirite chaunged, and out went there	But whither went his Soul, let such relate
Whether warde I cannot tell, ne where	Who search the Secrets of the future State:
Therefore I stint, I am no diuinistre	Divines can say but what themselves believe;
Of soules finde I not in this registre	Strong Proofs they have, but not demonstrative:
Ne me leste not thilke opinion to tell	For, were all plain, then all Sides must agree,

in 'The Politics of Providence in Dryden's *Fables Ancient and Modern*', *Translation and Literature*, 17 (2008), 1–20.

[47] Morell, pp. 392–3.

Of hem, though they writen where thei dwell
Arcite is cold, that Mars his soule gie.

(*KnT*, 2809–15; Speght 1598, Fol. 10ʳ)

And Faith itself be lost in Certainty.
To live uprightly then is sure the best,
To save ourselves, and not to damn the rest.
The Soul of *Arcite* went, where Heathens go,
Who better live than we, tho' less they know.

(*Palamon and Arcite*, 3. 843–53;
Dryden, *Works*,7. 177)

Dryden's handling of the question 'whither went his Soul?' had a curious reception history, sometimes being treated solemnly, sometimes being used for the purposes of burlesque.[48] Though Dryden supposed Chaucer to have a fondness for the opinions of Wycliffe, and so presumably did not see the old poet as a fellow Catholic, his responses to Chaucer's religion overall would seem to imply that he imagined his poet-predecessor to have been—rather as he saw himself—profoundly sincere, but superior to most members of the clerical profession. The literary corollary of Dryden's theological position—and perhaps Chaucer's as he saw it—is to acknowledge that there might have been, as it were, pre-Christian fathers; that not all the thoughts of those denied the revelation of Jesus Christ were incapable of human wisdom—a wisdom that had not been purely or simply replaced by revealed inspiration.

Egeus and the Wisdom of Ages

There are many reasons for thinking that the passages of Chaucer that pleased most and pleased longest were those that were grounded upon commonplaces—metaphors that had occurred to many generations, particularly when faced with the inevitabilities of the human condition. One interesting elaboration of the common thought that life is a journey is the speech given by Dryden to old Egeus on the untimely death of Arcite:

No man maie glad Theseus
Sauing his old father Egeus
That knewe this worlds transmutacion
As he had seen it, bothe up and doun,
Joie after wo, and wo after gladnesse
And shewed him ensamples and likenesse

Good after Ill, and after Pain, Delight;
Old *Aegeus* only could revive his Son,
Who various Changes of the World had known;
And strange Vicissitudes of Humane Fate,
Still alt'ring, never in a steady State:
Alternate, like the Scenes of Day and Night:

---

[48] The first eight lines of the passage were included (s.v. '*Futurity*') in editions of Bysshe's *Art of Poetry* from 1705 to 1762. The whole passage was printed as an epigraph to Chapter VII of Anne Plumptre's novel *The Rector's Son*, 3 vols (London, 1798) . Elsewhere, it was read less solemnly. See 'An Elegy upon The Death of The Most Renown'd General War, By a Disbanded Officer' in *A New Voyage to the Island of Fools* (London, 1713), p. 60. The first six lines were stolen almost *verbatim* for a curious mock elegy consisting largely of passages from Dryden's poems but pretending to have been composed by Walpole on the death of George I: 'Glubech Digbeye', *Robin's Pathetick Tale, an Heroic Poem* (London, 1727), Sig. A2. In a slightly more serious vein, Thomas Johnson's 'Westminster Abbey, A Masonic Poem', in *Summer Productions; Or Progressive Miscellanies* (London, 1788) contains, among lines on the death of kings, a couplet derived from Dryden: 'But whither went their Souls, let those relate, / Who search the Secrets of a future State' (p. 14).

Right as there died never man, quod he
That he ne liued in yearth in some degree
Right so there liued neuer man, he saied
In this world, that sometime he ne deied
This world is but a throughfare full of wo
And we been pilgrimes, passing to and fro
Death is an end of euery worldes sore.

(KnT, 2837–49; Speght 1598, Fol. 10ʳ)

Since ev'ry Man who lives, is born to die,
And none can boast sincere Felicity.
With equal Mind, what happens, let us bear,
Nor joy, nor grieve too much for Things beyond our Care.
Like Pilgrims, to th'appointed Place we tend;
The World's an Inn, and Death the Journeys End.
Ev'n Kings but play; and when their Part is done,
Some other, worse or better, mount the Throne.

(Palamon and Arcite, 3. 877–90; Dryden, Works, 7. 179)

Like much else in *Palamon and Arcite*, Dryden's version of Egeus's speech was found memorable almost independently of his poem as a whole, and of its Chaucerian original. The passage appears in a large number of anthologies, dictionaries, novels, and memoirs (even an *Ephemeris*), published for a wide range of readers of diverse kinds.[49] In the case of the anthologies, novels, and memoirs, Egeus's words are adduced, without reference to context of any kind, as a memorable description of the common state of life. Johnson drew citations from this passage for his *Dictionary* (1755) in his entries on *after, beyond, grieve, inn, pilgrim,* and *to revive*—where those on *grieve, inn,* and *pilgrim* perhaps testify to the essential elements.

Dryden, whose genius, according to Johnson, was one that 'collects, combines, amplifies and animates', has chosen a vocabulary for Egeus's speech that expresses a common thought in common terms, and the key comparisons in his passage (humanity as pilgrims, the world as an inn, death as a journey's end, kings as actors in a drama) can be paralleled in the writings of many predecessors. Thomas Morell—who read Chaucer in manuscript, but with Dryden's version in his memory—thought that Chaucer's mind was resting on the stability of truth in Egeus's speech. For him, this was one of the many moments when Chaucer struck the Homeric note, in touching on the essential passions of the human heart:

> Since our Author compares the Mourning of the *Athenians* at the Death of *Arcite*, to the Mourning of the *Trojans* upon the Death of *Hector*, I think I may very properly quote that beautiful Passage in *Homer*, wherewith *Achilles* endeavours to comfort old *Priam*, upon the Death of his Son, and which I doubt not but our Author had in View, when he makes old *Ægeus* reason after the same Manner.[50]

It is, however, the peculiarity and the interest of his version that, although Dryden had given Egeus's consolations the accretions of 300 years so that Egeus speaks 'full

---

[49] The passage appears in the poetical commonplace books of Edward Bysshe and Charles Gildon, in *The Beauties of Poetry Display'd* (London, 1757) and *The Beauties of the English Drama* (London, 1777). An amalgamation of the words of Egeus and Theseus is made to serve as a moral commentary on astrological change in Edmund Weaver's ephemeris, *The British Telescope* (London, [1743]). The passage was also quoted in historical narratives and memoirs by Thomas Nugent and James Lackington, and in fictions by A. Woodfin and Eliza Haywood.

[50] Morell, p. 416.

wisely', he also hints, in the authorial remarks that follow, that Egeus's wisdom is merely commonplace, a collection of platitudes to please the crowd, which could be made to serve any turn:

And ouer all this yet saied he moche more
To this effect, full wisely to exhort
The people, that they should hem recomfort.

(*KnT*, 2850–2; Speght 1598, Fol. 10ʳ)

With Words like these the Crowd was satisfi'd,
And so they would have been, had *Theseus* dy'd.

(*Palamon and Arcite*, 3. 891–2; Dryden, *Works*, 7. 179)

Chaucer, as Dryden read him, had not merely *reproduced* the common thoughts and common metaphors of mankind, but had exposed their inevitable limitations. In this light, it is telling that many eighteenth-century readers who quoted the speech should ignore the apparently dismissive comment and amalgamate Egeus's sentiments with the words of Theseus, his son. Egeus's words are passive and melancholy, accepting vicissitudes that bring woe rather than, as Theseus recommends, seizing those that bring joy.

Theseus and the *Metamorphoses*

Morell seems to have composed some of his annotations to Chaucer's text on the conviction that Theseus's speech constituted one of the supreme moments in poetry and encapsulated some kind of eternal wisdom. Morell expands upon Chaucer's passage as Dryden had done, perhaps on the assumption that readers' minds might make connections similar to those suggested by Dryden's treatment. Alongside references to Boethius and Gower, Morell draws parallels with Spenser and with Homer, particularly as rendered by Pope. For Morell as for Dart, and perhaps for Dryden, the similarity between Chaucer and Homer and Virgil is clearest in the sentiments of this passage and provides significant support for Dryden's conviction that *The Knight's Tale* is a poem of epic stature.

As Morell appears to have seen it, Chaucer in this poem presented an essentially Homeric view of life. For example, when Theseus describes how the 'Movere'

> of his wise purueyaunce,
> He hath so well beset his ordinaunce,
> That spaces of things and progessions
> Shullen edure by <u>successiouns</u>
> And not eterne
>
> (*KnT*, 3011–15; Speght 1598, Fol. 10ᵛ)

—which Dryden had translated—

> This Law th' Omniscient Pow'r was pleas'd to give,
> That ev'ry Kind should by <u>Succession</u> live;

> That Individuals die, his Will ordains;
> The propagated Species still remains.
>
> (*Palamon and Arcite*, 3. 1054–7; Dryden, *Works*, 7. 189)

—Morell quotes from Pope's *Iliad*, providing at once an illustration of the sentiment and a genealogy of the poetic history of the terms *succession* and *successive*:

> Like Leaves on Trees the Race of Man is found,
> Now green in Youth, now with'ring on the Ground
> Another Race the following Spring supplies,
> They fall <u>successive</u>, and <u>successive</u> rise.
> So Generations in their Course decay,
> So flourish these, when those are past away.
>
> (*The Iliad of Homer*, 6. 181–6; Pope, *Poems*, 7. 334–5)[51]

Similarly, when Theseus emphasizes the inevitability of death, Morell quotes Hector's celebrated expression of a similar sentiment from the sixth book of Pope's *Iliad*.[52] Theseus's preference for a short life with honour over a long life of ignoble ease is another passage which Dryden had expanded,[53] and as a parallel for which Morell quotes, from Pope's *Iliad*, a couplet from Priam, eight lines from Hector, and finishes with the comment: 'Such too was *Achilles's* Choice, who was so possessed with the Love of Glory, that he preferred it to Life itself', referring the reader to Pope's annotations.[54] It is very much to the present point that Morell should, as it were, reverse the process in the annotations to his translation of Seneca's *Epistles*, where Chaucer and Dryden's versions of Chaucer are occasionally cited in support of the wisdom of the Roman writer.[55] For Morell, as for Dryden, the dominant and determining notion seems to have been that Chaucer was a 'perpetual fountain of good sense'.

In the 1714 edition of his *Art of English Poetry*, Edward Bysshe quoted (s.v. *Death*) the whole of the passage in which Dryden's Theseus describes the course of life and death in the natural and human world:

Lo the oke, that hath so long a norishing,	The Monarch Oak, the Patriarch of the Trees,
Fro the time that it beginneth fyrst to spring,	Shoots rising up, and spreads by slow Degrees:
And hath so long a life, as ye may see	Three Centuries he grows, and three he stays,
Yet at the last wasted is the tree	Supreme in State; and in three more decays:
Considereth eke, how that the hard stone	So wears the paving Pebble in the Street,
Under our feete, on which we tread and gone,	And Towns and Tow'rs their fatal Periods meet.
Yet wasteth it, as it lieth in the weie,	So Rivers, rapid once, now naked lie,
The brode river somtime wexeth drie	Forsaken of their Springs; and leave their Channels dry.
The great touns, se we wane and wend	So Man, at first a Drop, dilates with Heat,

---

[51] See ibid. p. 422.
[52] Ibid. p. 423; *The Iliad of Homer*, 6. 628–31; Pope, *Poems*, 7. 358.
[53] *Palamon and Arcite*, 3. 1088–101. Dryden, *Works*, 7. 178–9.
[54] Morell, pp. 423–4.
[55] Thomas Morell, trans. and ed., *Th Epistles of Lucius Annaeus Seneca*, 2 vols (London, 1786), 1. 74.

Than ye see that all this thing hath end
And man and woman see shall we also
That endeth in one of the terms two
That is to sain in youth or els in age
He mote be dedde, a king as well as a page.
Some in his bed, some in the deepe see
Some in the large field, as ye may see
It helpeth not, al goeth that ilke weie
Than maie you see that al thing mote deie
What maketh this but Jupiter the king
That is prince, and cause of al thing
Converting al to his proper will
From which it is deriued soth to tell.

(KnT, 3017; Speght 1598, Fol. 11^r)

Then form'd, the little Heart begins to beat;
Secret he feeds, unknowing in the Cell;
At length, for Hatching ripe, he breaks the Shell,
And struggles into Breath, and cries for Aid;
Then, helpless, in his Mothers Lap is laid.
He creeps, he walks, and issuing into Man,
Grudges their Life, from whence his own began.
Retchless of Laws, affects to rule alone,
Anxious to reign, and restless on the Throne:
First vegetive, then feels, and reasons last;
Rich of Three Souls, and lives all three to waste.
Some thus; but thousands more in Flow'r of Age:
For few arrive to run the latter Stage.
Sunk in the first, in Battel some are slain,
And others whelm'd beneath the stormy Main.
What makes all this, but *Jupiter* the King,
At whose Command we perish, and we spring?

(Palamon and Arcite, 3. 1058–83; Dryden, Works,
7. 189–91)

The account of inevitable decay in human beings is here to some degree counteracted by the loving treatment of the physical facts of conception, womb-life, and birth. One line in that description ('At length, for Hatching ripe, he breaks the Shell') appealed to William Blake, who used it as the title of a plate in *The Gates of Paradise* (1793) (see Fig. 3.5). Dryden's account of the ages of man represents a considerable addition to the words of Chaucer's Theseus, for whom the human resemblance to the wasted oak, the wasted stone, and the dried river is exclusively that human lives will end 'in youth or els in age'. Dryden has made his Theseus give a comprehensive picture of the rising and falling of human lives that equals that of the Monarch Oak. It is as if Theseus, like Chaucer, had a 'comprehensive soul'.

The frontispiece to the second edition of *Fables Ancient and Modern* shows streams of light from the volumes of Chaucer and Ovid, held by cherubs in the

Fig. 3.5 'At length for hatching ripe he breaks the shell'. Engraving and etching by William Blake from *The Gates of Paradise* (London, 1793).

clouds, *combining* in a mirror held by an almost fully grown angel, near the quill-holding hand of Muse. The illustrator may have had passages such as this in mind. Dryden's Theseus gives an account of the course of human life that combines Chaucer's sentiments with a passage from Ovid's *Metamorphoses* which Dryden translated, and also included in *Fables*, under the title *Of the Pythagorean Philosophy; From the Fifteenth Book of Ovid's Metamorphoses*.[56] (See Fig. 2.1) In his headnote, Dryden described Ovid's account of Numa's meeting with Pythagoras and the subsequent exposition of 'the Moral and Natural Philosophy of Pythagoras' as 'the most learned and beautiful Parts of the whole *Metamorphoses*':

> Time was, when we were sow'd, and just began
> From some few fruitful Drops, the promise of a Man;
> Then Nature's Hand (fermented as it was)
> Moulded to Shape the soft, coagulated Mass;
> And when the little Man was fully form'd,
> The breathless Embryo with a Spirit warm'd;
> But when the Mothers Throws begin to come,
> The Creature, pent within the narrow Room,
> Breaks his blind Prison, pushing to repair
> His stifled Breath, and draw the living Air;
> Cast on the Margin of the World he lies,
> A helpless Babe, but by Instinct he cries.
> He next essays to walk, but downward press'd,
> On four Feet imitates his Brother Beast:
> By slow degrees he gathers from the Ground
> His Legs, and to the rowling Chair is bound;
> Then walks alone; a Horseman now become,
> He rides a Stick, and travels round the Room:
> In time he vaunts among his Youthful Peers,
> Strong-bon'd, and strung with Nerves, in pride of Years,
> He runs with Mettle his first merry Stage,
> Maintains the next, abated of his Rage,
> But manages his Strength, and spares his Age.
> Heavy the third, and stiff, he sinks apace,
> And tho' 'tis down-hill all, but creeps along the Race.
> Now sapless on the verge of Death he stands,
> Contemplating his former Feet, and Hands;
> And Milo-like, his slacken'd Sinews sees,
> And wither'd Arms, once fit to cope with Hercules,
> Unable now to shake, much less to tear the Trees.

(Of the Pythagorean Philosophy, 324–53; Dryden, Works, 7. 493–4)

---

[56] Dryden's use of Ovid in this passage is discussed by Paul Hammond in 'The Interplay of Past and Present in Dryden's *Palamon and Arcite*', pp. 67–8.

Dum Vivimus, Vivamus

Although Dryden's Theseus, like Chaucer's, attributes the Laws of Life to '*Jupiter the King*', in his injunction to thankfulness he returns to plural and unspecified deities:

What may conclude of this long storie
But after sorow, I rede vs be merie
And thank Jupiter of all his grace.

(*KnT*, 3067–9; Speght 1598, Fol. 10ʳ)

What then remains, but after past Annoy,
To take the good Vicissitude of Joy?
To thank the gracious Gods for what they give,
Possess our Souls, and while we live, to live?

(*Palamon and Arcite*, 3. 1111–14; Dryden,
Works, 7. 193)

A great deal is packed into Dryden's four lines. The equivalent of Chaucer's 'What may conclude of this long storie' is 'What then remains, but ...', a common locution in both secular contexts and sermons. Dryden had used it most memorably towards the end of his translation of Juvenal's tenth satire:

What then remains? Are we depriv'd of Will,
Must we not Wish, for fear of wishing Ill?
Receive my Counsel, and securely move;
Intrust thy Fortune to the Pow'rs above.
Leave them to manage for thee, and to grant
What their unerring Wisdom sees thee want.

(*The Tenth Satyr of Juvenal*, 533–8;
Dryden, *Works*, 4. 239)

Though the characters in *The Knight's Tale* are pagans, and therefore cannot express themselves in explicitly Christian terms, Dryden's diction in his version of Theseus's speech combines elements of the secular and the divine. 'Past annoy' and 'vicissitude of Joy' may be Dryden's coinages. The governing idea, however, is biblical: 'In your patience possess ye your souls.'[57] And it is telling that George Stanhope's translation of Simplicius's commentary on Epictetus's *Enchiridion*, published six years before Dryden's *Fables*, maintained that 'the Practice of Vertue and a Good Life is the ultimate Design of all Study, and all Instruction' and exhorted himself and his readers to a conviction 'of the Excellence, and the Necessity of being Vertuous' so that we may 'possess our Souls with a lively and vigorous Sense of our Duty'.[58]

Theseus's injunction to 'Possess our Souls' is combined with a close translation of the Latin tag *dum vivimus, vivamus*: 'while we live, let us live'. The tag

---

[57] Luke 21:19.
[58] George Stanhope, trans., *Epictetus His Morals, with Simplicius His Comment, Made English from the Greek* (London, 1694), p. 545.

often appeared in vaguely Epicurean contexts almost as if it were an Horatian recommendation of love and wine, but was often denounced on explicitly Christian occasions.[59] Sir Thomas Browne cited it in a sidenote in support of the contention that 'Antiquity held too light thoughts from objects of mortality, while some drew provocatives of mirth from anatomies, and jugglers showed tricks with skeletons.'[60] Robert South, in 1694, had complained against 'some Men', who, 'after an ingenuous Education in Arts, and Philosophy' nevertheless, 'place their Summum Bonum upon their Trenchers, and their utmost felicity in Wine and Women': '*Dum vivimus vivamus*; *Let us eat and drink to day, for to morrow we must die*'.[61]

But the injunctions of Chaucer's Theseus to 'thank Jupiter of all his grace' and Dryden's to 'thank the gracious Gods for what they give, / Possess our Souls, and while we live, to live' are by no means exhortations either to surrender to Fate alone, or to indulge in the pleasures of the bed or the table. Dryden's Theseus puts his faith in that easy combination of Roman and Christian sentiment characteristic of the poem as a whole.

What Dryden had perhaps demonstrated in his version of *The Knight's Tale* was that the reading experience of Chaucer was to stimulate *thought*, that Chaucer's powers as a poet were to quicken contemplation and excite the memory—the memory of other poets, as much as of human events and emotions. Dryden's version, like the poetic translations of many of his imitators, including Pope, do not attempt to reproduce the original but present traces of the original in the company of other thoughts that arise and other poems that are recalled when contemplating his subject matter. Dryden's critical and creative act was a demonstration that Chaucer was not dead, not limitedly of antiquarian interest, but as living as Ovid, Homer, Virgil, Spenser, Milton—or as his contemporaries Congreve and Prior. For that reason, perhaps, it seemed proper for Palamon to quote Juvenal and draw on Lucretius and Spenser, and for Dryden to have followed Chaucer in drawing on Statius when describing the Temple of Mars. Dryden appears to have convinced the majority of his readers that these are all things that Chaucer would have done

---

[59] According to Boswell, Samuel Johnson considered the following verses by Philip Doddridge, the Independent minister, to be 'one of the finest epigrams in the English language:

> Live, while you live, the *epicure* would say,
> And seize the pleasures of the present day.
> Live, while you live, the sacred preacher cries,
> And give to GOD each moment as it flies.
> Lord, in my views let both united be;
> I live in *pleasure*, when I live to *thee*.

See James Boswell, *Life of Samuel Johnson*, ed. George Birkbeck Hill, rev. L. F. Powell, 6 vols (Oxford, 1934–50), 5. 271.

[60] Sir Thomas Browne, *Hydriotaphia, Urn-Burial* (London, 1669), p. 39.

[61] Robert South, *Twelve Sermons Preached upon Several Occasions* (London, 1694), p. 351.

if he were living in 1699—since he, clearly, had the capacity and ability to deploy a range of tonal reference that made him a peer rather than merely a precursor, and a poet whose depictions of human 'Manners' and of the conditions governing human life in all ages justified *The Knight's Tale* being considered a poem 'of the Epique kind' that had 'followed Nature everywhere'.

4

The Cock and the Fox

Apologue, Amplification, and Embellishment

In an essay introducing his version of *The Clerk's Tale* that was included in his collection of modernizations from *The Canterbury Tales*, George Ogle included some general remarks on Dryden's dealings with Chaucer. Ogle had found it 'not easy to determine' whether Dryden's 'chief Excellence' lay in 'the talents of Criticism, or Poetry', but considered that, especially where principles of translation were concerned, Dryden's 'Practice and Example' were of 'greater Prevalence and Force than any Argument'. Ogle considered 'Mr. Dryden to have been the first, who put the Merit of Chaucer into its full and true Light, by Turning Some of the *Canterbury Tales* into our Language as it is now refin'd, or rather as He himself refin'd it'.[1] Ogle's remark is paradoxical. The 'full and true Light' by which Chaucer's 'Merit' has been revealed is something very different from the original poems themselves: Dryden, Ogle suggests, has revealed the essence of Chaucer's poems *because* he has changed them.

'Foolish If Not Worse'? The Peculiarities of Dryden's Poem

Ogle was not singular in his opinion. As we have already seen, Dryden's critical remarks about, and translation of, Chaucer's *The Knight's Tale* were widely persuasive and influential. But *The Cock and the Fox*, Dryden's version of the tale of Chaucer's Nun's Priest about the farmyard cock Chanticleer, and his narrow escape from the 'col fox' Reynard, might seem, on the face of it, less likely to appeal to an eighteenth-century readership. The anonymous hand-written emendations in a copy of Dryden's *Fables* in the British Library, for example, condemn the poem outright, asserting that *The Cock and the Fox* 'is so foolish, if not worse, that I omit it entirely notwithstanding it has some good lines. It adds little to Chaucer's

---

[1] Ogle, 3. 15–16.

Chaucer in the Eighteenth Century. David Hopkins and Tom Mason, Oxford University Press.
© David Hopkins and Tom Mason (2022). DOI: 10.1093/oso/9780192862624.003.0005

Reputation that he was the original Author of it.'[2] And in his *Life of Dryden*, Samuel Johnson dismissed 'the tale of the Cock' as 'hardly worth revival.'[3]

In *The Cock and the Fox*, Dryden has indeed accentuated every element in his original that challenged conventional notions of poetical propriety, decorum, homogeneity, good sense, common decency, and the proper disposition of parts. Chaucer's own range of reference and allusion in *The Nun's Priest's Tale* is, as Thomas Warton was to observe, remarkable—and remarkably miscellaneous,[4] and Dryden seems to have seen this promiscuity of allusion as an essential element in the method of the tale, seizing any and every opportunity to follow and extend Chaucer's parallels and allusions. In Dryden's poem, a cock—likened variously to Adam, a mermaid, an astronomer, an angel, a beau, a saint in rapture, St Cecilia, Virgil, Pindar, Horace, an Olympic contender, several heroes, and a long line of kings, including both the first and the second Charles—quotes Homer and discusses theology while pecking his corn. He is a cock who reads the stars, and—in full view of his and her six sisters—feathers his hen-wife. She, in turn, is compared variously to the much-rivalled wife of a king, an ideal courtly beloved, a dutiful and loving helpmeet, a nagging and bullying archwife, a lay doctor, Eve, and an heroic suicide. The cock is then seduced by a fox, who resembles a clerical hypocrite, an heroic traitor, a common murderer, a court flatterer, a poetical encomiast, a puritan, a papist priest, the Devil, and a regicide. This is a poem which disregards chronology even more completely than had *Palamon and Arcite*, ranging in its references from Homer to recent anti-Catholic proclamations, digressing at length and in a way that furthers neither action nor argument, and yet concluding, in complete disregard of its own miscellaneous nature, with the audacious claim that the critical principles followed in this 'plain Fable' have been those of Quintus Horatius Flaccus, and the exemplary literary model that was provided by Jesus Christ:

> Who spoke in Parables, I dare not say;
> But sure, he knew it was a pleasing way,
> Sound Sense, by plain Example, to convey.
> And in a Heathen Author we may find,
> That Pleasure with Instruction should be join'd:
> So take the Corn, and leave the Chaff behind.
>
> (*The Cock and the Fox*, 816–21; Dryden, *Works*, 7. 335)

Despite the echo here of Horace's celebrated injunction to writers to combine pleasure and utility,[5] *The Cock and the Fox* would seem almost to offer a textbook

---

[2] See Caroline Spurgeon, *Five Hundred Years of Chaucer Criticism and Allusion, 1357–1900*, 3 vols (Cambridge, 1925), 1. 480–1. Spurgeon attributes the annotations to William Bell of Uscombe, Kent, and assumes that the notes were made in preparation of a new edition of Dryden's *Fables*. The annotations include the following instruction at the beginning of 'The Cock and the Fox': 'The Printer is desired to omit this Tale'.

[3] Johnson, *Works*, 21. 481.

[4] Warton, *History*, 1. 420–1.

[5] *Ars Poetica*, 1. 243.

example of the 'incoherent Stile' that 'mixes all Extreams' which is condemned elsewhere by that Roman poet.[6] Dryden's poem follows Chaucer in mingling the vocabularies of solemn and detailed philosophical discussion of predestination and freewill,[7] with equally specific accounts of laxative and emetic cures and the language of herbal and astrological medicine,[8] where the specialized terms of astrology[9] co-exist with those of Christianity,[10] where various forms of heroic diction (including quotations from and allusions to Homer, Virgil, Spenser, and Milton) are mingled with the language of the farm[11] and the farmyard,[12] where a vocabulary of the pecking, spurning, feathering, and treading of poultry takes turns with solemn descriptions of 'Deeds of Night', of 'Filth', 'Ordure' and 'Dung', of murdered corpses ('Pale, naked, pierc'd with Wounds, with Blood besmear'd'), of shipwreck and of suicide, of anti-French riots and the massacre of Jews—all interwoven by a narrator who becomes entangled in his own implications, by which he is apparently bewildered, and from which he can extricate himself only with difficulty and by deception.

And yet the poem seems to have been read with care and delight during the whole of the following century. Despite his dismissive verdict, quoted above, Samuel Johnson included a great many passages from *The Cock and the Fox* in his *Dictionary*, and the poem was frequently quoted and alluded to in a wide variety of poems, novels, and essays over the following century.[13]

John Miller and Sir Walter Scott on *The Cock and the Fox*

It is sometimes difficult to estimate the extent to which pleasure in *The Cock and the Fox* encouraged readers to turn to Chaucer's *The Nun's Priest's Tale*. But two

---

[6] See Wentworth Dillon, Earl of Roscommon, trans. *Horace's Art of Poetry*, (London, 1680), pp. 1–2.

[7] e.g. 'agent', 'Prescience', 'foresight', 'inevitable Fate'.

[8] e.g. 'Repletion', 'Complexion', 'boiling Choler', 'abounding Bile', 'yellow Gaul', 'peccant Humors', 'Tertian Ague'.

[9] e.g. 'vernal Equinox', 'rays', 'exalted', 'Ephemeris', 'scheme', 'Patron-Planet', 'solar-people'.

[10] e.g. 'boundless Grace', 'Mercy to Mankind', 'devout Intent', 'Holy Dispensation', 'Omnipotence', 'the Maker's Image'.

[11] e.g. 'parlour-beam', 'Kitchin-fire', 'Quarter-Rent', 'parlour-window', 'maple dresser'.

[12] e.g. 'dry Ditch', 'dunghill', 'perch', 'colworts', 'Snout', 'Grunt', 'Beagle's Whelp' and 'a ewe called *Mally*'.

[13] Many passages were quoted in the poetic commonplace books of Edward Bysshe and Charles Gildon. The poem was praised in *The Spectator*. It was borrowed from by John Smith in *Poems upon Several Occasions* (London, 1713), and quoted in several poems by Samuel Wesley. It was cited as an authority in learned commentaries upon Lucretius by John Digby (1714) and on the religious poems of Vida by Thomas Morell (*Poems on Divine Subjects, Original and Translated from the Latin of M. H. Vida and M. A. Flaminio* (London, 1732)). It was praised by John Oldmixon in *An Essay on Criticism* (London, 1728), and by the author of *The Beeriad* (London, 1736). The lines from the poem describing dreams were quoted by Eliza Haywood in *The Female Spectator*, 4 vols (London, 1745) and *Epistles for the Ladies*, 2 vols (London, 1749–50), and praised in Richard Lobb's, *The Contemplative Philosopher* (London, 1800). The lines on free will were quoted approvingly in *The Egg, or the Memoirs of Gregory Giddy* (London, ?1772). Lovelace alludes to the poem in Samuel Richardson's *Clarissa* (London, 1748). It was given political application in *Letters of the Late Thomas Rundle* (Dublin, 1789).

notable accounts of Dryden's poem involved detailed consideration of Chaucer's original and are, therefore, of special interest in the present context. The first occurs in *A Course of the Belles Letters: or the Principles of Literature* (1761) by John Miller, a free adaptation of *Les beaux arts réduits à un même principle* (1746) by the French philosopher and aesthetician, the Abbé Charles Batteux (1713-1780).[14] The second appears in the commentary on *The Cock and the Fox* provided by Walter Scott in his edition of Dryden's works.

In Miller's account of the poem and its relation to Chaucer's original, the most extensive in the eighteenth century, *The Cock and the Fox* is paraded as the supreme English example of the *apologue*: a moral fable where words and actions of animals or even inanimate objects are, as Johnson put it in the *Dictionary*, 'contrived to teach a moral truth'. In his account of 'the apologue or fable', Miller supplements his translation of Batteux's text—in accord with the principles adopted throughout his translation—with English examples, in this case using *The Cock and the Fox* as a foil to Batteux's discussion of the works of the acknowledged master of the form, Jean de La Fontaine. The clear implication of Miller's discussion is that the tale of the Nun's Priest is Chaucer's masterpiece and that *The Cock and the Fox* is Dryden's most characteristically excellent work.

Scott's account of *The Cock and the Fox* is particularly interesting for what it suggests about the effects of Dryden's additions to Chaucer's original. Scott's estimation of Chaucer's poem was very high, and he believed that his pleasure in Dryden's version was continuous with the intense pleasure he discovered in Chaucer, and that he imagines Chaucer found in the short poem by Marie de France that had been quoted by Tyrwhitt as Chaucer's source:

> [T]he hand of genius gilds what it touches; and the naked Apologue [...] was amplified by Chaucer into a poem, which, in grave, ironical narrative, liveliness of illustration, and happiness of humorous description, yields to none that ever was written. Dryden [...] has executed a version at once literal and spirited, which seldom omits what is valuable in his original, and often adds those sparks which genius strikes out when in collision with the work of a kindred spirit.[15]

As Scott sees it, the form of the 'apologue' has been 'amplified' first by the 'genius' of Chaucer, and then, in turn, by the 'kindred spirit' and 'genius' of Dryden. But in maintaining that Chaucer's is a work which 'yields to none that ever was written', Scott appears to be assuming that the tale of the Nun's Priest has transcended its genre and entered into successful competition, as it were, with all other poems that employed 'grave, ironical narrative, liveliness of illustration, and happiness of humorous description'.

---

[14] The Abbé Batteux was professor at Paris of the humanities and rhetoric and a member of the Academy of Inscriptions and of the Académie Française.
[15] *Works of John Dryden*: ed. Walter Scott, 11. 326.

The paradox in Scott's position is most strongly marked in his contention that Dryden's version of the tale of the Nun's Priest is 'at once literal and spirited'. The 'literal' nature of his version is shown by the fact that he 'seldom omits what is valuable in his original'. Its 'spirited' qualities are provided by Dryden's addition of 'those sparks which genius strikes out when in collision with the work of a kindred spirit'. In stories 'of a light and ludicrous kind, as the Fable of the Cock and the Fox', Scott says, Dryden 'displays all the humorous expression of his satirical poetry, without its personality. There is indeed a quaint Cervantic gravity in his mode of expressing himself, that often glances forth, and enlivens what otherwise would be mere dry narrative'.[16] Scott's suggestion is that Dryden had produced a true translation of Chaucer's poem by expanding it. Dryden's version, Scott believes, is a peculiarly lively representation, exemplification, and embodiment of the reading process, which Scott sees as necessarily comparative, associative, and speculative. Such a process is particularly strong in the case of the tale of the Nun's Priest, where readers must consider at every moment the many and various ways in which the words, actions, and sentiments of the cock, fox, and hen resemble the words, actions, and sentiments of their own species.

John Miller's account of *The Nun's Priest's Tale* suggests that he may have come to Chaucer with somewhat conventional assumptions about the 'barbarism' and 'grossness' of the poet's art, but was won over by a careful reading of Dryden's version to see something close to what Ogle had described as the 'full merit' of Chaucer's original. It is particularly striking that Miller's discussion of the 'apologue' is made to culminate in the discussion of *The Nun's Priest's Tale* and *The Cock and the Fox* when Batteux had stressed 'brevity, clearness, and probability' as the essential features of the 'apologue' form.[17] *The Cock and the Fox* would seem, on the face of it, to violate Batteux's principles blatantly and absolutely. 'The stile of fable', Batteux maintained, 'should be familiar, plain, sprightly, pleasing, natural, easy, and simple'. The plain style 'consists in expressing in as few words as possible, and in the common terms', while nothing 'is so prejudicial to fable as an air of ... parade'.[18] But Chanticleer and Partlet are the most garrulous of birds, Chanticleer in particular being given to every kind of 'parade'. The tale's narrator is hardly less loquacious, a comic master of an impressive range of rhetorical tropes, ancient, medieval, and modern.

There appear to have been be two notions in the light of which—despite Batteux's contrary principles—Miller was able to find merit in Chaucer's poem and in Dryden's version. One was Miller's appreciation of 'just thoughts' in contradistinction to 'false glare'. The other was his own notions of translation and of poetical history. He has, he says, no more attempted literal translation of Batteux than had

[16] Scott, 1.500; Ibid.; Scott, 11. 435.
[17] Charles Batteaux, *A Course of the Belles Letters: or the Principles of Literature*, trans. John Miller, 4 vols (London, 1761), 1. 206.
[18] Ibid. 1. 215.

Dryden in the case of Chaucer, and has 'here and there substituted some passages in the room of the original ones, where [he] thought it was necessary, in order to adapt the whole more particularly to the meridian of our own nation and language'.[19] Miller sees the history of the fable as essentially a series of retellings, in which copies may actually excel the original, just as La Fontaine had excelled his sources in Aesop, Phaedrus, and others. In his rendering of Chaucer, Miller notes, 'Mr. Dryden',

> to use his own words, has not tied himself to a literal translation; but has often omitted what he judged necessary, or not of dignity enough to appear in company of better thoughts, adding at times such of his own as he thought requisite to give a new lustre to his author, confined by the indigence of words in the age he lived in. 'And to this I was the more emboldened (adds he) because, if I may be permitted to say it of myself, I found I had a soul congenial to his, and that I had been conversant in the same studies'.[20]

Miller, Chanticleer, and Partlet

There are in fact a number of passages in Chaucer's poem and some in Dryden's that could be seen to exhibit the 'nature, plainness, and simplicity of stile' desiderated by Batteux, particularly since the French critic had allowed that the 'narration' of an 'apologue' may receive several kinds of legitimate 'ornaments or embellishments'.[21] One such instance, Miller thought, occurred in Dryden's description of 'the body' of Chanticleer, where Dryden follows Chaucer quite closely:

His come was redder than the fine corall,	High was his Comb, and Coral-red withal,
And battelled, as it had be a castell wall	In dents embatteld like a Castle-Wall:
His bill was blacke as any iet it shone;	His Bill was Raven-black, and shon like Jet,
Like asure were his legges and his tone	Blue were his Legs, and Orient were his Feet:
His nailes whiter than the lilly floure	White were his Nails, like Silver to behold,
And like the burned gold was his colour.	His Body glitt'ring like the burnish'd Gold.
(*NPT*, 2859–64; Speght 1598, Fol. 85ᵛ)	(*The Cock and the Fox*, 49–54; Dryden, *Works*, 7. 289)

The comparative plainness of this passage is highlighted if one compares it with the later version by William Lipscomb, who 'embellished' his description with the suggestions that Chanticleer's comb 'menac'd fate to all', that his bill was 'like ripen'd sloe' and that his 'toe' was 'taper'.[22]

---

[19] Ibid. 1. iii.
[20] Ibid. 1. 262–3.
[21] Ibid. 1. 207.
[22] Lipscomb, 3. 317.

There are, however, not many passages where Dryden has followed Chaucer as closely as in his description of Chanticleer, and Lipsomb's embellishments are therefore in line with Dryden's more characteristic and expansive practice. Miller was able to praise many of Dryden's 'decorative' passages partly because they had been sanctioned by Batteux's belief that 'the rules relating to the apologue are included in those of the epopoia and drama'.[23] Such 'rules' included the use of direct speech. When coming to the initial event of the narrative, it is, significantly, the remarks—and the tone of the remarks—of Partlet the hen to which Miller draws particular attention:

And it so fell, that in the dawning	It happ'd that perching on the Parlor-beam
As Chaunteclere, among his wiues all,	Amidst his Wives, he had a deadly Dream;
Sat on his perch, that was in the hall	Just at the Dawn, and sigh'd, and groan's so fast,
And next him sat his faire Pertelote	As ev'ry Breath he drew wou'd be his last.
This Chaunteclere gan to grone in his throte,	Dame Partlet, ever nearest to his Side,
As a man in his dreme is drenched sore	Heard all his piteous Moan, and how he cry'd
And whan that Pertelote thus herd him rore	For Help from Gods and Men: And sore aghast
She was agast, and said, hert dere	She peck'd, and pull'd, and waken'd him at last.
What eyleth you to grone in this manere.	Dear Heart, says she, for Love of Heav'n declare
	Your Pain, and make me Partner to your Care.
	You groan, Sir, ever since the Morning-light,
	As something had disturb'd your noble Spright.
(*NPT*, 2882–90; Speght 1598, Fol. 85ᵛ)	(*The Cock and the Fox*, 93–104; Dryden, *Works*, 7. 293)

'The hen addresses the cock in this place', Miller comments, 'as if he was a person of great importance; which forms an agreeable figure in the stile. And we shall accordingly find in the course of the fable, that he deems himself an animal of no small consequence.'[24] Chanticleer's self-importance is of the utmost importance to Miller. In accordance with Batteux's willingness to permit, within direct speech, 'allusions; or certain strokes, which form either a serious or comic figure with the subject of the narration',[25] Miller points to the moment in *The Cock and the Fox* when 'dame Partlet and the cock in Dryden [...] discourse on the subject of dreams', and quotes the words of the hen:

Lo Caton, which that was so wise a man	*Cato* was in his time accounted Wise,
Said he not thus, do not force of dremes.	And he condemns them all for empty Lies.
(*NPT*, 2940–1; Speght 1598, Fol. 85ᵛ)	(*The Cock and the Fox*, 162–3; Dryden, *Works*, 7. 297)

'This speech, and the following', Miller observes, 'present us with fine instances of the sprightly and entertaining stile of this author; and of humorous allusions, producing images serious or comic, with the matter of the fable'. For Miller, this

---

[23] Batteux, *Course of the Belles Letters*, 1. 203.
[24] Ibid. 1. 274.
[25] Ibid. 1. 209.

allusion constituted 'an elegant satyr on those pedantic spirits, who are for ever puzzling their own brains, and deafening their hearers with learned reasonings upon the most trivial circumstances':[26]

Madame (qd. he) gramercy of your lore	Madam, quoth he, Grammercy for your Care,
But nathelesse, as touching dan Caton	But *Cato*, whom you quoted, you might spare.
That of wisdome hath so great renoun	'Tis true, a wise and worthy Man he seems,
Though he bade no dremes for to drede	And (as you say) gave no belief to Dreams;
By God, men may in olde bookes rede	But other Men of more Authority,
Of many a man, more of auctoritie	And by th'Immortal Pow'rs, as wise as He,
Than euer Caton was, so mote I thee.	Maintain, with sounder Sense, that Dreams Forebode;
	For *Homer* plainly says, they come from God.
	Nor *Cato* said it: but some idle Fool,
	Impos'd in *Cato's* Name on Boys at School.
(*NPT*, 2970–6; Speght 1598, Fol. 86ʳ)	(*The Cock and the Fox*, 95–204; Dryden, *Works*, 7. 297–9)

Here, Dryden has seized the opportunity to allow Chanticleer to allude to the moment in Book 1 of the *Iliad* where Achilles addresses Agamemnon—and which in Dryden's version might have acted as a particular warning to the cock:

> Consult, O King, the Prophets of th'event:
> And whence these Ills, and what the Gods intent,
> Let them by Dreams explore; for Dreams from *Jove* are sent.
> (*The First Book of Homer's Ilias*, 91–3; Dryden, *Works*, 7. 263)

At the same time, he gives his cock an opportunity to display his pedantry and attempt to humble his hen-wife by distinguishing between Cato the Censor and 'Dionysius Cato', the supposed author of the still-popular school text *Disticha de Moribus ad Filium*.[27] Miller does not present these 'ornaments' as contradictions of the model Fable. For him, the momentary allusion supplies or contributes to a satirical reflection that is subsidiary to the governing moral.

'A Large and Inclusive Moral'

Of all Batteux's propositions, Miller seems to have been most influenced by the French critic's proposition that an 'apologue' is justified by the potential inclusiveness and general applicability of its moral—in this case, the injunction that 'we are not to exalt ourselves above our condition'.[28] Miller apparently recalled this

---

[26] Ibid. 1. 275–6.

[27] The distich to which Partlet refers is *Somnia ne cures; nam mens humana, quod optat, / Dum vigilat, sperat; per somnum cernit id ipsum* ('Don't pay attention to dreams; for the human mind hopes for that which it wishes when it is awake; in sleep it discerns that thing [which it hopes for]').

[28] Batteux, *Course of the Belles Letters*, 1. 203.

proposition when he came to the moment in the tale when the cock, having finally descended from the beam in the hen house, his heart light with the confidence of intellectual triumph, addresses his wife on the subject of the glories of Nature and the superiority of cocks over all other forms of creation—a passage where Dryden had extensively elaborated his original:

When the moneth in which the world began	'Twas now the Month in which the World began,
That hight March, that God first made man	(If *March* beheld the first created Man:)
Was complete, and passed were also,	And since the vernal Equinox, the Sun,
Sith March began, twenty daies and two	In *Aries* twelve Degrees, or more had run,
Befill that Chaunteclere, in all his pride	When casting up his Eyes against the Light,
His seuen wiues walking him beside	Both Month, and Day, and Hour he measur'd right;
Cast vp his eyen to the bright Sunne	And told more truly, than th' Ephemeris,
That in the signe of Taurus was yrunne	For Art may err, but Nature cannot miss.
Fourty degrees and one; and somwhat more	Thus numb'ring Times, and Seasons in his Breast,
He knew by kinde, and by none other lore,	His second crowing the third Hour confess'd.
That it was prime, & crew with a blissful seuen	Then turning, said to Partlet, See, my Dear,
The sunne he saide is clombe vp to heuen	How lavish Nature has adorn'd the Year;
Fourty degrees & one, & somwhat more ywis,	How the pale Primrose, and blue Violet spring,
Madame Pertelot, my worldes blisse,	And Birds essay their Throats disus'd to sing:
Herken how these blisful birdes sing	All these are ours; and I with pleasure see
And see the fresh floures how they spring:	Man strutting on two Legs, and aping me!
Full is mine hert of reuel and solas	An unfledg'd Creature, of a lumpish frame,
	Indew'd with fewer Particles of Flame:
	Our Dame sits couring o'er a Kitchin-fire,
	I draw fresh Air, and Nature's Works admire:
	And ev'n this Day, in more delight abound,
	Than since I was an Egg, I ever found.
(*NPT*, 3187–203; Speght 1598, Fol. 87ʳ)	(*The Cock and the Fox*, 445–66; Dryden, *Works*, 7. 313–15)

'There cannot be a more noble lecture of morality, nor a finer satyr on vanity and self-sufficiency' comments Miller, than is to be found within these lines:

> How beautiful a picture has the poet drawn of the absurd and arrogant thoughts which men are so apt to entertain of their own importance in the creation; as that the stars in the firmament, and all the glories of nature, were created only to please their eyes, and amuse their imaginations.[29]

Miller is here in effect quoting the similar comment on the same lines by Thomas Tickell in *The Spectator*. From the general proposition that human pride 'flows from want of Reflection, and Ignorance of ourselves' and that 'Knowledge and Humility come upon us together', Tickell had been led to consider the pride of brute creatures:

[29] Ibid. 1. 276.

we might imagine, from the Gestures of some of them, that they think themselves the Sovereigns of the World, and that all Things were made for them. Such a Thought would not be more absurd in Brute Creatures than one which <u>Men are apt to entertain</u>, namely, That all the <u>Stars in the Firmament were created only to please their Eyes, and amuse their Imaginations</u>. Mr. *Dryden*, in his Fable of the *Cock and the Fox*, makes a Speech for his Hero the Cock, which is a pretty instance for this Purpose.[30]

So close is Miller's wording, that one suspects that the *Spectator* piece may have first drawn his attention to Dryden's poem.

At any rate, there are reasons for thinking that Miller and Tickell were reading Dryden very much as Dryden had read Chaucer—bringing to or discovering in his poem large reflections on the human condition. In the passage just quoted, Dryden has amplified Chaucer's original with ornaments and allusions borrowed from various poetical sources to sharpen our sense of the paradoxical connections between the thoughts and behaviour of the cock—who 'deems himself an animal of no small consequence' and considers himself as occupying the central place in his farmyard universe—and those of human beings, who similarly think of themselves as being at the centre of the larger scheme of things.

When Chanticleer describes the poor widow who owns his farmyard as 'couring by the kitchen fire' and as 'Indew'd with fewer <u>Particles</u> of Flame', Dryden recalled the '<u>particles</u> of Heav'nly Fire' that at the opening of his own version of Book 1 of Ovid's *Metamorphoses* distinguish Man from beast—Man who is there described as 'of a more Exalted Kind' than the rest of creation by virtue of being 'Conscious of Thought', and who is distinguished from other creatures precisely and principally because of his upright stature, and ability to cast his eyes towards the heavens:

> while the mute Creation downward bend
> Their Sight, and to their Earthy Mother tend,
> Man looks aloft; and with erected Eyes
> Beholds his own Hereditary Skies.
> (*The First Book of Ovid's Metamorphoses*, 107–10;
> Dryden, *Works*, 4. 379)

Both the cock's speech, in which he makes himself the sun and sum of his own world, and Miller's and Tickell's interpretations of that speech are in consonance with thoughts suggested in two passages in Montaigne's *Apology for Raimond de Sebonde*, which Dryden himself may have remembered as he read Chaucer. In the first passage, Montaigne, with considerable solemnity, questions the grounds for the belief that humans have in 'their own importance in the creation', as Miller

---

[30] *The Spectator*, No. 621 (Wednesday 17 November 1714), in Donald F. Bond, ed., *The Spectator*, 5 vols (Oxford, 1965), 5. 124–5. Bond notes the 'striking parallels' to Pope's *Essay on Man* in this (originally anonymous) essay, but supports Tickell's authorship on the grounds that notes for the essay exist among Tickell's extant papers.

was to put it, and in particular the assumption 'that the stars in the firmament, and all the glories of nature, were created only to please their eyes, and amuse their imaginations':[31]

> Let him make me understand by the force of his Reason, upon what Foundations he has built those great Advantages, he thinks he has over other Creatures: Who has made him believe, that this admirable Motion of the Celestial Arch, the Eternal Light of those Tapers that roll over his Head, the wonderful Motions of that infinite Ocean should be established and continue so many Ages, for his Service and Convenience? Can any thing be imagined so ridiculous, that this miserable and wretched Creature, who is not so much as Master of himself, but subject to the Injuries of all things, should call himself Master and Emperour of the World, of which, he has not power to know the least part, much less to command the whole. And this Priviledge which he attributes to himself, of being the only Creature in this vast Fabrick, that has the Understanding to discover the Beauty, and the Parts of it ... Who I wonder, seal'd him this Patent?[32]

Montaigne transforms his own question in a comic direction when he returns to it later in his essay in a passage that may have prompted Dryden to paint a cock who, in appreciating the gifts of 'Lavish Nature', has some better reasons to believe himself to be the centre of the universe than might his owner:

> For why may not a *Goose* say thus, All the part of the Universe I have an Interest in, the Earth serves me to walk upon, the Sun to light me, the Stars have their Influence upon me: I have such Advantage by the Winds, and such Conveniences by the Waters: There is nothing that yond heavenly Roof looks upon so favourably as me; I am the Darling of Nature? Is it not Man that treats, lodges and serves me? 'Tis for me that he both sows and grinds.[33]

When Dryden's Chanticleer expresses his appreciation of the world around him, his reference to 'lavish Nature' which 'has adorn'd the Year', might indicate that he and Dryden were recalling another literary 'Lord of all the workes of Nature', Spenser's 'ioyous Butterflie' in *Muipotmos* who appreciates the 'Fat Colworts, and comforting Perseline, / Colde Lettuce, and refreshing Rosmarine' that 'lauish Nature' has provided for his delight.[34] Chanticleer, it seems, is viewing nature through the spectacles of books. He is conversant with the best authors.

---

[31] Batteux, *Course of the Belles Letters*, 1. 276.

[32] Michael Seigneur de Montaigne, *Essays*, trans. Charles Cotton, 3 vols (London, 1685–86), 2. 195–6.

[33] Montaigne, *Essays*, 2. 348. The passage was remembered and alluded to by Pope in the *Essay on Man*, Epistle 3, lines 45–6 (see Pope, *Poems*, 3i. 96).

[34] Spenser, *Muipotmos*, 161–4, 209–14, in Edmund Spenser, *Shorter Poems*, ed. Richard A. McCabe (London, 1999), 296–7.

'The Latter End of Joy Is Woe'

But, despite his learning and refined sensibility, Dryden's cock is, of course, making a mistake of mock-heroic proportions, which will have—or so it seems at this point in the narrative—mock-tragic consequences. In an interjection immediately following the cock's delighted contemplation of the circumambient world—

> The time shall come when Chanticleer shall wish
> His Words unsaid, and hate his boasted Bliss.
> (*The Cock and the Fox*, 467–8; Dryden, *Works*, 7. 315)

—Dryden drew on Virgil's comment on the fate of Turnus in pillaging the 'shining Belt' from the corpse of Aeneas's friend, Pallas:

> The Time shall come, when *Turnus*, but in vain,
> Shall wish untouch'd the Trophies of the slain:
> Shall wish the fatal Belt were far away;
> And curse the dire Remembrance of the Day.
> (*The Tenth Book of the Aeneis*, 700–3; Dryden, *Works*, 6. 699)

The error of the cock, however, exceeds even the hubris of Turnus when ignoring Fate and dishonouring Pallas's corpse. Dryden's Chanticleer is labouring under the delusion that he stands in the place occupied in Milton's version of Ovid's lines on the creation of Man:

> the Masterwork, the end
> Of all yet don; a Creature who not prone
> And Brute as other Creatures, but endu'd.
> With Sanctitie of Reason, might erect
> His Stature, and upright with Front serene
> Govern the rest, self-knowing.
> (*Paradise Lost*, 7. 505–10)

'Self-knowing' Chanticleer is not. His delusion is absolute. In both Dryden and Chaucer, the cock is speaking in ignorance of the laws of life. In Dryden's version, the necessary reminder of his true station will come from the gods.

ever the latter ende of ioy is wo	The crested Bird shall by Experience know, ⎫
God wote, worldly ioye is soone ago	*Jove* made not him his Master-piece below; ⎬
And if a rethore coud faire endite	And learn the latter end of Joy is Woe. ⎭
He in a chronicle might safely write	The Vessel of his Bliss to Dregs is run,
As for a soueraine notabilitie.	And Heav'n will have him tast his other Tun.
(*NPT*, 3205–9; Speght 1598, Fol. 87ʳ)	(*The Cock and the Fox*, 469–73; Dryden,
	Works, 7. 315)

If Dryden's mind turned to Milton at this point (in calling Chanticleer a 'crested Bird', for example, where Milton had mentioned a 'crested Cock')[35], his thought might have been that Milton was a 'rethore' of precisely the kind described by Chaucer. As Dryden seems to have seen it, Milton had showed himself, extraordinarily, to be the poetic 'son' of Chaucer at the moment when his Satan interspersed a vision of a happy couple with a sudden moment of regretful tenderness and the reminder that 'the latter ende of <u>ioy</u> is <u>wo</u>' and that 'worldly <u>ioye</u> is soone ago':

> Ah gentle pair, yee little think how nigh
> Your change approaches, when all these delights
> Will vanish and deliver ye to <u>woe</u>.
> More <u>woe</u>, the more your taste is now of Joy.
>
> (*Paradise Lost*, 4. 366–9)

When lamenting Chanticleer's near fatal error later in the poem, Dryden's apostrophe echoed Adam's condemnation of Eve in *Paradise Lost*:

> <u>O</u> Chaunteclere, accursed be the morowe
> That thou in thy yerde flew from the bemes.
>
> (*NPT*, 3230–1; Speght 1598, Fol. 87ʳ)

> <u>O</u> Chaunticleer, <u>in</u> an unhappy <u>Hour</u>
> <u>Did'st thou</u> forsake the Safety of thy Bow'r.
>
> (*The Cock and the Fox*, 504–5; Dryden, *Works*, 7. 317)

> O *Eve*, in evil hour thou didst give eare
> To that false Worm.
>
> (*Paradise Lost*, 9. 1067–8)

Dryden, however, has given the cadence of his couplet, perhaps, the more regretful tone of Milton's own apostrophe: 'O much deceav'd, much failing, hapless *Eve*'.[36]

Satan and St Reynard

In his discussion of *The Nun's Priest's Tale* and *The Cock and the Fox*, John Miller appears to be seeing both Dryden and Chaucer before him as 'embellishing' rather than deserting the form of the apologue. Batteux had maintained that the 'sprightly or humorous stile in fable consists in bestowing such appellations and qualities on animals, as only properly belong to men'. In this connection, Miller, as well as enjoying Chaucer's and Dryden's depiction of Chanticleer who 'deems himself an animal of no small consequence' noted that 'Saint Reynard is put

---

[35] *Paradise Lost*, 7. 443. For the presence of Milton in *The Cock and the Fox*, see Taylor Corse, 'Dryden and Milton in "The Cock and the Fox"', *Milton Quarterly*, 27 (1993), 109–18.
[36] *Paradise Lost*, 9. 404.

for an hipocritical fox' and obviously relished Dryden's substantial expansion of Chaucer's depiction of his Chanticleer's adversary:[37]

A col fox (full of sleight and iniquitie)	A Fox full fraught with seeming Sanctity,
That in the groue had wonned yeres three	That fear'd an Oath, but like the Devil, would lie,
By high imagination aforne caste	Who look'd like Lent, and had the holy Leer,
The same night, through the hedge braste	And durst not sin before he say'd his Pray'r:
A col fox (full of sleight and iniquitie)	This pious Cheat that never suck'd the Blood,
That in the groue had wonned yeres three	Nor chaw'd the Flesh of Lambs but when he cou'd,
By high imagination aforne caste	Had pass'd three Summers in the neighb'ring Wood;
The same night, through the hedge braste	And musing long, whom next to circumvent,
Into the yerde, there Chaunteclere the faire	On Chanticleer his wicked Fancy bent:
Was wont and eke his wiues to repaire:	And in his high Imagination cast,
And in a bedde of wortes still he lay	By Stratagem to gratify his Tast.
Til it was passed vndren of the day	The Plot contriv'd, before the break of Day,
Waiting his time, on Chaunteclere to fall	Saint Reynard through the Hedge had made his way;
As gladly done these homicides all	The Pale was next, but proudly with a bound
That in a waite lie to murdre men.	He lept the Fence of the forbidden Ground:
	Yet fearing to be seen, within a Bed
	Of Colworts he conceal'd his wily Head;
	There skulk'd till Afternoon, and watch'd his Time,
	(As Murd'rers use) to perpetrate his Crime.
(*NPT*, 3215–25; Speght 1598, Fol. 87ʳ)	(*The Cock and the Fox*, 480–98; Dryden, *Works*, 7. 315–17)

Miller noted that Dryden's portrait is drawn 'in the true spirit of fable, and conveys the most lively idea of the manners, as well as exterior deportment of this subtle beast'.[38] Dryden had expanded his description of his fox's 'manners' by drawing again on Milton. Reynard's 'manners' remind us in several respects of those of Milton's Satan. Reynard, 'Full fraught with seeming sanctity', for example, resembles Satan at the end of Book 2 of *Paradise Lost*, where 'Accurst, and in a cursed hour' he approaches the 'pendant world' 'full fraught with mischievous revenge'. So Reynard's chawing the flesh of Lambs recalls Milton's Satan upon the first convex of the world, when the Fiend 'bent on his prey', and 'walking at large in spacious field', is compared to a 'Vultur' intending to 'gorge the flesh of Lambs or yeanling Kids'.[39] And when Dryden's Reynard bursts through the hedge into the farmyard, Dryden remembered that Chanticleer's yard had a fence, at the same time as recalling Satan before the gates of Eden, when 'Due entrance he disdained, and in contempt, / At one slight bound high over leap'd all bound', and is compared to 'a prowling Wolfe' that 'Leaps o'er the fence with ease into the Fould'.[40] Dryden's Reynard, similarly, 'proudly with a bound ... lept the Fence of the forbidden Ground'. Dryden does not, however, appear to have been using Chaucer to parody Milton or to align

[37] Batteux, *Course of the Belles Letters*, 1. 201–8, 216.
[38] Ibid. 1. 277.
[39] *Paradise Lost*, 3. 430–41.
[40] Ibid. 4. 179–96.

Chaucer's fox straightforwardly with Milton's Satan. If Reynard's proud bound is like Satan's, his entry of the 'forbidden ground' of females 'and eke his wiues' recalls Virgil's comparison of Turnus to a 'wanton Courser' who 'in the Pride of Youth o'releaps the Mounds/ And snuffs the Females in forbidden Grounds'.[41]

Reynard and Satan's Flattery

Miller's pleasure in the depiction of the 'manners' of the 'hipocritical fox' does not cause him to ignore or lose sight of the larger dramatic situation. When he came to the meeting between the Cock and the Fox, Miller attended equally to the human and the animal realities. Chanticleer reacts purely as a bird. Reynard, although limited by the size of his animal body, responds as a man. This is another passage where Dryden was able to adopt many of Chaucer's words and rhythms:

And so befell as he cast his eye	And so befel, that as he cast his Eye,
Among the wortes on a butterflie	Among the Colworts on a butterfly,
He was ware of the foxe that laie full lowe	He saw false *Reynard*, where he lay full low,
Nothing than list him for to crowe	I need not swear he had no list to Crow:
But cryed cock cocke, and up he stert	But cry'd, Cock, Cock, and gave a suddain start,
As one that was affraide in his hert	As sore dismaid and frighted at his Heart.
For naturally beastes desireth to flie	For Birds and Beasts, inform'd by Nature, know
For her contrarie, if he may it see	Kinds opposite to theirs, and fly their Foe.
Tho he neuer erst had seen it with his eye.	So, Chanticleer, who never saw a Fox,
This Chaunteclere, wen he gan him espie	Yet shun'd him as a Sailor shuns the Rocks.
He would have fled, but the foxe anone	… But the false Loon who cou'd not work his Will
Said gentle sir, alas: what woll ye done?	By open Force, employ'd his flatt'ring Skill;
Be ye affrayd of me, that am your frende?	I hope, my Lord, said he, I not offend,
	Are you afraid of me, that am your Friend?
(*NPT*, 3273–85; Speght 1598, Fol. 87ʳ⁻ᵛ)	(*The Cock and the Fox*, 579–92; Dryden, *Works*, 7. 321)

On this occasion, Miller's remarks might apply equally to Dryden and to Chaucer.[42] 'How admirable well imagined', Miller comments on Reynard's speech which follows,

> is this exordium to the speech of the fox; nothing less than this humility in his approach and address, together with the seasoning of flattery, and air of consequence, reflected on Chanticleer, by giving him the title of my lord! could have been supposed capable of reconciling the cock to the least conference with a creature, whose appearance answered so exact to the image that had filled him with such apprehensions in his dream the night before. The Poet appears to have been fully sensible of this, and has with great art supplied every exigence of the subject.[43]

---

[41] *The Eleventh Book of the Aeneis*, 745–6; Dryden, *Works*, 6. 744.
[42] The first couplet and the last line of this passage represent instances where Dryden was able to incorporate and integrate lines from Chaucer in his translation with minimum alteration.
[43] Batteux, *Course of the Belles Letters*, 1. 278–9.

The art by which Dryden 'supplied' the 'exigence' of the subject was again partly borrowed from *Paradise Lost*:

Now certes, I were worse than a fende	I come no Spy, nor as a Traytor press,
If I to you would harme, or villanie	To learn the Secrets of your soft Recess:
I am not come your counsaile to espie	Far be from *Reynard* so prophane a Thought,
But truely the cause of my comming	But by the sweetness of your Voice was brought:
Was only to here howe ye sing	For, as I bid my Beads, by chance I heard,
For sothly ye haue as mery a steuen	The Song as of an Angel in the Yard:
As any angel hath, that is in heuen	A Song that wou'd have charm'd th'infernal Gods,
Therewith ye haue of musicke more feling	And banish'd Horror from the dark Abodes:
Than had Boece or any that can sing.	Had *Orpheus* sung it in the neather Sphere,
	So much the Hymn had pleas'd the Tyrant's Ear,
	The Wife had been detain'd, to keep the Husband there.
(*NPT*, 3286–94; Speght 1598, Fol. 87ᵛ)	(*The Cock and the Fox*, 597–607; Dryden, *Works*, 7. 323)

When Chaucer's fox mentions the 'fende', claiming that he had not come to 'espie' Chanticleer's 'counsaile', Dryden thought of Milton's Satan—in this instance addressing beguiling words to the powers of darkness—

> Ye Powers
> And Spirits of this nethermost Abyss,
> Chaos and ancient Night, I come no Spy
> With purpose to explore or to disturb
> The secrets of your Realm.
>
> (*Paradise Lost*, 2. 968–72)

—and also recalled another moment in Milton which prompted him to make his fox call Chanticleer's abode a *recess*:

> Such Pleasure took the Serpent to behold
> This Flourie Plat, the sweet recess of Eve
> Thus earlie, thus alone.
>
> (*Paradise Lost*, 9. 455–7)

Again, though, Dryden does not suggest any simple or consistent parallel between his deceiver and Milton's. If the fox resembled a puritan on his first appearance, Dryden also here equips Reynard with a rosary and a high strain of neo-classical flattery.

Chanticleer's Seduction: 'A Fine Picture of Human Nature'

When Chanticleer succumbs to the flattery of the fox, Miller attends both to moral and to narrative, and his sense of the point of the moment has clearly been shaped by Dryden's version:

We have a fine picture of human nature presented us in the character of the cock; imbecility of body and of mind could not convince this little vain trifler of his own insignificance, and the little title he had to the extravagant encomiums lavished on him by the fox.[44]

Dryden's additions to this part of the poem stress the Vanity of Cockly Aspirations, but, in achieving this effect, he displays a lightness of touch that makes his additions 'rather seem to rise of themselves, than to be the effects of choice or study':[45]

This Chauntecleer his wings gan to bete As a man that could not his treson aspie So was he rauished with his flaterie. (*NPT*, 3322–4; Speght 1598, Fol. 87ᵛ)	The Cock was pleas'd to hear him speak so fair, And proud beside, as solar People are: Nor cou'd the Treason from the Truth descry, So was he ravish'd with this Flattery: So much the more as from a little Elf, He had a high Opinion of himself: Though sickly, slender, and not large of Limb, Concluding all the World was made for him. (*The Cock and the Fox*, 651–8; Dryden, *Works*, 7. 325)

Miller believes that the 'fine picture of human nature' that Chaucer's and Dryden's narratives suggest and on which it depends is displayed to particular advantage in the 'extremely fine' 'application' 'of the moral to princes and great men':[46]

Als ye lordes, many a false flaterour Is in your courte, & many a false lesingour That plese you well more, by my faith Than he that sothfastness unto you saith Redeth Ecclesiast of flaterie Bewar ye lordes of her trecheeerie. (*NPT*, 3325–30; Speght 1598, Fol. 87ᵛ)	Ye Princes, rais'd by Poets to the Gods, And *Alexander'd* up in lying Odes, Believe not ev'ry flatt'ring Knave's report, There's many a *Reynard* lurking in the Court; And he shall be receiv'd with more regard And list'ned to, than <u>modest Truth</u> is heard. (*The Cock and the Fox*, 659–64; Dryden, *Works*, 7. 325)

Dryden, in naming poets as principle among 'lesingours', includes himself in the general indictment. Where Chaucer had invoked Ecclesiaticus, Dryden's mind returned to some thoughts he had first expressed in his 'Prologue to His Royal Highness'. There, he had compared courtiers to foxes, 'That crafty kind' who possess 'seeming Innocence':

> Still we are throng'd so full with *Reynard's* race,
> That Loyal Subjects scarce can find a place:
> Thus <u>modest Truth</u> is cast behind the Crowd:
> Truth speaks too Low; Hypocrisie too Loud.[47]
>
> ('Prologue to His Royal Highness 14–17;
> Dryden, *Works*', 2. 193–4)

---

[44] Ibid. 1. 280.
[45] Ibid. 1. 215.
[46] Ibid. 1. 280.
[47] The Prologue was spoken on 21 April 1682.

The Hens' Lament, the Village in Pursuit, and Chanticleer's Great Escape

Again, however, neither Dryden nor Miller confined their attention to the moral, however 'fine'. Among the passages that pleased Miller best and most particularly are those where 'a comparison' is made 'of small things, with great' and where effects are produced 'by measuring, affecting and interesting incidents, by the most trivial and insignificant; so that the whole together forms a kind of grotesque'. The particular passage that prompted these remarks is the lament of the hens, in which Miller found 'a vast fund of elegant irony'. But Miller was also greatly taken by the description of the chase after the fox (see Fig. 4.1):[48]

Fig. 4.1   The village in pursuit of the fox. Drawn by Thomas
Stothard and engraved by Robert Cromek. From John
Dryden, *Fables from Boccacio and Chaucer*, ed. John Aikin
(London, 1806).

[48] Batteux, *Course of the Belles Letters*, 1. 216, 281–3.

These twelve lines convey a very humorous and natural description of a village fright; the painting is so lively, that we are in a manner transported into the midst of the hurry and confusion, and hear the squeaking of the pigs, the cackling of the geese, &c. &c.

Again, if the finishing of the 'painting' is Dryden's, the groundwork is Chaucer's:

Aha the Foxe, and after hem they ran
And eke with staues, many another man
Ran, Coll our dogge, Talbot, & eke garlonde
And Malkin, with her distaffe in her honde
Ran Cowe & Calfe, and eke the verie hogges
For they so sore aferde were of the dogges
And shouting of men, and of women eke
They ran so, her hert thought to breke
They yellen as fendes do in hell.

(*NPT*, 3381–9; Speght 1598, Fol. 87ᵛ)

The Fox, the wicked Fox, was all the Cry,
Out from his House ran ev'ry Neighbour nigh:
The Vicar first, and after him the Crew,
With Forks and Staves the Felon to pursue.
Ran *Coll* our Dog, and *Talbot* with the Band,
And *Malkin*, with her Distaff in her Hand:
Ran Cow and Calf, and Family of Hogs,
In Panique Horror of pursuing Dogs,
With many a deadly Grunt and doleful Squeak
Poor Swine, as if their pretty Hearts would Break.
The Shouts of Men, the Women in dismay,
With Shrieks augment the Terror of the Day.

(*The Cock and the Fox*, 724–35; Dryden, *Works*, 7. 329–31)

Miller's appeal here is to the simple but fundamental claim that poetry approximates the remote: the readers is 'transported' into a scene which is 'painted' in 'so lively' a way as to create in his or her mind the illusion of hearing the very sounds of the pursuers—'the squeaking of the pigs', which is explicitly mentioned, and 'the cackling of the geese', which is only implied.

Miller's reading of Dryden follows Dryden's reading of Chaucer in that the moral is extended in various ways and in several directions but is never entirely out of sight. Nor is the narrative sacrificed to the moral. Everything so far has been suggesting that Chanticleer's pride will lead to an irrevocable fall and that he will indeed be plucked and eaten to the bone. But the fable then returns upon itself, and its moral is complicated by the cock's ability to learn from his mistake, not by rejecting flattery, but by instantly becoming himself an absolute master of the art. This was a moment and a movement that interested Dryden particularly. He had added the Vicar to the crowd of men, women, and animals who rush out in pursuit of the fox, and returned to this little joke when inspiration saves Chanticleer from the Jaws of Death:

Lo how fortune tourneth sodainly
The hope and the pride of her enemy
This Cocke that laie vpon the Foxe backe
In all his drede, vnto the Foxe he spake
And saied, sir, if I were as ye
Yet should I saie, as wise God helpe me
Tourneth ayen, ye proude churles all
A very pestilence vpon you fall
Now am I come vnto this woods side

But see how Fortune can confound the Wise,
And when they least expect it, turn the Dice.
The Captive Cock, who scarce cou'd draw his Breath,
And lay within the very Jaws of Death:
Yet in this Agony his Fancy wrought
And Fear supply'd him with this happy Thought:
Yours is the Prize, victorious Prince, said he,
The Vicar my defeat, and all the Village see.
Enjoy your friendly Fortune while you may,

Maugre your hed, the Cocke shall here abide	And bid the Churls that envy you the Prey,
I woll him eate in faith, and that anon.	Call back their mungril Curs, and cease their Cry,
	See Fools, the shelter of the Wood is nigh,
	And Chanticleer in your despight shall die.
	He shall be pluck'd, and eaten to the Bone.
(*NPT*, 3403–13; Speght 1598, Fol. 88ʳ)	(*The Cock and the Fox*, 753–66;
	Dryden, *Works*, 7. 331)

Scott commented on this passage in a footnote: 'This excellent parody upon Virgil is introduced by Dryden, and marks his late labours.'[49] The speech that Scott and Dryden had in mind is Turnus's final and vain prayer for mercy from Aeneas, which Dryden had rendered as follows:

> I know my Death deserv'd, nor hope to live:
> Use what the Gods, and thy good Fortune give ...
> The Latian Chiefs <u>have seen</u> me beg my Life;
> <u>Thine is the Conquest</u>, thine the Royal Wife:
> Against a yielded Man, 'tis mean ignoble Strife.
>
> (*The Twelfth Book of the Aeneis*, 1349–59; Dryden,
>
> *Works*, 6. 806)

For Scott, it is presumably 'one of the sparks which genius strikes out when in collision with the work of a kindred spirit' that Chanticleer should present himself in the guise of Turnus, and the Fox in that of Aeneas. Dryden's fox had seduced the cock in the manner of Milton's Satan, the '<u>Artificer of</u> fraud',[50] and Dryden's depiction of Chanticleer had been coloured by terms originally applied to Turnus. Chanticleer's education in the 'Liberal Arts' now allows him to turn the tables, almost as if he had learnt from his own narrator:

And as he spake the worde, all sodainly	This *Reynard* said: but as the Word he spoke,
This Cock brake from his mouth deliuerly	The Pris'ner with a Spring from Prison broke:
And high vpon a tree he flewe anon	Then stretch'd his feather'd Fans with all his might,
And whan the Foxe saw that he was gon	And to the neighb'ring Maple wing'd his flight.
Alas (qd he) O Chaunteclere alas	Whom when the Traitor safe on Tree beheld,
I haue (qd he) doe to you trespass.	He curs'd the Gods, with Shame and Sorrow fill'd;
	Shame for his Folly; Sorrow out of time,
	For Plotting an unprofitable Crime:
	Yet mast'ring both <u>th'Artificer of Lies</u>,
	Renews th'Assault, and his last Batt'ry tries.
	Though I, said he, did ne'er in Thought offend,
	How justly may my Lord suspect his Friend?
(*NPT*, 3415–20; Speght 1598, Fol. 88ʳ)	(*The Cock and the Fox*, 768–79; Dryden,
	Works, 7. 333)

When Dryden embellishes Reynard's final rhetorical onslaught on Chanticleer, he recalls the language employed by those parliamentarians of the 1640s who insisted

---

[49] Dryden, *Works*, ed. Scott, 11. 351.
[50] *Paradise Lost*, 4. 121.

they were not fighting against the sacred person of the King. Dryden's Reynard declares that he had no intention to 'bear' Chanticleer from his 'Palace-yard', and was merely acting like those 'loyal subjects' who 'often seize their Prince ... / Yet mean his sacred Person not the least Offence'.[51]

Decorations, Digressions, and Exempla

The echoes of Virgil, Montaigne, and Milton in *The Cock and the Fox*, and the references in the poem to specific historical events, though notable, are not so much allusions in the modern sense as the vestigial traces of Dryden's process of thought as he read and recomposed Chaucer's poem. It was John Miller's conviction that, whatever sources Dryden had drawn upon while composing his poem, everything had served a single purpose: to show the effects of 'fond Credulity' and to encourage readers 'of Flatt'rers to beware'. In this respect, Miller believed, Dryden's poem provided a perfect exemplum of the 'apologue', as defined by Batteux.

And yet, while Miller had admired Dryden's various 'extensions' of the tale's moral, he passes over many passages in silence and excises much from the texts of both Chaucer's original and Dryden's version that he prints in his book. He reduces Chaucer's description of the 'pore wedow' to three lines and excises Pertelote's medical observations and laxative recipe. Chanticleer's long series of exempla proving that dreams presage is completely removed, together with the speech in which the cock provides amorous reasons for ignoring his own intellectual conclusions and defying 'bothe vison and dreme'. Miller also removes Chaucer's comments on the knowledge of birds. Narratorial comments not immediately bearing on the moral are removed or reduced. Miller curtails the description of 'Chanticleer in all his pride', removes the interjection of the narrator on the claims to truth of his own story, the exclamations against murder, traitors, the discussions of freewill and the responsibility of women for the fall of man, the invocations of destiny, Venus and Vinsauf, and the references to Nero, to Jack Straw, and the flight of ducks.

Here, Miller and Dryden part company since many of the passages Miller removed were those where Dryden seems to have found himself most engaged and having most to add. Of passages in *The Cock and the Fox* that contain substantial original additions, Miller omitted from his abridged version remarks on incestuous kings, Partlet's list of female requirements in the ideal male, Chanticleer's diatribe against doctors, some of Reynard's more obviously clerical attributes, Reynard's leap into the yard, the list of historical hypocrites and traitors, the whole of

---

[51] *The Cock and the Fox*, 784, 790–2; Dryden, *Works*, 7. 333. Compare *The Humble Petition of the Maior, Aldermen, and Common Councell, of the Citie of London* (London, 1641), pp. 2–4; Gerard Langbaine, *A Review of the Covenant* (Oxford, 1645), p. 47; *A Just Defence of the Royal Martyr, K. Charles I* (London, 1699), p. 165.

the very extended discussion of free will, Reynard's exempla of remarkable cocks, and Dryden's remarks on 'modest truth'. Miller appears to have thought that the comments, in both Chaucer and Dryden, on the 'liberal arts' and on educated poultry, the attribution of hands to birds, and the description of cocks and hens singing in harmony were deviations from the decorum of the apologue. Gone too are the initially unobserved escape of the fox, Reynard's comments on the laws of hospitality, and the references to anti-French and anti-Jewish riots.

Sir Walter Scott, in contrast, relished the full variety of Dryden's expanded digressions and exempla,[52] welcoming Dryden's invitations to compare, associate, and speculate, which, for him, represented an exemplification and embodiment of the reading process itself. For Scott, Dryden had 'put the Merit of Chaucer into its full and true Light' by producing a version enlivened by the spirit or 'spiritedness' but not the letter of his original.[53]

A notable instance of the intermingling of past and present in *The Cock and the Fox* that Scott so admired is to be found in the passage depicting the hue and cry after the fox. Noticing that Chaucer had, on this rare occasion, made a clear contemporary reference to the Peasant's Revolt of 1387, and believing he had a soul congenial to Chaucer's and that poets can divine one another's thought, Dryden added references peculiar to his own times, including one most particularly affecting his immediate friends and family. In his version, the ducks hear 'a Proclamation cry'd / And fear'd a Persecution might betide' (736–7). The language here is close to that of a letter by Dryden to Elizabeth Steward, written at the same time as *Fables* was being prepared:

> We poor Catholiques daily expect a most Severe Proclamation to come out against us, & at the same time are satisfyed, that the King is very Unwilling to persecute us, considering us to be but an handfull, & those disarmd; But the Archbishop of Canterbury is our heavy Enemy; & heavy He is indeed, in all respects.[54]

The fears, although experienced by ducks, are described by Dryden in solemn terms and with what Scott called 'Cervantic gravity', a gravity that rises to apocalyptic proportions when we are told that such was the commotion that 'Earth seem'd to sink beneath, and Heav'n above to fall' (748). Dryden appears to have

---

[52] Dryden refers to Garth's *Dispensary*, the story of Tristram, Foxe's *Actes and Monuments*, and *Paradise Lost*, together with a long series of historical and mythical names: 'Kenelm the Son of Kenulph', 'Quenda', 'venerable Bede', 'Macrobius', 'Scipio', 'Charlemaign', 'Daniel', 'Joseph', 'Craesus', 'Hector', 'holy Austin', 'Bradwardin', 'sweet Cecilia', 'Mercia's King', 'Orpheus', 'the Ptolemy's', 'Jack Stawe', 'Priam', 'Ganelon', 'Lancelot', 'Sinon', 'Brennus and Benlius', 'Pyrrus', 'Asrubal', 'Venus', 'Mars', 'Jove', 'Mercury the God of Gain', 'Nero', 'Richard Ceur de Lion'. Some of these names are derived directly from Chaucer.

[53] Interestingly, and despite the dismissiveness of his summary account of *The Cock and the Fox* in his 'Life of Dryden', Samuel Johnson also seems to have been another admirer of Dryden's additions and expansions in this poem, and quoted from several of them in his *A Dictionary of the English Language*, 2 vols (London, 1755). Sometimes, the citation provides instances of otherwise unexampled words. On other occasions, the passages seem to have been chosen as offering an acute observation upon human life.

[54] John Dryden, *Letters*, ed. Charles E. Ward (Durham, NC, 1942), p. 112.

seen this moment in Chaucer as a depiction of the fears of many times, including his own, and of various kinds of riots of all ages. So rich was Chaucer's account that it had served, as it were, to predict the future. Dryden has not simply applied Chaucer to the present, but here, as so often, has conflated historical periods and combined the historical and the fictional. When Dryden refers to the time when 'the Welkin rung with *One and all* / And Echoes bounded back from *Fox's Hall*' (746–7), he 'alludes', as Scott noted, 'to the riots of his own time, whose gathering cry used to be "one and all"'.[55] The medieval mob moves into the immediate present, its echoes sounding both from Reynard's imaginary country seat and from the notoriously riotous Vauxall (popularly known as 'Foxhall') gardens in Dryden's London. Dryden appears to be operating in the belief that the governing principle of this part of the tale of the Nun's Priest is the joining of the most ludicrous behaviour of animals and birds and the most terrible of human events.

In Praise of Venus: Incest and Holy Dispensations

But if Dryden's reworking of Chaucer is imbued, in part, by his sense of his precarious position in William III's England, he showed no inclination to turn the tale of the Nun's Priest into a poem in defence of Stuart Kings. It seems to be the principle on which this poem is based that one movement in one direction is followed by a contrary movement in another. If there may be some hints of satirical reflections upon the regicides and King William's regime, the Stuart kings are hardly treated in a flattering light. As Dryden describes him, the royalty of Chanticleer is most clearly and emphatically displayed in his marital arrangements. When Dryden came to Chaucer's description of a 'gentel cocke' who had 'Seuen hennes' to 'done his plesaunce' and who were 'his susters and his paramours', and noticed that the cock with his hens scurrying around him is also described as 'royal as a prince in his hall', his mind seems to have returned to the most notable fact about one monarch known to him, which was that when 'Nature prompted' and 'and no law deny'd / Promiscuous use of Concubine and Bride', he 'variously' imparted 'his vigorous warmth' / To Wives and Slaves'.[56]

   Chanticleer, that is, is most like a King in his royal adultery and expedient incest. In animals and Kings, it seems, incest and adultery are blessed:

This gentel cocke, had in gouernaunce	This gentle Cock for solace of his Life,
Seuen hennes, to done his plesaunce	Six <u>Misses</u> had beside his lawful Wife;
Which were his susters and his paramours	Scandal that spares no King, tho' ne'er so good,
And wonder like to him, as of colours.	Says, they were all of his own Flesh and Blood:
	His Sisters both by Sire, and Mother's side,
	And sure their likeness show'd them near ally'd.

---

[55] Dryden, *Works*, ed. Scott, 9. 350.
[56] *Absalom and Achitophel*, 5–9; Dryden, *Works*, 2.5.

> But make the worst, the Monarch did no more,
> Than all the *Ptolomeys* had done before:
> When Incest is for Int'rest of a Nation,
> 'Tis made no Sin by Holy <u>Dispensation</u>.
> Some Lines have been maintain'd by this alone,
> Which by their common Ugliness are known.

(*NPT*, 2865–8; Speght 1598, Fol. 85ᵛ)   (*The Cock and the Fox*, 55–66; Dryden,
                                                                                          Works, 7. 289–91)

The resonances of Dryden's presentation, however, are complex and equivocal. His reference to 'Holy Dispensation', for example, is reminiscent of anti-papist tracts of the early seventeenth century, in which papal dispensations of incestuous unions are offered as proof positive that the Pope was the Anti-Christ.[57] But Dryden's reference to the '*Ptolomeys*' serves as a reminder that repugnance towards incest had not been universal. Nathaniel Wanley, for example, had attributed the taboo on incest to religion alone.[58] Thomas Tenison, later Archbishop of Canterbury, had the 'Student of Religion' in his *The Creed of Mr. Hobbes Examined* (1670) argue against the efficacy of natural law as a basis for society by maintaining that there is no law of nature prohibiting the case of 'promiscuous mixtures', including incest.[59] And Nourmahal, in Dryden's *Aureng-Zebe*, had argued, similarly, that 'Promiscuous Love is Nature's general Law', since 'whosoever the first Lovers were, / Brother and Sister made the second Pair, / And doubled, by their love, their piety'.[60]

In *The Cock and the Fox*, the balance between Chanticleer's claims and those of humanity is in constant flux. At some moments, Chanticleer's pride is pure folly; at others, his claims are stronger than those of man. The immediate prompter for Dryden's thoughts about Chanticleer's incest was probably his own translation of the episode of Cinyras and Myrrha from Book 10 of Ovid's *Metamorphoses*. In that poem, Myrrha ponders at length whether her passion for her father is a sin or a crime. Like Tenison's controversialist, she argues that 'the Country makes the Crime' and recalls that there are some 'Nations' among which 'happy Daughters with their Sires are join'd'. Most pertinently in the present context, she argues that the 'envious Laws' forbidding incest were 'Made not for any other Beast, but Man'. Among the examples she draws from the animal world, one appears to be almost an anticipation of *The Nun's Priest's Tale*:

---

[57] See, e.g. George Downame, *A Treatise Concerning Antichrist Divided into Two Bookes* (London, 1603), 77–78.
[58] See Nathaniel Wanley, *The Wonders of the Little World* (London, 1673), p. 453.
[59] See Thomas Tenison, *The Creed of Mr. Hobbes Examined* (London, 1670), p. 139.
[60] *Aureng-Zebe*, IV. i. 132–5; Dryden, *Works*, 12. 213.

The Hen is free to wed the Chick she bore,
And make a Husband, whom she hatch'd before.[61]

(*Cinyras and Myrrha*, 46–7, Dryden, *Works*, 7. 249–50)

In Praise of Venus: The Passive Doctrine

Among Dryden's contemporaries, the conventional wisdom appears to have been that husbands were, in sexual terms, fonder of their 'misses' than their wives.[62] The case of Chanticleer, particularly in Speght's text, partly contradicts such a notion—with some energy:

... the fayrest hewed in the throte	But passing this as from our Tale apart,
Was called faire Damosell Pertelote	Dame Partlet was the Soveraign of his Heart:
He fethered her a hundred times a day,	Ardent in Love, outragious in his Play,
And she him pleseth, all that euer she may[63]	He feather'd her a hundred times a Day:
Curteis she was, discrete, and debonaire	And she that was not only passing fair,
And compeneable, and bare herself so faire	But was withal discreet, and debonair
Sens the time that she was seuenight old.	Resolv'd <u>the passive Doctrin</u> to fulfil
That truelich, she hath the hert in hold	Tho' loath: And let him work his wicked Will.
Of Chaunteclere, loking in euery lith.	<u>At Board and Bed</u> was affable and kind,
	According as their Marriage-Vow did bind,
	And as the Churches Precept had enjoin'd ...
	Ev'n since she was a Sennight old, they say
	Was chast, and humble to her dying Day,
	Nor Chick nor Hen was known to disobey.

(*NPT*, 2869–75; Speght 1598, Fol. 85ᵛ)   (*The Cock and the Fox*, 67–80; Dryden, *Works*, 7. 291)

In describing Partlet's attitude to her husband as obeying 'the passive doctrine', Dryden is alluding to a specific and controversial issue in contemporary politics. In his *Reflections on the History of Passive Obedience* (1689), the passionate Whig Samuel Johnson, the 'Benjochanan' of *Absalom and Achitophel*, commented on the

---

[61] For further discussion, see David Hopkins, 'Nature's Law and Man's: Dryden's "Cinyras and Myrrha"', in *Conversing with Antiquity: English Poetry and the Classics from Shakespeare to Pope* (Oxford, 2010), 177–201.

[62] In Nathaniel Lee's *The Princess of Cleve*, for example, St André declares that

Misses are really more pleasant than a Wife can be, *Probatum est*. A Wife dares not assume the Liberty of pleasing like a Miss, for fear of being thought one. A Wife may pretend to dutiful affection, and bustle below, but must be still at night. 'Tis Miss alone may be allow'd Flame and Rapture, and all that.

Nathaniel Lee, *The Princess of Cleve* (London, 1689), p. 20.

[63] Thomas Tyrwhitt noted that the couplet on the cock feathering and the fair damsel pleasing could be found 'in only two Mss. HA. and D', and commented that he 'was glad to leave them out as an injudicious interpolation' (Tyrwhitt 1798, 2. 499). However, Dryden and the scribe who composed the couplet in Speght's copy text might be seen as responding to the Epilogue to the tale, where the Nun's Priest is called a 'treadfoule' by the Host.

potential 'mischievous Consequence' of the 'Passive Doctrine' which binds subjects 'not to Resist, but to Assist [their] Prince, though a Tyrant'. If, Johnson argues, the 'passive doctine' embraced by some Protestant clergy during the reign of James II had prevailed after William III's accession, it would have consituted 'a standing Common-place-Book for Treasonable Practices'. It would have 'for ever inslaved the Nation', and prevented William from 'rescuing' 'these three Kingdoms ... from their own chosen and voluntary Bondage'.[64]

But if the relationship of Chanticleer and Pertelote is momentarily likened to one possible relationship between a contemporary monarch and his subjects, Dryden also likens it to a marriage sanctioned by the Christian Church, since in referring to Pertelote being 'affable and kind' 'At Board and Bed', Dryden echoes the words of the medieval marriage vow, in which the wife promises to be 'buxum in bedde and at the borde tyll deathe us departhe'.[65] To this troth-plight Partlet adheres, apparently with remarkable strictness.

In Praise of Venus: Recreant Knights, Baffled Knight, and Dunghill-Cocks

Partlet, however, includes among her wifely duties the obligation to keep her husband up to the mark. In Chaucer, Pertelote consistently addresses her husband in the second person plural. Dryden's Partlet here uses the *thou* form, often used for rebuke or reproach:

Away (qd. she) fie for shame hertlesse	Now fy for Shame, quoth she, by Heav'n above,
Alas (qd. she) for by God aboue	Thou hast for ever lost thy Ladies Love;
Now haue ye lost my hert, and all my loue	No Woman can endure a <u>Recreant Knight</u>,
I cannot loue a coward by my faith:	He must be bold by Day, and free by Night:
For certes, what so any woman saith,	Our Sex desires a Husband or a Friend,
We all desire, if that it might be	Who can our Honour and his own defend;
To haue husbondes, hardie, wise, and fre,	Wise, Hardy, Secret, lib'ral of his Purse:
And secrete, and no nigard, ne no fole	A Fool is nauseous, but a Coward worse:
Ne him that is agast of euery tole	No bragging Coxcomb, yet no <u>baffled Knight</u>,
Ne none auantour, by that God aboue	How dar'st thou talk of Love, and dar'st not Fight?
How durst ye say for shame, vnto your loue	How dar'st thou tell thy Dame thou art affer'd,
That any sweuen might make you a ferd?	Hast thou no manly Heart, and hast a Beard?
Haue ye no mannes hert, and haue a berd?	If ought from fearful Dreams may be divin'd,
Alas, and con ye be aferd of sweuenis?	They signify a <u>Cock of Dunghill-kind</u>.
Nothing but vanite God wotte in sweuen is	
(*NPT*, 2908–21; Speght 1598, Fol. 85ᵛ)	(*The Cock and the Fox*, 126–39; Dryden, *Works*, 7. 293–5)

---

[64] Samuel Johnson, *Reflections on the History of Passive Obedience* (London, 1689), 3–4.
[65] Henry Barclay Swete, *Church Services and Service-Books before The Reformation* (London, 1896), p. 152.

In maintaining that no female can endure a 'Recreant Knight', Partlet is recalling the chivalric ethos of Spenser's *Faerie Queene*.[66] But her second reference to a 'baffled' knight appears to come from a very different world. Chaucer's term 'auantour' was happily matched by 'bragging Coxcomb', but Dryden apparently thought that something more than mere cowardice was hinted at in 'him that is agast of euery tole'. A 'baffled' knight was one who had been disgraced, often for cowardice.[67] It is used in the ballad the goes under the title *The Baffled Knight*, in which a knight 'drunk with wine' meets a fine lady and proposes to 'lay her down', but is 'by the lass', who is astonished at the knight's punctilious over-restraint, 'Ingeniously outwitted'.[68]

The movement from a chivalric to a sexual world is repeated when Partlet turns to the consideration of poultry. Partlet's rebuke of her husband—that, in showing his fears, Chanticleer is revealing himself to be a 'Cock of Dunghill-kind'—is heavily loaded. A *dunghill cock*, in seventeenth-century terms, is precisely what Chanticleer *is*.[69] In books of husbandry, the term is descriptive and in no way derogatory. Yet, despite the observation that the dunghill cock is 'strong in the Art of generation', the term had derogatory sexual connotations when applied to humans. Dryden had used it thus in *Amphitryon*.[70] There is also a poem by John Eliot which describes 'a Lady that went to Tunbridge Wells' to 'cure her wombs sterillity' and was there 'delivered of a goodly daughter', an event that 'bred about the court much mirth and laughter'—Eliot's own mirth taking the form of a series of turns on the term 'cock':

> 'Twas not the water, they that say so mock,
> It was the pipe, rather the water cock;
> Nor think it was a dunghillcock, for shame,
> O noe, it was a lusty cock o'th game.
>
> (John Eliot, *Poems* [London, 1658], p. 58)

---

[66] See, e.g. Edmund Spenser, *The Faerie Queene*,II. vi. 28 (Chymochles to Guyon and Phaedra); VI. iii. 35 (Calepine to Turpine) . Richard Hurd noted how the term 'Recreant Knight' was regularly used by the 'old Romancers', to express their 'disdain of a dastard or vanquished knight', particularly those who, 'falling into the hands of the Saracens' had been 'induced to renounce their faith, in order to regain their liberty'. See *Letters on Chivalry and Romance* (2nd edn, London, 1762), p. 21.

[67] See *Oxford English Dictionary, baffled* 1.

[68] Francis James Child, ed., *The English and Scottish Popular Ballads*, 5 vols (Boston, MA, 1884–98), 2. 485.

[69] In *Cheape and Good Husbandry for the Well-Ordering of All Beasts, and Fowles* (London, 1614, p. 110), Gervase Markham describes a 'dunghill cock' as 'a Fowle of all other birds the most manliest; stately and maiesticall, very tame and familiar with the Man, and naturally inclined to liue and prosper in habitable houses: he is hot and strong in the Art of generation, and will serue tenne Hennes sufficiently, and some twelue and thirteene'.

[70] *Amphitryon*, II. i. 217; Dryden, *Works*, 15. 262.

Chanticleer, unsurprisingly, adopts the aristocratic and chivalric account of himself. When he finally tries to resolve the dispute with his wife with an extraordinary mixture of flattery and condescension, Dryden apparently thought he had nothing to add—that his task was to emulate. His cock, like Chaucer's cocksure but really subservient male, speaks with the voice of a beguiler self-beguiled, so animating that most Chaucerian of thoughts: that true husbandly happiness is only found by the well ruled and well deceived. A great deal is condensed when, at the moment of crisis, the poet invokes the Goddess of Love:

O Venus that art goddesse of pleasaunce	On *Friday*-morn he dreamt this direful Dream,
Sithens y^t thy seruant was this chaunteclere	Cross to the worthy Native, in his Scheme!
And in thy seruice did all his powere	Ah blissful *Venus, Goddess of Delight*.
More for delite, than the worlde to multiplie	How cou'd'st thou suffer thy devoted Knight,
Why woldst thou suffer him on thy dai to die?	On thy own Day to fall by Foe oppress'd,
	The wight of all the World who serv'd thee best?
	Who true to Love, was all for Recreation,
	And minded not the Work of Propagation.
(*NPT*, 3342–6; Speght 1598, Fol. 87^v)	(*The Cock and the Fox*, 685–92; Dryden, *Works*, 7. 327)

Prescience and Predestination: 'Lighter Rhimes Ill Suit Such Deep Debate'?

And yet, if Venus approves of Chanticleer's absolute devotion to his hen-wife, it is less clear that the poem does. Dryden reproduces but does not comment on Chanticleer's (mistranslated) Latin remark that woman is the confusion of man, and in one place Dryden, or Dryden's narrator, describes the cock as one 'Who had not run the hazard of his Life / Had he believ'd his Dream, and not his Wife' (58–9). But that remark, like so many in this poem, raises more questions than it answers. Chanticleer *did* believe his dream. He just ignored it. If the dream should have been believed, it must have come from God. If it came from God, the outcome was foreknown and could not have been avoided.

In the abridged version of *The Cock and the Fox* which accompanies his commentary, John Miller omitted the digression in which Dryden elaborates at great length Chaucer's discussion of the nature of the divine and human (or cockly) agency which might be in play in the action of his tale. And in his later version of Chaucer's tale, William Lipscomb passed rapidly over the passage, merely inserting a remark to the effect that 'deep debate' about 'How God's decrees the powers of man restrain' 'ill suit' such 'lighter rhimes'.[71] But Dryden, despite his narrator's expressed 'fear of splitting on a Rock' (551), chose to treat Chaucer's passage almost as if it was the centre of the tale, and expanded upon it with considerable

---

[71] Lipscomb, 3. 328–9.

energy and engagement, displaying to the full the ratiocinative and argumentative powers that Samuel Johnson thought were his particular *forte*.

Dryden had reflected on questions of 'liberty and necessity, destiny and contingence' on several previous occasions.[72] He was not, however, singular in his predilection for this subject. The debate that Chaucer attributed to 'an hundred thousand men' had not declined in the intervening years and had been reinvigorated in the 1670s.[73] In his digression, Dryden makes a point of combining the English and the Latinate terms of the European debate on the subject ('absolute Predestination', 'Foresight', 'Prescience'):

O Chaunteclere, accursed be the morowe	O Chanticleer, in an unhappy Hour
That thou in thy yerde flew from the bemes	Did'st thou forsake the Safety of thy Bow'r:
Thou were ful wel warned by thy dremes	Better for Thee thou had'st believ'd thy Dream,
That ilke day was perillous to thee	And not that Day descended from the Beam!
But what y^t God afore wote, must nedes bee	But here the Doctors eagerly dispute:
After the opinion of certaine clerkes	Some hold Predestination absolute:
Witnesse of him, that any clerke is	Some Clerks maintain, that Heav'n at first foresees,
That in schole is great altercation	And in the virtue of Foresight decrees.
In this matter, and great disputacion	If this be so, then Prescience binds the Will,
And hath ben, of an hundred thousand men.	And Mortals are not free to Good or Ill:
	For what he first foresaw, he must ordain,
	Or its eternal Prescience may be vain:
	As bad for us as Prescience had not bin:
	For first, or last, he's <u>Author of the Sin</u>.
	And who says that, let the blaspheming Man
	Say worse ev'n of the Devil, if he can.
	For how can that Eternal Pow'r be just
	To punish Man, who Sins because he must?
	Or, how can He reward a vertuous Deed,
	Which is not done by us; but <u>first decreed</u>?
(NPT, 3230-9; Speght 1598, Fol. 87^r)	*(The Cock and the Fox, 503-22; Dryden, Works, 7. 317)*

Dryden's elaboration supplies the opinions of Chaucer's 'certaine clerkes'. One group maintained that life is completely, simply, and inexorably predetermined. Another held that Heaven foresees what will happen, and that this foreknowledge in itself determines events and constrains the human will. This second case interests Dryden particularly—and is particularly problematic. By this account, the good or evil actions of humanity are not the result of free will but are determined by God's foreknowledge. If God foresees that something will happen, he must also cause it to happen. The position of both groups of theologians has blasphemous

---

[72] See, e.g. *The Tempest*, III. v. 157–62 (Dryden, *Works*, 10. 64); *The Spanish Fryar*, III. iii. 161–8 (Dryden, *Works*, 14. 154); *Absalom and Achitophel*, 252–9 (Dryden, *Works*, 2. 13).
[73] See, e.g. *De causa Dei, or, A Vindication of the Common Doctrine of Protestant Divines Concerning Predetermination* (London, 1678).

implications that are as unwelcome as would be the complete denial of divine fore-knowledge, since it appears to follow that God is the cause of sin and is unjust both in reward and in punishment.

It is not clear whether these comments are to be attributed to the poet or to the Nun's Priest, or how the remarks of either might bear on the contemporary debate. One extra-literary hypothesis might be that Dryden, as a convert to Roman Catholicism, was invoking Chaucer as an exponent of an earlier orthodoxy against extreme Protestant determinism. Dryden's charge that, according to both arguments, God becomes the '<u>Author of the Sin</u>' might seem to point securely in such a direction. But the case is further complicated by the fact that, in the eyes of some of his contemporaries, Dryden was a notorious denier of the freedom of the human will. Dryden's enemy Tom Brown, for example, constructed a dialogue in the course of which Dryden, as 'Mr Bayes', is asked why he is 'so great an enemy to Freewill?'[74] In his response, 'Mr Bayes' quotes four lines from *The Spanish Fryar*:

> The Priesthood grosly cheat us with Free-will:
> <u>Will</u> to doe what, but what Heaven <u>first decreed</u>?
> Our Actions then are neither <u>good</u> nor <u>ill</u>,
> Since from eternal Causes they proceed.
> *(The Spanish Fryar*, II. iii. 161–4; Dryden, *Works*, 14. 154)

In *The State of Innocence*, Adam debates the issue with Gabriel and Raphael. Adam engages the two angels by a series of questions in a near dispute on the status of his own free will. Raphael tells Adam that God formed him free, 'With <u>will</u> unbounded as Deity'. Adam, however, wonders if freedom can be 'by finite man possest'. Conceding that God might have originally given man liberty, he then asks:

> Are we not bounded now, by firm <u>decree</u>,
> Since what so e'er is pre-ordained must be?
> Else Heav'n for man events might preordain,
> And man's free <u>will</u> might make those orders vain.
> *(The State of Innocence*, IV. i. 42–5; Dryden, *Works*, 12. 124)

At the end of the debate, Adam is left to soliloquize unresolved, uncertain, and unsatisfied:

> Hard state of life! Since Heav'n foreknows my <u>will</u>,
> Why am I not ty'd up from doing ill?
> Why am I trusted with myself at large,
> When he's more able to sustain the charge?
> Since angels fell, whose strength was more than mine,
> 'Twould show more grace my frailty to confine.

---

[74] Thomas Brown, *The Reasons of Mr. Bays Changing His Religion* (London, 1688), 20–1.

> For-knowing the success, to leave me free,
> Excuses him, and yet supports not me.
>
> (*The State of Innocence*, IV. i.
> 113–20; Dryden, *Works*, 12. 126)

It is not certain, then, that Dryden's questions in *The Cock and the Fox*—on whether or not the '<u>will</u>' of man is 'free to <u>Good</u> or <u>Ill</u>', and on the justice of rewarding 'a vertuous Deed' which was '<u>first decreed</u>'—are intended as *entirely* rhetorical. On the one hand, Dryden's question 'For how can that Eternal Pow'r be just / To punish Man, who Sins because he must?' resembles, in point as it does in form, the remarks to Adam of Milton's Raphael, who claims that God requires 'voluntarie' rather than 'necessitated' service:

> for how
> <u>Can</u> hearts, not free, be tri'd whether they serve
> Willing or no, who will but what they must,
> By Destinie. and can no other choose?
>
> (*Paradise Lost*, 3. 112–19)

On the other hand, Dryden seems to have written with much less certainty about the easy coexistence of foreknowledge and free will than that expressed by Milton's God when he claims that Adam and Eve could not

> justly accuse
> Thir maker or thir making, or thir Fate.
> As if predestination over-rul'd
> Thir will, dispos'd by absolute Decree
> Or high foreknowledge; they themselves decreed
> Thir own revolt, not I: if I forknew,
> Foreknowledge had no influence on thir fault,
> Which had no less prov'd certain unforeknown.
>
> (*Paradise Lost*, 3. 112–19)

'The Tale I Tell Is Only of a Cock'

Dryden's method of conducting his digression resembles a tightrope act, with the poet carefully stepping his way across an abyss of blasphemy. Throughout his expansion of Chaucer's original, Dryden elucidates, elaborates, and illustrates problems that in the end prove to be, as for Chaucer and Dryden's Adam, intractable and insoluble:

But I ne can nat boulte it to the bren	I cannot boult this Matter to the Bran,
As can the holy doctour saint Austin	As *Bradwardin* and holy *Austin* can:
Or Boece, or the bishop Bradwardin	If Prescience can determine Actions so
Whether that goddes worthy foreweting	That we must do, because he did foreknow.
Straineth me nedely to do a thing	Or that foreknowing, yet our choice is free,

(Nedely clepe I simple necessitie)
Or if the free choice be graunted me
To do the same thing, or do it nought
Though God forewote it, er it was wrought
Or of his weting straineth neuer a dele
But by necessitie condicionele.
I wol not haue to done of such mattere
My tale is of a cocke, as ye shall here
That toke his counsaile of his wife with sorow
To walke in the yerde vpon the morow,
That he had met the dreme, as I you tolde.

(NPT, 3240–55; Speght 1598, Fol. 87ʳ)

Not forc'd to Sin by <u>strict necessity</u>:
This <u>strict necessity</u> they simple call,
Another sort there is conditional.
The first so binds the Will, that Things foreknown
By Spontaneity, not Choice, are done.
Thus Galley-Slaves tug willing, at their Oar,
Consent to work, in prospect of the Shore;
But wou'd not work at all, if not constrain'd before.
That other does not Liberty constrain,
But Man may either act, or may refrain.
Heav'n made us Agents free to Good or Ill,
And forc'd it not, tho' he foresaw the Will.
Freedom was first bestow'd on human Race,
And Prescience only held the second place.
    If he could make such Agents wholly free,
I not dispute; the Point's too high for me;
For Heav'n's unfathom'd Pow'r what Man can sound,
Or put to his Omnipotence a Bound?
He made us to his Image all agree;
That Image is the Soul, and that must be,
Or not the Maker's Image, or be free.
    But whether it were better Man had been
By Nature bound to Good, not free to Sin,
I wave, for fear of splitting on a Rock,
The Tale I tell is only of a Cock;
Who had not run the hazard of his Life
Had he believ'd his Dream, and not his Wife.

(*The Cock and the Fox*, 523–54; Dryden,
Works, 7. 317–19)

The difficulties are increased when the digression is applied to the narrative. The last line of the passage above suggests that Chanticleer did have free will to act or to refrain in that, had he trusted in his vision of the night, he might not have descended from the beam to the yard, and might have defied his wife. And yet, the narratorial comment on Chanticleer's decent from the beam declares, apparently with absolute finality, that the event was predestined from, or before, the creation of the universe. In suggesting that Chanticleer's 'Doom was written' and 'the Decree was past, / E'er the Foundations of the World were cast' (677–8), Dryden appears to have recalled not only two passages in Scripture referring to the Kingdom of Heaven and Christ,[75] but also the seventeenth of the Thirty-Nine Articles of the Church of England, in which it is declared that 'Predestination to Life' is 'the everlasting Purpose of God' established 'before the Foundations of the World were laid'. At the same time, Dryden's use of

---

[75] 1 Peter 20; Matthew 25:34.

the verb 'cast' may suggest that he had also recalled Milton's account of Hell, wishing but not able to flee from 'Heav'n ruining from Heav'n' since Fate had '<u>cast</u> too deep / Her dark <u>foundations</u>.'[76]

Dreams: Mimic Fancy and the Reasonable Soul Run Mad

The suggestion that Chanticleer might have 'believ'd his Dream, and not his Wife' entails further complications. If the possibility that the cock might not have descended from his beam and met the fox implies that destiny is not fixed, accurately presaging dreams would seem to be one expression of divine foreknowledge not constraining the will. Dryden's response to Chaucer's four lines on this subject was to expand and elaborate every possible side of the question. Chanticleer's faith that dreams are sent by God as warnings of almost irrevocable fate is given as weighty force as Partlet's contrary proposition that dreams are the result of a disordered body and have only medical significance. In addition, Dryden found an opportunity to elaborate upon a third possibility: that dreams are essentially psychological in origin. The case is put by the sceptical merchant rejecting a vision presaging drowning in one of Chanticleer's cautionary tales:

His felowe that lay by his beddes side
Gan for to laugh, and scorned him full faste
No dreme (qd he) may so my herte agaste
That I woll let for to do my thinges
I set not a strawe for thy dreminges
For sweuens ben but vanities and iapes
Men meten all day of oules and of apes
And eke of many a mase therewithall
And dremen of thing that neuer was, ne shall.

His Friend smil'd scornful, and with proud contempt
Rejects as idle what his Fellow dreamt.
Stay, who will stay: For me no Fears restrain,
Who follow Mercury the God of Gain:
Let each Man do as to his Fancy seems,
I wait, not I, till you have better Dreams.
Dreams are but Interludes, which Fancy makes,
When Monarch-Reason sleeps, this Mimick wakes:
Compounds a Medley of disjointed Things,
A Mob of Coblers, and a Court of Kings:
Light Fumes are merry, grosser Fumes are sad;
Both are the reasonable Soul run mad:
And many monstrous Forms in sleep we see,
That neither were, nor are, nor e'er can be.
　　Sometimes, forgotten Things long cast behind
Rush forward in the Brain, and come to mind.
The Nurses Legends are for Truths receiv'd,
And the Man dreams but what the Boy believd.
Sometimes we but rehearse a former Play,
The Night restores our Actions done by Day:
As Hounds in sleep will open for their Prey.
In short, the Farce of Dreams is of a piece,
Chimeras all; and more absured, or less:

---

[76] *Paradise Lost*, 6. 867–70.

You, who belive in Tales, abide alone,

What e'er I get this Voyage is my own.

(*The Cock and the Fox*, 319–43; Dryden,

Works 7. 305–7)

(*NPT*, 3086–94; Speght 1598, Fol. 86ᵛ)

Again, rendering Chaucer led Dryden to draw on a wide range of authors, ancient and modern, including Shakespeare and Lucretius.[77] But if a passage from Lucretius provided the form of a particular line in the merchant's argument, the overall shaping was the memory of a scene from the *State of Innocence*, where Lucifer comes across 'a pleasant Bower' in which Adam and Eve are asleep:

> Their <u>Reason</u> sleeps, but <u>Mimick Fancy</u> wakes;
> Supplies her parts, and wild Idea's takes
> From Words and things ill-sorted and mis-joyn'd;
> The Anarchy of Thought and Chaos of the Mind.
>
> (*The State of Innocence*, III. iii. 5–8; Dryden, *Works*, 12. 118)

Dryden's lines have their origin in the moment in *Paradise Lost* when Adam comforts Eve after her nightmare by explaining the workings of the mind:

> know that in the Soule
> Are many lesser Faculties that serve
> <u>Reason</u> as chief; among these Fansie next
> Her office holds; of all external things,
> Which the five watchful Senses represent,
> She forms Imaginations, Aerie shapes,
> Which <u>Reason</u> joyning or disjoining, frames
> All what we affirm or what deny, and call
> Our knowledge or opinion; then retires
> Into her private Cell when Nature rests.
> Oft in her absence <u>mimic Fansie</u> wakes
> To imitate her; but misjoyning shapes.
> Wilde work produces oft, and most in dreams,
> Ill matching words and deeds long past or late.
> Some such resemblances methinks I find
> Of our last Evenings talk, in this thy dream,
> But with addition strange; yet be not sad.
> Evil into the mind of God or Man
> May come and go, so unapprov'd and leave
> No spot or blame behind.
>
> (*Paradise Lost*, 5. 100–19)

Milton had suggested that Reason 'retires / Into her private Cell when Nature rests'. Dryden's sceptical merchant is more extreme. For him, dreams are examples of 'the reasonable Soul run mad'.

---

[77] Shakespeare, *Julius Caesar*, II. ii. 99–100; Dryden, *Translation of the Latter Part of the Third Book of Lucretius: Against the Fear of Death*, 225; Dryden, *Works*, 3. 54.

Readers of Dryden's poem are thus bound to ask, as Montaigne asked, whether it is possible for them to be sure that they possess their own souls:

> 'Tis not only Feavers, Debauches and great Accidents that overthrow our Judgements; the least things in the World will do it. We are not to doubt, though we are not sensible of it, but that if a continued Feaver can overwhelm the Soul a *Tertian* will in some proportionate measure alter it. If an *Apoplexy* can stupifie, and totally extinguish the sight of our Understanding, we are not to doubt but that a great Cold will dazzle it. And consequently there is hardly one single hour in a Man's whole Life, wherein our Judgement is in its due place and right condition.[78]

The poem has offered physical or mental disorder as a possible cause of dreams. If this explanation is adopted, it follows that we have such a fragile possession of our souls that we lose them every time we sleep, catch a cold, or eat the wrong food. Chanticleer's alternative explanation is that dreams are warnings from a foredooming God and man is an automaton.

Murders and the Mercy of God

The questions are left hanging—although reasons for believing that it might have been better if man had been bound to good and not free to sin are suggested by the picture of human life represented by Chanticleer's grim exemplary tales. Dryden's treatment of these tales implies that he thought there was nothing quaint or simply benign about Chaucer's poem. He has worked to compel his readers to pay the greatest attention to at least the first two of these stories—the one about a murder and the other of a shipwreck. In the first place, he has added enough detail to give the stories a life independent of their teller or their immediate purpose. But he has also taken such care over his versification that these tales are more rapid than even the lightest or tightest prose—as in these lines, for example, which describe the night spent by a pilgrim forced for the first time to sleep apart from his best friend:

And so befel, long er it were day	Supine he snor'd; but in the dead of Night,
This man mette in his bedde, there as he lay	He dreamt his Friend appear'd before his Sight,
How that his felowe gan vpon him call,	Who with a ghastly Look and doleful Cry,
And said (alas) for in an oxes stall	Said help me Brother, or this Night I die:
This night shal I be murdered, there I lie	Arise, and help, before all Help be vain,
Now helpe me dere brother er I die,	Or in an Oxes Stall I shall be slain.
In al haste, come to me (he said)	Rowz'd from his Rest he waken'd in a start,
This man out of his slepe for feare abraid	Shiv'ring with Horror, and with aking Heart;
But when he was waked of his slepe,	At length to cure himself by Reason tries;
He turned him, and tooke of this no kepe	'Twas but a Dream, and what are Dreams but Lies?
Him thought his dreme was but a vanite	So thinking chang'd his Side, and clos'd his Eyes.
Thus twise in his slepe dremed he	His Dream returns; his Friend appears again,

---

[78] Montaigne, *Essays*, 2. 389.

And at third time, yet his felawe
Cam as him thou3t, & said I now am slawe
Beholde my bloudy woundes, depe and wide
Arise vp erly, in the morow tide
And at the west gate of the toun (qd he)
A carte full of dong there shalt thou see
In which my body is hid ful priuely
Do thou that carte arest boldly
My golde caused my deth, soth to saine
And told him euery point how he was slaine
With a full petous face, pale of hewe.

(NPT, 3001–23; Speght 1598, Fol. 86)

The Murd'rers come; now help, or I am slain:
'Twas but a Vision still, and Visions are but vain.
He dreamt the third: But now his Friend Appear'd
Pale, naked, pierc'd with Wounds, with Blood
                                   Besmear'd:
Thrice warn'd awake, said he; Relief is late,
The Deed is done; but thou revenge my Fate:
Tardy of Aid, unseal thy heavy Eyes,
Awake, and with the dawning Day arise:
Take to the Western Gate thy ready way,
For by that Passage they my Corps convey:
My Corpse is in a Tumbril laid; among
The Filth, and Ordure, and enclos'd with Dung.
That Cart arrest, and raise a common Cry,
For sacred hunger of my Gold I die;
Then shew'd his grisly Wounds; and last he drew
A piteous Sigh; and took a long Adieu.

(The Cock and the Fox, 229–56; Dryden, Works, 7.301)

The solemnity with which Dryden was treating this passage is most strongly suggested by the claim that the man is murdered for 'sacred hunger' of his gold. Dryden here remembered Virgil's lament over Polydorus, the son of Priam, in Book 3 of the *Aeneid*, sent for his own protection from Troy but murdered 'for his wealth' by a 'faithless Tyrant', as a result of the 'sacred hunger of pernicious gold'.[79]

But if the murder is described in heroic terms, the reaction to the atrocity is conducted unequivocally by a 'mob', the action of which is interpreted by Dryden (281–2) as a manifestation of God's 'boundless Grace and Mercy to Mankind' (282), as well as justice. As to the human consequences of God's 'Grace and Mercy', however, Dryden's account is specific and unflinchingly brutal:

And right anon, the ministers of the toun
Haue hent the carter, and sore him pyned
And eke the hosteler so sore engyned
That they beknow her wickednesse anone
And were honged by the necke bone.

(NPT, 3058–62; Speght 1598, Fol. 86ʳ⁻ᵛ)

                              in the present Case; ⎫
The Criminals are seiz'd upon the Place: ⎬
Carter and Host confronted Face to Face.   ⎭
Stiff in denial, as the Law appoints
On Engins they distend their tortur'd Joints:
So was Confession forc'd, th'Offence was known,
And publick Justice on th'Offenders done.

(The Cock and the Fox, 289–95; Dryden, Works, 7. 303)

'Glad Poverty'

If Chanticleer's *exempla* are taken together with the mentions of riots, of suicides, of betrayals, the sackings of cities, and the death of kings, it is hard to reconcile

---

[79] *The Third Book of the Aeneis*, 75–80; Dryden, *Works*, 5. 419.

the view of human life surrounding the farmyard with any notion that this is the best of all possible worlds. Balancing such purely sceptical or dispiriting notions, however, is the opening description of the contented life of a poor widow, which forms a measure against which the cock, half-mistakenly, measures himself and his vision of the world. The widow, more than anything else in the poem, establishes a notion of the potential worth of humanity that contradicts or counteracts the tales of human brutality and the extravagancies of Chanticleer's vanity (see Fig. 4.2). Chaucer's priest appears to suggest that the widow will be the *subject* of the tale. Dryden presents his description rather as the tale's *foundation*. He has attempted a version of these lines in verse that is neither condescending nor sentimental, neither strained nor facile, but free, relaxed, and apparently at peace with its subject:

This wedowe, of which I tell you my tale
Sens the day that she was last a wife
In pacience, led a full simple life
For litell was her catell and her rent;
By husbondry, of such as God her sent
She fond her self, & eke her daughters two
Thre large sowes had she, and no mo
Thre kine, and eke a shepe that hight Mall
Well sooty was her boure, and eke her hall
In which she ete many a slender mele
Of poinant sauce, ne knew she never a dele
Ne deinty morcell passed through her throte
Her diet was accordaunt to her cote
Replection ne made her never fike
A temperate diete was her Phisike
And exercise, and hertes suffisaunce
The gout let her nothing for to daunce.

(NPT, 2824–40; Speght 1598, Fol. 85ᵛ)

This Dowager, on whom my Tale I found,
Since last she laid her Husband in the Ground,
A simple sober Life, in patience led,
And had but just enough to buy her Bread:
But Huswifing the little Heav'n had lent,
She duly paid a Groat for Quarter-Rent;
And pinch'd her Belly, with her Daughter two,
To bring the Year about with much ado.
    The Cattle in her Homestead were three Sows,
An Ewe call'd *Mally*; and three brinded Cows.
Her Parlour-Window stuck with Herbs around,
Of sav'ry Smell; and Rushes strew'd the Ground.
A Maple-Dresser, in her Hall she had,
On which full many a slender Meal she made:
For no delicious Morsel pass'd her Throat;
According to her Cloth she cut her Coat:
No poignant Sawce she knew, no costly Treat,
Her Hunger gave a Relish to her Meat.
A sparing Diet did her Health assure;
Or sick, a Pepper-Posset was her Cure.
Before the Day was done, her Work she sped,
And never went by Candle-light to Bed:
With Exercise she sweat ill Humours out;
Her Dancing was not hinder'd by the Gout.
Her Poverty was glad, her Heart content,
Nor knew she what the Spleen or Vapors meant.

(The Cock and the Fox, 5–30; Dryden, Works, 7. 287–9)

Dryden's homely particulars subserve a general point. In describing the life and mind of this poor widow, Dryden has chosen a vocabulary that is at once specific and general and that had at one and the same time Christian and classical associations. Dryden appears to have been the first writer to combine the terms

Fig. 4.2 The poor widow's daughters. From John Dryden, *The Fables … Ornamented with Engravings from the Pencil of the Right Hon. Lady Diana Beauclerk* (London, 1797).

'simple' and 'sober' in description of a *life*. A purely '<u>sober</u>' life is often found in Christian contexts.[80] But a 'sober' life was not exclusively Christian, particularly if, as in this case, the simplicity was, partly or largely, a matter of diet. On

[80] See, e.g. Donald Lupton, *The Glory of Their Times, or The Lives of the Primitive Fathers* (London, 1640), p. 481.

the other hand, the apparently practical suggestion that the widow 'cut her Coat' 'according to her Cloth' may have had religious overtones.[81]

The description of the widow would appear to be epitomised in the line 'Her Poverty was glad, her Heart content'. Although the ideal of contented poverty was a commonplace, both classical and Christian, that Dryden had discussed on many occasions, he seems here, as it were, to have used Chaucer to fortify Chaucer, by drawing on the crone's words in *The Wife of Bath's Tale*, to which he gave the fullest extension in his version:

> Philosophers have said, and Poets sing,
> That a glad Poverty's an honest Thing.
> Content is Wealth, the Riches of the Mind;
> And happy He who can that Treasure find.
>
> (*The Wife of Bath Her Tale*, 465–7; Dryden, *Works*, 7. 477)

When the cock at the very moment of his highest self-conceit (half-mistakenly) prefers his lot to that of his keeper ('Our Dame sits couring o'er a Kitchin-fire; / I draw fresh Air, and Nature's Works admire'), a great many contradictory notions of the pride, glory, and foolishness of poultry and of mankind are admitted into harmonious (if not resolved) co-existence. As Dryden presents it, the contrast between Chanticleer and the poor widow might be one of the possible examples of the closing proposition of Montaigne's *Essays*:

> 'Tis an absolute, and as it were, a Divine Perfection, for a Man to know how loyally to enjoy his Being: We seek other conditions, by reason we do not understand the use of our own; and go out of our selves, because we know not how there to reside. 'Tis to much purpose to go upon stilts, for when upon stilts, we must yet walk upon our Legs; And when seated upon the most elevated Throne in the World, we are but seated upon our Breech. The fairest Lives, in my opinion, are those which regularly accommodate themselves to the common and human model: but without miracle, and without extravagance.[82]

Chaucer's Comprehensive Soul

The 'fond Credulity', the effects of which Dryden suggested in 'The MORAL' the poem demonstrated, extends far beyond the cock's deeming himself 'an animal of no small importance' (as Miller put it), to any belief that humanity might be raised on stilts beyond the simple life lived by the poor widow. Similarly, the 'Flatt'rers' of which the reader of Dryden's fable should learn 'to beware' are not limited to those resembling Reynard the fox. They are 'most pernicious when they speak too fair',

---

[81] See, e.g. Thomas Draxe, *The Christian Armorie* (London, 1611), 62–3; Richard Younge, *A Christian Library* (London, 1660), p. 13.

[82] Montaigne, *Essays*, 3. 572–3.

and include poets in their ranks—particularly perhaps poets given to aggrandizing the rationality and centrality of Mankind.

In the Preface to *Fables*, Dryden, comparing Ovid and Chaucer, had maintained that both poets were 'well-bred, well-natur'd, amorous, and Libertine, at least in their Writings' and that their 'Studies were the same' including, particularly, 'Philosophy'.[83] Following as it does the word 'amorous', the first implication of 'Libertine' would seem to imply an absence of moral restraint in sexual matters, i.e. 'dissolute', 'licentious'. In the light of his versions, however, it would seem that Dryden was using the word in the wider sense of one who holds free or sceptical opinions about religion and received morality.

But while some of the *procedures* by which the questions—of predestination and free will, of the relations between body and mind, of possibility of possession of the mind and rational soul—are discussed might look like some of the sceptical methods of Bayle's *Dictionary*, there is nothing systematic in *The Cock and the Fox*. Chaucer's poem appears, rather, to have provided Dryden with an unparalleled and otherwise unexampled opportunity to achieve the supreme felicity of having things both ways. The poet's is and is not the voice of the poem. Love is and is not the greatest happiness. Marriage and unbridled sexuality may and may not be reconciled. Females are and are not the cause of all male woe and all male folly. Cocks and kings do and do not have a deal in common. Incest is and is not natural. The soul is and is not dependent on the body. Dreams do and do not presage. Actions and events, in the farmyard and in the greater world, are and are not determined by the stars, or by ill-digestion. God's foreknowledge does and does not constrain the human will. Chanticleer was and was not predestined to descend from his beam. His will is and is not free. His pride is and is not punished by the Fox. Self-pride is as foolish as it is glorious. Cocks and men have an equal, and equally weak, claim to consider themselves God's masterworks on earth. A man and a cock ('Though sickly, slender, and not large of Limb') might be seen to have equal, and equally weak, reasons for 'Concluding all the World was made for' them. Mankind is and is not a rational species.

In the Preface to *Fables*, Dryden illustrates the proposition that Chaucer 'must have been a Man of a most wonderful comprehensive Nature' primarily with reference to 'the various Manners and Humours' displayed in his characterisation.[84] Such a 'comprehensiveness' would seem to extend to the sheer quantity of human events and human sentiments to which Chaucer had given room and voice.

Even more, perhaps, than in the case of *The Knight's Tale*, Dryden may have found the Chaucer of *The Nun's Priest's Tale* to be a poet with a 'soul Congenial' who shared his profoundest preoccupations—particularly with free will and the relations between human and non-human creatures. If that is the case, he

---

[83] Dryden, *Works*, 7. 30.
[84] Ibid. 7. 37.

would have been seeing the poetic past as a present potentiality. For Dryden, the questions that Chaucer asked, and his means of asking them, were not obsolete. They had gained acuity rather than being obscured by the passage of time. Chaucer's sceptical good sense was, in that sense, 'perpetual'. For although Dryden had brought to the poem a wealth of distinctly seventeenth-century thought, and peculiarly seventeenth-century emphases, that thought and those emphases had been arranged and transformed by the application to Chaucer's tale of a cock and a hen.

PART II

COMIC AND NATURALISTIC TALES

5

Chaucer's Characters, Chaucer's Character, and the Character of Chaucer's Verse

Dryden's great hope had been that his versions of some of Chaucer's poems would lead to a revival of interest in Chaucer himself: 'I seriously protest, that no Man ever had, or can have, a greater Veneration for Chaucer than my self. I have translated some part of his Works, only that I might perpetuate his Memory, or at least refresh it amongst my Countrymen.'[1] Dryden's hope was indeed fulfilled in the remarkable burgeoning of Chauceriana that occurred from the early eighteenth century onwards.

Few of the poets who contributed to *Luctus Britannici*, the volume of elegies on Dryden's death published in 1700, could resist implying that there had been a particular significance in the poet's having been buried in Chaucer's tomb. One suggested that 'the Sacred Shade' of Chaucer 'makes room' for Dryden, since 'Souls so like should take but up one tomb'. Another maintained that, before the publication of *Fables Ancient and Modern*, Chaucer's 'Language with its Master lay for Dead'; but Chaucer 'shall again with Joy be Read', with '*Dryden*, striving His Remains to save, / Sunk in His *Tomb*, who *brought* him from his *Grave*'.[2] In 1706, the civil servant and amateur poet, Jabez Hughes expressed a common reaction to Dryden's versions from Chaucer:

> cloath'd by Thee, the burnish'd Bard appears
> In all his Glory, and new Honours wears.
> Thus *Ennius* was by *Virgil* chang'd of old;
> He found him Rubbish, and he left him Gold.
>
> (Jabez Hughes, *Verses Occasion'd by Reading Mr. Dryden's*
> *Fables* [London, 1721], p. 4)

The desire in the period to see Chaucer 'made new' took a variety of forms. The decision of Dryden, or his publisher Jacob Tonson, to present the original Chaucerian texts included in *Fables Ancient and Modern* in modern typeface (rather than in the antiquated gothic form in which they had previously appeared) was also

---

[1] Dryden, *Works*, 7. 42.
[2] *Luctus Britannici, or The Tears of the British Muses for the Death of John Dryden* (London, 1700), pp. 18, 55.

Chaucer in the Eighteenth Century. David Hopkins and Tom Mason, Oxford University Press.
© David Hopkins and Tom Mason (2022). DOI: 10.1093/oso/9780192862624.003.0006

adopted in the Urry edition of Chaucer's *Works*, and in all subsequent eighteenth-century editions of the poet's work.[3] There were also various poetic productions based on different aspects of Chaucer's poetry and language. An antique, pseudo-Chaucerian style was adopted by several early eighteenth-century poets, in poems with an essentially modern purpose.[4] Other writers broadly followed the example of Dryden and produced modern translations or imitations of particular Canterbury Tales, including some of the more risqué stories that had been deliberately avoided by Dryden.[5] A third category of eighteenth-century Chauceriana consisted of versions of poems that were included in early editions of Chaucer but are no longer considered to be his work.[6] Finally, though the overwhelming concentration in the period was on the *Canterbury Tales* or works contained in what later scholars would call the Chaucer Apocrypha, there were a few engagements with Chaucer's other works.[7]

That pleasure in translations accompanied a growing interest in Chaucer's originals—or that the two interacted—is clear from the edition by Thomas Morell. In Morell's presentation, Chaucer's text is edited afresh from manuscripts, and accompanied by newly written notes. The texts of the *General Prologue* and *The*

---

[3] Urry's original intention, however, had been to present Chaucer's works in black-letter.

[4] See, e.g. *Two Imitations of Chaucer, 1. Susannah and the Two Elders, II. Earl Robert's Mice* (London, 1712), published in the same volume as Samuel Cobb's version of Chaucer's *Miller's Tale* (see below) and attributed to Matthew Prior. The second poem was itself imitated by Giles Jacob in 'A Tale in Imitation of Mr. Prior's Earl Robert's Mice', in Jacob's *A Miscellany of Poems* (London, 1718). See also Elijah Fenton's 'A Tale, Devised in the Plesaunt Manere of Gentil Maister Jeoffrey Chaucer' in his Elijah Fenton's 'A Tale, Devised in the Plesaunt Manere of Gentil maister Jeoffrey Chaucer', in *Poems on Several Occasions* (London, 1717) and John Gay's 'An Answer to the Sompner's Prologue of Chaucer in Imitation of Chaucer's Style', in *Poems on Several Occasions, By His Grace the Duke of Buckingham and Other Eminent Hands* (London, 1717), 147–51.

[5] Many of these versions were incorporated in the compendia of versions of the *Canterbury Tales* edited by George Ogle (*The Canterbury Tales of Chaucer: Modernis'd by Several Hands*, 3 vols (London, 1741)) and William Lipscomb (*The Canterbury Tales of Chaucer Completed in a Modern Version*, 3 vols (London, 1795)), discussed in the present study. Most of the translations are reprinted, with full bibliographical references, in Betsy Bowden, ed., *Eighteenth-Century Modernizations from 'The Canterbury Tales'* (Woodbridge, 1991). See also https://chaucerlibrary.com/modernizations-adaptations-translation/.

[6] See Arthur Maynwaring, trans., 'The Court of Love. A Tale from Chaucer', in *Ovid's Art of Love in Three Books* (London, 1709; eleven reprints by 1850), and by Alexander Stopford Catcott in *The Court of Love, a Vision, from Chaucer* (London, 1717); John Dart, trans., *The Complaint of the Black Knight from Chaucer* [now attributed to John Lydgate] (London, 1720) (the opening of which is closely modelled on Dryden's *The Flower and the Leaf*); George Sewell, *The Proclamation of Cupid; or, a Defence of Women. A Poem from Chaucer* [actually by Thomas Hoccleve] (London, 1718); William Cooke, 'The Cuckow and the Nightingale. Modernized from Chaucer', [now attributed to Sir John Clanvowe] in *Poetical Essays on Several Occasions* (London, 1774).

[7] Most notably, Alexander Pope's *The Temple of Fame, A Vision* (London, 1715) (discussed above, and further in Chapter 11 below); Captain Phillips's, *The Romance of the Rose. Imitated from Chaucer* (London, 1709); Walter Harte's, 'To My Soul, from Chaucer', in *Poems on Several Occasions* (London, 1727) (discussed below); 'The Song of Troilus', a rare imitation of a passage from Chaucer's longest poem, *Troilus and Criseyde*, in George Sewell, *A New Collection of Original Poems* (London, 1720); Jane Brereton, 'The Dream: In Imitation of Some Parts of Chaucer's Second and Third Book of Fame', in *Poems on Several Occasions* (London, 1744) (discussed in Chapter 11).

Knight's Tale are followed by translations of both, the latter being that of Dryden.[8] Where most of the Chaucerian items cited above consisted of versions of single works without much reference to context or provenance, Morell's edition was intended to be a complete representation of the *Canterbury Tales* as a single interconnected work—interest in which was apparently increasing. In 1739, George Ogle published *Gualtherus and Griselda: or, The Clerk of Oxford's Tale*, which, although taking its main lines from Chaucer, also drew on versions of the tale by Boccaccio and Petrarch, but was accompanied by a discussion of the character of the Clerk.[9] Ogle was attempting to do two things at once. He was providing a classic composite version of the famous story of patient Griselda at the same time as locating the tale and its interpretations within the larger context of *The Canterbury Tales*.

In 1741, Ogle went on to edit *The Canterbury Tales of Chaucer, Modernis'd by Several Hands*. This volume included, alongside a rewriting of Spenser's continuation of *The Squire's Tale*, versions—some of them already published separately—of various *Canterbury Tales* (and the spurious *Tale of Gamelyn*) by Thomas Betterton, Samuel Cobb, Samuel Boyse, Henry Brooke, Dryden, Ogle himself, Pope, John Markland, and 'Mr. Grosvenor'. Ogle's own versions, particularly of the passages joining the Tales, contain many perceptive insights into Chaucer's design and intentions.

Chaucer's Characters: Thomas Betterton and Alexander Pope

Ogle was not the first to show interest in the characters of Chaucer's pilgrims as represented in the *General Prologue* to *The Canterbury Tales* (see Fig. 5.1). In most copies of *Miscellaneous Poems and Translations by Several Hands*, published by Bernard Lintott in 1712, two poems are given special title pages: the first version of Alexander Pope's *The Rape of the Locke* and *Chaucer's Characters or the Introduction to the Canterbury Tales. By Mr. Thomas Betterton*. The volume also includes a poem entitled *The Miller of Trompington, or, the Reve's Tale from Chaucer. By Mr. Betterton*. Thomas Betterton, the most successful actor of the later seventeenth-century, had died in 1710, and it has been argued that Pope may have served in some kind of editorial capacity in the assembly of the miscellany, perhaps editing

---

[8] The first and only volume of this edition, published 'for the Editor' was published in 1737 and reissued in 1740. It seems from an unpublished letter of Morell to James West of 1771 (BL Add. MS 34728) that Morell had actually completed the rest of the edition, and that it was 'ready for the Press' but that he had 'found it too expensive to go on with it on [his] own bottom'. His intention in 1771 was 'to contrive ere long, some way to reassume the work'. But no more was ever published. See Ruth Smith, 'Thomas Morell and his Letter about Handel', *Journal of the Royal Musical Association*, 127 (2002), 191–225 (p. 212).

[9] To this Ogle added '*A letter to a friend, with the Clerk of Oxford's character, &c. The Clerk of Oxford's Prologue, from Chaucer. The Clerk of Oxford's conclusion, from Petrarch. The declaration, or L'envoy de Chaucer a les maris de notre temps, from Chaucer. The Words of our host, from Chaucer*'.

Fig. 5.1 Departure of the Canterbury Pilgrims, by John Hamilton Mortimer (engraved
1787).

or modifying Betterton's versions of Chaucer, or even substantially writing them
himself.[10] The truth of the matter is difficult to determine.

---

[10] Norman Ault argued for Pope's 'editorship' of *Miscellaneous Poems and Translations*: see Norman
Ault, *New Light on Pope* (London, 1949), pp. 27–48; James McLaverty has suggested a looser, more
purely advisory, connection: see James McLaverty, *Pope, Print and Meaning* (Oxford, 2001), pp. 17–18.
In his 'Life of Pope', Samuel Johnson remarked that Pope

One problem in ascribing 'Chaucer's Characters' to Pope alone is their unevenness.[11] It is hard to imagine Pope at any age writing a couplet such as 'Then came a *Dartmouth* Seaman far from *West*, / A very awkard Rider at the best'.[12] All eighteenth-century versions of Chaucer, to be sure, are uneven and irregular in their relation to the original. They adopt none of the standard categories—imitation, paraphrase, literal translation—systematically, or for long. Characteristically, a line closely modelled on the original is followed by a wild departure or allusion to an entirely different work. *Chaucer's Characters* is closer to Chaucer than many, and the verse, despite local lapses, is in fact often easy and unstrained. Allusions, interpretations, and interjections are intermittent, although the occasional moral is drawn. Morell, in the otherwise largely deferential reprinting of the *Characters* in his edition, put into corrective parentheses an interjected anticlerical comment on offerings at Becket's shrine: '[For Priests with empty thanks are never shamm'd; / The rich buy Heaven, and ragged Rogues are damn'd]'.[13] Some of Betterton's interjections are at once commentary and allusion. To the account of the Manciple's cheating of the lawyers, for example, is appended a moral: 'In Life's long Course, such diff'rent Ways we run, / *Some to undo, but most to be undone*'. This addition is a direct echo of a line in Sir John Denham's *Cooper's Hill*, which had itself been re-used in Dryden's translation of Book 1 of *Ovid's Art of Love*.[14] But the echo, though witty in itself, closes a paragraph that included some awkwardness—a run-on line interrupted by a parenthesis—and was considered to require further revision by Morell, who at the same time brought the passage closer to his own text of Chaucer:[15]

appears to have regarded Betterton with kindness and esteem; and after his death published, under his name, a version into modern English of Chaucer's *Prologues*, and one of his *Tales*, which, as was related by Mr. Harte, were believed to have been the performance of Pope himself by Fenton, who made him a gay offer of five pounds, if he would shew them in the hand of Betterton.

See Johnson, *Works*, 23. 1065. Johnson's remarks were endorsed by Joseph Warton, by Betterton's nineteenth-century biographer, Robert W. Lowe, and, in our own time, by Betsy Bowden: see *The Works of Alexander Pope*, ed. Joseph Warton, 9 vols (London, 1797), 2. 166; Robert W, Lowe, *Thomas Betterton* (London, 1891), p. 186; Betsy Bowden, *Chaucer Aloud: The Varieties of Textual Interpretation* (Philadelphia, PA, 1987), pp. 221–4. But 'Chaucer's Characters' has never been included in editions of Pope's work.

[11] It was partly on these grounds that Elwin and Courthope suggested that 'the internal evidence supports the conclusion that Betterton composed the translation, and that Pope merely revised it'. See Alexander Pope, *Works*, ed. Whitwell Elwin and William John Courthope, 10 vols (London, 1886), 1. 160; 6. 157. And while advancing the claims of Pope's authorship, Betsy Bowden concedes that the poems attributed to Betterton are 'less artistically polished' than those in Pope's acknowledged Chaucer versions: 'Images are developed, but mechanistically. Allusions remain allusions, without reaching the smoother fusion that Pope would attain' (Bowden, *Chaucer Aloud*, p. 221).

[12] *Miscellaneous Poems and Translations* (London, 1712), p. 266.

[13] Morell, p. 310.

[14] See Sir John Denham, *Poetical Works*, ed. Theodore Howard Banks (2nd edn, Hamden, CT, 1969), p. 65; Dryden, *Works*, 4. 483.

[15] Morell's text of this passage in Chaucer (GP, 573–6) runs: 'Now is not that of God a ful fayr Grace, / That swiche a lewdé Manys Wit schal pass / The Wisdom of an heap of larnid Men? / Of Maystres had he mo than that thryes ten' (Morell, p. 52).

Some wonder much, how an unletter'd Man,	Some wonder much, how with his shallow Wit,
Of such low, sordid Education, can	This man, of sordid Education, bit
(Who is but One to more than three times Ten)	So many grave, and wise, and learned Men;
O'er-reach so many Grave, Wise, Learned Men?	For Masters had he more than three times Ten.
A practis'd Lawyer all things understands,	A practis'd Lawyer all things understands,
Th'Affairs of half the Nation pass their Hands.	Th'Affairs of half the Nation pass their Hands.
We praise unjustly, partially condemn,	We praise unjustly, partially condemn,
As the Cheat others, others Cozen them.	As the Cheat others, others Cozen them.
By various Methods all Professions live;	By various Methods all Professions live;
By *Their* wise Management *He* learn'd to thrive	By *Their* wise Management *He* learn'd to thrive
In Life's long course such diff'rent Ways we run	In Life's long course such diff'rent Ways we run
Some to undo, but most to be undone.	*Some to undo, but* most *to be undone.*

(*Miscellaneous Poems and Translations*
by Several Hands [London, 1712],
pp. 274–5)

(Morell, p. 237)

The author of *Chaucer's Characters* was well read in Dryden and clearly translated Chaucer in the belief that the vocabulary and phrasing most proper for rendering the work of the Father of English Poetry was that selected by his latest son. The description of the entirely admirable Knight as 'Plain and Sincere, observant of the Right; / In Mien and Manners, an accomplish'd Knight'[16] echoes the praise of Aeneas by his followers in Dryden's translation of Book 1 of the *Aeneid*: 'a juster lord, / Or nobler warrior, never drew a sword / Observant of the right, religious of his word'.[17] And in Dryden's version of Ovid's story of *Cinyras and Myrrha*, Myrrha describes her father as 'observant of the right'.[18] Similarly, Betterton's description of the '*Pardon-monger*' as having a 'Patriarchal Face, and Holy Leer'[19] employs a favourite phrase of Dryden's, which he had used to delineate Chaucer's 'Fox full fraught with seeming Sanctity' who 'look'd like Lent; and had the holy Leer',[20] to describe the 'Midnight Parson' in *The Wife of Bath Her Tale*, who approaches a 'Country-Girl' with a 'holy Leer',[21] and, more solemnly, when painting the Temple of Mars in *Palamon and Arcite*, where 'stood Hypocrisie, with holy Lear: / Soft, smiling, and demurely looking down, / But hid the Dagger underneath the Gown'.[22]

---

[16] Thomas Betterton, 'Chaucer's Characters, or the Introduction to the Canterbury Tales' in *Miscellaneous Poems*, p. 259.

[17] *The First Book of the Aeneis*, 767–9; Dryden, *Works*, 5. 367.

[18] *Cinyras and Myrrha*, 100; Dryden, *Works*, 7. 251.

[19] *Miscellaneous Poems and Translations*, p. 279.

[20] *The Cock and the Fox*, 482; Dryden, *Works*, 7. 315.

[21] *The Wife of Bath Her Tale*, 39; Dryden, *Works*, 7. 453.

[22] *Palamon and Arcite*, 2. 564; Dryden, *Works*, 7. 121.

Dryden's Good Parson, Betterton's Monk, and Pope's January

Paradoxically, the most telling tribute to Dryden in *Chaucer's Characters* may be the omission of any account of the Parson. Dryden's *Character of a Good Parson* stands apart from his other Chaucerian versions and had by 1712 established a reputation of its own, independently of *Fables* and of Dryden's other poems.[23] Morell, Ogle, and, later, William Lipscomb were all to produce a composite version of the Prologue to *The Canterbury Tales* by including Dryden's *Good Parson* alongside Betterton's *Characters*—and, in the case of Morell and Ogle, adding further characters and linking passages of their own. The resulting composite work was always a strange mixture. Not only was Dryden's *Good Parson* much longer than the other characters, but it also bore a different relation to Chaucer's original than that adopted by any other translator, or by Dryden himself in his other Chaucer versions.

When Dryden described his poem as 'Imitated from CHAUCER, And Inlarg'd', he was presumably using the term *imitation* to suggest not merely 'free translation' but—in the sense that became most common during the eighteenth century from such poems as Johnson's *Vanity of Human Wishes*—translation that applies its original, at least in part, to the translator's own times. Dryden's version of the portrait of the Good Parson is very much 'Inlarg'd'. Dryden is attempting to describe an ideal priest by thinking equally about Chaucer's fictional example and that provided by the non-juring clergyman Thomas Ken (1637–1711), whose admirers were happy to see the poem as a tribute to their beloved bishop. One writer ended his biographical preface to Ken's *Expostulatoria* (1711) with a printing of Dryden's poem, introduced thus: '*take his Character from the following Lines, in which Mr.* Dryden *has very accurately and justly drawn his Picture*'.[24]

Dryden's poem might be described as a meditation upon, rather than a representation of, Chaucer's 'character'. Chaucer's sentiments are selectively *applied* to a specific modern figure rather than being allowed a larger general resonance. The passages in Chaucer's poem which Dryden has followed most closely were often those where various observations were presented in, or might be collected into, a single paragraph, culminating in a line of primarily metaphorical import, as in the following passage:

---

[23] Dryden's *Character of a Good Parson*, had (surprisingly) been reprinted in *Mirth Diverts All Care, being Excellent New Songs* (London, 1708), pp. 100–3. The full text of Chaucer's original account of the Parson is printed (in black-letter) in Lancelot Addison, *A Modest Plea for the Clergy* (London, 1709), pp. 132–5, and (in Roman type) in *A Letter of Advice to a Young Clergy-Man* (London, 1709), pp. 18–20. In that work, it is given 'in *Chaucer*'s own Words; for it is not to be improved by any *Modern* Stile' (p. 18). No poet attempted to rival Dryden's *Good Parson* until William Dunkin, 'The Character of a Good Parson. From Chaucer', in *Selected Poetical Works*, 2 vols (Dublin, 1769–70), 2. 480–1. Dunkin's 'Character of a Good Parson, from Chaucer' is shorter than Dryden's, but not, in fact, consistently closer to the original.

[24] Thomas Ken, *Expostulatoria, or, The Complaints of the Church of England* (London, 1711), Sig. A4ᵛ.

Wide was his parish, and houses fer asonder	Wide was his Parish; not contracted close
But he ne lefte neither for raine ne thonder	In Streets, but here and there a straggling House;
In siknes ne in meschiefe for to uisite	Yet still he was at Hand, without Request
The farthest in his parish, muche or lite,	To serve the Sick; to succour the Distress'd:
Upon his feet, and in his hand a stafe	Tempting, on Foot, alone, without affright,
This noble ensample, to his shepe he yafe …	The Dangers of a dark, tempestuous Night.
He set nat his benefice to hire	All this, the good old Man, perform'd alone,
And leet his shepe, acomber in the mire	Nor spar'd his Pains; for Curate he had none.
And renne to London to sainct Poules	Nor durst he trust another with his Care;
To seken him a Chauntery for soules	Nor rode himself to *Pauls*, the publick Fair,
Or with a brotherhed to be withhold	To chaffer[25] for Preferment with his Gold,
But dwelte at home, and kept well his fold	Where Bishopricks, and *sine Cures* are sold.
So that the Wolfe, ne made hem iscarry	But duly watch'd his Flock, by Night and Day;
He was a shepherd, and not a mercenary	And from the prowling Wolf, redeem'd the Prey;
	And hungry sent the wily Fox away.
(*GP*, 491–514; Speght 1598, Sig. A, iiii^v)	(*The Character of a Good Parson*, 60–74;
	Dryden, *Works*, 7. 507–8)

Chaucer's 'characters' are presented by Dryden in the Preface to *Fables* as prime examples of Chaucer's excellence. But Dryden's account appears to point in two directions at once. On the one hand, as we saw in Chapter 2, he had claimed of Chaucer's characters that 'All his Pilgrims are severally distinguish'd from each other, and not only in their Inclinations, but in their very Phisiognomies and Persons. *Baptista Porta* could not have describ'd their Natures better, than by the Marks which the Poet gives them.'[26] On the other hand, he had maintained that the characters described in the Prologue somehow constitute 'general Characters' which 'are still remaining in Mankind'. The significance of 'general Characters' is, it appears, independent of particular circumstance, 'For Mankind is ever the same, and nothing lost out of Nature, though every thing is alter'd'.[27]

Baptista della Porta, to whose treatise *De Humana Physiognomia* (1586) Dryden referred when discussing Chaucer, had concentrated particularly on illustrating similarities between the faces of men and the heads of animals, an emphasis that Dryden had sometimes himself evoked.[28] But when Dryden writes of 'the Descriptions of Persons' in which Chaucer excelled, he included not merely human/animal resemblances, but stressed the wide range of ways in which the detailed depiction of bodies, of faces, of clothes might reveal inward states of mind and ways of being.

---

[25] 'To treat about a bargain; to haggle; to bargain' (Samuel Johnson, *Dictionary*, citing this couplet).
[26] Dryden, *Works*, 7. 37.
[27] Ibid. 7. 37–8.
[28] See, e.g. *An Evening's Love*, V. i. 294 (Dryden, *Works*, 10. 303), where Bellamy explicitly evokes Della Porta to explain the 'leer' of the 'lewd debauch'd Spirit', Wildblood. In this connection, it is perhaps significant that Dryden's Fox, Friar, and Hypocrisy all have the same 'holy leer'.

When comparing Chaucer's characterization with that of Ovid, Dryden chose as his principal example Ovid's depiction of Baucis and Philemon, who are described in minute circumstantial detail and yet represent a human ideal:

> Both of them understood the Manners; under which Name I comprehend the Passions, and, in a larger Sense, the Descriptions of Persons, and their very Habits: For an Example, I see *Baucis* and *Philemon* as perfectly before me, as if some ancient Painter had drawn them; and all the Pilgrims in the *Canterbury Tales*, their Humours, their Features, and their very Dress, as distinctly as if I had supp'd with them at the *Tabard* in *Southwark*: Yet even there too the Figures of *Chaucer* are much more lively, and set in a better Light.[29]

Chaucer's characters were, of course, not all such types of ideal humanity as Baucis and Philemon in Dryden's eyes. It followed from Chaucer's 'Comprehensive Nature' that 'Some of his Persons are Vicious, and some Vertuous'.[30] The problem for translators after Dryden was how to present mixed characters—but, above all, of how to convey that Chaucer's characters, in both the *General Prologue* and in the *Tales*, are at once created out of circumstantial detail (or the traditions of 'estates satire')[31] and, in some way, the perpetual characters of the species:

> We have our Fore-fathers and Great-Grand-dames all before us, as they were in *Chaucer*'s days; their general Characters are still remaining in Mankind, and even in *England*, tho' they are call'd by other Names than those of Monks and Fryars, and Chanons, and Lady Abbesses, and Nuns: for Mankind is ever the same, and nothing lost out of Nature, tho' every thing is alter'd.[32]

Dryden appears not to have been troubled by his own paradox—any more than William Blake, when making similar points with a similar vocabulary:

> The character of Chaucer's Pilgrims are the characters which compose all ages and nations: as one age falls, another rises, different to mortal sight, but to immortals only the same; for we see the same characters repeated again and again, in animals, vegetables, minerals, and in men; nothing new occurs in identical existence; Accident ever varies, Substance can never suffer change nor decay.
> Of Chaucer's characters, as described in his Canterbury Tales, some of the names or titles are altered by time, but the characters themselves for ever remain unaltered, and consequently they are the physiognomies or lineaments of universal human life, beyond which Nature never steps. Names alter, things never alter. I have known multitudes of those who would have been monks in the age of monkery, who in this deistical age are deists.[33]

---

[29] Dryden, *Works*, 7. 31–2.
[30] Ibid. 7. 37.
[31] As argued by Jill Mann, *Chaucer and Medieval Estates Satire: The Literature of Social Classes and the General Prologue to the 'Canterbury Tales'* (Cambridge, 1973).
[32] Dryden, *Works*, 7. 37–8.
[33] William Blake, *'Seen in My Visions': A Descriptive Catalogue of Pictures*, ed. Martin Myrone (London, 2009), p. 49.

The paradoxical combination of particularity and generality, however, was difficult to resolve in modern verse. Here is Chaucer's Monk, juxtaposed with Betterton's:

A Monke there was, fair for the maistry,	Next these a merry Monk appears in place,
An outrider, that loued venery:	Who follow'd Hunting, more than saying Mass.
A manly man, to been an Abbot able,	As bravely mounted, as a Lord from Court;
Ful many a deinty horse had he in stable:	No well-fed Abbot bore a comelier Port.
And when he rode, men might his bridle here	And when in State he ambled, all might hear
Gingling in a whistling wind as clere	The Gingling of his Bridle, loud and clear,
And eke as loud as doth the chappel bell	As far, almost, as any Chappel Bell.
There as this lord was keeper of the sell,	This lordly Monk, once Keeper of a Cell,
The rule of sainct Maure and of saint Benet	Held good St. *Bennet*'s Order too severe;
Because it was old somedele streit,	St. *Maure* to his nice Judgement did appear
This ilke Monke did letten olde things passe,	Too strict, and rigid; for old Dotards fit,
And held after the new world the pace	But scorn'd by Priests of *Spirit*, and of *Wit*.
(*GP*, 165–75; Speght 1598, Sig. Aii^{r})	(*Miscellaneous Poems and Translations*, p. 256)

In some respects, Betterton's version follows the rhetorical shaping of Chaucer's original closely. But towards the end of this passage, he exercises some imaginative interpretation. The tension between the two tendencies gets him into certain difficulties. As is frequently the case in Betterton's *Characters* (and is rarely the case in any poem printed as Pope's), changes of subject occur mid-couplet. In this example, the mid-couplet opening of a new paragraph in Speght's text is followed slavishly, but requires explanation: this monk *once* lived in a cell but has now relinquished the teaching of his order. It was not until Urry's edition that the sense of Chaucer's couplet was reconnected: 'And eke as lowd, as doth the Chappell bell / There as this Lord was keper of the Cell'.[34] And it was not until Tyrwhitt published his Glossary that it was explained that the monk was keeper of a subordinate monastery: '*Celle*: A religious house'.[35] There is also some taming in the interests of decorum: Betterton's Monk is as stout as an abbot, not as *capable*; his bridle is only *almost* as loud as a chapel bell.

Betterton has allowed himself some freedom in the representation of the Monk's mind and thoughts. The Monk's considering himself a priest of *spirit* and of *wit* suddenly attributes to him the psychology of the eighteenth century.[36] Authorial complicity with the opinions and words of the character is an occasional but recurring feature of Betterton's characters, as it is a constant feature of Pope's Chaucer versions. And yet, were Betterton's Monk to be thought to suggest the hand of

---

[34] Urry, p. 2.

[35] Tyrwhitt 1775–78, 5. 33.

[36] In Pope's *Epistle to Bathurst: Of the Use of Riches*, the 'Tempter' gives Sir Balaam riches and so secures his soul. Sir Balaam now becomes 'a man of spirit', who 'Ascribes his gettings to his parts and merit' and considers 'God's good Providence, a lucky Hit' (Pope, *Poems*, 3ii. 120).

Pope, it may be observed that even at this point Morell thought that the lines required slight revision. Objecting, perhaps, to the useless 'expletive' 'did', or in a desire to replace irony with authorial mock complicity, he altered Betterton's 'St. *Maure* to his nice Judgement did appear / Too strict', to 'St. *Maure's* Rule seem'd to his nice-judging Ear/Too strict'.[37] For Morell's Monk, to choose or reject the rule of St *Bennet* or St *Maure* becomes almost a matter of musical taste. For all these reasons, both Betterton's and Morell's portraits—and Dryden's own *Character of a Good Parson*—fall short of achieving the fusion of generality and specificity that Dryden thought to be so characteristic of Chaucer's portrayal of his various pilgrims and fictional creations.

Pope's methods in representing the minds of Chaucer's fictional characters are very clearly on display in his opening description of January in *January and May*. Pope offers a large number of possibilities as to the worth, intelligence, virtue, and folly of the old man, but holds back final decision or the adoption of a fixed point of view. His version is as intriguing and unsettled as are the character and motives of January himself. Information that might seem miscellaneous and contradictory falls effortlessly into sentences, and those sentences into seamless paragraphs:

Whylom there was dwellinge in Lumbardy	There liv'd in *Lombardy*, as Authors write,
A worthy knight, that born was at Pauye	In Days of old, a wise and worthy Knight;
In whych he liued in greet prosperite	Of gentle Manners, as of gen'rous Race,
And sixty yere a wifeles man was he	Blest with much Sense, more Riches, and some
And folowed aye his bodely delite	Grace.
On women, ther as was his appetite	Yet, led astray by *Venus* soft Delights,
As don these foles that ben seculeres	He cou'd not rule his Carnal Appetites;
And when that he was past sixty yeres	For long ago, let Priests say what they cou'd,
Were it for holinesse or dotage	Weak, sinful Laymen were but Flesh and Blood.
I can nat sain, but such a great corage	But in due Time, when Sixty Years were o'er,
Had this knight to ben a wedded man	He vow'd to lead that Vicious Life no more;
That day and night he doth all that he can	Whether pure Holiness inspir'd his Mind,
To espye where that he wedded might be	Or Dotage turn'd his Brain, is hard to find;
Praying our lord to graunten him that he	But his high Courage prick'd him forth to wed,
Mighten ones knowen of that blissfull lif	And try the Pleasures of a lawful Bed.
That is bitwixt an husbond and his wife.	This was his nightly Dream, his daily Care,
	And to the Heav'nly Pow'rs his constant Pray'r,
	Once, e're he dy'd, to taste the blissful Life
	Of a kind Husband, and a loving Wife.
(*MerT*, 1245–60; Speght 1598, Fol. 27ʳ⁻ᵛ)	(*January and May*, 1–18; *Poetical Miscellanies* (1709), pp. 177–8)

Although some borrowed rhymes ('Delights / Appetites', 'Life / Wife') are traces of Pope's attention to the letter of Chaucer's text, the parts have been reassembled in the service of a governing idea and an elusive but pervasive and coherent tone. The allusions, if they are such, are so fused and interwoven with the dominant subject as to constitute private, secret, half-jokes. When Pope describes January

---

[37] Morell, p. 216.

as 'Of gentle Manners, as of gen'rous Race', he may have been recalling Canto 3 of
Book 6 of Spenser's *The Faerie Queene*, which opens with the proposition that

> True is, that whilome that good Poet sayd,
> The gentle minde by gentle deeds is knowne,
> For a man by nothing is so well bewrayd,
> As by his manners, in which plaine is showne
> Of what degree and what race he is growne,

and goes on to assert 'That gentle bloud will gentle manners breed'. January's long-
ings for a wife ('This was his nightly Dream, his daily Care') echo Dryden's version
of Dido's lament in Ovid's seventh Epistle:

> *Æneas* is my thoughts perpetual Theme,
> Their daily longing, and their nightly dream.
>
> (*Dido to Aeneas*, 27–8; Dryden, *Works*, 1. 133)

Pope printed *January and May* in pride of place in his *Works* of 1717.[38] There, he
made only one improvement to his text. Where in 1709 the authorial voice observes that January 'cou'd not rule his Carnal Appetites', the 1717 version offers
the reader a glimpse of what might have been January's own characterization of
his weakness: 'He scarce could rule some idle appetites'. Chaucer was, for Pope, a
poet whose means of characterization were of a subtlety that require the highest
sophistication of answering poetic art.

Chaucer's Character

Art, it was commonly felt, characterized both Chaucer's descriptions and any adequate renderings of them because Chaucer's characters were drawn with the eye of
wisdom—a wisdom that was the result of the largeness and equanimity of his view.
Chaucer's inclusivity, and tolerance were assumed to be the quality of the man as
much as the poet. His judgement as an artist was an expression of his judgement
in life. Most eighteenth-century biographical accounts of Chaucer are essentially
responses to his poems, in that they attempt to invent a life that would explain the
poems.

Writing of his 'Life of Geoffrey Chaucer' which was prefixed to Urry's edition,
John Dart described himself as 'having spar'd no Pains', and as having been 'at very
extraordinary Expence to collect Records, and write as particular and full a Life as
possible, of a Name I ever reverenc'd'.[39] There is no reason to doubt any part of that

---

[38] James McLaverty (*Pope, Print and Meaning*, p. 73) argues that the presence of section titles and
engraved headpieces is an indication of Pope's fondness for a particular poem.
[39] *Westmonasterium*, 2 vols (London, 1723) 1. 88, quoted in Caroline Spurgeon, *Five Hundred Years
of Chaucer Criticism and Allusion* 1. 365.

statement. But the difficulty for Dart, as for other eighteenth-century biographers of Chaucer, was that the available records were so few and so unrevealing that the desire to express 'reverence' for the poet in a Life that was both 'particular' and as 'full as possible' inevitably led to a highly inventive reading of the primary texts. Dart wanted to see Chaucer as if alive, and to reinvent and in part re-animate the person who wrote the poems that excited his 'reverence'. But his enterprise, like that of the other eighteenth-century biographers, is both critical and circular in that it attempted to invent a life that would explain the poems, and to read the poems in such a way as would construct a life.

If love and veneration prompted scrupulous care, they also encouraged inclusiveness. No writing that *might* be Chaucer's, no biographical detail that might possibly have authority, no anecdote however far-fetched could be abandoned. Some passages in *The Complaint of the Black Knight*, now ascribed to Lydgate but admired by Dart as genuinely Chaucerian, were taken as certain evidence that Chaucer's poems contained 'frequent descriptions' of the park at Woodstock.[40] Chaucer's walks had been re-imagined, even re-traced (again, on the strength of verse that was not his work): 'In his *Cuckow and Nightingale*, the *Morning Walk* he takes was such as this day may be traced from his House through part of the Park, and down by the Brook into the Vale under *Blenheim Castle*'.[41]

Such notions remained constant throughout the century. In his substantial two-volume *Life* of Chaucer (1803), the philosopher William Godwin took it that *The Complaint of the Black Knight* was addressed to Anne of Bohemia who at that time 'resided at Woodstock', and that the poem had been composed when Chaucer 'was "old and unlusty"'. The work was an 'exquisite example' of one particular 'feature of the poet's mind':

> The customary cheerfulness and serenity of the mind of Chaucer is particularly conspicuous in his delineations of nature. They all take their hue from the mind of the beholder, and are gay, animated and fresh. He usually sets out upon his walk early in the morning, when the world has been refreshed by repose, when the grass is impearled with dew, and when the delicious scents of field and tree and flower are yet unpolluted by the beams of the flaring sun.[42]

The difference between Dart and Godwin is slight. Dart thinks the descriptions are accurate depictions of still-existing features of landscape: he mentions a particular maple. Godwin thinks they record the impressions of real walks and feels the descriptions (which are, in fact, very conventional) to be coloured by the combination of animation and maturity in Chaucer's mind.

---

[40] Urry, Sig. b1ʳ. Dart published his own modernised version of *The Complaint of the Black Knight* (discussed in Chapter 9) in 1720.

[41] Urry, Sig. b1ʳ.

[42] William Godwin, *The Life of Geoffrey Chaucer, The Early English Poet*, 2 vols (London, 1803), 2. 567. This work is discussed further in Chapter 12.

The 'Life of Chaucer' by Robert Shiels included in Volume 1 of Theophilus Cibber's *Lives of the Poets of Great Britain and Ireland* (1753) combines Dart's assessment of Chaucer's temperament—based on early testimonies as well as the poems, genuine and spurious, where Chaucer was thought to have described himself—with Dryden's assessment of his artistic character:

> I cannot better display the character of this great man than in the following words of Urry. 'As to his temper, says he, he had a mixture of the gay, the modest and the grave. His reading was deep and extensive, his judgement sound and discerning; he was communicative of his knowledge, and ready to correct or pass over the faults of his contemporary writers. He knew how to judge of and excuse the slips of weaker capacities, and pitied rather than exposed the ignorance of that age. In one word, he was a great scholar, a pleasant wit, a candid critic, a sociable companion, a stedfast friend, a great philosopher, a temperate oeconomist, and a pious christian.' As to his genius as a poet, Dryden (than whom a higher authority cannot be produced) speaking of Homer and Virgil, positively asserts, that our author exceeded the latter, and stands in competition with the former.[43]

But the two accounts are significantly dissimilar. Dryden had assumed that Chaucer's character 'at least in' his 'Writings' and perhaps also in his life, had resembled the 'well bred, well natur'd, amorous, and Libertine' character of Ovid.[44] Dart depicts a more philosophical figure, partly drawn from *The Canterbury Tales*, but also from other works, so that the invented personality is truly capacious. Dart's conception is remarkably vivid and full of confident detail. Chaucer, Dart is sure, was

> of a middle stature, the latter part of his Life inclinable to be fat and corpulent, as appears by the Host's bantering him in the Journey to *Canterbury*, and comparing shapes with him. His face was fleshy, his features just and regular; his complexion fair, and somewhat pale, his hair of a dusky yellow, short and thin; the hair of his beard in two forked tufts, of a wheat colour; his forehead broad and smooth; his eyes inclining usually to the ground, which is intimated by the Host's words; his whole face full of liveliness, a calm easy sweetness, and a studious venerable aspect. As in the Characters of his Pilgrims he so naturally described them, that the nicest pencil could not possibly give us so full an Idea of them as his words; so likewise he has given us as just a Picture of himself.[45]

Were it not for the mention of his sources, the impression might be given that the subject was personally known to his biographer. Dart draws his details from passages in *The Canterbury Tales*, and from an early manuscript portrait of Chaucer. But the suggestion that Chaucer's 'whole face' was 'full of liveliness, a calm easy

---

[43] Theophilus Cibber, ed., *The Lives of the Poets of Great Britain and Ireland*, 5 vols (London, 1753), 1. 13.
[44] Dryden, *Works*, 7. 30.
[45] Urry, Sig. e2ᵛ.

sweetness, and a studious venerable aspect' would seem to be an inference depending upon arts of portraiture *un*common in the fourteenth century—to be an account, rather, of the portraits of Chaucer by George Vertue, one of which was specially commissioned for Urry's edition (see Fig. 5.2).

The process by which personality is read *from* or read *into* physical appearance was, for Dart, itself distinctly Chaucerian. In *A Poem on Chaucer and his*

Fig. 5.2 Portrait of Chaucer by George Vertue. From *The Works of Geoffrey Chaucer*, ed. John Urry (London, 1721).

Writings (1722), he suggested that the method of characterization in *The Canterbury Tales* is one by which 'We see the Person, and we read his Mind.' Such a process, Dart thought, was particularly in evidence in *The Testament of Love*, a work now attributed to Thomas Usk:

> [O]ne may from the *Testament of Love* conceive as perfect an Idea of *Chaucer's* behaviour and actions in conversation, as if one were sitting in the Prison with him, while he discoursed with Philosophy. The down-cast look, the strict attention, the labouring thought, the hand waving for silence, the manner of address in speaking, the smooth familiar way of arguing, the respectful way of starting his objections, and in short every expression in that dispute figures a lively Image of him in the mind of the Reader.[46]

John Campbell's *Life* of *Chaucer* in *Biographia Britannica* similarly draws on *The Testament of Love*, to offer an almost tragic depiction of Chaucer's reaction to the supposed events and tribulations of his late middle age. In *The Testament*, Campbell claims

> one plainly sees a great Philosopher broken by misfortunes, deserted by companions, and exposed to the censures of an evil world, delivering himself in prison with freedom and spirit, though in a melancholy mood, and in the language of sorrow; and painting in the boldest colours his own mistakes as well as those of others, and pointing out the sole remedies that are left, when a man is abandoned by fortune and by friends. Such is the picture of this performance in which we have a clear and perfect representation of his condition and may enter fully into all the causes of his private griefs, which were also those of the publick disorders of the time, as if we actually sat by him in the prison, and heard him utter those complaints, which, with equal force of fancy, and elegance of expression, he has committed to the perusal of posterity, and therby transmitted the fairest evidence of a spirit, which, though calamity might tame, yet it could not injure, much less destroy.[47]

From the diverse materials available to them, the eighteenth-century biographers constructed an imaginary Chaucer. Educated at Oxford, at Cambridge at the Inns of Court, and perhaps also in Paris, he had a house at Woodstock and a castle at Donnington, and, according to Godwin, had long and intimate conversations with Petrarch and Boccaccio. The invented personality is comprehensive. His mind as Godwin describes it possesses 'elasticity'. In 'almost every one' of Chaucer's 'productions we recognise the elasticity of his spirit, and the healthful temper of his soul' and 'that muscular and elastic character, which are peculiarly the inheritance of great minds'.[48] Chaucer, it was thought, must have been a man of extraordinary poetical and general wisdom.

---

[46] Ibid. Sig. e1r.
[47] *Biographia Britannica, or The Lives of the Most Eminent Persons Who Have Flourished in Great Britain and Ireland, from the Earliest Ages, Down to the Present Times*, 7 vols (London, 1748), p. 1301.
[48] Godwin, *Life*, 2. 94, 204.

The Gode Counsaile of Chaucer

One of the poems Godwin praised—and which helped to form his notion of Chaucer's wise equanimity—was that which he entitled 'Gode Counsaile of Chaucer', a poem that Urry claimed had been written in Chaucer's 'last hours' and showed 'a scorn of worldly affairs'.[49] Godwin was convinced by the 'phraseology' of one line ('Forth, pilgrim, forthe, o best out of thy stall'), 'which has no strict connection with the preceding part of the composition', that the poem had indeed been composed on Chaucer's deathbed and was 'expressive of that serene frame of temper, that pure and celestial equanimity, which so eminently characterised the genius of Chaucer and of Shakespear'.[50] On grounds such as these, the poem attained an enormous importance. Here, Chaucer was thought to have been speaking without irony in his own voice and expressing the sum of his own troubled experience. It also gave permission to 'the pleasure of believing' in a good death:

> Chaucer died, at the venerable age of seventy-two, in the same happy frame of mind in which he had lived, cheerful, composed and serene, at peace with the world, and philanthropically disposed with his dying breath to speak counsels of prudence and contentment to those who survived.[51]

Godwin, like others, found serenity in the poem, but assumed that it was addressed to others. He imagines that Chaucer was attended at his death by his son who was 'nearly everything the fondest father could have wished'.[52] Pope's friend, Walter Harte, however, had made clear, in his version of the poem published in his *Poems on Several Occasions* (1727), his belief that Chaucer was addressing his own inner being. Here is Harte's version, alongside Urry's text:

Gode counsaile of Chaucer.

Flie fro the prese and dwell with sothfastnesse,
  Suffise unto thy gode though it be small,
For horde hath hate, and climbyng tikilnesse,
  Prece hath envie, and wele it brent oer all,
  Savour no more then The bihovin shall,
    Rede wel thy self, that othir folke canst rede,
    And trouthe The shall delivir it'is no drede.

Painè The not eche crokid to redresse,
  In trust of her that tournith as a balle,
Grete reste standith in litil business,
  Beware also to spurne again a nalle,
  Strive not as doth the crocke with a walle,
    Demith thy self, that demist othir's dede,
    And trouthe The shal delivere, it'is no drede.

To my Soul. From *Chaucer*

I.

FAR from mankind, my weary soul retire,
Still follow truth, contentment still desire.
Who climbs on high, at best his weakness shows,
Who rouls in riches, all to fortune owes.
Read well thy self, and mark thy early ways,
Vain is the muse, and envy waits on praise.

II.

Wav'ring as winds the breath of fortune blows,
No pow'r can turn it, and no pray'rs compose.
Deep in some hermit's solitary cell
Repose and ease and contemplation dwell.
Let conscience guide thee in the days of need;
Judge well thy own, and then thy neighbour's
deed.

---

[49] Urry, Sig. c1ᵛ.
[50] Godwin, *Life*, 2. 553–4.
[51] Ibid. 2. 555.
[52] Ibid. 2. 555.

That The is sent, receve in buxomnesse;
  The wrastlyng for this worlde askith a fall;
Here is no home, here is but wildirnesse:
  Forthe pilgrim, forthe o best out of thy stall,
  Loke up on high, and thanke thy God of all;
  Weivith thy luste and let thy ghost The
                      lede,
And trouthe The shall delivir, it'is no
                      drede.
      Explicit.

        (Urry, p. 548)

III.

What Heav'n bestows with thankful eyes receive;
First ask thy heart, and then thro' faith believe.
Slowly we wander o'er a toilsome way,
Shadows of life, and pilgrims of a day.
'Who wrestles in this world, receives a fall;
'Look up on high, and thank thy God for all!

      FINIS.

  (Walter Harte, *Poems on Several*
           Occasions, pp. 243–4)

Here is a clear instance of the circular interrelation between versions of Chaucer's poems and his biography, each informing the other. Harte's version—a meditation on Chaucer's poem, rather than a translation—has the poet bidding farewell to his art: 'Vain is the muse, and envy waits on praise'. His rendering may be compared with the version of Chaucer's poem that was printed—along with Urry's text of the original, with an occasional emendation and without pronunciation marks—in *Biographia Britannica*. John Campbell had taken this version from an essay, 'Some Account of the Life and Writings of Chaucer', that had appeared in *The Universal Visiter and Monthly Memorialist* in 1756. The essay, and almost certainly the poem, had been written by Christopher Smart.[53] In a sidenote, Campbell recorded the supposed circumstances of the poem's composition: 'In a MS in the Cotton Library … this title is inserted: *A Balade made by* Giffrey Chaucyer, *upon his Dethe Bedde lying in his grete Anguysse*'. But his reasons for printing the poem and the translation were as much aesthetic as biographical: 'This *Sonnett* or *Ode* consists of no more than three stanzas, and as well for the beauty of the piece, as for the extraordinary occasion on which it was written, I think it very well deserves a place here.' According to Campbell's reimagining, Chaucer bore 'the near approach' of death 'with Christian patience'.[54] The poem although '"composed in his last agonies", very plainly proves that his senses were perfectly sound, and the faculties of his mind not in the least impaired'.[55] This is Christopher Smart's version as it had

---

[53] For Smart's involvement with *The Universal Visiter*, see Claude Jones, 'Christopher Smart, Robert Rolt, and *The Universal Visiter*', *The Library*, 4th series, 18 (1937), 212–14; Roland B. Botting, 'Johnson, Smart, and the "Universal Visiter"', *Modern Philology*, 26 (1939), 293–300; Robert Brittain, 'Christopher Smart in the Magazines', *The Library*, 4th series 21 (1940), 320–35; Arthur Sherbo, 'Christopher Smart and *The Universal Visiter*', *The Library*, 5th series, 10 (1955), 203–5. For his authorship of the essay, see Trevor Ross, *The Making of the English Literary Canon* (Montreal and London, 1998), pp. 3–4 and Robert Mahony and Betty W. Rizzo, *Christopher Smart: An Annotated Bibliography, 1743–1983* (New York and London, 1984), 551–2. For his authorship of the Chaucer translation, see David Hopkins and Tom Mason, 'Two Uncollected Poems by Christopher Smart', *Notes and Queries*, 67 (2020), pp.504–6.

[54] This partly echoes Dart, who had observed: 'he fell sick, and with a truly Roman Courage, and at the same time with a calm and Christian resignation, ended his days in the Seventy second year of his age, and left the World as tho' he despised it, shewing a scorn of worldly affairs in the Song of *Flie fro the prese*, &c. which he wrote in his last hours.' (Urry, Sig. e^v).

[55] *Biographia Britannica*, 2. 1303.

appeared in *The Universal Visiter*, where it is presented as evidence that Chaucer died 'with a true *Roman* intrepidity, and, what is infinitely greater, a true Christian resignation':[56]

> *Good Councils of* Chaucer, *written in the Agonies of Death.*
>
> I
>
> Flee from the croud, and be to virtue true,
> Content with what thou hast, tho' it be small,
> To hoard brings hate; nor lofty thoughts pursue,
> He, who climbs high, endangers many a fall.
> Envy's a shade that ever waits on fame,
> And oft the sun, that raises it, will hide;
> Trace not in life a vast expensive scheme,
> But be thy wishes to thy state ally'd:
> Be mild to others, to thyself severe;
> So truth shall shield thee, or from hurt or fear.
>
> II
>
> Think not of bending all things to thy will,
> Nor vainly hope that fortune shall befriend;
> Inconstant she, but be thou constant still,
> What'er betide, unto an honest end.
> Yet needless dangers never madly brave,
> Kick not thy naked foot against a nail;
> Or, from experience, the solution crave,
> If well and pitcher strive which shall prevail,
> Be in thy cause, as in thy neighbour's, clear;
> So truth shall shield thee, or from hurt or fear.
>
> III
>
> Whatever happens, happy in thy mind
> Be thou, nor at thy lot in life repine;
> He 'scapes all ill, whose bosom is resign'd,
> Nor way, nor weather, will be always fine.
> Beside, thy home's not here, a journey this,
> A pilgrim thou, then hie thee on thy way;
> Look up to GOD, intent on heav'nly bliss,
> Take what the road affords, and praises pay.
> Shun brutal lusts, and seek thy soul's high sphere;
> So truth shall shield thee or from hurt of fear.
>
> (*The Universal Visiter for the Year 1756*, pp.11–12)

Harte, in his freer imitation, had assumed that Chaucer in this poem was addressing his own soul first, and only secondarily the world. Smart has seen Chaucer as offering advice to the generality of mankind, and has perhaps read Chaucer's last words partly in connection with the wisdom discovered in Horace by late

---

[56] Christopher Smart, 'Some Account of the Life and Writings of Chaucer', in *The Universal Visiter and Monthly Memorialist* (London, 1756), p. 11.

seventeenth-century and early eighteenth-century poets.[57] Smart's 'pilgrim' and 'journey' may also recall Egeus's speech in *Palamon and Arcite*, which, as we saw in Chapter 3, was much remembered and highly regarded. It is only in his final couplet ('Who wrestles in this world, receives a fall; / "Look up on high, and thank thy God for all!"') that Harte comes close to Chaucer's words.

When reprinting Smart's poem, Campbell introduced one tiny emendation. He replaced Smart's self-injunction or Chaucer's warning to the world ('Trace not in life a vast *expensive* scheme') with 'a vast *expansive* scheme'. He may have been thinking of the incomplete *Canterbury Tales*. Several writers expressed astonishment and admiration at Chaucer's having attempted such a scheme in what they thought to be his extreme and possibly troubled old age. For Campbell, *The Canterbury Tales* was an arduous undertaking:

> The scheme of this work is in every respect very extraordinary, and of so vast an extent, that at first sight, one would be apt to pronounce it absolutely impracticable, from a persuasion that it must surpass the powers of any single mind to paint the different lineaments, and call out to view the various faculties of every mind.[58]

For Smart, Chaucer was 'one of the greatest and most universal genius's that ever the world produced', and again, 'without controversy, the most universal genius that ever was'.[59]

The Character of Chaucer's Verse

The debate, discussed in Chapters 1 and 2, as to whether Chaucer had adorned or corrupted the language rumbled on throughout the century. Equally debated was the question of Chaucer's invention of the ten-syllable rhyming couplet. There was no doubt that he had provided models for later poets. The debate was about whether or not he himself had adhered to those models consistently. Many thought that Chaucer's contributions to the more general reform of literature gave him a claim to timeless value. Literature before Chaucer, in their opinion, had been monkish, gothic, fanciful, extravagant, shapeless. Chaucer had restored or introduced Nature, for which deity he remained a primary spokesman. The Father of English Poetry had laid down laws of poetry (restraint, naturalness, the importance of remaining *nimis poeta*) which had, in the eyes of many, permanent validity. But to what extent and how consistently, it was asked, were such principles mirrored in the detailed verbal and metrical textures of his work?

---

[57] In recognizing Chaucer's 'her that tournith as a balle' as Fortune and calling her 'Inconstant', Smart seems to recall Horace's lines as translated by Dryden: 'Fortune, that with malicious joy, / Does Man her slave oppress, / Proud of her Office to destroy, / Is seldome pleas'd to bless / Still various and unconstant still; / But with an inclination to be ill; / Promotes, degrades, delights in strife, / And makes a Lottery of life' (*Horace. Ode 29. Book 3*, 73–80; Dryden, *Works*, 3. 83–4).

[58] *Biographia Britannica*, 2. 1306.

[59] *The Universal Visiter*, pp. 9, 12. Smart's essay is discussed further in Chapter 8.

Christopher Smart's version of the 'Gode Counsaile of Chaucer' pays rather more attention to Chaucer's vocabulary and metre than had Harte's, but makes little attempt to echo the string of imperatives, the repeated and interlocking rhymes (*sothfastnesse*; *tickelnesse*; *redresse*; *businesse*; *buxomnesse*; *wildernesse*; *small*; *all*; *shall*; *balle*; *nalle*; *walle*; *fall*; *stall*; *all*), or the high number of inverted first feet. In the eyes and ears of Harte, Smart, and Campbell, the gentle, rather mournful *sentiments* of Chaucer's poem were, perhaps, beautiful, but with a kind of beauty that could not be accommodated in modern verse. The lines of Chaucer's poem were probably easy enough to scan as consisting of ten syllables with eighteenth-century pronunciation—or could be when reshaped by John Urry, where, for example, Speght's 'Savour no more than the bihoue shall' becomes 'Savour no more then The bihov_in_ shall'. But although ten syllables could generally be found, several lines as rendered by Urry are neither elegant nor musical—at least, to eighteenth-century tastes. Neither Dryden nor Pope would happily place an accent on an elision in the fourth foot of an iambic line—as seems to be the case in the recurring refrain of Chaucer's poem in Urry's text: 'And trouthe The shall delivir, *it'is* no drede'. It may be telling that Harte avoided this line completely. A slightly awkward metrical pattern was forced on the line by Urry's insistence, marked by his spelling, that *deli̱vir* is trisyllabic. Some years later, Henry Todd came across a manuscript[60] where the refrain ran 'And trouthe shall deliver, it is no drede'. But he re-introduced a *thee* (which was 'wanting in MS')—perhaps, like others, wishing to retain the echo of John 8:32, where Jesus said 'to those Jews which believed on him', 'ye shall know the truth, and the truth shall make you free'.[61]

Despite such uncertainties over the shaping of particular lines, many readers and writers in the period would have endorsed Thomas Warton's striking judgement, discussed in Chapter 3, that in 'improving' Chaucer's verse, later poets had both embodied and demonstrated qualities that were genuinely there in Chaucer's originals, and that without the presence of the 'nervous and flowing numbers' which 'we are surprised to find in a poet of such antiquity' it would not have been possible for Dryden to make his 'paraphrase' of *The Knight's Tale*, 'the most animated and harmonious piece of versification in the English Language'.

There were, however, also some readers who thought that Dryden's modern verse was inappropriate for Chaucer's sentiments. In *Woodstock Park* (1706), the Oxford poet William Harrison suggested that there is a peculiarly close, almost erotic, relation between a poet and his inspiration. Woodstock, Harrison wrote, is the place

> Where *Chaucer* (sacred Name!) whole Years employ'd,
> Coy Nature courted, and at length enjoy'd;

---

[60] MSS Cotton.A.xviii.
[61] Henry J. Todd, *Illustrations of The Lives and Writings of Gower and Chaucer* (London, 1810), p. 132.

> Mov'd at his Suit, the naked Goddess came,
> Reveal'd her Charms, and recompenc'd his Flame.

It is thanks to this conjunction that in Chaucer's verse

> Each lively Image makes the Reader start,
> And Poetry invades the Painter's Art.
> This *Dryden* saw, and with his wonted Fate
> (Rich in himself) endeavour'd to translate;
> Took wond'rous Pains to do the Author Wrong,
> And set to modern Tune his antient Song.
> Cadence, and Sound, which we so prize, and use,
> Ill suit the Majesty of *Chaucer*'s Muse;
> His Language only can his Thoughts express,
> And honest *Clytus* scorns the *Persian* Dress.[62]
>
> (William Harrison, *Woodstock Park. A Poem*
> [London, 1706], p. 4)

The debate between admirers of Dryden and those who thought Chaucer's language was the perfect dress or embodiment of his thoughts often centred on the description in *Palamon and Arcite* of a lark greeting the morning and the rise of the sun. This was seized upon by Philip Neve, in his *Cursory Remarks on some of the Ancient English Poets, particularly Milton* (1789) as an example of Dryden's over-decoration. In support of his proposition that 'if in any one passage, or even couplet, the harmony and flow of this antient poet's lines will stand in compare with those, from the polished pen of Dryden, he is not surely to be called "obsolete"', Neve offered his readers a comparison of Chaucer's description of the morning in *The Knight's Tale* with Dryden's version of the same passage, using in his quotations some scansion marks for Chaucer's original, and italics for words and letters in Dryden's version to which he wanted to draw particular attention:

The besy larke,[63] the messager of day,	The *morning* lark, the messenger of day,
Saleweth in hire song the morwe gray;	Saluteth in her song the *morning* gray;[65]
And firy Phebus riseth up so bright,	And soon the sun arose with beams so bright,
That all the orient[64] laugheth of the sight,	*That all th'horizon laugh'd to see the joyous sight*;
And with his strēmĕs drieth in the greves	He with his tepid rays the *rose renews*,
The silver drōpĕs, hanging on the leves.	And licks the *dropping* leaves, and *dries* the *dews*.
(KnT, 1491–6; Neve, *Cursory Remarks on Some of the Ancient English Poets, Particularly Milton* [London, 1789], p. 7)	(*Palamon and Arcite*, 2. 37–42; Neve, *Cursory Remarks*, pp. 7–8)

Neve commented that

---

[62] Clytus was executed for mocking Alexander's claims to divinity and his effeminate Persian attire.
[63] Neve was using Tyrwhitt's text (1. 59). Dryden's texts read 'merie lark'.
[64] Dryden's texts of Chaucer read 'all the orisont'.
[65] Here, Neve was conflating Chaucer and Dryden. All texts of Dryden read *Saluted* where Neve prints *Salueth*.

In *Dryden*'s verses, the double use of '*morning*,' in the first couplet; the ragged alexandrine, in the second; and the *Pierce-Plowman*-like alliteration, in both the verses of the third, seem to leave the point of harmony (to any one who will so far accustom himself to Chaucer's words) entirely in favour of the old poet.

The criticism went to the heart of the matter. These lines of Dryden had been much admired and were frequently anthologized throughout the eighteenth century. They appear in all editions of Bysshe's *Art of Poetry* and in its rivals and imitators, and were sometimes cited in the footnotes to editions of classical poets.[66] In contrast, editors of Milton made a point of referring to Chaucer's original, pointing to his lines when describing the moment in *Paradise Regain'd* when 'the herald lark / Left his ground-nest, high tow'ring to descry / The morn's approach, and greet her with his song'.[67] In his edition of Milton's poem, Thomas Newton compared Milton's 'beautiful thought' to Chaucer's passage, in which, he says, 'Chaucer leads the way to the English poets, in four of the finest lines in all his works'.[68] And in his edition of 1800, Charles Dunster endorsed Newton's judgement, commenting, in addition, that 'Dryden, in his PALAMON AND ARCITE, has paid [these lines] the compliment of preserving the three first unaltered, considering them, we may suppose, as rising to that degree of excellence, which, under any advancement of language, it is not easy to improve'.[69] In a similar vein, John Dart had maintained in his *Life* of Chaucer that the medieval poet's language is 'in some places ... so smooth, concise, and beautiful, that even Mr. Dryden would not attempt to alter it, but has copied some of his Verses almost *literatim*'.[70] In his account of Chaucer's and Dryden's description of the lark, Dunster goes on, however, to observe, much in Neve's vein, that in 'altering *orient* to *horizon*, and extending the verse to "a needless Alexandrine"', Dryden has 'certainly [...] not improved' Chaucer's original. Dryden's reproduction and disfiguring of Chaucer provided for some critics equally powerful illustrations of the beauty of Chaucer's verse.

Chaucer's Prosody

It may be useful at this point to return to the discussion of eighteenth-century perceptions of Chaucer's metre in Chapter 2 and to subject some passages to the

---

[66] See, e.g. Thomas Creech, trans. *T. Lucretius Carus, Of the Nature of Things*, 2 vols (London, 1714), 2. 474.

[67] John Milton, *Paradise Regained*, 2. 279–81.

[68] John Milton, *Paradise Regained*, ed. Thomas Newton (London, 1752), p. 72.

[69] John Milton, *Paradise Regained, With Notes of Various Authors*, ed. Charles Dunster (London, [1800]), p. 92.

[70] Urry, Sig. f1^r.

kind of minute examination that may necessitate the kind of advance apology that Samuel Johnson offered for his detailed discussion of the prosody of *Paradise Lost*:

> However minute and trivial the employment may appear, of analysing lines into syllables, and whatever ridicule may be incurred by a solemn deliberation upon accents and pauses, it is certain that without this petty knowledge no man can be a poet; and that from the proper disposition of single sounds results that harmony that adds force to reason, and gives grace to sublimity; that shackles attention, and governs passion.[71]

It was with beliefs similar to Johnson's that Thomas Morell (see Fig. 5.3) and Thomas Tyrwhitt (see Fig. 5.4) objected vehemently to Urry's text of Chaucer, Morell on the grounds that there was no manuscript that presented the consistent ten-syllable lines that Urry wanted, Tyrwhitt because Urry's ten-syllable lines had been manufactured by illegitimate intrusions. The complaint of both was essentially that Urry's lines were clumsy, ugly, and unmusical. It was inconceivable, thought Tyrwhitt, that abilities and mental capacities such as Chaucer's could have

Fig. 5.3 Portrait of Thomas Morell. Engraved by John Moore 'from the original picture by Hogarth'.

[71] *The Rambler*, No. 88; Johnson, *Works*, 4. 99.

Fig. 5.4 Portrait of Thomas Tyrwhitt. From his edition of Chaucer's
Canterbury Tales (London, 1798 edition).

'failed so grossly and repeatedly, as is generally supposed, in an operation, which
every Balladmonger in our days, man, woman, or child, is known to perform with
the most unerring exactness, and without any extraordinary fatigue'.[72]

As was noted in Chapter 2, Dryden had offered in the Preface to his *Fables*
a passage from the *General Prologue* to the *Canterbury Tales* (in which Chaucer
had attempted to excuse the 'gross' 'Ribaldry' to be found in some of the tales) as
'*Specimen* of *Chaucer*'s Language' which presented 'more than one Example of his
unequal Numbers'.[73] Part of the difficulty for Dryden and other readers, perhaps,
was that of knowing the tone of Chaucer's passage, and, since tone is difficult to determine where prosody is uncertain, the degree of seriousness or solemnity with
which Chaucer was offering his remarks. That difficulty would be compounded
with those which faced every reader of Chaucer's verse in determining where elisions were to be made and guessing at the number of syllables and seat of the accent
in polysyllabic words.

---

[72] Tyrwhitt 1775–78, 4. 91.
[73] Dryden, *Works*, 7. 38–9.

Some notion of which lines might have been for Dryden examples of 'unequal Numbers' may be gathered from a comparison of the passage as Dryden quotes it in his Preface with Urry's text—Urry's ambition having been to 'restore Chaucer to his feet again'. The two are set out in parallel below, with underlining added to indicate the more significant differences:[74]

But first, I pray you, of your courtesy,	But first I pray you of your courtesie,
That ye ne arrete it nought my villany,	That ye n'arrett it nought my villanie,
Though that I plainly speak in this mattere	Though that I pzlainely speak in this mattere,
To tellen you her words, and eke her chere:	To tellin you ther words, and eke ther chere,
Ne though I speak her words properly,	Ne though I speak ther wordis properly.
For this ye knowen as well as I,	For this ye knowin al as well as I,
Who shall tellen a tale after a man	Whoso shall telle a tale after a man,
He mote rehearse as nye, as ever He can:	[He]Mote rehearse, as nygh as ever he can,
Everich word if it been in his charge,	Evèrich word, if it been in his charge,
All speke he, never so rudely, ne large.	Al speke he nevir so rudely ne large:
Or else he mote tellen his tale untrue,	Or ellis he mote telle his tale untrewe,
Or feine things, or find words new:	Or feynè thingis, or find wordis newe:
He may not spare, altho he were his brother,	He may not spare [al]tho he wer his brother,
He mote as well say o word as another.	But [He mote] as wele say o word as another.
Christ spake himself full broad in holy Writ,	Christ speke himself full brode in holie writ,
And well I wote no Villany is it.	And wele ye wote no villanie is it.
Eke Plato saith, who so can him rede,	Eke Plato sayith, whoso can him rede,
The words mote been Cousin to the dede.	The wordis mote be Cosin to the dede.
(*GP*, 725–42; Speght 1598, as quoted	(*GP*, 725–42; Urry, p. 7)
in Dryden, *Works*, 7. 38–9)	

Urry contracts several lines that in seventeenth-century pronunciation might be supernumerate, but it appears that, for Dryden, it was, rather, a syllabic *deficiency* that was the problem. As was observed in Chapter 2, Dryden had complained of the impossibility of discovering 'Ten Syllables in a Verse where we find but Nine': 'It were an easie Matter to produce some thousands of his Verses, which are lame for want of half a Foot, and sometimes a whole one, and which no Pronunciation can make otherwise.'[75] Elisions were, of course, common in seventeenth-century verse.[76] It seems likely that neither Dryden nor Urry read line 726 (*That ye ne arrete it nought my villany*) as having eleven syllables: Urry avoids possible redundancy by marking the elision: 'ye n'arrete it nought'.[77] In contrast, line 732 (*He mote*

---

[74] The first ten lines of this extract were quoted by Francis Beaumont in a passage added in Speght's edition of 1602. In l. 726, Dryden's 'villany' follows Speght 1598, rather than the 'follie' of Speght 1602. The phrase 'of it' is Dryden's mistake for 'if it'.

[75] Dryden, *Works*, 7. 34.

[76] Edward Bysshe (*The Art of English Poetry* [London, 1702], p. 11) regarded the observation of the proper elisions as one of the ways in which English poetry had been 'very much polish'd and refin'd since the days of Chaucer, Spenser, and the other Ancient Poets'. Eleanor Prescott Hammond (*Chaucer: A Bibliographical Manual* [New York, 1933], p. 496) provides a list of elision or 'slurring' found in Chaucer's accepted texts almost as comprehensive as that given by Bysshe.

[77] The elision was not marked by Tyrwhitt 1775–78, 1. 30, but was readopted by Charles Cowden in Geoffrey Chaucer, *The Riches of Chaucer*, ed. Charles Cowden Clarke (London, 1835), p. 81, and by several twentieth-century editors.

rehearse as nye, as ever He can) presented Urry with a particular problem since he apparently could not conceive of possible elisions in this place, and so dropped the initial *He*. Unlike Dryden, who was perfectly happy with eleven-syllable double-rhyme lines,[78] Urry, whose concern was for ten syllables at any price, read both lines 738 and 739 as containing a supernumerary syllable and contracted accordingly: 'He may not spare [al]tho he wer his brother, / But [He mote] as wele say o word as another'. Urry has removed the *al* from *altho* in one line, and the first syllable *He* from the other—presumably forcing the accent and the rhyme onto the last syllable of *brothER* and *anothER*.

That couplet of Urry's would have been as metrically incomprehensible to Dryden as it was to Morell and, later, to Tyrwhitt. It was Chaucer's practice—as it was of almost every succeeding writer of rhyming iambic pentameter—to allow eleven syllables to lines ending in a double rhyme. In the last line of the passage quoted above ('*The words mote been Cousin to the dede*') Urry's spelling of 'wordis' introduces the missing syllable. In the line (*For this ye knowen as well as I*), a similar deficiency has been supplied with the introduction of an '*al*'.[79] The following line could be completed by indicating that 'Evèrich' was trisyllabic. Line 736 ('*Or feine things, or find words new*') presented more difficulties, since Urry had to find three syllables. In the light of the common nineteenth-century assumption that the discovery of a sounding *-e* solved all problems, it is remarkable that this is the *only* line in the passage where Urry considered it fitting that an *-è* be pronounced: 'Or feynè thingis, or find wordis newe'.

Thomas Morell cites the ten-syllable double-rhyming couplet from this passage as a particular instance of his many disagreements with Urry. Having complained that 'the Apostrophe or Elision is not observed' by Urry 'when it is necessarily required', he goes on to confess to being 'surpriz'd' that 'Mr. Urry very often disallows, the *double Rhime*' than which, in his opinion, 'nothing can be more absurd'.[80] The return of these lines to eleven syllables is Morell's most substantial metrical difference from Urry:

But first I pray you of your courtesie,	But ferst, I pray you of your Curtesye,
That ye n'arrett it nought my villanie,	That ye nearrete it not myn Velanye,
Though that I plainely speak in this mattere,	Thow that I pleynly speke in this Matere,
To tellin you ther words, and eke ther chere,	To tellen you her Wordis and her chere
Ne though I speak ther wordis properly.	Ne thow I speke her Wordis properly;
For this ye knowin al as well as I,	For this ye knowen als so well as I,

---

[78] Bysshe (*Art of English Poetry*, p. 21) maintained of 'Double Rhyme' that 'All words that are accented on the last save one, require the Rhyme to begin at the Vowel of that Syllable, and to continue to the end of the word' instancing Dryden couplet: '*Then all for Women, Painting, Rhyming, Drinking, / Besides ten Thousand freaks that dy'd in thinking*'.

[79] Tyrwhitt also adopted an *al* in this place, but also emended the following word: *al so well as I*.

[80] Morell, p. xxvii.

Whoso shall telle a tale after a man,	Whoso schal telle a Tale aftir a Man,
Mote rehearse, as nygh as ever he can,	He mote reherse as nigh as ever he can,
Evèrich word, if it been in his charge,	Everyche Word, yif it be[en] in his Charge
Al speke he nevir so rudely ne large:	Al speke he never so rewdely and large
Or ellis he mote telle his tale untrewe,	Or ellis he mote telle his Tale ontrewe
Or feynè thingis, or find wordis newe:	Or feiné Thyngys, or fynden Wordys Newe;
He may not spare tho he wer his brother,	He may not spare al thof he were his Brothir,
But as wele say o word as another.	He mot as well seyn o Word as another.
Christ speke himself full brode in holie writ,	Christ spake hymself full brode in holy Wryt,
And wele ye wote no villanie is it.	And well ye wote no Velanye is it:
Eke Plato sayith, whoso can him rede,	Eke Plato seyth, hoso can hym rede,
The wordis mote be Cosin to the dede.	The Wordys mot ben Cousyn to the Dede.
(*GP*, 725–42; Urry, p. 7)	(*GP*, 725–42; Morell, pp. 63–4)

Unlike Urry, Morell was suspicious of the *eke* in the line 'To tellin you her words, and eke ther chere', deleting the *eke* and finding the missing syllable in the plural *Wordis*. The line (in Speght 1598: 'Or feine things or find words new') that caused most trouble to Urry (solved with a final *è*: 'Or feynè thingis, or find wordis newe') is rendered grammatical by Morell ('Or feiné Thyngys, or fynden Wordys Newe'), as it was to be with greater strictness by Tyrwhitt ('Or feinen thinges, or finden wordes newe').

In his edition, Morell moves in several near-contradictory directions, possibly with several rather different readerships in mind. On the one hand, he has used a modern typeface and early eighteenth-century capitalization. On the other, he has preserved MS spelling, including some difficult forms (e.g. *hoso* in l. 741 of the passage quoted above). Some of his choices are explained in footnotes.[81] Some spellings seem to have been chosen to draw attention to their difference from the modern sense.[82] Some notes show wide reading in Chaucer. To explain the reference to Plato in Chaucer's penultimate line, for example, Morell quotes (p. 64) from Chaucer's *Boethius*: 'thou heard lernede by the Sentence of *Plato*, that nedes the Wordis mote bene Cosyns to thingys of whiche they speken'.

Thomas Tyrwhitt was unwilling to deface his text with accentual marks as an aid to pronunciation. But in the Glossary that he added in his fifth volume in 1778, he explained several words from this passage helpfully: 'Chere, *n*. Fr. Countenance, appearance'; 'Cosin, *n*. Fr. A cousin, or kinsman. It is sometimes used *adjectively*. Allied, related'. 'Vilanie, *n*. Fr.' is glossed as 'Any thing unbecoming a gentleman'. Tyrwhitt's text of this passage scans fairly easily, even without pronunciation marks. As with Morell, the major difference between Tyrwitt's text and Urry's lies

---

[81] e.g. 'Narette, ne arette, *i.e.* Judge not, determine not. *Fr. arrester*, to judge, to decide a Cause, *&c*' (Morell, p. 63).

[82] The 'Velanye' of which there is none in '*holy Wryt*' gets a long note (drawing on Skinner's *Etymologicon*): '*i.e.* any rude or dishonourable thing either in Word or Deed. Fr *Villain*. Ital *Villano*. Lat *Villanus*; properly signifying a rustic Servant, but now generally used in a bad Sense; because these Slaves were formerly no better than Rogues and Thieves'.

in his restoration of the eleven-syllable couplet: 'He may not spare, <u>although</u> he were his brother, / <u>He moste</u> as wel <u>sayn</u> o word as an other'.[83]

'Not in Purgatory, But in Hell'

And yet, in larger ways Thomas Morell and Thomas Tyrwhitt held widely divergent notions of Chaucer's versification. Morell followed Dryden in doubting that Chaucer wrote consistently 'in equal measure'. John Dart held similar views, as did Timothy Thomas in the Glossary to Urry's edition. The entry there, under *Missemetre*, is particularly interesting and almost constitutes a miniature essay on the subject. Chaucer admits, Thomas claims (citing the opening of Book 3 of *The House of Fame*), that he 'chose sometimes to leave a Verse too short by a Syllable, where he had a greater regard to the sense than the Metre'.

On the other hand, Timothy Thomas suggests, Chaucer 'was not so loose in his Metre, as some may imagine; for by collating any part of his works with MSS. or old Editions, it will appear, that Verses, which in one Copy or Edition are defective, may out of others be made compleat'. This is the policy employed by Morell and Tyrwhitt, as by most subsequent editors, and, Timothy Thomas maintains, it makes unnecessary the expedients so often resorted to by Urry. Chaucer's metre, Thomas argues, may frequently be restored 'very often without the use of *i* or *y* prefixt to Verbs, the distinct pronunciation of the final *in* or *é*, or useless <u>Expletives</u>'.[84] Thomas's charge against the original and senior editor of the edition to which he contributed is that Urry had restored Chaucer not to his own feet but those supplied by his (Urry's) own invention (and bad ear), and in so doing had made Chaucer resemble the feeble prosodists condemned by Alexander Pope:

> These *Equal Syllables* alone require,
> Tho' oft the Ear the *open Vowels* tire,
> While *Expletives* their feeble Aid *do* join,
> And ten low Words oft creep in one dull Line.[85]
> (*An Essay on Criticism*, 344–47; Pope, *Poems*, 1. 277–8)

An 'exact numerosity', Morell concluded, was not Chaucer's main Care; but […] he had sometimes a greater Regard for the Sense, than the Metre'. It is Morell's leading suggestion, however, that such a neglect of 'exact numerosity' is not a *defect*: 'His Numbers […] are, by no Means so rough and inharmonious as some People imagine; there is a charming Simplicity in them, and they are always musical, whether they want or exceed their Complement'.[86]

---

[83] Tyrwhitt 1775–78, 1. 30.
[84] Urry, Glossary, p. 46.
[85] Timothy Thomas wrote of '*useless* Expletives'. Pope called them *feeble*. In the same passage, however, he wrote (356) of *needless* alexandrine.
[86] Morell, p. xxvi.

The difference between Morell and Tyrwhitt can be observed in the textual transmission of a single line in *The Knight's Tale*. It occurs when Arcite, freed from prison against his will, and compelled to see Emily no more, weeps, wails, and contemplates suicide:

> And said / alas the day that I was borne
> Nowe is my prison worse than beforne
> Nowe is me shappen eternally to dwell
> Nought in purgatory / but in hell.

(*The Workes of Geffray Chaucer, Newly
Printed*, ed. William Thynne [London, 1532], Sig. L. iii^r)

The fourth line of this passage remained in this form though every transmission, appearing for example, with modern punctuation, in the text of Chaucer's poem included in Dryden's *Fables*: 'Nought in purgatory, but in hell'. Urry, however, found the need to add a syllable, the deficiency being in his view, again, one that no pronunciation could overcome:

> Nought in Purgatorie, but <u>right</u> in Hell.

'Mr. *Urry*', Morell complained, 'to make out his ten Syllables, reads it, *right* in Hell, which right, tho' I am no great Admirer of a Pun, is *wrong*, as it render the Verse very harsh and dissonant', whereas Chaucer's genuine lines are 'always musical'.[87] Morell regards it as an allowable, and often beautiful, latitude in Chaucer's verse to drop an unaccented syllable 'at the Beginning of a Verse, when a Pause is to be made, or rather two Times to be given to the first Syllable'.

Tyrwhitt was firmly opposed to Morell's conclusions on this subject: 'I have no conception myself', he comments acidly, 'that an heroic verse, which wants a syllable of its complement, can be musical, or even tolerable.'[88] Tyrwhitt, who was prepared to allow what he calls the 'Diameter Trochaic Catalectic' as an occasional variant in iambic octosyllabic verse (e.g. 'God of science and of Light', as opposed to the 'unnecessary' Urry emendation '*Thou* God of science and of light'), thought that 'no such liberty can be taken in the Heroic measure without totally destroying its harmony'. He therefore assumed that 'the learned Editor'—as he calls Morell—had been 'carried too far' by his 'partiality for' Chaucer.

Tyrwhitt claims that the line '*Not* in purgatory but in helle', where he observes the italicization of the first word as quoted in Morell's Preface but neither Morell's capitalization nor his spelling

> however you manage it; (whether you make a pause; or give two times to the
> first syllable, as he rather advises;)—can never pass for a verse of any form.

---

[87] Ibid. Urry may have scanned the line something like this—NOUGHT in | PURgat | ORie, | but RIGHT | in HELL—which would give him ten syllables, but a line containing three trochaic feet.
[88] Tyrwhitt 1775–78, 4. 82.

Nor did Chaucer intend that it should. He wrote (according to the best Mss.)—
Not *only* in purgatory but in helle.[89]

Tyrwhitt's line adds two syllables to Morell's version, and that found in almost all manuscripts. He was counting perhaps on an elision between *only* and *in*.[90] Or he may have been taking *purgatory* as trisyllabic (*purgat'ry*) a form which—although the syllabic value of the word does not seem to have been firmly established— sometimes appears in late-seventeenth-century verse.[91] Alexander Pope, following Chaucer, gave the four-syllable form, and the same emphatic effect, to the Wife of Bath when discussing her fourth husband: 'His Soul, I hope, enjoys eternal Glory; / For here on Earth I was his Purgatory'.[92]

Tyrwhitt's line ('Not *only* in purgatory but in helle') may provide ten syllables— but also turns Arcite's words to nonsense. In giving these words to Arcite, the ancient Theban, Chaucer was wildly anachronistic, but it would be hard to envisage a theology which permitted simultaneous, or even sequential, residence in both places of torment. As Robert Bell was to explain in a footnote to the line: 'In purgatory there is hope of redemption; not so in hell.'[93]

In the light of the evidence surveyed above, it is apparent that it was—albeit in very different ways—Tyrwhitt and Urry, rather than Morell and Dryden, who were insistent that Chaucer should scan according to the criteria provided by heroic couplets written since Cowley. Dryden was prepared to live with what he saw as the 'lame' and 'unequal Numbers' of some of Chaucer's lines because he thought it was amply compensated for by the larger virtues of Chaucer's work—including the 'natural and pleasing' (if 'not perfect') 'rude Sweetness' of his versification. Morell insisted that Chaucer's verse had its own musicality, which at its best was different from, but certainly not inferior to, that of the verse of George Sandys, Edmund Waller, or John Denham. In this, he anticipated the findings of Skeat and some more recent prosodists.[94]

---

[89] Ibid.

[90] Cowden Clarke was to mark such an elision in his *Riches of Chaucer*: 'Not on̲l̲y̲'̲i̲n̲ purgatory but in hell' (*The Riches of Chaucer*, ed. Cowden Clarke, 1. 95).

[91] In Pope's *The Fourth Satire of Dr. John Donne*, the word appears to have a full four syllables with an accent on the penultimate: 'I've had my *Purgatory* here betimes, / And paid for all my Satires, all my Rhymes' (5–6; Pope, *Poems*, 4.27). Abraham Cowley, who was, as Morell observed, notorious for the freedom of his versification, in his *Ode upon His Majesties Restoration and Return*, rhymes on the word, procuring one nine-syllable and one thirteen-syllable line: Charles and 'his *Royal Brothers*' gain 'New marks of *honour* and of *glory* ... / And look like *Heavenly Saints* even in their *Purgatory*' (Abraham Cowley, *Poems*, ed. A. R. Waller (Cambridge, 1905), p. 429.

[92] *The Wife of Bath, Her Prologue*, 237–8; Pope, *Poems*, 2. 68.

[93] *The Poetical Works of Geoffrey Chaucer*, ed. Robert Bell, 4 vols (London, 1878–80), 1. 128. Versions of the line struggled with each other in editions later than those of Urry, Morell, Tyrwhitt, and Cowden Clarke already cited. Yet another variant ('Nat in my purgatorye, but in helle') was given in Geoffrey Chaucer, *The Knight's Tale*, ed. J. A. W. Bennett (2nd edn, London, 1974), p. 45.

[94] Modern support for Morell's argument of the existence of headless lines in all manuscripts of Chaucer's poems can be found in Derek A. Pearsall, 'Chaucer's Meter: The Evidence of the Manuscripts',

Informing the judgement of Morell and other Chaucer enthusiasts was their conviction that 'Wordis mote bene Cusyns to thingys of whiche they speaken.'[95] There were, therefore, many places where Chaucer's 'Language only can his Thoughts express.'[96] If the vocabulary itself continued to present difficulties, the 'point of harmony' might be heard or felt to excel 'to any one who will so far accustom himself to Chaucer's words.'[97] Chaucer's works contain 'all the beauties that can be wished for or expected, in every kind of composition', largely because as 'no man understood human nature better so it may be truly said that no writer in any language has either painted it with greater force, exactness, or judgement.'[98] Chaucer's language 'in some places' is 'smooth, concise, and beautiful'. There is 'a charming Simplicity' in his lines: 'they are always musical, whether they want or exceed their Complement.'[99] Thomas Morell is likely to have used the word 'musical' with care. He worked closely with Handel, providing the librettos for four of Handel's oratorios,[100] and carefully underlaying new words to Handel's music in three *pasticcio* oratorios put together after Handel's death by Handel's former assistant, John Christopher Smith Junior.[101]

Appreciation of Chaucer's peculiar musicality—and its relation both to his narrative gifts and to his insights into the human heart—is perhaps clearest in the eighteenth-century imitations of those moments when his defence of speaking 'rudely' and 'large' was particularly necessary, and where there was much *vilanie*—language and behaviour 'unbecoming a gentleman' in any age. The enormous attractions of such moments form the subject of Chapter 6.

---

in *Medieval Literature: Texts and Interpretation*, ed. Tim W. Machan (Binghamton, NY, 1991), 41–57 and Ad Putter, 'In Appreciation of Metrical Abnormality: Headless Lines and Initial Inversion in Chaucer', in *Engaging with Chaucer Practice, Authority, Reading*, ed. C. W. R. D. Moseley (New York and Oxford, 2021), 55–75: the crucial headless line discussed above, '*Noght* in purgatorie, *but* in helle.' (*KnT*, 1226), is analysed by Putter on p. 63.

[95] Morell (p. 64) quotes this phrase from Chaucer's translation of Boethius.

[96] William Harrison, *Woodstock Park. A Poem* (London, 1706), p. 4.

[97] Philip Neve *Cursory Remarks on Some of the Ancient English Poets, Particularly Milton* (London, 1789), p. 8.

[98] Campbell, in *Biographia Britannica*, pp. 1304–5.

[99] Morell, p. xxvi.

[100] *Judas Maccabeus* (1747), *Alexander Balus* (1748), *Theodora* (1750), and *Jephtha* (1752).

[101] *Nabal* (1764), *Tobit* (*c.* 1764?), and *Gideon* (1769). Morell's scrupulous attention to scansion, elision, and the 'harmoniousness' of verse is very clearly in evidence in a detailed letter to Rev. Robert Cory Sumner about the versification of Sophocles, preserved in the Archives Centre at King's College, Cambridge, Morell's old college (Coll. 34/11). The care exercised by Morell in fitting texts to music in the pasticcio oratorios is documented and discussed by Richard G. King in 'John Christopher Smith's Pasticcio Oratorios', *Music and Letters*, 79 (1998), 190–218.

6

The True, Enlivened, Natural Way

The Monk and the Merchant's Wife, January and May,
Phoebus and the Crow, The Carpenter of Oxford, and
The Miller of Trompington

Edmund Curll, Jeremy Collier, and Chaucer's 'Native Obscenity'

Perhaps the most curious mention of Chaucer's works in the eighteenth century occurs in *The Humble Representation of Edmund Curll, Bookseller and Citizen of London, concerning Five Books, Complained of to the Secretary of State*, which was probably published in 1725.[1] This piece is halfway between a defence of and an advertisement for five books that the notorious publisher Edmund Curll had published in the previous seven years, and that had been charged with obscenity. Curll defends four of the books—on 'the Uses of FLOGGING in Physical and Venereal Affairs', on the 'lewd Practices of *Nuns and Fryars* in Monasteries and Convents', on 'the Necessity of frequently getting Drunk', and on 'The Mysteries of Human generation'—on the grounds both that they are translations and have ancient and honourable precedents, and that they are morally or medically instructive. But his defence of the fifth volume, *Three New Poems* (1721), takes a different form, and one that is particularly pertinent to the present enquiry. The first two of Curll's *Three New Poems* are: '*Family Duty*: Or, The Monk and the Merchant's Wife; being the *Shipman's* Tale from *Chaucer* modernized, by Mr. John Markland of St. *Peter's* College *Cambridge*', and 'The *Curious Wife*, a tale devised in the Manner of *Chaucer*. By Mr. Fenton. Modernized by the same Hand'. Rather than denying the obscenity and lewdness of the poems as printed, Curll appeals to the precedent of similar Chaucerian lewdness already in print, and extends the charge as widely as possible to poets, to publishers, and to venerable institutions:

> THESE Performances of Mr. *Markland* and Mr. *Fenton* have not any Thing more criminal in them, than several of *Chaucer's* Tales which have been modernized by Mr. *Dryden*, and published by Mr. *Tonson*, among which is the *Wife of Bath's* Tale, but the Prologue to it Mr. *Dryden* declared he could not attempt on Account of its Obscenity;

[1] See Paul Baines and Pat Rogers, *Edmund Curll, Bookseller* (Oxford, 2007), pp. 159, 166, 181.

Chaucer in the Eighteenth Century. David Hopkins and Tom Mason, Oxford University Press.
© David Hopkins and Tom Mason (2022). DOI: 10.1093/oso/9780192862624.003.0007

yet this *lewd Prologue* has been modernized by Mr. *POPE* and likewise published by Mr. *Tonson*. And the whole Works of *CHAUCER*, have been lately given us in their *native Obscenity*, after the most *correct Manner*, by the Society of *Christ Church* College *Oxford*, in a pompous Folio Edition, published by Mr. *LINTOT*; the Profits arising from the Sale of which, he assured me are to be applied to the Finishing of *Peckwater* Quadrangle, belonging to that College.[2]

Despite the broadness of his brush, and the disingenuousness of his apparent condemnation of recent Chaucerian publications,[3] Curll had a point—or, rather, two points. There was considerable Chaucerian activity at this time from all sections of the literary world. Loud voices had been raised against literary indecency generally, and several commentators had accused some of Chaucer's poems in particular of what Curll calls 'native Obscenity'. Curll both invokes and abuses Dryden's authority in his defence of *Three Poems*. His implication is, first, that Dryden's version of *The Wife of Bath's Tale* is itself 'lewd', but, second, that more recent writers and publishers had ignored the false boundary Dryden had set himself, and had translated the 'native obscenity' of the most excessive tales.

Dryden's case was symptomatic of a common difficulty at the turn of the century. Among the many causes for Dryden's turning to Chaucer in his *Fables* was a desire to answer the attacks mounted on himself and others in *A Short View of the Immorality, and Profaneness of the English Stage* (1698) by the non-juring clergyman Jeremy Collier. Included amongst the '*Liberties*' of Dryden and others that Collier regards as 'intolerable' are 'Their *Smuttiness* of *Expression;* Their *Swearing, Profainness,* and *Lewd Application of Scripture;* Their *Abuse* of the *Clergy;* Their *making* their *Top Characters Libertines,* and giving them *Success* in their *Debauchery*'.[4] Collier objected particularly to Dryden's mixing of sexual obscenity with profanity, as, for example, in *Absalom and Achitophel*, where Dryden wonders whether the outstanding qualities of the Duke of Monmouth might be attributable to the fact that 'inspired with a diviner Lust, / His Father got him with a greater gust':

> This is down right Defiance of the Living God! Here you have the very Essence and Spirit of Blasphemy, and the Holy Ghost brought in upon the most hideous Occasion. I question whether the Torments and Despair of the Damn'd, dare venture at such Flights as these. They are beyond Description, I Pray God they may not be beyond Pardon too.[5]

Collier maintained that 'Ribaldry is dangerous under any Circumstances of Representation', and that 'to represent' women without the quality of 'Modesty'

[2] *The Humble Representation of Edmund Curll, Bookseller* (London, 1725), pp. 10–11.
[3] Curll was quite happy to print what amount to advertisements for these publications. In Giles Jacob, *An Historical Account of the Lives and Writings of Our Most Considerable English Poets* (London, 1720), pp. 159, 166, 181 issued by Curll in 1720, Urry's edition and Chaucerian versions by Pope and Samuel Cobb are specifically mentioned and commended (see pp. 30, 148, 149).
[4] Jeremy Collier, *A Short View of the Immorality, and Profaneness of the English Stage* (London, 1698), p. 2.
[5] Ibid. pp. 184–5.

'is to make Monsters of them, and throw them out of their Kind'.[6] Dryden—who seems to have taken Collier at least in part seriously, and who would also have been mindful of condemnations of 'Ribaldry' by the Earl of Mulgrave (in his *Essay on Poetry*), of 'Want of Decency' by the Earl of Roscommon (in his *Essay on Translated Verse*), and of the 'Dross' 'At which a Virgin hides her face' by Abraham Cowley (in his *Ode of Wit*)—was at pains to assure his readers that all his *Fables*, including his versions from Chaucer, had an 'instructive moral'.

In Speght's edition of Chaucer, however, Francis Beaumont had offered a defence of Chaucer's indecency which was substantially followed and extended by Dryden in the Preface to *Fables*. Beaumont had excused the 'vndecent' nature of some of Chaucer's speeches, arguing that Chaucer's practice was no different from that of the Roman poets, who had observed decorum by 'giuing to their comicall persons such manner of speeches as did best fitt their dispositions'. In 'purposing', Beaumont maintained, 'to describe all Englishmens humors liuing in those days', Chaucer had no alternative but to describe their 'filthy delights' and 'desires'—a task that, as Chaucer himself had pointed out, could not be accomplished 'without some of their words'.[7]

In his Preface, Dryden expanded on Beaumont's position. It is very much part of his praise of Chaucer's comprehensiveness that 'Even the Ribaldry of the Low Characters is different: the Reeve, the Miller, and the Cook are several men, and distinguish'd from each other, as much as the mincing Lady Prioress and the broad-speaking gap-tooth'd Wife of *Bathe*'.[8] Dryden, as we saw in Chapter 5, quoted Chaucer's own defence of the 'gross' 'Ribaldry' in *The Canterbury Tales*. But, he nevertheless conceded that

> if a man should have inquired of *Boccace* or of *Chaucer* what need they had of introducing such Characters, where obscene Words were proper in their Mouths, but very undecent to be heard; I know not what Answer they could have made: For that Reason, such Tales shall be left untold by me.[9]

If, however, Dryden says, he had 'desir'd more to please than to instruct, the *Reve*, the *Miller*, the *Shipman*, the *Merchant*, the *Sumner*, and above all, the *Wife of Bathe*, in the Prologue to her Tale, would have procur'd me as many Friends and Readers, as there are *Beaux* and Ladies of Pleasure in the Town'.[10] The implication is that some of Chaucer's tales were suitable only for a young and dissolute readership. As Edmund Curll noted, several writers—mostly, but not exclusively, young—were happy to supply such a dissolute audience by composing versions of *precisely* the list proscribed by Dryden. Indeed, it could be said that many early eighteenth-century works inspired by Chaucer reacted to earlier strictures on Chaucer's indecency in a spirit of near-defiance.

[6] Ibid. pp. 11, 118.
[7] Speght 1602, Sigs. Aiii[r–v].
[8] Dryden, *Works*, 7. 37.
[9] Ibid. 7. 38–9.
[10] Ibid. 7. 38.

Alexander Pope was given a copy of Speght's 1598 edition of Chaucer in 1701, when he was thirteen. Looking back in 1736, he suggested that the appearance of Dryden's *Fables* had been the cause of his translating Chaucer. His *January and May* had probably been composed in 1704–05 and was published in 1709. His version of *The Wife of Bath from Chaucer* appeared in 1714. Pope's example prompted an extraordinary publishing explosion. Thomas Betterton's version of *The Reeve's Tale* was published in 1712, the same year as Samuel Cobb's rendering of *The Miller's Tale*. Other versions of the comic tales included John Smith's *Miller's Tale* (1713); a much-expanded anonymous version of *The Reeve's Tale* (1715); John Markland's *Shipman's Tale* (1721) and *Friar's Tale* (1723); Henry Travers's *Shipman's Tale* (1731) and *Reeve's Tale* (1740); 'Mr. Grosvenor' [= Eustace Budgell]'s *Summoner's Tale* (1733); George Ogle's *Cook's Tale* (1741); Andrew Jackson's *Shipman's Tale, Manciple's Tale*, and *Wife of Bath's Prologue* (1750); George Ellis's lascivious *The Wife of Bath's Tale from Chaucer* (1777); an equally lascivious (anonymous) *Miller's Tale* (1791); William Lipscomb's *Shipman's Tale* and *Manciple's Tale* (1795), and William Wordsworth's *Phoebus and the Crow*—a version of *The Manciple's Tale* (composed 1801; published 1841).[11]

Such a level of interest in Chaucer's more indecent poems requires explanation. Why did so many aspiring poets turn specifically to *Chaucer's* indecency in the face of clerical and critical disapproval of what was seen as witless smut? Jeremy Collier had observed that 'we have … Lewdness enough of our own Growth, without Importing from our Neighbours'.[12] The same argument might reasonably be applied to the past. If mere sexual obscenity in verse was what was desired, Curll was able to supply his readership with 'Lewdness enough' either in the form of translations or of poems with an English provenance. What were the specific attractions of native obscenity, *antiquated* obscenity, and of pseudo-Chaucerian indecency subsequently modernized?

'In The Pleasaunt Manere of Gentil Maister Jeoffrey Chaucer'

As so often with Edmund Curll, there is some deception and some sleight of hand in his defence of his publication of *Three New Poems*. He could safely attribute the obscenity of John Markland's *Family Duty* to its close following of its Chaucerian

---

[11] *The Miller of Trompington, Being an Exercise upon Chaucer's Reeve's Tale* (London, 1715) is rather different from the other versions. Betsy Bowden describes this vastly expanded version in brisk octosyllabics as 'mock heroic'. It actually resembles *Hudibras* a little more closely than *Le Lutrin, Mac Flecknoe*, or *The Rape of the Lock*, and includes debates on verse and verse translation, praise of *Paradise Lost* (825–99), and some knowing mockery of 'the Honour and Dignity / Of Cambridge University'. In an Epilogue, the author describes the limits of his poetic ambition: '*I never aim'd at being truly / A Milton*, Butler, Ben *or* Cowley' (2561–2). The version is included (pp. 33–54), along with most of the others, in Betsy Bowden, *Eighteenth-Century Modernizations from 'The Canterbury Tales'* (Woodbridge, 1991).
[12] Collier, *Short View*, p. 71.

source, *The Shipman's Tale*, where Markland's interest is evenly distributed, and focuses as much on the financial as the sexual dealings of the lecherous Monk, the honest Merchant, and his expensively wayward wife.[13] The adultery between the Monk and the Merchant's Wife is described with some distance and restraint:

> The *Monk* and Wife a hasty Bargain wrought,
> That for these hundred Crowns so duely brought,
> He should enjoy her Company in Bed.
> This they perform'd, a busy Life they led,
> And *stock'd the Cattle on the Merchant's Head.*
>
> (John Markland, 'The Shipman's Tale', in *Three New Poems*
> [London, 1721], pp. 19)

But the lovemaking of the married couple is, though euphemistically described, rather more salacious:

> So all that Night, for Joys, they set apart,
> For he was Fresh, and Merry at the Heart.
> At Morning he renew'd his *warm Embrace*,
> And kiss'd her Lips, and sooth'd a *better Place.*
>
> (*Three New Poems*, p. 23)

Although there are no lewd words here, Collier might have objected to Markland and Chaucer giving their 'Libertine' characters '*Success* in their *Debauchery*'. Similarly, the shameless wife of Markland's poem violates Collier's demand that writers should not make 'Monsters' of women by representing them without 'Modesty'. Markland's wife, like Chaucer's, is not condemned by the teller or by the tale for her exercise of total sexual control of her husband:

> No *more* (*said she*) in truth *you've had enough.*
> Then wantonly she play'd, and *egg'd him on*,
> Till all his *Force* was lost, and *Strength* was gone
>
> (*Three New Poems*, p. 23)

The second of Curll's *Three New Poems*, *The Curious Wife* cannot be so easily defended on grounds of its antiquity, since it is a modernization not of a genuine Chaucerian poem but of an 'imitation' in pseudo-medieval English of 'Chaucerian' style—an imitation, moreover, that shares neither plot nor sentiment with anything written by or attributed to Chaucer himself. The original, 'A TALE, Devised

[13] Henry Travers's, 'The Shipman's Tale, from Chaucer', in *Miscellaneous Poems and Translations* (London, 1731) appears to be more interested in the relations between the Monk and the Merchant, than those between either man and the Wife. Andrew Jackson, in contrast, employs equine terms to describe (or not describe) the Monk's sexual activity: 'That night he rode, as Monks devoutly ride. / The Leagues he journey'd, or how oft he baited / I do not find by Lady *Fame* related'. At the end of the tale, the Merchant 'feasted on the honey' of his wife's 'lips' and 'Stroak'd the dear Pad' (see Andrew Jackson, *Matrimonial Scenes … Modernized from Chaucer* (London, 1750), pp. 15, 18.

in the plesaunt manere of gentil Maister Jeoffrey Chaucer', had been composed by Pope's friend Elijah Fenton, and published by Lintot in *Poems on Several Occasions* (London, 1717). Unabashed by complaints, Curll reprinted Markland's version of the poem in some issues of *The Altar of Love* (1727).

The nature of the pleasure that the pseudo-Chaucerian language of Fenton's *Tale* is designed to provoke is not obvious. At one point in the tale, there is a passage describing the relations between a priest and a 'doxy'. In Fenton's poem, as it appeared in 1717, the passage reads as follows:

> Thilke Clerke echaufed in the Groyne,
> For a yonge Damosell did pyne,
> Born in East-Cheape; who, by my Fay,
> Ypert was as a Popinjay:
> Ne Wit, ne Wordes did she waunt,
> Wele cond she many a Romaunt;
> She carrold soote as Nightingale;
> Ore Muscadine, or spiced Ale.
>
> (Elijah Fenton, *Poems on Several Occasions*
> [London, 1717], pp. 171–2)

In Markland's version (as reprinted in 1727), this becomes:

> This Priest, as modern stories teach,
> For a young Doxie, felt an Itch,
> A cockney of no scanty Fame,
> Whose ev'ry Grace her Worth proclaim;
> Was Brisk, and Buxom, Blyth, and Gay,
> And Pert as any *Popping-jay*;
> Had Wit at Will, of Tales was fond,
> For ev'ry *New Romance* she conn'd;
> Had CURLL's *Letchery* by Heart,
> Which he in *Tryals* does impart:
> O'er Racy-Sack, and Nut-brown Ale,
> Would sing like any *Nightingall*.
>
> (*The Altar of Love* [London, 1727], pp. 29–30)

Presumably persuaded by his publisher, Markland has replaced Fenton's account of his 'Damosell's' reading habits with an advertisement for Curll's publications.[14] The indecency extends to the footnotes, partly perhaps because there is not much in the original. Neither Fenton nor Markland have used many lewd words in their tale. Reference to the sexual act is largely restricted, in Markland's case, to a euphemistic replacement of Fenton's reference to 'blissful Consummation' by a

---

[14] To the line referring to Curll's 'Letchery' and 'Tryals' is appended a footnote listing Curll's titles: 'Case of *Impotency* and *Divorce*. Treatise of *Flogging. Eunuchism* and *Onanism Display'd*'. This is one of Curll's favourite titles. The contents of the book, and its subtitles, varied enormously—sometimes in the same year.

description of the 'young Doxie' as 'a Well-wisher to—*that same*'. The overall intention of Markland's imitation seems to have been to amuse and charm rather than to shock or arouse. Fenton's reference to 'the plesaunt manere of gentil Maister Jeoffrey Chaucer' perhaps reflects a belief that Chaucer had a civilized and agreeable manner of evoking the oddities of human sexuality—particularly female perceptions of their own sexuality and that of men. For Fenton, the fake-antique language and the protecting and softening shade of antiquity that it provided, was essential to the charm. Curll and Markland appear to have considered that pleasure to be doubled by setting a faux-antique original against a version in the modern idiom.

Curll had been curiously silent in his *Humble Representation* about his own earlier 'Chaucerian' publications. In the same year as Samuel Cobb's *The Carpenter of Oxford, or, The Miller's Tale, from Chaucer* (1712), Curll added to his list *Two Imitations of Chaucer, 1. Susannah and the Two Elders, II. Earl Robert's Mice*, attributed to Matthew Prior.[15] Again, it is not easy to see exactly what was appealing about the much-reprinted first poem of this pair. The editor of *A Collection of Epigrams* (1727), in which *Susannah and the Two Elders* was reprinted, regarded the poem's 'raillery' as too 'easy', but judged that its lines 'have some merit for the antique stile, which is so well imitated in them'. The poem's 'raillery' of *Susannah and the Two Elders* might be thought 'easy' in that it consists entirely in the observation that, if an *old* Susannah had been confronted by *young* gallants, the preservation of her chastity would have constituted a miracle. The poem's popularity was perhaps partly attributable to its 'antique style'—its pretended relation to Chaucer's work. Curll had, interestingly, presented it to the public in 1712 in black-letter dress (see Fig. 6.1). Matthew Prior had, at this time, a considerable reputation for elegant indecency. He was the author of *Hans Carvel's Ring; or a Charm against Cuckoldom*, a version in adroitly insinuating octosyllabics of the indecorous and witty tale told by Rabelais and La Fontaine, where the only certain prevention of cuckoldom is a husband's finger inserted permanently into his wife's vagina. Henry Felton maintained that 'since Chaucer's Days none hath told a merry ... Tale so well' as Prior.[16]

Although they may not have known it, Fenton and Prior (if it was he), in writing mildly indecent poems in the manner of Chaucer, were following Alexander Pope, who had composed an octosyllabic 'imitation' of Chaucer—perhaps when younger than sixteen. This poem was first printed anonymously as 'A Tale of Chaucer. Lately found in an old Manuscript' in Swift's *Miscellanies: The Last Volume* (1728), and first acknowledged by Pope in his *Works* of 1736. Pope's imitation was itself translated in a similar manner to that deployed by poets when rendering

---

[15] Prior's modern editors omit the first poem, noting that it is attributed to Samuel Cobb in *Poems on Several Occasions, By the Earls of Roscommon and Dorset* (1721) (see Matthew Prior, *Literary Works*, ed. H. Bunker Wright and Monroe K. Spears, 2 vols [2nd edn, Oxford, 1971], 2. 928).

[16] Henry Felton, *A Dissertation on Reading the Classics, and Forming a Just Style* (London, 1713), 210–11.

SUSANNAH and the Two ELDERS,

IN

Imitation of *CHAUCER*.

By Mr. PRIOR.

FAIR SUSAN did her Wifehode
    (Well maintaine,
Algates assaulted sore by Leachers
    (twaine:
Now, an' I reade aryghte that auncient
    (Song,
The Paramours were Olde, the Dame
    (was Yong.

Had thilke same Tale in other guise
    (bene tolde,
Had they been Yong (pardie) and she bene
    (Olde,
Sweet Jesu! that had bene much sore
    (Trevaile;
Full Marvaillous, I wot, were such
    (Devaile!

H   SU.

SUSANNAH and the Two ELDERS,

Attempted in a

MODERN STILE.

WHEN Fair SUSANNAH in a cool retreat
    Of shady Arbours shun'd the Sultry heat.
Two wanton Lechers to her Garden came,
And, rushing furious, seiz'd the trembling Dame.
What Female Strength could do, her Arms perform,
And guarded well the Fort they strove to Storm.
The Story's ancient, and, if rightly told,
Young was the Lady, but the Lovers Old.

Had the Reverse been true, had Authors Sung,
How that the Dame was *Old*, the Lovers *Young*.
If She had then the blooming Pair deny'd,
With tempting Youth and Vigour on their side,
Lord! How the Story would have shock'd my
    (Creed!
For that had been a Miracle indeed.

Fig. 6.1 From 'Susannah and the Two Elders', attributed to Matthew Prior, and printed in black letter in *The Carpenter of Oxford … and Two Imitations of Chaucer …* (London, 1712).

Chaucer's genuine poems. Here is Pope's original, from the 1728 text, alongside the anonymous translation from *A New Miscellany in Prose and Verse* (1742). The translator has curtailed the narrative but extended the moral:

A Tale of Chaucer. Lately found in an old Manuscript.

Women, tho'nat sans Leacherie,
Ne swinken but with Secrecie:
This in our Tale is plain y-found,
Of Clerk, that wonneth in *Irelond*:
Which to the Fennes hath him betake,
To filch the gray Ducke fro the Lake.
Right then, there passen by the Way
His Aunt, and eke her Daughters tway.
Ducke in his Trowzes hath he hent,
Not to be spied of Ladies gent.
'But ho! our Nephew, (crieth one,)
'Ho! quoth another, Cozen *John*;
And stoppen, and lough, and callen out,—
This sely Clerk full low doth lout:

A Translation, in modern English, of Mr. P—'s Imitation of Chaucer

An *Oxford* Scholar made a Goose his Prize,
And hid it where the Garb invests his Thighs;
Too weak the Buttons prov'd the Goose too strong,
And burst its Jail as Ladies past along;
The Bill came bolting forth, a ruddy Sight,
The neck came after, long, and round, and white;
The Creature cackling, pertly rais'd its Head,
The Lad look'd foolish, and the Women fled.
'O Jesu! Sister *Moll*, said wanton Miss,
'Is this the Thing wherewith they use to p—-?
''Tis better far to feed on Coals, on Chalk,
'Than trust to faithless Man who's Tail can *talk*.'
Thus *Chaucer* whilom did the Fair advise,
That Maids should never sport but with the Wise.

They asken that, and talken this,
'Lo here is *Coz*, and here is *Miss*.
But, as he glozeth with Speeches soote,
The Ducke sore tickleth his Erse Roote:
Fore-piece and Buttons all-to-brest,
Forth thrust a white Neck, and red Crest.
Te-he <u>cry'd</u> Ladies: Clerke nought spake:
Miss star'd; and gray Ducke crieth *Quaake*.
'O Moder, Moder, (quoth the Daughter,)
'Be thilke same Thing Maids longer a'ter?
'Bette is to pyne on Coals and chalke,
'Then trust on Mon, whose yerde can *talke*.

With sly Conceit, the Bard his Story told,
Then left this Moral, worth its Weight in Gold:
'*Pardie*, Miss *Betty*, thou didst reason well;
'They bear the Goose about that love to *tell*.

(*Miscellanies* (1728), p. 44; Pope,
Poems, 6. 41–2)

(*A New Miscellany in Prose and Verse*
[London, 1742], pp. 51–3)

Two of Pope's lines echo genuine Chaucerian poems. One ('His Aunt, and <u>eke her Daughters tway</u>') is a close reflection of the description of the old woman in *The Nun's Priest's Tale* ('She fond her self, & <u>eke her daughters two</u>'). In the other, the Ladies' exclamation *Te-he* recalls that of Alison in *The Miller's Tale*. Joseph Warton described Pope's imitation as 'A gross and dull caricature of the father of English poetry, and very unworthy of our author at any age'.[17] Valerie Rumbold observes that this 'anecdote' 'transgresses accepted norms in every way [the young Pope] can devise: its plot is disjointed, its subject indecent, its syntax and reflections chaotic, and its metre hobbling'.[18] But in Rumbold's view the incoherence of 'A Tale of Chaucer' was deliberate: a caricature of 'Gothic' art which at the same time was perhaps designed to convey some sense of its exuberance.

Alexander Pope, *January and May*

No two poems, however, could be more unlike than Pope's pseudo-Chaucerian imitation and *January and May, or, The Merchant's Tale from Chaucer*, parts of which were included in the 'Popeana' section in Curll's *The Altar of Love* (London, 1727), but which had been initially published in its entirety in the Sixth Part of Tonson's *Poetical Miscellanies* (1709), as well as in *The Works of Mr. Alexander Pope* (1717), where it was sumptuously presented and headed by an illustrative fleuron, to the design of which Pope himself may have contributed (see Fig. 6.2). Although in a later printing of 1736 the poem is classed with Pope's other imitations (of Spenser and Waller and Cowley), this was clearly a poem of a different kind. Where *A Tale of Chaucer* suggests that Chaucer's poetry was non-sequential,

[17] *The Works of Alexander Pope*, ed. Joseph Warton, 9 vols (London, 1797), 2. 276.
[18] Valerie Rumbold, 'Pope and the Gothic Past', unpublished PhD dissertation, University of Cambridge, 1983, 77–8.

Fig. 6.2 A fleuron, engraved by Simon Gribelin, and possibly based on Pope's own design, for *January and May*, in Pope's *Works* (London, 1717).

awkward in movement, and broadly obscene, *January and May* points in a quite different direction, signalling that Chaucer was highly sophisticated, a master of sustained irony, who deployed the whole range of poetic tones and could mingle indecency of action with surprising profundity of thought.

Pope's version of *The Merchant's Tale* is characteristic of many of the eighteenth-century versions (as opposed to 'imitations') of Chaucer, in that the poet's main attention is devoted to vividly rendered *deeds*—presented in the fulness of their absurdity—rather than to replicating Chaucerian *diction*. In the case of *The Merchant's Tale,* Pope's interest in low words or indecent sexual detail was markedly less than that of one earlier reader of Chaucer's poem—the scribe who, assuming that *throng* ('thrust') was transitive, provided the lines in Speght's text—now rejected by editors—which contain the youthful May's precise physical comparisons between the genital tumescence of her young lover and January, her decrepit husband:

> & in he throng
> A great tent,[19] a thrifty and a long
> She said it was the merriest fit
> That euer in her life she was at yet
> My lordes tent serueth me nothing thus
> It foldeth twifolde by swete Jesus
> He may nat swiue woth a leke
> And yet he is full gentil and ful meke
> That is leuer to me than an euensong.
>
> (*MerT*, 2350–3; Speght 1598, Sig.32ʳ⁻ᵛ)

---

[19] *tente:* 'A probe. Also fig. Obs' (*OED*).

Pope is at this moment far more decorous:

> But sure it was a merrier Fit, she swore,
> Than in her Life she ever felt before.
>
> *(January and May*, 746–7; Pope, *Poems*, 2. 51)

And yet, while better mannered than the scribe, Pope seems to have taken the scribal *merriest fit* as the key note, adopting the scribe's curious and fanciful notion that the narrator has been told by May at some unspecified later date what her impressions were at the time. Pope's emphasis in his retelling of the tale is on the sexual act as a contribution to *merriment*, both of some of the participants in the action and of his readers. He has also rendered the indecency less conventional than the scribe, in that what makes January's love-making intolerable is not impotence—the usual story—but relentless insatiability. When the married couple are brought to bed, Pope refuses to comment: 'What next ensu'd beseems not me to say; /'Tis sung, he labour'd 'till the dawning Day'.[20]

When, at the tale's climax, January reacts to May's suggestion that her current position is the result of her having been told that she would restore her husband's sight 'By Struling with a Man upon a Tree', (see Fig. 6.3) a scribe whose wording is again preserved in Speght's edition—but is again rejected by modern editors—felt an irresistible itch to elaborate—and Pope again retrenched:

Strogle (qd he) ye algate in it went	If this be Struggling, by this holy Light,
[Stiffe and rounde as any bell	'Tis Struling with a Vengeance, (quoth the Knight:)
It is no wonder though thy bely swell	So Heav'n preserve the Sight it has restor'd,
The smocke on his brest lay so thecke	As with these Eyes I plainly saw thee whor'd;
And euer me thought he pointed on ye Breche]	Whor'd by my Slave—Perfidious Wretch! may Hell
God giue both on shames deth to dieen	As surely seize thee, as I saw too well.
(*MerT*, 2376–7; Speght 1598, Fol. 32ʳ)	*(January and May*, 766–71; Pope, *Poems*, 2. 52)

January is given a pithy and witty response. But Pope's main emphasis is on May's extraordinary powers of self-exculpation, which are revelled in and almost applauded, than on the indecency and outrageousness of the adulterous act itself. January has had more immediately visual evidence than would be possible in almost any other situation. His certainty is absolute (even if not quite as graphically verified as in Speght's text), but he is talked out of that certainty with remarkable ease—though in Pope's version with the addition of some tears from May:

Ye mase ye mase, good sire (qd she)	By all those Pow'rs, some Frenzy seiz'd your Mind,
This thanke haue I for that I made you se	(Reply'd the Dame:) Are these the Thanks I find?
Allas (qd she) that euer I was so kinde	Wretch that I am, that e'er I was so Kind! ...
Now dame (qd he) let all passe out of minde	She said; a rising Sigh express'd her Woe,
Come doun my lefe, and if I haue missaide	The ready Tears apace began to flow,

---

[20] *January and May*, 383–4; Pope, *Poems*, 2. 33.

Fig. 6.3 'January and May, Damien in the Tree', by John Hamilton Mortimer
(engraved 1787).

God helpe me so, as I am yuel apaide
But by my fathers soule, I wende haue seyn
How that this Damian had by the lyen
And that thy smoke had lien upon his brest

And as they fell, she wip'd from either Eye
The Drops, (for Women, when they list, can cry.)
The Knight was touch'd, and in his Looks appear'd
Signs of Remorse, while thus his Spouse he chear'd:
Come down, and vex your tender Heart no more:
Excuse me, Dear, if aught amiss was said,
For, on my Soul, amends shall soon be made:

Let my Repentance your Forgiveness draw,
By Heav'n, I swore but what I *thought* I saw.

(*MerT*, 2387–95; Speght 1598, Fol. 32ᵛ)

(*January and May*, 780–94;
Pope, *Poems*, 2. 52–3)

Pope has given all his young skill and the benefit of his already extensive reading (along with one alexandrine) to young May in her appeal to January's Reason to reject the evidence of his eyes:[21]

May as Pope recreates her is inspired. She speaks and acts exactly as she has been prompted to act by the presiding deity, the Queen of the Fairies:

… be my mothers soule sir I swere …	For her, and for her Daughters I'll ingage, …
That though they been in any gilt itake	And all the Sex in each succeeding Age,
With face bolde, they shullen hem selue excuse	Art shall be theirs to varnish an Offence,
And bere hem down, that would hem accuse	And fortify their Crimes with Confidence.
For lacke of answere, non of hem shull die,	Nay, were they taken in a strict Embrace,
All had he sey a thing with both his eyen	Seen with both Eyes, and pinion'd on the Place,
Yet should we women so uisage is hardely	All they shall need is to protest, and swear,
And wepe and swere, and chide subtelly	Breathe a soft Sigh, and drop a tender Tear;
That ye shall ben as leude as gees	'Till their wise Husbands, gull'd by Arts like these,
	Grow gentle, tractable, and tame as Geese.

(*MerT*, 2265–75; Speght 1598, Fol. 32ʳ)   (*January and May*, 659–68; Pope, *Poems*, 2. 46–7)

The power of easy exculpation even from the most incriminating of circumstances, the Queen declares, is granted to all women of all times.

The Fairie Way of Writing

Pope has curtailed Chaucer's poem in several places. But he has elaborated with some pleasure the role of the divinities that control the outcome. One of the places where Pope seems to have considered Chaucer to be entering into conversation with other poets of earlier and later times occurs in the description of January's garden—and, most importantly, its inhabitants. Thomas Tyrwhitt, in uncharacteristically fanciful mood, made a connection between the fairy gods of *The Merchant's Tale* and those of *A Midsummer Night's Dream*—a connection in which he was anticipated by Pope, who had removed the names of the classical deities:

Whatever was the real original of this Tale, the Machinery of the Faeries, which Chaucer has used so happily, was probably added by himself; and indeed, I cannot

---

[21] For May's reference to the 'Imperfect Objects' that can 'beguile' the 'Sense' (798), compare Canto 4 of Samuel Garth, *The Dispensary* (London, 1714), p. 49; for January's 'swimming Eyes' (803), compare Dryden, *The State of Innocence*, III. i. 44; Dryden, *Works* 12. 114 (Eve describing her first sexual ecstasy); for possible sources for the mock-heroic effect of her description of how 'dusky Vapors rise, and intercept the Day' (801), see Book 4 of *Aeneid* in Richard Maitland, Earl of Lauderdale, trans., *The Works of Virgil* (London, [1709]), p. 156 ('dusky vapours' also feature in Shakespeare (*1 Henry VI*, I. ii. 27) and Richard Blackmore, *Prince Arthur* (4th edn, London, 1714), p. 139.

help thinking, that his *Pluto* and *Proserpina* were the true progenitors of *Oberon* and *Titania*, or rather, that they themselves have, once at least, deigned to revisit our poetical system under the latter names.[22]

Taking his hint from the suggestion that a goddess was accompanied by a fairy band, Pope brings together Chaucer, Spenser, Shakespeare, Milton, and Dryden in a description of what he is unable to describe. January's 'spacious Garden' is evoked by Pope as:

> A Place to tire the rambling Wits of *France*
> In long Descriptions, and exceed *Romance*;
> Enough to shame the gentlest Bard that sings
> Of painted Meadows, and of purling Springs.
>
> *(January and May,* 452–5; Pope, *Poems,* 2. 36–7)

Pope's declared avoidance of 'long Descriptions' that 'exceed *Romance*' and would 'tire the rambling Wits of France' alludes to Boileau's advice to avoid the 'barren Superfluity' of lengthy descriptive passages, to Pope's own mock-commendation of 'long Descriptions' in *A Receit to Make an Epic Poem*, and to Joseph Addison's declaration in his *Letter from Italy* that his 'softer theme' demands 'A painted meadow, or a purling stream'.[23]

Fairies are not diminutive creatures in medieval writing. In his description of the inhabitants of the garden, Pope combines echoes of the 'pert Fairies' and 'dapper elves' of Milton's *Comus* with the 'gambolling' of the fairies from the opening of Dryden's version of *The Wife of Bath's Tale*.[24] Similar powers of poetic assimilation by Pope are present when the gods are finally encountered more intimately:

Bright was the day, & blew the firmamēt	'Twas now the Season, when the glorious Sun
Phebus of gold doun hath his streames sent	His Heav'nly Progress thro' the *Twins* had run;
To gladen euery flour with his warmenesse	And *Jove*, Exalted, his mild Influence yields,
He was that time in Gemini, as I gesse	To glad the Glebe, and paint the flow'ry Fields.
But little fro his declination	Clear was the Day, and *Phoebus* rising bright,
The causer of Iouis exaltacion	Had streak'd the azure Firmament with Light;
And so befell that bright morow tide	He pierc'd the glitt'ring Clouds with Golden Streams,
That in the garden, on the further side	And warm'd the Womb of Earth with Genial Beams.
Pluto, that is the king of Fayrie	It so befel, in that fair Morning-tide,
And many a ladie in his companie	The Fairies sported on the Garden's Side,
Following his wife, the quene Proserpine	And, in the midst, the Monarch and his Bride.
[Ech after other right as a line]	So featly tripp'd the light-foot Ladies round,
Whiles she gadred floures in a mede	The Knights so nimbly o'er the Greensward bound,

---

[22] Tyrwhitt 1775–78, 4. 161.

[23] See *The Art of Poetry*, trans. Sir William Soame and John Dryden (1683) (1. 59–60; Dryden, *Works*, 2. 125); *The Guardian*, No. 78 (Alexander Pope, *Prose Works*, ed. Norman Ault and Rosemary Cowler, 2 vols (Oxford, 1936–86), 1. 117; Joseph Addison, 'A Letter from Italy', in *Poetical Miscellanies: The Fifth Part* (London, 1704), p. 12.

[24] See *A Maske Presented at Ludlow Castle, 1634* [*Comus*], 118; Dryden, *The Wife of Bath Her Tale*, 3–4 (Dryden, *Works*, 7. 451).

In Claudian ye may the story read,	That scarce they bent the Flow'rs, or touch'd the Ground.
How in his grisely cart he her fette	The Dances ended, all the Fairy Train
This king of Fayry doune him sette	For Pinks and Daisies search'd the flow'ry Plain:
Vpon a bench of turues fresh and greene	While on a Bank reclin'd of rising Green,
And right anon thus said he to his queen.	Thus, with a Frown, the King bespoke his Queen.
My wife (qd. he) that may nat say nay	'Tis too apparent, argue what you can,
Experience so proueth it euery day	The Treachery you Women use to Man.
The treason, which that women doth	
to man.	
(MerT, 2219–39; Speght 1598, Fol. 31ᵛ)	(January and May, 609–28; Pope, Poems, 2. 44–5)

Observing that Chaucer's 'Phebus … hath his streames sent' to 'gladen euery flour with his warmenesse', Pope recalled the opening of Dryden's *The Flower and the Leaf*, 'Where Venus from her Orb descends in Show'rs / To glad the ground and paint the Fields with Flow'rs'.[25] Pope's 'light-foot Ladies' trip 'featly' like the Ladies in Dryden's *The Wife of Bath Her Tale*.[26] The 'Womb of Earth' that is warmed with 'genial Beams' may owe something to Cowley, who in his Ode 'The Resurrection' had described '*Showers*' parenthetically as '*Heav'ens* vital *seed* cast on the *womb* of *Earth* / To give the *fruitful Year a Birth*'.[27] To this, Dryden, in his translation of Virgil's Second Georgic, had added that the seeds were 'genial' ('fecund, propagative'): 'The spring adorns the woods, renews the leaves; / The womb of earth the genial seed receives'.[28]

Similar poetic care on Pope's part is evident when the gods now speak. To have pagan gods dispute the Old Testament had struck some readers as deeply improper. It is hardly less so to hear Solomon abused by the Queen of the Fairies, who speaks, at this moment, almost as the sister of the Wife of Bath. This is an extreme example of Collier's 'Lewd Application of Scripture':

I wote well this Iewe, this Salomon	What tho' this sland'rous *Jew*, this *Solomon*,
Fonde of us women, foles many one	Call'd Women Fools, and knew full many a one?
But though he ne fonde no good woman	The wiser Wits of later Times declare
Yet there hath ifonde many another man	How virtuous, chast, and constant, Women are …
Women ful true, full good, & full virtuous.	
(MerT, 2277–81; Speght 1598, Fol. 32ʳ)	(January and May, 669–72; Pope, Poems, 2. 47)

The indecorum of *January and May* at such moments is an indissoluble compound of levity and near profanity. Obscenity resides only in the Fairy Queen's calling King Solomon 'a rank Leacher', and (an addition of Pope's) in praising the amorous propensities of King David. She speaks self-declaredly and unashamedly

[25] Dryden, *The Flower and the Leaf*, 5–6; Dryden, *Works*, 7. 365.
[26] Dryden: 'He saw a Quire of *Ladies* in a round, / That featly footing seem'd to skim the Ground' (*The Wife of Bath Her Tale*, 215–16; Dryden, *Works*, 7. 463); cp. Ariel in Shakespeare, *The Tempest*, I. ii. 380.
[27] Abraham Cowley, 'The Resurrection', in *Poems*, ed. A. R. Waller (Cambridge, 1905), p. 182, stanza 1.
[28] Dryden, *The Second Book of the Georgics*, 438–9; Dryden, *Works*, 5. 195. George Ogle (1. 1) was to draw on Pope's spring to open his version of the *General Prologue* in an invocation to 'April! That bathes the teeming Womb of *Earth*, / And gives, to Vegetation, kindly Birth!'

as a woman—constitutionally unable to hold her tongue and an enemy of all constraint:

Eye, for very God that nis but one
What make ye so much of Salomon?
What though he made a tēple goddes house?
What though he were rich and glorious?
So made he a temple of false goddes
How might he don a thing, y[t] more forbod is
Parde as faire as ye his name emplaster
He was a lechour, and an idolaster,
And in his elde, very God forsooke
And if that God nadde (as saith the boke)
Yspared him for his fathers sake, he should
Haue lost his reigne soner than he wolde
  I set nat of all the villany
That ye of women write, a butterflie
I am a woman, needs mote I speke
Or els swell, til that mine hert breke
For sithen he said, that we been iangleresses
As euer mote I hole broke my tresses
I shall not spare for no curtesy
To speke hem harme, that would us villany
  Dame (qd this Pluto) be no lenger wroth,
I giue it up ...

But grant the worst, shall Women then be weigh'd
By ev'ry Word that *Solomon* has said?
What tho' this King (as *Hebrew* boasts)
Built a fair Temple to the Lord of Hosts;
He ceas'd at last his Maker to adore,
And did as much for Idol-Gods, or more.
Beware what lavish Praises you confer
On a rank Leacher and Idolater,
Whose Reign Indulgent God, says Holy Writ,
Did but for *David's* Righteous Sake permit;
David, the Monarch after Heav'ns' own Mind,
Who lov'd our Sex, and honour'd all our Kind.
  Well, I'm a Woman, and as such must speak;
Silence wou'd swell me, and my Heart wou'd break.
Know then, I scorn your dull Authorities,
Your idle Wits, and all their Learned Lies.
By Heav'n, those Authors are our Sexe's Foes,
Whom, in our Right, I must, and will oppose.
  Nay, (quoth the King) dear Madam be not wroth;
I yield it up ...

(MerT, 2291–312; Speght 1598, Fol. 32[r])   (*January and May*, 682–701; Pope, *Poems*, 2. 48)

One large difference between *January and May* and *The Merchant's Tale* is the quantity of argument and thought given in the former to the Fairy Queen and the young wife, without obvious disapproval or blatant mockery, while January's thoughts are mocked continuously, if obliquely. In the Fairy Queen's praise of David, Pope was recalling Dryden's *Absalom and Achitophel*.[29] In both poems, 'Heavn's own Mind' is to be followed in a generous bestowing of love on women. The indecorum and indecency reside principally in Pope's hint that the young of either sex are everywhere preferable to the old, and that young women prefer young lovers to old husbands. The conventional decencies are transformed when the tale ends with an apparently unalloyed happiness that is in fact grounded in deception—a conclusion that, in its comic challenge to conventional notions of the relative importance of things—is as satisfying as it is surprising:

> With that, she leap'd into her Lord's Embrace,
> With well-dissembl'd Virtue in her Face:
> He hugg'd her close, and kiss'd her o'er and o'er,
> Disturb'd with Doubts and Jealousies no more:
> Both, pleas'd and blest, renew'd their mutual Vows,
> A fruitful Wife, and a believing Spouse.

[29] Dryden, *Absalom and Achitophel*, 7–10; Dryden, *Works*, 2. 5.

Thus ends our Tale, whose Moral next to make,
Let all wise Husbands hence Example take;
And pray, to crown the Pleasures of their Lives,
To be so well deluded by their Wives.

(*January and May*, 811–20; Pope, *Poems*, 2. 54)

This prayer for happy delusion is more extreme than the interjection of the Wife of Bath at the end of her tale as rendered by Dryden—of which Pope's lines are an echo:

And so may all our Lives like their's be led;
Heav'n send the Maids young Husbands, fresh in Bed:
May Widows Wed as often as they can,
And ever for the better change their Man.
And some devouring Plague pursue their Lives,
Who will not well be govern'd by their Wives.

(*The Wife of Bath Her Tale*, 541–6; Dryden, *Works*, 7. 481–3)

Pope's description of January as a 'believing Spouse' and his suggestion that husbandly pleasures are crowned by being 'well deluded' have put many readers in mind of 'A Digression Concerning the Original, the Use and Improvement of Madness in a Commonwealth', in Jonathan Swift's *A Tale of a Tub* (1704):

When a Man's Fancy gets *astride* on his Reason, when Imagination is at Cuffs with the Senses, and common Understanding, as well as common Sense, is Kickt out of Doors; the first Proselyte he makes, is Himself ... Those Entertainments and Pleasures we most value in Life, are such as *Dupe* and play the Wag with the Senses ... what is generally understood by *Happiness ... is a perpetual Possession of Being well Deceived.*[30]

It has been suggested, however, that a closer match to the ending of *January and May*, and thus to the poem as a whole, may be found in *Witt against Wisdom* (1683), White Kennett's translation of the *Praise of Folly*, by Desiderius Erasmus, an author whom Pope greatly admired. Particularly pertinent are the moments when Folly praises her own essential role in the origination, preservation, and continuance of marriage. 'Good God!', she cries,

What frequent divorces, or worse mischief, would oft sadly happen, except man, and wife were so discreet as to pass over light occasions of quarrel with laughing, jesting, dissembling, and such like playing the fool? Nay, how few matches would go forward, if the hasty lover did but first know how many little tricks of lust, and wantonness (and perhaps more gross failings) his coy, and seemingly bashful Mistress had oft before been guilty of? and how fewer marriages, when consummated, would continue happy, if the husband were not either sottishly insensible of, or did not purposely wink at, and pass over the lightness and forwardnes of his good-natur'd wife?[31]

---

[30] Jonathan Swift, *A Tale of a Tub and Other Works*, ed. Marcus Walsh (Cambridge, 2010), 110–11.
[31] See Philip Smallwood, 'Great Anna's Chaucer: Pope's *January and May* and the Logic of Settlement', in *Queen Anne and the Arts*, ed. Cedric D. Reverand II (Lewisburg, PA, 2015), 99–117. For Pope's admiration of Erasmus, see *An Essay on Criticism*, 693–6; Pope, *Poems*, 1. 318–19.

The sting in Pope's description of May as a now 'fruitful Wife' may be a reflection of Folly's contention that 'This peace and quietnes is owing to my management, for there would otherwise be continual jars, and broils, and mad doings, if want of wit only did not at the same time make a contented cuckold, and a still house.'[32] Pope recounts (813–14) how January 'hugg'd' May 'close, and kiss'd her o'er and o'er, / Disturb'd with Doubts and Jealousies no more'. Erasmus's Folly describes a similar state of happy delusion:

> if the *Cuckow* sing at the back door, the unthinking Cornute takes no notice of the unlucky *omen* of *others eggs being laid in his own nest*, but laughs it over, kisses his dear spouse, and all is well. And indeed it is much better patiently to be such a hen-peckt frigot,[33] than alway to be wrack'd and tortur'd with the grating surmises of suspicion and jealousie.[34]

Such thoughts, such attitudes are only to be found in comic expression—most effectively of all, perhaps, when emerging from a comic narrative poem. Although Collier might have been appalled at the suggestion that inspired artfulness rather than 'Modesty' is 'the *Character* of Women', it seems to have been wildly fanciful comedy rather than obscenity that Pope was (re)producing in *January and May*. Although Pope makes no attempt to avoid or palliate the central event—an act of adulterous fornication in a tree—which is indeed the poem's comic core, there is little in fact in the language of *January and May* at which an eighteenth-century virgin need hide her face.

True Humour, Merriment, and Indecency in *The Miller's Tale*

That this was the case is suggested by the inclusion of Pope's poem in the Rev. William Lipscomb's collected *Canterbury Tales of Chaucer* (1795). In his preliminaries, Lipscomb expressed his intention of 'purging [Chaucer] from his impurities' and 'exhibiting him free from stains'.[35] The Miller and the Reeve have simply vanished from his volume, but *January and May* appears ungelded and complete, suggesting that, unlike Pope's version of *The Wife of Bath's Prologue*, it was felt to be unexceptionable, indeed unsurpassable.

In his *History of English Poetry*, Thomas Warton observed that Dryden and Pope had translated *The Nun's Priest's Tale* and *The Merchant's Tale* as examples of the best of Chaucer's tales in the 'comic species'. He suggested, however, that *The Miller's Tale* 'has more true humour' than either of these tales. But he immediately

---

[32] White Kennett, *Witt against Wisdom, or a Panegyrick upon Folly, Penn'd in Latin by Desiderius Erasmus* (Oxford, 1683) 25–6.
[33] A person of cold or passive temperament.
[34] Kennett, *Witt against Wisdom*, p. 26.
[35] Lipscomb, 1. ix.

qualified that claim, saying that he will not 'palliate the levity of the Story', which reflects 'the prevailing manners of an unpolished age', and is 'agreeable to ideas of festivity not always the most delicate and refined'.[36] Warton shies away from the contemplation of this tale even in the process of enjoying it. His detailed comments on *The Miller's Tale* draw attention to the 'lively circumstances' in the description of Nicholas, and the 'elegance with a mixture of burlesque allusions' in the description of 'the young wife'. Although maintaining that 'the humour of the characters is made subservient to the plot', Warton is unable to speak of the 'humorous contrivance' which 'crowns the scholar's schemes with success': it 'cannot be repeated here'.[37]

There were, however, several attempts to translate *The Miller's Tale* in the eighteenth century, and the translators' responses show that the pleasures they found in this obviously indecent tale were continuous with those experienced by several of their predecessors.[38] In 1687, a drastically shortened version of *The Miller's Tale* had been included in a volume entitled *Canterbury Tales: Composed for the Entertainment of all Ingenuous Young Men and Maids at Their Merry Meetings ... By Chaucer Junior*. Despite its brevity, this version does include some salient details. 'Chaucer Junior' employs direct speech at the point at which Nicholas deceives the carpenter:

> It happened that the Carpenter miss'd his Boarder upon a time, and searching about, found him in a Cock-loft, looking up towards the Skie: what's the matter, quoth he? Oh says the Gentleman, I find by Astrology that on Monday next at quarter-night, there will fall such a Prodigious Rain that *Noah*'s Flood was not half so great; therefore get quickly three Bucking-Tubs that we may get into them, and tye them to the top of the Garret, that we may save our Lives.

There is also some descriptive specificity. The carpenter falls asleep 'after much sighing'. And 'Chaucer Junior' expands on Chaucer's original to suggest how the conjunction between Alison's posterior and Absalom's lips was made:

> At length, she opens the Window, and desires what he does to do quickly: now the night was very dark, and she felt about till she found him.

Some hint of an apology is provided for one central incident: 'and to tell the Tale neither better nor worse; he very savourly kiss'd her bare Arse'. The only detail entirely added is the somewhat cruel one that the carpenter, having fallen from the rafters to the floor, 'be[pi]ss'd his Breeches'.[39]

---

[36] Warton, *History*, 1. 423.

[37] Warton, *History*, 1. 425, 426, 431.

[38] For a useful discussion of various reactions to *The Miller's Tale*, and particularly the indecency therein (and ways of avoiding it), see Mary Flowers Braswell, '"A Completely Funny Story": Mary Eliza Haweis and The Miller's Tale', *Chaucer Review*, 42 (2008), 244–68.

[39] *Canterbury Tales: Composed for the Entertainment of all Ingenious Young Men and Maids at their Merry Making Meetings...by Chaucer Junior* (London, 1687) Sigs A4ᵛ–A5ʳ.

Such tiny additions, however, represent a common reaction. Many readers seem to have enjoyed Chaucer's indecent poems by adding little jokes of their own, drawing attention to details and to *sententiae*, and sometimes relishing the very profanity so vehemently deplored by Collier. In his retort to the Reeve during their interchange following *The Knight's Tale*, Chaucer's Miller, voicing sentiments not unlike those that conclude *January and May*, asserts that 'An husband should not been inquisitife / Of Goddes privete; ne of his wife / For so he find Goddes foison [plenty] there, / Of the remnaunt nedeth not to enquere'. Though the effrontery of the comparison, like the Queen of the Fairies' complaints against Solomon in *January and May* is self-evident, Alexander Pope, in his copy of Speght's edition, marked this passage for special approval.[40]

Richard Brathwaite, in his *Comment upon the Two Tales of Our Ancient, Renowned, and Ever-Living Poet Sir Jeffray Chaucer* (1665), had praised the same lines as follows:

> An excellent Rule of direction, including a twofold Precept. First, Not to pry too curiously into the secret Cabinet of God's Divine Will. Secondly, Not to be too jealously inquisitive after the Actions of his Wife. For the former, as it is an Argument of too daring presumption; so the later, of weakness and indiscretion.[41]

In Deuteronomy (29:29), it is said that 'the secret things belong unto the Lord our God', but Collier would no doubt have considered it outrageously profane for Brathwaite to have spoken of 'the secret Cabinet of God's Divine Will' in the particular context of Chaucer's bawdy tale.

Samuel Cobb, *The Carpenter of Oxford, Or The Miller's Tale from Chaucer* (1712)

Samuel Cobb's version of *The Miller's Tale* expands upon almost every detail of Chaucer's original, while respecting the connotations of Chaucer's words. When the carpenter is in Oseney, Nicholas, in Cobb's version 'Began to sport and wanton with his Dame'

And priuily he caught her by the queint	And privily he caught her by *That same*.
And saied: I wis but I haue my will,	My Lemman dear (quoth he) I'm all on fire,
For derne loue of thee lemman I spill:	And perish, if you grant not my desire.
And held her full fast by the haunch bones,	He claspt her round, and held her fast, and cry'd
And saied: lemman loue me well at ones,	O let me, let me—never be deny'd.
Or I woll dien also God me saue.	
(*MilT*, 3276–81; Speght 1687, p. 27)	(Samuel Cobb, *The Carpenter of Oxford*, [London, 1712], p. 7)

---

[40] See Maynard Mack, *Collected in Himself: Essays Critical, Biographical, and Bibliographical on Pope and Some of His Contemporaries* (Newark, DE, 1982), p. 187.

[41] Richard Brathwaite, *A Comment upon the Two Tales of Our Ancient, Renowned, and Ever-Living Poet Sr Jeffray Chaucer* (London, 1665), p. 5.

It is difficult to gauge the level of indecency attaching to Cobb's phrase '*That same*', which could be used apparently for both the male and female sexual parts, or for the sexual act itself. Cobb was perhaps attempting to maintain a kind of equilibrium, suggesting that Nicholas's *act* is indecent, while avoiding the indecent *language* of Chaucer's original.

Other versions, however, saw the Miller as *insufficiently* indecent. In the only-would-be-delicate mouth of John Smith's Nicholas, the language of and delicate love becomes something altogether lascivious:

> For Love of You (says he) I inly mourn,
> All night I languish, and all day I burn.

At the same time, Smith has made Nicholas's wooing more openly and elaborately physical and sexual, and draws attention to this in what he appears to see as the centre of the tale. In his version, Nicholas 'squeez'd her heaving Breast' and then 'wantonly he stole down by degrees' pressing her 'swelling Thigh then grasp'd her knees / Till his impatient Hand like Lightning flew / To a strange Place—which scarce her Husband knew'. Here Smith elaborates:

> (There He had been indeed, but been in vain,
> Gave Her small Pleasure, and Himself much Pain)
>> (John Smith, *Poems upon Several Occasions*
>> [London, 1713], pp. 315–16)

The anonymous author of *The Miller's Tale from Chaucer* (1791) expands Chaucer's original even further than had Smith:

And prively he caught her by the queint,	They kiss'd, caress'd—the mounting blood grew warm—
And sayde; Ywis, but if I have my will,	Beneath her stays he thrust his lecherous arm—
For derne love to thee, lemman, I spill.	Fast round her supple loins one hand he prest,
And helde hire fase by the haunche bones,	And with the other grasp'd her heaving breast—
And side; Lemman, love me wel at ones,	And 'bless me now,' he cried, 'with all your charms
Or I wol dien, al so God me save.	'Meet all my wishes with luxurious arms—
	'Or kill me with your frown—
(*MilT*, 3276–81; Tyrwhitt 1775–78, 1. 128)	(*The Miller's Tale from Chaucer*, 85–91; Bowden,
	Eighteenth-Century Modernizations, p. 17)

At the moment of consummation itself, the old and deluded carpenter has been working all day at the weary business of constructing three great tubs which he has suspended from the rafters of his house, and in one of which he is situated. His wife, Alison and her would-be lover, Nicholas, are in adjacent tubs. Here is this moment in Cobb's version:

The deed sleep, for wery besinesse	And now at *Curfew* time, dead Sleep began
Fel on this carpenter, right as I gesse	To fall upon this easy, simple Man.
About curfewe time, or litell more	Who, after so much care and business past,
For trauaile of his goste he groneth sore	And spent with sad concern, was quickly fast.
And eft he routeth, for his heed mislay	Soft down the Ladder stole this Loving Pair,
And doun of ỹ ladder than stalketh Nicholay	Good NICHOLAS, and ALISON the Fair;

And Alisoun ful softe after she spedde	Then without speaking to the Bed they creep
Without words mo they went to bedde	Of JOHN, poor Cuckold! Who was fast asleep.
Ther as the carpenter was woned to lye	There all the Night they revel, sport, and toy,
There was the reuel, and the melody	And act the merry Scene of Amorous Joy:
And thus lyeth Alison and Nicholas	Till that the Bell of *Lauds* began to ring,
In besinesse of mirthe and solas	And the fat Fryars in the Chancel sing.
Til that the bel of laudes gan to ring	
And freres in the chauncell gan sing.	
(*MilT*, 3642–56; Speght 1598, Fols 13ᵛ–14ʳ)	(Cobb, *The Carpenter of Oxford*, pp. 31–2)

Cobb's treatment of the scene is indecorous, in that it records an act of adultery emphasized by the interjection 'JOHN, poor Cuckold!', which reinforces Chaucer's observation that the place of sin is the bed where, very specifically, the carpenter was wont to lie. Cobb appears to have read two of Chaucer's lines, which in many modern editions are separated by a full stop, as a couplet: 'Ther as the carpenter was woned to lye / Ther was the reuel, and the melody'. Cobb's version is perhaps most strikingly indecent because of the complete absence, of condemnation (as in Chaucer) as the adulterous couple 'act the merry Scene of Amorous Joy'.

John Smith is more interested in the carpenter at this point, incorporating John's snoring and the travails of his ghost. But he then elaborates, with obvious excitement at what he calls 'the melting Pastime':

The dead sleepe, for wery businesse	In Death-like Sleep the *Carpenter* soon lay,
Fell on this carpenter, right as I gesse	Fatigued with toilsome Labours of the Day;
About curfewe time, or little more:	Much about Curfew-time, or little more,
For trauaile of his ghost he groneth sore,	His troubl'd Ghost in Travail groan'd full sore,
And eft he routeth, for his head mislay:	His Head mis-laid upon the naked Board,
And doune the ladder stalketh Nicholay,	Made him uneasy, and he soundly snor'd:
And Alison full soft after she sped:	Which fairly seem'd the friendly Husband's Cue,
Withouten words mo they went to bed	T'instuct the Lovers what they ought to do.
There as the carpenter was wont to lie,	
There was the reuell, and the melodie.	When Gentle *Nicholas* perceiv'd him fast,
And thus lieth Alison and Nicholas	Down by the *Ladder* he descends in Haste;
In businesse of mirth and solas,	Then *Alison* full softly after sped,
Till that the bell of laudes gan to ring,	And both *sans* Ceremony went to Bed.
And Freres in the chaunsell gone to sing.	What wanton Revellings! What am'rous Feats
	Were play'd between the Matrimonial Sheets!
	What breathless Extasies! What dying Charms!
	And how they curl'd in one another's Arms!
	In melting Pastime, Solace, and Delight,
	They pass'd the pleasing Hours, and entertain'd
	the Night;
	Till ev'n the *Bell* of *Lauds* began to ring,
	And *Friars* to the *Chancells* went to sing.⁴²
(*MilT*, 3642–56; Speght 1687, p. 30)	(Smith, *Poems upon Several Occasions*, p. 343)

---

⁴² That Speght 1598 was used by Cobb and Speght 1602 or 1687 by Smith is suggested by the different readings 'freres in the chauncell gan sing' in 1598 and 'Freres <u>to</u> the *Chancells* gone to sing' in 1602/87, which account for the difference between Cobb's 'Till that the Bell of *Lauds* <u>began to</u> ring, / And the

Some of Chaucer's lines here are reproduced almost verbatim. As in the original, the Friars ('fat Fryars' in Cobb) seem almost to join in the revelry, with no hint of condemnation.

The Ending of *The Miller's Tale*

As with Chaucer, none of the renderings of *The Miller's Tale* side with Absalom or John rather than with Alison. Each, however, draws different conclusions from the action. In John Smith's version, even though 'the Good Wife had Plenty of that Same', punishments are dealt to all, and all are discontented. Absalom is left to his resentment, 'The injur'd Husband to his Discontent, / The *Philomath* and Wife for ever to repent'.[43] Smith's punishments are awarded on partly religious grounds.

Samuel Cobb took an almost opposite line. Coming to the Miller's summary of the tale ('Thvs swyved was this carpenteris wyf / Fo al his kepyng and his jalusye'), he shaped his moral—if such it may be called—from the sixteenth Ode in Horace's Third Book. This poem tells the story of King Acrisius shutting his daughter Danae in a brazen tower, where, despite his care, she was visited by Zeus in the form of a shower of gold, and so (as Cowley put it in the most popular version) 'Melted the Maiden-head away, / Even in the secret scabbard where it lay'. For Cobb, this stanza served almost as a commentary on Chaucer's tale:

> A Tower of <u>Brass</u>, one would have said,
> And Locks, and Bolts, and Iron <u>Bars</u>,
> And Guards, as strict as in the heat of wars,
> Might have preserv'd one innocent Maiden-head.
> The <u>jealous</u> Father thought he well might spare
>   All further <u>jealous</u> Care.
> And as he walkt, t'himself alone he smil'd,
>   To think how *Venus* Arts he had beguil'd.
>   (Abraham Cowley, *Essays, Plays, and Sundry Verses*, ed. A. R. Waller
>   [Cambridge, 1906], p. 441)

Cobb draws on Horace to describe Alison:[44]

> Thus Doors of <u>Brass</u>, and <u>Bars</u> of Steel are vain
> And watchful <u>Jealousie</u>, and carking Pain

---

fat Fryars in the Chancel sing', and Smith's 'Till ev'n the *Bell* of *Lauds* began to ring, / And *Friars* to the *Chancells* went to sing'.

[43] Smith, *Poems upon several Occasions*, p. 357. Nicholas is called a *Philomath*, presumably as he pretended to be an astrologer or prognosticator, rather than a more generalized seeker of knowledge.

[44] Erasmus's Folly speaks similarly: 'how fewer marriages, when consummated, would continue happy, if the husband were not either sottishly insensible of, or did not purposely wink at, and pass over the lightness and forwardnes of his <u>good-natur'd</u> wife?' (*Witt Against Wisdom*, p. 25).

> Is fruitless all, when a good-natur'd Spouse
> Designs Preferment for her Husband's Brows.
>> (Cobb, *The Carpenter of Oxford*, p. 46)

This Horatian moral does not, however, quite fit Chaucer's tale. We have heard little in the story about the carpenter's 'watchful Jealousie and carking Pain'. And the degree of irony in Cobb's description of Alison as 'good-natur'd' seems uncertain. But Cobb's presentation of Alison as happily triumphant did not hinder him from following Chaucer's Miller in ending the poem with a sudden leap, as it were, from Nicholas's burning buttocks to a kind of prayer:

> Thus ALISON her Cuckold does defye,
> And ABSOLON has kiss'd her nether Eye;
> While NICOLAS is scalded in the Breech,
> My Tale is done, God save us all, and each!
>> (Cobb, *The Carpenter of Oxford*, p. 46)

Cobb's response again appears to have half-overlapped with that of Brathwaite, for whom the ending had been simply comic—and therefore *merry*:

> The Cloud's dispers'd, the Floud or Deluge past,
> And *Absolon* of wanton become chast,
> *John* to his *Alyson* is reconcil'd,
> And Shee, perhaps, by *Nicholas* with Child,
> *John* doth his jealous humor quite disdain,
> What *Alice* did, she will not do again.
> "Heav'n Smiles, Earth joyes, when all things fall amending,
> "And Tragick Acts have such a Comick ending.[45]
>> (Brathwaite, *A Comment Upon the Two Tales*, p. 59)

Much of Brathwaite's ending, however, is his own invention—or is the report of an invention. It is clear enough why Absolon has ceased to be wanton. But quite when or how '*John* to his *Alyson*' was 'reconcil'd' is not explained. Are we to imagine John, like January in *The Merchant's Tale*, rejoicing in his wife's pregnancy? Despite the promise that 'What *Alice* did, she will not do again', it was daring of Brathwaite to suggest that 'Heav'n Smiles' at 'such a Comick ending'. Such a reaction, however, seems to determine many eighteenth-century accounts of this poem and of Chaucer's indecency generally. It is an indecency that issues in *merriment*, for the reader if not for the fictional personages. Neither the indecency nor the merriment is seen as an addition to Chaucer. The events of the tale *itself* are humorous, rather than merely being told in a humorous *manner*. It follows that merriment, indecency, and humour cannot be separated. The ending is comic *because* it is indecent; it is only by these indecent means that the happy ending invented by Brathwaite could have been achieved.

---

[45] Roman and italics reversed.

George Ogle, who printed Cobb's version in his collected *Canterbury Tales* of 1741, seems to have recorded what he imagined to be a common eighteenth-century reaction to the poem, while translating the imagined response of the fourteenth-century Pilgrims to Chaucer's Miller:

> The *Miller* ceas'd, exulting at the Close,
> And, as He ceas'd, a gen'ral Laugh arose;
> For hum'rous was the Tale, tho' low the Stile,
> Ev'n They, that blush'd to laugh, agreed to smile.

The laugh is general, the smile perhaps to be seen only on the faces of the women, but each pilgrim finds a different episode of particular interest:

> Each, various, variously discuss'd the Case;
> The *Scholar*'s Payment, and the *Clerk*'s Disgrace!
> The frisky *Wife*'s Elopement in the Dark,
> And the dull *Husband*, lodg'd in *Noah*'s Ark!
>
> (Ogle, 1. 229)

The mention of the dull husband and Noah's ark as the crowning joke is a reminder that for some readers the profanity was as essential as the obscenity, and that the indecencies of the tale were multiple.

One reader of Cobb's *Miller's Tale* as printed in Ogle's collection, however, did not think that version was sufficiently indecent. In one copy of Ogle's volume,[46] where Cobb had written of Absolon's misplaced kiss and reaction to it: 'He curst the Hour, and rail'd against the Stars, / That he was born to kiss my Lady's —', an anonymous wag emended the couplet by hand, to read: 'Ye cruel Gods have I deserv'd the affront / Why was I born to kiss my Lady's —'. The annotator has increased the obscenity, but with the enhanced obscenity has achieved a kind of precision—particularly when the lines are transformed as they are by Cobb from Chaucer's indirect speech to the *ipsissima verba* of Absalom himself. The emendation is attentive to the narrative, but not to Chaucer's words. The impulse behind the handwritten addition would seem to be broadly similar to that which motivated some scribes to increase the sexual performances of Chanticleer, or to provide a precise and tactile comparison of the sexual organs of Damon and January.

In Cobb's version, Absalom is convinced that the event is an affliction visited upon him by the heavens, cruel fate, or the gods themselves—while for Alison, physical conjunction is a matter of pure merriment. The comic effect is achieved in Chaucer's original by the juxtaposition of Alison giggling while Absalom invokes the devil and hell, and meditates revenge, with Nicholas's mockery ('A Beard! A Beard!') of the physical specifics of Absalom's plight. Cobb and (even more so)

---

[46] In a private collection.

his anonymous emender combine an attentiveness to physical particulars with an appreciation of the larger comic situation. The anonymous composer of the version of 1791 concentrates on the former, and defends Chaucer's reference to specific features of female anatomy by an appeal to the different attitudes of the Middle Ages and those of 'this age of refinement':

> In Geoffrey's time, the features of Nature, as they were as universally known, so they were not so partially treated as by our modern writers. Our forefathers thought beauty was beauty, wherever they found it; and would pay their tribute of adoration to it, wherever their experience assured them of is existence … . The most mincing prude is not only herself conscious that the structure of her body differs in some particulars from that of her brother's body, and that Nature has not restrained the growth of hair to the scalp alone: but she knows that every reasonable creature, past the age of puberty, in the room where she sits, is as thoroughly possessed of those circumstances as herself: I cannot therefore be made to think that any allusion, like that of our poet, to the limbs which few see, but all know to exist, is by any means a more flagrant outrage upon good manners, than the common hackneyed allusions to *events*, which arise from the equally well-authenticated difference between the two sexes.[47]

The end of the translator's version take up the issue:[48]

> Thus was the beauteous Alison enjoy'd,
> Tho' John had all his jealous cares employ'd,
> Thus on that part the clerk his passion seal'd,
> 'Which modest Nature keeps from sight conceal'd.'
> Thus hath, alas! The crafty scholar sped,
> His wiles at length retorted on his head:
> Thus ever hath the jealous husband far'd,
> And still deceit shall bring its own reward.
>
> (Bowden, *Eighteenth-Century Modernizations*, p. 176)

The Manciple's Tale

The 1791 *Miller's Tale*, in its exultant indecency and in its commitment to modern idiom, was the last of its kind. Many later eighteenth-century writers argued that greater concessions should be paid to the antiquity of Chaucer's vocabulary and syntax on the one hand, and, on the other, to modern delicacy and decency.

We have already witnessed how William Lipscomb, in his attempt to 'purge' Chaucer 'from his impurities', 'wholly omitted' translations of the Miller's and

---

[47] Bowden, *Eighteenth-Century Modernizations*, pp. 169–70.
[48] The quotation marks belong to the poem and signal a quotation from Dryden's *Theodore and Honoria*, when the living mortals are invaded by ghosts including 'a beauteous maid, / With hair dishevelled, issuing through the shade; / Stripped of her clothes, and even those parts revealed / Which modest nature keeps from sight concealed' (Dryden, *Theodore and Honoria*, 107–10; Dryden, *Works*, 7. 339).

Reeve's tales on the grounds that they were 'highly indelicate, as well in the sentiments as in the language'.[49] Some other stories also faced Lipscomb with difficulties: *The Manciple's Tale*, for example, in which a crow, initially white in hue, tells its master Phoebus of his wife's infidelity in his absence. Phoebus kills his wife, but angrily turns on the crow and changes its plumage black. A potential problem was created for readers and translators by the explicit directness with which the crow reports on the conduct of Phoebus's wife. The brutality of the crow's report had been exaggerated in the version of the tale composed by Andrew Jackson as one of his *Matrimonial Scenes* (London, 1750):

... so mote I thrive:	So may I relish all the Joys of Life,
For on thy bedde thy wif I sawe him swive.	As on that Bed I saw him dight thy Wife!
What wol you more? The crowe anon him told,	Saw the bivalvous[50] End expanding lay'd,
By sade tokinis, and by wordis bold,	With an exub'rant *Paphian* scene disply'd,
How that his wife had doen her lecherie ...	Which suddenly was hidden from my View;
	For over all the Cuckow-Maker flew.
(*ManT*, 255–9; Urry, p. 176)	(Andrew Jackson, *Matrimonial Scenes*, p. 28)

This is gross indecency of image, if not of word. William Lipscomb, in marked contrast, gave an *account* of the crow's words, merely and very distantly reported, rather than the words themselves:

... so mote I thrive:	Whence this new song? His master soon enquir'd,
For on thy bedde thy wif I saw him swive.	And herd in answer more than he desir'd;
What wol you more? The crowe anon him told,	Nought, like a faithful friend, the crow conceal'd,
By sade tokenes, and by wordes bold,	But all he heard, and all he saw reveal'd.
How that his wif had don hire lecherie ...	
(*ManT*, 255–9; Tyrwhitt 1775–78, 3. 134)	(Lipscomb, 3. 387)

The difficulty with this moment was faced by William Wordsworth when he turned to the tale in 1801.[51] Writing six years after Lipscomb, Wordsworth exceeded his predecessor in a belief that Chaucer required minimal translation, but would not take Lipscomb's way out of the difficulty of the Crow's direct speech.[52] Much later (in March 1840), he told his friend Barron Field that 'He wished the delicacy of modern ears would allow him to translate the whole of this tale.'[53] In Wordsworth's version, *Phoebus and the Crow*, the bird does speak directly, but speaks the language of lawyers: 'For I full plainly as I hope for life / Saw him *in guilty converse* with thy wife.'[54] Even so, Wordsworth withdrew the poem from

---

[49] Lipscomb, 1. vi–viii.
[50] *Bivalvous,* having two valves like an oyster.
[51] See William Wordsworth, *Translations of Chaucer and Virgil*, ed. Bruce E. Graver (Ithaca, NY, 1988). p. 11.
[52] He had some difficulties earlier in the tale: 'They took their fill of love and lovers rage' (l. 135), becomes 'In loves delights themselves they did engage'.
[53] Wordsworth, *Translations*, ed. Graver, p. 26.
[54] Wordsworth, *Translations*, ed. Graver, p. 97.

publication, informing a correspondent that 'I could not place my version at the disposal of the Editor, as I deemed the subject somewhat too indelicate for pure taste to be offered to the world at this time of day.'[55]

The Miller of Trompington (1712)

In *The Miller of Trompington*, his version of Chaucer's *Reeve's Tale*, Thomas Betterton had to handle indecencies of a slightly different kind from those contained in *The Miller's Tale*. This tale may contain humorous episodes, but, like *The Manciple's Tale*, it is rarely good- humoured. Where Chaucer's Miller had referred to 'revel' and 'solas', the verb 'swive' is used by Chaucer's Reeve with almost as much freedom as it was by Rochester. The machinations that take place in the Mill ('in low and plashy ground') are near-farcical, but the setting and circumstances are attractively vivid and seem life-like. As much attention has been paid by Betterton to Chaucer's details in *The Miller of Trompington* as is visible in John Hamilton Mortimer's illustration (see Fig. 6.4).[56] The main personages are evoked with economy and with much reference to animals and birds. Simkin the Miller is 'proud as a Peacock, subtle as a Fox'; his wife 'Walk'd like a Duck, and chatter'd like a Pye'. Some circumstances have been added. The 'Two poor Scholars' who take upon themselves the safety of the corn of 'Scholars Hall' at Cambridge are 'hungry' because, thanks to the Miller's thefts, 'Their Bread fell short'. The young men's scheme of watching the milling at both ends is accurately depicted. Even their horse which 'makes to the Fenns, where Mares and Fillies feed' plays his proper part. The only substantial omission is the passage recounting the priestly father-in-law's reasons for keeping his grand-daughter unmarried—and therefore, perhaps, an only-half-unwilling victim to Allen.

There are moments of great liveliness, as when the miller's wife, either pre-instructed or in a moment of inspiration, dupes the young scholars with a vivid account of their run-away horse:

> Out bolts *Sim*'s Wife, and (with a ready Lie)
> She cries, I saw him toss his Head and play,
> Then slip the loosen'd Reins, and Trot away.
> Which Way? they both demand—With wanton Bounds,

---

[55] Letter to Henry Reed, quoted in Wordsworth, *Translations,* ed. Graver, p. 27. In Steve Ellis, ed. *Chaucer: An Oxford Guide* (Oxford, 2005), David Matthews argues that Wordsworth's increasing squeamishness would 'seem to reflect a double standard: a disjunction between what is seemed acceptable, on the one hand, for private reading by educated people and, on the other, for presentation to a general readership through publication' (p. 533).

[56] See Betsy Bowden, 'Tales Told and Tellers of Tales: Illustrations of the Canterbury Tales in the Course of the Eighteenth Century', in *Chaucer Illustrated*, ed. William Finley and Joseph Rosenblum (Newcastle, DE and London, 2003), 121–90 (137–9).

Fig. 6.4 'The Miller of Trompington and Two Scholars'. Illustration to *The Reeve's Tale* by John Hamilton Mortimer (engraved 1787).

> I saw him scamp'ring tow'rd yon Fenny Grounds;
> Wild Mares and Colts in those low Marshes feed.
>
> (*Miscellaneous Poems and Translations by Several
> Hands* [London, 1712], p. 308)

Betterton's efforts in this version have been unfairly denigrated. Thomas R. Louns-bury observed acidly that Betterton's poem constituted evidence that 'poetry suffered no loss by his having made acting a profession and not literature', and included the work in his general judgement that 'Chaucer was not so much translated as he was transmogrified.'[57] A hundred years later, Derek Brewer, accepting Betsy Bowden's case for Pope's authorship of *The Miller of Trompington*, wrote: 'This is a fairly close [translation], which loses nothing of its bawdiness ... It is told with a touch of typically eighteenth-century antifeminism.'[58]

A number of positive features of Betterton's version are by-passed in these rapid dismissals. The contention that the translation is 'fairly close', for example, obscures the remarkably varied degrees of adherence to the letter of the original—from near-word-for-word to completely fresh invention. And the observation that Betterton's version 'loses nothing' of the 'bawdiness' of Chaucer's original needs some qualification. *The Miller of Trompington* curtails, but does not neglect or much soften, the events on which the catastrophe turns:

Alein uprist and thought, er it dawe	Now *Allen* softly feeling for his Bed,
He would go crepe in by his felawe	By chance his Hand laid on the Cradle-head,
And found the cradell with his hande anon	And shrinking from it, said (with no small Fear)
By God thought he, al wrong I haue I gon	That Rogue the Miller and his Wife lie there.
My hedde is tottie of my swinke to night	Turning, he finds *Sim*'s Palate, in he crept;
That maketh me that I go nat aright	I'm right, he says, dull *John* all Night has slept.
I wot wel by the cradel I haue missego	Then shaking him—Wake, Swineherd, *Allen* cries,
Here lieth the Miller and his wif also	I've joyful News—What? grumbling *Sim* replies.
And foorth he goeth on twentie deuill waie	I am the luckiest Rogue—by this *No Light*,
Unto the bedde, ther as the Miller laie	I have had full Employment all the Night.
He wende haue cropen by his felawe John	The Daughter kindly paid her Father's Score,
And by the Miller he crept in anon	All Night I have embrac'd her.—O the Whore!
And caught hym by the necke, & soft he spake	O thou false Traytor, Clerke! thou hast defil'd
He saied: John, thou swineshed awake	Our honest Family, deflower'd our Child![59]
For Christes soule, and here a noble game	Thy Life shall answer it ...
For by that lorde, that called is sainct Jame	
As I haue thrise in this short night	
Swiued the Millers doughter bolt upright,	
Whilest thou hast, as a coward ben agaste.	
Ye false harlot (qd the Miller) haste?	
A false traitour, false clerke (qd he)	
Thou shalt be dedde, by Goddes dignite ...	
(*RvT*, 4249–70; Speght 1598, Fol. 16ᵛ)	(*Miscellaneous Poems and Translations*, p. 317)

Betterton's Allen's 'All Night I have embrac'd her' is a euphemistic version of Chaucer's Alein's callous boast: 'I haue thrise in this short night / Swiued the Millers doughter bolt upright'. On the other hand, Betterton's assumption that the 'harlot' referred to by Chaucer's miller is the daughter rather than the student

[57] Thomas R. Lounsbury, *Studies in Chaucer, His Life and Writings*, 3 vols (London, 1892). 3. 187.

[58] Derek Brewer, 'Modernising the Medieval: Eighteenth-Century Translation of Chaucer', in *The Middle Ages after the Middle Ages*, ed. Marie-Françoise Alamichel and Derek Brewer (Martlesham, 1997), 103–20 (p. 112) .

[59] Ogle, in reprinting Betterton's version, represents this word with two elisions: *deflow'r'd*.

helps to make Simkin's potentially murderous reaction no less brutal than in the original—while making his pride in his daughter's 'lineage' an integral part of his initial shock. Betterton's Allen also emphasizes, with a multiple pun on 'kindly', that the whole business had been matter of redress and revenge: 'The Daughter kindly paid her Father's Score'.

In *The Miller of Trompington*, the parting between Allen and the miller's daughter Grace—the occasion, as in Chaucer, when she reveals her father's secrets—has been significantly altered. Some sentiments exchanged between Allen and Grace have been added:

Alein waxe werie in the dawnyng	Now *Allen* fancied Light would soon appear,
For he had swonken all the long night	He kiss'd the Wench, and said, 'My *Grace*, my Dear;
And saied, fare wel, Malin swete wight	Thou kindest of thy Sex, the Day comes on,
The daie is comen, I maie no lenger bide	And we must part—Alas, will you be gone,
But euermo, whereso I go or ride	She said, and leave poor harmless me alone?—
I am thine owene clerke, so haue I heel.	If I stay longer, we are both undone;
Now dere lemman (quod she) go, farewele	For should your Father wake and find me here,
But er thou go, one thyng I wol thee tel	What will become of me, and you, my Dear?
When thou wendest homward by the Mell	That dreadful Thought (she cries) distracts my Heart,
Right at the entre of the doore bihinde	Too soon you won me, and too soon we part.
Thou shalt a cake of half a busshel finde	Then clinging round his Neck, with weeping Eyes,
That was imaked of thyne owne meale	She says, Remember me! *Allen* replies,
Which that I helpe my sire for to steale	I'll quickly find occasion to return;
And good lemman God thee saue and kepe	You shall not long for *Allen*'s Absence mourn.
And with that worde she gan almost to wepe	Farewel, she cries! But, Dearest, one Word more;
	You'll find upon a Sack behind the Door
	A Cake, and under it a Bag of Meal:
	The Flour my Father and my self did steal
	Out of your Sack; but take it, 'tis your own;
	Be careful, Love,—not a Word more, be gone.
(*RvT*, 4234–48; Speght 1598, Fol. 16ᵛ)	(*Miscellaneous Poems and Translations*, pp. 315–16)

Most eighteenth-century commentators, following Speght's suggestion in his 'Arguments to euery Tale and Booke', assumed that the source for (rather than merely an analogue of) *The Reeve's Tale* was to be found in the Sixth Story of the Ninth Day in Boccaccio's *Decameron*. The added sentiments uttered by Allen and the miller's daughter in *The Miller of Trompington* may indeed owe something to Boccaccio's story where the couple have hitherto been unconsummated lovers and at this moment 'proceeded to take their fill of that sweet pleasure for which they yearned above all else'.[60]

In Boccaccio's tale, the wife was decidedly the heroine and her intelligence central to the story. In *The Miller of Trompington*, the wife 'crept' close to John 'full harmlessly'. John, more gently than in Chaucer, 'takes her in his Arms' and 'treats

---

[60] Giovanni Boccacio, *The Decameron*, trans. G. H. McWilliam (2nd edn, London, 1995), p. 679.

her with unusual Charms'. In Chaucer, the sentiments of the wife are limited to a brief reference to her 'merry fit'.[61] But in Betterton:

> She thought (strange fancies working in her Mind)
> Some *Saint* had made her Husband over-kind,
> Propitious Stars this Fortune did bestow
> On both …
>
> (*Miscellaneous Poems and Translations*, p. 315)

It may have been a memory of Boccaccio that prompted Betterton's expansion and humanization of the wife's pleasures.

Betterton's Clever Wife

Perhaps the most interesting part of *The Miller of Trompington* is its ending—though it is an ending very different from that of Chaucer's *Reeve's Tale*. Chaucer's story concludes with the two Cambridge students beating the miller and retrieving their flour. Both actions receive the teller's endorsement: 'Thus is the proud Miller well ybete / And hath ylost the grinding of the whete'. In Speght's edition of 1602, the 'prouerbes' which receive the adornment of the pointing hand are of the 'do-as-you-would-be-done-by' and 'swindlers-are-always-swindled' kind:

> Him dare not well ween that euill dooth: 🖛
> A guilour shall himselfe beguiled be. 🖛
>
> (Speght 1602, Fol. 16ʳ)

And the Reeve ends his tale with a conclusion that is exclusively devoted to the humiliation of the Miller, at which the humiliations of the wife and daughter are aimed. Betterton's version, in marked contrast, contrives a happy ending (of sorts) for all the personages—both, as in Chaucer, for the students who ride back to Scholar's Hall 'Pleas'd with the strange Adventures of the Night', and also for the miller and his wife and daughter: 'And thus the Miller of his Fear is eas'd, / The Mother and the Daughter both well-pleas'd'. Attention in this version has been turned from the students to the miller, and, most importantly, his wife:

> The Wife the Scholars curses, binds his Head,
> Then lifts him up, and lays him on the Bed.

The miller tells his grief:

> O Wife, says *Sim*, our Daughter is defil'd!
> That Villain *Allen* has debauch'd our Child.

---

[61] In the line (4230) remembered by Pope and by the scribe whose insertion of it into *The Merchant's Tale* is preserved by Speght.

> Mistaking me for *John*, he told me all;
> Ten thousand Furies plague that *Scholars-Hall!*

The miller's wife has to think quickly. It is a concomitant of the close attention given to circumstances in this poem that it seems at this point inevitable that Sim the miller will eventually work out exactly what had been going on, and—what the reader knows so clearly—who had been in which bed, at what time, and therefore with whom. Betterton's wife, demonstrating true motherly care, at one stroke exculpates herself and her daughter:

> O false abusive Knave! (the Wife reply'd)
> In ev'ry Word the Villain spake he ly'd.
> I wak'd, and heard our harmless Child complain,
> And rose, to know the Cause, and ease her Pain.
> I found her torn with Gripes, a Dram I brought,
> And made her take a comfortable Draught.
> Then lay down by her, chaff'd her swelling Breast,
> And lull'd her in these very Arms to Rest.
> All was Contrivance, Malice all and Spite,
> I have not parted from her all this Night.

To her husband's direct question, she is able to reply with (almost) complete truth:

> *Then is she Innocent?* Ay, by my Life,
> As pure and spotless—as thy Bosom Wife.
> *I'm satisfied*, says *Sim*. O that damn'd *Hall!*
> I'll do the best I can to starve 'em All.
> And thus the Miller of his Fear is eas'd,
> The Mother and the Daughter both well-pleas'd.
> (*Miscellaneous Poems and Translations*, pp. 319–20)

This follows Boccaccio's version of the story quite closely. In the anonymous translation of Boccaccio published in 1702, the wife at the same juncture makes the same answer: 'He lies like a Rogue, says the Wife, I have lain with her all this night, and she has done nothing worse than I my self.'[62]

The ending of *The Miller of Trompington* could only have been written by someone who had entered into Chaucer's story imaginatively, at several points, and from several different perspectives. Betterton has drawn on Boccaccio to produce a comic effect that counterpoises the churlish brutality of the Reeve's narrative. This seems to be a translation conducted not just in response to the particular original, which is its main concern, but in the light of a sense of the 'Chaucerian' derived from several of his other comic works.

As we saw in Chapter 5, it has been suggested that Alexander Pope may have had a hand in Betterton's Chaucer translations. The handling of the ending of *The*

---

[62] Giovanni Boccacio, *Il Decamerone. One Hundred Ingenious Novels*, 2 vols (London, 1702), 2. 189.

Reeve's Tale in *The Miller of Trompington* does not resolve one way or the other the question of Pope's possible involvement. Betterton did not write enough—or enough that is sufficiently similar in character—for any conclusion to be drawn about his methods or the extent of his unaided abilities. Nor, for that matter, do we have much idea of how Pope might have written had he been composing fast to help a friend. Like Betterton's other versions from Chaucer, *The Miller of Trompington* contains too many redundant phrases, verbal infelicities, and uncertainties of versification to have easily passed under Pope's name. Yet the general quality of the Betterton versions—and of *The Miller of Trompington*, in particular—is superior to that of most of the eighteenth-century 'modernizations' of Chaucer. The conduct of its narrative is unusually clear. The writer has a firm grip on all the details and conveys an exact sense of who was sleeping where, with whom, at what time, with what outcome. Pope's *January and May* has strikingly similar virtues. It is possible to speculate that Betterton, having retired, 'spent some of his leisure hours modernizing Chaucer … encouraged his young friend to do the same, and Pope, who was willing to try his hand at anything that would help him acquire poetic skill, produced versions of the *Merchant's Tale* and the *Wife of Bath's Prologue*'.[63]

Pope, in conversation with Spence, praised Chaucer's enduring power of pleasing:

> I read Chaucer still with as much pleasure as almost any of our poets. He is a master of manners, of description, and the first tale-teller in the true enlivened natural way.[64]

The key terms in Pope's remarks are 'manners', 'description', 'enlivened' and 'natural'. Chaucer, according to Pope, pleases us with the liveliness and truthfulness of his characterizations and descriptions, and with the power of his narratives to hold our attention and make us anxious for the event. For eighteenth-century writers and readers, the pleasure to be found in translating and adapting Chaucer's comic tales does not seem to have been primarily a pleasure in writing about sexuality and obscenity under the cover of reproducing the work of a great and almost canonical poet. Their interest seems have been focused, rather, on discovering, and partially reliving, ways of depicting human life in all its variety that were at once different from prevailing conventions and restrictions and yet thrillingly ancient. Many of the writers of modern versions of those tales that seemed to revel in 'native obscenity' appear to have given almost as much energy to the descriptions of people and places as to the moments of purely sexual comedy. Many, too, appear to have taken pleasure in mingling sexual comedy with religious—as opposed to merely anti-clerical—concerns. In this they may have been finding in Chaucer's poems something that was not to be easily had elsewhere.

---

[63] Netta Murray Goldsmith, *Alexander Pope: The Evolution of a Poet* (Aldershot, 2002), p. 41.

[64] Joseph Spence, *Observations, Anecdotes and Characters of Books and Men*, ed. James M. Osborn 2 vols (Oxford, 1966), 1. 179.

It is noticeable that great attention is paid in many of the eighteenth-century imitations and translations of Chaucer to the remarks of very young women, whether extremely naïve, like the 'wanton Miss' of Pope's 'Tale of Chaucer' or the outrageously sophisticated heroine of his *January and May*. As in Chaucer, women are often left the last, and often triumphant, word. Their direct speech—even if it is only the *tee hee* of Alison in *The Miller's Tale*—tends to set the tone of the whole. It is to the most outrageous and loquacious of all Chaucer's female figures that Chapter 7 is devoted.

7

Some Eighteenth-Century Wives of Bath

In the introductory note to Byron's *The Vision of Judgment* as it appeared in *The Liberal* (1822), 'Quevedo Redivivus' (Byron, pseudonymously) noted wryly that it is 'possible that some readers may object, in these objectionable times, to the freedom with which saints, angels, and spiritual persons, discourse in this "Vision"'. In defence of such freedoms, Byron adduces several literary works. He explains that the 'whole action passes on the outside of heaven; and Chaucer's Wife of Bath, Pulci's Morgante Maggiore, Swift's Tale of a Tub ... are cases in point of the freedom with which saints, etc., may be permitted to converse in works not intended to be serious'.[1] The mention of 'Chaucer's Wife of Bath' here is odd. There is not much conversation by 'saints etc.' in any of the several works by Chaucer in which the Wife of Bath makes an appearance, tells a tale, or recounts the words of others. Little that is associated with Chaucer's character can be paralleled with the debates in Byron's satire over the destination of King George's soul between Lucifer, St Peter, the archangel Michael, and the devil Asmodeus. Byron, moreover, was by no means an admirer of Chaucer.[2] On this occasion, indeed, he may actually have been thinking not of Chaucer, but of a ballad which is set, like Byron's, outside the gates of heaven and in which divine and human elements are brought into a vertiginous combination. In it, the 'Wanton Wife of Bath' disputes with a variety of biblical figures—Jacob, Judith, David, Solomon, Jonas, St Thomas, Mary Magdalene, St Paul, and St Peter himself—shaming them all into abject capitulation.[3]

---

[1] *The Liberal: Verse and Prose from the South* (London, 1822), 1. iv–v.

[2] 'Chaucer, not withstanding the praises bestowed on him, I think obscene and contemptible: he owes his celebrity merely to his antiquity, which does not deserve so well as Piers Plowman or Thomas Erceldoune' (from a memorandum book dated 30 November 1807, in Lord Byron, *Letters and Journals*, ed. Moore (London, 1830), p. 36).

[3] Thomas Percy included *The Wanton Wife of Bath* 'from an ancient copy in black-print, in the Pepys Collection' in Vol. 3 of the first edition of his *Reliques of Ancient English Poetry*, 3 vols (London, 1765), observing that 'Mr. Addison has pronounced this an excellent ballad.' Perhaps because he deemed the Wife's irreverence and *post obitum* repentance unsuitable for publication by a rising cleric, it was removed in the second and subsequent editions. Percy was ordained Bishop of Dromore in County Down in 1782. The many appreciative references to Chaucer in the *Reliques*, along with the 'rondeau' ('Youre two eyn will sle me sodenly') which Percy was the first to print 'from an ancient MS in the Pepysian Library', and a long quotation from the opening of *The Wife of Bath's Tale* in support of Corbett's *The Fairies Farewell*, all remained in the collection.

Chaucer in the Eighteenth Century. David Hopkins and Tom Mason, Oxford University Press.
© David Hopkins and Tom Mason (2022). DOI: 10.1093/oso/9780192862624.003.0008

The Wanton Wife of Bath

That, more or less, is the pattern of events and interactions in the ballad in all its versions and variants,[4] several of which were shocking to the sensibilities of early generations.[5] The ballad presents itself almost as a *report* of Chaucer's *Wife of Bath's Prologue*:

> IN *Bath* a wanton Wife did dwell,
>   As *Chaucer* he doth write;
> Who did in Pleasure spend her Days,
>   In many a fond Delight.

The anonymous editor of the ballad in 1723 made a slightly ambiguous attribution to Chaucer: 'I need not acquaint my Readers that the following Story is borrow'd from old Chaucer', but relies on a critical endorsement rather than venerable antiquity to justify the poem's appearance in his volume: 'The Ballad it self has always been esteem'd, and even Mr. Addison has commended it, whose Judgment in Poetry, I believe never was disputed'.

In No. 247 of *The Spectator*, Joseph Addison had described the 'excellent old Ballad of The Wanton Wife of Bath', pointing to 'the following remarkable Lines':

> *I think, quoth* Thomas, *Womens Tongues*
> *Of Aspen Leaves are made.*

Addison is here endorsing a comfortably patronizing account of the irrepressible talkativeness of women.[6] The 'tongue' of the Wanton Wife in the ballad is, however, like that of some of the Chaucerian heroines discussed in Chapter 6, all-conquering: 'Thou unbelieving Wretch, quoth she' to Saint Thomas, the 'Doubter', 'All is not true that's said'—at which point, Thomas gives way to 'Mary Magd'len', who is assumed to be the woman taken in adultery but not condemned by Jesus.[7]

---

[4] Though the ballad was clearly in early circulation (see n 5) the first extant version is datable to *c.* 1665. Quotations below are from *The Wanton Wife of Bath* in *A Collection of Old Ballads: Corrected from the Best and Most Ancient Copies Extant, with Introductions Historical, Critical, or Humorous. Illustrated with Copper Plates*, 2 vols (London, 1723), 2. 173–8.

[5] See Caroline Spurgeon, *Five Hundred Years of Chaucer Criticism and Allusion, 1357–1900*, 3 vols (Cambridge, 1925), 3.54. Spurgeon records that in 1600 one version of the ballad was 'brought in and burnt' and the printers fined, and that in 1632 Henry Goskin was sent to Bridewell for printing a ballad 'wherein the histories of the Bible are scurrilously abused'. A work entitled *The New Wife of Beath*, printed (apparently) in Glasgow, is a considerable expansion of the ballad, and is noticeable for making explicit the theological difficulty of the *posthumous* date of the Wife's repentance. There is no evidence to suggest which version of the ballad Byron might have seen.

[6] Donald F. Bond, ed., *The Spectator*, 5 vols (Oxford, 1965), 2. 461. Addison's discussion moves from the ballad to Ovid, who 'in the Description of a very barbarous Circumstance, tells us, that when the Tongue of a beautiful Female was cut out, and thrown upon the Ground, it could not forbear muttering even in that Posture'.

[7] John 7:53–8:11.

The composer of the ballad has remembered all the moments when Chaucer's Wife had abused leading figures in the Old and New Testaments. This Wife is irresistibly loquacious and undaunted, even in the presence of Solomon. Here, she has just humiliated King David by mentioning his adultery with Bathsheba:

> The Woman's mad, said *Solomon*,
>   That thus doth taunt a King.
> Not half so mad as you, she said,
>   I know in many a thing.
>
> Thou haddest seven Hundred Wives,
>   For whom thou did'st provide,
> Yet for all this, three hundred Whores,
>   Thou did'st maintain beside.
>
> And those made thee forsake thy God,
>   And worship Stocks and Stones,
> Besides the charge they put thee to
>   In breeding of young Bones.
>
> Had'st thou not been besides thy Wits,
>   Thou would'st not thus have ventur'd;
> And therefore I do marvel much,
>   How thou this Place hast enter'd.

A similar assault upon the authority of Solomon, as we have seen, had been expressed with force by the Queen of the Fairies in Pope's *January and May*. In *The Wife of Bath, from Chaucer*, Pope's version of the Wife's *Prologue*, first printed in Steele's *Poetical Miscellanies* (1713, dated 1714) and reprinted with some pomp in his *Works* of 1717, Pope's Wife had been more restrained, and he had retrenched Chaucer's Wife's happy imaginings of Solomon's many sexual delights:

Lo he the wise king Salamon	More Wives than One by Solomon were try'd,
I trow had wiues mo than on	Or else the Wisest of Mankind's bely'd.
As would God it lefull were to me	I've had, my self, full many a merry Fit,
To be refresshed halfe so oft as he	And trust in Heav'n I may have many yet.
Which a gift of God had he, for all his wyuis	For when my transitory Spouse, unkind
No mã hath such that in this world a liue is	Shall die, and leave his woful Wife behind,
God wote this noble king, as to my witte	I'll take the next good Christian I can find.
The first night had many a merry fitte	
With ech of hem, so well was him aliue	
Blessed be God, I have had fiue	
(*WBP*, 35–44; Speght 1598, Fol. 33ʳ)	(*The Wife of Bath, from Chaucer*, 21–7; Alexander Pope, *Works* [London, 1717], pp. 248–9)

It may have been one of the reasons that the ballad was seen as a poem 'wherein the histories of the Bible are scurrilously abused' that the Wanton Wife had gone behind Chaucer, as it were, to the biblical evidence for Solomon's womanizing: 'King Solomon loued many strange women, (together with the daughter of Pharaoh) women of the Moabites, Ammonites, Edomites, Sidonians & Hittites ... And he had seuen hundred wiues, Princesses, and three hundred concubines: and his wiues turned away his heart.'[8]

All the accusations of the Wanton Wife have biblical support. She ignores any palliating glosses. Not until she meets Christ does she repent with any seriousness, and wins entry into heaven by citing the Good Thief and the Prodigal Son:

> Then up starts Peter at the last,
>   And to the Gate he highs,
> Fond Fool, quoth he, knock not so fast,
>   Thou weariest Christ with Cries.
>
> *Peter*, said she, content thy self,
>   For Mercy may be won,
> I never did deny my Christ,
>   As thou thy self hast done.
>
> When as our Saviour Christ heard this,
>   With heavenly Angels bright,
> He comes unto this sinful Soul,
>   Who trembled at his Sight.
>
> Of him for Mercy she did crave,
>   Quoth he, thou hast refus'd,
> My proffer'd Grace, and Mercy both,
>   And much my Name abus'd.
>
> *Sore have I sinn'd, O Lord, she said,*
>   *And spent my time in vain.*
> *But bring me like a wand'ring Sheep,*
>   *Into thy Flock again:*
>
> *O Lord my God, I will amend*
>   *My former wicked Vice.*
> The Thief at these poor silly Words,
>   Past into Paradice.
>
> My Laws and my Commandments,
>   Saith Christ, were known to thee,
> But of the same in any wise,
>   Not yet one Word did ye.

---

[8] 1 Kings 11:1 and 3 (AV).

Grant the same, O Lord, quoth she,
    Most lewdly did I live,
But yet the loving Father did
    His prodigal Son forgive.

So I forgive thy Soul, he said,
    Through thy repenting Cry,
Come you therefore into my Joy,
    I will not thee deny.

The ballad's outrageous, mingling of biblical accuracy with human shrewdness clearly appealed to readers in the eighteenth century and beyond. Versions appeared in one form or another well into the 1800s.[9] Betsy Bowden records fifty-four separate printings, including one that makes the necessary point with some emphasis: *The Wife of Beith: Being an Allegorical Dialogue. Containing Nothing But What Is Recorded in Scripture.*[10]

Chaucer's Incensed Ghost

In 1732, a poem was reprinted in *Phœnix Britannicus*, a 'miscellaneous collection of scarce and curious tracts, historical, political, biographical', in which 'Chaucer's Incensed Ghost' complains about the prevailing trivialization of his work. 'How light soe're, or wantonly' his tales might appear to modern readers, 'Chaucer' declares, 'Yet they in very Deed are nothing so'. If 'the Marke they aim'd at' could be 'descryd', then 'Even in these Dayes they would be verify'de'. In support of this contention, the ghost of Chaucer calls to witness 'The am'rous Stories of my Wife of Bath / Which such Variety of Humours hath' and which, 'tho'' moulded in a distant Age; / Still raise new Structures both for Press and Stage'.[11] The anonymous poem was in fact the work of Richard Brathwaite, whose version of *The Miller's Tale* we encountered in Chapter 6. It had first appeared over a century earlier in *The Smoaking Age* (1617). But 'Chaucer's ghost' would have had more grounds for complaint in 1732 than on its first visit, and would continue to be provided with further grounds for the rest of the eighteenth century.

Of all Chaucer's tales, the 'am'rous Stories' of the Wife of Bath prompted more 'new Structures both for Press and Stage' than any other. She is the most frequently mentioned of Chaucer's characters in print in the eighteenth-century (see

---

[9] Several stanzas of 'The Wanton Wife' were sung on stage in Thomas Jevon's, *The Devil of a Wife: or, A Comical Transformation.* This play, originally printed in 1686, was much reprinted in the early eighteenth century. Some quotations from the ballad, together with some touches from Chaucer's poem, were worked into what is in effect a verse narrative version of Jevon's play, *The Conjurer; or Metamorphoses of Pride and Humility* (London, ?1770), pp. 67–8.

[10] Betsy Bowden, *The Wife of Bath in Afterlife: Ballads to Blake* (Bethlehem, PA, 2017), pp. 2, 6.

[11] *Phoenix Britannicus … Collected by J. Morgan* (London, 1732), pp. 543–4.

Fig. 7.1). In *The Wanton Wife of Bath*, all the saints and patriarchs in heaven instantly know who and what she is. Alongside the frequent reprintings of the ballad, Chaucer's Wife appears in plays, versions of Chaucer's original, imitations, dictionaries, anthologies, poetical commonplace books, and in the footnotes to

Fig. 7.1 A young and flirtatious Wife of Bath. Drawn by Thomas Stothard and engraved by Jean Marie Delattre for Vol. 14 of John Bell's *British Poets* (Edinburgh, 1782–83).

editions of Spenser, Shakespeare, Milton, and occasionally Horace and Juvenal.[12] There is a particularly interesting note in Volume 2 of Thomas Newton's edition of *Paradise Lost* (1749), a propos of Eve's wish, after eating the apple, to be 'sometime / superior' to Adam (9. 823–5):

> There is a very humorous tale in *Chaucer*, which is also versify'd by *Dryden*, wherein the question is propos'd, what it is that women most affect and desire? Some say wealth, some beauty, some flattery, some in short one thing, and some another; but the true answer is sovranty. And the thought of attaining the superiority over her husband is very artfully made one of the first, that Eve entertains after eating of the forbidden fruit.[13]

Interest in Chaucer's figure extended beyond the literary. Historians of dress were interested in the Wife's clothes,[14] historians of the theatre in her fondness for miracle plays; students of religious customs in her marriages at the church door, or the burial of her fourth husband under the rood beam.[15] In no two instances, however, do the interests of different kinds of reader appear exactly to coincide. Only in the ballad, for example, is she both a believer in and receiver of infinite mercy.

Richard Brathwaite's enthusiasm for Chaucer, evidenced in 'Chaucer's Incensed Ghost', had, as we have seen, been amply demonstrated in his *Comment upon the Two Tales of ... Sr. Jeffrey Chaucer* (1665). It is significant that in 'Chaucer's Incensed Ghost' Brathwaite has Chaucer call to witness 'The am'rous Stories of my Wife of Bath' in the plural, and on the title page of his *Comment* subsumes both the Wife of Bath's *Prologue* and her *Tale* under her name. *The Wife of Bath's Prologue* was sometimes called a 'tale' and her story of the knight and the Crone was as popular as the story of her matrimonial experiences. Brathwaite pays equal attention to the Wife's account of her husbands and to the Arthurian story, regarding them as a single tale, and attends equally to words spoken by the Wife *in propria persona* and those in which she voices the words of others.

The blurring of distinctions between the Wife's *Prologue* and her *Tale*, and the variety of ways in which her words were understood is paralleled in the various attitudes taken towards both the Wife and her stories. Some writers, such as Brathwaite, describe her, with only the lightest of irony, as 'jolly', a 'charitable old Trader'

---

[12] There are several references to *The Wife of Bath's Tale* in Zachary Grey's, *Critical, Historical, and Explanatory Notes on Shakespeare* (London, 1754), and in John Upton's edition of Edmund Spenser, *The Faerie Queene, A New Edition*, 2 vols (London, 1758). There is a long quotation (on fairies and King Arthur) from her tale in Thomas Warton's *Observations on The Fairy Queen of Spenser*, 2 vols (2nd edn, London, 1762). The Wife is also cited by Thomas Newton as a source for Milton's 'thick ... As the gay motes that people the sun-beams' (*Il Penseroso*, 7–8) in his edition of *Paradise Regained, Samson Agonistes, and Poems on Several Occasions* (London, 1760), p. 36.

[13] John Milton, *Paradise Lost: A Poem*, ed. Thomas Newton, 2 vols (London, 1749), 2. 185.

[14] In *A Complete View of the Dress and Habits of the People of England*, 2 vols (London, 1796–99), 2. 168, Joseph Strutt, comments on the Wife's *wimple*.

[15] For burials under the rood beam, see William Stukeley, *Palæographia Britannica* (London, 1743), p. 56. For marriages at the church door, see William Gostling, *A Walk In and About the City of Canterbury* (Canterbury, 1774), p. 126.

(*Comment upon the Two Tales*, p. 105), and as 'this merry *Wife of Bath*' (p. 123). For others, she was the embodiment of all that was detestable in woman. For still others, she was a frank confessor of the faults of her sex—faults of which she is cheerfully conscious and by which she is frequently amused. Several readers saw Chaucer as using the Wife as a satirical mouthpiece expressing his own opinion of friars, false nobility, disbelief in incubi, and only slightly less malevolent fairies. For others, again, many of her points are to be taken seriously, either as an account of the miseries of matrimony, both for husbands and wives, or as a just revolt against male writings. For many, her obscenity was unacceptable. Samuel Wesley, for example, in 'Advice to One who was about to Write, to avoid the Immoralities of the Ancient and Modern Poets', warned against imitating her combination of obscenity and profanity: 'Sing not loose Stories for the Nonce, / Where Mirth for Bawdry ill attones, / Not long-tongu'd Wife of *Bath*, at once / On Earth and Heaven jesting.'[16] For others, her speeches were examples of admirable plain speaking.[17] Her attitudes to sexuality were endorsed by some.[18] Thomas Warton wrote of 'the genial WIFE of BATH', all the 'more amiable for her plain and useful qualifications', concluding 'She is a respectable dame.'[19] His brother Joseph called her 'a jocose old woman.'[20]

   Though all these responses refer to the Wife of Bath as a creation of Chaucer's, and though her *Prologue* and *Tale* were available in the collected editions of his work, both poems were, until publication of cheaper complete editions of English poets towards the end of the century, most often printed and read in the versions by Dryden and Pope. Their versions, moreover, were both excerpted in popular anthologies, and were conflated in many minds with the Wife's appearance in *The Wanton Wife of Bath*, which, as we have seen, was popular both via cheap reprints and by being sung on the stage as an integral part of plays. The Wife thus became a figure who both had many husbands in life, and who, after life, argued her own way into heaven. It is thus often difficult, in any given instance, to be sure which aspect of the Wife of Bath is determining readers' overall memories and responses, and precisely which version of her sayings and actions is being alluded to (see Fig. 7.2).

   The most famously adverse account of the Wife of Bath was that of William Blake:

> The characters of Women Chaucer has divided into two classes, the Lady Prioress and the Wife of Bath. Are not these leaders of the ages of men? The lady prioress, in some ages, predominates; and in some the wife of Bath, in whose character Chaucer has been equally minute and exact; because she is also a scourge and a blight. I shall say

---

[16] *Miscellaneous Poems by Several Hands* (London, 1726), p. 229.
[17] See, e.g. William King, *The Toast: An Heroick Poem in Four Books* (London, 1736), pp. 96–7.
[18] See William Hayley, *A Philosophical, Historical, and Moral Essay on Old Maids* (London, 1785), p. 129.
[19] Warton, *History*, 1. 236, 436.
[20] Joseph Warton, *An Essay on the Genius and Writings of Pope*, 2 vols (London, 1782), 2. 10.

no more of her, nor expose what Chaucer has left hidden; let the younger reader study what he has said of her: it is useful as a scare-crow. There are of such characters born too many for the peace of the world.[21]

Many writers, often young, were happy to 'expose what Chaucer has left hidden', but frequently with some palliation of what might have made Chaucer's Wife of Bath 'a scourge and a blight' or a threat to 'the peace of the world'. Some, indeed, found, or made, her charming.

John Gay's *Wife of Bath*

In the revised version of John Gay's comedy, *The Wife of Bath* (1730),[22] the Wife is described as 'talkative' and 'carnal' (I. ii. 17) and as one who 'was always a zealous advocate for the liberties of women' (I. vi. 8), but is most often portrayed by Gay as the provider of wry observations, where wit overrides bile or regret. Despite the exigencies of a complicated plot, Gay's Wife of Bath returns again and again to the topic of her five husbands: 'I have had some love, 'tis true; but then I have run the risque of a few husbands for it; they indeed had their crosses, for I was always a woman of spirit' (I. viii. 60–2). Throughout the play, she is presented as desiring yet another husband: 'Look ye, my dear, thanks to my lucky planets, I have made a shift to dispatch five good men already, and welcome the sixth, say I!' (II. i. 56–8). She convinces one young woman that marriage is preferable to a nunnery, but varies in her estimate of the degree of amorousness likely to follow in the marital state: 'I ever thought sleep so much time lost; but I never could perswade any one of my five husbands to be of this opinion' (II. vii. 3–5). Her dominant tone is taken almost straight from Chaucer—as when describing her 'constitution, which, in troth, hath worn out two brace and a half of brave jolly husbands already, and yet never the worse for it. A-lack and well-aday, that ever love was sin, say I!' (III. ix. 27–30).

In the 'Epilogue. By a Friend' to Gay's play, the Wife presents herself initially as an old soldier:[23]

> *The Toil of Wedlock five Times bravely past,*
> *You'll say,'twas cruel to be baulk'd at last.*
> *Grown old in* Cupid's *Camp—long vers'd in Arms,*

---

[21] William Blake, *'Seen In My Visions': A Descriptive Catalogue of Pictures*, ed. Martin Myrone (London, 2009), pp. 57–8.

[22] The first version of Gay's play was first performed at Drury Lane on 12 May 1713 and published on 22 May. The revised version was first performed at Lincoln's Inn Fields on 19 January 1730 and published on 3 February. The wife, although frequently on stage, is not the leading figure in either play. The play is quoted here from the text based on the revised version in John Gay, *Dramatic Works*, ed. John Fuller, 2 vols (Oxford, 1983), with line references in parenthesis.

[23] The Epilogue is the only part of Gay's play to be untouched in the revised version. John Fuller (*Dramatic Works*, 1. 412–13) suggests that the 'Friend' was Alexander Pope.

> *I from my Youth have known the Pow'r of Charms:*
> *Was I to single Combat ever slow?*
> *Did I e'er turn my Back upon the Foe?*
>
> (1–6)

The innuendo is not very subtle. Later, however, she sees herself as Triumphant Woman epitomized:

> *I danc'd, I sung, I smil'd,—I look'd demure,*
> *And caught each Lover with a diff'rent Lure:*
> *In frequent Wedlock join'd, was Woman still,*
> *And bow'd subservient Husbands to my Will.*
> *If Reason governs Man's superior Mind,*
> *A ready Cunning prompts the Female Kind.*
>
> (13–18)

Chaucer's Wife only *pretends* to believe in the superiority of male reason as the basis for her contention that males should, as reasonable beings, give way on every point. A 'ready Cunning', however, is an accurate term for what many readers took to be the determining characteristic of Chaucer's Wife—much as it had been that of the young wife in *January and May*.

Where Chaucer's Wife describes her obligatory mourning at the death of a husband, Gay's 'friend' elaborates:

> *When-ever Heav'n was pleas'd to take my Spouse,*
> *I never pin'd on Thought of former Vows;*
> *'Tis true, I sigh'd, I wept, I sobb'd at first.*
> *And tore my Hair—as decent Widows—Must:*
> *But soon another Husband dry'd mine Eyes;*
> *My Life, my Dear!—supply'd the Place of Sighs.*
>
> (25–30)

As John Fuller has observed, this is a close reproduction of Alexander Pope's *The Wife of Bath her Prologue*, given here as presented in his collected *Works* of 1717:

Whan that my fourth housbond was on bere	Thus day by day, and month by month we past;
I weep algate, and made sorie chere	It pleas'd the Lord to take my spouse at last!
As wiues moten, for it is usage	I tore my gown, I soil'd my locks with dust,
And with my kerchefe couered my visage	And beat my breasts, as wretched widows—must.
But for that I was purueied of a make	Before my face my handkerchief I spread,
I wept but small, and that I undertake.	To hide the flood of tears I did—not shed.
(WBP, 587–92; Speght 1598, Fol. 35ᵛ)	*(The Wife of Bath Her Prologue, 307–12;* Pope,*Works* [1717], p. 263)

The similarity between the Epilogue and Pope's version of the Wife's *Prologue* is partly that both Pope and Gay's 'friend' have imagined the Wife of Bath as an accomplished *performer*. As she was skilful in managing her husbands, she is skilful now in describing her past deceptions with wit, detachment, and untroubled shamelessness.

A Tale of Five Husbands: Alexander Pope, *The Wife of Bath Her Prologue*

David Nokes has suggested that Gay's *Wife of Bath* is 'closer, in both vocabulary and tone, to Chaucer's original than to Pope's refinement'. While Gay's Wife, in Nokes's view, 'has an instinctive colloquial turn of phrase, reducing principles to proverbs', Pope's Wife of Bath is 'a town-rake, sophisticated in her maxims and worldly in her views'. As an illustration, Nokes points to the moment in the 1713 version of Gay's play when the Wife 'expresses her contempt for a jealous husband': 'Would he, an old Niggard, have had ever the less Light for letting a Neighbour light a Candle at his Lanthorn?'(I. i. 176–8). This, Nokes observes, 'is taken directly from Chaucer: "He is to greet nygard that would werne /A man to lighte a candle at his lanterne; / He shal have never the lasse light, pardee"'. Gay's lines, suggests Nokes, are 'strictly localized in the domestic comedy of a *ménage à trois*', while in Pope, 'the Wife's aphorism becomes an ironic instance of self-love and social being the same':[24]

Haue thou inow, what dare the recke or care	Lord! when you have enough, what need you care
How mereley that other folke fare	How merrily soever others fare?
For certes, old dotard by your leue	Tho' all the day I take and give delight,
Ye shall haue queint inow at eue	Doubt not, sufficient will be left at night.
He is to great a nigard that woll werne	'Tis but a just and rational desire,
A man, to light a candle at his Lanterne	To light a taper at a neighbour's fire.
He shall haue neuer the lesse light, parde	
Haue thou inogh, thou darst nat plain thee:	
(*WBP*, 329–36; Speght 1598, Fol. 34ʳ)	(*The Wife of Bath Her Prologue*, 134–9; Pope,*Works* [1717], p. 254)

Pope was most concerned to maintain the rapidity of his narrative and the clarity of his irony—both when directed *by*, and *at* the Wife of Bath. In the passage quoted, his aim is more than merely a sophisticated and worldly 'refinement'. While only a 'niggard', as in Chaucer and Gay, would refuse to allow a man to light a candle at his lantern, in Pope's version the 'just and rational desire' would seem to be Alison's, to take and give delight all day—rather as Chanticleer in Dryden's *The Cock and the Fox* 'took by turns and gave so much delight' to Partlet that 'Her sisters pin'd with envy at the sight'. The Wife's aphorism is pure sleight of hand—preposterous, and of absolutely no comfort to a jealous husband. Neither Gay nor

---

[24] David Nokes, *John Gay, A Profession of Friendship* (Oxford, 1995), p. 126.

Fig. 7.2 Illustration by J. Wale, engraved by G. Mosley, of 'The Wife of Bath Her Tale' strangely retitled to illustrate lines from Pope's version of her *Prologue*: 'Ye sovereign Wives! Give ear and understand, / Thus shall ye speed and exercise Command.' From Vol. 2 of the 1753 edition of Pope's *Works*.

Pope permit themselves the indecent brutality of Chaucer's Wife ('For certes, old dotard by your leue / Ye shall haue queint inow at eue'), but in Pope the essential boast, threat, or promise, despite the more mannerly surface, is palpable: 'Doubt not, sufficient will be left at night'. But while Pope refashioned, he did not replace

Chaucer's text. The first couplet in the passage above is closer to the original than anything in Gay.

Like Dryden in his versions of Chaucer, Pope on occasion made his own paragraphs culminate in a line closely modelled on Chaucer's, and, like Gay, sometimes makes much of an archaic word. Here is his Wife of Bath recalling some husbandly abuse:

Thou saiest also, I was lyk a Catte	There's danger too, you think, in rich array,
For who so would senge the Cattes skinne	And none can long be modest that are gay.
Than would the Catte dwellen in his Inne	The Cat, if you but sindge her tabby skin,
And if the Cattes skinne be slicke and gay	The chimney keeps, and sits content within;
She nill nat dwell in hous halfe a day	But once grown sleek, will from her corner run,
But forth she woll or any day be dawed	Sport with her tail, and wanton in the sun;
To shew her skin and gon a Catrewawed.	She licks her fair round face, and frisks abroad
	To show her furr, and to be catterwaw'd.
(*WBP*, 348–54; Speght 1598, Fol. 34ʳ)	(*The Wife of Bath Her Prologue*, 140–7; Pope, *Works* [1717], pp. 254–5)

The concluding word in this passage—*catterwaw'd*—was given in italics in the first edition of Pope's version, in Steele's *Poetical Miscellanies* (1713; dated 1714). The editors of the Longman Annotated English Poets edition suggest that the italics 'emphasise an overt archaism and bawdy suggestion'.[25] In Chaucer, however, the female cat will herself *catterwaw*, while in Pope she will *be catterwaw'd*—presumably by the local tomcats.[26] This is the wife reporting, very vividly, the words of one of her stupid husbands, who had himself given a vivid account of feline sexuality. She is a superb mimic or ventriloquist. She enjoys giving the husbands the best lines she has.[27] Here, both the Wife and her husband, ostensibly the original speaker, have been temporarily forgotten. Pope has directed attention almost entirely to the cat sporting with her tail, and wantoning in the sun.

In Pope's version, we get almost equal quantities of reported speech from the Wife—whether or not noticeably coloured by her own attitude—and direct speech in the Wife's own voice. In the following passage, the Wife is giving the imagined speech of what her husbands *should have* said, but did not. The marginal quotation marks are present both in the first edition, and in the text included in Pope's *Works* (1717):

---

[25] Alexander Pope, *Poems, Vol. 1*, ed. Paul Baines and Julian Ferraro (London, 2019), p. 664.

[26] The same mistaken passive use of the verb 'catterwawe' (if mistake it is) was made by Andrew Jackson (whose cat 'Gets Catterwawl'd'; *Matrimonial Scenes*, p. 46), but not by Richard Braithwait: 'You say a sleek-skinned Cat will ever go a Caterwawing; she cannot abide keeping at home. No more will I … I must needs be shewing my gay Cloaths, there is no remedy' (*A Comment upon the Two Tales of Our Ancent, Renowned, and Ever-Living Poet Sr Jeffray Chaucer*, p. 94).

[27] In the Speght edition of 1602, there are as many approving manicules pointing to the comments of the husbands as there are to the Wife's reports.

wife, go where you list
Take your disport, I woll leue no tales
I know you for a true wife dame Ales

(WBP, 318–20; Speght 1598, Fol. 34^r)

'Go where you will,
'Dear spouse, I credit not the tales they tell.
'Take all the freedoms of a married life;
'I know thee for a virtuous, faithful wife.

(The Wife of Bath Her Prologue, 130–3;
Pope, Works [1717], p. 254)

And here she is recalling in Pope's version (though more elegantly), her very intimate words to her husband *verbatim*—and dramatizing the source of her power:

What aileth you to grutch thus and grone?
Is it for ye would haue me queint alone?
Why take it all, lo, haue it eyery dell
Peter beshrew you but you loue it well.
For if I would sel my belchose
I couth walke as fresh as any rose,
But I woll kepe it for your own toth
Ye be to blame by God, I say you soth.

(WBP, 443–50; Speght 1598, Fol. 34^v)

'Fye, 'tis unmanly thus to sigh and groan;
'What? wou'd you have me to your self alone?
'Why take me, Love! take all and ev'ry part!
'Here's your revenge! you love it at your heart.
'Would I vouchsafe to sell what nature gave,
'You little think what custom I could have?
'But see! I'm all your own—nay hold—for shame!
'What means my dear—indeed—you are to blame.[28]

(The Wife of Bath Her Prologue, 197–204;
Pope, Works [1717], pp. 257–8)

Although much abbreviated from Chaucer's original, the husbands' appearance and speeches are both strongly evoked by Pope and Pope's Wife:

Thou comest home as drunken as a Mouse
And preachest on thy bench with yuel prefe
Thou saiest to me, it is a great mischefe
To wedde a poore woman for costage
And if that she be rich of high parage
Than saiest thou, it is a very tourmentry
To suffer her pride and her Malancoly
And if that she be faire, thou very knaue
Thou saiest that euery holour woll her haue
She may no while in chastite abide
That is assailed on euery side

(WBP, 246–56; Speght 1598, Fol. 34^r)

But you reel home, a drunken beastly bear,
Then preach till midnight in your easy chair;
Cry Wives are false, and ev'ry woman evil,
And give up all that's female to the devil.
    If poor (you say) she drains her husband's purse;
If rich, she keeps her Priest, or something worse;
If highly born, intolerably vain;
Vapours and pride by turns possess her brain:
Now gaily mad, now sourly splenatic,
Freakish when well, and fretful when she's sick.
If fair, then chaste she cannot long abide,
By pressing youth attack'd on ev'ry side.
If foul, her wealth the lusty lover lures,
Or else her wit some fool-gallant procures.

(The Wife of Bath Her Prologue, 82–95;
Pope, Works [1717], pp. 251–2)

There is no end to the complaints of the husbands—or those of the Wife—and therefore there can be no happy ending to *The Wife of Bath Her Prologue*. Pope, who had worked so hard to bring *January and May*—and also, if he had some hand in the poem, *The Miller of Trompington*—to a pleasing conclusion, seems

---

[28] Andrew Jackson at this point has his Wife remember herself saying to a suddenly amorous husband (as if a mock-heroic version of Juno to Jupiter) 'Psha, pish, what in the Face of Day,—and here!' (*Matrimonial Scenes*, p. 49).

not to have been able to credit or re-imagine the events with which Chaucer's Wife of Bath ends her tale. The domestic violence between Alison and Jankin is only slightly less comically brutal in his version than in Chaucer's—though there are fewer mentions of Alison's permanent deafness resulting from her husband's beating.[29] Pope has truncated the whole business—but most particularly the words of the terrified husband:

... at the laste out of my swoun I braid	I groan'd, and lay extended on my Side;
Oh, hast thow slain me false thefe I saied	Oh! thou hast slain me for my wealth (I cry'd)
For my lond thus hast thou murdred me?	Yet I forgive thee—take my last embrace.
Er I be dedde, yet woll I ones kisse thee	He wept, kind soul! and stoop'd to kiss my face;
And nere he came, and kneled faire adoun	I took him such a box as turn'd him blue,
And saied: deere suster, swete Alisoun	Then sigh'd and cry'd, Adieu my Dear, adieu!
As help me God I shal thee neuer smite	
That I have doen it is thy self to wite	
Foryeve it me, and that I thee beseke	
And yet eftsones I hitte hym on the cheke	
And saied: thefe, thus moch am I bewreke Now	
Now woll I die, I may no lenger speke.	
(WBP, 799–810; Speght 1598, Fol. 36ᵛ)	(The Wife of Bath Her Prologue, 419–24; Pope, Works [1717], pp. 268–9)

By means of her final deception, the Wife of Bath in Pope's version achieves an unconditional triumph, expressing herself in almost political terms, and assuming 'government' and 'empire' with 'absolute command':

But at the laste, with mikell care and wo	But after many a hearty struggle past,
We fell accorded within our seluen two	I condescended to be pleas'd at last.
He yaf me all the bridell in myne hond	Soon as he said, My mistress and my Wife,
To haue the gouernaunce of hous and lond	Do what you list, the term of all your life:
And of his tongue, and of his hond also	I took to heart the merits of the cause,
And made hem brenne his booke anon tho	And stood content to rule by wholsome laws;
And whan I had gotten unto me	Receiv'd the reins of absolute command,)
By maistry, all the souerainete	With all the government of house and land;)
Than he saied: mine owne true wife	And empire o'er his tongue, and o'er his hand.)
Doe as thou list, the terme of all thy life	As for the volume that revil'd the dames,
Kepe thyne honour, and eke mine estate	'Twas torn to fragments, and condemn'd to flames.
After that day we had neuer debate	
God helpe me so, I was to him as kinde	
As any wife fro Denmarke unto Inde	
And also true, and so was he to me	
I pray to God, that sitte in Maiestie	
So blesse his soule, for his mercy dere.	
(WBP, 811–26; Speght 1598, Fol. 36ᵛ)	(The Wife of Bath Her Prologue, 427–38; Pope, Works [1717], p. 269)

---

[29] Andrew Jackson's Wife of Bath (Matrimonial Scenes, p. 63) seems to hit her husband rather feebly compared with Chaucer's. This weakens the tale and makes the ending (which explains how she wins sovereignty) unclear.

In the early decades of the eighteenth century, 'wholesome laws' were often said to have been established by ancient, rather than contemporary, sovereigns.[30] Pope's Wife is giving away *nothing*.[31] Richard Brathwaite, on the other hand, who had *invented* a more pleasing conclusion for *The Miller's Tale* than Chaucer had provided, was, on this occasion, content to paraphrase. The bargain as described in Chaucer constituted, as Brathwaite read it, a 'very beneficial Peace for Jenkin'—'a shrewd Dame to a peaceable Wife changed':

> Never from that time did any Wife from *Denmark* to *India* (to take her own Compass) live with Husband in more Unity … and all this without Hypocrisie … One True-Love Knot betwixt them both: So faithful was his Love to her till the End, as she cannot chuse but remember his Soul in her Prayers after his end.[32]

The Wife, Brathwaite observes at this point, 'thinks he had his Purgatory of Earth, and consequently, without any Rub or Stay in his way, he may go directly to Heaven' (p. 108). In Pope, the Wife prays with marked irony. Her husbands may be in Heaven only because she gave them Purgatory on Earth:

> Now heav'n on all my husbands gone, bestow
> Pleasures above, for tortures felt below:
> That rest they wish'd for, grant them in the grave,
> And bless those souls my conduct help'd to save!
>
> *(The Wife of Bath Her Prologue*, 439–41;
> Pope, *Works* [1717], p. 269)

Pope, that is, has taken the dominating thought from earlier in the Wife's own *Prologue*: 'By God, in yearth I was his purgatorie / For which I hope his soul be in glory'.

Like *January and May*, *The Wife of Bath Her Prologue* passed unmodified into the collection of the slightly squeamish Lipscomb—as well it might. Thomas Tyers recounted the reaction of John Hughes, the editor of Spenser: 'Hughes, the agreeable poet and prose-writer, hearing this prologue was to be inserted, which, as the editor of his life says, was inconsistent with his ideas of decency, withdrew his name and his contribution of pieces.'[33] Tyers himself, however, was of a different opinion:

---

[30] See Charles Davenant, *Essays upon I. The Ballance of Power. II. The Right of Making War, Peace, and Alliances. III. Universal Monarchy* (London, 1701) p. 237; John Seller, *The History of England* (London, 1703), p. 67; George Smalridge, *Twelve Sermons Preach'd on Several Occasions* (Oxford, 1717), p. 212.

[31] The triumph of Andrew Jackson's Wife's is similarly political ('When like a Monarch, seated on his Throne, / I found the sov'reign Pow'r was all my own; / And when my subject Spouse, cry'd dearest Wife, / Do as you list the Term of all your Life, / Take to thy Charge my Honour and Estate, / We from that Moment never had Debate') but is, like Chaucer's, generous in victory: 'So help me Heav'n, as I was kind and true, / As any Wife from *England* to *Peru*' (Jackson, *Matrimonial Scenes*, pp. 63–4).

[32] Richard Brathwaite, *A Comment*, pp. 144–5.

[33] Thomas Tyers, *An Historical Rhapsody on Mr. Pope* (London, 1782), p. 39.

> Pope modernised the prologue to Chaucer's Wife of Bath ... which Dryden says, he durst not adventure because it was too licentious. Whatever may be in the original text, the translator had pretty well disguised it. The *old Crone*, if not over modest, is not very barefaced.[34]

From Pope's version, it was hard to deduce quite what Dryden had found in the poem that deserved such a warning. Joseph Warton wondered at Pope's choice of this poem of Chaucer's, which 'perhaps nothing but his youth could excuse', but observed that the lines of the poem 'are spirited and easy, and have, properly enough, a free colloquial air'. He noted that Pope had 'omitted or softened the grosser or more offensive passages'.[35] Pope had reduced Chaucer's poem by almost half and had apparently excised all that had caused offence. At times, particularly during the first 150 lines of his poem, he seems almost to be composing a decent summary of the Wife's words. Although they are often replaced with innuendo of various kinds, Pope had removed a great many instances when the wife refers to her own body as a whole or to some of its parts.[36] Gone, for example, are the Wife's speculations on the intended function of 'membres of generation', 'our bothe things small', or her husbands' 'seley instrument'. If the 'queynte's' were clearly taboo, Pope was no less abstemious with the Wife's euphemisms: her 'belle chose', and her 'quoniam'.

The greatest difference between *The Wife of Bath Her Prologue* and *January and May* is the absence in the former of the divinities whose presence lifts the poem into a magical realm in which a comic perspective on the action is made possible and outrageous behaviour is made to seem delightful. Although they are coloured by her prevailing attitudes and exaggeration, there is no escape in the *Prologue* from the quotidian realities of the Wife's domestic life on the one hand, and the tales of murderous and incestuous wives in Jankin's book, on the other. The unrelenting scepticism of Chaucer's Wife towards anything expounded by 'clerkes' of any religion is, in Pope, replaced by nothing. From Pope's point of view, perhaps, the Wife's final trick did not seem sufficiently or outrageously clever, and only some extra-human comic force could bring into being Jankin's complete, sudden, and unprepared change of tone: 'Deere suster, swete Alisoun', 'mine owene treue wife / Doe as thou list, the terme of all thy life'. For readers of Pope's version of the Wife's *Prologue*, as it was combined with Dryden's version of her *Tale* in the collected and connected versions of *The Canterbury Tales* of 1741 and 1795, that situation would be remedied.

---

[34] Ibid. pp. 38–9.
[35] Joseph Warton, *An Essay on Pope*, 2.10, 6–7.
[36] W. H. Dilworth, *The Life of Alexander Pope* (London, 1759), p. 36 observed that both *January and May* and *The Wife of Bath Her Prologue* 'tend a little to obscenity, or to use the softest terms, strongly abound with warm *double entendre*. But the Fault being originally Chaucer's, it is not to be solely imputed to his imitator.'

Dryden's Version of *The Wife of Bath's Tale*

In George Ogle's collected *Canterbury Tales* of 1741, immediately following Alexander Pope's account of the *Wife of Bath's Prologue*, which itself immediately follows *January and May*, the Friar makes the joking observation that 'twas a long Preamble of a Tale'. Having 'chuckled' at his own 'Speech so smart', he then quarrels with the Sumner, until brought to silence by 'our Lordly Host', who, with respectful politeness, asks the Wife of Bath to continue. The Wife is surprisingly acquiescent, her irony only emerging in one word in italics:

> I'll do the best to please you that I can,
> If I have Licence[37] from this *worthy* Man.

Then, on the next page, follows the poem entitled, in Ogle's collection, 'The Desire of Woman: or, the Wife of Bath's Tale. By Mr. Dryden'.[38]

Dryden's version, of course, had first appeared long before Ogle's collection. In his *Fables*, its title had been given as *The Wife of Bath, Her Tale, from Chaucer*, and on the half title to the poem itself as *The Wife of Bath Her Tale*. Dryden was presenting the tale as spoken by the 'the broad-speaking gap-tooth'd Wife of *Bathe*', a woman who said much that savoured of 'Immodesty' 'in the Prologue to her Tale' on which he had not dared 'to adventure ... because 'tis too licentious'.[39] In the Preface to *Fables*, Dryden had noted that the 'Matter and Manner' of each of the tales told by Chaucer's pilgrims 'are so suited to their different Educations, Humours, and Callings, that each of them would be improper in any other Mouth'.[40] But when turning to Chaucer's Wife of Bath, Dryden, mindful of the criticisms surveyed in Chapter 6, was aware of the need for caution. In concentrating attention on the tale itself, Dryden successfully avoided renewed accusations of obscenity. His version was included alongside Pope's version of *The Wife of Bath's Prologue* in William Lipscomb's composite translation of the *Canterbury Tales* (1795), from which, as we have seen, the tales of the Miller and the Reeve were omitted altogether.

The Voices of the Wife of Bath

Although Dryden may have seen *The Wife of Bath's Tale*, in broad terms, as suited to its teller, he clearly thought that it had an intrinsic interest which went far beyond a mere exhibition of the Wife's 'character', or a mere 'fictional fulfilment of the

---

[37] The (ecclesiastical) term is also used ironically by Chaucer.
[38] Ogle, 3. 73–5.
[39] Dryden, *Works*, 7, 37, 38, 43.
[40] Ibid. 7, 37.

wife's fantasy of female power'.[41] There are, indeed, vivid and vigorous moments in Dryden's version of the tale, as in Chaucer's original, where the Wife steps in to interrupt or contradict her own tale. When one female witness in the tale maintains that women like to keep secrets, the Wife, thinking the notion absurd, recasts Ovid's tale of Midas so that it is the royal wife, rather than his barber, who blabs the truth about Midas's ass's ears. Most strikingly of all, it is the Wife of the *Prologue* whose defiant voice ends the tale—in Chaucer ('I pray to God to shorte her liues / That will not be gouerned by her wiues')—and in Dryden:

> And so may all our Lives like their's be led;
> Heav'n send the Maids young Husbands, fresh in Bed:
> May Widows Wed as often as they can,
> And ever for the better change their Man,
> And some devouring Plague pursue their Lives,
> Who will not well be govern'd by their Wives.
>
> (*The Wife of Bath Her Tale*, 541–6; Dryden, *Works*, 7.481, 483.)

But elsewhere Dryden's Wife of Bath presents a narrative that is independent of her 'personality'—perhaps not surprisingly, considering that, as Pope demonstrated, the Wife of Bath is a speaker who is *ondoyant et divers*, who articulates a kaleidoscopic variety of sentiments and attitudes that are actually not always consonant or consistent with one another. The prevailing impression of Dryden's version of her tale is one of constant surprise.

Fiends, Imps, Fryars, and a Midnight Parson

The very first lines of *The Wife of Bath's Tale*, which contrast country life in 'Days of Old, when *Arthur* fill'd the Throne' with that of more recent times, constitute one such surprising moment. Here, Dryden seems to have attempted to match the Wife's wit, if not her psychology. The Wife's most recent enemy, the Friar, is included in the picture. Dryden has slightly increased the satire by making his friars run to '*wealthy* Regions' and 'Farmers rich'—where Chaucer's Wife had seen them in 'euery land and euery streme / As thicke as motes in the Sunne beme'. But in Dryden's version, the friars are surrounded by an astonishing number of clerical and supernatural beings, helping or preying upon dairy-maids, country girls, and late-returning labourers. Dryden partly mimics the mercurial activity of all these beings in an unusually long run of rapidly moving triplets.

---

[41] Geoffrey Chaucer, *The Canterbury Tales*, ed. A. C. Cawley, intro. by Derek Pearsall (New York, London, Toronto, 1992), p. xv.

The passage was extraordinarily popular, both in the original and in Dryden's version, and deserves quoting in full:

In the old daies of King Artour	In Days of Old, when *Arthur* fill'd the Throne,
(Of which the Bretōs speakē greet honour)	Whose Acts and Fame to Foreign Lands were blown;
Al was this lond fulfilled of fairy	The King of Elves, and little Fairy Queen
The Elfe quene, with her ioly company	Gamboll'd on Heaths, and danc'd on ev'ry Green.
Daunsed full oft in many a grene mede	And where the jolly Troop had led the round
This was the old opinion as I rede	The Grass unbidden rose, and mark'd the Ground:
I speake of many an hundred yere ago	Nor darkling did they dance, the Silver Light
But now can no man se none elfes mo	Of *Phœbe* serv'd to guide their Steps aright,
For now the great charite and praiers	And, with their Tripping pleas'd, prolong'd the night.
Of limitours and other holy Freres	Her beams they follow'd, where at full she plaid,
That serchen euery land and euery streme	Nor longer than she shed her Horns they staid,
As thicke as motes in the Sunne beme	From thence with airy Flight to Foreign Lands convey'd.
Blissing halles, chambers, kitchenes, & boures,	Above the rest our *Britain* held they dear,
Citees, borowes, castelles, and hie toures	More solemnly they kept their Sabbaths here,
Thropes, Bernes, shepens, and Deiries	And made more spacious Rings, and revell'd half the Year.
This maketh, that there been no faieries	I speak of ancient Times, for now the Swain
For there as wont to walke was an Elfe	Returning late may pass the Woods in vain,
There walketh now the limitour hymselfe	And never hope to see the nightly Train:
In undermeles, and in mornynges	In vain the Dairy now with Mints is dress'd,
And saieth his Mattins, & and his holy things	The Dairy-Maid expects no Fairy Guest,
As he goeth in his limitacioun	To skim the Bowls and after pay the Feast.
Women may go safely vp and doun	She sighs and shakes her empty Shoes in vain,
In euery bush, and under euery tre	No Silver Penny to reward her Pain:
There nis none other incubus but he	For Priests with Pray'rs, and other godly Geer,
And he ne will doen hem no dishonour	Have made the merry Goblins disappear;
	And where they plaid their merry Pranks before,
	Have sprinkled Holy Water on the Floor:
	And Fry'rs that through the wealthy Regions run
	Thick as the Motes, that twinkle in the Sun;
	Resort to Farmers rich, and bless their Halls
	And exorcise the Beds, and cross the Walls:
	This makes the Fairy Quires forsake the Place,
	When once 'tis hallow'd with the Rites of Grace:
	But in the Walks where wicked Elves have been,
	The Learning of the Parish now is seen,
	The Midnight Parson posting o'er the Green.
	With Gown tuck'd up to Wakes; for *Sunday* next,
	With humming Ale encouraging his Text;
	Nor wants the holy Leer to Country-Girl betwixt.
	From Fiends and Imps he sets the Village free,
	There haunts not any Incubus, but He.
	The Maids and Women need no Danger fear
	To walk by Night, and Sanctity so near:
	For by some Haycock or some shady Thorn
	He bids his Beads both Even-song and Morn.

(*WBT*, 857–81; Speght 1598, Fol. 36ᵛ) (*The Wife of Bath Her Tale*, 1–44; Dryden, *Works*, 7. 451–3)

Dryden's passage, as so often in his Chaucer versions, expands his original considerably, and makes explicit and emphatic sentiments and observations that are more discreetly and implicitly signalled in the original. But the additions here, and elsewhere in *The Wife of Bath Her Tale*, can be seen to be 'growing out of' rather than 'stuck into' his original.[42]

In this opening, Dryden has responded fully to the poised play of wit that is pervasive in Chaucer's tale. He has transformed the 'fairy-tale' element in Chaucer's opening, building in echoes of the diminutive (and thus un-Chaucerian) fairies' 'merry Pranks' and Puck's milk-skimming from Shakespeare's *A Midsummer Night's Dream*, and from his own description of fairy rings in *The Hind and Panther* (which itself had been prompted by the 'green ... ringlets' of Shakespeare's *The Tempest*),[43] adding references to folk superstitions about fairies,[44] and incorporating touches from the celebrated evocation of a lost fairy realm in Richard Corbett's 'A Proper New Ballad, Intituled The Faeryes Farewell': 'When *Tom* came home from labour, / Or *Cisse* to milking rose, / Then merrily merrily went their Tabour / And nimbly went their Toes'.[45]

The effect is to reinforce Chaucer's, or the Wife's, setting of the tale in an imaginary realm, removed in crucial ways, like the garden in *January and May*, from the everyday realities and mundanities of the present. But the effect is not merely to encourage nostalgia for a Land of Lost Content. The fairies, it is made clear, were mischievous as well as beneficent, and included 'Fiends', 'Imps' and 'Incubi'. And their replacement by 'Priests', 'Fryars', and 'Limitours' is not portrayed as a matter for straightforward lament. Even the ample girth of the much-famed King Arthur is momentarily and gently mocked when we are told that 'In Days of Old' he '*fill'd* the Throne'. The new-style priests come in for some of the strokes of anti-clerical satire which are pervasive in Dryden's work. But, at the same time, the resemblance of the 'Fryars' to 'Motes, that twinkle in the Sun' and the image of the 'Midnight Parson' 'posting o'er the Green, / With Gown tuck'd up to Wakes; for *Sunday* next, / With humming Ale encouraging his Text' is presented in a manner somewhere between genial amusement and satirical animus. Dryden renders the Wife of Bath's attitude towards both the fairies and the priests who have replaced them as *simultaneously* satirical and appreciative, her usual persistent anti-clericalism issuing on this occasion into comic creation.

---

[42] See Dryden's description of the additions in his translation of Virgil (*Dedication of the Aeneis*; Dryden, *Works*, 5. 329).

[43] See *The Hind and Panther*, 1. 212–15; Dryden, *Works*, 3. 129 (and note at p. 365, referring to *The Tempest*, V. i. 36).

[44] See the passages from Robert Burton, John Gerarde, and Richard Brathwaite cited in John Dryden, *Poems*, ed. Paul Hammond and David Hopkins, 5 vols (Harlow, 1995–2005), 5.499–500.

[45] See Richard Corbett, *Poems*, ed. J. A. W. Bennett and H. R. Trevor-Roper (Oxford, 1955), pp. 49–52, cited by Tom Mason, 'Dryden's Version of The Wife of Bath's Tale', *Cambridge Quarterly*, 6 (1975), 240–56.

The Rape—According to Voltaire and 'Sir Gregory Gander'

The most striking and starkest emphasis in the tale on the brute reality that coun-
terpoints the fairy activity is the description of the rape of the country girl by
the young knight—so unlike his Spenserian counterpart, as Dryden signals by an
immediately recognizable echo of the opening of *The Faerie Queene* ('A Gentle
Knight was pricking on the plaine').[46] In Dryden's version, we are allowed to see
the knight's lust for the 'Damsel gay' almost from his own point of view:

And so fell it, that this king Artour	It so befel in this King *Arthur*'s Reign, ⎫
Had in his house a lusty bacheler,	A lusty Knight was pricking o'er the Plain; ⎬
That on a day come riding fro the riuer	A Batchelor he was, and of the courtly Train. ⎭
And happed, that alone as he was borne	It happen'd as he rode, a Damsel gay
He saw a maid walkyng him biforne	In Russet-Robes to Market took her way;
Of which maid anon, maugre her hed	Soon on the Girl he cast an amorous Eye,
(By very force) he biraft her maidenhed	So strait she walk'd, and on her Pasterns high:
For which oppression was soch clamour	If seeing her behind he lik'd her Pace:
And soch pursute vnto king Artour	He lights in hast, and full of Youthful Fire,
That dampned was this knight to be dedde	By Force accomplish'd his obscene Desire:
By course of law, & should haue lost his hed	This done away he rode, not unespy'd,
	For swarming at his Back the Country cry'd;
	And once in view they never lost the Sight,
	But seiz'd, and pinion'd brought to court the Knight.
(WBT, 882–92; Speght 1598, Fol. 36ᵛ)	*(The Wife of Bath Her Tale*, 46–60;
	Dryden,*Works*, 7. 453)

Dryden's semi-projection into the Knight's consciousness, however, in no way
inclines him to pardon the Knight's actions.[47] The Knight's 'Desire' is clearly
registered—in an addition by Dryden—as 'obscene' (56). He is a 'brutal Ravisher'
(72) who is condemned to death according to the Law of King Arthur.

The distinctive emphases of Dryden's reworking of *The Wife of Bath's Tale* are
thrown into relief by a consideration of the only other two eighteenth-century versions of Chaucer's tale. One is by Voltaire; the other, 'The Wife of Bath's Tale. From
Chaucer', first published in *The New Paradise of Dainty Devices*' (London, 1777)
and reprinted with revisions, in *Poetical Tales. By Sir Gregory Gander* (Bath, 1778),
is the work of the miscellaneous author and scholar George Ellis (1753–1815).[48]
Ellis treats Chaucer's original in a flippant, almost burlesque manner, playing the

---

[46] Dryden alludes to the opening of Spenser's *Faerie Queene* in his replacement of Chaucer's 'lusty
batcheler ... riding fro the riuer' with 'lusty Knight ... pricking o'er the Plain'.

[47] *Pace* A. C. Spearing, who, in saying that 'the initial rape is ... seen through the rapist's eyes', seems to
imply that this necessarily involves *approval* of the knight's actions. See 'Rewriting Romance: Chaucer's
and Dryden's *Wife of Bath's Tale*', in Ruth Morse and Barry Windeatt, eds., *Chaucer Traditions: Studies
in Honour of Derek Brewer* (Cambridge, 1990), pp. 234–48 (p. 242).

[48] *The New Paradise of Dainty Devices* is said to be 'By Different Hands', but is attributed, in its
entirety, by ESTC and ECCO to the minor poet, Sir John Henry Moore (1756–80). The volume in
which the revised version of 'The Wife of Bath's Tale. From Chaucer' was published, however, was immediately identified as the work of George Ellis, whose later work included a substantial and popular

action consistently for laughs, and only slightly mollifying in his revised text the coarse touches of his original poem. Both of Ellis's versions, for example, make light of the rape. In the unrevised version, it is said that the knight 'took it in his head / To womanize a maid'. In the revised version, he made 'one mistake': 'for want of time' he 'never ask'd the Lady's leave' and his action thus 'appear'd to all the quorum / A most prodigious indecorum'. In the earlier version, his action had been

> a breach of all decorum,
> A violation o'th' *sanctum sanctorum*
>   A crime for which there could be no remission,
> Thus to enter
>   Without permission
> A lady's venter.
>
> (*Dainty Devices*, p. 16)

Ellis uses *The Wife of Bath's Tale* as an excuse for ribald and somewhat facile raillery, rather than engaging with Chaucer's tale—in which the rape is the primary event from which all else follows—at any deeper level.

A far more artistically serious engagement with Chaucer's tale is to be found in the French verse tale by Voltaire, *Ce qui plaît aux dames*, first published separately but then given wider currency in *Contes de Guillaume Vadé* (1764).[49] This poem was directly based on Dryden's version rather than Chaucer's original, but is significantly different from both in its main emphases.[50] If the voice of the Wife of Bath is by no means consistently or obtrusively present in Chaucer and Dryden, it is entirely absent in Voltaire, who adopts a suave, gentlemanly narrative

---

contribution to the study of earlier English literature, *Specimens of the Early English Poets*, 3 vols (London, 1801) (to be discussed in Chapter 12). Since the poems in *The New Paradise of Dainty Devices* were, as we have seen, described as 'by different hands', and since the version of *The Wife of Bath's Tale* does not appear in any of the later editions of that collection, it seems reasonable to suppose that Ellis gave permission for his poem to be included in *The New Paradise* before his own slightly revised version of the following year. (An alternative explanation is that the inclusion of the poem in *The New Paradise* was unauthorized, and represents an earlier state of a text that was revised by Ellis before he published it in his own collection of 1778). In the discussion below, use is made of both texts, neither of which is included in Bowden, ed., *Eighteenth-Century Modernizations*, but quoted consistently from *The New Paradise of Dainty Devices*.

[49] 'Guillaume Vadé' was a name adopted by Voltaire as a *nom de plume*. For the early separate editions of Voltaire's tale, see Voltaire, *Les Oeuvres Completes de Voltaire*, Vol. 57B (Oxford, 2014), pp. 32–35. For Dryden as Voltaire's source, see Donald Clive Stuart, 'The Source of Two of Voltaire's 'Contes en Vers', *Modern Language Review*, 12 (1917), 177–81. Voltaire's poem was translated into English, closely and elegantly, in Vol. 25 (1765) of *The Works of M. de Voltaire*, ed. Tobias Smollett and Thomas Francklin, 35 vols (London, 1761–65). It is not known precisely who was responsible for the translation of 'Ce qui plaît aux dames', but Eugène Joliat suggests that the translations from Voltaire's verse in the Smollett/Francklin edition were (like those of Voltaire's plays) likely to have been the work of Francklin. See Eugéne Joliat, 'Smollett, Editor of Voltaire', *Modern Language Notes*, 54 (1939), 429–36. Quotations in English above are taken from the translation in Smollett/Francklin, and in French from the edition cited above, with page and line references given in the text.

[50] For an itemization of printings of versions of Dryden's poem in France, Germany, and Denmark, see Bowden, *The Wife of Bath in Afterlife*, p. 135.

persona very close to his own voice in other works. The incident, moreover, with which Voltaire's tale begins, is significantly different from that in its Drydenian source. The young girl, called Marton by Voltaire, is not raped by the 'chevalier' Robert, but submits voluntarily to his advances, for a payment of 'vingt écus'. During their encounter, the eggs which she is carrying to market are broken, and Robert's horse and Marton's payment are purloined by a passing monk, and it is the loss of her 'vingt écus' that takes precedence over other any other considerations when making her complaint against Robert to King Dagobert.

Courts of Kings

The 'chevalier' is, however, condemned to death—until the condemnation is suspended, as in Chaucer and Dryden, by the Queen, on condition that he discovers what women most desire. In Dryden, the court of King Arthur had been explicitly—and favourably—contrasted, in lines that have no equivalent in Chaucer, with those of the late seventeenth century:

> Then Courts of Kings were held in high Renown,
> E'er made the common Brothels of the Town:
> There, Virgins honourable Vows receiv'd,
> But chast as Maids in Monasteries liv'd.
>
> (*The Wife of Bath Her Tale*, 61–4; Dryden, *Works*, 7. 453–5)

Dryden's account had then incorporated a glance at the court of Charles II, when the poets, although living in 'a vicious age', were in themselves 'not bad', but had 'debauch'd the Stage' in order to 'please the Prince'. Dryden was here drawing on his own body of reflections on the courts he had served, and with whose corrupt values he felt he had become complicit. Such feelings found expression on several occasions in his later work,[51] but were perhaps most forcibly voiced when comparing his own work, and that of some of his dramatist contemporaries, with the poems of the young Anne Killigrew. There, Dryden confesses that, 'hurry'd down' a 'lubrique and adult'rate age', the playwrights of Charles's court had 'Debas'd' the 'Heav'nly Gift of Poesy' to 'each obscene and impious use', and had increased 'the steaming Ordures of the Stage'.[52]

One important difference between the Court of King Arthur, as described by Chaucer, and that of King Charles is that women play a crucial judicial role. The knight gains a temporary reprieve by courtesy of the Court Ladies, to whose petitions Arthur, a 'slave' to 'Nuptial Ties', yields, and who establish themselves

---

[51] See David Hopkins, *John Dryden* (Cambridge, 1986), pp. 90–4.
[52] *To the Pious Memory of … Mrs Anne Killigrew*, 56–65; Dryden, *Works*, 3. 111.

temporarily as a 'Female Parliament'. He is sent by the Ladies on his quest to discover what it is that women most desire. In Dryden (Chaucer is silent on the point), the Ladies' actions are as much prompted by romantic sentiment as by humanitarian principle. They 'thought it much a Man should die for Love' and cover 'their Kindness with dissembled Hate' (78, 80). In Voltaire, the ladies remark that the chevalier is notably handsome. In Ellis's version, the Queen engineers the knight's reprieve partly because she understands 'The force of youthful flesh and blood' and partly because she would frequently herself, out of weariness with 'the pomp of pow'r', 'pass a leisure hour / In cuckolding the King'.

The Women's Answers

Missing from Voltaire's tale is any equivalent to the lengthy passage in which Dryden's knight, in an expansion of Chaucer, is given a procession of diverse and contradictory answers to the question of what women most desire. Robert's doubts are not so much about what answer he should give to the question, as about how he might present his answer tactfully to the queen:

'Comment nommer, disait-il en lui-même,	How can I in plain terms declare
Très nettement ce que toute femme aime,	What 'tis that pleases all the fair,
Sans la fâcher?	And not her majesty offend?
(106–8)	(p. 15)

In Voltaire, there is no disagreement about the answer to the question. It is simply that Robert's witnesses will not come clean on the matter:

Toutes mentaient; nulle n'allait au fait.	All gave evasive answers, none
	The real truth wou'd fairly own.
(116)	(p. 15)

For Ellis, the quest to find 'The object of all womankind's desire' is an opportunity for salacious obscenity—but of the kind, as we have seen, common in versions of Chaucer's comic tales, where the taboo word is avoided at the very moment that the thing, action, or event being depicted is expanded upon with apparent relish. Ellis passes over several of the knight's witnesses quickly until he dwells at length on 'some' who 'pretended in one spot to find / The great controuler of the female mind'. He does not evaluate this suggestion, but claims with mock coyness that his 'muse is so extremely modest / She swears she will not name the place', and instead gives the following:

> 'Tis that which *Venus* shew'd to *Paris*—
> It is a kind of secret locket,
> A locket which my lady carries

For her virginity to sleep in,
> It sleeps as if 'twas in her pocket
Till she marries,
When 'tis no longer worth the keeping.
> (*Dainty Devices*, p. 18)

In Dryden, as in Chaucer, it is far otherwise. The various responses of the various ladies are of no use to the troubled knight because each 'answer'd ... according to her Mind; / To please her self, not all the Female Kind'. The collected testimony is presented as a comical cacophony, a miscellaneous account of the anarchic range of individual female desires:

> One was for Wealth, another was for Place:
> Crones old and ugly, wish'd a better Face.
> The Widow's Wish was oftentimes to Wed;
> The wanton Maids were all for Sport a Bed ...
> One thought the Sexes prime Felicity
> Was from the Bonds of Wedlock to be free:
> Their Pleasures, Hours, and Actions all their own,
> And uncontroll'd to give Account to none.
> (*The Wife of Bath Her Tale*, 125–8, 135–8;
> Dryden,*Works*, 7. 457–9)

Chaucer's Wife of Bath offers occasional assessment of the answers; on the opinion that women do not like to have their vices pointed out, she says:

> For trewly there nis none of us all,
> If any wight wol clawe us on the gall,
> That we nil kike, for that he saith us sothe
> Assaye, and he shall finde it, that so dothe.
> (*WBT*, 939–42; Speght 1598, Fol. 37ʳ)

For Dryden's Wife, that last threat becomes a prediction of endless and unremitting hostility:

> Some wish a Husband-Fool; but such are curst,
> For Fools perverse, of Husbands are the worst:
> All Women wou'd be counted Chast and Wise,
> Nor should our Spouses see, but with our Eyes;
> For Fools will prate; and tho' they want the Wit
> To find close Faults, yet open Blots will hit:
> Tho' better for their Ease to hold their Tongue,
> For Womankind was never in the Wrong.
> So Noise ensues, and Quarrels last for Life;
> The Wife abhors the Fool, the Fool the Wife.
> (*The Wife of Bath Her Tale*, 139–48; Dryden, *Works*, 7. 459).

Fig. 7.3 The knight and the crone, with fairies dancing in the background. From John Dryden, *The Fables ... Ornamented with Engravings from the Pencil of the Right Hon. Lady Diana Beauclerk* (1797).

The Wedding Night

When the knight, baffled by his unsuccessful quest to discover 'What the Sex of Women most Desire' (97), comes upon the 'Quire' of dancing ladies, the 'fairy' element is again enhanced in Dryden's version, when, as was noted in Chapter 6, the 'featly footing' of the ladies is evoked with a noticeable echo of Ariel in *The Tempest* (I. ii. 380):

> He saw a Quire of Ladies in a round
> That <u>featly footing</u> seem'd to skim the Ground:
> Thus dancing Hand in Hand, so light they were,
> He knew not where they trod, on Earth or Air.
>
> (*The Wife of Bath Her Tale*, 215–18; Dryden Works, 7. 463)

But the knight sees only a group of women, one of whom might solve his quest. (See Fig. 7.3) The grotesqueness of the 'Hag' who remains when the fairies have gone ('fowler far / Than Grandame Apes in *Indian* Forests') is emphasized by Dryden with a borrowing from Juvenal's Tenth Satire.[53] The ugliness of the old woman is further emphasized by Ellis and Voltaire—is, indeed crucial to the point of their versions (see Fig. 7.4).

In Dryden, as in Chaucer, there is no hint of the Crone's true intentions in coming to agreement with the knight: 'Plight me thy faith, quoth she, that what I ask, / Thy danger over, and perform'd thy task, / That thou shalt give for hire of thy demand' (247–9). In Voltaire, when the Crone offers to help Robert declare the secret to the Queen, her offer is conditional—and full of hints as to the eventual outcome:

'Mais jurez-moi qu'en me devant la vie	But swear that for the life you owe,
Vous serez juste, et que de vous j'aurai	Becoming gratitude you'll shew;
Ce que me plaît et que fair mon envie;	That from you I shall have with ease
L'ingratitude est un crime odieux.	What never fails our sex to please.
Faites serment, jurez par mes beaux yeux,	An oath then from you I require
Que vous ferez tout ce que je desire.'	That you'll do all that I desire.
(162–7)	(pp. 16–17)

All is revealed when, having rescued Robert, the Crone refuses the Queen's offer of Robert's now-recovered horse as her reward, insisting that it is Robert's person, rather than his possessions, that she desires:

Rien de ROBERT ne me plaît que lui-même;	'Tis Robert's person I desire,
C'est sa valeur et ses graces que j'aime:	His grace and valour I admire:
Je veux régner sur son Coeur amoureux:	I o'er his am'rous heart would reign,
De ce trésor ma tendresse est jalouse:	That's all the prize I wish to gain;
Entre mes bras ROBERT doit vivre heureux;	Robert with me must pass his life,
Dès cette nuit je pretends qu'il m'épouse.	This day must take me for his wife.
(219–24)	(p. 18)

In all the versions the 'liquorish Hag' speaks the language of love, but in Dryden, the language, specifically, of a loving *wife*:

---

[53] See Dryden's version, 311; Dryden, *Works*, 4. 225.

Fig. 7.4 The crone claims the knight as her bridegroom. Drawn by Thomas Stothard
and engraved by James Fitter for Dryden, *Fables from Boccacio and Chaucer*,
ed. John Aikin (London, 1806).

> Not all the Wealth of Eastern Kings, said she,
> Have Pow'r to part my plighted Love, and me;
> And, Old and Ugly as I am, and Poor,
> Yet never will I break the Faith I swore;
> For mine thou art by Promise, during Life,
> And I thy loving and obedient Wife.
>
> (*The Wife of Bath Her Tale*, 321–6; *Dryden Works*, 7. 469)

In all the versions, the knight's abhorrence of marriage to the Crone provides a central scene and a turning point in the narrative, culminating when the ill-matched couple are brought to bed. Dryden expands Chaucer's description of the knight's behaviour on his wedding night ('He waloweth, and turneth to and fro' (*WBT*, 1085)) to comic effect:

> Restless he toss'd and tumbled to and fro,
> And rowl'd and wriggled further off; for Woe.
>
> (*The Wife of Bath Her Tale*, 344–5; Dryden, *Works*, 7. 471)

Ellis offers a description of the Crone on her wedding night which far exceeds Chaucer—who in fact offers little or no description of her—in its grotesqueness:

> Her nose—you'd swear had been forgot,
>   But thro' her nostrils without pain
>   You might look into her brain
> And trace each wand'ring thought.
> Her eyes—but they long since had fled,
> And taken refuge in her head;
> So I can't tell with much precision
>   Whether they were black or blue;
>   Her eye-lids like the foreskin of a Jew
> Seem'd just escap'd from circumcision.
>
> (*Dainty Devices*, p. 22)

This, according to Ellis, is 'a face and shape as / Would damp the vigor of a young Priapus'. The man Ellis calls 'our hero' is now 'in some danger of a rape' and has to apologize for his 'redundancy of vigour'. His eventual capitulation—'The only way to show my wit / Is to submit'—is attributed not to any comprehensive display of wisdom from the Crone but to the mere fact that 'the fatal knot is tied'.[54]

In Voltaire's tale, the Crone gives an abbreviated defence of age and poverty before the Queen, in a successful attempt to convince the court that she should have the chevalier as her husband. Voltaire has avoided Dryden's emphasis on the Crone as a powerfully persuasive figure, to whose philosophical, religious, and scientific authority the knight has to submit. As a consequence, the story is re-orientated from one which culminates, in Chaucer and Dryden, in an acknowledgement of the *mutual* 'surrender' that is necessary if the sexes are to live in harmony, to one in which the main concern is with—in the words of Voltaire's modern editors— the 'insatiabilité sexuelle des femmes' even in extreme old age, and with men's inability to rise to the occasion. Voltaire's Crone insists on Robert's surrender to

---

[54] Ellis's grotesque depiction of the Crone may have been inspired by the version of the story included (as the tale of Florent) in John Gower's *Confessio Amantis*. Ellis included Gower's tale in Volume 1 of his *Specimens of the Early English Poets*, 3 vols (London, 1801), pp. 178–98, where he says (p. 179) that it is 'generally supposed to be the original of Chaucer's Wife of Bath's Tale'. Gower's descriptions of the Crone appear on pp. 190–1 and 194–5 of Ellis's collection.

her sexual desires. Even when lauding the virtues of poverty, and appealing to the example of Baucis and Philemon, the aged couple who offer hospitality to the gods in Ovid's *Metamorphoses*, Voltaire's Crone (255–6) emphasizes Baucis's and Philemon's continuing sexual union (in the English version, 'old Philemon's flame / For Baucis'),[55] and voices her own plea to Robert in openly sexual terms:

De ma pudeur les timides accents,	The timid voice of struggling shame
Sont subjugués par la voix de mes sense.	Is stifled by my am'rous flame;
Régnez sur eux ainsi sur mon âme;	Reign o'er my sense without control,
Je meurs, je meurs! ciel! à quois réduis-tu	Since you reign pow'rful o'er my soul;
Mon naturel qui combat ma vertu!	I die! just heaven say to what end
Je me dessous, je brûle, je me pâme,	With virtue must our love contend?
Ah! Le Plaisir m'enivre malgré moi.	I'm quite dissolv'd in love's bright flame,
	Pleasure thrills thro' my vitall frame;
	Must I, alas! without thee die?
(352–8)	(p. 22)

Robert has been charmed by the Crone's thoughts and anecdotes, which include, *pace* her celebration of Love in a Cottage, a eulogy on her own aristocratic ancestors. When he eventually manages to respond adequately, he is motivated by pity and by a chivalrous sense of sexual duty rather than by any change of heart about her person and appearance. But his decision is rewarded by her transformation—she is, it emerges, Urgelle, the fairy queen—and their union is likened to the highly erotic congress of Venus and Mars.

The two post-Drydenian versions of *The Wife of Bath's Tale* take Chaucer's tale in two very different directions—in the case of Ellis towards bawdy burlesque, in the case of Voltaire towards an acknowledgement—almost at times a celebration—of ungovernable female sexual need, even in extreme old age. Neither is close in substance or spirit to Dryden or Chaucer. The demands made on Robert are, though, perhaps a more fitting punishment for a rapist than anything provided by Dryden or Chaucer.

The Moral?

Ellis has no moral at all. Voltaire ends with some lines lamenting the loss of *contes de fées* from common entertainments. Did Dryden derive a moral from *The Wife*

---

[55] Dryden's translation of the story of Baucis and Philemon appeared in the same volume as *The Wife of Bath Her Tale*, and therefore may perhaps have been known by Voltaire. Dryden describes the couple as 'Now old in Love' and as 'long marry'd and a happy Pair' (33–4), but a greater stress is placed on the couple's specifically amatory attachment in the version of the same tale by Jean de La Fontaine upon which Dryden drew when making his translation from Ovid. La Fontaine writes of Baucis and Philemon that 'Ni le temps ni l'hymen n'éteignirent leur flame' and that 'L'amitié modéra leurs feux sans les détruire'. See Jean de La Fontaine, *Fables, contes et nouvelles*, ed. René Groos and Jacques Shiffrin (Paris, 1954), p. 323. For Dryden's use of La Fontaine, see Dryden, *Poems*, ed. Hammond and Hopkins, 5. 249, 251, 255, 256.

of Bath's Tale? In the Preface to *Fables*, he claimed that in his choice of poems for his final volume

> I have endeavour'd to chuse such Fables, both Ancient and Modern, as contain in each of them some instructive Moral, which I could prove by Induction, but the Way is tedious; and they leap foremost into sight, without the Reader's Trouble of looking after them.[56]

Readers, however, were mystified by quite what the moral of many of Dryden's Fables might be, or, where there is a declared moral, how that might square with the rest of the poem.[57] The 'moral' of Chaucer's poem might, some thought, be divined by way of comparison with similar concerns that are in evidence elsewhere in his work. Throughout the eighteenth century, the most famous Chaucerian pronouncement on *maistrie* was that uttered by Chaucer's Franklin near the beginning of his tale, here set against the version by William Lipscomb:

Love will not be constreined by maistrie.	Love ne'er by tyrant force will be confin'd;
Whan maistrie cometh, the God of love anon	And, when he sees prepar'd the galling ties,
Beteth his winges, and farewel, he is gon.	'Spreads his light wings, and in a moment flies:'
Love is a thing, as any spirit free.	Hateful alike to every generous soul,
Women of kind desiren libertee	To women as to men, is harsh controul.
And not to been constreined as a thral;	
And so don men, if sothly I say shal.	
(*FranT*, 764–70; Tyrwhitt 1775–78, 2. 130ʳ)	(Lipscomb, 3. 110)

Lipscomb's quotation marks signal his borrowing of a line spoken by the heroine in Alexander Pope's *Eloisa to Abelard* first published in Pope's *Works* of 1717.[58] Eloisa is proclaiming her contempt for the constraints of marriage:

> How oft', when press'd to marriage, have I said,
> Curse on all laws but those which love has made?
> Love, free as air, at sight of human ties,
> Spreads his light wings, and in a moment flies.

Eloisa is expanding and elaborating on Chaucer's declaration: 'Love is a thing, as any spirit free':

---

[56] Dryden, *Works*, 7. 27.

[57] Dryden's remarks are paralleled, and were perhaps prompted, by Cervantes's Prologue to his *Novelas Ejemplares*, a series of tales each of which, Cervantes claims, has an obvious moral. See Dryden, *Poems*, 5. 54. The 'morals' of Cervantes *Novelas* have proved as elusive to interpretation as those of Dryden's *Fables*.

[58] The popularity of this line (and its Spenserian antecedent) is discussed in Chapter 11.

> If there be yet another name more free,
> More fond than mistress, make me that to thee!
> Oh happy state! when souls each other draw,
> When love is liberty, and nature, law:
> All then is full, possessing, and possess'd,
> No craving Void left aking in the breast:
> Ev'n thought meets thought, e're from the lips it part,
> And each warm wish springs mutual from the heart.
> This sure is bliss (if bliss on earth there be)
> And once the lot of Abelard and me.
>
> (Pope, *Works* [1717], pp. 421–2)

But Eloisa's world, like that of Dorigen, Arveragus, Aurelius, and the gentle Magician in *The Franklin's Tale*, is very different from both of the worlds depicted by the Wife of Bath—the world of woe with her five husbands, or the world of King Arthur with its rapists, sometimes-evil fairies, incubi, prisons, executions, quarrels that last for life, and women for whom complete domination is a cherished, if secret, desire, and who are surrounded by men who have absolute power already—or so they think. The great difference between *The Franklin's Tale* and that told by the Wife is that her tale is essentially comic. The Wife herself, with her final wish that 'Heav'n send the Maids young Husbands, fresh in Bed' and that widows may 'Wed as often as they can' seems determined to keep it so.

There is, indeed, very little in the action of *The Wife of Bath's Tale* that is not enlivened by comedy. In Voltaire, the comedy is broad and constantly alive to sexual innuendo. In Ellis, it is largely dependent on his tale's flippant and raffish style. Dryden's comedy is more various and concentrated on the ill matching of the strange couple and the mutual resignations at the ending of the *Tale*—which mirrors the ending of Chaucer's (but not Pope's) *Wife of Bath's Prologue*. After the 'rambling garrulity'[59] of her account of her dealings with her first three husbands, Chaucer's Wife gains 'maistrye' over her fifth husband by means of some extravagantly turbulent comic combat, and some outrageous deception. This absolute rule she then resigns, to become a perfectly loving wife to a perfectly loving husband. This reversal is repeated in the *Tale*, where the male surrenders, completely, abjectly:

This knight auiseth him, and sorely siketh	Sore sigh'd the Knight, who this long Sermon heard,
But at the last, he said in manere:	At length considering all, his Heart he chear'd:
My lady and my loue, and wife so dere	And thus reply'd, My Lady, and my Wife,
I put me in your wise gouernaunce	To your wise Conduct I resign my Life.
(*WBT*, 1228–31; Speght 1598, Fol. 38ᵛ)	(*The Wife of Bath Her Tale*, 509–12; Dryden, *Works*, 7. 481)

---

[59] Helen Cooper, *Oxford Guides to Chaucer: The Canterbury Tales* (2nd edn, Oxford, 1996), p. 147.

But his lady and his wife responds in kind, asking, indeed, for *his forgiveness*:

Than haue I got of you yᵉ mastry (qd she)	Then thus in Peace, quoth she, concludes the Strife,
Sin I may chese, and gouerne as my list	Since I am turn'd the Husband, you the Wife:
Ye certes wife (qd he) I hold it for the beste	The Matrimonial Victory is mine,
Kisse me (qd she) we be no longer wrothe	Which, having fairly gain'd, I will resign;
	Forgive, if I have said or done amiss,
	And seal the Bargain with a Friendly Kiss.
(*WBT*, 1236–9; Speght 1598, Fol. 38ᵛ)	(*The Wife of Bath Her Tale*, 519–24; Dryden, *Works*, 7. 481)

Although the knight cannot know what lies ahead when he asks his wife, 'Choose you for me, for well you understand / The future Good and Ill, on either Hand (512–14), it is his handing over to her the decision as to whether she will be foul and faithful, or fair and faithless that produces the magical outcome. It is significant that the Crone speaks of 'matrimonial *victory*'. Rapprochement, mutual surrender, and a refusal of either partner to dominate the other, is the result of long struggle—in this case a *very* 'long Sermon'.

The Wife of Bath's Christian Wisdom?

In Ellis, and in Voltaire, the omission or curtailment of the curtain lecture delivered by the Crone on her wedding night, after the knight's release from his death sentence, takes the tale away from Chaucer, refusing what seems to be the point of his whole tale. For Dryden, the speech was at the centre of *The Wife of Bath's Tale*: the episode that transforms everything.

In his tale, Dryden writes:

> *Chaucer* introduces an old Woman of mean Parentage, whom a youthful Knight of Noble Blood was forc'd to marry, and consequently loath'd her: The Crone being in bed with him on the wedding Night, and finding his Aversion, endeavours to win his Affection by Reason, and speaks a good Word for her self, (as who could blame her?) in hope to mollifie the sullen Bridegroom. She takes her Topiques from the Benefits of Poverty, and Advantages of old Age and Ugliness, the Vanity of Youth, and the silly Pride of Ancestry and Titles without inherent Virtue, and which is the true Nobility.[60]

After having written *The Wife of Bath Her Tale*, Dryden turned to Boccaccio's story of Sigismonda and Guiscardo, only to be reminded that it contains 'the same Argument of preferring Virtue to Nobility of Blood, and Titles' that is found in the speech of Chaucer's Crone. He would, he says 'certainly have avoided' Boccaccio's tale 'for the Resemblance of the two Discourses, if [his] Memory had not fail'd

---

[60] Dryden, *Works*, 7. 43.

[him]'. As things stand, he encourages his readers to 'weigh them both' and to 'right *Boccace*' if they think he has, in his preference, been 'partial to *Chaucer*'.[61]

Telling testimony to the intrinsic power of both the Crone's and Sigismonda's speeches is found in Edward Bysshe's poetical commonplace books, where passages from both speeches are juxtaposed, in the spirit of Dryden's invitation to compare the two. Quotations from the Crone's speech are increased in number between the 1702 and 1718 editions of Bysshe's *Art of English Poetry*, and a further substantial extract is included in *The British Parnassus* (1714), bringing the total of lines from the speech quoted across Bysshe's two books to over two-thirds of the whole.

In her soliloquy, Dryden's Crone, like Chaucer's, lifts the tale beyond the immediate circumstances of her marriage to the unwilling knight, to consider fundamental questions about the material universe and the nature of human descent and inheritance.[62] But even here, there are flashes of comedy. Some of the arguments are clever defences of the indefensible: 'Age and Ugliness, as all agree, / Are the best Guards of Female Chastity' (491–2). Dryden expands both the playful and solemn elements in Chaucer's original, emphasizing and extending the ways in which the Crone adduces, and fuses, both Christian and pagan wisdom to support her argument—in the face of the knight's snobbish complaint that she is 'descended from so mean a Race, / That never Knight was match'd with such Disgrace' (368–9)—that true nobility 'comes not by Inheritance' (395). Lineage, the Crone argues, is regularly 'tainted' in transition, and 'seldom three Descents continue Good' (403). True nobility, rather, 'proceeds from God' and is 'giv'n / By Bounty of our Stars, and Grace of Heav'n' (446–7), and the true model of virtue and nobility, she argues, is to be found not in the wealth, power, and status of aristocracy, but in the life of Christ. The Crone exhibits the same ease of transition from secular to divine as is found everywhere in the Wife's words—though the Crone and the Wife use it to very different ends:

Christ wuld we claimed of him our gětilnesse,	The Nobleman is he whose noble Mind
Not of our elders, for our old richesse	Is fill'd with inborn Worth, unborrow'd from his
For though they yeue us all her heritage	Kind.
For which we claymen to ben of hie parage	The King of Heav'n was in a Manger laid;
Yet may they not byqueth, for nothing	And took his Earth but from an humble Maid:
To none of us, her virtuous liuing	Then what can Birth, or mortal Men bestow,
That made hem gentilmen icalled be	Since Floods no higher than their Fountains flow?
And bad us folowen hem in such degre.	We who for name, and empty Honour strive,
	Our true Nobility from him derive.
(*WBT*, 1117–24; Speght 1598, Fol. 38ʳ)	(*The Wife of Bath Her Tale*, 384–91; Dryden, *Works*, 7. 473)

---

[61] Ibid. 7. 43–4.

[62] Paul Davis observes that 'what Dryden's hag opposes to the knight's snobbishness is not lumpen moralizing but a yeasty vision of human changefulness, a vision Dryden rises to the task of realising in couplets strikingly various and liquid in their movement'; see Paul Davis, 'After the Fire: Chaucer and Urban Poetics, 1666–1743', in *Chaucer and the City*, ed. Ardis Butterfield (Martlesham, 2006), 177–92 (p. 185).

Dryden's Crone, however, does not merely rest her case on religious faith, but draws (in lines that have no equivalent in Chaucer's original) on the materialist philosophy of Lucretius to support her contention that human lineage is to a large extent dependent on the operations of chance:

> Chance gave us being, and by Chance we live.
> Such as our Atoms were, ev'n such are we,
> Or call it Chance, or strong Necessity.
> Thus, loaded with dead weight, the Will is free.
> And thus it needs must be: For Seed conjoin'd
> Lets into Nature's Work th' imperfect Kind
>
> *(The Wife of Bath Her Tale, 421–6; Dryden, Works, 7. 475)*

And in her lines on the virtues of poverty, Dryden's Crone revisits the example of Christ, again linking his example to the teachings of the pagan world—only to return at the end of the passage to invoke the knowledge of 'The hie God on whom that we bileue', 'the great Controller of our Fate':

And there as ye of povertie me repreue
The hie God on whom that we bileue
In wilful pouerte chese to lede his life
And certes euery man, maide, and wife
May understond, Jesu heuen king
Ne would not chese a viciouse liuing.
  Glad pouerte is an honest thing certaine
This wold Seneck and other clerkes saine
Who so would holde him paide of his pouert
I holde him riche, all had ne not a shert
He that couciteth is a full poore wight
For he wold han, that is not in his might
But he yᵗ nought hath, ne coueiteth to haue,
Is rich, although ye hold him but a knaue
Very pouert is sinne properly
  Juuenal saith of pouert merily
The poore man, whan he goeth by the way
Biforne theues, he may sing and play.
Pouert is hatefull good: and as I gesse,
A full great bringer out of business
A great amender eke of sapience
To him that taketh it in patience
Pouert is, although it seme elenge
Possession, that no wight wol chalenge.
Pouerte ful often, whan a man is lowe
Maketh his god, and eke himselfe to knowe.

(WBT, 1177–202; Speght 1598, Fol. 38ʳ)

If Poverty be my upbraided Crime,
And you believe in Heav'n; there was a time,
When He, the great Controller of our Fate
Deign'd to be Man; and liv'd in low Estate:
Which he who had the World at his dispose,
If Poverty were Vice, would never choose.
Philosophers have said, and Poets sing,
That a glad Poverty's an honest Thing.
Content is Wealth, the Riches of the Mind;
And happy He who can that Treasure find.
But the base Miser starves amidst his Store,
Broods on his Gold, and griping still at more
Sits sadly pining, and believes he's Poor.
The ragged Beggar, tho' he wants Relief,
Has not to lose, and sings before the Thief.
Want is a bitter, and a hateful Good,
Because its Virtues are not understood:
Yet many Things impossible to Thought
Have been by Need to full Perfection brought:
The daring of the Soul proceeds from thence,
Sharpness of Wit, and active Diligence:
Prudence at once, and Fortitude it gives,
And if in patience taken mends our Lives;
For ev'n that Indigence that brings me low
Makes me my self; and Him above to know:
A Good which none would challenge, few
                     would choose,
A fair Possession, which Mankind refuse.

(The Wife of Bath Her Tale, 458–84;
Dryden, Works, 7. 477–9)

Dryden has here followed Chaucer's lead, in combining Christian sentiments with those of Seneca[63] and Juvenal,[64] and has added colourings from his own earlier translation of an Ode by Horace, and from a poem by his son, Charles.[65] In his references to 'the ragged Beggar' and to the 'Content' which constitutes true 'Wealth', Dryden recalls the wording of his translation of Horace, Odes 3. 29, at the point where the speaker expresses his readiness to accept the vicissitudes of fortune with equanimity:

> Content with poverty, my Soul I arm;
> And Vertue, tho' in rags, will keep me warm.
>
> (*Horace. Ode 29. Book 3, Paraphras'd in*
> *Pindarique Verse*, 86–7;Dryden, *Works*, 3. 84)

One notable 'moral' of *The Wife of Bath Her Tale* is contained in the Crone's definition of true nobility, which includes all sexes, all ages, all positions in life—and which makes questions of sovereignty irrelevant, and the need for mutual forgiveness acute:

> And Noble then am I, when I begin
> In Virtue cloath'd, to cast the Rags of Sin.
>
> (*The Wife of Bath Her Tale*, 456–7; Dryden, *Works*, 7. 477)

It is, admittedly, unlikely that the Wife of Bath would or could ever say this—or anything like this—in her own voice:

> Yet may that hie god, and so hope I
> Graunt me grace to liue vertously:
> Than am I gentil, whan I beginne
> To liue vertuously, and leuen sinne.
>
> (*WBT*, 1173–6; Speght 1598, Fol. 38ʳ)

If Ellis and Voltaire provided comparatively superficial responses to the Wife of Bath, there was one treatment of Chaucer's Wife current in the eighteenth century that might be thought to have something in common with Dryden in its ultimate response to *The Wife of Bath's Tale*. Though the ballad of *The Wanton Wife of Bath*, with which this chapter began, is far distant in its narrative design and conclusion from Dryden's *Wife of Bath Her Tale*, its spiritual and emotional upshot are perhaps not that remote from Dryden's understanding of Chaucer's intentions. For, in its final lines, the Wanton Wife, however outrageous her conduct and arguments

---

[63] Seneca, *Epistulae Morales*, 2. 4, cited by Speght (Sig. Bbbb vʳ).

[64] Juvenal, *Satires*, 10. 22 (Dryden's translation, 33–4; Dryden, *Works*, 4. 209).

[65] In his lines about the 'base Miser', Dryden quotes, almost verbatim, a couplet from Charles Dryden's poem, 'On the Happyness of A Retir'd Life': 'This Wretch, like *Croesus*, in the midst of Store / Sits sadly Pyning, and believes he's Poor' (*The Annual Miscellany: for the Year 1694* (London, 1694), pp. 195–201).

might have seemed up to this point, is welcomed into heaven by Christ in the same way as the Prodigal Son was welcomed and forgiven by his father. The divine and the human are brought together in a surprising alliance. The ballad ends with an affirmation of the all-embracing sympathy and forgiveness that Dryden seems to have thought were present in the resolution of *The Wife of Bath's Tale*. Helen Cooper has observed that *The Wanton Wife of Bath* 'represents the most attentive and responsive reading of Chaucer between 1395 and 1670' and that 'the ballad reading populace of England had their last sight of the Wife of Bath entering the gates of Heaven; and Chaucer, one suspects, would have approved'.[66] Chaucer would perhaps have also approved, on not entirely dissimilar grounds, of Dryden's reworking of *The Wife of Bath's Tale*.

---

[66] Helen Cooper, 'The Shape-Shiftings of the Wife of Bath, 1395–1670', in *Chaucer Traditions*, ed. Ruth Morse and Barry Windeatt, pp. 168–84 (p. 182).

8

Samuel Johnson and Chaucer

'The First of Our Versifyers Who Wrote Poetically'

Dryden's critical and creative responses to Chaucer were, as we have seen, much read and quoted during the first half of the eighteenth century. What kind of interest in Chaucer can be discovered in the work of the most influential critic of the century's second half? What, in particular, can be learnt from Samuel Johnson's great *Dictionary of the English Language* (1755; rev. edn, 1773) about the perpetuation of Chaucer's presence in the English language and in English literature by the mid-eighteenth century, and, in particular, about the continuance of the idea of Chaucer as the 'father' of the language of English poetry? What can be discovered from the *Dictionary* about Johnson's own engagement with Chaucer, both linguistic and literary? The evidence in the case of both questions is complex and somewhat elusive, and has to be pieced together with some care, and in some detail. That will be the purpose of the present chapter.

The significance of Chaucer for Johnson has been assessed in very different ways. The Chaucer scholar Derek Brewer has written that Johnson, 'our greatest Neoclassical critic, is evidently unsympathetic' to Chaucer.[1] The Johnson scholar, Amanda Leff, however, has drawn attention to the considerable extent of Johnson's knowledge of Chaucer.[2] Both views, as we shall see, have some evidence to support them. But both also need qualifying in various ways. We will begin our investigation of Johnson's response to Chaucer with one of the most famous of Johnson's reported conversational exchanges, one that involves a passage from *The Wife of Bath's Tale* quoted and discussed in Chapter 7.

The Knee of a Horse

'Ignorance, Madam, pure ignorance': Johnson's explanation for his having misdefined the word 'pastern' in his *Dictionary* is among the most notorious of

---

[1] Brewer, *Chaucer: The Critical Heritage*, 1. 13.
[2] Amanda Leff, 'Johnson's Chaucer: Searching for the Medieval in *A Dictionary of the English Language*', *The Age of Johnson*, 21 (2012), 1–20. The present chapter is heavily indebted throughout to Leff's essay.

Chaucer in the Eighteenth Century. David Hopkins and Tom Mason, Oxford University Press.
© David Hopkins and Tom Mason (2022). DOI: 10.1093/oso/9780192862624.003.0009

the many Johnson sayings reported by Boswell and requoted in many books of quotations.[3] Johnson had mistakenly defined 'pastern' as 'the knee of an horse' in an entry that contains an extremely oblique Chaucerian presence. Johnson's exclamation had been, at least partly, *created* by Boswell, who had *imagined* the expectations of the female questioner and Johnson's unconcern.[4] For Boswell, the anecdote is interesting in relation to other mistakes in Johnson's *Dictionary*. For Frances Reynolds, the original source, it was one of a series of stories about Johnson's unconventional behaviour in the presence of women.

The story has been dismissed as a 'piece of third-hand hearsay'.[5] The underlying facts, however, are clear. The first edition of Johnson's *Dictionary* defines—or, to use the word Johnson preferred, 'explains'—'pastern' as 'the knee of an horse'. This is a particularly surprising mistake, in that perfectly serviceable definitions of the term had been given in the earlier dictionaries of Thomas Blount (1656), John Kersey (1702), and Nathan Bailey (1736). On most occasions when he was aware of his own ignorance, Johnson turned for equine information to the works of the knowledgeable, sometimes allowing a professional quotation to serve as his 'explanation'.[6]

Johnson's procedures and intentions in the *Dictionary* and the interconnections between his 'technical' definitions of words and his memories of the uses of those words in poetic contexts are not always easy to reconstruct. But in the present instance, the underlying facts seem certain enough. In his revised edition of 1773, the explanation of 'pastern' is corrected to read 'that part of the leg of a horse between the joint next the foot and the hoof', but that is the only emendation made to this entry. Johnson retains a confused quotation from Nehemiah Grew's *Musaeum Regalis Societatis* (1685)—from which his mistake may have derived in the first place—designed to demonstrate 'the Providence of Nature' in giving to each animal precisely the parts it needs, in engineering terms. And he ignores Nathan Bailey's suggestion that the word 'pastern' might refer to 'a Shackle for a Horse'—a usage of which the *OED* provides many examples.

In offering his 'explanation' of 'pastern', Johnson was perhaps less interested in equine anatomy—the parts of a *horse* ('A neighing quadruped')—than in two

---

[3] James Boswell, *Life of Samuel Johnson*, ed. George Birkbeck Hill, rev, L. F. Powell, 6 vols (Oxford, 1934–50), 1. 293.

[4] The story was first told to, and then by, Frances Reynolds, Johnson's friend and the painter's sister, in a version where the questioner asks about the mistake 'with a very audible voice' and Johnson's reply is even blunter: 'Ignorance, Madam, ignorance' (Frances Reynolds in *Johnsonian Miscellanies*, ed. George Birkbeck Hill, 2 vols (Oxford, 1897), 2. 278).

[5] See Paul J. Korshin, 'The Mythology of Johnson's Dictionary', in *Anniversary Essays on Johnson's Dictionary*, ed. Jack Lynch and Anne McDermott (Cambridge, 2005), pp. 10–23 (p. 16) .

[6] For 'fetlock', for instance, he used Thomas Wallis's *The Farrier's and Horseman's Complete Dictionary* (London, 1759): 'A tuft of hair as big as the hair of the mane that grows behind the pastern-joint of many horses: horses of a low size have scarce any such tuft.'

(related) quotations from Dryden. One is from Dryden's translation of Virgil's *Georgics*:

> The colt that for a stallion is design'd,
> Upright he walks on *pasterns* firm and straight,
> His motions easy, prancing in his gait.

The other is from *The Wife of Bath, Her Tale*:

> So straight she walk'd, and on her *pasterns* high:
> If seeing her behind, he lik'd her pace,
> Now turning short, he better lik'd her face.

The second passage is offered in support of an otherwise unexampled use: '2. The legs of an human creature in contempt'. Though Johnson changes the definition of 'pastern' from the equine 'knee' (in 1755) to 'That part of the leg of a horse between the joint next the foot and the hoof' (in 1773), the reference to human *legs* is retained. Particularly striking here is the last phrase of Johnson's definition: 'in contempt'. This phrase depends upon Johnson's memory of the passage in Dryden's version of Chaucer's *Wife of Bath's Tale* discussed in Chapter 7, in which, it will be remembered, a 'lusty knight' casts an 'amorous eye' upon 'a damsel gay', who 'In russet robes to market took her way'.

Elsewhere in his *Dictionary*, Johnson explained 'contempt' as 'the act of despising others; slight regard, scorn'. But in the passage from *The Wife of Bath Her Tale*, as we have seen, the contempt is unconscious. The knight is (or thinks he is) *appreciative* of the 'damsel's' attractions. Dryden, or Dryden's Wife of Bath, is almost looking through the eyes of the violator, whose horse-appreciating view reveals itself also in his appreciation of the human female's 'pace'.[7] Johnson's conviction that the use is *contemptuous* seems to depend partly upon a general notion that *any* comparison of the ankles of a woman to the pasterns of a horse must reveal an underlying 'slight regard' and partly on an attentive reading of this particular poem—where the attitude of the man results in rape, and his punishment in his ultimate subjection to the will and wisdom of an old and ugly woman. For Johnson, the word, when transferred from horse to woman, clearly carried particular connotations about the speaker of that word, connotations that are here made clear by the juxtaposition between Dryden's appreciative account of Virgil's appreciative account of the 'colt that for a stallion is design'd' who walks 'Upright' 'on *pasterns* firm and straight, / His motions easy, prancing in his gait', and the country girl as perceived in the mind of Chaucer's rapist: 'straight she walk'd, and on her *pasterns* high'.

A notable feature of Johnson's 'pastern' entry is that it depended upon a close, careful, and engaged reading of a poem, Dryden's *The Wife of Bath Her Tale*, which

---

[7] Defined by Johnson as 'a particular movement which horses are taught, though some have it naturally'.

Johnson did not even bother to mention in his 'Life of Dryden' when speaking slightingly of the versions of Chaucer included in *Fables Ancient and Modern*. This oddity is compounded by the many other citations from this poem, and from all Dryden's Chaucer poems, in the *Dictionary*—and by the various presences and traces in the *Dictionary* of Chaucer's works themselves. The *Dictionary* entry on 'pastern' shows that Johnson had engaged in detail with one of Chaucer's tales. But, as we have seen (and this is a theme to which we will return later in this chapter), it was Dryden's version of *The Wife of Bath's Tale* rather than Chaucer's original that Johnson knew so well.

Johnson, Chaucer, and the History of the English Language

Johnson's reading of his critical predecessors presented him with wildly contradictory views of Chaucer's linguistic and poetic powers. There were some who still regarded the antiquity of Chaucer's language as an insuperable obstacle, while a few expressed the judgement that Chaucer was in some ways the greatest of all modern, as opposed to classical, poets. John Dart, as we have seen, had called Chaucer 'the greatest Poet that *England* (or perhaps the World) ever produc'd'. And, as we saw in Chapter 3, Walter Harte had observed in his commentary upon his translation of the sixth book of Statius—as if it were an entirely uncontentious assertion—that 'Chaucer, who was perhaps the greatest poet among the moderns, has translated these verses almost word for word in his *Knight's Tale*.'[8]

There is substantial evidence to support Derek Brewer's assertion that Johnson was generally 'unsympathetic' to Chaucer. The 'History of the English Language' which occupies twenty-six double-column pages of the *Dictionary*, for example, seems almost designed to question Chaucer's position as the father of English poetry—apparently transferring the honorific title to John Gower: 'The first of our authours, who can be properly said to have written *English*, was Sir *John Gower*, who, in his *Confession of a Lover*, calls *Chaucer* his disciple, and may therefore be considered as the father of our poetry.'[9]

Johnson was relying here on a misreading of some lines spoken by *Venus*, rather than by the poet himself, in Gower's *Confessio Amantis*, in which the goddess addresses Chaucer as 'mi disciple and my poete'. Gower's passage is quoted, and correctly ascribed to Venus, in the 'Testimonies of Learned Men' included in Urry's edition of Chaucer. Johnson owned Urry's volume, but only occasionally consulted it.[10] In writing that Gower should be 'considered as the father of our poetry',

---

[8] See Walter Harte, *Poems on Several Occasions* (London, 1727), p. 189. This is the volume that includes Harte's version of 'To my Soul. From *Chaucer*' discussed in Chapter 5.

[9] Johnson, *Works*, 18. 180.

[10] For Johnson's ownership of Urry's Chaucer, see Donald J. Greene, *Samuel Johnson's Library: An Annotated Guide* (Victoria, BC, 1975), p. 48. Henry Todd complained that the same mistake had been

Johnson seems to be using the term 'father' as it had been applied to Ennius rather than to Homer—as a harbinger who provided occasional *glimpses* of what was to come. In No. 63 of *The Idler* (June 1759), Johnson compounded the error about poetic precedence by writing of 'Gower, whom Chaucer calls his master'. There, too, Johnson is apparently concerned to deny Chaucer the title which Dryden and many others had awarded him, but the point is made with some ambiguity: Gower 'however obscured by his scholar's popularity, seems justly to claim the honour which has been hitherto denied him, of showing his countrymen that something more was to be desired, and that English verse might be exalted into poetry'.[11] This account possibly suggests that Gower did little more than *gesture* towards a glorious poetic future.

The account of, and short quotation from, Gower in 'The History of the English Language' in the *Dictionary* is immediately followed by a sentence which—if the word 'perhaps' is passed over rapidly—appears to be more clearly definitive:

> The history of our language is now brought to the point at which the history of our poetry is generally supposed to commence, the time of the illustrious *Geoffry Chaucer*, who may, perhaps, with great justice, be stiled the first of our versifyers who wrote poetically.[12]

Johnson here seems to be distinguishing Gower, who was (supposedly) the first to write *verse in English*, from Chaucer, who was the first to write *poetically*. Philip Neve reported that 'Dr. *Johnson* has said of *Chaucer*, "that he was the first English versifier, who wrote poetically"', thinking this an 'expression, taken from that excellent treatise, *The Defense of Poesy*, by Sir *Philip Sidney*; who says, "one may be a poet, without versing, and a versifier, without poetry"'.[13] It is not certain whether or not that was Johnson's distinction here. One difficulty is that Johnson is running the history of the language and the history of poetry together, as one process.

Johnson accused Dryden of doing something similar, when he maintained that Dryden, 'mistaking genius for learning', had:

> ascribed to *Chaucer* the first refinement of our language, the first production of easy rhymes, and the improvement of our language, by words borrowed from the more polished language of the continent ... But he that reads *Gower* will find smooth numbers and easy rhymes, of which Chaucer is supposed to be the inventor ... The works

made on the same (bad) grounds by Ellis and Ritson: 'This is a grievous blunder: It is Venus, whom Gower describes, at the close of his *Confessio Amantis*, claiming Chaucer as her scholar and her bard, and as having distinguished himself in her service by his literary compositions' (see Henry J. Todd, *Illustrations of the Lives and Writings of Gower and Chaucer*, p. xxxiii).

[11] Johnson, *Works*, 2, 197–8.

[12] Ibid. 18, 182.

[13] Philip Neve, *Cursory Remarks*, p. 4. Neve maintained of Chaucer (p. 3) that 'from a close study of *Dante*'s sublimity, the elegance of *Petrarca*, and the style and manners of *Boccaccio*, he gained copiousness, harmony, and whatever was formed to give poetical expression'.

of *Gower* and *Lydgate* sufficiently evince, that his diction was in general like that of his contemporaries.[14]

Quoting this passage from Johnson, George Ellis was to complain in his *Specimens of the Early English Poets* (1801) that 'the severe and unnecessary censure of Dryden exhibits a strong instance of the very haste and inaccuracy which it condemns'. Ellis thought it

> scarcely credible that Dryden, while he was employed in paraphrasing the Knight's Tale, and the Flower and the Leaf, which are perhaps the most finished specimens of his poetry, and at the same time very faithful copies of his original, should have entirely neglected to consult the cotemporary poets, whose works were necessary to the explanation of Chaucer's language.[15]

Johnson's paragraph both was and was not *quite* a refutation of Dryden. When, discussing vocabulary and syntax, Dryden had written that 'With Ovid ended the golden age of the Roman tongue; from Chaucer the purity of the English tongue began', the mention of gold may suggest that *purity* is a matter of removing impurities. On the other hand, Chaucer 'first adorn'd and amplified our barren tongue from the Provençal'. For Dryden, there was no doubt that Chaucer's verse was more musical than Gower or Lydgate:

> The verse of *Chaucer*, I confess, is not Harmonious to us; but 'tis like the Eloquence of one whom *Tacitus* commends, it was *auribus istius temporis accommodata* [suited to the ears of that time]: They who liv'd with him, and some time after him, thought it Musical; and it continues so even in our Judgment, if compar'd with the Numbers of *Lidgate* and *Gower*, his Contemporaries.[16]

As Johnson presents the matter in the *Dictionary*, Chaucer's innovations distinguish his verse only slightly from the 'smooth numbers and easy rhymes' of Gower: 'some improvements he undoubtedly made by the various dispositions of his rhymes, and by the mixture of different numbers in which he seems happy and judicious'.[17] For Johnson, writing *poetically*, it seems, involves writing with greater metrical sophistication and freedom of rhyme than mere versifiers—but no more. For Dryden, *poetry* had quite other connotations.

Johnson's position can be clarified by comparison with Thomas Warton's *Observations on the Faerie Queene of Spenser* (1754), which Johnson may well have

---

[14] Johnson, *Works*, 18. 182–3.
[15] George Ellis, *Specimens of the Early English Poets*, 1. 206–7.
[16] Dryden, *Works*, 7. 34.
[17] Johnson, *Works*, 18. 183. George Ellis was again to protest at Johnson's account:
> From a critic so intimately acquainted with the mechanism of language we should have expected to learn, whether Chaucer had in any degree added to the precision of our English idiom by improvements of its syntax, or to its harmony by the introduction of more sonorous words; or whether he was solely indebted for the beauty and perspicuity of his style to that happy selection of appropriate expressions which distinguished every writer of original thinking and real genius.
> (Ellis, *Specimens of the Early English Poets*, 1. 208).

had by him while composing his 'History'. Warton, like Johnson, can find no absolute differences between the vocabulary of Gower and Chaucer, running them together as writers 'who sought to reform the roughness of their native tongue, by naturalising many words for the Latin, French and Italian'.[18] On the other hand, Warton has different notions about the claims of both to be primary among writers of English poetry: 'Gower and Chaucer were reputed the first English Poets, because they first introduc'd INVENTION into our poetry; they MORALISED THEIR SONG, and strove to render virtue more amiable, by clothing her in the veil of fiction.'[19] In addition, Chaucer 'deserves to be rank'd as one to the first English poets' on account of 'his admirable artifice in painting the manners, which none before him had ever attempted even in the most imperfect degree; and it should be remember'd to his honour, that he was the first who gave the English nation, in his own language, an idea of HUMOUR':[20]

> When I sate down to read Chaucer with the curiosity of knowing how the first English poet wrote, I left him with the satisfaction of having found what later and more refin'd ages could hardly equal in true humour, pathos, or sublimity.[21]

Johnson was perhaps responding to similar notions of Chaucer's poetic scope in giving very much more space to his works than to those of Gower in the 'History of the English Language', and, as Amanda M. Leff has observed, in the body of the *Dictionary* itself.[22] And any full assessment of the nature of Johnson's interest in Chaucer would have to take on board the presence in the 'catalogue of publications projected by [Johnson] at different periods', which Sir John Hawkins had 'lying before [him]' when writing his *Life* of *Johnson* (1787), of a detailed and carefully considered plan—far more ambitious than that of Urry's venture—for a new edition of Chaucer

> from manuscripts and old editions, with various readings, conjectures, remarks on his language, and the changes it had undergone from the earliest times to his age, and from his to the present. With notes explanatory of customs, &c. and references to Boccace and other authors from whom he has borrowed, with an account of the liberties he has taken in telling the stories, his life, and an exact etymological glossary.[23]

The large number of quotations from Chaucer in the Preface to Johnson's *Dictionary* is partly accounted for by the fact that the extracts from Chaucer's *Boethius,*

---

[18] Warton, *Observations on the Fairy Queen of Spenser* (London 1754), p. 90.
[19] Thomas Warton, *Observations*, p. 228. Warton is referring to the opening of Spenser's *Faerie Queene* ('Fierce warres, and faithful love shall moralize my song'), and probably also to Alexander Pope's claim in his *Epistle to Arbuthnot* (340–1) that 'Not in Fancy's maze he wander'd long / But stoop'd to Truth, and moraliz'd his song' (Pope, *Poems*, 4. 120).
[20] Warton, *Observations*, p. 228.
[21] Ibid. p. 141.
[22] See Leff, 'Johnson's Chaucer', p. 13.
[23] Sir John Hawkins, *The Life of Samuel Johnson*, ed. O. M. Brack (Athens, GA, 2009), p. 52. See also Boswell, *Life of Johnson*, ed. Hill, rev. Powell, 4. 381.

from his *Treatise on the Astrolabe*, and from the *Prologue* to *The Testament of Love*—a work actually not by Chaucer anyway—are in prose, and are intended primarily to illustrate developments in the history of the language, and to demonstrate its lack of agility and elegance in Chaucer's day. Johnson's verse extracts from Chaucer are carefully transcribed from Urry's edition and illustrate what Johnson calls the 'the mixture of different numbers in which' Chaucer 'seems happy and judicious'.[24]

'Some Account of the Life and Writings of Chaucer by Dr. Samuel Johnson'

Whatever the ultimate balance of his sympathies with regard to Chaucer, it is clear that Johnson was not widely perceived during the eighteenth century as having lessened Chaucer's reputation as the father of English poetry. A strange piece of evidence to support this suggestion is to be found in a work that was attributed to him in his lifetime.

The European Magazine and London Review for February 1785 mentions a 'Life of Chaucer', which 'as Dr. Johnson's sentiments on this poet will be new to most of our Readers, we shall reprint in our Magazine of next Month'.[25] Duly, in March 1785, there appeared in the *Magazine* 'Some Account of the Life and Writings of Chaucer by Dr. Samuel Johnson'. This piece had originally been published in the *Universal Visiter* in 1756,[26] and in that magazine is accompanied by the three asterisks that often mark Johnson's contributions. But Boswell questioned Johnson's authorship of the 'Life',[27] and recent scholarship has suggested that it is almost certainly the work of one of the editors of *The Universal Visiter*: the poet, Christopher Smart.[28]

The attribution of this piece to Johnson is surprising both in the light of the uncritical, adulatory sentiments, and in the repetitiousness of their exclamatory expression: Chaucer is here 'one of the greatest and most universal geniuses that

[24] Johnson, *Works*, 18. 183.
[25] The 'Some Account of the Life and Writings of Chaucer'. also appeared in *The Edinburgh Magazine or Literary Miscellany* April (1785) 298–302 and in *The Universal Magazine of Knowledge and Pleasure* (1766), 38 (Issue 273), 141–9 (pp. 142–3).
[26] *The Universal Visiter and Memorialist. For the Year 1756*, pp. 9–15. Quotations in the text are from this version.
[27] Boswell, *Life of Johnson*, ed. Hill, rev. Powell, 1. 306.
[28] Robert Mahony and Betty W. Rizzo note that the 'Life' is part of a sequence of Lives of the poets displayed in the poem beneath the frontispiece to the 1756 volume of *The Universal Visiter*, of which only the first three (Chaucer, Spenser, Shakespeare) were completed. The last was signed 'S' (one of the usual marks of Smart's authorship of pieces in the magazine) and Mahony and Rizzo conjecture that all three Lives were almost certainly Smart's work (see Robert Mahony and Betty W. Rizzo, *Christopher Smart: An Annotated Bibliography, 1743–1983* (New York and London. 1984), item 551, pp. 206–8. For Smart's authorship of the poem 'Good Councils of Chaucer' included in 'Life of Chaucer', see Chapter 5.

ever the world produced'; 'If not the greatest, he was, without controversy, the most universal genius that ever was'; 'There is not a single species of poetry in which this great man has not left some specimens of his excellency.' The assessment of Chaucer's contribution to the history of the language is almost directly in contradiction to Johnson's account: 'when we reflect that [Chaucer] had the language in a manner to make as he wrote it in, what manner of amazement does it afford?' Dryden's remarks on Chaucer are treated with uncritical respect: 'We are assured, from no less authority than that of Mr. Dryden, that his "Knight's Tale" is a perfect epic poem.' Smart's account also resembles Thomas Warton's more closely than Johnson's in its emphasis on Chaucer's humour: 'That he was capable of writing as excellent comedy, appears from his "Canterbury" Tales which work indeed is a kind of dramatic performance: and the character of the Host or Landlord in particular, is supported with as much humour and propriety as Shakespeare's Sir John Falstaff.'

The mention of Dryden and Shakespeare was not accidental. *The Universal Visiter* was, from the outset, devoted to presenting English poetry as a continuum.[29] The frontispiece to the first issue depicted an author at a desk gazing upwards towards shelves holding the works of the English poets (see Fig. 8.1).[30] Under the engraving were printed the following lines describing the progress of the language, lines which, if Smart's authorship of the Lives of Chaucer, Spenser, and Shakespeare in *The Universal Visiter* is accepted, are also likely to be his work:

> To CHAUCER! Who the English Tongue design'd:
> To SPENCER! Who improv'd it, and refin'd:
> To Muse-fir'd SHAKEPEAR! who increas'd its Praise
> Rich in bold Compounds, & strong-painted Phrase,
> To WALLER! Sweet'ner of its manly Sound:
> To DRYDEN! Who its full Perfection found.

This is the standard eighteenth-century history of the language of *poetry*, placing Chaucer clearly at the head and culminating in Dryden '*Who its full Perfection found*'. Chaucer was probably important to Smart's plans for *The Universal Visiter* from its inception. The compilers of the journal proclaim themselves as 'glad to give instruction' as they will 'be proud of receiving it'—'a lesson which was taught them by those two excellent lines of Chaucer, which they have chosen for their

---

[29] In the first issue, the Life of Chaucer follows 'Some Thoughts on the English Language', which concludes with a poem beginning 'Hail, Energeia! hail my native tongue'. Both 'Some Thoughts' and the poem are listed by Mahony and Rizzo as certainly Smart's work.

[30] For the engraving, see Alok Yadav, *Before the Empire of English* (New York, 2004), pp. 27–30. For the lines beneath the engraving, see Trevor Ross, *The Making of the English Literary Canon* (Montreal and London, 1998), pp. 3–5 and Richard Terry, *Poetry and the Making of the English Literary Past, 1660–1781* (Oxford, 2001), pp. 58–60. Ross suggests that the author depicted in the frontispiece is to be seen as Smart himself.

Fig. 8.1 Venerating English poets from Chaucer to Dryden.
Frontispiece to the first issue of *The Universal Visiter and
Memorialist for the Year 1756*.
Reproduced by permission of the Bodleian Library, Oxford.

motto'. The motto on the title page of all issues of the *Universal Visiter* was adapted
from Chaucer's character of 'The Clerke of Oxenford':

> *Sounding with Moral Virtue was his Speech,*
> *And gladly would he learn, and gladly teach.*

Johnson's leading suggestion in the *Dictionary* that Chaucer might 'be stiled the
first of our versifyers who wrote poetically' had became part of the staple praise

of the poet and was repeated in many general accounts. It is therefore perhaps not surprising that the 'Life of Chaucer' printed in the *Universal Visiter*, despite its inconsistency with his other writings, was assumed to be a representation of 'Dr. Johnson's sentiments on this poet'. Though Johnson might have been thought, in some of his remarks, to have taken away the 'fatherhood' claim of Chaucer, it also seemed that he had, in others, given it back again. Even if Chaucer may not have invented the common language, or even affected it strongly in any particular direction, and may not even have invented English verse, he was the first who wrote *poetically*.

Indeed, Johnson's *Dictionary* was thought by many readers to have contributed to the elevation of Chaucer's fame and as having endorsed Dryden's praise of his great predecessor. Robert Anderson describes Chaucer as 'the father of the English heroic verse, and the first English versifier who wrote poetically'.[31] In *The Biographical Magazine, Containing Portraits & Characters of Eminent and Ingenious Persons* (1794)—to take another example almost at random—the entirely conventional entry on Chaucer begins by describing the poet as 'the father of English poetry', and ends by running together Johnson's remarks from the *Dictionary* and Dryden's from the Preface to *Fables*: 'Dr Johnson observes, that Chaucer was the first English poet who wrote poetically; and Dryden holds him in the same degree of veneration, as the Grecians held Homer, or the Romans Virgil.' Most striking of all is the opening sentence of Thomas Warton's chapter on Chaucer in his *History of English Poetry*:

> The most illustrious ornament of the reign of Edward the third, and of his successor Richard the second, was Jeffrey Chaucer; a poet with whom the history of our poetry is by many supposed to have commenced; and who has been pronounced, by a critic of unquestionable taste and discernment, to be the first English versifier who wrote poetically.[32]

Chaucer in Johnson's *Dictionary*

Despite such affirmations, it is, however, difficult to determine precisely what 'Dr. Johnson's sentiments' on Chaucer ultimately amounted to. There are apparently insurmountable difficulties in reconciling Johnson's remarks on Chaucer in the *Lives of the Poets*, his plan for a new edition of Chaucer's works, and the Chaucerian traces to be found in different parts of the *Dictionary*. In the *Lives*, Johnson, as we have seen, expressed opinions directly contrary to those of most of his friends, considering anachronism in *Palamon and Arcite* a serious blemish, whereas others rejoiced in it, regarding the 'tale of *The Cock*' as 'hardly worth revival', and

---

[31] Robert Anderson, ed., *A Complete Edition of the Poets of Great Britain*, 14 vols (Edinburgh, 1793), 1. iii.
[32] Warton, *History*, 1. 342.

setting his face against the revival of the medieval past by any means—with some consistency, pertinacity, and even animus.

It seems significant that Johnson should include, under his entry for 'survive', a quotation that is longer than strictly necessary from Pope's *Essay on Criticism* on the decay of language:

> No longer now that golden age appears,
> When patriarch-wits *surviv'd* a thousand years;
> Now length of fame, our second life, is lost,
> And bare threescore is all ev'n that can boast;
> Our sons their father's failing language see,
> And such as Chaucer is, shall Dryden be.
>
> *Pope.*

That thought was disquieting for all lexicographers. Benjamin Martin, the publication of whose *Lingua Britannica Reformata* in 1749 may have thrown Johnson into depression, predicted that Addison and Pope 'may appear to our posterity in the same light as Chaucer, Spenser, and Shakespear do to us; whose language is now grown old and obsolete; read by very few, and understood by antiquarians only'.[33]

Telling, too, but in a different way, is a quotation in Johnson's entry on 'mist' ('A low thin cloud; a small thin rain not perceived in single drops') from Sir John Denham's poem *On Mr Abraham Cowley*:

> Old Chaucer, like the morning star,
> To us discovers day from far;
> His light those *mists* and clouds dissolv'd
> Which our dark nation long involv'd.
>
> *Denham*

One difficulty for later readers, as we saw in Chapter 1, was that there was, in their perception, a gap both in the development of the English language and in the process of poetical transmission or tradition after Chaucer. If Chaucer 'may perhaps, with great justice, be stiled the first of our versifyers who wrote poetically', his work was, as almost everybody saw it, not equalled until Spenser. It is significant that the poem of Denham's from which Johnson quotes continues thus:

> But he descending to the shades,
> Darkness again the Age invades.
> Next (like *Aurora*) *Spencer* rose,
> Whose purple blush the day foreshows.
>
> Denham, *Poetical Works*, ed. Theodore Howard Banks
> (2nd edn, Hamden, CT, 1969), p. 149

---

[33] Benjamin Martin, *Lingua Britannica Reformata: or, a New English Dictionary* (London, 1749), p. 111. Johnson's reactions to Martin's work are described by Allen Reddick in *The Making of Johnson's Dictionary 1746-1773* (Cambridge, 1996), pp. 51–3.

Johnson's *Dictionary* entries show him to have paid particular attention to Dryden's Preface to *Fables Ancient and Modern*, and within that Preface, to Dryden's remarks about poetic inheritance and the course of English poetry. Under 'clan', for example, Johnson quotes Dryden's statement that 'Milton was the poetical son of Spenser, and Mr. Waller of Fairfax; for we have our lineal descents and *clans* as well as other families'. And under 'master', he quotes Dryden's remark that 'Spenser and Fairfax, great *masters* of our language, saw much farther into the beauties of our numbers than those who followed.'

Johnson dated the start of the English language to be included in his *Dictionary* more or less from the period of Spenser's youth: 'I have fixed *Sidneys's* work, for the boundary, beyond which I make few excursions.'[34] Surprising as it may seem to us, such an early starting date was highly unusual. Benjamin Martin referred his 'Reader for *old and obsolete Words* to the *Glossaries* on *Chaucer, Spenser,* &c.' and, in the body of his Dictionary, included a few words found only in Milton, but none from Spenser.[35]

It is perhaps principally for lexicographical rather than literary reasons that there is relatively little Chaucer in Johnson's *Dictionary*.[36] Johnson had decided that the English language emerged properly in the works of Sidney, Shakespeare, Hooker, and Spenser. He was able, in writing from this period onwards, to deduce the meaning of any given word from the words that surround it and expected his readers to be able to do the same. It appears to have been for reasons of intelligibility that he makes few excursions across the boundary marked by Sidney's work: 'I have been cautious lest my zeal for antiquity might drive me into times too remote, and croud my book with words now no longer understood.'[37] Johnson's general method was to give an explanation inferred from his examples, and then to provide the evidence on which that inference had been made. In the case of some technical words, the citation *is* the definition. He did not want his readers to have to take his mere say-so for the meaning of words but invited them to perform the process of inference themselves, particularly in detecting 'shades' of meaning. Many Chaucerian passages would have faced his readers with too many unknown words together. Spenser and Shakespeare he might save from obsolescence by these methods. Further back he could not go.

---

[34] Johnson, *Works*, 18. 96.
[35] Martin, *Lingua Britannica Reformata*, p. iv.
[36] There is, however, more reference to Chaucer than has often been allowed:

> The surprisingly strong presence of Chaucer in Johnson's work is important both because it undercuts the critical remarks about Chaucer that Johnson makes in the History of the English Language and elsewhere in his oeuvre, particularly with regard to the relative merit of Chaucer and Gower, and because it would have given eighteenth-century users of the Dictionary far more opportunities than we have imagined of encountering the medieval.
>
> (Leff, 'Johnson's Chaucer', p. 2).

[37] Johnson, *Works*, 18. 96.

Chaucer in Johnson's *Etymologies*

It would not, in fact, have been difficult for Johnson to represent and illustrate a substantial part of Chaucer's vocabulary in his *Dictionary* had he so wished. The glossary provided by Timothy Thomas for Urry's edition is much more extensive and precise than anything existing before. Johnson, however, appears to have consulted it only occasionally. His main source for information about Chaucer's vocabulary was Franciscus Junius's *Etymologicum*.[38] Johnson had constant recourse to this volume: it was the source for many of the etymologies in the *Dictionary*. Much of Johnson's Chaucer in the *Dictionary* is, in fact, *Junius's* Chaucer because Johnson was, during the work's composition, thinking of Chaucer in primarily etymological terms. For Johnson, the proper place for Chaucer was confined, as it were, to the square brackets that follow the headword where etymology, orthography, and the *past* history of the word are discussed, and precede the definitions and illustrations. Even when, as in the entry on 'coy', lines from Chaucer break out from the square brackets to become supporting illustrations, the reason for this is often historical. From the various Chaucerian illustrations offered by Junius, Johnson chose one that allowed a mid-eighteenth-century reader to infer something of the meaning from the surrounding words.

On some occasions, as, for example, in the entry on 'dam', a description of alterations between a Chaucerian and a modern sense is necessary if the modern use is to be fully understood. Johnson's point is that the word had *once* signified a human mother, and had *then* come to mean 'the mother: used of beasts, or other animals not human', so that its application to 'a human mother' in 'Shakespeare's *Winter's Tale*' was clearly made 'in contempt or detestation' ('This brat is none of mine; / It is the issue of Polixenes: / Hence with it, and, together with the *dam*, / Commit them to the fire').[39] In contrast to the use of 'pasterns' in *The Wife of Bath Her Tale*, the contempt and detestation in the Shakespeare passage is both stronger and something which the speaker consciously intends. Johnson helps his readers to recall the context by providing full details of the work from which the lines are taken, rather than merely giving the lines' author, his usual practice.

There are some instances, however, where fragments of Chaucer's text break out of the historical brackets for apparently inexplicable reasons, and where Johnson is violating his own procedures without obvious cause. The most peculiar of these occasions is the entry for 'erke' ('idle; lazy; slothful'). This Johnson observes is 'an old word' and his only illustration is from *The Romance of the Rose*: 'For men therein should hem delite; / And of that dede be not *erke*, / But oft sithes haunt

---

[38] Franciscus Junius [Francis Du Jon], *Etymologicum Anglicanum*, ed. Edward Lye (Oxford, 1743). Amanda Leff notes ('Johnson's Chaucer', pp. 4–5): 'A second group of Chaucer references, twenty in all, can be found in the *Dictionary*'s etymological notes, in which Johnson cites Chaucer as an authority for earlier uses or forms of words but does not quote Chaucer's poetry.'

[39] *The Winter's Tale*, II. iii. 92–5.

that werke'. That Johnson was regarding the entry as a contribution to the history of the language is suggested by the addition in 1773 of the comment 'whence we now say *irksome*'. But it is hard to see why he would make such a comment and *not* move his quotation to the entry for the current word *irksome*. The difficulty is accentuated by Johnson marking the word as a noun while explaining it as an adjective. Johnson probably looked up 'erke' in Junius—where the word is given a long note discussing various possible Anglo-Saxon derivations—and took his illustration from there.

Chaucer as a Simple Gloss for the Bible, and Spenser, and Milton

When lines by Chaucer, or lines assumed to be Chaucer's, are quoted in Johnson's *Dictionary*, they are often quoted not so much for their own sake, but in order to preserve some other text from obsolescence and unintelligibility. One such text was the Bible as represented in the Authorized Version of 1611. Johnson, for example, illustrates the word 'grin' ('a snare; a trap') with a fragment from the pseudo-Chaucerian *Remedy of Love*: 'Like a birde that hasteth to his *gryn*, / Not knowinge the perile'. The almost self-defining Chaucerian quotation and the etymology ('*gryn, gyrene*, Saxon') are necessary to illustrate the sentence from Job also given by Johnson: 'The *grin* shall take him by the heel, and the robber shall prevail against him' [Job 18:9]. They also seem designed to preserve the word 'grin' from contamination from the much more common term 'gin', similarly glossed in the *Dictionary* as 'a trap; a snare', which Johnson derived from 'engine', and which, as the *OED* observes, replaced 'grin' in some printings of the Bible. In the Authorized Version, 'grin' is found in certain passages (Job, 18:9; Ps. 140:5; 141:9) where modern editions read 'gin'. Where Johnson was able to provide examples of 'gin' from Sidney, Shakespeare, Milton, Butler, and Ben Jonson, he had perhaps come across no other instances of 'grin' in the sense of a trap. It does *not* seem to have been the case, however, that Johnson had trawled through Chaucer's works to find his quotation. He had presumably marked 'grin' in a copy of the Bible and then turned to Junius, where the lines from *The Remedy of Love* are quoted, as by Johnson, from Speght's edition.

Similarly, it seems to have been in order to explain the use of 'conne' ('to know') in Spenser's *The Shepherds Calendar* that Johnson cited Chaucer: '*connan*, Sax. to know; as in Chaucer, *Old wymen connen mochil thinge*; that is, *Old women have much knowledge*'. On this occasion, Johnson does seem to have turned to Chaucer himself—or, rather, turned to his *memories* of Chaucer: the fragment as he gives it does not occur in any text of Chaucer's works. Johnson's '*Old wymen connen mochil thinge*' is probably misremembered from 'Thise <u>olde</u> folk can <u>muchel thing</u>' (*The Wife of Bath's Tale*, 1004). The line, however imprecise—indeed, *because* imprecise—perhaps indicates that Johnson was working from memory. It may indeed be the only certain indication in the *Dictionary* that Johnson had read in Chaucer's works for himself.

If Johnson turned to Junius when wanting to gloss the word 'defended' in Milton,[40] he would have discovered only that the term in this sense was common in Chaucer. He was thus left to find an illustrative example for himself. A passage from *The Wife of Bath's Prologue*, provides the illustration of Johnson's fourth definition of 'defend' ('to prohibit; to forbid'): 'Where can you say, in any manner, age, / That ever God *defended* marriage?' Johnson, however, may here not have gone to Chaucer directly, but to a note in Thomas Newton's edition of *Paradise Lost*, where Milton's 'defended fruit' is illustrated by the same lines from Chaucer.[41]

Welkin: Chaucer and Poetic Genealogies

In all the instances so far discussed, Chaucer is referred to in illustration of the history of the common, rather than the specifically poetic, language. However, one reason for the inclusion of a proliferation of supporting examples in the *Dictionary* offered by Johnson in the Preface to the work is to provide a history of poetic diction, or, as Johnson puts it, 'a genealogy of sentiments':

> I have sometimes, though rarely, yielded to the temptation of exhibiting a genealogy of sentiments, by shewing how one authour copied the thoughts and diction of another: such quotations are indeed little more than repetitions, which might justly be censured, did they not gratify the mind, by affording a kind of intellectual history.[42]

The inclusion of a line from *The Book of the Duchess* in the entry for 'welkin' ('The visible regions of the air. Out of use, except in poetry') may be explained as an example of such a process. In Johnson, Chaucer's line ('Ne in all the *welkin* was no cloud') is followed by examples from Spenser, Shakespeare, Milton, and J. Philips.

This is a lonely instance of Johnson presenting Chaucer as the father of what became a distinctly poetical form. But once again, the example was probably not Johnson's own discovery. In some editions of John Gay's *Pastorals*, illustrating the third line from 'Monday, or the Squabble' ('No chirping lark the welkin sheen invokes') is a note on 'welkin': '*Welkin the same as* Welken, *an old Saxon word signifying a* Cloud, *by poetical licence it is frequently taken for the* Element *or*

---

[40] 'O sons! like one of us, man is become / To know both good and evil, since his taste / Of that *defended* fruit' (*Paradise Lost*, 12. 86).

[41] John Milton, *Paradise Lost: A Poem*, ed. Thomas Newton, 2 vols (London, 1749), 2. 311; Newton attributes his note to Patrick Hume and Jonathan Richardson. The Chaucerian couplet is also quoted s.v. 'defend' in John Cowell, *The Interpreter of Words and Terms, Used Either in the Common or Statute Laws of This Realm, and in Tenures and Jocular Customs* (London, 1701) .

[42] Johnson, *Works*, 18. 98.

Sky *as may appear by this Verse in the Dream of Chaucer.* Ne in all the Welkin was no cloud.'[43]

Chaucerian Absences

Despite this entry on 'welkin', and despite Amanda Leff's demonstration that Chaucer features more largely in Johnson's work than has been traditionally allowed, the most striking feature of Chaucer's role in the *Dictionary* remains the poet's relative *absence*. Most strangely, but characteristically, Chaucer does not appear in the *Dictionary* as an illustration either of the history of poetic or common language on several occasions when he might—or *should*. Such is the case with Johnson's entry for 'hight' ('was named; was called'), where an example from Spenser is followed by one from Dryden's *The Cock and the Fox*: 'Within this homestead liv'd, without a peer / For crowing loud, the noble Chanticleer, / So *hight* her cock'. Why, we might ask, did Johnson not cite Chaucer's poem, of which Dryden's is, in this instance, a close reflection: 'In whiche she had a cocke, <u>hight</u> chauntecleer, / In al the lande of crowing n'as his peer'?[44] The case is complicated by the fact that Johnson, as in the quotation from *The Winter's Tale* mentioned earlier cites the title of the poem ('*Dryden's Nun's Priest*') from whence his illustration came, rather than just its author.

Much the same could be said of Johnson's 'illustrations' of 'debonair' ('elegant; civil; well bred; gentle; complaisant'), where Spenser, Milton, and Dryden are cited, but where the last, again from *The Cock and the Fox*, might have been the first, since Dryden is, again, close to Chaucer's original: Dryden's lines 'And she that was not only passing fair / But was withal discreet and *debonair*, / Resolv'd the passive doctrine to fulfil' preserve Chaucer's *debonair* intact: 'Curteis she was, discrete and <u>debonaire</u>, / And compenable, and bare her self so fair'.[45]

On some occasions, Chaucer's words appear in the *Dictionary* without Johnson fully noticing it. Such is the case with his definition of the adverb 'sore', a word Johnson observes that 'is now little used'. This is illustrated by two quotations from Dryden's versions of Chaucer, the first of which, from *Palamon and Arcite*, resembles the original text closely:

> So that, if Palamon were wounded *sore*,
> Arcite was hurt as much.

In Urry's text of Chaucer, the lines read:

> That, if that Palamon was woundid sore,
> Arcit' was hurt as much as he, or more.[46]

[43] John Gay, *The Shepherd's Week. In Six Pastorals. By Mr. J. Gay* (London, 1714), p. 3.
[44] Urry, p.169.
[45] Ibid. p. 169.
[46] Ibid. p. 10.

As was the case with quotations from *The Nun's Priest's Tale*, Johnson's extended title ('*Dryden's Knights Tale*') refers a reader beyond Dryden to Chaucer, in that the poem was commonly known by Dryden's title, *Palamon and Arcite,* rather than Chaucer's.

There is, however, no indication that the next 'illustration' under 'sore' is to be attributed to Chaucer's Wife of Bath, where the quotation from Dryden's version of her *Tale* is not as close to Chaucer's original:

> *Sore* sigh'd the knight, who this long sermon heard:
> At length, considering all, his heart he chear'd.   *Dryden.*

> This knight avisith him, and <u>sore</u> he siketh,
> But at the last he said in this manere.

> (Urry, p. 10)

The case against Johnson having any acute sense of the place of Chaucer's works in the language of poetry is clearest in Johnson's entry on 'observance'. Here, Johnson's quotation from Dryden's *Palamon and Arcite* ('Arcite left his bed, resolv'd to pay / *Observance* to the month of merry May') half-acknowledges and half-denies Chaucer's role in fathering the sentiment that young people—particularly lovers—might pay observance to the month of May. The quotation from Dryden is, as with the use of *Palamon and Arcite* cited above, closely related to its original, as Johnson might have found it in Urry's edition: 'And Arcite ... / Is rise, and lookith on the mery day, / And to don his observauncis to May'.[47]

Continuities in Poetic Diction

It may have been a fondness for Dryden's Chaucer poems, and for *Palamon and Arcite* in particular, that explains Johnson's entry for 'gladder' ('one that makes glad; one that gladdens'). Here, Johnson seems primarily concerned to provide a gloss for the line that he quotes from *Palamon and Arcite* ('Thou *gladder* of the mount of Cytheron, / Have pity, goddess'). But Johnson gives no indication or betrays no knowledge of the fact that the lines are almost *verbatim* from Chaucer. He gives no indication that the agent noun is now an archaism or poeticism.[48]

But the most striking instance of the absence of Chaucer in Johnson's *Dictionary* where one might expect his presence is Johnson's entry on 'armipotent'. Again, Johnson hints at a genealogy, providing illustrations from Shakespeare's *All's Well That Ends Well*, from Edward Fairfax's translation of Tasso, and from a work he calls '*Dryden's Fab*': 'Beneath the low'ring brow, and on a bent, / The temple stood of Mars *armipotent*'. Here again, the last item in the genealogical succession, in strictly chronological terms, should have been the first. The target word 'armipotent' (and

---

[47] Ibid. p. 12.
[48] Johnson might have noticed the use of the word in John Dart's *Westminster-Abbey. A Poem* (London, 1721): 'O sacred Liberty, of heavenly Birth! / Joy of Mankind, and <u>Gladder</u> of the Earth!'

the rhyme and the shape of the couplet) is clearly Chaucer's rather than Dryden's, and the original lines are not difficult: 'And downward from an hill undir a bent / There stode the temple' of Mars armipotent.'[49]

The *poetic* genealogy of 'armipotent'—particularly as an epithet for Mars—is an instance, if ever there was one, of poetic 'fathering', with Chaucer's *Knight's Tale* as its ancestral source. Johnson, that is, *might*, have provided an entry for the word rather like this:

ARMI'POTENT.*adj.* [*armipotens*, Lat.] Powerful in arms; mighty in war.

There stode the temple' of Mars *armipotent*	*Chaucer Knight's Tale*
Mars the stierne God *armypotente*	*Chaucer Knight's Tale*
The myghty lorde, the god *armypotent* Thare saw I Mars, the god *armypotent*,	*John Lydgate, Troy Book*
At this tyme Mars, the god *armypotent*	*Gavin Douglas, Virgil's Aeneid*
The *Armipotent* Mars, of Launces the almighty,	*Loves Labour's Lost*
For if our God the Lord *Armipotent*, Those armed Angels in our aid down send, That were at Dothan to his Prophet sent, Thou wilt come down with them, and well defend Our host.	*Edward Fairfax, Godfrey of Buloigne*
Mars *armipotent* with his Court-of-guard, *giue sharpnes to my Toledo*	*Thomas Dekker, Blurt Master-constable*
Here Mars *armipotent* pour'd courage great Into the Latines hearts, and Martiall heat.	*John Vicars, The XII Aeneids of Virgil,*
Beneath the low'ring brow, and on a bent, The temple stood of Mars *armipotent*.	*Dryden's Fab.*
So Mars *Armipotent* invades the Plain (The wide destroyer of the race of man)	*Pope, The Iliad of Homer*

Although in his entry Johnson provides only Dryden's uses of 'Mars armipotent', he may have admired the phrase. In his entry on 'bent' ('declivity'), Johnson extended a quotation from *Palamon and Arcite* beyond the point strictly necessary for the definition, to include Dryden's mention of 'Mars armipotent', perhaps because, like other poets, he found it memorable. On this occasion, although the target word 'bent' is Chaucer's, the reference given is to '*Dryd. Pal. and Arc*'— Johnson being, again, apparently more interested in *Dryden's* words than in their Chaucerian antecedents.

---

[49] Urry, p. 16.

Dryden's Chaucer in Johnson's *Dictionary*

Given how cruelly dismissive are Johnson's remarks upon *Palamon and Arcite* in his *Lives of the Poets*, it is remarkable, and remarkably inexplicable, how often it provides illustrations in the *Dictionary*.[50] Johnson's entry on 'oak', for example, intermingles several botanical accounts of the tree with illustrations from Shakespeare, Dryden, and Pope that seem to be there because of their poetic attractiveness alone. These include an extract from Theseus's speech at the end of *Palamon and Arcite*:

> The monarch *oak*, the patriarch of the trees,
> Shoots rising up and spreads by slow degrees:
> Three centuries he grows, and three he stays
> Supreme in state, and in three more decays.   *Dry.*

This passage was of interest to Johnson for words *added* to Chaucer by Dryden, and is cited in his definitions of 'monarch', 'patriarch', 'shoot', 'supreme', and 'decay', as well as 'oak'. The frequency with which words in the passage must have been underlined by Johnson and copied out by his amanuenses may reflect his sense that the words were mutually illuminating within Dryden's lines, but also that they were intrinsically impressive. Johnson's interest in Dryden's oaks extended to another passage in *Palamon and Arcite* where Dryden coined the epithet 'doddered' for the oak branches brought by the local peasants for use in the funeral of Arcite. In this instance, Johnson's fondness for Dryden's usage seems to have overridden any desire for botanical accuracy, and was severely criticized by the authors of the *OED*:

> Johnson explained it as 'Overgrown with dodder: covered with supercrescent plants'; and this explanation, which was manifestly erroneous, since neither dodder nor any plant like it grows upon trees, has been repeated in the dictionaries, and has influenced literary usage, in which there is often a vague notion of some kind of parasitical accretion accompanying or causing decay.

The Cock and the Fox and the *Dictionary*

Dryden's *The Cock and the Fox* is frequently cited in the *Dictionary*. While it cannot be assumed that frequent citation inevitably implies Johnson's approbation, his citations of this poem suggest an unusually deep and thorough knowledge of it—and perhaps, behind it, some shadowy knowledge of Dryden's original. In Johnson's entry under 'Chanticleer', for example, quotations from Spenser, Shakespeare, and Ben Jonson are followed with an account from Camden's *Remains* of

---

[50] As Roger Lonsdale observes in his edition of *The Lives of the Most Eminent English Poets; with Critical Observations on Their Works*, 4 vols (Oxford, 2006), 2. 366.

Chaucer's poem of 'the description of the sudden stir, and panical fear, when *Chanticleer* the cock was carried away by Reynold the fox'. And the entry closes with a quotation from *The Cock and the Fox* ('Within this homestead liv'd without a peer, / For crowing loud, the noble *chanticleer*').

Chanticleer's hen-wife Partlet gets an entry of her own in the *Dictionary*, and passages relating to her are included in Johnson's entries on 'debonair', 'passing', 'chicken', and 'feather' ('to tread as a cock'). In the last instance, the illustrative quotation includes a line ('He *feather'd* her a hundred times a day'), which Dryden reproduced almost exactly from Speght's text of Chaucer. The line was also included by Urry. But Thomas Tyrwhitt noticed that the line could be found 'in only two' manuscripts, and commented that he 'was glad to leave them out as an injudicious interpolation'.[51] The presence of this line might serve as a telling instance of Chaucer's general role in the *Dictionary*: Chaucer's verse is *gestured towards* rather than clearly *present*, and gestured towards as it had been influential on the minds of others rather than as a *direct* and *active* element in the mind of Johnson himself.

Dryden's Good Parson

Readers of Johnson's *Dictionary* would have encountered in the entry on 'comprehensive' Dryden's judgement that Chaucer 'must have been a man of a most wonderful *comprehensive* nature, because he has taken into the compass of his Canterbury tales the various manners and humours of the whole English nation in his age'. And in the entry on 'sup' they would have read Dryden's affirmation that he saw 'all the pilgrims in the Canterbury tales as distinctly as if [he] had *supped* with them'. It is, indeed, to the characters in *The Canterbury Tales* that readers of the *Dictionary* would be most often referred. They are invoked in some detail, Johnson managing to include all the adjectives which Dryden had deployed when describing Chaucer's characters. In his entries for 'mince', 'prioress', 'broad and gap-tooth'd', Johnson quotes Dryden's description of five of Chaucer's characters: 'The reeve, miller, and cook, are distinguished from each other as much as the mincing lady prioress and the broad-speaking gap-toothed wife of Bath.' And in the entry for 'ever', readers would have met the paradoxical generalization with which Dryden summed up his experience of reading and translating Chaucer's poems: 'Mankind is *ever* the same, and nothing lost out of nature, though every thing is altered.'

One of Dryden's versions of Chaucer cited most frequently by Johnson is *The Character of a Good Parson*. Johnson cites this poem in the course of no less than fifteen definitions, with the effect that all the salient elements in Dryden's portrait

---

[51] Tyrwhitt 1775–78, 3. 288.

are given in the *Dictionary*.[52] But this poem, as we saw in Chapter 5, stands apart from Dryden's other Chaucerian translations, in that Dryden has introduced into Chaucer's portrait reflections on the qualities of a particular clergyman of his own day. The presence of Chaucer behind Dryden is therefore in this instance even more shadowy and distant than elsewhere.

The Inevitability of a Chaucerian Presence?

Johnson's sense of Chaucer's importance to English poetry is suggested by a minute correction made for the 1773 edition to the fourth meaning of 'to hold'. In 1755, the illustration read: 'As he is the father of English poetry, so I *hold* him in the same degree of veneration as the Grecians *held* Homer, or the Romans Virgil.' This was an accurate transcription from Dryden's Preface to *Fables Ancient and Modern*, but in 1773 Johnson amended the text, while still attributing his quotation to Dryden, to make clearer who it was that Dryden so venerated: 'As Chaucer is the father of English poetry, so I *hold* him in the same degree of veneration as the Grecians *held* Homer, or the Romans Virgil.'

It is clear that, despite his later dismissive remarks in the *Life of Dryden*, Johnson had, at one time in his life, read both the Preface and the Chaucerian poems in *Fables Ancient and Modern* with great attention, and perpetuated many of its leading contentions. In the *Dictionary*, Chaucer is a presence in his own voice in occasional citations within the *Dictionary* itself, as well as in the passages—from *The House of Fame*, *Boethius*, 'Flee from the press', etc.—included in the Preliminaries that illustrate the history of the language. He is a presence most often as mediated by others—Denham, Dryden (most often), Pope, and even Betterton[53]—both in the form of versions of his poems and in references to fictional personages, not only the characters on the pilgrimage but those within the tales, Arcite, Palamon, Chanticleer, and Partlet.

In his Preface to Shakespeare, Johnson offered high praise for Chaucer—at the same time as denying his relevance to Shakespeare:

> There is a vigilance of observation and accuracy of distinction which books and precepts cannot confer; from this almost all original and native excellence proceeds. Shakespeare must have looked upon mankind with perspicacity, in the highest degree curious and attentive. Other writers borrow their characters from preceding writers, and diversify them only by the accidental appendages of present manners; the dress is a little varied, but the body is the same. Our authour had both matter and form to provide; for except the characters of Chaucer, to whom I think he is not much indebted,

---

[52] *The Character of a Good Parson* is cited under the following words: accomplice, affright, aspect, benefice, brilliant, call, chaffer, churchman, creation, crowd, commission, curate, diffuse, exhale, harsh, innate.

[53] Johnson cites Betterton's version of *The Reeve's Tale* once in 1773, under 'clack' ('A bell that rings, when more corn is required to be put in').

there were no writers in English, and perhaps not many in other modern languages, which shewed life in its native colours.[54]

To have 'shewed life in its native colours' was for Johnson the highest of possible literary attainments. To say that Shakespeare was 'not much indebted' to Chaucer was to overlook the suggestions of Pope and Theobald concerning *Troilus and Cressida* and Chaucer's *Troilus*, and *A Midsummer Night's Dream* and *The Knight's Tale*. But Johnson's clear implication, nevertheless, is that Chaucer's ability to 'shew life in its native colours' did not fall much short of Shakespeare's. When all Johnson's references to Chaucer are taken together, they suggest some acquaintance with Chaucer's work, but of a highly unschematic and arbitrary kind. The frequent replacement of Chaucer with Dryden in the *Dictionary* may be explained by an observation that Johnson made in the *Lives of the Poets* immediately after his dismissal of Dryden's Chaucer translations: 'Whatever subjects employed [Dryden's] pen he was still improving our measures and embellishing our language.'[55] Despite Johnson's declared hostility to Dryden's *Fables*, the frequent citation of the volume and its Preface in the *Dictionary* can be seen, in fact, as amounting to a tacit endorsement of Dryden's judgement as a critic and as a poet. In several instances, Dryden is shown by Johnson to have revived an old word or phrase with success ('gladder', 'Mars armipotent'), or to have formed part of a continuing poetic genealogy. As well as displaying his respect for Dryden, Johnson's *Dictionary* records and responds to Chaucerian presences in the writings of Edmund Spenser, Alexander Pope, John Hughes, Thomas Newton, John Gay, Zachary Grey, Thomas Warton, and many other writers, and thus testifies, implicitly but powerfully, to the enduring presence of Chaucer as a linguistic and poetical father-figure.

In the *Dictionary*, the entry on 'particularly' ('in an extraordinary degree') contains the following citation from Dryden: 'With the flower and the leaf I was so *particularly* pleased, both for the invention and the moral, that I commend it to the reader.' Under the entries both for 'door' ('entrance; portal'), and 'to doubt' ('to hesitate; to be in suspense'), appear the following lines:

> At first the tender blades of grass appear,
> And buds, that yet the blast of Eurus fear,
> Stand at the *door* of life, and *doubt* to clothe the year.

Johnson's entry on 'gem' ('the first bud') is illustrated thus:

> Embolden'd out they come,
> And swell the *gems*, and burst the narrow room.

---

[54] Johnson, *Works*, 7. 88.
[55] Ibid. 21. 482.

Both passages are attributed to Dryden. Both come from *The Flower and the Leaf*, and provide evidence of Johnson's response to the strong eighteenth-century interest and delight in the extraordinarily miscellaneous group of poems once attributed to Chaucer but now often known as 'The Chaucerian Apocrypha'. These poems form the subject of Chapter 9.

PART III
GOTHIC, ROMANTIC, AND VISIONARY POEMS

9

Visions, Proclamations, and Courts of Love

George Ellis, as we have seen, expressed mild disappointment at Johnson's treatment of Chaucer in his *Dictionary*. Others, however, were roused to something very like fury in response to his animadversions upon Dryden's *Fables* in his *Lives of the Poets*. Joseph Warton, who had at one time been a close friend of Johnson's, observing that *The Flower and the Leaf* 'has received a thousand new graces from the spirited and harmonious Dryden', wrote that

> It is mortifying and surprising to see the cold and contemptuous manner in which Dr. Johnson speaks of these capital pieces, which he says require little criticism, and seem hardly worth the *rejuvenescence* (as he affectedly calls it) which Dryden has bestowed upon them. It is remarkable that, in his criticisms, he has not even mentioned the Flower and the Leaf.[1]

It is, however, neither surprising nor accidental that Joseph Warton should have singled out from several 'capital pieces' *The Flower and the Leaf* in reference to which Samuel Johnson had been so unaccountably and unforgivably silent. For Warton, that poem was both an 'exquisite VISION' in itself, and one that had been beautifully embellished by Dryden.[2] Warton was far from alone in his admiration for this poem. One reader who agreed with him about Johnson and Chaucer was the translator of Aeschylus, Robert Potter, who in his *The Art of Criticism* observed of Johnson:

> Chaucer is no favourite with our author; but his wit was brilliant, and his humour powerful; too hostile to the chicanery of priestcraft for Johnson, and very extraordinary at that time of day; but sometimes indecent. Dryden is probably partial in setting *Palamon* and *Arcite*, on a level with the *Eneid*; yet Chaucer was a great genius and deemed the primo-genitor of English poetry. His *Flower and Leaf*, past over by the smoak-loving Johnson, is charmingly modernized: the nineteen first lines in particular are so delightful, and contain so incomparable a sketch of the beauty of Spring, that they should charm all readers.[3]

---

[1] *The Works of Alexander Pope*, ed. Joseph Warton, 9 vols (London, 1797), 2. 165–6.
[2] Joseph Warton, *An Essay on the Genius and Writings of Pope*, 2 vols (London, 1782), 2.12.
[3] Robert Potter, *The Art of Criticism; As Exemplified in Dr Johnson's Lives of the Most Eminent English Poets* (London, 1789), pp. 60–1. See Herbert G. Wright, 'Robert Potter as a Critic of Dr. Johnson', *Review of English Studies*, 12 (1936), 305–21.

Chaucer in the Eighteenth Century. David Hopkins and Tom Mason, Oxford University Press.
© David Hopkins and Tom Mason (2022). DOI: 10.1093/oso/9780192862624.003.0010

There are many reasons for thinking that, after *The Canterbury Tales*, *The Flower and the Leaf* was the most loved and therefore most influential of all the poems included in editions of Chaucer's *Works* since 1598—or *became* so after Dryden had drawn attention to it with his version and in the Preface to his *Fables*. Responses to the poem took several forms. Many, such as Joseph Warton and Robert Potter, were charmed by Dryden's 'harmonious' version. Others, like Keats, praised the original, but may not have read it had Dryden, and before him Speght, not rescued it from oblivion.[4] It led others to look at poems by Chaucer, or included in collections of his work, that seemed to be broadly similar in their descriptions of the natural world, or in their possession of visionary or dream-like qualities. Alexander Pope connected *The Flower and the Leaf* with other Chaucerian and European visions, particularly *The House of Fame* and Petrarch's *Trionfi*. Others placed the poem in the company of works of what Thomas Warton described as a 'general romantic and allegoric vein'.[5]

Enduring Pleasures

For commentators in the closing years of the nineteenth century—most notably Walter W. Skeat—it counted heavily against eighteenth-century readers and critics that they could not tell the genuine work of Chaucer from the apocryphal works that were included in the editions of Chaucer available to them. But a taste for the Chaucer Apocrypha was by no means merely a fad of the eighteenth century. Several fifteenth-century manuscript collections attest to both the popularity of some of the apocryphal poems and their close association with genuine Chaucerian works. They were loved long and late, and with some intensity, and were sometimes abandoned with reluctance. *The Flower and the Leaf* remained the most popular of the apocryphal poems (see Fig. 9.1). In 1859, indeed, *The Dublin University Magazine* described it as 'the most beautiful and pure of all Chaucer's works'.[6] Thomas R. Lounsbury accepted that the poem was not genuinely Chaucerian, but nevertheless praised its 'beauty and grace' and judged that 'no small share of the master's mantel has fallen upon his nameless follower'.[7] Most remarkably, in lectures delivered as late as 1880, and printed in 1902, the American poet Sidney

---

[4] For the suggestion that Keats was influenced both by the original *Flower and the Leaf* and by Dryden's version, both in his sonnet on the poem and in the 'Ode to a Nightingale', see Kathleen Forni, *The Chaucerian Apocrypha. A Counterfeit Canon* (Gainesville, FL, 2001), pp. 132–6. Speght's edition is the unique source for the poem. No manuscripts have survived.

[5] Warton, *History*, 1. 465.

[6] See Forni, *The Chaucerian Apocrypha*, pp. 135–6.

[7] Thomas R. Lounsbury, *Studies in Chaucer, His Life and Writings*, 3 vols (London, 1892), 1. 496.

Fig. 9.1 The lady in the arbour, knights fighting, trees beyond.
Illustration by Thomas Stothard, engraved by Robert Cromek, in
John Dryden, *Fables from Boccacio and Chaucer*,
ed. John Aikin (London, 1806).

Lanier wrote: 'I do not hesitate to pronounce [*The Flower and the Leaf*] a far finer poem than any of the *Canterbury Tales*—in fact, to my thinking, worth all the *Canterbury Tales* put together.'[8] An illustration of *The Flower and the Leaf* formed

[8] See Sidney Lanier, *Shakspere and his Forerunners* (London, 1902), quoted in Forni, *The Chaucerian Apocrypha*, p. 138.

the centre-piece of the Chaucer window installed at Westminster Abbey in 1868 (see Fig. 9.2).[9]

But although it was the most enduringly popular, *The Flower and the Leaf* was only one of a group of poems—some thought to be by Chaucer, others included in editions of his work but clearly signalled as the work of others—that attracted both poets and general readers during the eighteenth century. These poems are various in nature, but often share one or other of two features, sometimes in combination: a 'visionary' or allegorical design, and the presence of passages expressing pathetic laments or complaints, often—though not always—voiced by women. Some of these features, of course, were to be found in genuine Chaucerian works, and the

Fig. 9.2 Design (1868) by J. G. Waller for the Chaucer window in Westminster Abbey, featuring *The Flower and Leaf*. The window itself was destroyed by bombing during the Second World War.

Reproduced by permission of the copyright holders, the Dean and Chapter, Westminster Abbey.

---

[9] See Forni, *The Chaucerian Apocrypha*, pp. 127, 138. The window, designed by J. G. Waller, was destroyed during the Second World War. Waller's design is preserved in the Library of Westminster Abbey.

apocryphal poems were not regarded as a separate group distinguishable from genuine Chaucerian poems such as *The House of Fame, The Parliament of Fowls, The Legend of Good Women, Anelida and Arcite,* or *The Book of the Duchess*.[10] It is perhaps surprising that some of these poems were bypassed by poetic imitators in favour of arguably inferior non-Chaucerian works. The taste for the apocryphal poems, however, was strong. Dryden's *Flower and the Leaf* was followed by two versions of *The Court of Love*: one by Arthur Maynwaring in 1709, and a second by Alexander Stopford Catcott in 1717.[11] George Sewell's *The Proclamation of Cupid; or, a Defence of Women, A Poem from Chaucer* (1718) was followed by John Dart's *The Complaint of the Black Knight* (1720). William Cooke's *The Cuckow and the Nightingale* (1774) was followed by William Wordsworth's version of the same poem (composed in 1801).[12]

What was the appeal of these poems at the time? What qualities in them seemed to offer particularly attractive possibilities for modern imitation and recreation? Many of the apocryphal poems that were admired and translated in the eighteenth century deal with a range of experiences associated with Love, seen from different viewpoints, often mingling pathos with something like satire, and implying a variety of attitudes to women that range from religious veneration to smiling contempt. Others are notable for their depictions of the natural world. In order to gain some sense of some of the features of the former kind that drew eighteenth-century poets to the Chaucerian apocrypha, it may be useful to begin our exploration with a version from the second half of the century of one of the least regarded of the poems. This version offers one of the clearest and simplest illustrations of the eighteenth-century taste for Chaucerian (or 'Chaucerian') pathos.

The Lamentation of Mary Magdalene

The history of the poem sometimes called *The Lamentatyon of Mary Magdaleyne* is slightly less convoluted than that of the other works in the Chaucerian Apocrypha—partly because it is something of an outlier. This poem was probably inspired by two lines in a genuinely Chaucerian work: the *Legend of Good Women*.

---

[10] Eighteenth–century versions of genuine Chaucer poems with a broadly 'visionary' nature are: Alexander Pope's *The Temple of Fame, A Vision* (London, 1715); Jane Brereton's 'The Dream: In Imitation of Some Parts of Chaucer's Second and Third Book of Fame', in *Poems on Several Occasions* (London, 1744); Thomas Godfrey's 'The Assembly of Birds; From Chaucer', in *Juvenile Poems, on Various Subjects* (Philadelphia, PA, 1775); and Robert, Marquis of Westminster's 'Annelida and Arcite. From Chaucer', in *Charlotte: An Elegy* (?London, ?1795). Pope's and Brereton's poems are discussed in Chapter 11 below.

[11] Arthur Maynwaring, trans., 'The Court of Love. A Tale from Chaucer', in *Ovid's Art of Love in Three Books* (London, 1709); Alexander Stopford Catcott, *The Court of Love, a Vision, from Chaucer* (Oxford, 1717).

[12] William Cooke, 'The Cuckow and the Nightingale. Modernized from Chaucer', in *Poetical Essays on Several Occasions* (London, 1774).

In that work, Cupid has charged Chaucer with slandering both women and the pursuit of love. Queen Alceste intercedes in Chaucer's defence, citing a list of his religious and philosophical works, including his translation of Boethius, and the narration of the life of St Cecilia (in *The Second Nun's Tale*), as well as a work entitled 'Orygenes upon the Maudeleyne'. Although there was no such work to be found in manuscript collections of Chaucer's works, a poem entitled *The Complaynte of the Louer of Chryst Saynt Mary Magdaleyn* appeared in the 1520s.[13] It was shortly attributed to Chaucer, found its way into William Thynne's edition of the poet's works (1532), and was included in the later editions of Chaucer by Speght and Urry. In the *Life of Chaucer* included in Urry's edition, it is suggested that *The Lamentation of Mary Magdalen* is, indeed, the poem mentioned in *The Legend of Good Women*, and the poem itself is described as a 'Treatise … taken out of St. *Origen* wherein *Mary Magdalen* lamenteth the cruell Death of her *Saviour Christ*'.[14]

Although he accepted that *The Court of Love* and the *Testament of Love* were genuine works by Chaucer, Thomas Tyrwhitt was sceptical about the *The Lamentation*, and thought it 'in every respect … infinitely meaner than the worst of [Chaucer's] genuine pieces'.[15] But Tyrwhitt's doubts were ignored. The *Lamentation* held its place in Bell's edition of 1782. And at the very time when Tyrwhitt was rejecting the poem from the Chaucerian canon, a modern poet was attempting to give it new life, in the form of *The Lamentation of Mary Magdalen from Chaucer* (1775).[16]

This version, like the original, has Mary speaking like a forlorn lover. She has come to the tomb apparently wanting to embalm the body of Jesus. Finding him gone, she laments for herself, and for Jesus's mother, recalling her pain at witnessing the crucifixion. Mary speaks directly in her own voice at all times: this is perhaps what, above all, appealed to the translator. He (or she) has opted for simplicity—both of expression and of feeling—and is often content to rest on the phrasing of the 1520s original. In the translation, as in the original, Mary sees herself as an abandoned lover, seeking comfort only in death. The women who will have visited her tomb are to wander the world in search of her lover—her 'royal Lord, and Friend' in the translation—to tell him that she died of love (underlinings here indicate words and phrases taken over directly from the original):

> And when the solemn rites are o'er,
>   And ye your mournful task have paid,
>   One thing, I beg, remember more,
>   In reverence to my hapless shade:

---

[13] *The Complaynte of the Louer of Cryst Saynt Mary Magdaleyn* (London, ?1520).
[14] Urry, p. 520.
[15] Tyrwhitt 1775–78, 5. 147.
[16] Anon, *The Lamentation of Mary Magdalen from Chaucer* (Nottingham, 1775). The author of this poem has never been identified. The book has no preface, dedication, or foreword of any kind.

> To ev'ry <u>village</u> let your search extend,
> And try to find my royal Lord, and Friend.
>
> > And if by <u>any grace at last</u>,
> > Ye hear where he may chance to dwell;
> > Inform him what has lately <u>past</u>,
> > And all my tender story tell.
> Say, how for him I <u>yielded up the ghost</u>,
> And dy'd to give him proof, <u>I lov'd him most</u>.

(The Lamentation of Mary Magdalen, p. 30)

In making his eighteenth-century Magdalene request that the virtuous women should 'all my tender story tell', the author recalls Alexander Pope's *Eloisa and Abelard*:

> <u>And</u> sure <u>if</u> fate some future Bard shall join
> In sad similitude of griefs to mine …
> Such if there be, who loves so long, so well;
> Let him our sad, our <u>tender story tell.</u>
> The well-sung woes will sooth my pensive <u>ghost</u>;
> He best can paint' em, who shall feel' em <u>most</u>.

(Eloisa to Abelard, 359–60, 363–6; Pope, Poems, 2. 348–9).

This echo indicates why the translator may have turned to the original poem in the first place, and may suggest the nature of their assumptions about the kind of poem it was. The author of the eighteenth-century *Lamentation of Mary Magdalen,* assuming that the poem was written by Chaucer, a supreme impersonator of characters, personalities, and circumstances unlike his own, has read the original as a sophisticated exercise in *pathos*. The poem is addressed to those 'in whose breast / Compassion bears a tender sway', those who will be prepared to accept the heroine's claim that she is *Christ's true lover, Mary Magdalen*. The assumption is that Mary's lament is an artistic expression of natural simplicity. For the author of the translation, Chaucer's art perhaps resembled that of Alexander Pope at his most sympathetic—particularly in giving voice to sorrowing women. It is even perhaps possible that Alexander Pope had himself recalled the '<u>And</u> … <u>if</u> …' and the '<u>ghost/most</u>' rhyme of the original pseudo-Chaucerian *Lamentation* when composing his own 'medieval' poem.

The afterlife of the *Lamentation* effectively terminated with Skeat's dismissal of the poem as the 'lugubrious' 'wail of a nun' that 'bears no resemblance to any work by Chaucer', and Lounsbury's assertion that it represents little more than the 'stammering' and 'feeble' 'utterances of a devout soul'.[17] In his essay on 'The Genius and Poetry of Chaucer' in Vol. 3 of his edition of *The Canterbury Tales of Chaucer* (1860), George Gilfillan had claimed that *The Lamentation of Mary*

---

[17] Lounsbury, *Studies in Chaucer*, 1. 478–9.

Magdalene for the Death of Christ is 'more interesting' than 'The Legend of Good Women', and that the twenty-eight lines he quotes from the poem are 'quaint but touching'.[18] But once dismissed by Skeat and Lounsbury, *The Lamentation* slipped entirely from notice.[19]

Arthur Maynwaring, *The Court of Love. A Tale from Chaucer*

The version by Arthur Maynwaring of *The Court of Love*, another poem from the Chaucer Apocrypha, was—after the Chaucer translations of Dryden and Pope— the most reprinted of all the Chaucerian versions in the period. This poem provides a very different view—or set of views—of woman than that represented by *The Lamentation of Mary Magdalene*. Its sophisticated artifice was self-evident to eighteenth-century readers. The poem depicts the visit of the young narrator, Philogenet, a clerk of Cambridge, to a Court of Love in which are displayed a set of statutes which all lovers are obliged to obey. The heading to the poem in Urry's edition indicated clearly that the poem was thought to be both fanciful and allegorical: 'This Book is an Imitation of the Romaunt of the Rose, shewing that all are subject to Love, what impediments soever to the contrary, containing also those 20 Statutes that are to be observ'd in the Court of Love'.[20] The poem was regarded as unquestionably Chaucer's, and, as was shown in Chapter 5, had become an essential source for his biography. It was said to have been written by Chaucer at the age of eighteen, when he was a student at Cambridge.[21] Its vocabulary and prosody presented fewer difficulties than other poems, but this was presented as evidence of Chaucer's extraordinary natural gifts, and the 'flow' and 'harmony' of the verse in *The Court of Love* was much admired.[22]

Maynwaring's *Court of Love* was an extraordinarily popular work, partly because it was included in the much-reprinted volume that contained the translation by Dryden and others of *Ovid's Art of Love* (see Fig. 9.3).[23] This volume combined pseudo-Chauceriana with versions of various Ovidian works, and its popularity was doubtless encouraged by memories of the close association of the two poets in

---

[18] Geoffrey Chaucer, *The Canterbury Tales*, ed. George Gilfillan, 3 vols (Edinburgh, 1860), 3. xxvi–xxvii.

[19] The afterlife and sudden death of all these works is documented in full detail by Kathleen Forni in *The Chaucerian Apocrypha*.

[20] Urry, p. 560. Urry prints the Middle English version of *Le Roman de la Rose* as Chaucer's, though his authorship (at least of the whole) is questioned by many modern Chaucer scholars.

[21] Urry, p. 560.

[22] See Thomas Campbell, ed., *Specimens of the British Poets*, 7 vols (London, 1819), 2. 16: 'As the earliest work of Chaucer, it interestingly exhibits the successful effort of his youthful hand in erecting a new and stately fabric of English numbers. As a piece of fancy, it is grotesque and meagre; but the lines often flow with great harmony.'

[23] The volume went through twenty editions by 1850, and constituted an 'erotic anthology' built round Dryden's translation of Book 1 of Ovid's *Ars Amatoria*, which the publisher Jacob Tonson already had in his possession. See John Dryden, *Poems*, ed. Paul Hammond and David Hopkins, 5. 623.

Fig. 9.3 Illustration for *The Court of Love, in Ovid's Art of Love, Together with the Remedy of Love. To Which Are Added, The Court of Love. A Tale from Chaucer. And the History of Love* (London, 1712 edition).

Dryden's Preface to *Fables*. Maynwaring's *Court of Love* received early and warm praise in John Oldmixon's biography of the author: 'Whoever will be at the Pains to compare this *Court of Love* with the Tale in *Chaucer*, from whence 'tis taken, will be extreamly well pleas'd to see how he has improv'd it.'[24]

---

[24] John Oldmixon, *The Life and Posthumous Works of Arthur Maynwaring* (London, 1715), p. 326.

Maynwaring's 'improvements' of his original were largely a matter of trunca-
tion, both of the poem as a whole and of local passages. But there are also witty
elaborations. In a reminiscence, for example, of Homer's and Virgil's celebrated
depiction of the adulterous liaison of Venus and Mars, Phoebus's past indiscretion
in 'unluckily' finding Mars in Venus's 'Arms', and the narrator's doubts about what
possible 'service *Venus* could receive' from 'Old Men', have been wittily intermin-
gled with the descriptions of the glorious Court, and tributes to the 'mighty Joys'
of love.[25] In places, however, Maynwaring's version is more chaste than the original. He has summarized 'those 20 Statutes that are to be observ'd in the Court of
Love' which Urry mentioned as a particular feature of the original. William Godwin thought that the sixteenth of the twenty statutes was 'particularly vulgar and
gross',[26] and this stanza, though marked with an approbatory asterisk in Speght's
edition (as a passage that a reader might like to commit to memory), leaves no
trace in Maynwaring:

> The xvi. statute keepe it if thou may,
> * Seuen sith at night thy lady for to please,
> And seuen at midnight, seuen at morrow day,
> And drinke a caudle earely for thine ease.
> Do this, and keep thine head from all disease,
> And win the garland here of louers all,
> That euer came in court, or euer shall.

On this the author of the original commented:

> Full few, think I, this statute hold & keep:
> But truely this my reason giueth me fele,
> That some louers should rather fall asleepe,
> Than take on hand to please so oft and wele.
>
> (*Court of Love*, 435–45; Speght 1687, p. 583)

Although, again, he summarizes, Maynwaring seems to have taken the full point
of the second set of rules—those of women which no man is ever allowed to see.
In the original there are, again, three passages marked with an asterisk:

> * For men shall not so nere of counsaile bene
> With womanhood, ne knowen of her guise,
> Ne w^t they think, ne of their wit then giue.

> * For it perauenture may right so befall,
> That they be bound by nature to deceiue,
> And spinne, & weep, and sugre strew on gall,
> The hert of man to rauish and to reiue.

---

[25] Maynwaring, 'The Court of Love', in *Ovid's Art of Love*, pp. 352–3.
[26] William Godwin, *The Life of Geoffrey Chaucer*, 1. 242.

> * Men may not wete why turneth <u>euery wind</u>,
> Nor waxen wise, nor been inquisitife
> To know secret of maid, widow, or wife,
> For they their statutes haue to them reserued,
> And neuer man to know them hath deserued.
>
>   (*Court of Love*, 533–5, 540–3, 549–53; Speght 1687, p. 584)

Maynwaring has compressed the point of each of these passages, grafting them on to the opening account which he has followed comparatively closely:

> I tourned leaues, looking on this booke,
> Where other statutes were of women shene,
> And rightforthwith Rigour on me gan looke
> Full angerly, and sayed vnto the queene
> I traitour was, and charged me let been,
> There may no man (qd. he) the statute know,
> That long to women, hie degree ne low.
>
>   (*Court of Love*, 519–25; Speght 1687, p. 584)

For Maynwaring, this joke—about the secret laws (hidden from men) which govern women in love—seems to constitute the poem's central point:

> … and as I turn'd the <u>Book</u>,
> On other Statues of the Realm to look.
> *Rigour* cry'd out, Hold, Traitor to the Queen,
> Those sacred Statues are not to be seen:
> Those are the Laws for Womankind ordain'd,
> That with Mens Eyes were never yet prophan'd;
> Not even with mine, though I on *Venus* wait,
> Long trusted with her deep Affairs of State;
> Believe me, Friend, Mankind must still despair
> To know the Rules and Maxims of the Fair;
> And when you see 'em change with <u>ev'ry</u> Wind,
> Themselves indulging, to their Slaves unkind,
> Conclude their Duty to these Laws they pay;
> Which, though unwillingly, they must obey.
>
>   (*Ovid's Art of Love*, pp. 359–60)

Maynwaring's near-comic tone is notable in the suggestion that women follow the secret laws '*unwillingly*'. It was perhaps the sense that Maynwaring had introduced too much levity into his narrative that prompted Alexander Stopford Catcott to publish a rival version of *The Court of Love* in 1717.[27] In some passages, Catcott was content to follow his predecessor closely, but in reducing the satire on women, he departed further from the original. Catcott often misses Maynwaring's

---

[27] *The Court of Love, a Vision from Chaucer* (Oxford 1717).

wit and plays down the suggestion (so clear in Maynwaring's version) that women's behaviour—however wayward-seeming to men—is prompted by a proper, if unwilling, duty to sacred Law.

Both poets narrate the poem in the first person. Maynwaring, though the older man, presents himself as a younger lover, whose desires are more candidly sexual. It is probably telling that one of Maynwaring's lines given in italics is 'A Fig for her, and all her Chastity' (p. 363). This comes as part of the apparently obligatory vows the dreamer makes to Venus in the course of a request for a woman to be 'Mistress, Empress, any thing but Wife':

> Helpe Lady goddesse, that possession
> I might of her haue, that in all my life
> I clepen shall my quene, and hearts wife.
>
> And in the court of Loue to dwell for aye
> My will it is, and done thee Sacrifice:
> Daily with Diane eke to fight and fraye,
> And holden werre, as might will me suffice:
> That goddesse chast, I keepen in no wise
> To serue, a Figge for all her chastity,
> Her law is for Religiousity.
>
> *(Court of Love, 677–86; Speght 1687, p. 585)*

It was passages like this in the original poem that seem to have contributed to the biographical accounts, mentioned earlier, of Chaucer's slightly wayward youth or to Dryden's notion that Chaucer was a 'libertine', at least in his writings. Maynwaring's *risqué* tone at such moments was perhaps one reason for his version's continuing popularity:

> So will I always Sacrifice to you,
> And with *Diana* constant War pursue;
> *A Fig for her, and all her Chastity,*
> Let Monks and Friars her Disciples be.
>
> *(Ovid's Art of Love, p. 363)*

Catcott at the same juncture addresses the same vow to Venus, but plays up the underlying metaphor of opposed religious cults:

> ... thy Pow'r I'll ever own,
> A Foe profest to chast *Diana* grown;
> Make thou the Joys, that bless thy Vot'ries mine,
> Let Monks, and Friars seek her barren Shrine.
>
> *(Catcott, Court of Love, p. 20)*

Where the original ends in birdsong and general celebration in which the troth-plighting is almost drowned, Maywaring ends with his beloved Rosalinda squeezing his hand, 'laughing' and saying,

> I know a Way thy Passion to appease,
> And soon will set thy simple Heart at Ease.
> But e'er she brought me to her promis'd Bed,
> The Rapture wak'd me, and the Vision fled.

(Ovid's Art of Love, p. 368)

Maynwaring ends there. Catcott's lover, like Philogenet in the original, has still to undergo further temptations and deliberations. In both versions, however, all is but a delicious dream. As Catcott puts it: 'O'erpower'd with Bliss, I woke to hated Light, / And all the Vision vanish'd from my Sight'.

George Sewell's *The Proclamation of Cupid; or, a Defence of Women, A Poem from Chaucer*

Some uncertainty about what in the eighteenth century was thought to constitute the 'Chaucerian' voice, tone, stance, or range of attitudes towards woman, to the love-tricks of men, and to the degree of sexual daring that was desirable in a love poem is evidenced in George Sewell's *The Proclamation of Cupid; or, a Defence of Women, A Poem from Chaucer*.[28] Sewell's title itself—and its claim to Chaucerian origin—was, as he well knew, contentious. His *Proclamation* was based on a poem, 'The Letter of Cupyde', that had been first included in Chaucer's works by William Thynne in 1532, but had been clearly attributed by Speght to Chaucer's admirer, Thomas Hoccleve—an attribution which, three years after the appearance of Sewell's poem, was confirmed in Urry's edition.

Sewell resisted the attribution to Hoccleve, on the grounds of the general similarity—particularly in its sympathy for the plight of women—between the *Letter of Cupyd* and other works of Chaucer, and, most strongly of all, on the evidence of Chaucer's supposed wisdom about relations between the sexes: '*Chaucer* knew the State of the Case between the Sexes as well as the best Poets of any Age, and in this Piece has plainly shewn what a Master he was of Human Nature'. Sewell's prefatory remarks constitute a notable simplification of Dryden's paradoxical proposition that though 'Mankind is ever the same' every aspect of human life and behaviour is 'alter'd' by the passing of time. In Sewell's account, *nothing changes*: in all ages women are maligned and lovers all untrue. The 'Subject' of his poem, he maintains, is 'adapted to all Times, Humours, and almost every Stage of Life': 'The Passion of *Love*, the conduct of young Lovers, and the Reflections of Old ones ... have been, are, and will continue to be the same to the End of Time.'

---

[28] George Sewell, *The Proclamation of Cupid; or, a Defence of Women. A Poem from Chaucer* (London, 1718). Sewell's poem has been reprinted in T. S. Fenster and M. C. Erler, eds, *Poems of Cupid, God of Love* (Leiden, 1990), pp. 219–37.

'Language indeed, and the Forms of Address', Sewell concedes, 'may alter, but Nature cannot'.[29]

Although Sewell's male lovers use contemporary 'Forms of Address', where the altered form of the language of love implies some altered notions of love itself, the transition did not prove difficult. Where Maynwaring and Catcott found parts of *The Court of Love* unusable, there was little in *The Letter of Cupyde* that had to be excised, and much that invited expansion.[30] Sewell frequently ends excursions of his own with a close approximation of his original. On the line, printed in italics, which concludes a paragraph on Satan's deliberate intention to deceive and the innocence of Eve, '*And so did not She* ADAM, *by your leave*', Sewell attached a footnote: '*This whole Line stands as in the Original*.'[31]

That relationship between the modern version and the medieval original is most evident in the treatment of the poem's central argument. *The Letter of Cupyde* is described in Urry's edition as 'a curious Defence of, and at the same time an artful Satyr upon Women'.[32] The latter was certainly not intended by the original female authoress. Cupid, indeed, attempts to defend women from the slanders of men, but, as is sometimes the case in the Wife of Bath's *Prologue*, the slanders are vigorously reported at great length. Sewell claims that he had 'often added a Word or two' in support of the women. In his version, a precarious balance is maintained between defence and abuse. Both are lively, and both extreme.

The case for the prosecution culminates in a passage that is reminiscent of, but does not actually recall, the sanguinary crimes attributed to women in Juvenal's Sixth Satire. Where the original spoke only briefly of what 'Clerkes saine' of 'womans wicked crabbidnesse', Sewell elaborated:

> And yet these Legendary Clerks devise,
> To blemish Woman with repeated Lyes.
> 'Hearken, they cry, ye bold Felonious Brood,
> 'Who live by Murder, and grow fat by Blood;
> 'Would you some new, some mighty Crime begin,
> 'Let *Woman* be a Sharer in the Sin.
> 'Do Tears and soft Compassion plead for Life?
> 'Give *Her* the fatal Sword, or murd'ring Knife:
> 'To all the gentle Ties of Nature blind,
> 'She'll stab—and justifie her wicked Kind.
>
> (Sewell, *The Proclamation of Cupid*, p. 14)

---

[29] Sewell, *The Proclamation of Cupid*, Sig. a[r].

[30] See Fenster and Erler, *Poems of Cupid*, p. 60. Sewell's treatment of his original is almost as freely expansive as, unbeknown to him, Hoccleve's had been of his source, Christine de Pizan's *Epistre au dieu d'Amours*.

[31] Sewell, *The Proclamation of Cupid*, p. 17. In fact, Sewell slightly alters the word order of the original: 'And so did she not Adam, by your leue'.

[32] Urry, Sig. e[r].

But that is almost the only Juvenalian note. Where Medea, for example, was an exemplary wicked woman for Juvenal, she is presented, as she regularly was in the Middle Ages, as the opposite in the *Letter* and in the *Proclamation*. Sewell's Medea is 'kindly'. 'Perjur'd Jason' was 'false' to the woman 'Who gave him Victory, and Fame, and Love'.[33] Cupid's case in the *Proclamation* (as in the *Letter*) is that only Malice can deny that female nature (unlike the male) abhors the cruel:

Malice of women what is it to drede,   Oh! to what Height Invention will arrive,
They slea no man, destroy no citees,   When Malice sows the Seed, and bids it thrive!
Ne oppresse folke, ne ouerlede,   Oppression is a Stranger to the Sex,
Betray Empires, Realmes, or Duchees,   They burn no Towns, no harrass'd Subjects vex;
Ne bireuen men her lands ne her mees,   No Instruments of War, or Fraud employ,
Enpoison folke, ne houses set on fire,   Betray no Empires, and no Kings destroy;
Ne false contracts make for no hire.   By them no Heirs are lost, no Bubbles made,
                                                   The Courtiers, Lawyers, and Physicians Trade.

(*Letter*, 330–6; Speght 1687, p. 555)   (Sewell, *Proclamation of Cupid*, pp. 14–15)

A willingness to follow his original into unfashionable regions, or to mingle the ancient and the modern, is characteristic of *The Proclamation* as a whole. In his Preface, Sewell saw it as 'strange' that Chaucer 'has mixed Fable and Truth, Heathen and Christian Stories indiscriminately together' in the poem. But this, says Sewell, '(if a Fault) has been followed by great Genius's since our Author, without the same Excuse'.[34] Sewell is unsure as to who is speaking at certain points in the poem: 'The Poet is not always just to his Design, for he sometimes speaks himself, and sometimes *Cupid*.'[35] It is, however, presumably Cupid who in Sewell's version refers to Chaucer by name. At this point, the argument is that one bad woman does not prove all to be so: 'Albeit that men find one woman nice, / Inconstaunt, rechlesse, and variable … Wicked, feirse, or full of cruelte / Yet followeth it not that soch all women be'.[36] Sewell translates:

Grant all these Follies in one Woman meet,
And shew the Vices of the Sex compleat:
Because one is, must ev'ry Fair be so?
The Fools say, Yes; but wiser *Chaucer*, No.
For sure one Woman cannot be a Test
To damn the Sex, and scandal all the rest.

(*Proclamation of Cupid*, pp. 8–9)

It has been said that in Sewell's 'urbane reading' of the *Letter* 'all trace of feeling has been translated into an elegant playfulness'.[37] But for Sewell the wisdom of Chaucer is sometimes expressed as a detailed sympathy with the position of

---

[33] Sewell, *The Proclamation of Cupid*, pp. 13–14.
[34] Ibid. Sig. aᵛ.
[35] Ibid. Sig. aᵛ.
[36] *Letter*, 148–9, 153–4; Speght 1687, p. 553.
[37] Fenster and Erler, *Poems of Cupid*, p. 219.

women beguiled, as all are, by the deceptions and self-deceptions of complicated human minds:

* Ful hard it is to know a mans herte,
For outward may no man the trouth deme,
When word out of mouth may none sterte,
But it by reson semed euery wight to queme,
So it is said of herte as it would seme,
O faithful woman full of innocence,
Thou art disceiued by false apparence.

  By processe moueth oft womans pite,
Wening all thing were as these men sey,
They graunt hem grace of her benignite,
For that men should not for her sake dey,
And with good hert sette hem in the wey
Of blisfull loue, keepe it if they conne,
And thus otherwhile women bethe ywonne.

(Letter, 36-49; Speght 1687, p. 552)

Full hard it is to search the secret Part,
And pierce the cover'd Foldings of the Heart.
Words sooth our Ear, and Persons please our Eye,
But none the Truth can by Appearance try.
Thus faithful *Woman,* innocently free,
Suspects no Falshood, where she none can see;
Led by fair Shows she hastens to her Fate,
Too soon believes them, and repents too late.
These said Degrees the Fair Ones often prove,
They pity first, and Pity kindles Love:
Fearful that Man to fierce Extreams may drive,
To stop his Ruin, they their own contrive,
To him resign their Love, their Fame, their All,
And *give the Gift they never can recall.*

(Sewell, Proclamation of Cupid, p. 3)

The close conjunction of pity and love may recall Chaucer's depiction of Dido's feelings for Aeneas in *The Legend of Good Women,*[38] but Sewell's emphasis throughout *The Proclamation of Cupid* is on 'Chaucer's' *balance.* Both when the poem was published on its own in 1718, and when he included it in *A New Collection of Original Poems* (1720), George Sewell appended a verse prefix 'To the LADIES'. There, it is claimed that Chaucer, '*now returns to shame this graceless Age, / Who Libel* Woman *from the Press, and Stage*'. As Sewell sees it, Chaucer's defence of women is mingled with tempered criticism: '*He knew, whate'er might be his secret Thoughts, / The Sex too well, to tell them half their Faults*':

> Chaucer, *who shuns the Folly of Extremes,*
> *With Wit and Truth records these common Themes;*
> *Not wholly to the Fair devotes his Pen,*
> *But wisely turns the Satyr on the Men:*
> *Their Arts, their Stratagems at large displays,*
> *And telling them, gives Women silent Praise.*
> *See! how he pities where he can't defend,*
> *The granting Mistress, and deceitful Friend:*
> *Alas! He knew the Torrent of Desire,*
> *When the Nerves tremble, and the Eyes shake Fire.*[39]

(George Sewell, A New Collection of Original Poems
[London, 1720], pp. 18–19)

Pity seems to be the controlling sentiment of *The Proclamation of Cupid*—a pity resulting from knowledge that is itself the result of fellow feeling.

---

[38] See *LGW*, 1078–81; Speght 1687, p. 342.
[39] Similar sentiments are given by Sewell to Cupid himself.

The Complaint of the Black Knight: An Elegiack Poem from Chaucer

There is some fellow feeling and cross-referencing, too, *between* translators of the Chaucerian apocrypha and of Chaucer's genuine poems. George Sewell's Cupid ends his Proclamation with the injunction that 'false men' should not 'dare again' to '*approach the Court of Love*'. John Dart, in the Preface to his version of *The Complaint of the Black Knight*, observes that 'Mr. Sewell' in 'his *Cupid's Proclamation*' had 'curiously exprest' Chaucer's 'Beauties, and the fine Turn and Genteel Sharpness of his Wit'. Dart claims that he has been incited by this example, and those of Dryden and 'Mr. Pope' (particularly 'that excellent Story of *January and May*'), 'to lend a Hand to the same Design'.[40] Dart provides a peculiarly interesting instance of the prevailing paradoxical response to Chaucer. He is fully convinced that Chaucer is 'the greatest Poet that *England* (or perhaps the World) ever produc'd', and, as such, is not limited by the time or language in which he wrote, but in the same breath maintains that Chaucer's greatness will only be widely appreciated when his whole works have been re-rendered in entirely modern verse:

> As the Works of this great and excellent Man are now in the Press at *Oxford*, in their genuine Language, so I could wish the Gentlemen would unite their Endeavours to dress him intirely in a more refin'd Habit.[41]

Dart's version of *The Complaint of the Black Knight* (a poem now attributed to John Lydgate) follows closely the structure of the original, but takes over less of its language than had the author of *The Lamentation of Mary Magdalene*. In *The Complaint*, the poet goes out into the woods—which are described at length—and finds in an arbour the prostrate figure of a knight who laments at length his sufferings in love, and the merciless conduct of his lady. Dart is sensitive to what he thinks are likely to be the reactions of his audience—which he assumes, or hopes, is likely to be partly female. He makes some apologies for his version and for the original, observing, for example, of the poem's very long descriptions that 'when *Chaucer* takes a Walk into a Wood, he is a long while e'er he gets out again'.[42]

What Dart does not apologize for is the extraordinary length and Petrarchan superfluity of the Black Knight's account of his 'world of woe':

---

[40] John Dart, *The Complaint of the Black Knight: An Elegiack Poem from Chaucer* (London, 1720), Sig. A2ᵛ.

[41] Ibid. Sigs. A5ʳ⁻ᵛ.

[42] Ibid. Sig. A4ʳ.

The brest is chest of dole and drerinesse,
   The body eke so feble and so fainte,
With hote and colde mine axis is so mainte,
    That now I chivir, for defaute of hete,
    And hote as glede nowe sodainly I swete.

Nowe hote as fire, nowe cold as ashis ded,
   Now hote for colde, now cold for hete again,
Now cold as yse, and now, as colis red,
    For hete I brenne, and thus betwixin twaine
    I possid am, and al forecaste in paine,
    So that my hete full plainly as I fele
    Of grevous colde is cause evèry dele.

This is the colde of inward hie disdaine,
   Colde of despite, and colde of cruil hate,
This is the colde that doth his besy payne,
   Ayenist trouthe to fight and to debate,
This is the colde that doth the fyre abate
   Of trewe mening, alas the hardè while,
   This is the coldè that wol me begile.

          (*Complaint*, 328–46; Urry, p. 453)[43]

My Body's weaken'd with perpetual Pain
Of Heat and Cold, that shoot thro' ev'ry Vein
Now Aguish Chills freeze o'er my vital Frame,
Now fev'rish Fires exert their raging Flame,
I glow, I burn, my stubborn Pulse beats high,
And now I chill with Cold, and trembling die,
As Ashes which the Flames no more supply,
Then Heat (repeated) reassumes its Place,
Cold dewy Drops run silent down my Face,
My Heart beats false, my Pulse forgets to beat,
While outward Sweats confess the inward Heat;
Alternately I'm wrack'd with equal Pain,
From Love the Fire proceeds, the Cold from her
                      Disdain.

      (Dart, *The Complaint of the Black Knight*,
                         pp. 12–13)

The Black Knight articulates the power of love to cause suffering, but in doing so raises the eternal problem: how is it that Venus allows the good to suffer and the wicked to prosper? How is it, asks the Black Knight, that he, who has 'practic'd many Years of Love' has found 'a Disappointment all his Gains', 'Whilst soothing Flatt'rers with deceitful Face / Flourish in Crimes and thrive in Actions base'?[44]

And yet the poem, in the original and the translation, includes playfulness as well as melancholy lament. Dart makes poor Adonis jealous of the handling of Venus by her blacksmith husband Vulcan, whose 'grizly Arms' and 'sooty Foulness' are described in some detail.[45] The plights of 'Lovely Adonis' and Mars, the 'Warriour-God', come together again in the closing paragraphs of the poem, when, the Black Knight having retired to his cottage, 'th'Ev'ning Star on high / Shot his clear Beams amid the western Sky', and the poet himself offers praise to Venus. At this point, Dart's admiration for Dryden's Chaucerian poems is pervasively evident. The model for his invocation was provided by Arcite's mention of Mars' love of Venus in his prayer to the warrior god in *Palamon and Arcite*:

> *Venus*, the Publick Care of all above,
> Thy stubborn Heart has softned into Love:
> Now by her Blandishments and <u>pow'rful Charms</u>

---

[43] Though Urry's text was not published until 1721, it had been edited long before that, and, since Dart was one of the team involved with the edition, quotations of *The Complaint of the Black Knight* and line numbering in this section are given from Urry.

[44] Dart, *The Complaint of the Black Knight*, p. 17.

[45] Ibid. pp. 20–1.

When yielded, she lay curling in thy Arms,
Ev'n by thy Shame, if Shame it may be call'd,
When *Vulcan* had thee in his Net inthrall'd;
O envy'd Ignominy, sweet Disgrace,
When <u>ev'ry God</u> that saw thee, <u>wish'd</u> thy <u>Place</u>!

Dart has mingled these lines with grammar taken from Palamon's prayer to Venus:

If e'er *Adonis* touch'd thy tender Heart,
Have pity, Goddess, for thou knowst the Smart.
(Dryden, *Works*, 7. 137, 147)

Venus's loves for Mars and Adonis are as crucial to Dart's invocation in *The Complaint of the Black Knight* as they had been for those of Palamon and Arcite. But Dart has introduced one distinctly original touch. The sexes of the divinities beholding Mars and Venus 'dissolv'd in Joys' have been reversed. In Dryden's poem, the *male* gods wished to be in the position of Mars, but in Dart 'ev'ry envious Goddess wish'd' to be in Venus's 'Place' beside the 'Warriour-God'. The underlinings in the passage below indicate Dart's borrowings from Dryden:

O lady Venus so feire on to see,
  Let not this sothfast man for his trouthe deye,
For that joy which thou haddist whan thou leye
  With Mars thy knight, when Vulcanus yfond,
And with a chaine unvisible you bonde

Togiþer bothè tway, in the same whyle
  That al the courte above celestial
At your shamè began to laugh and smyle,
  Ah, fairist lady willy fond at al,
  Comfort to careful Goddis immortal,
    Be helping nowe, and do thy diligence
    To let the stremis of thine influence

Discendin downe, in forthering of the trouth,
  Namely of hem that lye in sorowe bounde,
Shew now thy might, and on ther wo have routh,
  Ere that false daungir slè hem and confounde,
  And special let thy might in this be founde
    For to help and socour what that thou may
    The trewè man that in the herbir lay.

And all that trewe are forthir for his sake,
  O gladè sterre, O lady Venus myne,
And cause his lady him to grace to take,
  Her hert of stele to mercy so encline,
  Ere that thy bemis go up to declyne,
    And er that thou nowe go fro us adowne,
    For that love which thou haddist to Adowme.
(*Complaint*, 620–45; Urry, p. 456)

Hail beauteous Pow'r, whose influence soft
                can move
The Breasts of Gods and Men, and teach 'em
                Love,
Inform the coldest Bosom with a Flame,
And raise to Fondness the severest Dame.

If e'er the Warriour-God with <u>pow'rful Charms</u>,
And vig'rous Pleasure fill'd your lovely <u>Arms</u>;
When all dissolv'd in Joys you lay intwin'd,
By *Vulcan* guarded, and the Net confin'd;
Expos'd and laugh'd at in the loose Embrace,
While <u>ev'ry</u> envious <u>Goddess</u> wish'd <u>your Place</u>;
To this unhappy Suppliant favouring prove,
If e'er <u>*Adonis*</u> mov'd thy Breast to Love:
Now Goddess, now thy kind Indulgence show,
And be propitious to my eager Vow.
Thou can'st to Love the coldest Breast incline,
Thine is the Pow'r to move, and the kind Infl'ence
                thine:
Hither thy Carr and wanton Sparrows bring,
Hither may Love attend with easy Wing;
His kindly Torch with speedy Hand apply,
And her cold Bosom with new Fire supply.
So may all Nature thy kind Pow'r invoke,
And *Paphos* from a Thousand Altars smoak:
May suppliant Mortals bend before thy Shrine,
Serve thee alone, and know no Pow'r but thine.

(Dart, *The Complaint of the Black Knight*, pp. 34–5)

It may have been his impression of the closeness of *The Complaint* and *The Knight's Tale* that convinced Dart of the poem's essentially Chaucerian spirit. Dart's conviction would have been supported by the scholarship available to him. *The Complaint of the Black Knight* was accepted as genuinely Chaucerian not only by Speght and Urry, but also by Tyrwhitt, and was not ejected from the Chaucerian canon until the late nineteenth century. It is now known to be the work of John Lydgate, who was, of course, one of Chaucer's most enthusiastic early poetic 'sons'.

Of the Cuckowe and the Nightingale

No need was felt in the eighteenth century to argue for the Chaucerian qualities of *The Cuckoo and the Nightingale*—another poem influenced by *The Knight's Tale*. This poem, cast in debate form, is also centrally concerned with the experience and worth of Love, which is praised by the nightingale, but, in violent contrast, mocked by the cuckoo for the trouble it causes.[46] The poem, first printed by William Thynne in 1532, is headed in Urry's edition with a caption: 'CHAUCER dreameth that he heareth the Cuckow and the Nightingale contend for Excellency in singing'.[47] There are certain resemblances in the poem to the episode of Canace and the bird in *The Squire's Tale*, to *The Parliament of Fowls*, as well as to *The Flower and the Leaf* and *The Court of Love*. Most strikingly of all, the opening lines are identical with some lines spoken by Theseus in *The Knight's Tale* when he comes across Arcite and Palamon fighting in a grove: 'The God of loue, ah benedicite / Howe mighty and how great a lorde is he?'. In Dryden's version, Theseus praises a deity of extensive powers—both for good and ill:

The God of loue, ah benedicite	The Pow'r of Love,
How mighty, and how great a lorde is he,	In Earth, and Seas, and Air, and Heav'n above,
Again his might there gaineth no obstacles	Rules, unresisted, with an awful Nod;
He may be cleaped a God for his miracles	By daily Miracles, declar'd a God:
For he can maken at his owne gise	He blinds the Wise, gives Eye-sight to the Blind;
Of euerich heart, a him list deuise	And moulds and stamps anew the Lover's Mind.
(*KnT*, 1785–90; Speght 1598, Fol. 5ʳ)	(*Palamon and Arcite*, 2. 350–5; Dryden, *Works*, 7.109)

The God of Love in *The Cuckoo and the Nightingale,* having a bird to speak for him, is off-stage, and not acknowledged by the love-denigrating Cuckoo. The opening, and the poem as a whole, attracted two sharply contrasting translators: William

---

[46] The poem is now generally attributed to Chaucer's friend, Sir John Clanvowe (*c.* 1341–91). Walter W. Skeat described it as 'decidedly one of the best of the poems ... which have been wrongly associated with the name of Chaucer'. A modern edition is included in Sir John Clanvowe, *Works: The Boke of Cupide and The Two Ways*, ed. John Scattergood (Cambridge, 1975).

[47] Urry, p. 543.

Cooke in 1774,[48] and, in the winter of 1801, William Wordsworth.[49] Cooke followed his pseudo-Chaucerian original in making the power of love slightly less terrible and rather more comforting than it had been in the genuinely Chaucerian *Knight's Tale* and Dryden's *Palamon and Arcite*:

The God of Love, ah! *benedicite!*	The God of Love, whom all revere,
Howe mighty and howe gret a Lorde is he!	How absolute a Monarch here!
For he can makin of lowe heartis hie,	For He can raise the lowly heart,
And of hye lowe, and likè for to die,	And sink the lofty with his Dart;
And hardè hertis he can makin fre	To Softness melt the coldest Fair,
	And calm the frantic Madness of Despair.
(Cuckoo, 1–5; Urry, p. 543)	(Cooke, *Poetical Essays*, p. 85)

Neither in *The Knight's Tale*, nor in this poem is there much evidence that the God of Love can 'calm the frantic Madness of Despair'.

The lines from Chaucer's *Knight's Tale*, that had been copied out long before by the author of *The Cuckowe and the Nightingale*, were copied again by William Wordsworth:

The god of love, ah! *benedicite!*	The God of Love——*ah benedicite!*
Howe mighty and howe gret a lorde is he!	How mighty and how great a Lord is he!
For he can makin of lowe heartis hie,	For he of low hearts can make high, of high
And of hye lowe, and likè for to die,	He can make low, and unto death bring nigh;
And hardè hertis he can makin fre:	And hard hearts he can make them kind and free.
(Cuckoo, 1–5; Anderson, *Poets of Great*	(*Chaucer Modernized*, ed. Horne, p. 37)
Britain, 1. 498)	

Wordsworth is here clearly engaging in a different kind of translation from that of the eighteenth-century writers that are the main subject of this book. The last line of Wordsworth's stanza is as close to the original as the need to supply three syllables ('them kind and') would allow. For Chaucer and his contemporaries, the word 'fre' had a range of humanly powerful associations and connotations. The word is glossed by Tyrwhitt as 'willing, unconstrained, at liberty, liberal, bountiful'. It is not clear quite what force Wordsworth imagined that *his* word 'free' had in 1801, or what support he thought it might gain from being paired with 'kind'. Was he attempting to revive *lost* resonances in Chaucer's words? Or did he think the words would have the *same* implications for his readers as they had had for Chaucer's?

Wordsworth approached *The Cuckoo and the Nightingale* with greater veneration for the letter of the ancient text than that of any previous modernizer. His

---

[48] Cooke, 'The Cuckow and the Nightingale' in *Poetical Essays on Several Occasions* (London, 1774).

[49] Wordsworth's modernizations of Chaucer were first published in *The Poems of Geoffrey Chaucer Modernized*, ed. Richard H. Horne (London, 1841). For full details of their composition and publication, see William Wordsworth, *Translations of Chaucer and Virgil*, ed. Bruce E. Graver (Ithaca, NY and London, 1998). The text of *Of the Cuckowe and the Nightingale* used by Wordsworth (and cited here in connection with his version, as 'Anderson') was that printed in Vol. 1 of Robert Anderson, ed., *A Complete Edition of the Poets of Great Britain*, 14 vols (Edinburgh, 1792–1807).

process is closer to restoration than translation—literally so when he included three stanzas where the poet casts a stone at the cuckoo 'from a manuscript in the Bodleian'.[50] Many rewriters of Chaucer's poems had included a number of antiquated words, and had reproduced occasional lines almost exactly, but in their versions all words and every line were to be sounded as if being delivered in contemporary English speech. It is not clear what kind of pronunciation Wordsworth was envisaging or demanding for his version. He has followed the stanza of his original where the first, second, and fifth lines agree in one rhyme, the third and fourth in another. In the original, the chime of rhyme provides shape and is generally true. But in Wordsworth, 'rood' rhymes with 'good' in one place, and 'good' with 'mood' in another; 'dead' rhymes with 'heed', and 'note' rhymes with both 'brought' and 'out' in the same stanza; 'I wis' rhymes with 'is' in one stanza, and with 'bliss' in another; and 'alsó' (with an accent marked) rhymes with 'saw' and 'woe', and 'service' rhymes with 'wise'.

In a footnote to his Preface to *Lyrical Ballads* (1800), Wordsworth had observed that the 'affecting parts of Chaucer are almost always expressed in language pure and universally intelligible even to this day'.[51] But when, some years later, he offered his version of *The Prioress's Tale* to the public, he did so with a note drawing attention to, rather than apologizing for, the poem's antiquity. He was much less certain of Chaucer's intelligibility than he had been in 1800 and much more aware of the changes that had occurred in the sound of words. He was almost pulling in two directions—wanting fluent reading and instant understanding on the one hand, but requiring ancient accents on the other:

> In the following Piece I have allowed myself no further deviations from the original than were necessary for the fluent reading, and instant understanding, of the Author: so much however is the language altered since Chaucer's time, especially in pronunciation, that much was to be removed, and its place supplied with as little incongruity as possible. The ancient accent has been retained in a few conjunctions, as alsō and alwāy, from a conviction that such sprinklings of antiquity would be admitted, by persons of taste, to have a graceful accordance with the subject.[52]

A reviewer of *Chaucer Modernized* (1841), in which Wordsworth's *The Cuckoo and the Nightingale* first appeared in print, praised the poem's 'poetic faithfulness' to 'the original', and Walter W. Skeat judged that Wordsworth had 'fairly reproduced' the original's 'light and pleasing style'.[53] But Robert Bell's general comment

---

[50] *Chaucer Modernized*, ed. Horne, p. 47. As Bruce Graver has shown, Wordsworth had not himself seen this MS, and relied on an account of these stanzas provided in the *Gentleman's Magazine* for January 1839. See Wordsworth, *Translations*, ed. Graver, pp. 24–5.

[51] See Wordsworth, *Translations*, ed. Graver, p. 10.

[52] Ibid. p. 36.

[53] See *The English Journal*, Saturday, January 2, 1841, p. 8; Geoffrey Chaucer, *The Complete Works*, ed. Walter W. Skeat, 7 vols. (Oxford, 1894), 7. lix.

on nineteenth-century modernization pinpoints some of the difficulties involved in Wordsworth's distinctive and new methods of translation:

> In proportion as they preserve strictly [Chaucer's] exact phraseology, they become formal and cumbrous; for that which is perfectly easy and natural in its antique garb and association, acquires an obsolete and heavy air when it is transplanted amongst more familiar forms.[54]

Where Wordsworth followed closely the verse form of his original, William Cooke had evolved a new form consisting of two octosyllabic couplets, followed by a couplet consisting of one octosyllabic and one pentameter line. His desire appears to have been to emulate the pleasures felt by the birds themselves, as in Stanza 14:

> joy'd they seem
> To greet the Sun's returning Beam,
> And, vying in Devotion, strove,
> And fill'd with Harmony the vocal Grove.
>
> (Cooke, *Poetical Essays*, p. 90)

Wordsworth once criticized Dryden for failing to 'have his eye upon' the 'object' of his writing. But in *The Cuckoo and the Nightingale*, he seems more intent on rendering his impression of old verses than on conveying the impression of a happy imaginary walk in a real wood. Where Bell had found that Wordsworth's 'transplanting' of Chaucerian phraseology produced an 'obsolete' and 'heavy' effect, Wordsworth's own desire, it appears, was to look into the past and find in its very antiquity something strangely intelligible and modern. Some 'sprinklings of antiquity' are assumed by Wordsworth 'to have a graceful accordance' with a dream where birds sing of love. The 'accordance', however, does not closely resemble the agreement between the sound of water and the singing of birds in the poem. In this stanza, Wordsworth neither finds nor adds melody or harmony, whose final stresses (required by metre) are in possible defiance of phonetic change:[55]

And the rivir that I sat upon,	Meanwhile the stream, whose bank I sate upon,
It madin soche a noisè as it ron,	Was making such a noise as it ran on
Accordant with the birdis armony,	Accordant to the sweet Birds harmony;
Me thought that it was the best melody	Methought that it was the best melody
That mightin ben yherde of any man.	Which ever to man's ear a passage won.
(*Cuckoo*, 81–5; Anderson, *Poets of Great Britain*, 1. 495)	(*Chaucer Modernized*, p. 41)

---

[54] *Poetical Works of Geoffrey Chaucer*, ed. Robert Bell, 4 vols (London, 1878–80), 1. 62.
[55] It is hard to know at which point '—y' ceased to constitute an accented syllable. Dryden rhymes 'harmony' with 'sky'. Blake rhymes 'eye' and 'symmetry'.

William Cooke, in contrast, attempted to emulate in his verse an effect conducive to the 'cheerfulness and serenity of mind' attributed to Chaucer:

> The crystal River, by whose Side
> I sat, ran on with murm'ring Tide,
> And seem'd to join the Songsters all
> As with Consent reciprocal:
> And so accordant was the Whole,
> No sweeter Harmony could charm the Soul.
>
> (*Poetical Essays*, p. 91)

In Cooke's version, the state of the *soul* and the imagined poet's reactions to what he sees appear to be essential to his notion of the principles behind the old poem.

George Sewell, in the address 'To the LADIES' prefixed to his *Proclamation of Cupid*, had written that Chaucer '*knew the Torrent of Desire, / When the Nerves tremble, and the Eyes shake Fire*'. The speaker of *The Cuckowe and the Nightingale* records that though he is now 'olde and unlusty', he has himself in the past felt the 'axis'[56] of Love acutely. Wordsworth, for all his veneration of its original, softens its force, by making the speaker describe himself, euphemistically, as 'to genial pleasure slow' and describe his amorous feelings as 'heart-aches'. Cooke's narrator, in contrast, is more explicit in stressing his past passions:

> From dear Experience thus I speak:
> Tho' Age his Furrows on my Cheek
> Hath deep entrench'd, long since I knew
> What vernal Suns of MAY cou'd do;
> In early Manhood doom'd to prove
> The Colds and Heats, strong Ague-Fits, of Love.
>
> (Cooke, *Poetical Essays*, p. 88)

Cooke seems to be concerned here to represent Chaucer's personality rather than his own. Throughout the eighteenth century, *The Cuckowe and the Nightingale* was seen by many as autobiographical, and was thought to contain reminiscences of Chaucer's early love experiences, of his walks in Woodstock Park, of his fresh responses to nature in that setting, and of the 'customary cheerfulness and serenity of mind' that is 'particularly conspicuous in [Chaucer's] delineations of nature'.[57]

But there is little 'cheerfulness and serenity of the mind' in the words of the vile Cuckoo on the universal effects of Love:

> For therof commeth diese and heviness,
> So sorrow', and care, and many' a grete sickness
> Despite, debate, and angre, and envy,

---

[56] Cooke may here have been influenced by Urry's gloss on 'axis' ('Feaver, Ague, Fit').
[57] See Urry, p. 545; Fol. b1ʳ, Fol. 2ʳ; Godwin, *Life of Chaucer*, 2. 567.

> Depraving, shame, untrust, and jealousie,
> Pride, mischese, povertie, and wodènesse
>
> (*Cuckoo*, 171–5; Anderson, *Poets of Great Britain*, 1. 500)

Cooke adopted or adapted many of the nouns in his original for the ill results of love:

> "For thence low Spirits and Disease,
> "And sickly Nights, and careful Days,
> "Despight, Debate and Anger spring,
> "Distrust and Shame, and jealous Fears,
> "And Mischiefs wild, and Penury in Tears.
>
> (*Poetical Essays*, p. 96)

Wordsworth seems to have remembered the rhyme and cadence of the medieval poem in his own version of the same passage:

> For <u>thereof come</u> all contraries to <u>gladness</u>;
> Thence sickness comes, and overwhelming sadness,
> Mistrust and jealousy, despite, debate,
> Dishonour, shame, envy importunate,
> Pride, anger, mischief, poverty, and <u>madness</u>
>
> (*Chaucer Modernized*, p. 35)

Thinking of Chatterton and Burns in his *Resolution and Independence* (1807), Wordsworth wrote: 'We poets in our youth begin in <u>gladness</u> / But <u>thereof come</u> in the end despondency and <u>madness</u>'.[58] Wordsworth was here identifying himself with his unfortunate predecessors. The phrase 'thereof come', and the double rhymes perhaps convey for Wordsworth a distant flavour of the Chaucerian or pseudo-Chaucerian 'antique'. Although these particular rhymes do not appear in *The Cuckoo and the Nightingale* (where 'woodeness' is the term for madness), double rhymes are frequent.

The Flower and the Leaf, or, The Lady in the Arbour, A Vision

If the personality of Chaucer was thought to be of central relevance to a reading of *The Cuckowe and the Nightingale*, the identity of the speaker in *The Floure and the Leafe* proved to be of equal importance—though for very different reasons. Dryden drew attention to the fact that, as Speght had put it in his account of 'The Argument', the story is told not by a poet, but by '*A Gentlewoman out of an Arbor*'—wording picked up in the half-title of the poem in *Fables*: 'The Flower and

---

[58] *Resolution and Independence*, 48–49. The echo is noted by Bruce Graver (citing Anthony E. M. Conran) in Wordsworth, *Translations*, ed. Graver, p. 70.

the Leaf; Or, The Lady in the Arbour. A Vision'. Although he thought the poem was a genuine composition of Chaucer's, the fact that it offers a distinctly female experience was for Dryden clearly one of its attractions. A fascination and sympathy with womanly sentiments was, as we have seen, characteristic of several of the most admired poems in the Chaucer Apocrypha. William Godwin, indeed, thinking highly both of Dryden's version and its source, suspected that Chaucer had translated this poem from a work originally composed by a woman, a lost poetic mother, so that the work constituted 'the first example which occurs in the history of modern literature, of a lady having been the writer of a work of invention of so considerable extent'.[59] But other commentators found the poem's possible female origins more problematic. Walter W. Skeat became convinced that the poem as printed in Speght's edition was *in point of fact* composed by a woman. In the introduction to Volume 7 of his edition of *Chaucer Works*, Skeat included an outright and downright attempt to smear the poem by all possible means. It is difficult to escape the impression that chief amongst these was Skeat's belief that the poem is contemptible *because* it was written by a woman. 'All the principal characters are ladies', he declared, 'and the chief personages are queens, viz. the queen of the Leaf and the queen of the Flower.' The presence of a female authorial mind, in Skeat's view, is evident in 'the continual reference to colours, dresses, ornaments, and decorations', and 'very characteristic of female authorship is the remark that the ladies vied with each other as to which looked the best'.[60]

As can be seen from the prefatory directory in Urry's edition, Dryden and the poem became intimately, almost indissolubly, associated:

> The *Flower and the Leaf*, was written by him [Chaucer]; as appears by his own words in the Prologue to the *Legend of gode Women*. This is judged by Mr. Dryden to be of our Author's own invention, after the manner of the *Provençals*; and he was so particularly pleased with it both for the Invention and Moral, that he recommends it to the Reader in a modern Dress.[61]

Skeat, indeed, believed, or pretended to believe, that it was only Dryden's version (which, he said, is 'finer than the original') that had caused *The Floure and the Leafe* to give readers pleasure.[62] But a more considered account would have recalled that, while Dryden may have drawn attention to the poem, and while some readers had preferred his version, there were several readers—most notably, as we have seen, John Keats—who had a particular fondness for the original poem, and many who found equal, and related, pleasure in both original and translation.

---

[59] Godwin, *Life of Chaucer*, 2. 350.
[60] Chaucer, *The Complete Works*, ed. Skeat, 7. lxviii, lxv.
[61] Urry, Sig. f'.
[62] Chaucer, *The Complete Works*, ed. Skeat, 7. lxviii.

Thomas Warton expected the attractions of the medieval poem to be obvious from his account of its narrative—though, interestingly, he neglects to mention that the narrator of this poem is female:

The poet is happily placed in a delicious arbour, interwoven with eglantine. Imaginary troops of knights and ladies advance: some of the ladies are crowned with flowers, and others with chaplets of agnus castus, and these are respectively subject to a *Lady of the Flower*, and a *Lady of the Leaf*. Some are cloathed in green, and others in white. Many of the knights are distinguished in much the same manner. But others are crowned with leaves of oak or of other trees: others carry branches of oak, laurel, hawthorn, and woodbine. Besides this profusion of vernal ornaments, the whole procession glitters with gold, pearls, rubies, and other costly decorations. They are preceded by minstrels cloathed in green and crowned with flowers. One of the ladies sings a bargaret, or pastoral, in praise of the daisy.... In the mean time a nightingale, seated in a laurel-tree, whose shade would cover an hundred persons, sings the whole service, 'longing to May.' Some of the knights and ladies do obeysance to the leaf, and some to the flower or the daisy. Others are represented as worshipping a bed of flowers. Flora is introduced 'of these flouris goddesse.' The lady of the leaf invites the lady of the flower to a banquet. Under these symbols is much morality couched. The leaf signifies perseverance and virtue: the flower denotes indolence and pleasure.[63]

William Godwin was perhaps the warmest admirer of Dryden's version of *The Floure and the Leafe*. He maintained that, when seen 'as the exhibition of a soothing and delicious luxuriance of fancy', Dryden's version, 'may be classed with the most successful productions of human genius. No man can read it without astonishment, perhaps not without envy, at the cheerful, well-harmonised and vigorous state of mind in which its author must have been at the time when he wrote it.'[64] Henry Todd followed an extensive quotation of this passage from Godwin with the comment: 'What lover of the English language, I may add, can be otherwise than passionately grateful for the production of the *Flower and the Leaf*.'[65] He was writing there of Dryden's version, but included in his volume the original text of the poem, printed in its entirety.

Godwin's attribution to the author of the poem of 'a cheerful, well-harmonised and vigorous state of mind' might be applied accurately to the state of mind of the Lady in the Arbour herself:

> In that sweet Season, as in Bed I lay,
> And sought in Sleep to pass the Night away,
> I turned my weary Side, but still in vain,
> Tho' full of youthful Health, and void of Pain:
> Cares I had none to keep me from my Rest,
> For Love had never enter'd in my Breast.
> I wanted nothing Fortune could supply,
> Nor did she Slumber till that hour deny.
>
> (*The Flower and the Leaf*, 20–5; Dryden, *Works*, 7. 367)

---

[63] Warton, *History*, 1. 466–7.
[64] Godwin, *Life of Chaucer*, 2. 346.
[65] Henry J. Todd, *Illustrations of the Lives and Writings of Gower and Chaucer* (London, 1822), p. 282.

Both in Dryden's version and in the original, the Lady's vigour is marked—and, in Dryden's account, described in verse of elegant fluidity:

And vp I rose three houres after twelfe	When Chaunticleer the second Watch had sung,
About the springing of the day	Scorning the Scorner Sleep from Bed I sprung.
And on I put my geare and mine array	And dressing, by the Moon, in loose Array
And to a pleasaunt groue I gan passe,	Pass'd out in open Air, preventing Day,
Long or the bright sonne up risen was	And sought a goodly Grove, as Fancy led my way.
(*FL*, 24–8; Speght 1598, Fol. 365ᵛ)	(*The Flower and the Leaf*, 33–7; Dryden, *Works*, 7. 367)

Samuel Johnson praised Dryden for being '*always another and the same*, he does not exhibit a second time the same elegances in the same form'.[66] Dryden has given the Lady in the Arbour verse which, although vigorous, is notably more tranquil and less emphatic than that which he had given, say, to Palamon or Arcite, and considerably less allusive than that which is spoken by the Nun's Priest.

In his *Essay on Criticism*, Alexander Pope was to mock, in memorably self-illustrating lines, verses that 'ring round the same *unvary'd Chimes*, / With sure Returns of still *expected Rhymes*'.[67] But these are almost exactly the means that are employed in Dryden's *Flower and the Leaf*. Untroubled serenity is expressed in repeated and unsurprising rhymes, a scattering of alexandrines, and an overriding easiness of metre. Frequent exclamations of ecstasy and delight, for example, produce little disturbance in the equanimity of the verse.[68] Poetic and metrical energy is often centred in the middle of the line. The overall effect is, as several readers noticed, 'soothing' (particularly in response to the singing of birds), as when the Lady tells that that the goldfinch 'sooth'd my Soul, and pleas'd my Ear' (113).

In the following passage, the Nightingale responds to the song of the goldfinch, and the lady to both:

The Nightingale with so merry a note	Her short Performance was no sooner try'd,
Answered him that all the wood rong	When she I sought, the Nightingale reply'd:
So sodainly that as it were a sote	So sweet, so shrill, so variously she sung,
I stood astonied so was I with the song	That the Grove ccho'd, and the Valleys rung:
Thorow rauished that till late and long	And I so ravish'd with her heavnly Note
I ne wist in what place I was ne where …	I stood intranc'd, and had no room for Thought.
Whereof I had so inly great pleasure	But all o'er-pow'r'd with Extasy of Bliss,[69]
That as me thought I surely rauished was	Was in a pleasing Dream of Paradice.
Into Paradise where my desire	
Was for to be and no ferther passe …	
(*FL*, 99–104, 113–116; Speght 1598, Fol. 366ʳ)	(*The Flower and the Leaf*, 114–21; Dryden *Works*, 7. 371–3)

---

[66] Johnson, *Works*, 21. 443. Johnson here echoes Dryden's own description of the phoenix in *Of the Pythagorean Philosophy*, 581 (Dryden, *Works*, 7. 501).

[67] *An Essay on Criticism*, 348–9; Pope, *Poems*, 1. 278–9

[68] One exception might be the placing of *trembling* in this alexandrine: 'And the soft Lute trembling beneath the touching hand' (359).

[69] We have here reinstated the reading 'o'er-pow'r'd' (emended to 'o'er pou'r'd' in Dryden, *Works*) from the text of *FL* published in the first edition of Dryden's *Fables Ancient and Modern* (London, 1700).

Both the medieval and the modern lady are *ravished*, and think or dream they are in Paradise.[70] Taking a hint from the suggestion in his original that the wood was more beautiful than anything seen before by living creature ('Of the world was neuer seen or than / So pleasant a ground of none earthly man'), Dryden described a 'Fairy Place' in which his lady 'wish'd to dwell for ever' and of which she can take 'sweet Possession' entirely without company:

> Single, and conscious to my Self alone,
> Of Pleasures to th'excluded World unknown.
> Pleasures which no where else, were to be found,
> And all *Elysium* in a spot of Ground.
>
> (*The Flower and the Leaf*, 142–5; Dryden, *Works*, 7. 373)

When 'An Host of Saints' danced round her 'Arbour', Dryden's Lady 'shook with holy Fear'—but 'not so much' as to impede her acute appreciation of the beauty of their 'Song or Dance' (206–9).

The Flower and the Leaf presents a 'Vision' and not a sleeping dream. But it is dream-like in that a wonderous plethora of things are seen without obvious pattern or interpretable meaning. The elaborate details of dress, movement, sound, and their diverse accoutrements are presented to the senses without immediate significance. Many elements in the vision would seem to be highly disturbing and yet the whole experience was apparently as deeply calm and delightful for its readers as it was for the Lady in the Arbour herself.

Ghosts and Fairies

Dryden's largest departure from his original concerns the very nature of the beings that constitute the vision. William Godwin observed that Dryden

> has somewhat obscured the purpose of the tale, which in the original is defective in perspicuity; but he has greatly heightened the enchantment of its character. He had made its personages fairies who annually hold a jubilee, such as is here described, on the first of May; Chaucer has left the species of the beings he employs vague and unexplained.[71]

It was particularly the enchantment associated with fairies (but, as in Dryden's version of *The Wife of Bath's Tale* and Pope's of *The Merchant's Tale*, of a distinctly unmedieval kind) that seems to have contributed to the enthusiasm for the poem in the early years of the nineteenth century. Thomas Campbell considered that

---

[70] 'The narrator becomes rapt while sitting alone in the grove, listening to the nightingale, and drawn into a realm of heightened mental awareness unknown in the world': Helen Phillips, '"This Mystique Show": Dryden and the Flower and the Leaf', *Reading Medieval Studies*, 27 (2003), 29–50.

[71] Godwin, *Life of Chaucer*, 2. 346.

the 'two best of Chaucer's allegories, the Flower and the Leaf, and the House of Fame, have been fortunately perpetuated in our language: the former by Dryden, the latter by Pope':

> The Flower and the Leaf is an exquisite piece of fairy fancy. With a moral that is just sufficient to apologize for a dream, and yet which sits so lightly on the story as not to abridge its most visionary parts, there is, in the whole scenery and objects of the poem, an air of wonder and sweetness; an easy and surprising transition that is truly magical.[72]

Dryden's Lady in the Arbour seems to recognize a magical presence even before she meets the fairy beings. She discovers 'a Path' which 'seem'd to meet' in 'narrow Mazes' and 'look'd, as lightly press'd, by Fairy Feet' (55–7). And when she comes across an arbour, 'the sacred Receptacle of the Wood' (61), she somehow recognizes it: 'The Master Work-man of the Bow'r was known / Through Fairy-Lands, and built for *Oberon*' (78–9).

It is not until the speaker meets a straggling Lady in White that the nature of the fairy beings is explained. The dreamer is 'inquisitive to know / The secret Moral of the Mystique Show' (459–60) and finds, 'A Lady all in White with Lawrel crown'd / Who clos'd the Rear, and softly pac'd along, / Repeating to her self the former Song' (464–6). This Lady, both in Dryden and in his original, having described the origins of those beings who follow the Leaf, ends by saying 'and I my self am one':

And she ayen answered right friendly	Ev'ry Lady cloath'd in White,
My faire doughter all tho that passed hereby	And, crown'd with Oak and Lawrel ev'ry Knight,
In white clothing, be <u>seruants</u> euerichone	Are <u>Servants</u> to <u>the Leaf</u>, by Liveries known
Vn<u>to the Leafe, and I my self am one</u>	Of Innocence; <u>and I my self am one</u>.
(*FL*, 466–9; Speght 1598, Fol. 368ʳ)	(*The Flower and the Leaf*, 502–5; Dryden, *Works*, 7. 397)

Everything preceding this declaration in Dryden's version has, however, been altered, almost beyond recognition. To the human Lady's question, the fairy Dame now replies,

> Fair Daughter know
> That what you saw, was all a Fairy Show:
> And all those airy Shapes you now behold
> Were humane Bodies once, and cloath'd with earthly Mold:
> Our Souls not yet prepar'd for upper Light,
> Till Doomsday wander in the Shades of Night;
> This only Holiday of all the Year,
> We priviledg'd in Sun-shine may appear:
> With Songs and Dance we celebrate the Day,
> And with due Honours usher in the *May*.

---

[72] Campbell, *Specimens of British Poets*, 2. 18–19.

> At other Times we reign by Night alone,
> And posting through the Skies pursue the Moon:
> But when the Morn arises, none are found;
> For cruel *Demogorgon* walks the round,
> And if he finds a Fairy lag in Light,
> He drives the Wretch before; and lashes into Night.
>
> (*The Flower and the Leaf*, 480–95; Dryden, *Works*, 7. 395)

These 'Shapes' are not identical to the Fairies in *The Wife of Bath Her Tale*. They are condemned to 'wander in the Shades of Night' until 'Doomsday', and, if seen by daylight, are harried by *Demogorgon*, most terrible of devils. And yet they are universally beneficent:

> All Courteous are by Kind; and ever proud
> With friendly Offices to help the Good.
> In every Land we have a larger Space
> Than what is known to you of mortal Race:
> Where we with Green adorn our Fairy Bow'rs,
> And ev'n this Grove unseen before, is ours.
>
> (*The Flower and the Leaf*, 496–501; Dryden, *Works*, 7. 397)

Their lives when 'cloath'd with earthly Mold' have embodied the Christian virtues—including virginity. The 'Soveraign Lady of our Land' is '*Diana*', the 'Queen of Chastity' (508–9). The knights belonging to this group, however, were such as 'never broke their Vow: / Firm to their plighted Faith, and ever free / From Fears and fickle Chance, and Jealousy' (322–4).

The moral of the poem is outlined in Speght's 'Arguments to euery Tale and Booke', and is placed immediately before the reprinting of the original poem in *Fables Ancient and Modern*:[73]

> Those which honour the Flowere a thing fading with every blast, are such as looke after beautie and worldly pleasure. But they that honour the Leafe, which abideth with the root notwithstanding the frost and winter stormes, are they which follow vertue and during qualities without regard of worldly respects.[74]

Dryden, who recommended *The Flower and the Leaf* to his readers 'both for the Invention and the Moral', has made the contrast between the followers of the Leaf and the Flower marked, and apparently decisive:

And as for her that crowned is in greene	*Flora* commands, said she, those Nymphs and Knights,
It is Flora of these floures goddesse	Who liv'd in slothful Ease, and loose Delights:
And all that here on her awaiting beene	Who never Acts of Honour durst pursue,

---

[73] Speght's 'Argument' was repeated by Urry and Anderson, and also given in *Chaucer Modernized*, ed. Horne.

[74] Speght 1598, Sig. c.vi.

It are such that loued idlenes
And not delite of no busines
But for to hunt, and hauke and pley in medes
And many other such idle dedes
And for the great delite and pleasaunce
They haue to the floure, and so reuerently
They vnto it do such obeisaunce
As ye may se

(*FL*, 533–43; Speght 1598, Fol. 368ᵛ)

The Men inglorious Knights, the Ladies all untrue:
Who nurs'd in Idleness, and train'd in Courts,
Pass'd all their precious Hours in Plays, and Sports,
Till Death behind came stalking on, unseen,
And wither'd (like the Storm) the freshness of their
Green.
These, and their Mates, enjoy the present Hour,
And therefore pay their Homage to the Flow'r.

(*The Flower and the Leaf*, 560–70;
Dryden, *Works*, 7. 401)

The memorable alexandrine 'The Men inglorious Knights, the Ladies <u>all untrue</u>' resembles a line from Dryden's *Secular Masque* in *The Pilgrim*, probably written within months of the composition of *The Flower and the Leaf*. In that work, Venus sings that 'Calms appear, when Storms are past, / Love will have his Hour at last', and Chronos, the personification of Time, remembers when 'Joy rul'd the Day, and Love the Night'. But then Momus, the god of mockery, dismisses Mars with the observation: 'Thy Wars brought nothing about' and Venus with a comment 'Thy Lovers were <u>all untrue</u>'.[75] That is lightly put, but it has been suggested that Dryden, in *The Secular Masque*, was reflecting on the court of Charles II, or the earlier years of the seventeenth century more generally. A more solemn note is struck in *The Flower and the Leaf* when 'Death behind came stalking on, unseen' upon those who were 'nurs'd in Idleness, and train'd in Courts'.[76]

If Dryden's *Flower and the Leaf* hints at criticism of the 'inglorious Knights' and 'the Ladies all untrue' of the court of Charles II, criticism of knights is focused, by the Lady of the Leaf in both poems, on their changeability and lack of perseverance:

For knights euer should be perseuering,
To seeke honour without feintise or slouth

(*FL*, 548–9; Speght 1598, Fol. 368ᵛ)

But Knights in Knightly Deeds should persevere,
And still continue what at first they were;
Continue, and proceed in Honours fair Career.

(*The Flower and the Leaf*, 571–3;
Dryden, *Works*, 7. 401)

The knights who in Dryden belong to the Order of the Garter are held up as corrective examples. They are 'protectors of their Prince: / Unchang'd by Fortune, to their Sovereign true' (549–50).[77]

In both poems, too, the *laurel* is of the greatest importance—one leaf of which conveys immortality. The Nightingale is found 'on a laurel spray' at the start (127), and its 'lasting leaves' bind the brows of the virtuous (576). In the Preface to *Fables*, Dryden refers to Chaucer as his 'Predecessor in the Laurel'. The remarks of the Lady

---

[75] Dryden, *Works*, 16. 272–3.

[76] Dryden here perhaps recalls his version of *The Fifth Satire of Persius*, where a personified 'Voluptuousness' advocates a life of free indulgence, since 'Death stalks behind' us all (Dryden, *Works*, 4. 339).

[77] 'The knights of the Leaf are not simply industrious, sober and steadfast as in the original poem, but (lines 547–54) Royalist' (Phillips, '"This Mystique Show"', p. 58).

of the Leaf on the enduring laurel may be read as Dryden's self-assertion of his own continuing poetic power:[78]

In <u>signe</u> of which with leaues aye lasting	For this with lasting Leaves their Brows are bound; ⎫
They be rewarded after their degree,	For Lawrel is the <u>Sign</u> of Labour crown'd; ⎪
Whose lusty green May, may not appaired be	Which bears the bitter Blast, nor shaken falls to ⎬
	Ground: ⎭
But aye keping their beauty fresh and greene	From Winter-<u>Winds</u> it suffers no decay,
For there nis storme that may hem deface	For ever fresh and fair, and ev'ry Month is *May*.
Haile nor snow, wind nor frosts kene	Ev'n when the vital Sap retreats below,
Wherefore they haue this propertie and grace	Ev'n when the hoary Head is hid in <u>Snow</u>;
	The Life is in the Leaf, and still between
	The Fits of falling Snows, appears the streaky Green.
(FL, 551–7; Speght 1598, Fol. 368v)	*(The Flower and the Leaf, 579–86;*
	Dryden, Works, 7. 401)

There is one difficulty with the suggestion that in his presentation of the Lady's reflections on courts and courtiers Dryden was hinting at a sharp political distinction between faithful Jacobites, say, and treacherous followers of King William. In the narrative of this poem, the emphasis is on the *reconciliation* between the two factions:

And whan ŷ storm was cleane passed away	But as Compassion mov'd their gentle Minds,
Tho in white that stood vnder the tre	When ceas'd the Storm, and silent were the Winds,
They felt nothing of the great affray,	Displeas'd at what, not suff'ring they had seen,
That they in greene without had in ybe	They went to chear the Faction of the Green:
To them they yede for reuth and pite	The Queen in white Array before her Band,
Them to comfort after their great disease	Saluting, took her Rival by the Hand;
So faine they were the helplesse for to ease …	So did the Knights and Dames, with courtly Grace
	And with Behaviour sweet their Foes embrace.
… the knights in fere	Then thus the Queen with Lawrel on her Brow,
Began to comfort hem and make hem chere	Fair Sister I have suffer'd in your Woe:
	Nor shall be wanting ought within my Pow'r
The Queen in white, ŷt was of great beauty	For your Relief in my refreshing Bow'r.
Tooke by the hond the queen ŷt was in grene	
And said suster I have right great pity	
Of your annoy and of the troublous tene	
Wherein ye and your company haue bene	
So long alas, and if that it you please	
To go with me, I shall do you the ease,	
In all the pleasure that I can or may …	
(FL, 372–8, 384–93; Speght 1598, Fol. 367ᵛ)	*(The Flower and the Leaf, 393–404;*
	Dryden, Works, 7. 389–91)

---

[78] It has been suggested that Dryden is here reflecting on his own position: 'although deprived of the official Laureateship in 1689, his poetic status and achievement, based on a lifetime of hard works, are unshaken by adversity' (Dryden, *Poems*, 5. 426). See also Paul Hammond, 'Dryden and the Laurel', in *Literary Milieux: Essays in Text and Context Presented to Howard Erskine-Hill*, ed. David Womersley and Richard McCabe (Newark, DE, 2008), pp. 104–15.

There is one moment in Thomas Warton's account of the poem when he may have recalled Dryden's version (423–36) while ostensibly describing the original: 'The lady of the leaf invites the lady of the flower to a banquet.'[79] There is little mention of any food beyond some 'Pleasaunt salades' in the original poem. But in Dryden, 'The Lady of the Leaf ordain'd a Feast, / And made the Lady of the Flow'r her Guest' (423–4), and the moment is elaborated with a supernaturally provided banqueting 'Bow'r' (426). In Dryden's version, it is of the utmost importance that:

> The vanquish'd Party with the Victors join'd,
> Nor wanted sweet Discourse, the Banquet of the Mind.
> *(The Flower and the Leaf,* 431–2; Dryden, *Works,* 7. 393)

Those last phrases are Dryden's own, and proved memorable.[80] The medieval vision, it seems, provided Dryden with a locus in which he could imagine a resolution to the dissentions that had troubled the century past.

A Chorus of Poets in Celebration of Spring

In this connection, it is notable that the most-loved lines in *The Flower and the Leaf* concerned renewal, harmony, and a new Spring. John Aikin thought the opening lines of Dryden's version were remarkable and entirely original:

> The very beautiful introductory picture of spring, as influencing the vegetable creation, is … Dryden's own, and displays the power of a master to throw novelty upon a trite subject. The progress of the buds, which at first shrink from the cold blast, and stand 'doubting at the door of life,' till at length, filled with the genial spirit, they expand to the sun, and breathe out their souls of fragrance, is delineated with exquisite fancy and elegance.[81]

As so often, Dryden's throwing 'novelty upon a trite subject' has been effected by drawing upon, reconciling, and harmonizing poetic fragments of a great many others:

When that Phebus his chaire of gold so hie	Now turning from the wintry Signs, the Sun
Had whirled vp the sterry sky aloft	His Course exalted through the Ram had run:
And in the Boole was entred certainly	And whirling up the Skies, his Chariot drove
Whan shoures sweet of raine descended oft	Through *Taurus,* and the lightsome Realms of Love;
Causing the ground fele times and oft	Where *Venus* from her Orb descends in Show'rs,
Vp for to giue many an wholsome aire	To glad the Ground, and paint the Fields with Flow'rs:
And euery plaine was clothed faire	When first the tender Blades of Grass appear,
	And Buds, that yet the blast of *Eurus* fear,

---

[79] Warton, *History,* 1. 466–7.

[80] They are echoed, for example, in Pope's translation of *The Odyssey of Homer,* 4. 330 and 15. 433 (Pope, *Poems,* 9. 135; 10. 90).

[81] John Dryden, *Fables from Boccacio [sic] and Chaucer,* ed. John Aikin (London, 1805), pp. xix–xx.

With new greene and maketh small flours

To springen here and there in feld & in mede
So very good and wholsome be the shoures
That it reneueth, that was old and deede
In winter time and out of euery seede
Springeth the hearbe so that euery wight
Of this season wexeth glad and light

(*FL*, 1–14; Speght 1598, Fol. 365ᵛ)

Stand at the door of Life; and doubt to clothe
    the Year;
Till gentle Heat, and soft repeated Rains,
Make the green Blood to dance within their Veins:
Then, at their Call, embolden'd, out they come,
And swell the Gems, and burst the narrow Room;
Broader and broader yet, their Blooms display,
Salute the welcome Sun, and entertain the Day.
Then from their breathing Souls the Sweets repair
To scent the Skies, and purge th'unwholesome Air:
Joy spreads the Heart, and, with a general Song,
Spring issues out, and leads the jolly Months along.

(*The Flower and the Leaf*, 1–19; Dryden,
Works, 7. 365)

It is interesting that, although Dryden had no reason to disbelieve that this poem was by Chaucer, his first impulse was to 'fortify' the opening lines by turning to other poems included in Speght's edition, including *The Story of Thebes*, clearly attributed by Speght to Chaucer's poetic disciple, John Lydgate:

> When bright Phebus passed was <u>the Ram</u>,
> Midde of Aprill, and in the Bull cam ...
> When that flora, the noble mighty queen
> The soile hath clad, in new <u>tender</u> green
> With her <u>shoures</u>...

(Speght 1598, Fol. 370ʳ)

Sir Walter Scott speculated that one of the 'studies' that Dryden found that he shared with Chaucer was astrology. Dryden's governing idea in the opening passage of his poem seems have been that Spring in *The Floure and the Leafe* was being described first in astrological terms. The phrase 'wintry signs' appears to have been his own invention, but the 'Ram' is apparently owed to the *Prologue* to the *Canterbury Tales* where the 'yong <u>sonne</u> / Hath in the <u>Ram</u> his halfe <u>course</u> <u>yronne</u>', or to *The Squire's Tale,* where Canacee 'up riseth' as 'fresshe' and 'As ioly and bright, as the yong <u>sonne</u> / That in the <u>Ram</u> is four degrees up <u>ronne</u>'.[82]

Although astrological in the first place, Dryden represented his planets here (as in *Palamon and Arcite*) as both the heavenly bodies of astrology *and* the gods of Homer, Virgil, and Ovid. The opening lines of the *Floure and the Leafe* ('When that Phebus his <u>chaire</u> of gold / Had <u>whirled</u> <u>vp</u> the sterrie sky aloft') are themselves a reminiscence of the fragment that ends *The Squire's Tale*, where 'Appollo

---

[82] In his reference to 'the Ram', Dryden seems also to have recalled his own version of Book 3 of Virgil's *Georgics* where when '<u>winter's</u> drizzly reign' is over 'the new <u>Ram</u> receives the <u>exalted sun</u>' (477–8)—lines to which he had attached one of his own (very rare) footnotes: 'Astrologers tell us, that the Sun receives his <u>Exaltation</u> in the sign *Aries*: *Virgil* perfectly understood both Astronomy and Astrology'. Dryden's sun, that is, is *exalted* in the astrological sense: it is in the astrological position of greatest influence (Dryden, *Works*, 5. 224; 6. 815).

whirleth up his chare so hie'. Dryden has his sun drive his chariot through 'Taurus' remembering the moment in *The Nun's Priest's Tale* where the 'brighte Sunne … in the signe of Taurus was y-runne'. Throughout his poem, Dryden also recalled the poet whom he thought of as one of Chaucer's most illustrious sons. In *The Faerie Queene*, Spenser had given further currency to the 'whirling' 'chare', so in one place Phoebus 'leaues the welkin way' with 'whirling wheels',[83] and in another Neptune has a 'whirling charet'.[84]

In *The Floure and the Leafe*, there is no connection between Phoebus 'in the Boole' and the sweet showers that fall on earth. In Dryden's version, it is Venus who is made the presiding deity of the Spring. His description of the realm of her influence, the 'lightsome realms' and 'realms of love', recall Spenser's description of a 'lightsome world',[85] and Ariel in the Dryden/Davenant *Tempest*'s description of 'the lightsome Regions of the Air' as his 'native fields'.[86] Dryden's use of 'glad' as a verb to describe the effect of Venus's showers on the ground may have been influenced by a line from *The Knights Tale* which he preserved intact in his own *Palamon and Arcite*—where Chaucer's 'O lady myn Venus … Thow glader of the mount of Citheron' is retained as 'Thou gladder of the mount of Cytheron'—or by Spenser's description of 'a flowre, that feeles no heate of sunne, / Which may her feeble leaues with comfort glade'.[87]

In making the swelling gems 'salute' the sun, Dryden may have remembered another passage in *The Knight's Tale* where 'The bisy larke, messager of day, / Salueth' the grey morning. In making the flowers rather than the wind or the ground 'breathe' 'sweets', Dryden was again drawing on several poetic predecessors. Spenser, in *Prothalamion*, had 'Sweete breathing Zephyrus' softly playing 'through the trembling ayre', and Fairfax, in *The First Booke of Godfrey of Bulloigne*, has a 'A Pagan damsell' arrange her hair 'To catch sweete breathing, from the cooling aire'. Waller, in this instance, clearly Fairfax's poetical son, proclaimed (in 'On Her Coming To London') that 'To welcome her the Spring breathes forth / Elysian sweets, / March strews the earth / With violets and posies, / The sun renews his [da]rting fires, / April puts on her best attires, / And May her crown of roses'.

In making Venus 'paint' the fields with flowers, Dryden recalled *The Franklin's Tale*, where 'May had peynted with his softe shoures' a 'gardin ful of leves and of floures', Spenser's *Prothalamion*, where 'the rutty Bancke of silver streaming Themmes / Was paynted all with variable flowers / And all the meades adorned with daintie gemmes', or Joshua Sylvester, who in 'The Third Day of the First Week' in his *Du Bartas: His Divine Weekes And Workes* has 'Flowrs' 'Whose Colours now

[83] Edmund Spenser, *The Faerie Queene*, I. iv.9.
[84] Ibid. II. xii. 22.
[85] Ibid. III. vii. 48.
[86] *The Tempest*, IV. iii. 62–3; Dryden, *Works*, 10. 85.
[87] Spenser, *Faerie Queene*, VI. x. 44.

shall <u>paint the Fields</u> so trim'. Dryden's memory was again combining his classical and his early English reading—Chaucer, Spenser, or Sylvester with Persius, who, in his *First Satire* as rendered by Dryden, described a poet so bad that he cannot 'paint the flowery <u>Fields</u> that <u>paint</u> themselves before' (138).

Dryden's use of 'spread' in the phrase 'joy spreads the heart' is more unusual. The use seems to be that given in the *OED* (3.d): 'To extend, to make larger or wider'—a meaning that is described as 'rare'. It is not clear whose heart is affected. Dryden's general idea seems to have been to transfer the joy of Spring from the humans to the natural objects themselves. In Dryden's poem, it is Spring and the jolly months who join together to sing a hymn to *themselves*.

Dryden's Spring Procession was again in part prompted by Spenser. The phrase 'issues out' recalls the *Two Cantos of Mutabilitie* when 'forth <u>issew'd</u> the Seasons of the yeare; / First, lusty <u>Spring</u>, all dight in leaues of flowres / That freshly <u>budded</u> and new <u>bloosmes</u> did beare'.[88] The governing fancy by which Spring *leads* the jolly months along recalls Milton's sonnet to the Nightingale where the 'jolly hours <u>lead</u> on propitious *May*' (4), or *Comus*, where the 'starrie quire … in their nightly watchfull Spheares, / <u>Lead</u> in swift round the <u>Months</u> and Yeares' (111–14).

In this hymn to the Spring, Dryden was presenting himself as the inheritor of both the poetic families he described in the Preface to *Fables*—the lines from Chaucer to Spenser and Milton and that from Chaucer to Fairfax and Waller. He was also demonstrating that this was *inevitably* the case. His poetic vocabulary and his poetic mind had been formed by their influence. Dryden had also found himself, as Pope put it, tracing the Muses upward to their fountain head. His version of the Spring demonstrates that all English poetic roads led to back to Chaucer. The quotation from Virgil on the title page of *Fables*, that is, indicates Dryden's sense that to write poetry was to cooperate with a divinely inspired process, a necessary retracing of poetical history, where succession and inheritance are essential to *renewal*:

> Joy spreads the Heart, and, with a general Song,
> Spring issues out, and leads the jolly Months along.

The great pleasures that were given by this passage from the *Flower and the Leaf*, together with the dream-like and the fanciful aspects of the poem, are strongly present in the writing of both Thomas and Joseph Warton. They point to a strong developing interest in the more other-worldly potential of Chaucer's work—in the visionary, in the magical, in fairy worlds and fairy-inhabited places, often alongside depictions of purity and pathos. These preferences for works of a 'general romantic and allegoric vein', as Thomas Warton put it, form the subject of Chapter 10.

---

[88] Ibid. VII. vi. 28.

10

Pathos, Chivalry, and Romance

Chaucer and the Warton Brothers

In his *Essay on the Genius and Writings of Pope*, Joseph Warton observed that 'the character of a fond old dotard betrayed into disgrace by an unsuitable match' had been 'supported in a lively manner' in 'the story of January and May'. But he had doubts about *The Wife of Bath's Prologue*, and wished that Pope had chosen very different Chaucerian works for imitation:

> The Wife of Bath, is the other piece of Chaucer which Pope selected to imitate: One cannot but wonder at his choice, which perhaps nothing but his youth could excuse. Dryden, who is known not to be nicely scrupulous, informs us that he would not versify it on account of its indecency. Pope however has omitted or softened the grosser and more offensive passages. Chaucer afforded him many subjects of a more serious and sublime species; and it were to be wished, Pope had exercised his pencil on the pathetic story of the patience of Griselda, or Troilus and Cressida, or the complaint of the black knight; or, above all, on Cambuscan and Canace. From the accidental circumstance of Dryden and Pope's having copied the gay and ludicrous parts of Chaucer, the common notion seems to have arisen, that Chaucer's vein of poetry was chiefly turned to the light and the ridiculous.[1]

Warton's list of poems that Pope might have imitated is particularly interesting—not least because it has sometimes been thought to advocate an essentially different Chaucerian canon from that favoured in the earlier years of the eighteenth century. Joseph Warton's writings, together with those of his brother Thomas (see Fig. 10.1) and Richard Hurd's *Letters of Chivalry and Romance* (1762), have been seen by some commentators as signalling a 'developing Romantic taste for the literary Gothic'.[2] Of course, readers of Hurd and the Wartons need to remember that some of their key terms have resonances significantly different from those that they have acquired since the eighteenth century. For these critics, the term 'romantic' was primarily associated with the literary genre of 'romance', and the fantastical, magical, and exotic characters and situations associated with that genre. And 'gothic' was, for them, primarily a term used to describe an historical period (roughly

---

[1] Joseph Warton, *An Essay on the Genius and Writings of Pope*, 2. 7–8.
[2] Brewer, *Chaucer: The Critical Heritage*, 1. 220.

Chaucer in the Eighteenth Century. David Hopkins and Tom Mason, Oxford University Press.
© David Hopkins and Tom Mason (2022). DOI: 10.1093/oso/9780192862624.003.0011

Fig. 10.1 Joseph Warton, engraved by J. R. Smith (1777) and Thomas Warton, engraved by
E. Mackenzie (1808), both from paintings by Sir Joshua Reynolds.

equivalent to the modern 'Middle Ages') and the literary forms and styles associated with it. Both terms, as we shall see, were sometimes used in the eighteenth
century as terms of praise and sometimes of denigration. But their resonances
are far removed from those familiar to modern readers in such phrases as 'The
Romantic Poets' or 'The Gothic Novel'.[3]

Joseph Warton was no doubt genuine in his wish that Pope had produced
versions of what he thought were Chaucer's more 'serious', 'sublime' and 'pathetic' poems. He shared with his brother Thomas the conviction—as expressed
in the second edition of Thomas's *Observations on the Fairy Queen of Spenser*
(1762)—that Chaucer 'abounds not only in strokes of humour, which is commonly
supposed to be his sole talent, but of pathos, and sublimity, not unworthy of a
more refined age'.[4] And such remarks have prompted the suggestion that Thomas
Warton's tastes were even 'in some ways more Romantically Gothic' than those of
'Chaucer himself'.[5] But the Wartons' preferences were, in significant respects, continuous with, rather than a complete departure from, those of the earlier eighteenth

[3] On the changing resonances of the term 'Romantic', see David Perkins, *Is Literary History Possible?*
(Baltimore, MD and London, 1992), Chapter 5 ('The Construction of English Romantic Poetry as a
Literary Classification'). On 'gothic', see Valerie Rumbold, 'Pope and the Gothic Past', unpublished PhD
dissertation, University of Cambridge, 1983.

[4] Thomas Warton, *Observations on the Fairy Queen of Spenser*, 2 vols (2nd corrected edn, London,
1762), 1.197.

[5] Brewer, *Chaucer: The Critical Heritage*, 1. 226. The fondness of the Wartons for the Gothic is discussed by Joan Pittock in *The Ascendancy of Taste: The Achievement of Joseph and Thomas Warton*
(London, 1973), pp. 89–92.

century.[6] We saw in Chapter 9, for example, how warmly the 'pathetic' passages in *The Complaint of the Black Knight*, a poem believed to be by Chaucer, had been embraced by John Dart. Dart, to be sure, had felt some pressure to apologize in his Preface for the poem's 'romantic' and 'chivalric' elements. He guessed that some readers might find the style and genre of the poem *too* 'medieval'. 'Perhaps', he suggested, they might be 'shockt at the Romantick Title', and he conceded that 'not only the Title but the Complaint' itself 'carries with it a Spice of the Humour[7] of [Chaucer's] Times'. There was, nevertheless, for Dart no ultimate or decisive qualitative difference between 'romantic' and other literary forms. He observed, for example—in a way that was to be echoed by both Wartons—that there was no essential conflict between the 'Chivalry' and 'romance' to be found in Chaucer's *Knight's Tale* and its status, in Dryden's estimation, as 'one of the best Epick Poems extant'.[8] And as for Chaucer's 'gothic' elements, Alexander Pope, as we will see in Chapter 11, was profoundly impressed by the 'sublime' qualities of the quintessentially 'gothic' *House of Fame*. Ogle's composite translation of *The Canterbury Tales*, moreover, which contained work from the first half of the century, had included extraordinarily elaborate versions of two of the poems on which Joseph Warton had particularly wished that Pope had 'exercised his pencil': the 'pathetic story of the patience of Griselda', and the Squire's 'romantic' story of Cambuscan and Canace.

It was therefore their emphasizing and singling out of certain areas of the Chaucerian corpus for special praise, rather than any wholesale reorientation of perspective, that differentiated the responses of Hurd and the Wartons from those of their predecessors. Thomas Warton certainly believed that Chaucer's poems—and some medieval writing more generally—offered particular attractions not available elsewhere:

> [Chaucer's] old manners, his romantic arguments, his wildness of painting, his simplicity and antiquity of expression, transport us into some fairy region, and are all highly pleasing to the imagination.[9]

The 'fairy regions' that had particularly attracted earlier eighteenth-century readers in Chaucerian poems, as we have seen in earlier chapters, had been in evidence in *The Wife of Bath Her Tale* and *January and May*, where they co-existed with

---

[6] For a full account of the complexities of Joseph Warton's accounts of Dryden and Pope, see Adam Rounce, ed., *Alexander Pope and His Critics*, 3 vols (London, 2003), 1. xiii–lxvi. The index in Vol. 3 of this publication lists all the references to the Chaucerian poems in Joseph Warton's *Essay on the Genius and Writings of Pope*.

[7] Here, clearly, meaning 'spirit' or 'style' (*OED*, 7b), rather than 'comedy'.

[8] John Dart, *The Complaint of the Black Knight from Chaucer* (London, 1720), Sig. A3ᵛ. Dart, however, considered *modern* romances to be ridiculous: 'the Classic Authors of *France*, have lately taken not a little Pains, in their elaborate Romances, to pester the World, and bewilder the Ladies with their polite Trumpery' (Sigs A3ᵛ–A4ʳ). For Joseph Warton's defence of Dryden's *Palamon and Arcite* against the strictures of Samuel Johnson, see his *Essay on the Genius and Writings of Pope*, 2. 12–17.

[9] T. Warton, *Observations on the Fairy Queen of Spenser*, 1. 197.

'realistic' elements that were felt less desirable by both Wartons. Whereas earlier critics had stressed Chaucer's greatness 'in every species of poetry' and his mastery of 'every kind' of poetical 'excellence',[10] and whereas Chaucer had been seen as *both* a naturalistic observer of human 'manners' and a poet of the 'sublime', the 'gothic', the 'wild', and the 'pathetic', it was the latter set of qualities that Hurd and the Wartons tended to single out for particular praise.

George Sewell and *The Song of Troilus*

The most surprising of the suggestions made by Joseph Warton of Chaucerian poems on which Alexander Pope might have 'exercised his pencil' is 'the pathetic story of ... Troilus and Cressida'. Though *Troilus* had been admired by Sir Thomas Wyatt and his Tudor contemporaries and drawn on by Shakespeare, it had not fared well since around 1700, and indeed, as Derek Brewer has observed, was to remain 'relatively neglected well into the twentieth century'.[11] But though for many eighteenth-century readers *Troilus* had become regarded as merely ancillary to the *Canterbury Tales*, it was clearly read in some circles with considerable care.[12] And the critical remarks that were occasionally made about *Troilus* were often strikingly positive. George Ogle, for example, reprinted the *Life of Chaucer* from Urry's edition, where Chaucer was described as 'an excellent Master of Love-Poetry, having studied that Passion in all it's Turns and Appearances'. 'His *Troilus and Criseide*', the *Life* continues, 'is one of the most beautiful Poems of that Kind; in which Love is curiously and naturally described in it's early Appearance, it's Hopes and Fears, it's Application, Fruition, and Despair in Disappointment'.[13] The noun *pathos*, the adjective *pathetic*, and the adverb *pathetically*, for the manner of telling, were frequently applied to *Troilus*, particularly in the later years of the century. Thomas Warton considered that Chaucer had 'constructed a poem of considerable merit, in which the vicissitudes of love are depicted in a strain of true poetry, with much pathos and simplicity of sentiment'.[14] For him, *Troilus* was a demonstration that 'pathetic description', with its capacity to move the reader, 'is one of Chaucer's peculiar excellencies'.[15]

---

[10] John Berkenhout, *Biographia Literaria* (London, 1777), p. 312.

[11] Brewer, *Chaucer: The Critical Heritage*, 1. 17.

[12] In his *The Art of English Poetry* (London, 1702), Edward Bysshe included a discussion of the stanzas in which the poem is composed. *Troilus* was also cited in some of the notes to Richard Bentley's notorious edition of *Paradise Lost* (1732), in Thomas Newton's edition of *Paradise Regain'd*, 2 vols (London, 1753), and in Ralph Church's edition of *The Faerie Queene* (1757). The dedication to Gower at the end of *Troilus* was noticed in accounts of that poet. The first part (only) of an English version of Sir Francis Kynaston's Latin commentary on *Troilus* (1639) was published as *The Loves of Troilus and Creseid* (London, 1796).

[13] Ogle, 1. liv.

[14] Warton, *History*, 1. 385.

[15] Ibid. 1. 387.

Thomas Warton's comments were frequently repeated, becoming, indeed, the standard account of *Troilus*. The poet Thomas Campbell was led by Warton to pleasures of his own, remarking in 1819 that *Troilus* is 'a story of vast length and almost desolate simplicity', which 'abounds in all those glorious anachronisms which were then, and so long after, permitted to romantic poetry':

> The languor of the story is, however, relieved by many touches of <u>pathetic</u> beauty. The confession of Cresseide in the scene of felicity, when the poet compares her to the 'new abashed nightingale, that stinteth first ere she beginneth sing,' is a fine passage, deservedly noticed by Warton. The grief of Troilus after the departure of Cresseide is strongly portrayed in Troilus's soliloquy in his bed … .The sensations of Troilus, on coming to the house of his faithless Cresseide, when, instead of finding her returned, he beholds the barred doors and shut window, giving tokens of her absence, as well as his precipitate departure from the distracting scene, are equally well described.[16]

But the appeal of the poem's 'pathetic beauty', nevertheless, seems ultimately to have been, even for enthusiastic readers, comparatively limited. Thomas Warton devoted fewer pages to *Troilus* than to several individual Canterbury Tales.

Among poets, Chaucer's *Troilus* attracted only George Sewell, and, eighty years later, William Wordsworth.[17] Sewell, whose version of *The Letter of Cupyde* was discussed in Chapter 9, suggested that Dryden's knowledge of *Troilus and Criseyde* had been evident in his echo of Chaucer's description of Criseyde ('*That Paradis stood formed in her Eyen*') in his description of 'Absalom' in *Absalom and Achitophel* ('*And Paradise was open'd in his Face*').[18] In making his own version of Troilus's song in Book 1 of *Troilus and Criseyde*, Sewell hoped that the translation would contribute to the wider 'Acquaintance of the Polite World' with Chaucer's works which he hoped would be the result of the '*New Edition*' of Chaucer's Works: Urry's, which was to appear the following year.[19] Sewell's interest in the song of Troilus may have been prompted by an advanced sight of the *Life of Chaucer* in Urry's edition, where it is rightly proposed that 'the Song of *Troilus* in the First Book is a Translation of that Song in *Petrarch*, which begins, *S'amor non è, che dunquè quel ch'io sento?*' ['If it is not Love, what then is it that I feel?'].[20] Chaucer's achievement, Sewell thinks, has been to produce a passionate version of a commonplace: 'The Thought in this *Song* has been used, and diversified a hundred times since *Chaucer's* Days; and yet he seems to have said more, and that more pathetically than any of his Imitators.'[21] Sewell was clearly concerned to make his version turn on the very lines given marks of approval in Speght's

[16] Thomas Campbell, ed., *Specimens of the British Poets*, 7 vols (London, 1819), 2. 19.
[17] George Sewell's 'The Song of Troilus' appeared in *A New Collection of Original Poems* (London, 1720). Wordsworth's 'Troilus and Cresida: Extract from Chaucer' was probably composed in 1801 or early 1802, but was not published until 1841 in *The Poems of Geoffrey Chaucer Modernized*.
[18] Sewell, *A New Collection of Original Poems*, p. 83.
[19] Ibid. p. 83.
[20] Urry, Fol. F^v.
[21] Sewell, *A New Collection of Original Poems*, p. 83.

texts. (In the text below, the italics are Sewell's, the underlining intended to show shared phraseology):

The song of Troilus	The Song of *Troilus*
If no loue is, O God what feele I so?	If *no Love is*—O God what feel I so?
And if Loue is, what thing, and which is he?	And, if *Love is*—what Thing, and which is He?
If loue be good, from whence cometh my wo?	If Love be *good*, from whence proceeds my Woe?
If it be wicke, a wonder thinketh me,	If it be *Ill*? How can that *Ill* agree?
When euery torment and adversite	His bitter Potions I the sweetest think,
That cometh of him, may to me savery think:	And ever thirst *the more*, the more I drink.
*For aie thurst I, the more that iche it drinke.	
And if that at mine owne lust I brenne,	If *willingly* I bear the burning Charm,
From whence cometh my wailing & my plaint:	Whence are my Wailings, and my deep Complaint?
If harme agree me, whereto plaine I thenne,	If Harm is pleasing, why do I grieve the Harm?
I not, ne why, unwery that I feint,	Why with the Load unwearied, am I faint?
O quicke death, o sweet harme so queint,	*Sweet Harm*, how holds my Heart of thee so much,
How may of thee in me be such quantite,	But that my Heart consents it should be such?
But if that I consent that it so be?	
And if that I consent, I wrongfully	And if my Heart consent and I agree?
Complaine iwis, thus possed to and fro,	The Folly of Complaint fair Wisdom binds,
All stereless within a bote, am I	Thus like a Boat all steerless in the Sea,
Amidde the sea, atwixen windes two,	My Heart is toss'd betwixt two jarring Winds.
That in contrary stonden ever mo?	Alas! what wondrous Woe poor Lovers try?
Alas! what is this wonder maladie?	For Heat of Cold, for Cold of Heat I dye.
*For heat of cold, for cold of hete I die.	

(TC, 400–20; Speght 1687, pp. 261–2)

(Sewell, A New Collection of Original Poems,
pp. 84–5)

Sewell's pleasure in the passage, however, does not seem to be echoed in the responses of the brothers Warton. Of Troilus's song, Thomas Warton commented: 'There is not so much nature in the sonnet to Love … It is translated from Petrarch; and had Chaucer followed his own genius, he would not have disgusted us with the affected gallantry and exaggerated compliments which it extends through five tedious stanzas.'[22] Sewell had assumed that the song represented a skilful representation of inner debate—a process of reasoning, pathetically expressed, similar to the 'reasoning in Verse' that is to be found in Dryden's heroic plays—which itself, perhaps, had been learnt from Chaucer.[23] Petrarchan turns, Sewell assumes, are not empty paradoxes, but the definitive expression of a common human dilemma.

The main difference between Thomas Warton and George Sewell is that Warton associates 'pathos' with 'simplicity of sentiment'.[24] Among the passages in *Troilus*

---

[22] Warton, *History*, 1. 385–6.
[23] Sewell, *A New Collection of Original Poems*, p. 83.
[24] Warton, *History*, 1. 385.

that Warton *did* think were both 'natural' and 'pathetic' was the following 'comparison', where 'The doubts and delicacies of a young girl disclosing her heart to her lover, are exquisitely touched' (the text and notes are Warton's):

> And as the newe abashid nightingale
> That stintith[m] first, when she beginith sing,
> When that she herith any herdis[n] tale,
> Or in the hedgis anie wight stirring,
> And after sikir[o] doth her voice outring;
> Right so Cresseidè when that her drede stent[p]
> Opened her herte and told him her intent[q].

[m] Stops. [n] Herdsman. A Shepherd. [o] With confidence.
[p] Her fears ceased. [q] L. iii. v. 1239.
(Warton, *History*, 1, 386)

This comparison between Criseyde opening her heart and the out-ringing song of the 'newe abashid nightingale' met Warton's criteria.[25] Because it is drawn from the natural world, Warton assumes that the comparison may be appreciated by his readers directly from Urry's text, if accompanied with light glossing. Sewell, in his treatment of the song of Troilus (where Warton assumed that artifice rather than 'simplicity of sentiment' is the keynote), expressed his pride at the number of Chaucer's words that he had not had to change in his version.[26] Some key lines are given almost *verbatim*. While Sewell was forced to substitute a conventional periphrasis ('the burning Charm') for Troilus's 'at mine owne lust I brenne', he was able to revive the word *steerless*: 'Thus like a Boat all steerless in the Sea, / My Heart is toss'd betwixt two jarring Winds'—assuming that the word in this context would be immediately intelligible. Sewell, despite some archaism of syntax, had managed to reproduce more of Chaucer's words than most other translators—before Wordsworth.

William Wordsworth: Troilus Laments the Loss of Criseyde

Wordsworth, who rendered the episode in Book 5 of *Troilus and Criseyde* where Troilus laments the loss of Criseyde during the first ten days of her absence in the Greek camp, attempted to change as little as possible, producing a version that is metrically and semantically intermediary between medieval and modern. Wordsworth, as we saw in Chapter 9, had suggested in 1800 that pathos

---

[25] This passage was to become a favourite of many—including William Hazlitt, who cited the passage on two occasions, once praising 'the description of Cresseide's first avowal of her love' as 'One of the most beautiful passages in Chaucer's tale'; on another occasion, exclaiming 'This is so true and natural, and beautifully simple, that the two things seem identified with each other' (see Brewer, *Chaucer: The Critical Heritage*, 1. 278).

[26] Sewell, *A New Collection of Original Poems*, p. 83.

and intelligibility went hand in hand in Chaucer's poems: the 'affecting parts of Chaucer are almost always expressed in language pure and universally intelligible even to this day'.[27] This impression may have been half-confirmed in the winter of 1801, as the communal reading of his household turned from Dryden's versions of Chaucer to their originals. The veneration that had prompted Dryden to recast his original considerably pushed Wordsworth into the opposite direction—to transcribe as often as possible, rather than translate. The pathos of Troilus's situation for Wordsworth resided in the precise details of the words he uses. More than this, it resided in the *antiquity* of those words—even in their sound. Dryden, like Sewell, had revived old words for their 'significancy', but they were to be pronounced and accented *exactly* as if they were contemporary English.

Not so for Wordsworth. Even the names in his version are, it seems, to be pronounced in non-modern ways. 'Troilus' is (as in the original) given three syllables. 'Cresida' is made to rhyme with 'day' and 'say'. Pandarus has two syllables in one place, but three in another. Taking a cue from one instance ('his hert began to cold' (535)), Wordsworth preserves as many auxiliary ''gans' as possible, giving them an apostrophe, suggesting that they are contractions of 'began'. Some of the ''gans' may be preserved for metrical reasons—with Wordsworth finding himself a half or whole foot short on several occasions and forced into a roughness that is not present in his original. Some verbs are archaized: 'rode' (607) becomes 'forth did pass' (90) and 'went' (603) becomes 'did go' (85).

In the course of reproducing Chaucer's words rather than recreating the situation to which those words refer and describing *that* in his own terms, Wordsworth has sometimes allowed the words to suggest their nearest modern equivalent, not noticing that they were *faux amis*. As Bruce Graver noted, Anderson, in the text of Chaucer used by Wordsworth, had reproduced Tyrwhitt's definition of 'werrie' ('to make war against') in connection with Troilus's exclamation 'How thou me hast weried on every side'. Wordsworth's modern equivalent seems, on the face of it, close to his original, but has a quite different meaning: 'How thus has wearied me on every side'.[28]

Wordsworth's austere fidelity to the letter of Chaucer's text did not always constrain the eloquence of his version. When Troilus addresses Criseyde's now empty palace directly, Wordsworth's lines connecting the ownership of heart and house are perhaps no less elegant and forceful than those of the original. (Tyrwhitt's had glossed 'gie' as 'to guide'):

---

[27] Footnote to Preface to Lyrical Ballads (1800), quoted in William Wordsworth, *Translations of Chaucer and Virgil*, ed. Bruce Graver (Ithaca, NY and London, 1998), p. 10.
[28] Wordsworth, *Translations*, ed. Graver, p. 72. For other examples, see Edward Dowden, 'Wordsworth's Selections from Chaucer Modernised', in *Wordsworthiana: A Selection of Papers Read to the Wordsworth Society*, ed. William Knight (London, 1889), pp.21–2.

O paleis whilom day, that now art night!	O Palace whilom day that now art night,
Wel oughtist thou to fal and I to die	Thou ought'st to fall and I to die; since she
Sens she is went that wont was us to gie.	Is gone who held us both in sovereignty.
(TC, 5. 544–6;, Anderson, *Poets of Great Britain,* 1.397, p. 397)	*(Chaucer Modernized,* ed. Horne, p. 128)

And although in principle Wordsworth rejected the notion of compensation (the substitution in translation of a new for a lost 'beauty'), he sometimes, in practice, found it necessary. Very occasionally, Wordsworth replaced Chaucer's words entirely. For example, he connected Chaucer's authorial comment on Troilus's melancholy with Hamlet's conjecture that the 'Divil' might 'seeke to damne' him 'out of my weakenesse and my melancholy':

And al this n'as but his melancolie,	All which he of himself conceited wholly
That he had of him selfe such fantasie	Out of his weakness and his melancholy.
(TC, 5. 623–4; Anderson, *Poets of Great Britain* 1.398)	*(Chaucer Modernized,* p. 132)

In late 1839, Wordsworth was to write to Thomas Powell:

> [I]n respect to the Poems in stanza, neither in The Prioresses Tale nor in The Cuckoo and Nightingale have I kept to the rule of the original as to the form and number and position of the *rhymes*, thinking it enough if I kept the same number of lines in each stanza; and this I think is all that is necessary—and all that can be done without sacrificing the substance of sense, too often, to the mere form of sound.[29]

With *Troilus*, however, he found himself able to follow the stanza and the rhymes with remarkable fidelity:

And hardily this winde that more and more	And certainly this wind, that more and more
That stoundèmele encresith in my face	By moments thus increaseth in my face,
Is of my ladies depè sighis sore;	Is of my Lady's sighs heavy and sore;
I preve it thus, for in none othir space	I prove it thus; for in no other space
Of al this toun, save onely in this place,	Of all this town, save only in this place,
Fele I no winde that sounith so like paine,	Feel I a wind, that soundeth so like pain;
It saith, Alas! why twinid be we twaine.	It saith, Alas, why severed are we twain.
(TC, 5. 674–9; Anderson, *Poets of Great Britain* 1.398)	*(Chaucer Modernized,* ed. Horne, p. 134)

Criseyde's words carried on the wind ('Alas! why twinid be we twaine') depend in the original on two cognates. Tyrwhitt, citing an earlier instance of the phase, had glossed 'twinned' as 'separated'. 'Parted' would have preserved the metre, but Wordsworth, wanting to retain something of the play between 'twinid' and 'twaine', came up with 'severed' to render the extremity of Troilus's pain,

---

[29] *The Letters of William and Dorothy Wordsworth, Vol. 6: The Later Years, Part III: 1835–9,* ed. Ernest de Selincourt, rev. Alan G. Hill (Oxford, 1982), p. 756.

while still preserving Chaucer's metre. This stanza perhaps served as confirmation of Wordsworth's belief, quoted earlier, that the 'affecting parts of Chaucer' are expressed in language that is 'pure and universally intelligible even to this day'. But what precisely did Wordsworth mean by 'pure'? And in what sense are Wordsworth's terms in this passage—'increaseth', 'soundeth', and 'saith'—'pure', and not, in 1801 or 1841, antiquated poeticisms?[30]

Charlotte Lennox, William Godwin, and 'Troilus'

George Sewell and William Wordsworth represented only fragments of *Troilus*. A full and sensitive account of the whole was included in *Shakespear Illustrated* (1754), where Chaucer's poem was summarized in prose by Samuel Johnson's friend, Charlotte Lennox.[31] Lennox breaks into direct speech on several occasions—particularly when representing the vehemence of Cressida's reactions to the enormous pressures put upon her by Pandarus. When her uncle suggests that she should thank the gods at the news that she is beloved by 'the young, the brave, the lovely *Troilus*':

> Ah, me! Interrupted *Cressida*, and is it for a Lover then, that I must thank the Gods! Is this the glorious Fortune they have destined for me! And can you, Oh, my Uncle! Can you resolve to lead me through the dangerous Paths of Pleasure? You, who ought rather to watch over my unguarded Steps, and save me from the treacherous Baits of Love! Oh, *Pallas*! Guardian Goddess of my Youth, assist me now! Direct me in this doubtful Maze of Fate, and save thy wretched Votary![32]

But Lennox's account becomes increasingly distant as the poem's action progresses. Book 3 is so baldly and prudishly summarized that there is no indication that the love between the couple extends much beyond the exchange of passionate letters. It is not until Godwin's *Life of Chaucer* that an account of the poem appeared which paid attention to all its parts.

Godwin, Derek Brewer suggests, 'completed the turn away from *Troilus and Criseyde* by his adverse criticism of the poem'.[33] But while it is true that there are indeed some 'adverse' comments in Godwin, and a long list of 'defects', the balance of his criticism is in fact massively in favour of the poem. Chaucer's story is well told by Godwin. He praises many of Chaucer's delicate beauties, including

---

[30] In *The Riches of Chaucer*, ed. Charles Cowden Clarke, 2 vols (London, 1833), 2. 140, Charles Cowden Clarke, apart from modernizing the spelling and marking the accents, considered it necessary to gloss only two words in the stanza on the wind-borne lament: 'hardély' ('certainly') and 'stoundémele' ('every instant'). 'Twinned' is left to the reader's ingenuity.

[31] Charlotte Lennox, *Shakespear Illustrated*, 3 vols (London, 1754), 3. 55–87.

[32] Ibid. 3. 68–9.

[33] Derek Brewer, 'Modernizing the Medieval: Eighteenth-Century Translations from Chaucer', in *The Middle Ages after the Middle Ages in the English-Speaking World*, ed. Marie-Françoise Alamichel and Derek Brewer (Martlesham, 1997), p. 105.

the comparison, so beloved by Warton, of Criseyde to a nightingale—than which, Godwin says, 'nothing can be more beautiful'. In his final judgement, *Troilus* is

> a work interspersed with many beautiful passages of exquisite tenderness, of great delicacy, and of a nice and refined observation of the workings of human sensibility. Nothing can be more beautiful, genuine, and unspoiled by the corrupt suggestions of a selfish spirit, than the sentiments of Chaucer's lovers. While conversing with them, we seem transported into ages of primeval innocence. Even Cresiede is so good, so ingenuous and affectionate, that we feel ourselves as incapable as Troilus, of believing her false.[34]

It is pertinent to the subject of this chapter, however, that Godwin did not see *Troilus* as in any way *romantic*. On the contrary, for him the poem

> contained nothing but what was natural. Its author disdained to have recourse to what was bloated in sentiment, or <u>romantic</u> and miraculous in incident, for the purpose of fixing or keeping alive the attention. He presents real life and human sentiments, and suffers the reader to dwell upon and expand the operations of feeling and passion. Accordingly the love he describes is neither frantic, nor brutal, nor artificial, nor absurd.[35]

Despite such praise, it is strange that no one attempted anything even remotely like a full-dress rendering of *Troilus* in the eighteenth—or, indeed, nineteenth—centuries. That fact must militate, at least to some extent, against the notion that readers of Chaucer in this period were responsive to the full range of what the fourteenth-century poet had to offer. It is unlikely that even Alexander Pope would have undertaken a translation of *Troilus*, as Joseph Warton suggested he should. Wordsworth wrote to Thomas Powell, the editor of *Chaucer Modernized*, about a putative modern version of the poem that he calls '*Troilus and Cressida*': 'You ask my opinion about that poem. Speaking from a recollection only of many years past I should say it would be found too long—and probably tedious.'[36]

George Ogle and Patient Griselda

Joseph Warton did not elaborate on his reasons for wishing that Pope had composed a version of Chaucer's *Clerk's Tale*, although his adjectives provide a clear indication of the nature of his pleasure in that poem: 'it were to be wished, Pope had exercised his pencil on the pathetic story of the patience of Griselda.'[37] It is significant that Warton described *The Clerk's Tale* as a pathetic *story*. Where the pathos of *Troilus* was concentrated in the laments of the male protagonist, Griselda

---

[34] William Godwin, *The Life of Geoffrey Chaucer,* 1. 300.
[35] Ibid. 1. 302.
[36] *The Letters of William and Dorothy Wordsworth*, ed. de Selincourt, 6. 756.
[37] J. Warton, *Essay on the Genius and Writings of Pope*, 2. 7.

refuses to elaborate on her griefs. Joseph's brother, Thomas, expressed a similar admiration for *The Clerk's Tale*, but similarly laid his stress on the tale's *incidents* rather than on the sentiments of its characters:

> The pathos of this poem, which is indeed exquisite, chiefly consists in invention of incidents, and the contrivance of the story, which cannot conveniently be developed in this place: and it will be impossible to give any idea of it's essential excellence by exhibiting detached parts. The versification is equal to the rest of our author's poetry.[38]

A version of the tale, George Ogle's *Gualtherus and Griselda: or the Clerk of Oxford's Tale, from Boccace, Petrarch, and Chaucer* (1739), published three years before Ogle's collection of Chaucer translations 'by several Hands', is one of the more interesting eighteenth-century Chaucerian adaptations—partly because it is among the more unusual.

It was *The Clerk's Tale* that first attracted Ogle to Chaucer, and attracted him in a number of problematic and potentially contradictory ways. In the first place, his interest had been drawn to a story that had been told and retold in a semi-independent manner by a number of distinguished writers: Boccaccio and Petrarch, as well as Chaucer. Ogle was one of the first—perhaps, *the* first—to compare any of Chaucer's poems systematically with its sources. He saw the telling of the Tale of Patient Griselda as a process of continuing addition and extrapolation. Petrarch, he says, 'much amplified, and much improved' Boccaccio's earlier telling.[39] Ogle took his cue partly from Dryden's Preface to *Fables*, where Petrarch's and Boccaccio's connections with *The Clerk's Tale* are mentioned,[40] but also from Petrarch's letter to Boccaccio, which he prints in full. He noted the differences between the three medieval versions carefully, thinking that the story acquired useful accretions in the process of transmission—none of which he was willing to forego.

Interestingly, however, despite Ogle's expansion of the story of Griselda in non-Chaucerian directions, his version is accompanied by an account of the Clerk taken from the *General Prologue*, by the Clerk's own *Prologue*, and, more significantly, by an elaborate *Epilogue* in which the words of Chaucer the Pilgrim mingle with those of the Host. Such additions, as we shall see, show that Ogle was profoundly interested in Chaucer's placing of the poem in the *Canterbury Tales* and the consequent confusion or complication of its ostensible moral purpose.

A sense of pathos is clearly an important element in Ogle's response to the tale (See Fig. 10.2). Ogle imagines that Chaucer himself was the 'Person of so much

---

[38] Warton, *History*, 1. 318.
[39] George Ogle, *Gualtherus and Griselda: Or, The Clerk of Oxford's Tale. From Baccace, Petrarch and Chaucer* (London, 1739), p. v.
[40] Dryden, *Works*, 7. 31.

GUALTHERUS AND GRISALDA.

His Lord Gualtherus going at the Gate
Gave to a Squire, and bade the attendance wait;
Scarce had he entered, when Grisalda came!
At distance known; he call'd her by her name

She down her Pail, beside the Oxen stall;
Hastes to depose; and on her knew to fall;
And thus in humble guise, &c.
As one that waits to hear the Royal will.

From the Original Picture in the Collection of George Bowles Esq.
to whom this Plate is Dedicated by his most Obedient Humble Servants
W. Dickinson.

Fig. 10.2 'Gualtherus and Griselda'. Engraved by F. Bartolozzi from a painting by Angelica Kauffman and included as an illustration of Ogle's *Clerk's Tale* in *Angelica's Ladies Library* (London, 1794).

Humanity' who had been brought to tears, according to Petrarch, on reading the tale in the author's presence:

> This person had barely gone half way thro' it, when He was prevented by a Flood of Tears; that after a short Pause, He resumed it again, but with all his Recollection was not able to proceed.... I took This, adds PETRARCH, as an Instance of his great

Good-nature, for in the whole Circle of my Acquaintance, I never knew a Man of more Humanity.[41]

But the story of Griselda is also a work that deals with human emotions and psychology in a more searching and complex manner than one would associate with a mere tale of tearful pathos—or a straightforward moral fable. From the outset, Ogle is at pains to defend the poem, and 'the Name of *Grizelda*', and to counter any surprise 'that any Man of Common-Sense should waste his Time, and Study on Reviving an old Nursery-Ballad'.[42] In defence of Griselda herself, Ogle expands or supplies depictions of inward psychological states at all points in the narrative. For example, she and Gualtherus are well acquainted before the marriage proposal, with the result that Griselda has some complicated emotions on the prospect of watching his marriage procession from her cottage gate:

> Yet Something here She found, nor yet cou'd find
> The Cause that pain'd her Heart, and griev'd her Mind.
>
> (Ogle, *Gaultherus and Griselda*, p. 27)

Gualtherus's emotional states are similarly complex. He has been inventing excuses to visit Griselda's dwelling as if by chance, and, on noticing her virtues, has almost revised his many objections to marriage and to women.

A truncated version of Ogle's tale was printed in *Angelica's Ladies Library* (1794), where the story carries the subtitle 'Happiness Properly Estimated', and culminates in a perfect marriage, in which a Prince, justly despising the venal ladies of his court, finds true virtue and true love in a poor country girl:

> To such a husband added such a wife;
> What fairer scene cou'd yield domestic life?
> Each seems of each the fortune to controul,
> Each worthy each in body as in soul.
> So fair the road, and so direct to bliss,
> Their way a pair so form'd cou'd hardly miss.
>
> (*Angelica's Ladies Library*, p. 104)

Ogle had drawn a similar contrast, not drawn by Chaucer, earlier in the tale. In his version, Griselda insists on breastfeeding her newly born daughter, against the initial wishes of Gualtherus. Griselda, though 'Mistress of a Throne', 'Intrusted'

---

[41] Ogle, *Gaultherus and Griselda*, p. vi.

[42] Ibid. p. iv. There were several ballads telling the story of patient Griselda. The earliest extant is a broadside of about 1600, now in the British Library, which was reprinted with only minor variations throughout the next two centuries, the final version appearing at the end of the eighteenth century. See Anne M. Haselkorn and Betty Travitsky, eds, *The Renaissance Englishwoman in Print: Counterbalancing the Canon* (Amherst, MA, 1990), p. 214. Some versions of the ballad half-resolve some of the difficulties of the more literary versions. In them, both Griselda and Gualtherus (the Marquis) are more blameless; his tests are primarily necessary to convince the populace of her virtue and the wisdom of his choice. The plot is simplified by Griselda giving birth only once (to twins). There was also a chap-book version in prose, which is divided into short chapters more or less along the lines of Chaucer's divisions.

her daughter 'to no Care, beside her own'. Ogle has to explain at some length that this constituted 'No Matrimonial Jar' to the unalloyed happiness of marital bliss. Griselda argues her case with some vehemence: 'Of all the Habitants of Earth and Air, / Shall Human Kind take less that Savage Care?'. She admits that her demand may seem to reflect 'The Language of the Daughter of a Swain' and that 'Courtly Dames' may disapprove, but denounces aristocratic practice with unconcealed contempt: ''Tis Vice of Fashion! 'Tis Neglect of Kind! /'Tis Indolence! 'Tis Cruelty of Mind!'.[43] Griselda's notions of motherhood receive Gualtherus's and Ogle's endorsement.

In Chaucer's tale, Walter begins to think of testing his wife at the time when his baby daughter 'had *souked* but a throwe', but there is no indication that Griselda is doing the suckling herself. Later, her son is taken 'fro the brest ... of his *norice*' when his turn comes. Nor are there any hints of maternal breastfeeding in Petrarch's version of the story, or in the Italian text of Boccaccio's. The translation of Boccaccio published in 1721, however, adds:

> Altho' she knew well it must needs be a great deal of trouble to suckle a Child, and that Persons in her Station never us'd to do it, yet she esteem'd that Niceness as a sort to Cruelty in them, and her Duty and tender Affection made her resolve to nurse her Daughter her self.[44]

In a similar vein, Ogle's Griselda proudly asserts the customs and values of her country upbringing:

> The Point let Courtly Dames with Leave contest,
> This lovely Child shall never quit my Breast.
>
> (Ogle, *Gualtherus and Griselda*, p. 43)

In Ogle's version, but not Chaucer's, it is thus against the crowd of court ladies whose vanities almost justify Gualtherus's disdain for and fear of all women, that Griselda's heroic virtues emerge—particularly when tormented by her husband.

Ogle has not neglected the pathos of the reference to Job in her outburst on being sent home to her father to make way for a new bride ('Naked out of my faders hous, quod she / I cam, and naked moot I turne agayn') or the proverbial plea ('Lat me nayt lyk a worm go by the weye'), but elaborates on her 'submission':

> "Naked I came, and naked I return,
> "Nor must I, since It suits your Grandeur, mourn ...
> "An Outcast let me be. Yet This I pray,
> "Let me not, like a Worm, go by the Way.
>
> (Ogle, *Gualtherus and Griselda*, p. 76)

---

[43] Ogle, *Gualtherus and Griselda*, pp. 42–3.
[44] *Il Decamerone: or, Decads, Consisting of One Hundred Ingenious Novels Written by John Boccaccio*, 2 vols (London, 1712 [1721]), 2. 294. This addition to Boccaccio may reflect a detail in Charles Perrault's version of the story, *La Marquise de Salusses, ou la patience de Griselidis*, first printed in 1691, where Griselidis similarly expresses her determination to nurse her child herself.

Ogle's Griselda, like Chaucer's, is presented as a paragon, and perhaps has even greater strength of mind.

When the Clerk breaks out into praise, Ogle follows Chaucer quite closely—but with a series of oppositions in the manner of Alexander Pope:

Thus with hir fadir, for a certaine space,
  Dwellith this flower of wively pacience,
That nevir by hir worde, ne by her face
  Before the folke, ne eke in their absence,
  Shewid she that to her was done offence;
    Ne of her hie estate no remembraunce
    Had she, as by her manir countenaunce.
 	
No wondir is, for in hir grete estate
  Her ghost was ay in plaine humilite,
No tendir mouthe, ne yet herte delicate,
  Ne pompe, ne semblaunce of high roialte,
  But full of pacient benignite,
    Discrete, and prideless, and ay honurable,
    And to her husbonde evir meke and stable.
              (*ClT*, 918–31; Urry, p. 103)
	Here, for a Space, remain'd the Patient Wife,
	And, thrown from great, returns to vulgar Life.
	Yet never once was heard her Lord to blame,
	Tho' spirited by many a busy Dame.
	Above the Powr of Fortune, or of Fate,
	She rose, in Good, or Ill, alike sedate!
	In Good, against Distress, She arm'd her still,
	And still prepar'd Her, for Success, in Ill.
	This was her Character, by All allow'd,
	'Virtuous, tho' Beautiful! Tho' Great, not Proud!
	'Discreet, as Witty! Sprightly, as Serene!
	'Sage, but not Sad! And Humble, but not Mean!'
	
	     (Ogle, *Gualtherus and Griselda*, pp. 79–80)

Ogle is more expansive in his rendering of Chaucer's passage that compares Griselda with Job, and comments on the dissimilarities between Griselda's perpetual obedience and the conduct of Job's unfeeling wife:

Men speke of Job, and most for his humbless,
  As Clerkis (whan 'hem lest) can well endite,
Namely of men, but in gode soothfastnesse,
  Thogh Clerkis praisin wymen but a lite,
  There can no men in humblesse them acquite
    As wymen can, ne ben thei half so true,
    As wymen ben, but it befalle of-newe.
 	
        (*ClT*, 932–8; Urry, pp.103-4)
	On JOB, Priests flourish still, with wond'rous
	                        Ease,
	And Priests on JOB may flourish, if They please.
	We mean not, here, to enter the Dispute.
	Yet Priests can prove, a Woman is a Brute;
	And, (when it serves their Turn) a Man, a God:
	But 'tis the safest Way to kiss the Rod.
	Yet when the MAN OF UZ, whose perfect Life,
	They gloss, and blazon the intemp'rate Wife,
	Who bade Him to his Face, curse God and die;
	Mean They the Sex? Sure, Priests may err or lye!
	Yet, not to stab the Church, but gently probe,
	I say, GRISELDA far transcended JOB!
	And fast as Men, cou'd Women Texts expound,
	As many Female Suff'rers wou'd be found!
	Women than Men, more patient, and more true!
	This is my Faith,—But then, It holds of Few.
	     (Ogle, *Gualtherus and Griselda*, p. 80)

Though Ogle takes from Petrarch and Boccaccio whatever side swipes at common female behaviour he can, entering imaginatively, and with some delight, into the minds of the venal and the snobbish, the vacuous and the vain, his governing notion seems to be that Griselda is an example of female heroism, out-Jobing Job in patience. Her resolution in the face of her husband's cruelty is in marked contrast (a contrast not found in Chaucer) to the triviality, venality, materialism, and mendacity of all the other women in the poem. The pathos evoked by the suffering of the patient wife is mingled with admiration of her heroic self-possession. Her fortitude is almost Homeric. After the removal of her children, she is 'Collected in Herself', like Ulysses facing the Trojan army alone in Pope's *Iliad*.[45] And in reflecting, in her retirement, that 'Mind' 'Can make a Hell of Heav'n, a Heav'n of Hell', she echoes the heroic resolve of Milton's Satan, but entirely without any hint of Satan's self-delusion.[46]

In his moral to the tale, Ogle's clerk, like that of Petrarch and Chaucer, distinguishes between God's testing and temptation: God 'tempts not: tho' He tries'. The tale, on this reading, is a moral fable about the trials imposed on man and woman by an austere but just Deity. The Clerk offers, in conclusion, a 'Maxim': 'All, that fortunes, fortunes for the Best'.[47] But at this point in Ogle's version, the pilgrim 'Chaucer, who close attended, from the Ground / His musing Eyes uprais'd, and look'd around' and offers 'One Word of Epilogue'. Maintaining that 'A merry Moral suits a serious Tale', Ogle's Chaucer turns to support the Wife of Bath:

> Hence, let our Pray'rs the Wife of BATH befriend,
> Whose Life, and Sect, ye Pow'rs of Love defend.
> Still may her Tongue the sov'reign Rule maintain;
> And never may her Hand relax the Rein.
> Free may She live, in undisturb'd Delight,
> All Day in Revel, and in Bliss all Night.
>
> (Ogle, *Gualtherus and Griselda*, p. 105)

Chaucer's Clerk also moved from austere moralism to a cheerfully jesting song in support of the Wife of Bath and her doctrine. Ogle has transferred this move from pathos to humour from the Clerk to the fictional figure of Chaucer. In the fiction as now conducted, Ogle's Clerk smiles at Chaucer's merry remarks, but the Host takes offence: 'Roundly he spoke, and horribly he swore'. His complaint, as in Chaucer, is that his own wife is 'an errant Shrew'.[48] Ogle seems to have been entirely at ease with the multiple interpretations and applications of the tale—as he is with the counteracting of sustained pathos with a comic return to common life, within the pilgrimage and beyond.

It may be significant that the term *romantic* is applied to the poem only in the words ascribed to the pilgrim Chaucer:

> And You, ye Wives of Spirit, above Wrongs,
> Let no such mean Example nail your Tongues.

[45] *The Iliad of Homer*, 11. 511; Pope, *Poems*, 8. 56.
[46] Ogle, *Gualtherus and Griselda*, p. 82; cp. Milton, *Paradise Lost*, 1. 254–5.
[47] Ogle, *Gualtherus and Griselda*, p. 104.
[48] Ibid. pp. 108–9.

Let, never, moral Poet of your Age,
Fill, with your Duty, one Romantic Page.
(Ogle, *Gualtherus and Griselda*, p. 106)

The Clerk's tale itself is described as 'romantic'—the term being used here to suggest not so much a fantastical or magical story but a moral fable of an *idealizing* kind, conducted at some distance from 'real life'. But the 'moral' content of the tale has been complicated in Ogle's version by his enhanced psychological realism, which has given us deeper insights into Griselda's consciousness than we are allowed in Chaucer's original. And the different perspectives provided by Chaucer are sharpened by Ogle's assignment of them to different persons. Attention is diverted by the *Clerk* from the pathos at the centre of the tale to the Clerk's Christian injunctions to 'Mankind' as a whole, and then by the pilgrim *Chaucer's* comic reorientation of the tale to a broader consideration of the pains and pleasures of marriage, and by his placing of the Clerk, in calling him a 'Modest Scholar … Who with much Decency much Truth has told'. Ogle's collection of *The Canterbury Tales*, in which his version of *The Clerk's Tale* forms the final item, ends on a distinctly comic note, with the *Host* complaining that 'no tame *Griselda* is our Wife' and wishing 'some kind Priest' would 'forge the Papal Bull' to bring his marriage to an end: '*Annull*, should be my Instant Song, *Annull*.'[49]

William Wordsworth and the Prioress

There is, however, nothing remotely comic in William Wordsworth's reading of *The Prioress's Tale*. Wordsworth, as we have seen, accompanied the publication of this version with a note where he suggested that, while he had made 'no further deviation from the original' than the necessary changes in language, 'especially in pronunciation', it remained the case 'that much was to be removed'. The Chaucerian phrases retained, as well as some of the replacements, represented 'sprinklings of antiquity' that would, Wordsworth said, have 'a graceful accordance with the subject'.[50] Those last phrases are particularly significant. Wordsworth was presenting *The Prioress's Tale* as a voice from the distant past.

Wordsworth's choice of *The Prioress's Tale* was unusual. Though Warton and others had commented variously upon the character of the Prioress, her tale had caused little comment.[51] One reviewer of Wordsworth's version expressed his

---

[49] Ogle, 3. 251.

[50] Wordsworth's *Prioress's Tale* includes some attempts to use old words in defiance of their usual (for Wordsworth's readers) associations. Mindful perhaps of Tyrwhitt's gloss on 'Bote' ('Remedy; Help; Profit'), Wordsworth's Prioress praises Mary 'Maid and Mother free', with the claim that 'she herself is honour, and the root / Of goodness, next her Son, *our soul's best boot*' (ll. 13–14).

[51] The notable exception being the comments of William Hazlitt, in his *Lectures on the English Poets* (London, 1818). For discussion of Hazlitt's possible influence on Wordsworth's decision to publish his

dislike of the tale with some vehemence: 'It is horrible in its facts, disgusting in its narration, and odiously profane in its language.'[52] Another appears to have taken Chaucer's poem almost as a parody of Roman Catholic superstition and credulity, while recognizing that Wordsworth had found it full of pathos:

> The legend is so exquisitely absurd that it must have been designed as a burlesque on the lying martyrological wonders of the Romish priesthood … When Chaucer wrote, such fables were not too gross for the vulgar credulity; but we know not for what purpose they are transplanted into modern poetry. To Mr. Wordsworth, indeed, we can conceive that such tales would recommend themselves by their very puerility; that he would be even melted into tears by the affected solemnity of a sly old humorist like Chaucer; and that was meant by him for satire, might be mistaken by our Author for pathos.[53]

Reprinting his version in 1827 with no substantial alteration, Wordsworth added a half-concessionary, half-defiant note: 'The fierce bigotry of the Prioress forms a fine background for her tender-hearted sympathies with the Mother and Child; and the mode in which the story is told amply atones for the extravagance of the miracle.'[54] This comment represents a transference of central interest from the passions of the characters in the tale—the principal concern of most earlier readers of most of Chaucer's tales—to the tender-hearted passions of the teller herself.

Wordsworth's only significant colouring of Chaucer's poem comes in an inter-polated line (underlined below)—the single instance of his breaking the stanza form that is otherwise adhered to with unfailing scrupulousness:

Thus hath this widewe hire litel sone ytaught	This Widow thus her little Son hath taught
Oure blisful Lady, Cristes moder dere,	Our blissful Lady, Jesu's Mother dear,
To worship ay, and he forgate it naught:	To worship aye, and he forgat it not;
For sely childe wol alway sone lere.	For simple infant hath a ready ear.
But ay, whan I remembre on this matere,	Sweet is the holiness of youth: and hence,
Seint Nicholas stant ever in my presence,	Calling to mind this matter when I may,
For he so yong to Crist did reverence.	Saint Nicholas in my presence standeth aye,
	For he so young to Christ did reverence.
(PrT, 509–15, Tyrwhitt 1775–78, 2. 51)	*(Wordsworth, Translations, ed. Graver, p. 39)*

If the defining general comment, 'Sweet is the holiness of youth', may be attributed to William Wordsworth, the memory of Saint Nicholas comes, presumably, in the voice of Madame Eglantine the Prioress. In the version by William Lipscomb, there had been no first-person pronouns at all:

---

version of *The Prioress's Tale*, and of the relation of Wordsworth's translation to his other work at the time, see Bruce Graver, 'Why Chaucer's Prioress?', *The Wordsworth Circle*, 51 (2020), 92–103.

[52] *The British Review, and London Critical Journal*, 16 (September 1820), p. 52.

[53] *Eclectic Review*, August 1820, XIV (second series), p. 1803, cited in Wordsworth, *Translations*, ed. Graver, p. 18.

[54] Quoted in Wordsworth, *Translations*, ed. Graver, p. 36.

His mind by early grace aright endued,
Constant his mother's precepts he pursued;
And, like St. Nicholas, to the holy Maid
From earliest infancy due homage paid.

(Lipscomb 3. 196)

Much in Lipscomb's account is softened or flattened. The 'Jewerye' in which the boy
has his throat cut becomes 'one street (a fair and noble space)' assigned 'to Abram's
worldly race'.[55] On the other hand, at the end of the tale, 'vengence just' 'pursues'
the 'murderous Jews / And with wild horses each asunder draws'.[56] Wordsworth,
at the same juncture, is closer to the fierce bigotry of his original in both having his
'Provost' tear 'every one' of his 'bad Jews' apart with wild horses and then hanging
them:

Who will do evil, evil shall he bear;
Them therefore with wild horse did he draw,
And after he hung them by the law.

(Wordsworth, *Translations*, ed. Graver, p. 43)

Wordsworth finds a strange pathos in the amalgamation of—rather than contrast
between—'fierce bigotry' and 'tender-hearted sympathies with the Mother and
Child':

With Mother's pity in her breast enclosed
She goeth, as she were half out of her mind
To every place wherein she hath supposed
By likelihood her little Son to find:
And ever on Christ's Mother meek and kind
She cried, till to the Jewry she was brought,
And him among the accursed Jews she sought.

(Wordsworth, *Translations*, ed. Graver, p. 43)

While *The Prioress's Tale* may have constituted, at least for Wordsworth, a striking example of violent pathos, it contained nothing remotely corresponding to the
Wartons' category of 'the romantic'. For that we have to look elsewhere.

Cambuscan, Sir Thopas, and Don Quixote

Joseph Warton, as we have seen, wished that Pope had 'exercised his pencil ...
above all, on Cambuscan and Canace', and presumably included this poem, *The*

---

[55] Lipscomb, 3. 196.
[56] Ibid. 3. 201.

Squire's Tale, among those of the 'serious and sublime species'. On the contents page of Thomas Warton's *History of English Poetry*, it is described as '*Chaucer's capital poem*', and in the *History* itself Warton has high praise for

> a mode of fabling, whose sublime extravagancies constitute the marvellous graces of … CAMBUSCAN; a composition which at the same time abundantly demonstrates, that the manners of romance are better calculated to answer the purposes of pure poetry, to captivate the imagination, and to produce surprise, than the fictions of classical antiquity.[57]

The fondness of the Wartons for the 'sublime extravagancies' of *The Squire's Tale* was shared by many, particularly since it was seen to have been powerfully endorsed by the enthusiasm of two of Chaucer's most eminent sons, Edmund Spenser and John Milton. For some, 'Cambuscan', unfinished as it was, was *the* characteristic Chaucerian poem, and enthusiasm for it became particularly prominent in the later years of the eighteenth century.[58]

The peculiarity is that it was the *unwritten* rather than the extant *Squire's Tale* that most appealed to the imagination of readers. Such seems to have been the case even with John Milton, who, in *Il Penseroso*, invokes Chaucer as the poet

> … who left half told
> The story of *Cambuscan* bold,
> Of *Camball*, and of *Algarsife*,
> And who had *Canace* to wife,
> That own'd the vertuous Ring and Glass,
> And of the wondrous Hors of Brass,
> On which the *Tartar* King did ride;
> And if ought els, great *Bards* beside,
> In sage and solemn tunes have sung,
> Of Turneys and of Trophies hung;
> Of Forests, and inchantments drear,
> Where more is meant than meets the ear.
>
> (109–20)

In the existing fragment of *The Squire's Tale*, these matters belong to the future of the story, as summarized by its narrator just before the tale is aborted. The 'wondrous Hors of Brass', as Warton lamented, 'vanishes on a sudden, and we hear no more of him':

> Every reader of taste and imagination must regret, that instead of our author's tedious detail of the quaint effects of Canace's ring, in which a falcon relates her amours, and

---

[57] Warton, *History*, 1. iv, 434

[58] Anderson (*Poets of Great Britain*, 1.vii) explicitly endorsed Thomas Warton's judgement. John Penn, in the Preface to his Critical and Poetical Works (London, 1797), described *The Squire's Tale* as 'perhaps' Chaucer's 'principal poem' (p. iii). Samuel Egerton Brydges, in *Theatrum Poetrum Anglicanorum* (London, 1800) , judged that it was 'written in the higher strain of poetry' and noted that it was 'the poem by which Milton describes and characterises Chaucer' (p. 9).

talks familiarly of Troilus, Paris, and Jason, the notable atchievements we may suppose to have been performed by the assistance of the horse of brass, are either lost, or that this part of the story, by far the most interesting, was never written.[59]

For Warton, and for several others, the 'most interesting' part of the story, never having been written, is to be re-imagined by readers of taste. Chaucer's 'principal poem', that is, existed only as a speculation. But for some readers, the fact that Chaucer had left untold the tale of Cambuscan—an imaginary poem of 'Gothic chivalry'—acted precisely as a stimulus for creative activity of their own. While John Penn's version, first published in his privately printed *Poems* of 1794, reproduced *The Squire's Tale* as 'a fragment from Chaucer' (see Fig. 10.3), a fuller attempt at recreation is represented by the version of Samuel Boyse, which was accompanied in Ogle's collection of 1741 by a version by Ogle himself of Spenser's continuation of *The Squire's Tale* in Books 3 and 4 of *The Faerie Queene*.[60] Versions of Chaucer's poem reached their ultimate conclusion in Richard Wharton's *Cambuscan, an Heroic Poem, in Six Books: Founded upon and Comprizing a Free Imitation of Chaucer's Fragment on that Subject*.[61]

Earlier attempts to complete the poem by John Lane (1615; revised 1630) and even Edmund Spenser were not highly regarded by Thomas Warton. He imagined

Fig. 10.3 Illustration to 'The Squire's Tale Modernized', in John Penn,
Poems, In Two Volumes (London, 1801).

---

[59] Warton, *History*, 1. 414.

[60] The version was further extended in Joseph Sterling, *Cambuscan, or the Squire's Tale of Chaucer, Modernized by Mr Boyce; Continued from Spencer's Fairy Queen by Mr Ogle, and Concluded by Mr Sterling* (Dublin, 1785).

[61] Published in Volume 2 of Richard Wharton's, *Fables: Consisting of Select Parts from Dante, Berni, Chaucer and Ariosto*, (London, 1805).

a poem that would have been 'romantic', 'gothick' and 'chivalric' in a way that none of the extant poems in Urry's canon could claim to be. Cambuscan's 'notable atchievements' with 'the assistance of the horse of brass' would have provided a wonderful escape from the eighteenth century, and possibly a way forward for a 'higher' or 'purer' strain of modern poetry, in which there would be as little connection as possible with the common life of the modern world.

There was a difficulty, however. Warton thought the 'imagination' of the story told by the Squire 'consists in Arabian fiction engrafted on Gothic chivalry'.[62] But his admiration for other examples of 'Gothic chivalry' was limited. He described medieval tournaments as a 'strange mixture of foppery and ferocity', long descriptions of which were to be deplored.[63] When Chaucer, in *The Man of Law's Tale*, cuts short a description of a wedding, Warton commented:

> I suspect that Chaucer, not perhaps without ridicule, glances at some of these descriptions, with which his age abounded; and which he probably regarded with less reverence, and read with less edification, than did the generality of his cotemporary readers.[64]

Warton thought that some of the long descriptions in *The Knight's Tale* were also intended as parody, but the telling—and troubling—exhibit was the poem Warton called the 'Rime of Sir Thopas':

> Chaucer, at a period which almost realised the manners of romantic chivalry, discerned the leading absurdities of the old romances: and in this poem, which may be justly called a prelude to Don Quixote, has burlesqued them with exquisite passages.[65]

The mention of Cervantes, often repeated in discussions of the 'Rime of Sir Thopas', is significant. *Don Quixote* was for many readers the work that at one and the same time destroyed the claims of romance and demonstrated its delusionary attractions:

> Cervantes shews a man, who having, by the incessant perusal of incredible tales, subjected his understanding to his imagination, and familiarised his mind by pernicious meditation to trains of incredible events and scenes of impossible existence, goes out in the pride of knighthood, to redress wrongs, and defend virgins, to rescue captive princesses, and tumble usurpers from their thrones.[66]

There would seem to be some contradiction between the notion that Chaucer's genius had led him, as it was to lead Cervantes, to reject the follies of the old romances

---

[62] Warton, *History*, 1. 389.
[63] Ibid. 1. 332.
[64] Ibid. 1. 333.
[65] Ibid. 1. 433.
[66] Johnson, *Works*, 21. 215. Johnson had great sympathy with the Knight of Mournful Countenance: 'When we pity him, we reflect on our own disappointments, and when we laugh, our hearts inform us that he is not more ridiculous than ourselves, except that he tells what we have only thought' (*Works*, 3. 11).

in favour of truth to nature and common sense and the notion that *Cambuscan*, with its magic horse, talking birds, and apparently wandering indirection, was his 'principal poem'.

Richard Hurd and 'The Rime of Sir Thopas'

These apparently contradictory tendencies are clear in *Letters on Chivalry and Romance* (1762) by Richard Hurd, on which Thomas Warton was drawing. Hurd's desire was to convince his readers 'to think with more respect, than is commonly done of the Gothic manners … as adapted to the uses of the greater poetry'. He distinguished sharply between gothic *subjects*, of which he approved, and gothic *literary forms*, of which he did not. His leading contention was that 'these phantoms of chivalry had the misfortune to be laughed out of countenance by men of sense, before the substance of it had been fairly and truly represented by any capable writer'. The case is complicated, since for Hurd Chaucer was principal among the 'men of sense' who had 'laughed' the 'phantoms of chivalry out of countenance': Chaucer, for Hurd, is 'an immortal genius', 'sagacious' and vastly 'superior' to the 'age' in which he lived, a man who 'not only discerned the absurdity of the old romances, but has even ridiculed them with incomparable spirit'. As it was to be for Thomas Warton, Hurd's primary evidence of Chaucer's attitude was Chaucer's 'Rime of Sir Topaz', which he thought 'is a manifest banter on these books, and may be considered as a sort of prelude to the adventures of Don Quixot' (see Fig. 10.4). When 'the good sense of the Host is made to break in upon him', Chaucer 'approves his disgust' and tells '*a moral tale virtuous*' in order 'to shew, what sort of fictions were most expressive of real life, and most proper to be put in the hands of the People'.[67]

Fig. 10.4 Sir Thopas from *The Works of Chaucer: Compared with the Former Editions, and Many Valuable MSS*, ed. John Urry (London, 1721), the only poem to be illustrated in Urry's edition. In all other cases, it is the teller who is illustrated.

[67] Richard Hurd, *Letters on Chivalry and Romance* (2nd edn, London, 1762), pp. 59, 106–9 . Thomas Percy also read 'Sir Thopas' as a deliberate burlesque of metrical romances and therefore a tribute to

Such an understanding was common. William Lipscomb, who dedicated his collected *Canterbury Tales* to Joseph Warton, his old Headmaster, chose to render 'The Rime of Sir Topaz' as a mock-ballad—but not without some affection for the form:

> Now, lordlings all, and ladies free,
>   Attend with gracious ear;
> Love feats, and deeds of chivalry,
>   Delighted ye shall hear.
>
> Let others wondrous tales rehearse,
>   Of Bevis and Sir Guy:
> Sir Thopas swells my nobler verse,
>   (The flower of chivalry.)
>
> His steed he strode, and forth he flew,
>   Like sparkle out of brand;
> His crest a tower wav'd fierce to view,
>   The while he scour'd the land.
>
> Beneath the sky the night he pass'd,
>   His helm sustain'd his head,
> And with kind nature's rich repast
>   Himself his palfrey fed.
>
> He, like the good Sir Percival
>   Drank of the crystal stream,
> Till on a day——————

(Lipscomb, 3. 212–13)

At this point, Chaucer is interrupted by the Host, who complains of 'tedious rhiming': 'Fatigued already is each sated ear, / And more in truth we cannot, will not hear!'. As in the original, the mockery is directed at the doggerel verse more than the absurdities of the narrative, which contain no more improbabilities than *The Squire's Tale*. But for Richard Hurd, the conduct—or lack of direction—of the tale is to be distinguished from that of *The Squire's Tale*: 'The Rime of Sir Topaz' is 'managed with infinite humour to expose the leading impertinences of books of chivalry, and their impertinencies only; as may be seen by the different conduct of this tale from that of Cambuscan, which Spenser and Milton were so pleased with'.[68]

Chaucer's intelligence. Introducing 'The Turnament of Tottenham: Or, the Wooeing, Winning, and Wedding of Tibbe, the Reev's Daughter There', Percy wrote:
> It does honour to the good sense of this nation, that while all Europe was captivated with the bewitching charms of Chivalry and Romance, two of our writers in the rudest times could see thro' the false glare that surrounded them, and discover whatever was absurd in them both. Chaucer wrote his Rhyme of Sir Thopas in ridicule of the latter.
>   (Thomas Percy, *Reliques of Ancient English Poetry*, 3 vols (London, 1765), 2. 13).

[68] Hurd, *Letters on Chivalry*, p. 108.

The potential contradiction between admiration for *The Squire's Tale* and the burlesque *Rime* was not noticed. Robert Anderson's *Life of Chaucer*, prefixed to his edition of Chaucer's works, was in complete agreement with Hurd and Warton: 'In delineating Chaucer's talent for humour, Mr. Warton agrees with Dr. Hurd, who, in his "Letters on Chivalry," supposes that the *Rime of Sir Thopas*, was intended to expose the leading absurdities of the old romance ... and therefore the tale may justly be called a prelude to Don Quixote.' But at the same time, he observes that 'the *Squier's Tale* is considered by Mr. Warton as Chaucer's capital poem.'[69]

Thomas Tyrwhitt, however, while endorsing the suggestions of Hurd and Warton in some respects ('the Rime of Sire Thopas was intended as a burlesque of the old ballad romances'), was less inclined to support Warton's notion that *Cambuscan* was Chaucer's 'capital poem': 'in this age of levity, I doubt some Readers will be apt to regret that he did not rather give us the remainder of *Sir Thopas*.'[70]

George Ogle, Samuel Boyse, and *Cambuscan*

In August 1740, *The Gentleman's Magazine* printed a letter signed 'Alcæus', the usual pseudonym of the poet Samuel Boyse:

> Sir, as there is a very noble Edition of the Prince of our *English* Poets, in a modern Dress, preparing for the Publick, it may not be disagreeable to some of your Readers to present them with a Specimen of that Undertaking, which I hope the generous Editor will forgive me for, as it proceeds from an Apprehension you may receive the Part I send you, in more incorrect form from another Quarter.[71]

The letter served as an introduction to some stanzas representing '*The Character* and *Speech* of Cosroes *the Mede*. An Improvement in [sic] the *Squire's Tale* of Chaucer. In the Manner of Spenser. Inscribed to George Ogle, Esq'. The title is followed by an account of the 'Argument' of the relevant part of Chaucer's tale:

> *Cambuscan (King of* Tartary*) having received an inchanted brazen Horse (with other Presents) from the Arabian Caliph, and a Dispute arising about the secret Cause of his Qualities the King sends for* Cosroes, *a* Persian *Philosopher, whose Character and Speech follow.*

In September of the same year, *The Gentleman's Magazine* printed a reply: 'Verses occasioned by the Translation of Chaucer in your last Magazine.'[72] 'The Muse ordains', wrote the correspondent, that 'future bards' will, like 'Alcaeus' spread 'Chaucer's endless strains' from 'age to age, / Not by their own inferior thought, / But by restoring what he wrote'. This is a surprising comment, since the 'Character

[69] Anderson, *Poets of Great Britain*, 1. vii-viii.
[70] Tyrwhitt 1798, 2. 482; 1. 106.
[71] 'Alcæus', 'Letter', *The Gentleman's Magazine*, 10 (August 1740) 404.
[72] *The Gentleman's Magazine*, 10, (September 1740) 463.

and Speech' of 'Cosroes, a Persian Philosopher' were entirely of Boyse's invention. Insofar as Boyse might be thought to be responding to anything in *The Squire's Tale*, it would seem to reside in the respect and sympathy which are exhibited for the customs and religion of the Persian court of Cambuscan, which are expressed in attributing to 'Cosroes the Mede' the wisdom that while 'All that we see in Life's deceitful Dream' 'glides away', 'Only the great *Orosmanes* shines the same/ Unwasted Fountain of eternal Day'.[73]

A revised version of Boyse's 'Speech of Cosroe the Mede' was included, along with Boyse's version of *The Squire's Tale*, in the Ogle *Canterbury Tales*. The transition from the version of Chaucer's tale to Spenser's continuation is unsignalled. Even the stanza numbers run continuously. The only indication of change of authorships is a footnote: '*What follows is continued by* Mr. OGLE, *from the Fourth Book of* SPENSER's Fairy Queen.'[74] Ogle found it possible to represent Spenser's continuation of *The Squire's Tale* with fewer additions than Boyse had brought to Chaucer—particularly when Spenser presented him with large general statements on the human condition:

O why doe wretched men so much desire,	O! why do wretched Men so much desire
To draw their dayes vnto the vtmost date,	To draw their Days to the remotest Date?
And doe not rather wish them soone expire,	Why do not rather wish Them to expire,
Knowing the miserie of their estate,	Knowing the certain Mis'ry of their State?
And thousand perills which them still awate,	Tost like the Vessel on the surging Wave,
Tossing them like a boate amid the mayne,	What Ills await Them, threat'ning to devour!
That euery houre they knocke at deathes gate?	One Danger, from the Cradle to the Grave,
And he that happie seemes and least in payne	Attends; for Death attends Them ev'ry Hour!
Yet is as nigh his end, as he that most doth	And Who most happy seems, and least complains,
playne.	Is yet, as near his End, as He that suffers Pains!
(*The Faerie Queene*, IV. iii. 1)	(Ogle, 2. 288–9)

Not all eighteenth-century readers of *The Squire's Tale* were drawn to passages that might be seen in one way or another as 'extravagant' or 'magical'. Alexander Pope, for example, reading the poem as a boy in his copy of Speght's edition of 1598, marked lines of which he particularly approved with commas. One set of commas accompany lines generalizing from the wild speculations and confusions of the court when attempting to explain the existence and operation of the magic horse:

> As leude people demeth comenly
> Of things that ben made more subtelly
> Than they can in her leudnesse comprehende
> They demen gladly to the badder ende.
>
>   (*SqT*, 221–4; Speght 1598, Fol. 26ᵛ).

---

[73] In *The Gentleman's Magazine* version (but not in the revised text included in Ogle's *Canterbury Tales*) there is a footnote: 'great Orasmenes … *Under this Name the ancient* Persians *adored God*'. The speech is quoted above from the *Gentleman's Magazine* version.

[74] Ogle, 2. 277.

These are the lines, and this the impasse, that prompted Boyce to introduce 'Cosroes *the Mede*' into the poem. But the nature of Pope's rather different interest is suggested by a second marked passage, which describes a law common to birds and to humankind:[75]

> Men louen of kinde newfangelnesse
> As briddes don that men in cages fede
> For thogh thou nyght & day take of hem hede
> And strawe hir cage faire and soft as silke
> And giue hem sugre, hony, breed and milke
> Yet right anon as that his dore is up
> He with his fete wold sporne adoun his cup
> And to the wood he wold, and wormes eate
>
> (*SqT*, 610–18; Speght 1598, Fol. 26ᵛ)

Here, Pope seems drawn to a passage in *The Squire's Tale* that offers shrewd observation of the natural and human conduct rather than fantastical extravagance. Pope seems generally to have regarded romance with a degree of affectionate mockery. As we saw in Chapter 6, he described a 'spacious Garden' in *January and May* as 'A Place to tire the rambling Wits of *France* / In long Descriptions, and exceed *Romance*'. In *The Rape of the Lock*, the Baron builds an altar 'Of twelve vast French *Romances*, neatly gilt'. Later in the poem, when Clarissa gives the Baron a pair of scissors, Pope comments, 'So Ladies in Romance assist their Knight, / Present the Spear, and arm him for the Fight'.[76] At the same time, Pope took intense and recreative enjoyment in re-imagining the fairies, in a post-*Midsummer Night's Dream* spirit, as Sylphs. It is the *length* of the descriptions and the vast bulk of French Romances that are the butt of the jokes—as it was the 'frivolous descriptions, and other tedious impertinencies, so common in the volumes of chivalry with which his age was overwhelmed' that Warton thought Chaucer had mocked in 'Sir Thopas'.[77]

Thomas Warton, Alexander Pope, and Samuel Johnson on the 'Middle Ages'

For Thomas Warton, Chaucer's writings, in whatever form or genre, had transcended the 'times' in which they were composed, and which were not, as he saw it, propitious:

---

[75] See Maynard Mack, *Collected in Himself: Essays Critical, Biographical, and Bibliographical on Pope and Some of His Contemporaries* (Newark, DE, 1982), p. 188:
Pope's commas … seem intended to signal observations of psychological interest, the kind of thing that Pope must have had in mind in stressing Chaucer's mastery of 'manners'. The first notes the response of ignorance to whatever is unfamiliar or complex … the second … dwells on human nature's love of freedom and change.

[76] Pope, *Poems*, 2. 36, 161, 177.

[77] Warton, *History*, 1. 434.

Their luxury was inelegant, their pleasures indelicate, their pomp cumbersome and unwieldy. In the mean time it may seem surprising, that the many schools of philosophy which flourished in the middle ages, should not have corrected and polished the times. But as their religion was corrupted by superstition, so their philosophy degenerated into sophistry.[78]

Alexander Pope's survey of the years before Erasmus was broadly similar:

> With *Tyranny*, then *Superstition* join'd,
> As that the *Body*, this enslav'd the *Mind*;
> All was *Believ'd*, but little *understood*,
> And to be *dull* was constru'd to be *good*;
> A *second* Deluge Learning thus o'er-run,
> And the *Monks* finish'd what the *Goths* begun.
>
> (*An Essay on Criticism*, 690–5; Pope, *Poems*, 1. 317–18)

For Samuel Johnson, 'The *English* nation' as late as 'the time of *Shakespeare*, was yet struggling to emerge from barbarity'. By 'barbarity', Johnson was probably thinking particularly of ignorance of Greek, but such ignorance had literary consequences:

Nations, like individuals, have their infancy. A people newly awakened to literary curiosity, being yet unacquainted with the true state of things, knows not how to judge of that which is proposed as its resemblance. Whatever is remote from common appearances is always welcome to vulgar, as to childish credulity; and of a country unenlightened by learning, the whole people is the vulgar. The study of those who then aspired to plebeian learning was laid out upon adventures, giants, dragons, and enchantments.

'Adventures, giants, dragons, and enchantments' are, for Johnson, typical elements of old romance. Dramatists before Shakespeare, Johnson believed, had created 'hyperbolical or aggravated characters, by fabulous and unexampled excellence or depravity', just as 'the writers of barbarous romances invigorated the reader by a giant and a dwarf; and he that should form his expectations of human affairs from the play, or from the tale, would be equally deceived'.[79]

Admirers of Chaucer tended to place the revival of a literature concerned with 'human affairs' and 'the true state of things' rather earlier than Johnson. Many, like George Ogle, thought that a kind of Renaissance had occurred in the Italy of Petrarch and Boccaccio, and that it was from this that Chaucer had drawn his essential inspiration. For such readers, Chaucer was the supreme medieval poet largely because he had rejected the absurdities, extravagances, and 'barbarous romances' of his 'gothic' predecessors—and, in this, had anticipated Cervantes and Shakespeare.

[78] Ibid. 1. 139.
[79] Johnson, *Works*, 7. 82.

The differences between Johnson's account of Shakespeare and that of Chaucer's admirers did not merely turn on considerations of history and chronology, or on the *mere* presence, or absence, of fantastical elements in works of literature. And—despite some of the Wartons' more extreme hankering, on occasion, after a 'pure' or 'higher' form of poetry that had little connection with quotidian human realities—the criteria of literary excellence both for Johnson and Chaucer's admirers were not those of strict or mere naturalism or verisimilitude. Despite his celebrated praise, in No. 4 of *The Rambler*, of writing that eschews the 'machines and expedients of the heroic romance, and can neither employ giants to snatch away a lady from the nuptial rites, nor knights to bring her back from captivity' nor 'bewilder its personages in desarts, nor lodge them in imaginary castles',[80] Johnson was quite happy to affirm his admiration for several passages in Shakespeare 'where the agency is supernatural'.[81] The first note in his edition of Shakespeare reproduces, with approval, William Warburton's judgement that '*The Tempest* and *The Midsummer Night's Dream*, are the noblest efforts of that sublime and amazing imagination peculiar to Shakespeare, which soars above the bound of nature without forsaking sense: or, more properly, carries nature along with him beyond her established limits'.[82] In Johnson's view, human sentiments and human language could be discerned in Shakespeare's work, however 'unnatural' the setting:

> Shakespeare approximates the remote and familiarizes the wonderful; the event which he represents will not happen, but if it were possible, its effects would probably be such as he has assigned; and it may be said, that he has not only shewn human nature as it acts in real exigences, but as it would be found in trials, to which it cannot be exposed.[83]

Eighteenth-century readers of Chaucer found pleasure in his wilder imaginings both in the comic and more solemn modes, and discovered a wide variety of literary experiences that could not easily be found in contemporary or classical literature: in the fairies that dance in January's garden in *The Merchant's Tale*, at the start of *The Wife of Bath's Tale*, and in *The Flower and the Leaf*; in elaborate visions of Courts of Love; in tales that assume a high degree of sexual tolerance; in some kinds of pathos, in expression and in narrative—including the otherwise 'unexampled excellence' of Patient Griselda.

But, at its best, their pleasure in such features—like Johnson's pleasure in the 'supernatural' elements in Shakespeare—was by no means incompatible with or separable from a pleasure in those aspects of Chaucer that engaged conspicuously with immediately identifiable human susceptibilities and emotions and with

---

[80] Ibid. 3. 19.
[81] Ibid. 7. 64.
[82] Samuel Johnson and George Steevens, eds, *The Plays of William Shakespeare in Ten Volumes* (London, 1778), 1. 3.
[83] Johnson, *Works*, 7. 65.

the larger powers and forces that govern human life. In this respect, despite the Wartons' occasional expressions of longing for a 'pure' or 'higher' poetry removed from all the contingencies of quotidian life, which was sometimes bizarrely identified with the *unwritten* part of Chaucer's *Squire's Tale*, the shared admiration across the period for one of Chaucer's poems, particularly as rendered by Dryden, is of considerable significance. Alexander Pope and Thomas Warton agreed with Warton's brother Joseph that 'whoever will attentively consider the noble poem of Palamon and Arcite, will be convinced that' Chaucer 'excels in the pathetic and sublime'.[84] The 'pathetic' and the 'sublime', in inextricable combination with the 'true, enlivened, way of story telling' could, both Pope and the Wartons agreed, be found—given the right circumstances—in the literature of all periods, ancient and modern, and was a particularly conspicuous characteristic of the poetry of Chaucer, and of his poetical 'son' Dryden.

Quite how Pope reconciled his admiration for Chaucer's poems with his general notions of the Middle Ages is the subject of Chapter 11, which returns to *The Temple of Fame*—the most irregular (and, in that way, the most 'gothic' and 'romantic') of all the Chaucerian poems.

---

[84] J. Warton, *Essay on the Genius and Writings of Pope*, 1. 352.

11

Chaucer and The Temples of Fame

How is it that some poems have been revoiced by successive generations and have prompted new creations, while most are *ephemeroi*, phantoms of a day? This question was continuously on the mind of Alexander Pope in his early twenties. He pursued the matter in *An Essay on Criticism* and in *The Temple of Fame*, a poem where the question is brought into sharp focus by association with Chaucer's *House of Fame*. In this chapter, Pope's response to Chaucer is compared with that of Jane Brereton, in her poem *The Dream*,[1] in an attempt to assess how far the accounts in these poems of the processes by which fame is awarded or renewed might be applied more generally to the survival of Chaucerian poems in the eighteenth century.[2]

'And Such as *Chaucer* Is, Shall *Dryden* Be?'

There was in Pope's mind no doubt that some poets had achieved, and would continue to achieve, fame of an unquestionable kind. In a celebrated passage in his *Essay on Criticism*, lasting and future fame is celebrated as the possession of a few distinctly and explicitly *ancient* '*Bards Triumphant*', whose works, '*Secure from Flames*, from *Envy*'s fiercer *Rage*, / Destructive *War*, and all-devouring *Age*' would

---

[1] Jane Brereton's, 'The Dream: In Imitation of Some Parts of Chaucer's Second and Third Book of Fame', appeared in her *Poems on Several Occasions* (London, 1744), pp. 132–67 (referred to in our text as Brereton, *Poems*).

[2] There was a third version of *The House of Fame*: *The Court of Fancy*, by the young American poet Thomas Godfrey. This places an opposition between fancy and delusion at its centre. The poem has the following headnote:

> The learned reader need not be acquainted that the Author took the hint of the Transition from the Court of Fancy to that of Delusion, from Chaucer's Poem called the House of Fame, where the change is from the House of Fame to that of Rumour; and that he likewise had Mr. Pope's beautiful Poem on that subject in his eye, at the Time when he compos'd this Piece.

See Thomas Godfrey, 'The Court of Fancy', in *Juvenile Poems on Various Subjects* (Philadelphia PA, 1765), pp. 44–64 (p. 44) . Godfrey also composed a free version of *The Parlement of Foules* entitled *The Assembly of Birds*. See Henry Bosley Woolf, 'Thomas Godfrey: Eighteenth-Century Chaucerian', *American Literature*, 12 (1941), 486–90.

Chaucer in the Eighteenth Century. David Hopkins and Tom Mason, Oxford University Press.
© David Hopkins and Tom Mason (2022). DOI: 10.1093/oso/9780192862624.003.0012

be celebrated by 'the *Gen'ral Chorus* of *Mankind*' and whose 'Honours' would 'with Increase of Ages *grow*, / As Streams roll down, *enlarging* as they flow!'[3]

But such praise of the ancients had unfortunate implications for the poets of Pope's own day. One reason that the 'mighty Names' of Pope's '*Bards Triumphant*' would sound in 'Nations *unborn*' is that they wrote in literary languages which had become unchangeably frozen at a particular stage of development. In *The Temple of Fame*, there are no modern names. Modern poets are not likely to last longer than 'fading Beauty' or 'present love' (as Waller put it in his poem 'Of English Verse' quoted in Chapter 1), largely because they 'write in Sand' in a 'daily changing Tongue' that alters, expands, and 'o'er flows' their work 'like the Tide':

> Short is the Date, alas, of *Modern Rhymes*;
> And 'tis but just to let 'em live *betimes*.
> No longer now that Golden Age appears,
> When *Patriarch-Wits* surviv'd a *thousand Years*;
> Now Length of *Fame* (our *second* Life) is lost,
> And bare Threescore is all ev'n That can boast:
> Our Sons their Father's *failing Language* see,
> And such as *Chaucer* is, shall *Dryden* be.
>
> (*An Essay on Criticism*, 476–83; Pope, *Poems*, 1. 292–3)

Many of Pope's readers, however, may have understood Pope's prediction rather differently from the way it was understood by the poet himself. Pope's knowledge of Chaucer's work was unusually extensive for his time. He had been reading Chaucer since he was thirteen in Speght's edition, and probably also in the texts provided in Dryden's *Fables Ancient and Modern*. Where Dryden's engagement with English poetry had been backward, a movement, starting with Cowley and only later turning to Spenser, and then to Chaucer, Pope had been given his first copy of Chaucer in 1701, and he appears to have read it with considerable care. Dryden's Chaucerian versions had appeared in his final volume. The very first publication Pope set before the public was *January and May*, his sparkling version of *The Merchant's Tale*. His collected *Works* of 1717, published when he was only twenty-nine, presented *January and May*, *The Wife of Bath's Prologue,* and Pope's version of *The House of Fame* at its centre, each adorned with a fleuron in which he may have had a hand.

The overt sense of Pope's line, 'And such as *Chaucer* is, shall *Dryden* be' was that Dryden's poems would become as obsolete, as nearly unreadable, as Chaucer's were believed to be by many of Pope's contemporaries. In his *Reflections Critical and Satyrical, upon a Late Rhapsody Call'd An Essay upon Criticism* (1711) John Dennis objected, with characteristic virulence, to Pope's proposition. He suggested that Pope was predicting the future without solid evidence, and expressed his own

---

[3] *An Essay on Criticism*, 189, 183–4, 188, 191–2; Pope, *Poems*, 1. 261–3.

conviction that Dryden's language would never be 'as obsolete as is at present that of *Chaucer*':

> Mr. *Dryden* has one Quality in his Language, which *Chaucer* had not, and which must always remain. For having acquir'd some Justness of Numbers, and some Truth of Harmony and of Versification, to which *Chaucer* thro' the Rudeness of the Language, or want of Ear, or want of Experience, or rather perhaps a mixture of all, could not possibly attain, that Justness of Numbers, and Truth of Harmony and of Versification can never be destroy'd by any alteration of Language; and therefor Mr. Dryden whatever alteration happens to the Language, can never be like to *Chaucer*.[4]

Dennis's assumption that Dryden's 'Justness of Numbers', and 'Truth of Harmony and of Versification' would survive linguistic change was precisely what Pope—conscious from studying Chaucer that harmonious versification is partly dependent upon pronunciation—doubted. Dryden, after all, had himself predicted a time when his own poems might, like Chaucer's require renewal. But a remark in one of Pope's *Observations* on his *Iliad of Homer* might suggest that Pope's prediction was actually susceptible to a rather different interpretation from that of Dennis. In a note to the passage in Book 23 describing the 'felling the forests' for the funeral of Patroclus, Chaucer is named with Spenser as being 'two of the greatest poets of our own nation' who have imitated Statius's imitation of Homer.[5] The excellence of Chaucer's passage, Pope believes, is that in a few lines the epithets given to each tree suggest large areas of human life, and death: building, coffin making, olives of peace, aspen for war, and the drunken vine.[6] Pope here assumes, as if it were a matter beyond dispute, that Chaucer was a poet who belonged with classic figures like Homer, Statius, and Spenser, rather than being susceptible to dismissal as old and unformed. From this example, we might conclude that Pope's prophecy ('and such as *Chaucer* is, shall *Dryden* be?') was a potential prophecy of the *longevity* of both his great predecessors.

Tetrameter, Pentameter, Burlesque, and *The House of Fame*

It is of particular significance that Pope decided to meditate on the problems of enduring fame by renewing Chaucer's *House of Fame*, a poem that might have

---

[4] John Dennis, *Critical Works*, ed. Edward Niles Hooker, 2 vols (Baltimore, MD, 1939–43), 1. 410–11.

[5] In his own copy of Spenser (*Faerie Queene*, I. i. 8–9), Pope wrote 'This fine description of the trees is imitated from Chaucer's Assembly of Foules'. See Valerie Rumbold, 'Pope and the Gothic Past', p. 90 and Maynard Mack, *Collected in Himself*, pp. 295–6.

[6] Pope, *Poems*, 8. 494.

been thought to belong to an almost irredeemably ancient past, in its verse form, vocabulary, and genre.

Pope's major alteration to Chaucer's poem was to replace its octosyllabics with iambic pentameters. At the beginning of Book 3 of the *House of Fame*, Chaucer, having invoked Apollo 'God of Science and of light', declares that he has no wish to exhibit mastery of the arts of poetry and that he is more concerned with 'sentence' than with form:

> Not that I will for maistrye
> Here art potenciall be shewde
> But for the rime is light and lewde
> Yet make it somewhat agreable
> Though som vers fail in a sillable
> And that I do no diligence
> To shew craft, but sentence.
>
> (*HF*, 1094–100; Speght 1598, Fol. 279ᵛ)

Thomas Tyrwhitt, who was extremely reluctant to admit any syllabic uncertainty in Chaucer's iambic pentameters, was untroubled by the irregularity of versification in *The House of Fame*, which 'often consists of nine and sometimes ten syllables; but the eighth is always the last accented syllable'.[7] Where, as we saw in Chapter 5, Tyrwhitt was unwilling to allow a missing syllable in the first foot of an iambic pentameter, such an omission was acceptable, he thought, in Chaucer's octosyllabic lines because a 'Dimeter Iambic' line is transformed into another acceptable form, 'Dimeter Trochaic Catalectic'. So the catalectic line ('God of science and of light') 'sounds as well' to Tyrwhitt's ear as Urry's '*Thou* God of science and of light'.[8]

Tyrwhitt observed that in France the 'octosyllabic verse seems by degrees to have been confined to the several species of lighter compositions, in which it is still used'. This had also become the case in the early years of the English eighteenth century, when octosyllabic couplets had become strongly associated with 'light and lewde' verse. Chaucer's octosyllabics may thus have seemed to Pope to have become—at least for solemn purposes—unusable. The danger of the shorter line was of falling into unintentional burlesque. One child of Chaucer's poem was thought to be the description of the goddess of Fame in Butler's *Hudibras*, a 'dame' who deals both in truth and lies and whose trumpet sounding 'before' is hardly distinguishable from Fame's nether trump 'behind':

> There is a Tall Long-sided Dame,
> (But wond'rous light,) ycleped *Fame*,
> That, like a thin *Camelion* Bourds
> Her self on Ayr, and eats your words:
> Upon her shoulders wings she wears,

---

[7] Tyrwhitt, 1775–78, 1. 80. In Speght's text, there are lines varying from six (as in the last line of the passage quoted) to eleven syllables.
[8] Tyrwhitt, 1775–78, 1. 82.

Like hanging-sleeves, lin'd through with ears,
And eys, and tongues, as *Poets* list,
Made good by deep *Mythologist*.
With these, she through the Welkin flyes,
And sometimes carries *Truth*, oft *Lyes*; …
Two Trumpets she does sound at once,
But both of clean contrary tones;
But whether both with the same wind,
Or one before, and one behind,
We know not; onely this can tell,
The one sounds vilely, th'other well.
And therefore Vulgar *Authors* name
Th' one Good, the other Evil *Fame*.

(Samuel Butler, *Hudibras*, ed. John Wilders [Oxford, 1967],
Part 2 Canto 1, 45–54, 69–76, p. 102)

Pope may also have seen an uncomfortable resemblance between the octosyllabic evocation of Fame in Book 1 of Chaucer's *House of Fame* and the version of Virgil's description of Fame in Book 4 of the *Aeneid* which was included in Charles Cotton's popular burlesque *Scarronides: or, Virgile Travestie*. Cotton's poem had itself adopted the 'wilomes' and 'I weens' common in imitations of 'Chaucerian' style, and his Goddess of Fame grows from a 'little prating slut' to become a 'lusty strapping lass' and a 'baggage':

At this a wench call'd *Fame* flew out
To all the good-Towns round about.
This *Fame* was daughter to a Cryer,
That whilome liv'd in Carthage-Shire,
A little prating slut, no higher,
When *Dido* first arriv'd at *Tyre*,
Than this—But in a few years space
Grown up a lusty strapping lass.
A long and lasie quean I ween
She was, brought up to sow, nor spin,
Nor any kind of Housewifery,
To get an honest living by;
But sauntred idely up and down,
From house to house, and town to town;
To spie and listen after news
Which she so mischievously brews;
That still what ere she sees or hears,
Sets Folks together by the ears.

(Charles Cotton, *Scarronides*, IV. 453–70; *Poems*, ed. Paul
Hartle, 2 vols [Oxford, 2017], 2. 66–7)

Cotton's Fame is at worst an irritant. Though Pope did not ignore the many moments of comedy in *The Temple of Fame*, he clearly wished to recreate a more terrifying Goddess—the figure who had been found by Chaucer in Book 12 of Ovid's *Metamorphoses*, the poem which the guiding Eagle, in *The House of Fame*, calls Chaucer's 'owne booke'. The palace of Ovid's Fame, says the Eagle, stands 'Right euen a middes of the way / Bytwene heuen, yerth, and see'.[9] The Eagle thus 'places' Chaucer's House of Fame in both literary and spatial terms.

In abandoning Chaucer's octosyllabics in favour of the ten-syllable 'heroic' line, Pope may have been encouraged by Dryden's rendering of Ovid's description of Fame's dwelling which Dryden had found to be 'one of the most beautiful Pieces in the whole *Metamorphoses*'.[10] Dryden's version had itself a high reputation, particularly as a representation of sound—in which respect Joseph Warton thought it an improvement upon the original. It was to be taken by Samuel Johnson, in the *Grammar of the English Tongue* prefixed to his *Dictionary*, as a supreme example of the capabilities of the heroic couplet. Dryden's version of the situation of Ovid's 'Palace' of Fame 'in the midst of this Created Space, / Betwixt Heav'n, Earth, and skies'[11] is strikingly close to that of Chaucer's Eagle. At the start of *The Temple of Fame*, when describing his own position in his dream, Pope echoes Dryden's wording, along with Milton's description of the newly created earth.[12]

All this suggests that, for Pope, addressing past, present, and looking towards the future, Chaucer was a writer whose poetic thought had been supported and extended by his poetic sons—particularly Dryden and Milton—and could receive further support and extension from Pope himself. Chaucer's own fame and his poem about fame were highly mutable and therefore different in kind from those of the ancient poets whose names were inscribed on the mountain of ice—or even the statues in the Temple itself. To make a poem that might be current, and was at once Chaucer's and Pope's own, required some recasting or reshaping of almost every element of the original. At the same time, Pope's innovations embody and exemplify profound continuities between the visons of Fame by Ovid, Virgil, and Chaucer, and between Chaucer and his more modern imitators.

Jane Brereton's *Dream*

One cannot, however, generalize from the experience of Alexander Pope to wider eighteenth-century readerly and poetic responses to Chaucer. The posthumously published *Poems on Several Occasions* by Jane Brereton (1744) contains a poem, *The Dream, In Imitation of some Parts of Chaucer's Second and Third Book of Fame*,

[9] *HF*, 714–15; Speght 1598, Fol. 278ʳ.
[10] Dryden, *Works*, 7. 406.
[11] Ibid. 7. 408.
[12] Pope (*Temple of Fame*, 11–13; *Poems* 2. 254) describes himself as standing 'betwixt Earth, Seas, and Skies', and as seeing 'The whole Creation open to [his] Eyes' in which 'In Air self-ballanc'd hung the Globe below'. See Milton, *Paradise Lost*, 7. 242, where the newly created earth 'self-balanc'd on her Center hung'.

which is a lively response to Chaucer's poem—and to Pope's.[13] For Brereton, it appears, *The House of Fame* presented no difficulty—linguistic, generic, or metrical. It is hard to know if her opening comments in the poem are an accurate account of her reading habits, but they are presented as such:

> I Took up *Chaucer* t'other Day,
> To pass some irksome Hours away;
> When I his Book of Fame had read,
> (Which sure with Whimseys fill'd my Head,)
> *Morpheus*, the Sleep-compelling God,
> Soon charm'd me with his leaden Rod.
>
> (Brereton, *Poems*, p. 135)

Brereton describes herself as reading Chaucer as if it were the most easy and natural thing in the world. She imitates Chaucer's short lines delightedly. She also relishes Chaucer's talking Eagle (ignored by Pope), and the other peculiarities of the 'medieval' dream experience. She picks up the book—perhaps Urry's handsome edition—to pass the time, falls asleep, and her own dreams mingle with, or are dictated by, those of Chaucer. She mentions real places, including her own birthplace—the contemplation of which is so disturbing that she would have woken 'If Fancy had not chang'd the Scene' and introduced 'old *Jeffrey*'s Fable, /His wild Conceits, and speaking Eagle' (p. 137) into the dream. Jove's Eagle is given weaker reasons for visiting Brereton than Chaucer, and promises less, but Chaucer's domestic and personal note was clearly welcome to Brereton. She appears to see a resemblance between Chaucer's habitual self-depreciation and her own part-enforced, part-chosen expression of modesty as a provincial woman writer.[14] These are the Eagle's descriptions of the uneventful daily lives of Geoffrey Chaucer—customs officer and compulsive student of poetry—and of Jane Brereton—perpetual seamstress and reader:

For whan thy labour al done is,	Too much thou hast thyself confin'd;
And haste made al thy reckininges,	Thou seldom dost relax thy Mind:
In stede of reste and of newe thinges	Thy Book, and Needle can't delight,
Thou goest home to thy house anone,	From eight at Morn,' till nine at Night.
And al so dombe as any stone	T' amuse Thee now my Care must be;
Thou sittist at anothir boke,	(So *Jove*'s immutable Decree!)
Tyl fully dasid is thy loke,	
And lyvist thus as an Hermite,	
Although thine abstinence is lyte;	

---

[13] Jane Brereton was Pope's close contemporary, being three years older and dying four years before him. Almost all that is known about her derives from the *Account of the Life of Mrs Brereton* (presumably written by her daughter Charlotte) attached to *Poems on Several Occasions*.

[14] Most of Brereton's poems appear to be intended for a close circle of friends, both men and women. Although her works are interestingly various, her favourite stance is that of a woman who, although learned, displays that learning by adapting male tropes (such as those of Horace) to domestic female realities—particularly tea-drinking.

And therfore Jovis through his grace
Wil that I bere The to a place,
Whiche that yhight the house of Fame,
And for to doe The sporte and game ...

(HF, 652–64; Urry, p. 462)

(Brereton, Poems, p. 139)

Brereton has taken her cue from the Eagle's suggestion that the flight will provide 'The sporte and game', but the dream remains *her* dream and is intended to
amuse in both the modern and the eighteenth-century sense of the word. She takes
her tone from Chaucer's exuberance and rapidity, but sees what she would see,
and hears what she would hear in her own life. In giving a list of all that is to be
heard in the house of Rumour (a clamour of the present that might drown out
all purely poetic voices entirely), she is responsive to Chaucer's point by departing
from his instances, but within a metrical pattern closely emulating that of her original, thereby escaping the burlesque potential of Hudibrastics, and thus bringing
out the appropriateness of the metre rather than burlesquing it:

Of werres, of pece, of mariages,	Of various News I much did hear,
Of restes, of labour, of viages	Of Sickness, Health, of Peace and War;
Of abode, of dethe, and of lyfe,	Of Love and Hate, of Death and Life,
Of love, of hate, accorde, of strife,	Of Reconcilements, and of Strife;
Of losse, of lore, and of winninges,	Of rich exhaustless Minerals,
Of hele, of sickenesse, or lesinges	Of Shipwrecks, and of stranded Whales;
Of faire wethir, and tempestis	Of flaming Meteors which appear,
Of qualme, of folke, and of bestis	Like Armies fighting in the Air;
Of divers transmutacions	Of Towns, by Fire in Ashes lost,
Of estates, and eke of regions,	Of Navies on the Ocean tost;
Of trust, of drede, of jalousy	Of Famine, Plenty, Loss and Gain,
Of witte, of winninge, of foly,	Of Thunder, Hurricanes and Rain;
Of plenty, and of grete famine,	Of *India* Stock, and *South Sea* Schemes
Of chepe, of derthe, and of ruine	Of Apparitions, and strange Dreams;
Of gode or of misgovernement,	Of *Lilliputian* Potentate,
Of fyre, and of divers accident.	Of Broils, and Factions in the State;
	Of Miracles vouch'd by the Pope,
	Of Wives who from their Mates elope;
	Of jilted Swains, of Nymphs beguil'd,
	Of monstrous Births, and Men with Child:
	Of these they talk'd, with ceaseless Noise,
	And sometimes mingl'd Truth with Lies.

(HF, 1961–76; Urry, p. 471)[15]
(Brereton, Poems, pp. 163–4)

---

[15] Urry supplies the following glosses: Abode: delay (staying in one place?); Lore: direction, Rule;
Lesyng: Lying; Qualme: grief.

It is tellingly bold that Jane Brereton should, amongst the noise of the present, include news 'Of Wives who from their Mates elope', since that is almost exactly what she herself was reported to have done.[16]

The Practice of the Greatest Geniuses, Both Ancient and Modern

Jane Brereton's confidence and ease is possibly a result of Pope's having won the preliminary battles in seeing the modern potential of *The House of Fame*. The 1715 edition of Pope's *Temple of Fame: A Vision* had included extensive explanatory annotation, sometimes apologetic, sometimes combative. Pope presented his *Vision* as a representative of a newly revived genre, a new direction for new poetry. He described the poem as at one and the same time his own composition and as one that bears a significant, but not merely dependent, relation to Chaucer's. In his 'Advertisement' he wrote:

> *The Hint of the following Piece was taken from* Chaucer's House of Fame. *The Design is in a manner entirely alter'd, the Descriptions and most of the particular Thoughts my own … The Reader who would compare this with Chaucer, may begin with his Third Book of* Fame, *there being nothing in the Two first Books that answers to their Title.*[17]

At the same time as proclaiming his ownership of 'particular thoughts', Pope presented his poem as belonging to the same genre as Chaucer's, a genre that, as he saw it, had been improperly discredited, and to which, significantly, he did not apply the potentially pejorative epithets 'gothic' and 'romantic'. 'Some modern Criticks', he wrote in the first of his 'Notes' to *The Temple of Fame*, 'from a pretended Refinement of Taste, have declar'd themselves unable to relish allegorical Poems.' He then traced the history of the allegorical genre, from poetry 'in the old Provençal' to 'Our Contryman Spenser', and concluded:

> *Upon the whole, one may observe this sort of Writing (however discontinu'd of late) was in all Times … far from being rejected by the best Poets.… to infer … that Allegory it-self is vicious, is a presumptuous Contradiction to the Judgment and Practice of the greatest Genius's, both ancient and modern.*

It is not clear which poets are included in Pope's mention of the 'Judgment and Practice of the greatest Genius's, both ancient and modern'. In the notes to *The*

---

[16] The *Account of the Life of Mrs Brereton* records that 'all who had any Regard for her' advised her to leave her improvident and violent husband. Initially, 'she express'd great Reluctance at it, especially unless she could have her Children with her'. But when that was

> at last brought about, she left *London* about the Year 1721, and retired to her native Country *Wales*, where she led a solitary Life, seeing little Company, except some intimate Friends, Persons of great Merit; well knowing what a critical Case it is to behave without the Censure of the World, when separated from an Husband.

(Brereton, *Poems*, iv).

[17] Pope, *Poems*, 2. 250, 252.

Temple of Fame, Petrarch, Boccaccio, Chaucer, and Spenser are presented as a continuous tradition. Pope's notion that 'this sort of Writing' has been 'discontinu'd' contains the suggestion that it may be revivified—perhaps as a *series* of works. That project would also revive Chaucer's fame, since it was Chaucer—'whose *Romaunt of the Rose*, *Court of Love*, *Flower and the Leaf*, *House of Fame*, and some others of his Writings are Master-pieces of this sort'—who had provided the defining classics of the genre.[18] Pope's emphasis is on Chaucer's potential for shaping the *future* of poetry. In this respect, his thinking, although different from the later demands of the brothers Warton, is no less innovative.

The Animadversions of John Dennis

Just how bold was Pope's, and, later, Jane Brereton's, choice of *The House of Fame* on which to base their own poems can be seen from the response to Pope's poem in another book by John Dennis.[19] In his *Remarks upon Mr. Pope's Translation of Homer*, Dennis complains that Pope's calling the poem a *Vision* 'will apologize for every Extravagance with which he is pleas'd to blot his Paper'[20]—many of which 'extravagances' Dennis is happy to castigate in detail. But, as always, Dennis's objections are bafflingly miscellaneous. Some of his objections to Pope's poem are particularly surprising:

> … this Author has corrupted the Unity of his Design, by unexpectedly shifting his Scene, and deserting *The Temple of Fame* for the Temple of Rumour.[21]

In this, Pope is following his source, and in his copy of the pamphlet he underlined Dennis's 'this Author' and, in the margin, wrote 'Chaucer'.[22] It is remarkable that in the whole course of Dennis's animadversions there is not a single reference to the poem from which Pope had taken his 'hint'. It seems that though Dennis recognized the *name* of Chaucer, he had never actually looked into his works. Dennis's concern throughout is to demonstrate Pope's violation of the laws of nature—and occasionally the laws of poetry. In comparing Pope's description of Fame with that of Virgil, Dennis concedes that 'the Image of *Fame* in Virgil' is 'above Nature' as 'all the Machines of … great Poets are', but objects that Pope's 'Image of the *Temple of Fame*, is contrary to Nature, and to the Eternal Laws of Gravitation'.[23] To this,

---

[18] Ibid. 2. 251. That Pope and Lintott may having been hoping for a revival of Chaucer's currency is hinted by the advertisement for Urry's forthcoming edition (mentioned earlier in the present study) included in some copies of *The Temple of Fame*.

[19] *Remarks on Mr Pope's Translation of Homer. With Two Letters Concerning Windsor Forest, and the Temple of Fame. By Mr Dennis*, (London, 1727).

[20] Dennis, *Critical Works*, 2. 138.

[21] Ibid. 2. 139.

[22] By happy chance, the copy of Dennis's pamphlet recorded on Gale's Eighteenth-Century Collections Online is that marked by Pope.

[23] Dennis, *Critical Works*, 2. 140.

Pope's marginal note responded sardonically, 'which no dream ought to be'. Dennis objects to any sign of what he sees as 'wild', asking, for example, whether the 'Image of a Temple built on a Rock of Ice, self-suspended in the Air', be not 'one of those vain Ideas, or Ideas of Things' which 'never subsist together in Nature, and which are not to be found but in the disorder'd Brains of Men in Fevers, or Madmen, and of Poetasters'.[24]

'Wild Order' and an 'Intellectual Scene'

In all his remarks, Dennis ignored both Chaucer's original and Pope's careful description of the experience he recounts in *The Temple of Fame*. Two borrowed phrases in close conjunction at the start of the poem—'wild Order' and 'Intellectual Scene'—are of importance in defining the nature of Pope's dream and Chaucer's:

> A Train of Phantoms in wild Order rose,
> And, join'd, this Intellectual Scene compose.
> *(Temple of Fame, 9–10; Pope, Poems, 2. 253)*

Pope's couplet, cited together with the lines from Abraham Cowley's *The Complaint* on which he might here be drawing, provide the only citations under Johnson's third definition of the word 'intellectual' in his *Dictionary*: 'Ideal; perceived by the intellect, not the senses'. Pope may have found his 'wild Order' in Dryden's *Eleonora,* where it describes a succession of 'gentle dreams': 'So close they follow, such <u>wild Order</u> keep / We think our selves awake, and are asleep'.[25] Pope's Vision, like Chaucer's, consists of imaginary, non-existent things and is 'wild', but, in that wildness, is sufficiently ordered to present a comprehensible picture to the mind—even of the wild extravagances of the goddess Fame herself.

Pope was so interested in placing the 'wild Order' of his *Vision* in a long line of 'Master-pieces of this sort' that he replaced Chaucer's unconventional opening, where the poet is sleeping in bed in December, with a version modelled closely on the opening of Dryden's *The Flower and the Leaf*. But Pope makes clear that, if he had taken Dryden's rendering of *The Flower and the Leaf* as his model, it was one as much to be resisted as followed. As we saw in Chapter 9, the subtitle of Dryden's poem, *The Lady in the Arbour*, draws attention to the fact that the narrator's voice is that of a woman, and the dream her dream. But Pope is *himself* the dreamer of his 'mysterious Visions'. Several poets followed the example of *The Flower and the Leaf* in producing free modern versions of Chaucerian visionary poems that attributed personalities and an appropriate tone of voice to the dreamer. But in no case is that speaker to be closely identified with the named writer. No author had

[24] Ibid. 2. 140–1.
[25] *Eleonora*, 313–24; Dryden, *Works*, 3. 244.

applied a Chaucerian poem specifically to himself. Pope's example, as we have seen, was followed by Jane Brereton. Dryden had found that he had a 'soul congenial' with Chaucer's. Pope and Brereton took a step closer to the ideal recommended to translators by Wentworth Dillon, Earl Roscommon, who in his *Essay on Translated Verse* advised potential translators to

> seek a *Poet* who *your* way do's bend,
> And chuse an *Author* as you chuse a *Friend*,
> United by this *Sympathetic Bond*,
> You grow *Familiar*, *Intimate*, and *Fond*;
> Your *Thoughts*, your *Words*, your *Stiles*, your *Souls* agree,
> No Longer his *Interpreter*, but *He*.
>
> (Wentworth Dillon, Earl of Roscommon, *An Essay on Translated Verse* [London, 1684], p. 7)

Pope, Brereton, and the Pursuit of Fame

Both Pope and Brereton's versions move towards an ending. Chaucer's poem, in fact, breaks off unfinished, but in Urry's text, the poet suddenly awakes in a fright—which makes it look as if the poem *does* end, albeit inconclusively. Pope judged that Chaucer's poem ended too 'abruptly', and both Pope and Brereton chose to end their poems with an exploration of their own desire for fame—so summarizing all each has heard and seen in the Temple and in the House of Rumour (see Fig. 11.1). Pope reshaped Chaucer's ending by drawing on a passage from elsewhere in *The House of Fame* which, he said, was 'more naturally made the conclusion, with the addition of a *Moral* to the whole'.[26] In *The House of Fame*, Chaucer, on being asked his reason for visiting the House of Rumour, had stated emphatically—particularly in Urry's text, where he appears slightly incredulous—that he had not the slightest wish for Fame:

> With that I gan aboutin wende,
> For one that stode right at my bake
> Me thought ful godely to me spake,
> And sayid, frende, what is thy name?
> Arte thow come hiðer to have fame?
> Have Fame! nay for sothe, frend (quoð I)
> I come nat hithir, grant mercy,
> For no soche causè, by my hed,
> Suffisith me, as I were ded,
> That no wight have my name in honde,
> I wot my selfe best how I stonde,
> For what I drie, or what I thinke,
> I wol my selfin al it drinke,
> Certainly for the morè parte,
> As ferforth as I can mine arte.
>
> (*HF*, 1868–82; Urry, p. 471)

---

[26] Pope, *Poems*, 2. 287.

Fig. 11.1 'The Poet Outside the Temple of Fame'. Illustration by Thomas
Stothard, engraved by James Walker, in Vol. 3 of *The Lady's Poetical
Magazine; or, Beauties of British Poetry* (London, 1782).

Pope replaced Chaucer's firm denial of a wish for fame with a qualified partial ad-
mission that, like all 'youthful Bards', he must be fond of Fame.[27] Jane Brereton

---

[27] 'It is clear that Pope understood Chaucer's original as referring to the art poetical, for in his new
conclusion he speaks of his own person as one of the
  'youthful bards' of his day. ... Evidently Pope, looking back over more than three centuries,
  heard in Geoffrey's credo a voice from past time when English poets had not yet learned

responded to Pope in her reconstruction of the passage, but though her version is profoundly shaped by his version, she takes her own independent path. Her conclusion is closer to Chaucer both in its brevity and the absolute refusal of fame. Pope's and Brereton's versions are here given in parallel:

While thus I stood, intent to see and hear,	Intent I stood to hear, and see,
One came, methought, and whisper'd in my Ear;	When one, methought, thus whisper'd me—
What cou'd thus high thy rash Ambition raise?	"How didst Thou to yon Place ascend?
Art thou, fond Youth, a Candidate for Praise?	"Thou wilt not, sure! to Fame pretend?
'Tis true, said I, not void of Hopes I came,	"No;—let me have but a good Name;
For who so fond as youthful Bards of Fame?	"I will not make Pretence to Fame.
But few, alas! the casual Blessing boast,	"Would Heaven, indulgent to my Pray'r,
So hard to gain, so easy to be lost:	"Relieve my Mind from anxious Care;
How vain that second Life in others' Breath,	"A mod'rate Competency give,
Th'Estate which Wits inherit after Death!	"Obscure, unknown, I'd chuse to live.
Ease, Health, and Life, for this we Must resign,	"And if, unbent, my Thoughts sometime
(Unsure the Tenure, but how vast the Fine!)	"Should gently flow in harmless Rhyme:
The Great Man's Curse, without the Gains, endure,	"Let *Wymondsold* approve my Lays,
Be envy'd, wretched, and be flatter'd, poor;	"I'll court no Fame, nor wish for higher
All luckless Wits our Enemies profest,	Praise.
And all successful, jealous Friends at best.	
Nor Fame I slight, nor for her Favours call;	
She comes unlook'd for, if she comes at all:	
But if the Purchase costs so dear a Price,	
As soothing Folly, or exalting Vice:	
Oh! if the Muse must flatter lawless Sway,	
And follow still where Fortune leads the way;	
Or if no Basis bear my rising Name,	
But the fall'n Ruins of Another's Fame:	
Then teach me, Heaven! to scorn the guilty Bays;	
Drive from my Breast that wretched Lust of Praise,	
Unblemish'd let me live, or die unknown,	
Oh grant an honest Fame, or grant me none!	
(Pope, *Temple of Fame*, 497–524; Pope, *Poems*, 2. 287–9[28])	(Brereton, *Poems*, p. 167)

Brereton, with her desires for a 'mod'rate Competency', is entirely practical. Pope is a youthful bard and therefore inevitably fond of fame, but at the same time he does *now*, at the end of his poem, count the full cost in contemporary and highly personal terms: 'Ease, Health, and Life, for this we must resign'.

Joseph Warton had nothing but admiration for the ending of *The Temple of Fame*, agreeing with Pope that the poem was thereby provided with 'a *Moral* to

to seek 'large fame' for themselves or to display personal thoughts and experiences in their verse. … Accordingly, his response to the bystander's question, unlike Geoffrey's, is positive.

(John Burrow, 'Geoffrey's Credo: *House of Fame*, lines 1873–82', *Chaucer Review*, 48 (2014), 251–7 (p. 256)).

[28] With the 1715–17 readings at ll. 507 and 511 reinstated (see below).

the whole', and therefore constituted an improvement of Chaucer rather than a faithful rendering:

> This conclusion is not copied from Chaucer; and is judicious. Chaucer has finished his story inartificially, by saying he was surprized at the sight of a man of great authority, and awoke in a fright. The succeeding lines give a pleasing moral to the allegory, and the two last shew the man of honour and virtue, as well as the poet.

> > Unblemish'd let me live, or die unknown.
> > Oh grant an honest Fame, or grant me none![29]

Pope's editor, William Roscoe, was similarly impressed:

> This conclusion, in which the poet speaks in his own character, is peculiarly beautiful and appropriate; and the more so, as there is reason to believe it exhibits a faithful picture of his mind at an early period of his life; and whilst it shews that he was, even then, 'a candidate for praise,' demonstrated that he had already formed those many and independent principles, with respect to his literary productions, by which he was invariably actuated, and which obtained for him not only a distinguished niche in the 'Temple of Fame,' but what he still more highly valued, the esteem of the wise and virtuous, and the deserved reputation of a firm, consistent, and honest man.[30]

Many readers were convinced like Roscoe that this part of Pope's poem was 'descriptive of' Pope's mind at 'an early period of his own life'—an opinion he repeated several times.[31]

At this final point in Pope's poem, there occurs a full and prophetic account of some of the hazards that an eighteenth-century poet might expect when he submitted his work to the reading public. Writing poetry, in Pope's view, can easily seem—as a later English poet put it—a 'mug's game'.[32] In the 1736 edition of The Temple of Fame, Pope distanced himself from 'youthful Bards', changing 'we' in line 507 to 'they', and 'our' in line 511 to 'their'. But at the moment of the poem's composition (1704–09?), he had presented himself as both fond of fame and acutely aware of its concomitant miseries and inherent fragility. Pope's epithet for fame, 'casual', coming as it does at the end of this particular poem, combines several senses distinguished one from another in the OED: Pope's Fame is accidental, fortuitous, uncertain, unsettled, frail, and precarious. Fame, as Pope now describes it, is both produced by and subject to chance, and, because of the 'Great Man's Curse', 'jealous Friends' and the enmity of 'All luckless Wits', 'easy to be lost'. Jane Brereton's immediate 'No' to the offer would therefore seem to show her responding not only to Chaucer but also to Pope.

---

[29] Joseph Warton, An Essay on the Genius and Writings of Pope, 1. 413–14.
[30] The Works of Alexander Pope, ed. William Roscoe, 10 vols (London, 1824), 2. 292.
[31] Ibid. 2. 255.
[32] T. S. Eliot, The Use of Poetry and the Use of Criticism (London, 1933), p. 154.

What the Age Demanded?

A common assumption is often made that each 'age' invents or reinvents past authors to suit itself, and that that invention or reinvention will be broadly consistent within any particular 'period'. But Alexander Pope and Jane Brereton, though almost exact contemporaries, responded to Chaucer's *House of Fame* in conspicuously different ways. Brereton's response was directly and simply personal. Alexander Pope was embarking on a career in the full knowledge that the more famous his poems would become, the more he would be envied; Brereton claims to be writing for the pleasure of *one* reader (Mathew Wymondesold). It is not therefore the demands of their 'century' or 'age' to which, prompted by Chaucer, they are responding, but to their own particular authorial circumstances, which were, in turn, determined partly by their different genders. Neither seems assured that their poem will meet the demands of their own, or any future, age.

The Temples of both Pope and Brereton are partial responses—if only because they have only taken parts of Chaucer's long poem. But they are 'partial' in another sense, in that their fondness for their chosen parts of Chaucer's original is matched by a fondness for some poets who have been rewarded, against all the odds, with lasting fame. Brereton, for example, includes a particularly lively account of Anacreon. Both poets are applying the poem to their own lives, internalizing its implications, and looking at the world through it, or by its means. They are responsive to many of its poetic arts, structures, and allegories and to the shaping of particular lines. But they realize that, given the changes in language and convention since Chaucer's day, they cannot merely copy but must emulate in a changed medium.

It is hard to know whether either poem was precisely *predictive* in effect. But Jane Brereton's wish for *no* fame was, so far as can be found, largely granted, and Pope was attacked by envy and by ignorance more virulently than almost any other poet, ancient or modern.

Circles in the Lake and the Spread of Fame

One of Pope's most notable alterations to *The House of Fame* was to move a passage—where the Eagle expounds an elaborate and comprehensive theory of the circulation of sound—from Book 2 of Chaucer's poem (which he did not translate) to a later moment, since he wished to keep the image that Chaucer used there for the spread of fame. Valerie Rumbold has observed that Pope had made a note in his copy of Speght's 1598 edition 'to remind himself to insert into the description of the second house the lines from Book II which compare the movement of sound to the rippling of water'. 'This image', Rumbold continues, 'comprehends Pope's entire action: the focus moves first towards the temple, over its façades, through the concentric groups of the famous to the throne of Fame, just as, according to the eagle, sound travels from earth to the temple.'[33]

As we saw in the Introduction to this book, Pope's simile of the Ice Mountains was admired by Joseph Warton and by Byron. His simile of the stone in the lake was also widely and strongly praised, notably by his biographer Owen Ruffhead:

> From the Temple of Fame, the scene changes to that of rumour, of which the description is beautifully picturesque. The effects arising from the various sounds are illustrated by a simile so happily imagined, and expressed in such melodious versification, that no reader of taste will be tired with the length of it.[34]

The simile was the result of Pope's having compressed a great many Chaucerian octosyllabic lines, spoken by the garrulous Eagle, into six couplets of his own. While the terms 'stone' and 'circle' and the numbering of the ripples come from Chaucer, the ideas are developed in largely independent vocabulary: a 'lake' is put in 'motion' and moves 'trembling' in 'rings' and each circle 'impels' its successor 'undulating' to the 'margin':[35]

if that thou	As on the smooth Expanse of Chrystal Lakes,
Threwe in a water now a stone	The sinking Stone at first a Circle makes;
Wel wost thou it wil make anone	The trembling Surface, by the Motion stir'd,
A litel roundel as a cercle	Spreads in a second Circle, then a third;
Parauenture, as brode as a couercle[36]	Wide, and more wide, the floating Rings advance,
And right anon thou shalt see wele	Fill all the wat'ry Plain, and to the Margin dance.
That whele cercle wil cause another whele	Thus ev'ry Voice and Sound, when first they break,
And that the third, and so forth brother	On neighb'ring Air a soft Impression make;
Euery cercle causing other	Another ambient Circle then they move,
Broder than himselfe was	That, in its turn, impels the next above;
And thus from roundel to compas	Thro' undulating Air the Sounds are sent,
Ech about other going	And spread o'er all the fluid Element.
Causeth of others steringe	
And multiplying euermo	
Till it be so fare go	
That it at bothe brinkes bee.	
Although thou may it not se	
Aboue, yet goeth it alway under,	
Though thou thinke it a great wonder …	
Right so of eyre my leue brother	
Euerich eyre in other stereth	
More and more, and spech up bereth	

---

[33] Rumbold, 'Pope and the Gothic Past', p. 196.

[34] Owen Ruffhead, *The Life of Alexander Pope Esq* (London, 1769), pp. 177–8. The simile was also praised in the twentieth century by G. Wilson Knight, *The Poetry of Pope: Laureate of Peace* (London, 1965), p. 106.

[35] Pope later used the image of 'Wave impelling Wave' in 'The Second Epistle of the Second Book of Horace', 253 (Pope, *Poems*, 4. 183).

[36] Glossed by Urry as 'A Cover or Lid'.

Or voice or noise, word or sowne
Aye through multiplicaciowne
Til it be at the house of Fame.

(*HF*, 788–806, 816–21;   (*Temple of Fame*, 436–47; Pope,
Speght 1598, Fol. 278ʳ⁻ᵛ)   *Poems*, 2. 284–5)

Jane Brereton was impressed with this simile—and more, perhaps, by the simile as
rewritten by Pope than by its exposition by Chaucer's eagle. Pope compressed the
image into twelve lines. Brereton managed a similar degree of compression despite
using twenty-four fewer syllables. In her version, she adapts Pope as follows:

A Stone, when cast into a <u>Lake</u>,
Will strait a <u>trembling</u> Circle make;
The Water, by that <u>Motion</u> stir'd,
Will spread a Second, then a Third;
Still round each Ring another's made,
Till each the <u>Margin</u> does invade.
Thus Voice, or Sound, <u>impels</u> the Air,
And makes an ambient Ringlet there,
Which <u>undulating</u> will enforce
Another Circle in its Course;
Each Ring will still another drive,
At *Rumour's House* till all arrive.

(Brereton, *Poems*, 162–3)

This simile, in all its versions may serve, with some modification, as a part-analogy
for the progress of Chaucer's fame and poetical fatherhood in the eighteenth century. We have seen that encomia on Chaucer's position as the father of English
poetry spread during the centuries immediately after his death, from those closely
associated with the poet himself like Lydgate and Hoccleve to those, particularly
Spenser, who imitated his works some time later. And references to Chaucer's
name increase markedly in publications towards the end of the eighteenth century.
Some responses to Chaucerian poems caused circles of their own—as Dryden's *The
Flower and the Leaf* provided an impulse for Pope's *Temple of Fame*, which then
prompted much critical discussion as well as influencing Jane Brereton's *Dream*
and several other poems.

There is a difficulty, however, in applying the analogy systematically. In the simile, the circles in the water proceed untroubled and uninterrupted from initial
impulsion to the final lakeside. The passage of Chaucer's fame was far otherwise.
Pope's version of Chaucer's image was befouled—confirming Pope's worst fears—
in a scatological parody of *The Temple of Fame* by a 'Mr. Preston', where the ripples
caused by a 'sinking Stone' are compared to those caused by 'A T—d' falling from
'a House of Office e'er a Lake', causing the 'Excrements' to 'advance' to 'Fill all

the wat'ry Place, and to the Margin dance'.[37] Pope himself reused the simile to more savoury purposes when describing the spread of benevolence in *An Essay on Man*.[38] But—such are the peculiarities of poetic transmission—Pope was prepared to reuse his simile as it had been befouled by 'Mr. Preston' at the end of Book 2 of his own *Dunciad*, where a faint phantom-like fragment of Chaucer's *House of Fame* serves to describe the inexorable process whereby a reading of books inspired by the goddess Dulness inspires 'nutation': the tell-tale nodding of the head which denotes drowsiness:[39]

> Who sate the nearest, by the words o'ercome,
> Slept first; the distant nodded to the hum.
> Then down are roll'd the books; stretch'd o'er 'em lies
> Each gentle clerk, and mutt'ring seals his eyes.
> As what a Dutchman plumps into the lakes,
> One circle first, and then a second makes;
> What Dulness dropt among her sons imprest
> Like motion, from one circle to the rest;
> So from the mid-most the nutation spreads
> Round, and more round, o'er all the sea of heads.
>
> (*The Dunciad*, 2. 401–10; Pope, *Poems*, 5. 316–17)

The Wave Behind Impels the Wave Before

When, in the simile, Pope described the 'ambient Circle' of sound 'That, in its turn, impels the next above', and when, earlier in *The Temple of Fame*, he had described as 'ever new' the 'Names inscrib'd unnumber'd Ages past' on 'the Rock's high Summit' that 'From time's first birth, with time itself shall last',[40] he was recalling the passage from Dryden's version of Book 15 of the *Metamorphoses*, where Pythagoras compares the passage of time to a river:

> Nature knows
> No stedfast Station, but, or Ebbs, or Flows:
> Ever in motion; she destroys her old,
> And casts new Figures in another Mold.
> Ev'n Times are in perpetual Flux, and run

---

[37] Mr Preston, *Aesop at the Bear Garden; a Vision in Imitation of the Temple of Fame,* (London, 1715), p. 30.

[38] *An Essay on Man*, 4. 361–72; Pope, *Poems*, 3 i. 163–4.

[39] John Sitter and Paul Davis have argued that *The Dunciad* represents a substantial rethinking of Pope's opinions about his own claims to fame in relation to Chaucer's *House of Fame*. See John Sitter, *The Poetry of Pope's 'Dunciad'* (Minnesota MN, 1971), pp. 67–8; Paul Davis, 'After the Fire: Chaucer and Urban Poetics, 1666–1743', in *Chaucer and the City*, ed. Ardis Butterfield (Martlesham, 2006), pp. 191–2.

[40] *Temple of Fame*, 47–51; Pope, *Poems*, 2. 256.

Like Rivers from their Fountain rowling on;
For Time no more than Streams, is at a stay:
The flying Hour is ever on her way;
And as the Fountain still supplies her store,
The Wave behind impels the Wave before;
Thus in successive Course the Minutes run,
And urge their Predecessor Minutes on,
Still moving, ever new: For former Things
Are set aside, like abdicated Kings:
And every moment alters what is done,
And innovates some Act, till then unknown.

(*Of the Pythagorean Philosophy*, 262–77;
Dryden, *Works*, 7. 492)

The applicability of Ovid's analogy to the progress of literary fame is that it allows for the co-existence of perpetual change ('every moment alters what is done') and perpetual continuity from a common source ('The Fountain still supplies her store'). The presence of the past is an impulse to new creation. Every minute 'urges' its 'Predecessor' on. The process is extremely energetic: 'The Wave behind *impels* the Wave before' and 'every moment *alters* what is done, / And *innovates* some Act, till then unknown' [our emphases]. Eighteenth-century responses to Chaucer's work are not always, or often, mere repetition, but repetition with reaction, as Brereton both follows and resists Pope and Chaucer, and as Chaucer's circles end up in the *Essay on Man* and *The Dunciad*.

Though eighteenth-century poetic responses to Chaucer were often 'impelled' by previous responses, they were not *determined* by them. Pope may not have turned to Chaucer if Dryden had not done so before him. But he turned to different poems, and in ways of his own. The various editorial, biographical, and creative Chaucerian publications of the eighteenth century are often in part-agreement with their predecessors and, at the same time, impelled to modification. Dryden's and Pope's admiration for Chaucer is cited frequently in Urry's edition. Thomas Morell's part-edition of *The Canterbury Tales*, while attempting to improve on Urry's text, makes extensive use of his predecessor's glossary, cites Dryden liberally, and includes Dryden's version of *The Knight's Tale*. Thomas Tyrwhitt ('the scholar's scholar') despised Urry's text but owed much to the glossary by Timothy Thomas included in Urry's volume. Tyrwhitt disagreed with Morell's description of Chaucerian metrics but acknowledged a considerable debt to the textual method of Morell's edition. And, despite his reticence on specifically critical issues, Tyrwhitt is a highly literary reader. He relegates to notes, or excludes altogether, lines the authenticity of which he doubts—often on grounds of literary coherence—but also lines that he thinks genuine but badly judged later thoughts of Chaucer's. Tyrwhitt has ideas about the relative authority of his various manuscripts but is prepared to override them on purely poetical grounds.

Inseparable Now, the Truth and Lye

One memorable moment in 'The House of Rumour' occurs when 'Truth and lye' join together and fly out of the house of Rumour as such inseparable 'Companions' that 'no Mortal e'er shall find' them 'unmix'd':

And sometime I saw ther at ones
Aleasing, and a sad soth saw
That gonnen of auenture draw
Out at the window for to pace
And whan they metten in that place
They were achecked both two
And neither of hem might out go
For ech other they gon so croud
Til ech of hem gan crien loud
Let me be gone first, nay but let me
And here I wol ensuren thee
With nones that thou wolt do so
That I shal neuer fro thee go
But be thine own sworn brother
We wol meddle us ech in other
That no man be he neuer so wroth
Shal have one two, but both
At ones ...
Thus saw I false and soth compowned
Togider flie for o tiding.
(*HF*, 2088–105; 2108–9; Speght 1598, Fol. 283ʳ)

There, at one Passage, oft you might survey
A Lye and Truth contending for the way;
And long 'twas doubtful, both so closely pent,
Which first should issue thro' the narrow Vent:
At last agreed, together out they fly,
Inseparable now, the Truth and Lye;
The strict Companions are for ever join'd,
And this or that unmix'd, no Mortal e'er shall find.

(*Temple of Fame*, 489–96; Pope, *Poems*, 2. 287)

The conduct of Pope's Lie and Truth is rather like that of gentlemen decorously debating as to who should first pass through a door. Brereton's 'Struggle' is in some respects closer to the account given by Chaucer:

Oft in some narrow Passage there,
A Truth, and Lie, contending were;
So close were they together pent,
Dubious a while appear'd th' Event;
They Struggle' till at last they end,
And Truth, and Lie, together blend:
Inseparably now combin'd,
They fly together in the Wind.

(Brereton, *Poems*, 166)

In both eighteenth-century versions, as in Chaucer's original, truth and lie emerge as inseparable. Pope's concluding alexandrine makes the moral point. Brereton conveys the idea by combining Chaucer and Pope in an image: Truth and Lie 'fly together in the Wind'. Even of this passage we might observe that Pope and Brereton are reporting on Chaucer's poem rather than translating it. Both poets give third-person accounts of the argument between Truths and Lies 'contending for the way', where Chaucer had presented the comic dissent and eventual polite agreement between Truth and Lies verbatim. In Pope, Truth and Lie are described as 'Strict companions'. In Chaucer, one is *heard* promising the other to be his 'owne sworen brother'. In all three poems, the combination of Truth and Lie is closer and stronger than it had been for any predecessor—as, for example, in Virgil's account as represented in Dryden's translation, where, in a fourteener, Fame 'Things done relates, not done she feigns; and mingles Truth with Lyes'.[41] Here, truth and lies are only *mingled*. In the Chaucerian poems, they exist in an indissoluble compound.

The beauty of the House of Rumour analogy is that it describes truth and lies as finding *happiness* in their combination. In Brereton's version, they 'fly together'. Pope's and Brereton's versions of *The House of Fame Dream* are simultaneously faithful and unfaithful to their original. At times, Brereton can be seen to be reading Chaucer through Pope. At others, she reads Chaucer for herself, and almost *against* Pope. It would be absurd to suggest that each poet's version of *The House of Fame* was pure invention and entirely independent of Chaucer's poem, but equally absurd to claim that either was an accurate reproduction. Fidelity and infidelity to Chaucer 'fly together' in both versions.

It is characteristic of the eighteenth-century Chaucerian record that contrary opinions exist side by side—to such an extent that it is impossible to make a general assessment of Chaucer's fame or standing at any one time, or during the course of the century as a whole. Pope's *Temple of Fame* is one rare case over which the brothers Warton disagreed, Joseph considering that Pope's changes were improvements, Thomas thinking them excrescences imposed on medieval form. In his *History of English Poetry*, Thomas Warton gave a fine and full account of *The House of Fame,* before turning to Pope's version:

> Pope has imitated this piece with his usual elegance of diction and harmony of versification; but in the mean time, he has not only misrepresented the story, but marred the character of the poem. He has endeavoured to correct it's extravagancies, by new refinements and additions of another cast: but he did not consider, that extravagancies are essential to a poem of such a structure, and even constitute its beauties. An attempt to unite order and exactness of imagery and anomalies, is like giving Corinthian pillars to a Gothic palace. When I read Pope's elegant imitation of this piece, I think I am walking among the modern monuments unsuitably placed in Westminster-abbey.[42]

William Roscoe included Warton's account of Chaucer's poem in his edition of Pope's works but disagreed with his judgement of *The Temple of Fame*, claiming that Pope had 'so amalgamated and harmonized' elements from Chaucer's original that it 'would be impossible, without a close examination, to distinguish what passages are taken from Chaucer and what are originally his own'. Such a harmony between Pope and Chaucer, Roscoe believed, had been achieved because of the profound similarity between the 'genius and poetical character' of the two

---

[41] *The Fourth Book of the Aeneis*, 271; Dryden, *Works*, 5. 461.
[42] Warton, *History*, 1. 396.

writers.[43] Roscoe was not the only reader to suggest a special relationship between Pope and the Chaucer of *The House of Fame*. William Mason, in his *Musaeus: A Monody to the Memory of Mr. Pope, in Imitation of Lycidas* (1747), has Chaucer himself—and in an imitation of 'his' own style—praise Pope as the 'Grete clerk of Fame' is house, whose excellence / Maie wele befitt thilk place of eminence'.

Transformations: Chaucer in Pope's Later Poems

Much of this book has concentrated—albeit often by close concentration on specific textual detail—on what might broadly be called large-scale, eighteenth-century responses to Chaucer, both translations and adaptations of particular Chaucerian poems and critical, scholarly, editorial, and lexicographical engagements with Chaucer's work as a whole. Most of the present chapter has explored two full-scale recreations of Chaucer's *House of Fame*, both for their own sakes and for the light they cast on the ways that Chaucer's fame was transmitted, disseminated, and sometimes misrepresented in the centuries after his death.

But Chaucer's afterlife and poetic paternity is arguably as significantly visible in local, occasional moments in poetry as in larger-scale responses. As a conclusion to this discussion of Chaucer and Fame, we will offer some examples of the more oblique ways in which fragments of Chaucerian language and imaginings lodged themselves in the minds of later poets, and were incorporated, sometimes deliberately and self-consciously, sometimes as partial, subconscious, and perhaps confused memories, in those poets' own work. Such memories can be seen to advantage in four later works by Pope which have no wholesale or immediately obvious Chaucerian provenance.

1. Chaucer's Franklin On Love And Maistrie

Throughout the eighteenth century, the most famous Chaucerian pronouncement on the freedom demanded by Love was that uttered by Chaucer's Franklin near the beginning of his tale. A miniature history of the fortunes of this Chaucerian dictum was provided by Thomas Tyrwhitt in the entry on 'Maisterie' included in the glossary which he added to his edition of Chaucer in 1778:

> Love wol not be constreined by maistrie
> When maistrie cometh, the God of love anon
> Beteth his winges, and farewell! he is gone

> I cite these elegant lines, as I omitted to observe before, that Spenser has inserted them in his Faery Queen, B.2 C.i. St.25. with very little alteration, and certainly without any improvement.

---

[43] *The Works of Alexander Pope*, ed. Roscoe, 2. x–xi, 255, 297.

> Ne may love be compel'd by mastery;
> For, soon as mastery comes, sweet love anone
> Taketh his nimble wings, and soon away is gone.[44]

Tyrwhitt's gloss, however, tells only the bare bones of the story. These sentiments about the incompatibility of mastery and love had an extensive life, deriving both from Chaucer's version directly[45] and from Spenser's reworking of Chaucer's words.[46] In Samuel Butler's *Hudibras*, a widow draws on Chaucer's passage in expounding her notions of love and the reasons why she rejects marriage:

> Love, that's too generous, t'abide
> To be against its Nature ty'd:
> For where' tis of it self inclin'd,
> It breaks loose when it is confin'd:
> And, like the Soul its harbourer,
> Debar'd the freedom of the Air;
> Disdains, against its will, to stay,
> But struggles out, and flies away:
> And therefore, never can comply,
> T'indure the Matrimonial tye:
> That binds the Female, and the Male,
> Where th'one is but the other's Bail.
>
> (Butler, *Hudibras*, Part III, Canto 1. 553–61;
> Butler, *Hudibras*, ed. Wilders, p. 206)

As we saw in Chapter 7, Alexander Pope gave sentiments derived from *The Franklin's Tale* to the heroine of his *Eloisa to Abelard*:

> How oft', when press'd to marriage, have I said,
> Curse on all laws but those which love has made!
> Love, free as air, at sight of human ties,
> Spreads his light wings, and in a moment flies.
>
> (*Eloisa to Abelard*, 73–6; Pope, *Poems*, 2. 325–6)

In his edition of Pope, printed in 1751, William Warburton supplied at this point a footnote which gave the Chaucerian original on which Pope was drawing as follows:

> Love wol not be confin'd by maisterie
> When maisterie comes, the Lord of Love anon
> Flutters his wings, and forthwith is he gone.

---

[44] Tyrwhitt 1775–78, 5. 184.

[45] See, e.g. George Rogers, *The Horn Exalted. Or, Room for Cuckolds* (London, 1721), p. 60.

[46] See, e.g. *The British Muse* (London, 1738, reprinted as *The Quintessence of English Poetry*, 1740) quoting from Robert Nevile's, *The Poor Scholar: A Comedy* (London, 1662).

But as Philip Neve pointed out in 1789, the words 'confin'd', 'Lord', 'Flutters' and 'forthwith' in Warburton's quotation do not in fact occur in Chaucer's original.[47] Warburton's 'confin'd' seems to derive from Butler, but the other words cited by Neve have no obvious source. Warburton was perhaps relying on his memory of Chaucer's passage rather than on any printed edition.

In his version of *The Franklin's Tale* included in his completion of Ogle's collection of translated *Canterbury Tales*, and ostensibly based on Tyrwhitt's text of Chaucer's original, William Lipscomb signalled with inverted commas a verbatim borrowing from *Eloisa to Abelard*:

Love will not be constreined by maistrie.	For free as air, and fleeting as the wind,
Whan maistrie cometh, the God of love anon	Love ne'er by tyrant force will be confin'd;
Beteth his winges, and farewel, he is gon.	And, when he sees prepar'd the galling ties,
Love is a thing, as any spirit free.	"Spreads his light wings, and in a moment flies:"
Women of kind desiren libertee	Hateful alike to every generous soul,
And not to been constreined as a thral;	To women as to men, is harsh controul.
And so don men, if sothly I say shal.	
(*FranT*, 764–70; Tyrwhitt 1775–78, 2. 130)	(Lipscomb, 3. 110)

Lipscomb has recalled, and incorporated in his version, the non-Chaucerian observation of Pope's Eloisa that love is 'free as air', and antithetical to 'ties'. He has also taken 'confin'd' from Butler's reworking of Chaucer—or possibly from Warburton's footnote.

In these examples, intense and sustained attention to Chaucer's sentiment was accompanied by a remarkably free-and-easy attitude to textual detail, and included the intermingling of words that, as Philip Neve put it, 'do not belong to *Chaucer*'. In almost all cases, however, the mutations retain a common outline: Love, refusing to be compelled, confined, constrained, or tied, spreading, or beating, or fluttering his sometimes nimble, sometimes light wings, takes instant flight 'and soon away is gone'. Chaucer's words, in this tiny instance, appear to have made a crucial contribution to the common stock of notions on the nature and laws of human love.

2. The Hens' Lament for Chanticleer

Our second fragment is much slighter but may exemplify a different kind of impact of Chaucer on Pope's mind. Among the most popular passages from Dryden's *The Cock and the Fox* was that describing the lamentation of the hens at the abduction of Chanticleer. The passage was reprinted in several anthologies. It was singled

[47] Philip Neve, *Cursory Remarks on Some of the Ancient English Poets, Particularly Milton* (London, 1789), pp. 6–7. Neve attributed Warburton's misquotation to Urry's 'vile' edition, but Warburton was not following Urry's text.

out for particular praise by John Miller for its ironic comparison of 'affecting and interesting incidents' with 'the most trivial and insignificant', and by William Milns for the way in which the 'irony' of the passage even surpasses that to be found in Partlet's and Chanticleer's debates on the nature of dreams earlier in the poem.[48] Dryden's version of this passage is closer to Speght's text of Chaucer than are many in *The Cock and the Fox*:

Certes such cry, ne lamentacion	Not louder Cries when *Ilium* was in Flames,
Nas neuer of Ladies made, whan that Ilion	Were sent to Heav'n by woful *Trojan* Dames,
Was won, & Pirrus with his bright swerde	When *Pyrrhus* toss'd on high his burnish'd Blade,
Whan he hent King Priam by the berde	And offer'd *Priam* to his Father's Shade,
And slough him, (as saieth Eneidos)	Than for the Cock, the widow'd Poultry made.
As made all the hennes in the cloos	Fair Partlet first, when he was born from sight,
Whan they had loste of Chaunteclere ye sight	With soveraign Shrieks bewail'd her Captive Knight.
But souerainly dame Pertelot shright	Far louder than the *Carthaginian* Wife,
Well louder than did Hasdruballes wife	When *Asdrubal* her Husband lost his Life.
Whan that her husbond hath lost his life.	
(*NPT*, 3355–64; Speght 1598, Fol. 87ᵛ)	(*The Cock and the Fox*, 699–707; Dryden, *Works*, 7. 329)

Dryden's passage was reprinted under the heading 'SHRIEKS' in Bysshe's poetic commonplace book *The British Parnassus*, and it is the *noise* of the hens that seems to have struck many readers: Dryden had picked up 'louder' from the end of Chaucer's passage, repeating it at the start of his.

Bysshe's entry juxtaposes Dryden's passage with one from the early version of Pope's *The Rape of the Lock*, which suggests that Pope, like John Miller, appreciated the 'vast fund of elegant irony' in both Chaucer's original and Dryden's version and appreciated its potential for creating mock-heroic effects. In Pope's passage, Belinda's lock has been severed from her 'fair Head', the 'living Fires come flashing from her Eyes, / And Screams of Horror rend th'affrighted skies'. The lines open with Dryden's 'Not louder' and also include Dryden's 'Dames':

> Not louder Shrieks by Dames to Heav'n are cast,
> When Husbands die, or *Lap-dogs* breath their last,
> Or when rich *China* Vessels fal'n from high,
> In glittring Dust and painted Fragments lie![49]
>
> (*The Rape of the Locke*, 1. 121–4; Pope, *Poems*, 2. 130–1)

Pope's memory of Dryden and Chaucer here reinforces his comic suggestion that there is no difference in decibels between the lamentations of bereaved wives, hens deprived of their cock, or women mourning the death of a monkey or a lapdog.

---

[48] See Batteux, *A Course of the Belles Letters*, 1. 216, 281; William Milns, *The Well-Bred Scholar*, 4 vols (London, 1794), pp. 104–5.

[49] In the 1714 version of the poem, the same pattern is followed, but 'Lap-dogs' are replaced by 'Monkeys'. In the 1717 version, Dryden's 'Dames' have disappeared, but the 'Lap-dogs' have returned.

The ostensible gravity of tone in Chaucer and Dryden at this point is more sustained than in Pope's passage. Chaucer and Dryden had compared the cry of hens to truly heroic outcries—that of women at the death of Priam and with Hasdrubal's wife, who had flung herself into the flames of burning Carthage. But Chaucer's and Dryden's combination of the classically heroic and the apparently trivial has made a small but significant contribution to the mock-heroic comedy of *The Rape of the Lock*.

3. King Midas and His Wife

A more prominent instance of a Chaucerian transformation in Pope is provided by the Wife of Bath's story of King Midas. This story is told by the Wife in contemptuous reaction to women who think their sex want to be thought discreet. The passage had become popular as an independent entity. It was included, for example, in James Greenwood's anthology, *The Virgin Muse* (1717), where it is given both in Dryden's version and in Chaucer's original. Greenwood's book was ostensibly '*Designed for the Use of young Gentlemen and Ladies, at Schools*', but his inclusion of this passage suggests that he was perhaps more concerned, at least in this instance, to please the young than to instruct them. It is hard to imagine what profit—at least, as the term is conventionally understood—the boys and girls might derive from the tale of Midas. The tale displays the almost physical impossibility of the wife keeping the secret of her royal husband's asses' ears. Women's inability to hold by the standards of male morality is, as the Wife of Bath presents it, an *inevitable* part of their natures, and in his version (here given with Chaucer's original in the texts printed by Greenwood[50]), Dryden had responded gleefully to Chaucer's emphasis on the physical compulsion that impels Midas' wife:

Her thought it swole so sore about her Hert,	But ne'ertheless she pin'd with Discontent;
That nedely some worde she most a stert:	The Counsel rumbled till it found a Vent.
And sith she durst tellen it to no Man,	The Thing she knew she was oblig'd to hide;
Down to a Marris fast by she ran,	By Int'rest and by Oath the Wife was ty'd;
Tyll she came there, her Hert was on a Fyre:	But if she told it not the Woman dy'd.
And as a byttour bumbeth in the myre,	Loath to betray a Husband and a Prince,
She layde her Mouth unto the Water adown.	But she must burst, or blab; and no Pretence
Bewray me nat thou Water with thy sown	Of Honour ty'd her Tongue from Self-Defence.
Quod she, to the I tell it, and to no mo,	A Marshy Ground commodiously was near,
My Husbonde hath long Asses Eres Two.	Thither she ran, and held her Breath for fear,
Now is myn Hert all hole, now it is out,	Lest if a Word she spoke of any Thing,
I myght no lenger kepe it out of dout.	That Word might be the Secret of the King.
Here mowe ye se, though we a time abyde,	Thus full of Counsel to the *Fen* she went,
Yet out it mote, we can no counsayle hyde.	Grip'd all the way, and longing for a Vent:
The remnaunt of the Tale if ye wyl here,	Arriv'd, by pure necessity compell'd,

---

[50] It is not clear which texts of either Chaucer or Dryden Greenwood is using.

Redeth Ovyde, and there ye may it lere.

On her Majestick Marrow-Bones she kneel'd:
Then to the Waters-brink she laid her Head,
And, as a Bittour Bumps within a Reed,
To thee alone, O Lake, she said, I tell
(And as thy Queen command thee to conceal)
Beneath his Locks the King my Husband wears
A goodly Royal pair of Asses Ears:
Now I have eas'd my Bosom of the Pain
'Till the next longing fit Return again.

(*WBT*, 951–82; Greenwood, *The Virgin Muse*
[London, 1717], pp. 172–3).

(*The Wife of Bath Her Tale*, 157–200;
Greenwood, *The Virgin Muse*, p. 148)

In the 'Notes Explaining some difficult Places' in his anthology, Greenwood commented: 'To do Justice to the Ladies, and also to *Ovid*, we must take Notice, that *Midas* told this Secret to his *Barber*, and not to his *Wife*'.[51] But in some minds, the Chaucerian Wife of Bath's account of Midas, his wife, and his 'Asses Ears' displaced, or mingled, with the versions of the story provided by the classical poets. One such mind was that of Pope, who, when a pressing need to reveal a secret arose in *An Epistle to Dr Arbuthnot*, wrote:

'Tis sung, when *Midas*' Ears began to spring,
(*Midas*, a sacred Person and a King)
His very Minister who spy'd them first,
(Some say his Queen) was forc'd to <u>speak, or burst</u>.

(*Epistle to Dr Arbuthnot*, 69–72; Pope, *Poems*, 4. 100)

Pope seems uncertain whether all his readers were as conversant with Chaucer as he was and appends a footnote mentioning Chaucer but encouraging his readers to turn to Dryden: 'The Story is told by some of his Barber, but by *Chaucer* of his Queen. See Wife of Bath's Tale in *Dryden*'s Fables.' Pope has, however, mingled his account of the plight of Midas's Queen with the opening of Persius's first Satire as rendered by Dryden:

Then, then I say—or wou'd say, if I durst—
But thus provok'd, I must speak out, or burst.

(*The First Satyr of Persius*, 25–6; Dryden, *Works*, 4. 261)

Pope's *Epistle* continues with his interlocutor Arbuthnot, like Persius's friend, interjecting a warning: 'Good friend forebear! You deal in dang'rous things, / I'd never name Queens, Ministers, or Kings'. But Pope refuses to be quelled, and identifies himself firmly with the Queen in the Wife of Bath's version of the story:

Out with it *Dunciad*! let the secret pass,
That Secret to each Fool, that he's an Ass:
The truth once told (and wherefore should we lie?)
The Queen of *Midas* slept, and so may I.

(*Epistle to Dr Arbuthnot*, 79–82; Pope, *Poems*, 4. 101)

---

[51] Greenwood, *The Virgin Muse*, p. 181.

Ovid, Persius, the Wife of Bath, Chaucer, Dryden, and Midas's Queen have momentarily joined in Pope's comic portrait.

4. Pope, Bounce, and the Death of Arcite

Our final fragment comes from the very end of Pope's life. In a letter to John Boyle, the fifth Earl of Orrery on 10 April 1744, Pope reacted to an account of the death of his dog Bounce, which had been on loan to Orrery's family, and recalled a couplet from *The Knight's Tale* which appears to be poised somewhere between comedy and pathos:[52]

> I dread to enquire into the particulars of the Fate of Bounce. Perhaps you conceal'd them, as Heav'n often does Unhappy Events, in pity to the Survivors, or not to hasten on my End by Sorrow. I doubt not how much Bounce was lamented: They might say as the Athenians did to Arcite, in Chaucer,
>
> > Ah Arcite! gentle Knight! why would'st thou die,
> > When thou had'st Gold enough, and Emilye?[53]

Pope's 'Twickenham' editors note that 'the couplet which follows was probably the last he ever wrote':

> > Ah Bounce! ah gentle Beast! why wouldst thou dye,
> > When thou had'st Meat enough, and Orrery?
> > (Pope, Poems, 6. 405)

It is a couplet that gives equal value to both the folly and the reality of such grief for a much-loved pet. Is it a mark of truth and lies combined, of mutability, or of creative survival, that Pope has misremembered Chaucer's couplet while half-remembering the shape of Dryden's version of it? Here are Chaucer's lines (*KnT*, 2835–6) as given in the editions of Speght, Urry, Morell, and Tyrwhitt:

> > Why woldest thow be dedde, thus womê crie
> > And haddest gold inough, and Emelie.
> > (Speght, 1598, Fol. 10ʳ)
> > Why wuldist thow be dede, the wymin crie,
> > And haddist gold ynow, and Emelye?
> > (Urry, p. 21)
> > Whi woldist thou ben ded, these Wemen crye,
> > And haddist Gold ynow, and *Emelie!*
> > (Morell, p. 189)

---

[52] Thomas Morell's footnote to the couplet reads (p. 189): 'Whi woldist thou, &c. I would not be thought to burlesque my Author, if I should say this is a Strain of the *Irish* Howl. "— Hub-bub-bub-boo, / What made Thee die! oh, dear *Aroon*, / What made Thee go away so soon, / And leave the Wealth behind! &c." *Ward's* Reform. p. 310.'

[53] Alexander Pope, *The Correspondence*, ed. George Sherburn (Oxford, 1956), 5. 517.

> Why woldest thou be ded? thise women crie,
> And haddest gold ynough, and Emelie.
>
> (Tyrwhitt 1775–78, 1. 111)

Here is Dryden's version from *Palamon and Arcite*:

> Why would'st thou go, with one Consent they cry,
> When thou hast Gold enough and *Emily*?
>
> (Dryden, *Works*, 7. 179)

Here, again, is Dryden's couplet as misremembered by Pope:

> Ah Arcite! gentle Knight! why would'st thou die,
> When thou had'st Gold enough, and Emilye.

And, finally, once again, Pope's lines on Bounce:

> Ah Bounce! ah gentle Beast! why wouldst thou dye,
> When thou had'st Meat enough, and Orrery?

In these mutations, a Chaucerian core remains: 'Why woldest thow … '; 'haddest … inough, and … '. But Pope's memory—like that of most poets, perhaps—is endlessly malleable, often false, and never reliable but rich with interconnections.

Active poetic fathering, such examples suggest, involves, and to some extent depends upon, a connection with other images, rhythms, sentiments, and intuitions in a poetic descendant's mind—often working with the remembered or half-remembered co-presence of other poetic minds responding to the same initial stimulus. Pope's couplet on Bounce does not so much steer from grave to gay but combines them in a single compound. As with Pope's and Brereton's versions of *The House of Fame*, Pope's little poem on Bounce neither reproduces a Chaucerian original nor stands completely independent of Chaucerian influence. Malleable fragments of Chaucer in the minds of later poets, slight as they sometimes may be, provide the surest indication of Chaucer's enduring poetic afterlife.

That afterlife persisted beyond Pope's death into the later eighteenth and early nineteenth centuries. Chaucer's legacy in this period, and its continuities with, and differences from, eighteenth-century responses form the subject of our final chapter.

12

Poets and Antiquarians

The Eighteenth-Century Bequest

The moment of transition from one century to another tends to have an extraordinary power over the human mind, leading us to expect some momentous alteration in human and artistic affairs. But while it has been the sustained suggestion of the present study that the publication of Dryden's *Fables Ancient and Modern* in 1700 marked a significant moment in the course of Chaucer's afterlife, nothing similar can be said of the year 1800. It is not that *no* change occurred in the fortunes of Chaucer in the years from 1775 to 1855 (roughly the period covered in this chapter). But changes were counterbalanced by continuities, and responses to Chaucer at the end of the eighteenth and beginning of the nineteenth century, viewed as a whole, were as diverse—and sometimes as contradictory—as those from the closing years of the seventeenth with which this study began.

While there appears to have been a continuing assumption in many quarters that Chaucer was the first English poet to write 'poetically' and was therefore the 'father' of all poets who came after him, some readers in these years were unable to recapture the pleasure in his work that had been experienced by their predecessors. The poet Anna Seward, for example, felt no embarrassment in telling her friends how little she enjoyed Chaucer. She complained of the poet's 'obsolete, coarse and inharmonious diction', and accused William Godwin of 'insane partiality' for what in Chaucer is 'tedious, unnatural, conceited and obscure'.[1] The 'barbarity' of Chaucer's fourteenth century was often assumed, and some critics reiterated accusations that the poet's 'numbers' were 'harsh' and 'lame' and that some of his poems contained 'disgusting obscenity' and 'lowest ribaldry'.[2] But such views cannot be regarded as dominant or exclusive, and it is certainly not easy to point to any political or other non-literary pressures affecting the reading or the standing of Chaucer, or to account for features of Chaucer's reception by appealing to any of the conventional divisions of literary history into 'styles', 'periods', or 'epochs'. When defending his own decision to organize his *History of English*

---

[1] See letters of 1792 and 1806, in Anna Seward, *Letters*, 6 vols (Edinburgh, 1811) 3. 141; 4. 269.
[2] 'C. B', in *The Gentleman's Magazine*, 88 (1818), 295–6. This article is discussed by Thomas A. Prendergast in *Chaucer's Dead Body: From Corpse to Corpus* (London, 2004), p. 131.

Chaucer in the Eighteenth Century. David Hopkins and Tom Mason, Oxford University Press.
© David Hopkins and Tom Mason (2022). DOI: 10.1093/oso/9780192862624.003.0013

Poetry chronologically, rather than according to the 'schools' of poetry delineated by Alexander Pope and Thomas Gray, Thomas Warton noted the distorting effect of all such categorizations. Such divisions, he argued, seem 'only to substitute the merit of disposition, and the praise of contrivance' for 'that satisfaction which results from a clearness and a fulness of information' and destroy 'that free exertion of research' which displays 'that complication, variety, and extent of materials', which a literary history 'ought to comprehend'.[3]

Such thoughts are relevant when one considers the work of Thomas and Joseph Warton themselves. Although the two brothers are sometimes considered to be the fathers of 'Pre-romanticism', we have seen that Thomas Warton's conception of 'romance' was largely ideal: no single romance examined in his *History* lived up to his requirements. And as Derek Brewer has observed, Chaucer's poems—contrary to the assumptions of some commentators—did not play any large part during this period in encouraging or developing a more general fondness for things 'medieval'.[4]

It has often been observed how curious it was that Thomas Warton and Thomas Tyrwhitt should have devoted so much energy and such scrupulous attention to the verses of Thomas Chatterton's imaginary fifteenth-century poet, Thomas Rowley, at the same time as they were celebrating the exceptional merits of Geoffrey Chaucer.[5] The strangeness is all the greater in that both Wartons, along with Thomas Percy, though initially intrigued by 'Rowley's' works, had eventually arrived at the unshakable conviction that Chatterton's knowledge of genuine medieval poetry was minimal. Of the 'Lines' supposedly 'composed by JOHN LADGATE, a Priest in London, and sent to ROWLIE, as an Answer' to Rowley's 'preceding *Songe to Ælla*', Warton observed that the writer appears to assume that Chaucer 'lived in Norman tymes'.[6] Chatterton's 'Ladgate' praises Rowley on the grounds that 'Chaucer lyves / Ynne ev'ry lyne he wrytes'.[7] That was not Tyrwhitt's impression. Though Chatterton may have consulted the glossary in Speght's edition of Chaucer's *Works*, there was little evidence that he had studied any of the poems seriously: 'How much time he should be supposed to have spent in *reading* Chaucer, and in *acquiring a competent knowledge of the meaning of ancient words*', wrote Tyrwhitt, 'I cannot precisely determine. I have proved, I think, that he never had acquired a competent knowledge of the meaning of ancient words; and I cannot find any marks of his having been a diligent reader of Chaucer.'[8] Tyrwhitt, accordingly, never once mentions Rowley in his edition

---

[3] Warton, *History*, 1. v.
[4] See Brewer, *Chaucer: The Critical Heritage*, 2. 21.
[5] See, e.g. David Matthews, *Medievalism: A Critical History* (Martlesham, 2017) p. 171.
[6] Warton, *History*, 2. 148.
[7] Thomas Tyrwhitt, ed. *Poems, Supposed to Have Been Written at Bristol, by Thomas Rowley* (London, 1777), p. 27.
[8] Thomas Tyrwhitt , *A Vindication of the Appendix to the Poems, called Rowley's* (London, 1782), p. 154.

of Chaucer. In the minds of these scholars, there was a chasm between the medieval language-world invented by Chatterton and that to be found in Chaucer's poems.[9]

The common notion that the writings of the Wartons, followed by those of Wordsworth, marked the beginning of a general decline in the appreciation of Dryden and Pope is, as far as the two poets' Chaucerian translations are concerned, extremely misleading. Joseph Warton is sometimes described as a critic who endeavoured to *lower* Dryden and Pope in the estimation of his readers. But in the case of their Chaucerian renderings, the contrary proposition would seem to be more accurate. As we have seen, Joseph Warton considered Dryden's *Palamon and Arcite* to be among the finest poems ever written, and—in this instance, unlike his brother—actually judged Pope's *Temple of Fame* to be an *improvement* on Chaucer's *House of Fame*.

Dryden's Chaucer poems were particularly popular in the 1790s and in the early decades of the nineteenth century. In 1797, there appeared a handsome folio reissue of the Chaucer and Boccaccio items from Dryden's *Fables*, illustrated by Lady Diana Beauclerk. In 1800, Edmond Malone called for 'a perfect edition' of Dryden's Chaucer poems, which he considered the 'most popular, and perhaps the happiest, of all our author's poetical performances'. In this ideal edition, 'the most splendid passages of the original should be compared with the copy, and the judicious retrenchments, as well as the beautiful amplifications, made by Dryden in various places, should be distinctly penned out'.[10]

Though Sir Walter Scott, in his edition of Dryden's works, and the editors (Joseph and John Warton and others) of Dryden's *Poetical Works* (1811) drew attention to some 'splendid passages of the original' that they thought Dryden had failed to emulate, their dominant impression of Dryden's Chaucer translations was of similarity and continuity with their originals. 'The Knight's Tale', wrote Scott, 'whether we consider Chaucer's original poem, or the spirited and animated version of Dryden, is one of the finest pieces of composition in our language.'[11]

The most extensive praise of Dryden's Chaucer in the period is to be found in a series of articles by John Wilson ('Christopher North'), first published in *Blackwood's Edinburgh Magazine* in 1845 and collected in book form the following year.[12] Wilson, at one time a friend and passionate admirer of Wordsworth,

[9] See Nick Groom ed., *Thomas Chatterton and Romantic Culture* (Basingstoke, 1999), pp. 127, 153 (on Tyrwhitt), p. 154 (on Warton), pp. 13–16 (on Warton and Malone), and pp.188–205 (on Thomas Percy's involvement in the Rowley controversy).

[10] John Dryden, *Critical and Miscellaneous Prose Writings*, ed. Edmund Malone, 3 vols in 4 (London, 1800), I. i. 328.

[11] *The Works of John Dryden*, ed. Walter Scott, 11. 243.

[12] See John Wilson ['Christopher North'], *Blackwood's Edinburgh Magazine*, 57 (1845), 133–58, 369–400, 503–28, 617–46, 771–93, and 58 (1845), 114–28, 229–56, and 366–88. The book version, John Wilson ['Christopher North'], *Specimens of the British Critics*, was published in Philadelphia in 1846.

commends Dryden's Chaucer in the highest possible terms: 'The verse marches with freedom, fervour and power. ... The translator makes the matter his own, and writes as if from his own unassisted conception.' But if Dryden 'makes the matter his own', he also 'intends and conveys the impression purposed and effected by Chaucer', and occasionally surpasses it. Of Theseus's speech in *Palamon and Arcite*, Wilson writes: 'If there is in the fine original anything felt as a little too stiffly formal, this impression is wholly obliterated or lost in the streaming poetry of the translator.' Dryden's version, he wrote, 'is indeed what Warton has pronounced it to be "the most animated and harmonious piece of versification in the English Language"'.[13]

Pope's Chaucer versions were also remembered and admired, if not quite to the same extent. Twenty-three editions of Pope's collected poetical works were printed between 1790 and 1830, most of which included the Chaucer poems, in some cases—such as that of Joseph Warton's editions of 1797 and 1811—with extensive commentary. And, as we have seen, William Roscoe, in his edition of 1824, suggested that there was a particular poetic affinity between Chaucer, Dryden, and Pope himself.

In the light of such evidence, it is difficult to see how the afterlife of Chaucer accords with accounts of the so-called 'Romantic period' as somehow witnessing a wholesale rejection and repudiation of the aesthetic values and practices of the 'Neoclassical' period that preceded it.[14] No clear division can be drawn between a 'Neoclassical' interest in the Greek and Roman past, and a 'Romantic' preoccupation with matters medieval. Several of the writers most concerned with Chaucer's works, both before and after the century break, were equally interested in the poetry of classical antiquity, and produced numerous kinds of editions and translations of classical authors and commentaries on their works.[15] Their interest in Chaucer—who had, of course, himself been profoundly influenced by classical antiquity—and in the writers of Greece and Rome was interconnected and inextricable.

There are, moreover, very few early nineteenth-century responses to Chaucer that were not at the same time responses to the eighteenth-century critical and

---

Quotations are from this edition, which has been reprinted in facsimile, with an Introduction by D. W. Hopkins (Delmar, NY, 1978).

[13] Wilson, *Specimens*, pp. 202–3, 215, 226.

[14] See, e.g. the highly differentiated (and highly tendentious) definitions of these terms in M. H. Abrams's *Glossary of Literary Terms*, a book which first appeared in 1957 and had gone through eleven editions by 2015.

[15] John Dart translated Tibullus, Morell Seneca, Ogle Anacreon and the Catullus-inspired Johannes Secundus. Pope translated Homer and imitated Horace. Tyrwhitt translated Plutarch and Babrius from newly discovered manuscripts and edited Aristotle's *Poetics*. Joseph Warton edited and translated Virgil. Thomas Warton edited Theocritus. Wordsworth translated Virgil. Henry J. Todd published a study of Greek manuscripts. Leigh Hunt translated from Homer, Anacreon, Theocritus, Catullus, Lucretius, Horace, and Ovid.

poetic past, as may be suggested by an examination of a number of key volumes produced between 1775 and 1845.

1775–78: Thomas Tyrwhitt's *Canterbury Tales*

Tyrwhitt's edition, which has been frequently referred to in the present study, was highly influential on subsequent writers' engagements with Chaucer.[16] Tyrwhitt had supplied readers with what was taken to be a definitive text of *The Canterbury Tales*, and had offered by far the fullest and most intelligible explanation of much that was found difficult in that work, including Chaucer's prosody. Tyrwhitt's arduous undertaking was not repeated or emulated. Nor were his methods applied to the rest of Chaucer's poems outside *The Canterbury Tales*. For those, publishers, as we have seen, resorted to Urry's text, or—on account of Tyrwhitt's comment that 'Mr. Urry's edition should never be opened by any one for the purpose of reading Chaucer'[17]—to Speght's early seventeenth-century versions.

Careful attention to Tyrwhitt's edition was not always restricted to scholarly matters alone. In *The Poems of Geoffrey Chaucer Modernized* (1841), to take one small but significant example, Richard Hengist Horne drew on a note in Tyrwhitt's edition when arguing for the indebtedness of Thomas Gray's *Elegy in a Country Churchyard* to Chaucer's *Reeve's Tale*.[18] In most of Tyrwhitt's other annotations, poetical context is presented almost entirely as a matter of sources or of analogues, most of which are closely contemporaneous with Chaucer. But Horne's use of Tyrwhitt in this instance shows that Tyrwhitt's reading of Chaucer—like that of the Warton brothers—was closely interconnected with his interest in distinctly modern poetry, particularly that of Thomas Gray.

Tyrwhitt is concerned almost everywhere to present himself as a scholar. For example, he criticizes Thomas Warton's comments about the 'pedantic formality' and 'sententious style' of Chaucer's Clerk, on the grounds that they are prejudicial to 'the credit of good letters'.[19] But for all his scholarly scrupulousness, Tyrwhitt was at pains to avoid 'pedantic formality' of his own. His edition certainly is lacking in

---

[16] Tyrwhitt's second edition (1798), though sensibly rearranged and beautifully printed, contains few modifications. For a full account of Tyrwhitt's editions, see B. A. Windeatt's chapter in Paul Ruggiers, ed., *Editing Chaucer, The Great Tradition* (Norman, OK, 1984), pp. 117–43, 273–7.

[17] Tyrwhitt 1775–78, 2. 524.

[18] See *The Poems of Geoffrey Chaucer Modernized*, ed. Richard H. Horne (London, 1841), pp. 140–1. Tyrwhitt had been reluctant to describe Chaucer's passage as Gray's 'original' on the grounds that Gray himself had named a sonnet of Petrarch, rather than Chaucer's tale, as his source. Horne, however, was convinced of the close resemblance between Gray's lines and Chaucer's, and judged that Gray had acknowledged Petrarch rather than Chaucer as the 'father' of his lines because in Gray's day 'it was no doubt far more elegant' to cite the Italian than the English poet.

[19] See Tyrwhitt 1798, 2. 401, responding to Warton, *History*, 1. 451.

the declaredly and sustainedly encomiastic strains that characterize other editions and accounts of Chaucer. But he leaves us in no doubt as to his conviction that *The Canterbury Tales*, considered as a whole, presents a 'great picture of life and manners':

> The design of Chaucer was not barely to recite the Tales told by the Pilgrims, but also to describe their journey … If we add, that the Tales, besides being nicely adapted to the Characters of their respective Relaters, were intended to be connected together by suitable introductions, and interspersed with diverting episodes; and that the greatest part of them was to have been executed in Verse; we shall have a tolerable idea of the extent and difficulty of the whole undertaking: and admiring, as we must, the vigour of that genius, which in an advanced age coud begin so vast a work, we shall rather lament than be surprised that it has been left imperfect.[20]

Like Thomas Warton, Tyrwhitt believed that Chaucer's work is superior to the staple of medieval romance: 'His RIME OF SIRE THOPAS was clearly intended to ridicule the "palpable-gross" fictions of the common Rimers of that age, and still more perhaps, the meanness of their language and versification.'[21] The emphasis in many of the notes of his edition is on Chaucer's comedy. In the Preface to his edition of Shakespeare, Samuel Johnson had pointed to the ease and durability of Shakespeare's comic scenes and to Shakespeare's instinctive 'disposition' for comedy.[22] For Tyrwhitt, the evidence of Chaucer's similar disposition was the relative freedom with which he treated his sources in his comic work:

> In his serious pieces he often follows his author with the servility of a mere translator, and in consequence his narration is jejune and constrained; whereas in the comic, he generally is satisfied with borrowing a slight hint of his subject, which he varies, enlarges, and embellishes at pleasure, and gives the whole the air and colour of an original; a sure sign, that his genius rather led him to compositions of the latter kind.[23]

In the later years of the nineteenth century, some scholars complained that Tyrwhitt had failed to distinguish with sufficient acuity between Chaucer's genuine works and those that were apocryphal. He had certainly cast doubt on several works. But his acceptance of *The Court of Love* and *The Testament of Love* had, as we shall see, a profoundly misleading effect on most biographies of the earlier nineteenth century—exactly as it had had on those by their predecessors.

---

[20] Tyrwhitt 1798, 1. 73–4.
[21] Ibid. 1. 106.
[22] Johnson, *Works*, 7. 69.
[23] Tyrwhitt 1798, 1. 87.

1795: William Lipscomb's *Canterbury Tales*
(and the Pupils of Joseph Warton)

William Lipscomb (1754–1842) was an occasional poet and rector of what he de-scribed as 'a remote village, near 250 miles from London', where necessary books 'were not to be procured'.[24] He was forty-one when he published *The Canterbury Tales of Chaucer Completed in a Modern Version*, printed in three octavo volumes in Oxford in 1795. The book, as its title suggests, is a completion of George Ogle's collection of modern versions of the *Canterbury Tales* published over fifty years previously. Lipscomb rearranged the order of the tales; translated *The Franklin's Tale* and those that followed it, together with connecting passages; provided a *Dedicatory Letter*, a *Preface*, and a *Postscript*; and reprinted the whole of Tyr-whitt's *Introductory Discourse to the Canterbury Tales* from Tyrwhitt's first edition of twenty years earlier .

On the one hand, Lipscomb's collection is 'of its age' and seeks to appeal to an audience of 'the present day', by which he seems to mean his immediate contemporaries. His volumes, he says, are

> offered to the public, under the reasonable confidence, that the improved taste in po-etry, and the extended cultivation of that, in common with all the other elegant arts, which so strongly characterizes the present day, will make the lovers of verse look up to the old Bard, the Father of English poetry, with a veneration proportioned to the improvements they have made in it.[25]

But his claims are not that different from those made earlier in the eighteenth cen-tury. The *Life of Chaucer* which his volume includes is said in the Table of Contents and in Lipscomb's introductory remarks to be by Tyrwhitt. But in fact, the *Life* and its extensive notes are taken *verbatim* from John Campbell's *Life* of Chaucer in the second volume of *Biographia Britannica* (London, 1748).[26]

Lipscomb also relied to a great extent on Campbell for what he thought to be the necessary *critical* claims for his project. For Campbell, as presumably for Lip-scomb, the proof of Chaucer's merits as 'the Father of English Poetry, and perhaps the Prince of it', whose works have 'all the beauties that can be wished for or ex-pected, in every kind', was to be found in more modern performances, and most of all in the direct reflection of those merits in poems like Pope's *Temple of Fame*, which 'will probably be esteemed, as long as there is either Taste or Poetry in this nation'.[27] Campbell and Lipscomb see no significant distinction between the mer-its of eighteenth-century and medieval poetry. For them, the course of poetry is

---

[24] Lipscomb, 1. x.
[25] Ibid. 1. v.
[26] This biography is discussed in Chapters 4 and 5 above.
[27] Lipscomb, 1. 20.

essentially continuous, and that continuity had been most strongly marked by and in the work of three poets who had most judged Chaucer 'worthy of imitation and revival': Spenser, Dryden, and Alexander Pope.[28]

One reason for the confidence with which Campbell and Lipscomb regard the project of rewriting the *Canterbury Tales* is that almost all accounts of Chaucer had presented the poet not only as one whose works had been continued, refashioned, and completed by succeeding poets since the time of Lydgate, but also as *himself* a translator, refashioner, and modernizer. That aspect of his work had been re-emphasized in and by Dryden's *Fables*, the Preface to which had discussed both Chaucer's immediate and long-term past, comparing Chaucer with Boccaccio, and with Ovid, Virgil, and Homer. Chaucer's reworking of medieval sources, and particularly Boccaccio, were elaborately exemplified in Tyrwhitt's *Introductory Discourse*, which Lipscomb's collection included in full.

Lipscomb's volumes, nevertheless, as we have seen, did make a strong claim to be a modern work, finely tuned to contemporary sensibilities. Paradoxically, it is pleasure in *modern* poetry that, Lipscomb assumes, will make modern readers turn to Chaucer. The 'improvements' in poetry of more recent times are seen as likely to provoke 'veneration' for Chaucer as a direct 'father' of English verse.

The 'present day' evoked by Lipscomb is more recent than the first half of the eighteenth century. It is significant that Lipscomb dedicated his volumes to his schoolteacher 'the Rev. Dr. Warton, Late Head-Master of Winchester School'.[29] Lipscomb does not appear to have been eccentric or singular in his conviction that his collection will appeal to those readers whose poetic 'taste' in general, and admiration for Chaucer in particular, has been educated, directly or indirectly, by Joseph Warton.[30]

In one respect, however, Lipscomb presents himself as being in tune with the present 'taste' *in contradistinction to* that of his predecessors. He suggests in his Preface that, although assenting to the proposition that translation 'should be rather free then servile', he had attempted greater fidelity than his predecessors:

[28] Ibid. 1. 55–6. The pioneering Old English scholar, Elizabeth Elstob, in her defence of the 'Northern Languages' against the charge that they were 'made up of nothing else but Monosyllables, and harsh sounding consonants' had moved with similar ease between consideration of the Anglo-Saxon writing which she was championing and the felicitous use of monosyllables by the Greek poets and by English poets from 'Father Chaucer' to Dryden and Roscommon. See her Preface ('with an Apology for the Study of Northern Antiquities') to *The Rudiments of Grammar for the English-Saxon Tongue* (London, 1715), pp. i–xxxv.

[29] Lipscomb, 1. iii.

[30] John Wooll, Warton's pupil and biographer, recorded his particular admiration for Warton's accounts of Pope's *Temple of Fame* and of Dryden's Chaucer translations: John Wooll, *Biographical Memoirs of the Late Joseph Warton* (London, 1806), p. 66. Another of Warton's pupils, Richard Mant, praised both Warton's classes on English poetry and the versions of Chaucer by Dryden. Mant expressed the fervent wish that Warton had himself written versions of Chaucer 'with kindred flame' in express emulation of 'tuneful Dryden'. See Richard Mant, 'Verses to the Memory of Joseph Warton, D. D. Late Head Master of Winchester College', in *Poems* (Oxford, 1806), pp. 102–4. Mant affixed to the opening of his poem *A Father's Prayer* (in *The Slave* [1807]) a long quotation from Palamon's complaint from *Palamon and Arcite*, which he describes as *'Chaucer's Knight's Tale, by Dryden'*.

I have imposed it on myself, as a duty somewhat sacred, to deviate from my original as little as possible in the sentiment, and have often in the language adopted his own expression, the simplicity and effect of which have always forcibly struck me, whenever the terms he uses (and that happens not unfrequently) are intelligible to modern ears.[31]

In one particular respect Lipscomb was willing to abandon his stated principles. Though the versions which he added are not, in fact, markedly closer in practice to those that he had inherited from Ogle, Lipscomb unashamedly declared his intention to remove from his translations traces of 'the grossness and indelicacy of the times'[32] in which Chaucer lived. His hope was that his 'veneration' for Chaucer would be demonstrated by 'purging him of his impurities' and presenting him 'to a more refined age':

[I]t is hoped, as it is believed, that the pruning way of his indelicacies will not be found to have robbed him of any thing valuable … since the exhibiting him free from stains has been effected scrupulously by the omission of the offensive passages, and not by the presumption to substitute fresh matter.

Accordingly, the Miller and the Reeve disappear from the *General Prologue*—along with their tales, which Lipscomb sees as 'highly indelicate, as well in the sentiments as in the language'.[33] Lipscomb's delicacy was not restricted to indecency. In his version of *The Nun's Priest's Tale*, he omits Chaucer's discussion of whether Chanticleer's descent from beam to yard was predestined with the comment, 'These lighter rhimes ill suit such deep debate!'. And where Chanticleer in Dryden's version should have 'believed his dream, and not his wife', Lipscomb gallantly—but in direct contradiction of Chaucer's plot—reverses the proposition: 'Oh! Hapless Chanticleer, lamented bird, / Oh! Had the counsels of the wife been heard!'[34]

---

[31] Lipscomb, 1. vii.

[32] Ibid. 1. vii.

[33] Ibid. 1. viii. Lipscomb's prudery differentiated him from his admired Tyrwhitt, who was quite happy to gloss 'tout' as 'backside' (Tyrwhitt 1798, 2. 634) and to cross-refer to Franciscus Junius [Francis Du Jon], *Etymologicum Anglicanum*, ed. Edward Lye (Oxford, 1743) for definitions of 'queint' (2. 612) and 'swive' (2. 630).

[34] *The Canterbury Tales*, ed. Lipscomb, 2. 331. The early dissemination of Lipscomb's volumes is evident in Maria Edgeworth's *The Modern Griselda* (London, 1805), where the passage from *The Clerk's Tale* detailing the promise that Gualtherus exacts from his bride is read aloud, to the general indignation of 'the married ladies who were present', and it is agreed that had Chaucer 'lived in our enlightened times, he would doubtless have drawn a very different character', since 'the situation and understandings of women have been so much improved since his days. Women were then slaves, now they are free.' (Edgeworth, *The Modern Griselda*, pp. 47, 55). The version of *The Clerk's Tale* read aloud in Edgeworth's novel is that composed by George Ogle, but the text is from Lipscomb's collection.

1801: George Ellis's *Specimens*

We last encountered George Ellis in Chapter 7 as the twenty-four-year-old author of a facetious version of *The Wife of Bath's Tale*. Ellis was forty-eight when he returned to Chaucer, including extracts from Chaucer's poems in the second edition (1801) of his *Specimens of Early English Poets*.[35] Ellis expresses admiration for Tyrwhitt's edition, and Thomas Warton's *History*, which, he says, his own volumes are 'by no means intended to supersede' but to which they might serve as 'an useful index'.[36] Ellis's particular strength as an anthologist is in choosing examples that are at once capable of illustrating the common language and of providing poetical pleasure. He is particularly concerned to display connections between the poets he represents. He wishes, for example, to attract readers to Gower, and chooses from that poet's works the *Tale of Florent*, which he considers to have been 'the original of Chaucer's Wife of Bath's Tale'.[37] We saw earlier that Ellis had reservations about the discussion of Chaucer in Johnson's Preface to his *Dictionary*. Ellis regards Dryden's remarks on Chaucer as 'mistaken in his censure, not in his encomium', and makes the case for Chaucer's pre-eminence with characteristic clarity, revealing, incidentally, that he was unimpressed by the doubts that Tyrwhitt had raised about the authenticity of *The Floure and the Leafe*:

> Chaucer's reputation, as an improver of our versification principally rests on the invention, or at least on the first adoption of the ten-syllable, or heroic verse, of that verse which has been employed by every poet of eminence from Spenser to Dr. Johnson, and in which its original inventor he has left many specimens, both in the Knight's Tale and in the Flower and the Leaf, which Dryden despaired of improving.[38]

The short biography of Chaucer in Ellis's *Specimens* tends to avoid speculation about the poet's life. The same certainly cannot be said of the very much longer biography of Chaucer that was published only two years later.

1803: William Godwin's *Life of Chaucer*

On its appearance in 1803,[39] William Godwin's *Life of Chaucer* represented the most extensive discussion of Chaucer's life and work to date.[40] The intention of

---

[35] George Ellis, ed., *Specimens of the Early English Poets*, 3 vols (London, 1801) . The first, one-volume, edition of Ellis's collection (1790) had contained no Chaucer, and started with poets from the reign of Henry VIII.

[36] Ellis, *Specimens*, 1. viii.

[37] Ibid. 1. 179.

[38] Ibid. 1. 207–8.

[39] The full (and revealing) title is: *The Life of Chaucer, the Early English Poet: Including Memoirs of His Near Friend and Kinsman, John of Gaunt, Duke of Lancaster: With Sketches of the Manners, Opinions, Arts and Literature of England in the Fourteenth Century* (2 vols [London, 1803]) . References to the *Life*, by volume and page, are given in the text.

[40] A second, four-volume, edition followed in 1804.

his book, Godwin says, was to survey the 'manners, the opinions, the arts and the literature' of Chaucer's time, as a means to understanding his mind 'and the causes which made him what he was' (*Life*, 1. viii).

Godwin's *Life* has sometimes been seen as representative of a growing tendency in this period to 'glamorize' the Middle Ages, and to reject earlier condemnation of the period's 'barbarism'. It has also been suggested that his work represents a new kind of attempt to 'contextualize' literary works of the past and see them in the light of the circumstances in which they were produced and received.[41] But such suggestions are misleading on two fronts. Godwin's 'contextualizing' approach to a past writer in fact differs little from that advocated in the previous century by both Samuel Johnson and Alexander Pope.[42] And Godwin cannot easily be associated with any 'glamorization' of the Middle Ages. Indeed, he is at pains to contrast Chaucer's 'times of barbarism' with the 'refinement' of the Elizabethan period (*Life*, 1. vi–vii). Chaucer's work is, he says, tainted with 'licentious' descriptions which are 'characteristic of the imperfect refinements of the times in which he lived' (1. 441). Some of his comic tales, he says, are 'filthy, vulgar and licentious' (2. 573–4).

Godwin's attempt to view Chaucer's works in the light of his 'Life and Times' provides a vivid and extensive instance of the mixture of truth and lies that Pope and Jane Brereton saw as an inherent feature of all 'fame'. His *Life*, in fact, comprises several different books in one, the connections between which are not always entirely clear or cogent. The 'historical' sections of the *Life* seek to present a rich and detailed account of Chaucer's England, and include full and numerous descriptions of fourteenth-century English life, ranging from popular and courtly entertainment to education, monastic life, the activities of Wycliffe and the Lollards, and the horrors of the Black Death. Political and military machinations and developments are charted in great detail, and extensive character sketches are offered not only of Chaucer himself, but of those prominent public figures whose fortunes were closely related to those of the poet, especially the three kings under whom he served and John of Gaunt, whose patronage of and kindness towards Chaucer make him in some ways the secret hero of Godwin's *Life*.

Like the earlier biographies of Chaucer, though at considerably greater length, the biographical sections of Godwin's *Life* are fatally compromised by their dependence on poems now known not to be Chaucer's work. Like his predecessors, Godwin draws on such sources for supposed insights into Chaucer's amatory life, education, personal connections, places of residence, and for various incidents in

---

[41] Brewer, *Chaucer: The Critical Heritage*, 1. 25.
[42] See Johnson, *Works*, 21. 436; Pope, Preface to *The Iliad of Homer* (Pope, *Poems*, 7. 14). On Pope's intense involvement with the 'context' of the Homeric poems, see Dryden, *Critical and Miscellaneous Prose Writings*, ed. Malone, I. i. 328; David Hopkins, 'A Translator's Annotation: Alexander Pope's Observations on his *Iliad*', in *Annotation in Eighteenth-Century Poetry*, ed. Michael Edson (Bethlehem, PA, 2017), pp. 105–28.

which Chaucer was allegedly involved. Godwin is also given to free speculation about various aspects of Chaucer's conduct, beliefs, and psychology. Colourful passages, for example, describe Petrarch's reaction to meeting Chaucer (2. 152–3) and Chaucer's attitude to King Henry IV (2. 545)—for neither of which is there any documentary evidence. A particularly delightful passage (2. 162–72) describes in great detail a grant of wine made to Chaucer in April 1374, and speculates at length about the convivial and poetic effects on Chaucer of his consumption of this piece of royal beneficence.

In these respects, Godwin is true to his own precepts as a biographer. He is at pains to differentiate himself from the kinds of historian that he calls 'antiquarians': 'men of cold tempers and sterile imaginations, writers who by their phlegmatic and desultory industry, have brought discredit upon a science, which is perhaps beyond all others fraught with wisdom, moral instruction and intellectual improvement' (1. x). Tyrwhitt, Godwin argues, 'has endeavoured to reduce the life of the poet to a dry extract of the records of those of our English sovereigns whom Chaucer served'. Godwin's own intention, he says, will be 'to carry the workings of fancy and the spirit of philosophy into the investigation of ages past' (1. xi). 'It would be an idle and ruinous scepticism', he says, 'to blot out of our narratives every thing which is not to be found in official records and gazettes':

> When a man of sober and calculating mind reads the histories of Herodotus or Sallust, he knows that he is reading a tale, a multitude of the circumstances of which may be real, or may be imaginary. But he does not on that account regard them as unworthy of notice.[43]

What connections can be seen between the historical and biographical sections of Godwin's *Life* and the literary-critical sections—extracts from which have been quoted on several occasions in the present study—with which they are juxtaposed? The short answer seems to be that, despite his claim to have produced 'a work of a new species', in which historical information would offer an improved understanding of Chaucer's mind and work (viii–x), Godwin approaches Chaucer's works in a way that is essentially no different from that of eighteenth-century translators and critics. Sir Walter Scott, though, like other early reviewers,[44] contemptuous of the biographical sections of Godwin's *Life*, praised the critical sections as

---

[43] Godwin, *Life*, 1. 352. Such sentiments are closely related to those expressed by Godwin in an essay written a few years before the *Life of Chaucer*, in which he rejected the kind of history which is composed of a 'mere chronicle of facts, places and dates' in favour of a kind of narrative in which 'the writer interweaves a number of happy, ingenious and instructive inventions, blending them into one continuous and indiscernible mass': see William Godwin, 'An Essay of History and Romance', in *Political and Philosophical Writings of William Godwin: Vol. 5: Educational and Literary Writings*, ed. Pamela Clemit (London, 1993), pp. 291–301.

[44] See Robert Southey's review in *The Annual Review and History of Literature* (January 1803), pp. 462–73 and the anonymous review in *The Critical Review, or Annals of Literature* (January 1804), pp. 60–5, 144–50, 324–42.

'the production of a man who has read poetry with taste and feeling'.[45] God-win's judgements of particular poems sometimes differ in detail from those of his predecessors—as those predecessors sometimes differed between themselves.[46] He is, for example, dismissive of Dryden's epic claims for *The Knight's Tale* as a 'ridiculous and impertinent exaggeration'. But he nevertheless praises the poem—in ways that fully accord with Dryden's account and rendering—as 'full of novelty and surprise', says that it is 'every where alive' and 'comprises the most interesting turns of fortune', 'exhibits the most powerful portrait of chivalry that was perhaps ever delineated, and possesses every thing in splendour and in action that can most conspicuously paint out the scenes of the narrative to the eye of the reader' (1. 373). In the case of the pseudo-Chaucerian *Floure and the Leafe*, as we saw in Chapter 9, Godwin is critical of the way in which Dryden has, in his version, 'obscured the purpose of the tale, which in the original is defective in perspicuity'. But he nevertheless applauds the way in which Dryden has 'greatly heightened the enchantment of its character' by making its personages 'fairies', when Chaucer had 'left the species of the being he employs vague and unexplained'. If the original 'is in a very striking style of imagery, gay, variegated and diffuse', Dryden's version, says Godwin, is even more distinguished, and 'may be classed with the most successful productions of human genius' (2. 341, 344). Godwin's account of Dryden's version of *The Floure and the Leafe* was singled out for particular praise in later accounts of the poem by Sir Walter Scott and John Wilson.[47]

Godwin was forced to truncate his *Life of Chaucer* since his publisher would not allow him to extend the project beyond the originally agreed two volumes. His account of the *Canterbury Tales* in the final chapter of the book is therefore briefer and more summary than it would otherwise have been. But it is entirely in line with some of the earlier accounts that we have already encountered. The *Canterbury Tales*, Godwin affirms, is 'certainly one of the most extraordinary monuments of human genius'. Its *General Prologue* presents us with an 'infinite variety of character' and represents 'a copious and extensive review of the private life of the fourteenth century in England'. If Chaucer's very engagement with the tastes and *mores* of his period sometimes led him in the direction of 'licentiousness and coarseness', it also allowed him to exercise his unsurpassed 'talent for comic narrative'. *The Nun's Priest's Tale*, in particular, is praised for its 'liveliness of painting, in the comic demureness with which human sentiments are made to fall from the lips of animals' (2. 373–5).

Chaucer's poetry, according to Godwin, simultaneously embodies and speaks beyond both the life and times of its maker. Writing about *The Romaunt of the*

[45] Walter Scott, 'Godwin's Life of Chaucer', *Edinburgh Review*, (January 1804), 445.
[46] For a full survey of Godwin's account of specific Chaucerian and 'Chaucerian' poems, see Paul M. Clogan, 'Literary Criticism in William Godwin's Life of Chaucer', *Medievalia et Humanistica*, n.s. 6 (1975), 189–98.
[47] See, *Works of John Dryden*, ed. Scott, 11. 354–5; Wilson, *Specimens of the British Critics*, pp. 202–3.

Rose, the English translation of which he believes was Chaucer's work, Godwin notes that though 'the manners of England under the Plantagenets were in many respects extremely unlike our own … yet', in the *Romance of the Rose*

> it is only man with a little variety of garb, and exhibiting in the main the same passions and humours, human frailty and human kindness. When the men of former times are shown, as [*The Romance*] bring them to our view, the sacred awe with which we contemplate the airy shadows of the departed perishes from our bosoms, and they become to us our brother-men, living, moving and real.[48]

'With the poetical character of Chaucer', Godwin declares, 'we have more concern than with his personal qualities. It is because his works live, that we are curious about his dispositions and habits' (2. 571–2). As with Shakespeare, Chaucer 'does not describe … he waves his magic wand, and the personages themselves appear, and act over again at his command the passions, the impressions, and the sorrows of their former life. The past is present before us.' 'No writer', Godwin declares, 'has ever exhibited so great a variety of talent in so short a compass, as Chaucer has done' in 'the successive description of the several pilgrims in the Prologue to the Canterbury Tales' (2. 579–80). However, 'the wonder, and the degree of power displayed in any monument of literature, will often be greatly enhanced, when we come to be acquainted with the circumstances in which it was erected'.

The best works of Chaucer, Godwin says

> have an absolute merit, which stands in no need of extrinsic accident to show it to advantage, and no apology to atone for its concomitant defects. They class with whatever is best in the poetry of any country or any age. Yet when we further reflect that they were written in a remote and semi-barbarous age, that Chaucer had to a certain degree to create a language, or to restore to credit a language which had been sunk into vulgarity and contempt by being considered a language of slaves, that history and the knowledge of past ages existed only in unconnected fragments, and that his writings, stupendous as we find them, are associated as to the period of their production, with the first half-assured lispings of civilization and the muse, the astonishment and awe with which we regard the great father of English poetry must be exceedingly increased, and the lover of human nature and of intellectual power will deem no time misspent that adds to his familiar acquaintance with the history of such a man, or with writings so produced.[49]

1818: William Hazlitt's *Lectures on the English Poets*

A blend of continuity with and distance from eighteenth-century views of Chaucer similar to that found in Godwin's *Life* is in evidence in William Hazlitt's account

---

[48] Godwin, *Life*, 2. 16.
[49] Ibid. 2. 582–3.

of 'Chaucer and Spenser' in his *Lectures on the English Poets* (1818).[50] In contrast
with many of his predecessors, Hazlitt is critical of Dryden's *Palamon and Arcite*,
judging that 'the descriptions of the three temples of Mars, of Venus, and Diana, or
the ornaments and ceremonies used in each, with the reception given to the offerings of the lovers, have a beauty and grandeur, much of which is lost in Dryden's
version'. (In an earlier contribution to *The Examiner*, he had similarly compared
Dryden's rendering of *The Floure and the Leafe* unfavourably with its original.)[51]
And, having benefited from Tyrwhitt's improvement of Chaucer's texts, Hazlitt felt
able to pronounce, in the face of earlier criticisms of Chaucer's versification, that
Chaucer's verse 'has considerable strength and harmony' and that 'its apparent
deficiency in the latter respect arises chiefly from the alterations which have since
taken place in the pronunciation or mode of accenting the words of the language'.
'The best general rule for reading him', Hazlitt says, 'is to pronounce the final *e*, as
in reading Italian' (Hazlitt, *Lectures*, p. 64).

But Hazlitt's comments on Chaucer's character and work often closely resemble those of his eighteenth-century and earlier nineteenth-century predecessors.
Like them, he is misled by inaccurately sourced information about Chaucer's life
(pp. 40–2). Like them, he believes *The Floure and the Leafe* to be a genuinely and
particularly fine Chaucerian work, the opening of which displays to great advantage the 'truth and freshness' of the poet's 'descriptions of natural scenery' (p. 53).
Like Thomas Warton and Thomas Campbell, Hazlitt praises the 'true and natural,
and beautifully simple' qualities of the simile in which 'Cressid's first avowal of her
love' is compared with the song of a nightingale (pp. 42–3). Like George Ogle and
others, he praises the 'trust in nature' that is visible in Chaucer's depiction of 'the
grief and patience of Grisdelda' and the 'touching' quality of *The Prioress's Tale*,
which, he says, 'has all the spirit of martyrdom' (pp. 56–7; 63). Like the earlier
eighteenth-century translators, and unlike Lipscomb, Hazlitt reveals no embarrassment when contemplating 'the utmost licentiousness of comic humour' to be
found in Chaucer's bawdy tales, and which he attributes to 'the manners of [his]
time' (p. 63).

Hazlitt comes closest to his predecessors when considering Chaucer's characterization. Like Dryden and Blake, he believes that Chaucer's depiction of his
pilgrims combines precise delineation of particulars with a generality of implication and offers 'external appearances as indicating character, as symbols of internal
sentiment' (p. 46). 'Chaucer, it has been said' (and here Hazlitt echoes Blake)
'numbered the classes of men, as Linnaeus numbered the plants' (p. 50). Reflecting on Chaucer's depiction of the Summoner, Hazlitt remarks that 'it would be
a curious speculation, (at least for those who think that the characters of men

---

[50] William Hazlitt, *Lectures on the English Poets, Delivered at the Surrey Institution* (London, 1818),
referred to in the text by page numbers.
[51] See further below, in the discussion of Leigh Hunt.

never change, though manners, opinions, and institutions may) to know what has become of this character … in the present day'. Here, Hazlitt glances, in a way that at first sounds sceptical, at Dryden's celebrated remarks about mankind being 'ever the same' though 'every thing' in nature is 'alter'd'. But he then proceeds to speculate, in terms that clearly take their lead from Dryden's findings:

> whether or not [the character of the Summoner] has any technical representative in existing professions; into what channels and conduits it has withdrawn itself, where it lurks unseen in cunning obscurity, or else shews its face boldly, pampered into all the insolence of office, in some other shape, as it is deterred or encouraged by circumstances. *Chaucer's characters modernized*, upon this principle of historic derivation, would be a useful addition to our knowledge of human nature. But who is there to undertake it?
>
> (p. 51)

1835: Cowden Clarke's *Riches of Chaucer*

In his presentation of Chaucer's works in *The Works of the English Poets* (1810), Alexander Chalmers expressed doubts about whether Chaucer's poems could now be read with the 'easy unearned pleasure' that, according to John Wilson, was still enjoyed by readers of Dryden's versions:

> Mr. Warton laments that Chaucer has been so frequently considered as an old, rather than a good poet, and recommends the study of his works. Mr. Tyrwhitt, since this advice was given, had undoubtedly introduced Chaucer to a nearer intimacy with the learned public, but it is not probable that he can ever be restored to popularity. His language will still remain an unsurmountable obstacle with that numerous class of readers to whom poets must look for universal reputation. Poetry is the art of pleasing; but pleasure, as generally understood, admits of very little that deserves the name of study.[52]

It was in an attempt to overcome, for the benefit of ordinary readers, the 'unsurmountable obstacle' of Chaucer's language that various editions were produced which sought to represent Chaucer's text in its original form, but with modernized or regularized spelling. Of these, perhaps the most interesting was Charles Cowden Clarke's *The Riches of Chaucer* (1835).[53]

Innovation is evident both in Cowden Clarke's selection and in his manner of presenting Chaucerian texts—both of which owe much to Godwin:

---

[52] Alexander Chalmers, ed., *The Works of the English Poets*, 21 vols (London, 1810), 1. xv.

[53] *The Riches of Chaucer: In Which His Impurities Have Been Expunged, His Spelling Modernized, His Rhythm Accentuated, and His Obsolete Terms Explained. Also Have Been Added a Few Explanatory Notes and a New Life*, ed. Charles Cowden Clarke, 2 vols (London, 1835). References for quotations are given in the text.

Gateway to Donnington Castle, the last country residence of Chaucer.
p. 80.

Fig. 12.1 'Chaucer's Castle' from *The Riches of Chaucer*, ed. Charles Cowden Clarke (London, 1833).

The idea of accenting the lines of Chaucer did not originate with myself; it is a suggestion put forth by Mr Godwin in his noble history of the poet and his times —for it was a piece of modesty to call the work 'A Life of Chaucer,'—the life of the poet threads the volume like a silver stream through a rich champaign.[54]

Cowden Clarke goes even further than Godwin in his attempts to square the narrative and sentiments of Chaucer's poems with those attributed to Chaucer on the basis of spurious biographical evidence. Chaucer's application and dedication to his art in triumph over the supposed difficulties of his life is everywhere emphasized. For Cowden Clarke, the poet was clearly a great and wise man. A propos of *The Canterbury Tales*, 'one of the most splendid monuments of human genius', Cowden Clarke writes:

> That a book combining at one and the same time an extraordinary delineation of character, a delightful variety of incident, a richness of imagination, a vigour of style, and animation of manner almost beyond all precedent, should have been written by a man after he was sixty years old, fills the mind with wonder and admiration.[55]

It may have been partly in response to such 'wonder and admiration' that Cowden Clarke, like Godwin, makes the story of Chaucer's life end happily: Chaucer, he says, 'descended to his grave in the fulness of a high reputation as an extraordinary genius, and a generous and noble-minded man' (*Riches*, 1. 39). Cowden Clarke follows Godwin closely in recounting that 'we find Chaucer in possession of the castle and park of Donnington, the noble presentation of his princely brother-in law' (1. 33). A representation of this castle ruin is the single illustration to the *Memoir* (see Fig. 12.1).[56]

---

[54] *Riches*, ed. Cowden Clarke, 1. viii.
[55] Ibid. 1. 31.
[56] Chaucer's supposed possession of this castle has a long history. Paul Davis observes that:
Camden had recorded that Dennington (i.e. Donnington) Castle, near Newbury, once belonged to a 'Chaucer', and while the great antiquarian specifically did not say that this was

Fig. 12.2 Portrait of Chaucer printed in all editions of Cowden Clarke's *Riches of Chaucer*, including that of 1896. Attributed in 1835 to Edward Scriven, and in 1870 to W. H. Mote. The influence of Vertue's portrait of 1721 (Fig. 5.2) is clear.

Chaucer's experience, Cowden Clarke suggests, contributed to his wisdom, (see Fig. 12.2) and formed his attitude to women:

> He was a humanist, for he has ever at hand an apology for the frailties of our nature;— above all, when he would atone for the lapses of the most responsible and the least excused of our race—the women.[57]

Very high praise, much of it reflecting that of earlier critics, is given by Cowden Clarke to a large number of Chaucerian works. 'The story of the Cock and the Fox, in the Nun's Priest's Tale', he notes, 'is allowed by all judges to be the most

the poet, his readers were not so fastidious: passing the ruins of the castle on 9 June 1654, John Evelyn noted in his diary that it was 'the possession of old Geofrie Chaucer'.
See Paul Davis, 'After the Fire: Chaucer and Urban Poetics, 1666–1743', in *Chaucer and the City*, ed. Ardis Butterfield (Martlesham, 2006), pp. 178–9, citing William Camden, *Britannia* (1586), trans. Philemon Holland (London, 1637), p. 284 and *The Diary of John Evelyn*, ed. E. S. de Beer, 6 vols (Oxford, 1955), 3. 100.
   [57] *Riches*, ed. Cowden Clarke, 1. 43.

admirable fable (in the narration) that ever was written' (1. 46). Godwin is quoted in support of the opinion that the story of Patient Griselda 'is the most pathetic that ever was written' (1. 48). Cowden Clarke also gives considerable space to a number of poems, notably *Troilus and Creseida* and *The Legend of Good Women*, which had been comparatively neglected in the eighteenth century. His singling out of *The Floure and the Leafe* for special praise is coloured by memories which he recounts of his friend John Keats's composition of his sonnet on the poem, written on a blank space in Cowden's copy of Chaucer while Cowden Clarke himself was dozing (1. 53): in his sonnet, Keats had praised the 'honeyed lines' of *The Floure and the Leafe* and celebrated the 'mighty power' of 'this gentle story'.

Even more remarkable than Cowden Clarke's wide representation of Chaucerian works is his 'idea of accenting the lines' and of altering the spelling: 'Obsolete spelling ... though repulsive, is only a difficulty to the eye, and easily overcome' (1. 12–13). Chaucer's words are therefore spelled by Cowden Clarke in a form as near as possible to their modern equivalents. All syllables that are to receive nonstandard pronunciation are marked. Glosses are supplied at the foot of the page to avoid the distraction involved in 'poring over a closely printed dictionary in a separate volume' (1. vii).

Cowden Clarke's sensitivities about broad speaking are similar to Lipscomb's. The only comic tales included among the *Riches* are the 'Wife of Bath's Tale—Story of King Arthur's Court' and the 'Nun's Priest's Tale—Cock and the Fox'. Cowden Clarke informs his readers that, in his text, 'several passages ... have been excised and substituted with asterisks, and some single words have been replaced' whenever he came across 'words and phrases ... in the original text which modern refinement would discountenance'. Some otherwise unobjectionable passages he has 'softened, or paraphrased, taking care, however, to note the circumstance by means of the inverted comma' (1. vii). Cowden Clarke's Pardoner no longer suggests that a drunkard makes a 'privy' of his throat, nor does he exclaim 'O womb, O belly, stinking is thy cod'. On the other hand, presumably because of its unimpeachable biblical provenance, Cowden Clarke allows the Pardoner's version of the 'filthy incest' of Lot's daughters to remain untouched: 'Lo, how that drunken Lot unkindély / Lay by his daughters two unweetingly; / So drunk he was he n'isté what he wroght' (1. 208). Cowden Clarke assumes that modern refinement might be easily discountenanced—even when the story, in the case of *The Nun's Priest's Tale*, concerns poultry. The word 'laxatif' (*NPT*, 136) presents no difficulty, but 'purging' poses insuperable problems. So the ornaments of the civilized age are brought into play when Cowden Clarke's hen counsels the cock to 'clean' rather than 'purge' himself (*NPT*, 146), and attributes to her herbs the power 'To 'clean and purify you eke above' (1. 290), where readers of Tyrwhitt's learned of slightly different properties: 'To purgen you benethe and eke above'. The removal of mentions of the copulation of Chanticleer and his hen-wives in *The Nun's Priest's Tale*, however, did not prevent Cowden Clarke from giving this poem the warmest approbation:

The description of the birds, the delightful gravity with which they are invested with intellectual endowments, are conceived in the highest taste of true poetry and natural humour. How amusing is the classical tendency of Sir Chanticleer! And how playful and waggish his complimentary addresses to Dame Pertelote![58]

Although not reprinted until 1870, Cowden Clarke's *Riches* was used and praised by several writers on Chaucer's poems.[59] Extensive use of Cowden Clarke's volume, for example, was made several years later by the Scots Presbyterian minister George Gilfillan in his edition of *The Canterbury Tales of Chaucer* (1860).[60] Gilfillan took his text where possible from Cowden Clarke's *Riches*. He adopted Cowden Clarke's modernized spelling, and included the accent and final -*e* marks of which Tyrwhitt had actually expressed explicit disapproval.[61] But in other respects, Gilfillan drew fully on Tyrwhitt, taking his marginal notes from his glossary, and reprinting his essay on Chaucer's *Language and Versification* and his *Introductory Discourse* verbatim. Importantly, Gilfillan restored the passages bowdlerized by Cowden Clarke, and offered little apology for Chaucer's obscenity. The result was a complete edition of *The Canterbury Tales* that was distinctly more 'user-friendly' than any of its predecessors.

1841: *Poems of Geoffrey Chaucer, Modernized*

In 1841, exactly a hundred years after Ogle's collection of versions from the *Canterbury Tales*, there appeared a volume, edited by Richard Hengist Horne (1802–84), entitled *Poems of Geoffrey Chaucer, Modernized*.[62] This book declares itself to be even more sensitive than Lipscomb had been to the delicacies of contemporary manners, language, and poetic sensibility. Believing that 'only a very small class of his countrymen ever read' Chaucer's poems (*Chaucer Modernized*, ed Horne, p. v), Horne sought to produce versions of a selection of Chaucerian works that deviated as little as possible from the text of the original, but which would be immediately intelligible and delightful to contemporary readers.

The collection contained a diverse and unusual selection of Chaucerian works, including a version of *Queen Annelida and False Arcite* by Elizabeth Barrett (later Browning). The Irish writer Robert Bell (1800–67) modernized *The Complaint of*

---

[58] Ibid. 1. 46.

[59] See, e.g. John Saunders, *Cabinet Pictures of English Life: Chaucer* (London, 1845) p. 222. Leigh Hunt (see below) quoted Cowden Clarke's text when offering his selections from Chaucer in Leigh Hunt's *London Journal* (1835).

[60] Geoffrey Chaucer, *The Canterbury Tales*, ed. George Gilfillan, 3 vols (Edinburgh, 1860).

[61] Of the various attempts to mark pronunciation and aid scansion in Urry's edition, Tyrwhitt had observed that they must 'necessarily very much disfigure the orthography of the language so that no editor has a right to introduce it'. His final swipe is entirely typical of Tyrwhitt and the spirit of his edition: 'But, after all, a reader who cannot perform such operations for himself, had better not trouble his head about the versification of Chaucer' (Tyrwhitt 1798, 1. lxxxvi).

[62] *Chaucer Modernized*, ed. Horne, cited in text by page number.

Mars and Venus. Thomas Powell (1809–87), fraudster, and the original inspirer of the collection, contributed versions of the *Legends* of Ariadne, Philomene, and Phillis, as well as *The Flower and the Leaf.* A writer signing himself 'Z. A. Z' modernized *The Rime of Sir Thopas.* Leigh Hunt offered versions of the *Manciple's, Squire's,* and *Friar's Tales.* Wordsworth allowed the printing of his version of *The Cuckoo and the Nightingale* and of the *Extract from Troilus and Cresida* that he had composed forty years earlier.

In his Introduction, Horne offers his reflections on several earlier engagements with Chaucer. Lipscomb's versions are roundly condemned. Horne has clearly read Tyrwhitt's notes with appreciative attention, though he has his own notions about Chaucer's prosody. Godwin's 'voluminous labours' are praised both in the Introduction (p. xcii), and in the 'Life of Chaucer' (pp. cvii–cxxxviii) put together by the Prussian Classicist Professor Leonhard Schmitz. Cowden Clarke's *Riches* is treated with respect—though deemed to have 'received no adequate encouragement' (p. xxxi).

On the title page, the following verse printed as an epigraph and ascribed to Wordsworth:

> That noble Chaucer, in those former times,
> Who first enriched our English with his rimes,
> And was the first of ours that ever broke
> Into the Muse's treasure, and first spoke
> In weighty numbers; delving in the mine
> Of perfect knowledge.

These lines are in fact by Michael Drayton (1563–1631), but their misattribution to Wordsworth indicates that poet's central importance to Horne's project.[63] The poems in Horne's collection are presented as following the model of the version of *The Prioress's Tale* 'with which the public have become acquainted in the works of Mr. Wordsworth'.[64] That poem had been chosen as a model because 'the severe poetical fidelity of its execution has long since been recognized by all true lovers of Chaucer' (p. xxix).

As we saw in Chapters 6 and 9, Wordsworth accompanied his version of *The Prioress's Tale* with a note where he suggested that, while he had made 'no further deviation from the original' than the changes in language, 'especially in pronunciation', demanded, it remained the case 'that much was to be removed'. The phrases retained, and some of those substituted, represented 'sprinklings of antiquity' that would, Wordsworth said, have 'a graceful accordance with the subject'.

---

[63] The lines are from 'To my most Dearely-loved friend Henery Reynolds Esquire, Of Poets and Poesie', included in Michael Drayton, *The Battaile of Agincourt* (London, 1627). Drayton's poem is discussed in Chapter 1.

[64] The poem had appeared in William Wordsworth, *The River Duddon: A Series of Sonnets: Vaudracour and Julia: And Other Poems* (London, 1820).

There was no consensus, however, about the value of Wordsworth's Chaucerian renderings. Commenting on the version of *The Cuckoo and the Nightingale* that was included in Horne's collection, John Wilson observed that Wordsworth

> works reverently, lovingly, surely with full apprehension of Chaucer; and yet, at every word where he leaves Chaucer, the spirit of Chaucer leaves the verse. You see plainly that his rule is to change the least that can possibly be changed. Yet the gentle grace, the lingering musical sweetness, the taking simplicity, of the wise old poet, vanish—brushed away like the down from the butterfly's wing, by the lightest and most timorous touch.[65]

In fact, although several of the contributors to *Poems of Geoffrey Chaucer, Modernized* retained the 'ancient accent' as recommended by Wordsworth 'in a few conjunctions, as alsò and alwày', few were able to achieve for any length the 'severe poetical fidelity' desired. The different versions vary, both from one another and within each of them, in their degree of closeness to the phraseology and prosody of their originals. But they all appear to be convinced that they represent a significant improvement on their earlier predecessors. Horne's Introduction dismisses the versions of Dryden and Pope, which are not sharply distinguished from those of the other members of Ogle's team or Lipscomb's:

> The versions of Chaucer which have been given by Dryden and Pope, are elaborate and highly-finished productions, reading exactly like their own poems, and not bearing the slightest resemblance to Chaucer.

(pp. x–xi)

One reason for the variability of approach in the contributors to Horne's volume may be that Wordsworth was not their only model. While eighteenth-century versions are consistently denigrated by Horne, the versions of 'Lord Thurlow'[66] are praised, as if they were similar to Wordsworth's. 'The version given by Lord Thurlow of the "Flower and the Leaf"', Horne writes, 'is such, in its execution and fine appreciation, as might be expected of a true poet'. Thurlow's versions are praised on the grounds that their 'versification' does not resemble 'the model of that uniformity of syllables and position of accents which may be regarded as the school of Pope' (p. xxix).[67]

As we have seen, Chaucer's obscenity presented particular problems to poets attempting to preserve his prosody and vocabulary. After Horne's volume had

---

[65] Wilson, *Specimens of the British Critics*, p. 262.

[66] Edward Hovell Thurlow, second Baron Thurlow (1781–1829). Thurlow was the author of *Arcita and Palamon. After the Excellent Poet Geoffrey Chaucer* (London, 1822) and *The Knight's Tale and The Flower and the Leaf. After Geoffrey Chaucer* (2nd edn, London, 1822).

[67] Horne was by no means here in agreement with all contemporary opinion. In the *Edinburgh Review* of 1814, Thomas Moore had delivered a devastating critique of Thurlow's Chaucer translations, arguing that Thurlow's 'mimickry'of his 'mighty elders' 'keeps carefully wide of their beauties', is laboriously faithful 'to their defects alone', and 'represents the mere mouldering form of their phraseology, without any of that life-blood of fancy which played through it' : see Thomas Moore, 'Lord Thurlow's Poems', *Edinburgh Review*, 23 (September 1814), p. 424.

appeared, Wordsworth remarked that he had been unwilling to 'place' his own version of *The Manciple's Tale* 'at the disposal of the editor' as he 'deemed the subject somewhat too indelicate for pure taste to be offered to the world at this time of day'.[68] It was Horne's argument that Pope's removal of quaintness of expression and 'sprinklings of antiquity' had increased rather than diminished the obscenity of eighteenth-century versions. The 'licentious humour of the original being divested of its quaintness and obscurity', he says, becomes in Pope's versions 'yet more licentious in proportion to the skill with which it is brought into the light'. It follows that all versions 'done in the time of Pope' may be dismissed out of hand:

> They are *not* modernized versions—which implies modern delicacy, as well as modern language—they are vulgarised versions. The public of the present day would certainly never tolerate any similar proceeding, even were it likely to be attempted.
>
> (p. xvii)

Given the double, and contradictory, demand (on the one hand, to represent the versification and phraseology of the original more closely, and on the other, to avoid indecency and swearing), it was bold and foolhardy of Horne to include his own modernization of *The Reeve's Tale,* a work excluded altogether by Lipscomb and Cowden Clarke, in his 1841 collection.[69] Horne explains his reasons for choosing this poem in a prefatory note: 'It has been thought that an idea of the extraordinary versatility of Chaucer's genius could not be adequately conveyed unless one of his matter-of-fact comic tales were attempted.' *The Reeve's Tale* has therefore been chosen 'as presenting a graphic painting of characters ... displayed in action by means of a story which may be designated as a broad farce ending in a pantomime of absurd reality'. Some of the action, and some matters of narrative fact, were, however, clearly problematic. The note ends with the suggestion that 'to those who are acquainted with the original, an apology may not be considered inadmissible for certain necessary variations and omissions' (p. 138).

Horne's version attempts to convey the humour while, in the interests of 'modern delicacy', excluding the indecency. An absurd consequence of this strategy is that it is hard, if not impossible, to know what is happening in the tale. Horne may be close to some of Chaucer's words, but he has altered Chaucer's action entirely. Like Betterton before him, he is a little coy about the reasons for the Miller's wife rising in the night ('Sone after this the wif hire routing lete, / And gan awake, and

---

[68] William Wordsworth, *The Letters of William and Dorothy Wordsworth, Vol. 6: The Later Years, 1821–1850,* ed. Ernest de Selincourt, rev. Alan G. Hill, 4 vols (2nd edn, Oxford, 1978–88), 4. 165, quoted in William Wordsworth, *Translations of Chaucer and Virgil,* ed. Bruce E. Graver (Ithaca, NY and London, 1998), p. 27.

[69] Wordsworth (in the same letter quoted in n 68) expressed his disapproval of the inclusion of the tale in *Chaucer Modernized.*

went hire out to pisse').[70] Chaucer's wording, however, seems to be bizarrely hinted at in Horne's rhymes:

> she was pained
> With night-mare dreams of skies that madly rained.
> Eastern astrologers and clerks, I wis,
> In time of Apis tell of storms like this.
>
> (p. 156)

The nightmare is important, however, because much mirth is to be had from the silly Miller's silly Wife wandering around, unable to find the right bed. She never gets into bed with John, but is apparently—it is all confused—left 'still groping' in the dark, until her husband, leaping out of bed in a struggle with Allen, bumps into her and knocks her down. Since this happens when 'the third cock of the morn 'gan sing', Horne has lost the night—so eventful in Chaucer's version. And it is not at all clear what John might intend in moving the cradle to stand beside his own bed.

Charlotte Morse has observed that 'Horne makes the students' revenge on the miller unintelligible'.[71] An essential point in Chaucer's tale is the means by which Allein wins the heart of the daughter. But in Horne's version, not only is she not 'swived bolt upright', she is not 'swived' at all. Horne does manage to include a few more items of Chaucer's vocabulary and locutions than had any predecessor, but, in avoiding indecency he has had to invent a number of phrases, often, as in the Chaucerian 'imitations' of Fenton and 'Prior', in the 'antique' manner. In the quotation below, underlining represents phases that Horne has been able to take over relatively untouched from his original, italics those that are purely his own:

	Meantime was heard the beating of a wing,
	And then the third cock of the morn 'gan sing.
	Allen stole back, and thought 'ere that it dawn
Aleyn up rist and thought, er that it daw	I will creep in by John *that lieth forlorn.*
I wol go crepen in by my felaw:	He found the cradle in his hand, anon.
And fond the cradel at his hand anon.	'Gude Lord!'thought Allen, 'all wrong have I gone!
By God, thought he, al wrang I have	My head is dizzy with the *ale* last night,
misgon.	*And eke my piping,* that I go not right.
My hed is tottie of my swink to night,	Wrong am I, by the cradle well I know:
That maketh me that I go nat aright.	Here lieth Simkin, and his wife alsó.
I wot wel by the cradel I have misgo;	And, scrambling forthright on, he made his way
Heere lith the miller and his wif also.	Unto the bed where Simkin *snoring* lay!
And forth he goth a twenty divel way	He thought to *nestle* by his fellow John,
Unto the bed, ther as the miller lay.	And by the Miller in he crept, anon,
He wend have cropen by his felaw John,	And caught him by the neck, and *'gan to shake,*
And by the millere in he crept anon,	And said, 'Thou John! thou swine's head dull, awake!

[70] Tyrwhitt 1798, 1. 166.
[71] Charlotte C. Morse, 'Popularizing Chaucer in the Nineteenth Century', *The Chaucer Review*, 38 (2003), 99–125 (pp. 105–6) .

And caught him by the nekke, and gan him
              spake.
And sayd; Thou John, thou swineshed awake,
For Cristes saule, and here a noble game:
For by that lord that called is Seint Jame,
As I have thries as in this short night
Swived the millers doughter bolt-upright,
While thou hast as a coward ben agast.
    Ye, false harlot, quod the miller, hast?
A, false traitour, false clerk, (quod he)
Thou shalt be ded, by Goddes dignitee,
Who dorste be so bold to disparage
My doughter, that is come of swiche linage.

      (RvT, 4249–72; Tyrwhitt, 1798, 1. 167–8)

Wake, by the mass! and hear a noble game,
For, by St. Andrew! to thy ruth and shame,
I have been trolling roundelays this night,
And won the Miller's daughter's *heart outright,*
Who hath me told where hidden is our meal:
All this—and more—and how they always steal;
While thou hast as a coward lain aghast.'
    '*Thou slanderous ribald!*' quoth the Miller, 'hast?
A traitor false, false *lying* clerk!' quoth he,
'Thou shalt be slain by heaven's dignity.'

      (*Chaucer Modernized*, ed. Horne, pp. 157–8)

'I have been trolling roundelays this night': Horne's own version of *The Reeve's Tale* is presumably an attempt to apply 'modern delicacy'—where the word 'modern' serves as a distinguishing marker separating Horne's present both from the medieval and the eighteenth-century pasts.

John Wilson, reviewing Horne's volume in 1845, argued that the 'passages interpolated by Mr Horne's own pen are as bad as possible—clownish and anti-Chaucerian to the last degree'.[72] His objections to Horne's *Reeve's Tale*, however, focus on Horne's inaccuracy rather than on his prudishness or spurious antiquity of phrase:

> Mr Horne cannot read Chaucer. The Miller does not, as he makes him do, accuse the Cantab [Allein] of falsely slandering his daughter's virtue. He does not doubt the truth of the unluckily blabbed secret; false harlot, false traitor, false clerk, are all words that tell his belief; but Mr Horne, not understanding 'disparage,' as it is here used by Chaucer, wholly mistakes the cause of the father's fury... . And this is modernizing Chaucer?[73]

Wilson's general comment is also pertinent:

> A language that is half Chaucer's and half that of his renderer, is in great danger to be the language of nobody. But Chaucer's has its own energy and vivacity which attaches you, and as soon as you have undergone the due transformation by sympathy, carries you effectually with it.[74]

And, significantly, Wilson goes to some length to defend Dryden's versions against Horne's charges:

---

[72] Wilson, *Specimens of the British Critics*, p. 255.
[73] Ibid. p. 257.
[74] Ibid. p. 265.

Dryden boldly and freely gives you himself, and along you sweep, or are swept rejoic-
ingly along. 'The grand charge to which his translations are amenable,' says Mr Horne,
'is that he acted upon an erroneous principle.' Be it so. Nevertheless, they are among
the glories of our [poetical][75] literature. Mr. Horne's, literal as he supposes them to
be, are unreadable. He, too, acts on an erroneous principle; and his execution betrays
throughout the unskilful hand of a presumptuous apprentice.[76]

Leigh Hunt

In his account of Horne's volume, John Wilson does not mention the versions
by Leigh Hunt, who had probably thought as much about Chaucer as William
Wordsworth, and perhaps more than Horne's other contributors.[77] Of Hunt's versions 'as poems', T. R. Lounsbury had a high opinion, regarding Wordsworth's
versions as 'inferior to those of Leigh Hunt, who deviates much further from the
language of the original, but in some respects remains more faithful to its spirit'. He
found 'an ease and freedom of movement which reminds the reader remotely at
least of the great original'.[78] Caroline Spurgeon in her synoptic survey and collection of Chaucer criticism and allusion went even further. 'Perhaps', she wrote, 'the
most constant and enthusiastic lover of Chaucer in the early nineteenth century
was Leigh Hunt.'[79]

In his *Autobiography*, Hunt recorded that he 'was not acquainted with [Chaucer]
at school, nor till long afterwards'.[80] But once he did make the poet's acquaintance, his work reveals a regular and detailed involvement with Chaucer's work
and its reception over a period of more than four decades. *The Tapiser's Tale* (1858)
is an attempt at the Chaucerian 'manner' reminiscent of the eighteenth-century
'imitations' of Chaucerian style. Hunt also made verse translations of four of the
Canterbury Tales; one of them, as we shall see in two very different versions, composed a prose retelling of *The Pardoner's Tale*,[81] and included prose paraphrases

---

[75] Misprinted as 'political' in the book version of Wilson's essays.
[76] Wilson, *Specimens of the British Critics*, pp. 265–6.
[77] Wordsworth himself had a high opinion of Hunt, writing to Moxon, his publisher, on the 24
February 1840 apropos of a publication of

> some portions of Chaucer modernised, as far and no farther than is done in my treatment
> of 'The Prioress's Tale.' That will, in fact, be his model.—He will have Coadjutors, among
> whom, I believe, will be Mr. Leigh Hunt, a man as capable of doing the work well as any
> living Author.
>   (quoted in Wordsworth, *Translations*, ed. Graver, p. 21).

[78] Thomas R. Lounsbury, *Studies in Chaucer, His Life and Writings*, 3 vols (London, 1892), 2. 210–11.
[79] Caroline Spurgeon, *Five Hundred Years of Chaucer Criticism and Allusion, 1357–1900*, 3 vols
(Cambridge, 1925), 1. lxv.
[80] Leigh Hunt, *Autobiography* (London, 1860) p. 79.
[81] In *Ollier's Literary Miscellany* (1820).

to accompany the extracts from Chaucer included in his anthology, *Wit and Humour* (1846). Hunt's critical works include many references to Chaucer, and in six articles in the 1835 volume of his *London Journal* he offered, under the title 'Characteristic Specimens of the English Poets', an extensive anthology of 'beauties' from Chaucer's work, accompanied by an enthusiastic critical commentary.[82]

Hunt's enthusiasm for Chaucer was not unlimited. Like many others (as we have seen), he was troubled by the 'coarseness' to be found in some of Chaucer's works, which, he says, was 'that of his age'.[83] Hunt noted:

> The subjects with which the court and gentry of the times of the Henrys and Edwards could be entertained, are sometimes not only indecorous but revolting. It is a thousand pities that the unbounded sympathy of the poet with everything that interested his fellow-creatures did not know, in this instance, where to stop.[84]

'Yet', Hunt continues, 'we must be cautious how we take upon ourselves to blame him. Even Shakspeare [*sic*] did not quite escape the infection of indecency in a much later and highly refined age', and, for all we know, 'allusions and phrases which are thought harmless now' may come to 'be regarded by our posterity as the grossest and cruellest barbarisms'. Moreover, 'when Chaucer is free from this taint of his age, his humour is of a description the most thoroughly delightful; for it is at once entertaining, profound, and good-natured'.[85]

The version by Leigh Hunt—entitled *The Manciple's Tale; or Phœbus and the Crow*—which replaced that withdrawn by Wordsworth from the Horne collection may illustrate his means of coming to terms with 'the infection of indecency' at the same time as exemplifying the 'ease and freedom of movement' described by Lounsbury. The skill with which Hunt's Manciple hints at the word 'whore' may be compared with Horne's heavy handling of the suppressed word 'piss' (as quoted above):

> This wife, when Phœbus was from home one day,
> Sent for her lemman then, without delay.
> Her lemman!—a plain word, I needs must own;
> Forgive it me; for Plato hath laid down,
> The word must suit according with the deed;
> Word is work's cousin-german, ye may read:
> I'm a plain man, and what I say is this:
> Wife high, wife low, if bad, both do amiss:

---

[82] For a list of many of the works by Hunt which display contact with Chaucer, see Spurgeon, *Five Hundred Years of Chaucer Criticism*, Vol. 3 (Index, pp. 52–3). Extracts from these works are printed by Spurgeon in the main body of her book. For a useful general survey of Hunt's dealings with Chaucer, see Paul M. Clogan, 'Chaucer and Leigh Hunt', *Medievalia et Humanistica*, n.s. 9 (1979), 164–74.

[83] *Leigh Hunt's London Journal*, 13 June 1835, p. 180.

[84] Leigh Hunt, *Wit and Humour: Selected from the English Poets* (London, 1846), pp. 74–5.

[85] Ibid.

> But because one man's wench sitteth above,
> She shall be called his Lady and his Love;
> And because t'other's sitteth low and poor,
> She shall be called,—Well, well, I say no more.
>
> (*Chaucer Modernized*, ed. Horne, p. 100)

Wordsworth's friend, Barron Field, accused Hunt of 'emasculating the whole moral' of this poem by 'softening the adultery into a kiss'.[86] In fact, there is no kiss between Hunt's wife and her unworthy 'leman'. We saw in Chapter 6 that in Wordsworth's *Phoebus and the Crow* the bird does not describe the couple's behaviour with Chaucer's brutal directness ('so mote I thrive: /For on thy bedde thy wif I saw him swive'), but says more decorously: 'For I full plainly as I hope for life / Saw him in guilty converse with thy wife'.[87] The crow in Hunt's version merely tells the 'woeful god' that 'bleared is thine eye'—at which point, the poem adopts reported speech: 'What would you more? The crow hath told him all'. The Crow's blatant lack of delicacy is, however, clearly conveyed:

> Phœbus, quoth he; for all thy worthiness,
> For all thy beauty and all thy gentilesse,
> For all thy song and all thy minstrelsy,
> And all thy watching, bleared is thine eye;
> Yea, and by one no worthier than a gnat …
>
> (*Chaucer Modernized*, ed. Horne, p. 101)

It is in his discussions of the translation of Chaucer that Hunt might seem at first to differ most sharply from his eighteenth-century predecessors. In an essay first published in *The Examiner* in 1815 and later collected in *The Round Table* (1817), Hunt anticipated some of the sentiments expressed by Horne, in suggesting that Chaucer was not best served by the kinds of paraphrastic translations included in the collections by Ogle and Lipscomb. Hunt proposed that 'the best method of modernizing the Father of English Poetry' should be

> after the mode of the Italian *rifacimento*, altering only just as much as is necessary for comfortable intelligibility, and preserving all the rest, that which appears quaint as well as that which is more modern,—in short, as much of the author,—his nature,—his own way of speaking and describing, as possible.

Such a method, he thinks, will ensure that we 'keep the model of Nature, [Chaucer's] own model, before us, and make modern things bend to her,—not her, as is the custom of our self-love, bend to every thing which happens to be modern'.[88] In accordance with this principle, Hunt offers specimens of *The Squire's*

---

[86] See Wordsworth, *Translations*, ed. Graver, p. 26, quoting Field's memoir (BL Add. MS. 41, 325).

[87] Wordsworth, *Translations*, ed. Graver, p. 97.

[88] Leigh Hunt, 'On Chaucer', in *The Round Table*, 2 vols. (London and Edinburgh, 1817), 1. 136. In numbers of *The Tatler* for June and July 1831, Hunt was to offer minimally modernized versions of three

Tale, translated in the minimalist way he describes.[89] (When quoting Chaucer in his *London Journal* essays, Hunt avoided translation altogether and used texts with modernized spelling from Cowden Clarke's *Riches*.)

The three Chaucerian versions by Hunt included in *Poems of Geoffrey Chaucer Modernized* employ, broadly speaking, the *rifacimento* style recommended by Hunt in his *Round Table* essay. But the translation of *The Squire's Tale* included in Horne's collection was not the first rendering of Chaucer's poem that Hunt had composed. That version, first published in *The Liberal* in 1823, had adopted quite a different translating method.[90] In it, very few of Chaucer's lines were preserved in anything like their original form, and the poem is in many places highly paraphrastic, departing substantially, for example, from Chaucer's description of the puzzled reactions of the courtiers to the gifts presented to King Cambus (Chaucer's Cambuscan), and finally, like Spenser and others, leaving Chaucer's tale altogether, as Chaucer himself had done, to anticipate (as Hunt explains in a footnote) 'a continuation of the story, which [Chaucer] would willingly conclude, if he had health and leisure'.

Detailed examination, moreover, of the translations by Hunt in Horne's collection reveals that even within his self-imposed restraints Hunt will sometimes depart from Chaucer either for the sake of metrical regularity, or when he suspects that the original will puzzle modern readers, or where he thinks the narrative could do with an added touch of lively detail.[91] And we have already witnessed his ingenuity in coping with Chaucer's notorious 'indecency'.

Hunt's final verse translation from Chaucer, *Death and the Ruffians*, a version of *The Pardoner's Tale*, first published in the *New Monthly Magazine* in 1845, represents an approach that differs both from that of his first version of *The Squire's Tale* and from that of the three translations in Horne's collection. In this rendering, Hunt's method is much closer to that of the paraphrastic translations of Dryden and Pope in which the contours of the original are followed closely, but the expression is reconceived in an entirely modern narrative style. In this version, as in Hunt's first rendering of *The Squire's Tale*, comparatively few of Chaucer's lines and phrases are preserved intact, and Chaucer's text is often freely expanded and

---

short extracts from Chaucer: the portraits of the Knight and the Squire from the *General Prologue* and the simile in *Troilus and Criseyde* comparing Criseyde to a nightingale: see Spurgeon, *Five Hundred Years of Chaucer Criticism*, 2. 181–2.

[89] The passages were repeated almost verbatim in his complete translation of the Tale included in Horne's collection.

[90] See Leigh Hunt, 'The First Canto of the Squire's Tale of Chaucer, Modernized', *The Liberal*, 4 July 1823, 317–31. This version (rather than that of 1841, as suggested by Spurgeon, *Five Hundred Years of Chaucer Criticism* [Part II, p. 22]) was the one reprinted in Hunt's *Stories in Verse* (London, 1855), thus showing that the Hunt of the 1850s had by no means 'disowned' it after his more literal version of fourteen years before.

[91] An example of the last occurs when the fiend in 'The Friar's Tale' encourages his horses by repeating the phrases previously given by Chaucer to the carter whose cart has stuck in the mud: "*Heit* there." quoth he; "*heit, hiet;* ah, *matthy wo*' (*Chaucer Modernized*, ed. Horne, p. 206).

contracted for the easier understanding and greater pleasure of modern readers. The concentration is entirely on the main Tale. Hunt omits the Pardoner's lengthy digression (*PardT*, 483–660) on Biblical condemnations of swearing, gambling, and drunkenness.

When *Death and the Ruffians* was reprinted in his *Stories in Verse* (1855), Hunt supplied an introduction in which he returned to the question of translating Chaucer. His own experience as a translator—together with the appreciation of Chaucer's local verbal artistry evidenced in his detailed and perceptive close readings of particular Chaucerian lines and passages[92]—has caused him to relax his original advocacy of *rifacimento* to incorporate the suggestion that while *no* translation of Chaucer could ever replace the original, translations might have some virtue, whether in encouraging readers to turn to Chaucer's original texts, or by manifesting poetic virtues of their own:

> The reader will do me great injustice, if he thinks that modernizations like these are intended as substitutes for what they modernize. Their only plea for indulgence is, that they may act as incitements towards acquaintance with the great original … I heartily agree with those critics who are of opinion, that no modernizations of Chaucer, however masterly they might be, could do him justice; for either they must be little else but re-spellings … or, secondly, they must be something betwixt old style and new, and so reap the advantages of neither … or lastly, like the otherwise admirable versions by Dryden and Pope, they must take leave *in toto* of the old manner of the original, and proceed upon the merits, whatever these may be, of the style of the modernizers.[93]

It is significant that by 1855 Hunt could refer to Dryden's and Pope's versions of Chaucer as 'admirable'. On several occasions, Hunt had compared Dryden's versions of Chaucer unfavourably with their originals.[94] But he had never gone as far as his collaborator William Hazlitt, who, in one of his *Round Table* essays for *The Examiner*, had compared the opening of *The Floure and the Leafe* with Dryden's version of the 'Chaucerian' original and had commented: 'Dryden and the rest of that school were merely *verbal poets*. They had a great deal of wit, sense and fancy; they only wanted truth and depth of feeling.'[95] As early as 1815, Hunt had been convinced that 'the best parts of Dryden's versification are some of the best music of which English rhythm is capable; or, in other words, are imitated from the best part of the versification of Chaucer himself'.[96] Hunt had always preferred Dryden to Pope, and had modelled his own versification on what he considered to be the 'freer' couplet style of Pope's predecessor. He was instrumental in encouraging

---

[92] See, particularly, the discussion of two individual lines from *The Knight's Tale* and *The Squire's Tale* in the Preface to Hunt, *Stories in Verse*, pp. 24–30.

[93] Hunt, *Stories in Verse*, pp. 262–3.

[94] See, e.g. the comparisons between passages in *The Knight's Tale* and Dryden's *Palamon and Arcite* in Hunt, *London Journal*, 20 June 1835, pp. 187–8.

[95] *The Examiner*, 3 September 1815, pp. 570–1. Hazlitt dropped the comparison when his *Round Table* essays (together with Hunt's) were collected in book form in 1817, but reinstated it (along with the rest of the essay) as 'Essay IX: Matter and Manner' in William Hazlitt, *Winterslow* (London, 1839).

[96] Hunt, *The Round Table*, p. 133.

Keats to engage in a detailed study of Dryden before writing *Lamia*, where Dryden's influence is very clear.[97] It is perhaps only to be expected that Hunt would see traces of the influence of his much-admired Chaucer in his much-admired Dryden.

Like Dryden, Leigh Hunt believed that Chaucer's poetry could manifest a 'grand' and 'comprehensive' 'epic power', while also being able, on other occasions, to record 'the smallest matter of fact'.[98] Chaucer's 'graphic facility, and healthy sense of the material', Hunt says, 'strongly ally him to the painter; and perhaps a better idea could not be given of his universality than by saying, that he was at once the Italian and the Flemish painter of his time'. Chaucer attains this 'universality'—and here Hunt is again close to Dryden, as well as to Blake—by combining sharply observed details of contemporary *mores* with a generality of implication that raises them above the merely contingent or documentary:

> Classes must, of course, be drawn, more or less, from the individuals composing them; but the unprofessional particulars added by Chaucer to his characters (such as the Merchant's uneasy marriage, and the Franklin's prodigal son) are only such as render the portraits more true, by including them in the general category of human kind.[99]

Like the critics discussed in Chapter 10, Hunt believed that 'Chaucer's pathos is true nature's: it goes directly to its object',[100] and, like George Ogle, Hunt found particular support for this judgement in *The Clerk's Tale*, to substantial extracts from which he devotes the entirety of his fourth *London Journal* article.

Hunt agreed with some of his critical predecessors that Chaucer's genius, though sometimes—and sometimes justifiably—sharply satirical, was essentially genial and tolerant:

> The third great quality of Chaucer's humour is its fair play;—the truth and humanity which induces him to see justice done to good and bad, to the circumstances which make men what they are, and the mixture of right and wrong, of wisdom and folly, which they consequently exhibit. His worst characters have some little saving grace of good-nature, or at least of joviality and candour.[101]

Above all, and like Dryden and other writers already discussed in this book, Hunt was absolutely convinced that Chaucer deserved his reputation as the father of English Poetry, and that he should—along, he says, with Spenser, Shakespeare, and Milton—be classed as one of the very greatest English poets—perhaps of all poets.[102] Hunt's critical opinions, that is, did not differ in any essential respect from

---

[97] See Upali Amarasinghe, *Dryden and Pope in the Early Nineteenth Century* (Cambridge, 1962), pp. 165–71. Hunt's preference for Dryden has antecedents in the late eighteenth-century debate about the relative merits of Pope and Dryden: see Gretchen M. Foster, *Pope Versus Dryden: A Controversy in Letters to 'The Gentleman's Magazine', 1789–1791* (Victoria, BC, 1989) .

[98] Hunt, *London Journal*, 13 June 1835, p. 180.

[99] Hunt, Wit and Humour, p. 75.

[100] Hunt, *London Journal*, 27 June 1835, p. 195.

[101] Hunt, *Wit and Humour*, p. 77.

[102] Hunt, *London Journal*, 13 June 1835, p. 180.

those of John Dart, who in 1720, as we have seen, had described Chaucer as 'the greatest Poet that *England* (or perhaps the World) ever produc'd', and so one not limited by the time or language in which he wrote.[103] Seven years later, Walter Harte had described Chaucer as 'perhaps the greatest poet among the moderns'.[104] And Robert Potter, the translator of Aeschylus, considered that while 'Dryden is probably partial in setting *Palamon and Arcite*, on a level with the *Eneid*', nevertheless judged that 'Chaucer was a great genius and deemed the primo-genitor of English poetry'.[105]

Chaucer as Poetic Legislator

The difference, if there is one, between eighteenth-century and early-nineteenth-century veneration for Chaucer is that the poet had come to be seen by some—and particularly by William Godwin—as not only among the best, but the very *type* of The Poet. The distinction of Chaucer, Godwin believed, does not rest merely on his skill and responsiveness as a commentator on the personalities or values of his own age. Nor—despite Godwin's lengthy, and mostly misguided, attempts to trace the events of Chaucer's life—does it depend on the light that his work sheds on Chaucer the Man. Godwin's claims for Chaucer the Poet rest ultimately on a set of convictions about the nature and stature of great poetry which both look back to some of Godwin's distinguished critical predecessors and anticipate the sentiments of some of his heirs.

Godwin's idea of poetry can be seen as a bridge between that of Imlac in Samuel Johnson's *Rasselas* and that celebrated by his future son-in-law Percy Bysshe Shelley in his *Defence of Poetry*. A poet, according to Godwin, is a being 'whose judgement should be clear, whose feelings should be uniform and sound, whose sense should be alive to every impression and hardened to none, who is the legislator of generations and the moral instructor of the world'.[106] Johnson's Imlac had claimed that the poet

> must divest himself of the prejudices of his age or country; he must consider right and wrong in their abstracted and invariable state; he must disregard present laws and opinions, and rise to general and transcendental truths, which will always be the same … He must write as the interpreter of nature, and the legislator of mankind, and consider himself as presiding over the thoughts and manners of future generations; as a being superior to time and place.[107]

[103] John Dart, trans., *The Complaint of the Black Knight from Chaucer* (London, 1720), Sig. A5ᵛ.
[104] Walter Harte, *Poems on Several Occasions* (London, 1727), p. 189. This volume includes Harte's version of 'To My Soul. From *Chaucer*', discussed in Chapter 5.
[105] Robert Potter, *The Art of Criticism; As Exemplified in Dr Johnson's Lives of the Most Eminent English Poets* (London, 1789), pp. 60–1.
[106] Godwin, *Life*, 1. 370.
[107] Johnson, *Works*, 16. 44–5.

Shelley was to maintain, famously, that 'Poets are the hierophants of an unapprehended inspiration, the mirrors of the gigantic shadows which futurity casts upon the present ... Poets are the unacknowledged <u>legislators</u> of the World.'[108]

Godwin's Chaucer has that knowledge of the world deemed necessary by Imlac, who had described the need for poets to 'estimate the happiness and misery of every condition; observe the power of all the passions in all their combinations, and trace the changes of the human mind as they are modified by various institutions and accidental influences of climate or custom, from the spriteliness of infancy to the despondence of decrepitude'.[109] For Godwin, Chaucer 'was a poet; and no man can be worthy of that name, who has not attentively studied the sensations and modes of feeling which various external impressions are calculated to produce in the human mind'.[110]

Chaucer, as we have seen, was a central presence in the literary culture of the eighteenth century. Responses to him were complex and often contradictory. He was sometimes condemned for his obscenity, for his archaic language, and for the supposed crudeness and imperfections of his versification. Biographical accounts of the poet were derived from poems spuriously attributed to him—poems which were often esteemed as much as, or more than, some of his genuine work. On the other hand, many eighteenth-century critics of Chaucer gave strikingly positive accounts of his work, praising it for its pathos, its philosophical profundity, and its enduring insights into the human heart and the natural world, and judging that his verse—despite the corrupt texts in which it was preserved, and the imperfect execution that it sometimes manifested—offered invaluable models of 'harmony' to later poets.

The responses to Chaucer by the greatest critic of the period, Samuel Johnson, can seem somewhat puzzling. Johnson appears not to have had much sustained contact with Chaucer's work in its original form. But he planned an edition of the poet's work, and, though as a critic he dismissed Dryden's re-imaginings of several Chaucer's tales, his *Dictionary* shows him to have known them intimately. Moreover, Johnson's general account of the qualities required in a poet, as we have seen, was strikingly continuous with a number of descriptions of Chaucer's genius and attainments by Johnson's predecessors, contemporaries, and successors.

But it was in and through the work of his poetic descendants, rather than the testimonies of critics, however distinguished, that Chaucer's role as a 'legislator of mankind' was most fully felt and embodied. And it was as a poetic 'father' whose continuing influence was powerfully felt that the greatest veneration to him was paid. The full variety of Chaucer's observation of life had been expressed, it was

---

[108] Percy Bysshe Shelley, *The Major Works*, ed. Zachary Leader and Michael O'Neil (Oxford, 2009), p. 701.

[109] Johnson, *Works*, 16. 44.

[110] Godwin, *Life*, 2. 316.

felt, in an answering variety of expression in his poetic offspring. As with biological paternity, Chaucer's 'fatherhood' of later poets was manifested in inextricable patterns of sameness and difference. Some of the most successful responses to Chaucer's work, as we have seen, depart from its letter in striking ways. Chaucer's poetic 'sons' (and daughters) were no mere replicas or clones of their 'father'. But their debt to their progenitor can, nevertheless, be clearly traced.

Chaucer's inspirational power—despite all the features of his work that might make him seem antiquated and unpalatable to later tastes—was seen by his most enthusiastic and distinguished admirers as nothing less than supranatural. It was, at any rate, in such terms that the greatest poets from the beginning and end of the period covered by this book praised their poetic ancestor. Dryden wrote that as Chaucer 'is the Father of *English* Poetry, so I hold him in the same Degree of Veneration as the *Grecians* held *Homer*, or the *Romans Virgil*', and suggested that 'there is something in it like Fatality; that, after certain Periods of Time, the Fame and Memory of Great Wits should be renew'd, as *Chaucer* is'.[111] And Wordsworth wrote of his 'profound reverence' for Chaucer 'as an instrument in the hands of Providence for spreading the light of literature thro' his native land'.[112] Chaucer's achievement was thought of by both Dryden and Wordsworth as a mysterious and gracious blessing for which all future English poets should be profoundly grateful, and which would have miraculous, continuing life in their own work.

---

[111] Dryden, *Works*, 7. 33, 42.
[112] Letter to Henry Reed, 1841, quoted in Wordsworth, *Translations*, ed. Graver, p. 29.

Bibliography

Abrams, M. H., *A Glossary of Literary Terms* (London and New York, 1957).

Addison, Joseph, 'A Letter from Italy', in *Poetical Miscellanies: The Fifth Part* (London, 1704), pp. 1–12.

Addison, Launcelot, *A Modest Plea for the Clergy* (London, 1709).

'Alcæus', 'Letter', *The Gentleman's Magazine*, 10 August 1740, 404.

Alderson, William L. and Henderson, Arnold C., *Chaucer and Augustan Scholarship* (Berkeley, CA, 1970).

Alexander, Michael, *Medievalism* (New Haven, CT, 2007).

Amarasinghe, Upali, *Dryden and Pope in the Early Nineteenth Century* (Cambridge, 1962).

Anderson, David, *Before the Knight's Tale: Imitation of Classical Epic in Boccaccio's 'Teseida'* (Philadelphia, PA, 1988).

Anderson, Robert, ed., *A Complete Edition of the Poets of Great Britain*, 14 vols. (Edinburgh, 1793).

Angelica's Ladies Library: or Parents and Guardians Present (London, 1794).

The Annual Miscellany: for the Year 1694 (London, 1694).

Atterbury, Francis, ed., *The Second Part of Mr. Waller's Poems* (London, 1690).

Ault, Norman, *New Light on Pope* (London, 1949).

Baines, Paul and Rogers, Pat, *Edmund Curll, Bookseller* (Oxford, 2007).

Bancks, John, *Miscellaneous Works, in Verse and Prose*, 2 vols (London, 1738).

Batteux, Charles, *A Course of the Belles Letters: or the Principles of Literature*, trans. John Miller, 4 vols (London, 1761).

Beattie, James, *Essays on Poetry and Music* (Edinburgh, 1776).

The Beauties of Poetry Display'd (London, 1757).

The Beauties of the English Drama (London, 1777).

The Beeriad (London, 1736).

Bell, John, ed., *The Poets of Great Britain*, 109 vols (London, 1777–82).

Berkenhaut, John, *Biographia Literaria* (London, 1777).

Betterton, Thomas, 'Chaucer's Characters, or the Introduction to the Canterbury Tales' and 'The Miller of Trompington, or The Reeve's Tale from Chaucer', in *Miscellaneous Poems and Translations by Several Hands* (London, 1712), pp. 248–82, 301–20.

Biographia Britannica, or The Lives of the Most Eminent Persons Who Have Flourished in Great Britain and Ireland, from the Earliest Ages, Down to the Present Times, 7 vols (London, 1748).

Biographical Magazine, Containing Portraits & Characters of Eminent and Ingenious Persons (London, 1748).

Blackmore, Richard, *Prince Arthur* (4th edn, London, 1714).

Blake, William, *The Gates of Paradise* (London, 1793).

Blake, William, *'Seen In My Visions': A Descriptive Catalogue of Pictures*, ed. Martin Myrone (London, 2009).

Blount, Sir Thomas Pope, *De Re Poetica: or, Remarks upon Poetry, with Characters and Censures of the Most Considerable Poets, Whether Ancient or Modern, Extracted Out of the Best and Choicest Criticks* (London, 1694).

Boccaccio, Giovanni, *Il Decamerone. One Hundred Ingenious Novels*, 2 vols (London, 1702).

Boccaccio, Giovanni, *Il Decamerone: or, Decads, Consisting of One Hundred Ingenious Novels Written by John Boccaccio*, 2 vols (London, 1712 [1721]).

Boccaccio, Giovanni, *The Decameron*, trans. G. H. McWilliam (2nd edn, London, 1995).

Bond, Donald F., ed., *The Spectator*, 5 vols (Oxford 1965).

Bonner, Francis W., 'Chaucer's Reputation during the Romantic Period', *Furman Studies*, 34 (1951), 1–21.

Boswell, James, *Life of Samuel Johnson*, ed. George Birkbeck Hill, rev. L. F. Powell, 6 vols (Oxford, 1934–50).

Botting, Roland B., 'Johnson, Smart, and the "Universal Visiter"', *Modern Philology*, 26 (1939), 293–300.

Bowden, Betsy, *Chaucer Aloud: The Varieties of Textual Interpretation* (Philadelphia, PA, 1987).

Bowden, Betsy, ed., *Eighteenth-Century Modernizations from 'The Canterbury Tales'* (Woodbridge, 1991).

Bowden, Betsy, 'Four Eighteenth-Century Modernizations of *The Shipman's Tale* as Audio-visual Performance', *Translation and Literature*, 3 (1994), 30–46.

Bowden, Betsy, 'Tales Told and Tellers of Tales: Illustrations of the Canterbury Tales in the Course of the Eighteenth Century', in *Chaucer Illustrated*, ed. William Finley and Joseph Rosenblum (Newcastle, DE and London, 2003) pp. 121–90.

Bowden, Betsy, *The Wife of Bath in Afterlife: Ballads to Blake* (Bethlehem, PA, 2017).

Braswell, Mary Flowers, '"A Completely Funny Story": Mary Eliza Haweis and The Miller's Tale', *Chaucer Review*, 42 (2008), 244–68.

Brathwaite, Richard, *A Comment upon the Two Tales of Our Ancient, Renowned, and Ever-Living Poet Sr Jeffray Chaucer* (London, 1665).

Brereton, Jane, 'The Dream: In Imitation of Some Parts of Chaucer's Second and Third Book of Fame', in *Poems on Several Occasions* (London, 1744), pp. 133–67.

Brewer, Derek, ed., *Chaucer: The Critical Heritage*, 2 vols (London, 1978).

Brewer, Derek, 'Modernizing the Medieval: Eighteenth-Century Translations from Chaucer', in *The Middle Ages after the Middle Ages in the English-Speaking World*, ed. Marie-Françoise Alamichel and Derek Brewer (Martlesham, 1997), pp. 103–20.

The British Muse (London, 1738).

Brittain, Robert, 'Christopher Smart in the Magazines', *The Library*, 4th series 21 (1940), 320–35.

Brown, Peter, *A Companion to Chaucer* (Oxford, 2002).

Brown, Thomas, *The Reasons of Mr. Bays Changing His Religion* (London, 1688).

Browne, Sir Thomas, *Hydrotaphia, Urn-Buriall* (London, 1669).

Brydges, Samuel Egerton, *Theatrum Poetarum Anglicanorum* (London, 1800).

Burney, Charles, *A General History of Music, from the Earliest Ages to the Present Period*, 4 vols (London, 1776–89).

Burrow, John, 'Chaucer', in *The Spenser Encyclopedia*, ed. A. C. Hamilton et al. (London, 1996), pp. 144–8.

Burrow, John, 'Geoffrey's Credo: *House of Fame*, Lines 1873–82', *Chaucer Review*, 48 (2014), 251–7.

Butler, Samuel, *Hudibras*, ed. John Wilders (Oxford, 1967).

Byron, Lord, *Letters and Journals*, ed. Thomas Moore (London, 1830).

Byron, Lord, *The Complete Miscellaneous Prose*, ed. Andrew Nicholson (Oxford, 1991).

Bysshe, Edward, *The Art of English Poetry* (London, 1702).

[Campbell, John], 'Chaucer', in *Biographia Britannica*, 7 vols, (London, 1748), 2. 1293–308.

Campbell, Thomas, ed., *Specimens of the British Poets*, 7 vols (London, 1819).

Catcott, Alexander Stopford, *The Court of Love, a Vision, from Chaucer* (Oxford, 1717).

Chalmers, Alexander, ed., *The Works of the English Poets*, 21 vols (London, 1810).

Chatfield, Minotte McIntosh, 'Chaucer Translation in the Romantic Era', 2 vols, unpublished PhD thesis, Lehigh University, 1961.

Chaucer, Geoffrey, *The Workes of Geffray Chaucer Newly Printed*, ed. William Thynne (London, 1532).

Chaucer, Geoffrey, *The Workes of Our Antient and Learned English Poet, Geffrey Chaucer*, ed. Thomas Speght (London, 1598).

Chaucer, Geoffrey, *The Workes of Our Antient and Learned English Poet, Geffrey Chaucer, Newly Printed*, ed. Thomas Speght (London, 1602).

Chaucer, Geoffrey, *The Works of Our Ancient, Learned, and Excellent English Poet, Jeffrey Chaucer*, ed. Thomas Speght (London, 1687).

Chaucer, Geoffrey, *The Works of Geoffrey Chaucer: Compared with the Former Editions, and Many Valuable MSS*, ed. John Urry (London, 1721).

Chaucer, Geoffrey, *The Canterbury Tales of Chaucer, in the Original, from the Most Authentic Manuscripts, and as They Turn'd into Modern Language*, ed. Thomas Morell (London, 1737).

Chaucer, Geoffrey, *The Canterbury Tales of Chaucer: Modernis'd by Several Hands*, ed. George Ogle, 3 vols (London, 1741).

Chaucer, Geoffrey, *Matrimonial Scenes ... Modernized from Chaucer*, ed. Andrew Jackson (London, 1750) [includes versions of *The Shipman's Tale*, *The Manciple's Tale*, and *The Wife of Bath's Prologue*].

Chaucer, Geoffrey, *The Canterbury Tales of Chaucer*, ed. Thomas Tyrwhitt, 5 vols (London, 1775–78).

Chaucer, Geoffrey, *Works*, ed. Robert Anderson, 14 vols (Edinburgh, 1793).

Chaucer, Geoffrey, *The Canterbury Tales of Chaucer Completed in a Modern Version*, ed. William Lipscomb, 3 vols (Oxford, 1795).

Chaucer, Geoffrey, *The Canterbury Tales of Chaucer*, ed. Thomas Tyrwhitt, 2 vols (2nd edn, Oxford, 1798).

Chaucer, Geoffrey, *The Riches of Chaucer*, ed. Charles Cowden Clarke, 2 vols (London, 1835).

Chaucer, Geoffrey, *The Poems of Geoffrey Chaucer Modernized*, ed. Richard H. Horne (London, 1841).

Chaucer, Geoffrey, *The Canterbury Tales*, ed. George Gilfillan, 3 vols (Edinburgh, 1860).

Chaucer, Geoffrey, *Poetical Works of Geoffrey Chaucer*, ed. Robert Bell, revised with a preliminary essay by Rev. Walter W. Skeat, 4 vols (London, 1878–80).

Chaucer, Geoffrey, *Complete Works*, ed. Walter W. Skeat, 7 vols (Oxford, 1884–97).

Chaucer, Geoffrey, *The Knight's Tale*, ed. J. A. W. Bennett (2nd edn, London, 1974).

Chaucer, Geoffrey, *The Canterbury Tales*, ed. A. C. Cawley, intro. by Derek Pearsall (New York, London, Toronto, 1992).

Child, Francis James, ed., *The English and Scottish Popular Ballads*, 5 vols (Boston MA, 1884–98).

Chudleigh, Lady Mary, *Poems on Several Occasions* (London, 1703).

Cibber, Theophilus, ed., *The Lives of the Poets of Great Britain and Ireland*, 5 vols (London, 1753).

Clanvowe, Sir John, *Works:The Boke of Cupide and The Two Ways*, ed. John Scattergood (Cambridge, 1975).

Clogan, Paul M., 'Literary Criticism in William Godwin's *Life of Chaucer*', *Medievalia et Humanistica*, n.s. 6 (1975), 189–98.

Clogan, Paul M., 'Chaucer and Leigh Hunt', *Medievalia et Humanistica*, n.s. 9 (1979), 164–74.

Cobb, Samuel, *Poetæ Britannici* (London, 1700).

Cobb, Samuel, *The Carpenter of Oxford, or The Miller's Tale, from Chaucer* (London, 1712).

Coghen, Monika, 'Rewriting Chaucer's "Wife of Bath's Tale" from Dryden, through Voltaire to Niemcewicz: Medievalism or Modernization', *Studia Literaria Universitatis Iagellonicae Cravoviensis*, 12 (2017), 175–85.

Cokain, Sir Aston, *Small Poems of Divers Sorts* (London, 1658).

Collier, Jeremy, *A Short View of the Immorality, and Profaneness of the English Stage* (London, 1698).

The Complaynte of the Louer of Cryst Saynt Mary Magdaleyn (London, ?1520).

The Conjurer: or Metamorphoses of Pride and Humility (London, ?1770).

Cooke, William, 'The Cuckow and the Nightingale. Modernized from Chaucer', in *Poetical Essays on Several Occasions* (London, 1774), pp. 85–103.

Cooper, Helen, *Oxford Guides to Chaucer: The Canterbury Tales* (2nd edn, Oxford, 1996).

Cooper, Helen, 'The Shape-Shiftings of the Wife of Bath, 1395–1670', in *Chaucer Traditions, Studies in Honour of Derek Brewer,* ed. Ruth Morse and Barry Windeatt (Cambridge, 1990), pp. 168–84.

Cooper, Helen, 'Welcome to the House of Fame: 600 Years Dead: Chaucer's Deserved Reputation as "the Father of English Poetry"', *Times Literary Supplement*, 27 October 2000, pp. 3–4.

Corbett, Richard, *Poems*, ed. J. A. W. Bennett and H. R. Trevor-Roper (Oxford, 1955).

Corse, Taylor, 'Dryden and Milton in "The Cock and the Fox"', *Milton Quarterly*, 27 (1993), 109–18.

Cotton, Charles, *Poems*, ed. Paul Hartle, 2 vols (Oxford, 2017).

Cowell, John, *The Interpreter of Words and Terms, Used Either in the Common or Statute Laws of This Realm, and in Tenures and Jocular Customs* (London, 1701).

Cowley, Abraham, *Poems*, ed. A. R. Waller (Cambridge, 1905).

Cowley, Abraham, *Essays, Plays and Sundry Verses*, ed. A. R. Waller (Cambridge, 1906).

Creech, Thomas, trans., *T. Lucretius Carus, Of the Nature of Things*, 2 vols (London, 1714) [with commentary by John Digby].

Crystal, David, *The Stories of English* (London, 2005).

Cummings, R. M., ed., *Edmund Spenser: The Critical Heritage* (London, 1971).

Curll, Edmund, *The Altar of Love* (London, 1727).

Dane, Joseph A., *Who Is Buried in Chaucer's Tomb? Studies in the Reception of Chaucer's Book* (East Lansing, MI, 1998).

Daniel, George, *Poems*, ed. A. B. Grosart, 4 vols (n.p., 1878).

Dart, John, trans., *The Complaint of the Black Knight from Chaucer* (London, 1720).

Dart, John, *Westminster-Abbey. A Poem* (London, 1721).

Dart, John, *A Poem on Chaucer and His Writings* (London, 1722).

Davenant, Charles, *Essays upon 1. The Ballance of Power. II. The Right of Making War, Peace, and Alliances. III. Universal Monarchy* (London, 1701).

Davis, Paul, 'After the Fire: Chaucer and Urban Poetics, 1666–1743', in *Chaucer and the City*, ed. Ardis Butterfield (Martlesham, 2006), pp. 177–92.

De Causa Dei, or A Vindication of the Common Doctrine of Protestant Divines Concerning Predetermination (London, 1678).

Della Porta, Giambattista, *De Humana Physiognomia* (Vico Equense, 1586).

Denham, Sir John, *Poems, &c, Written upon Several Occasions* (London, 1668).

Denham, Sir John, *Poetical Works*, ed. Theodore Howard Banks (2nd edn, Hamden, CT, 1969).

Dennis, John, *Remarks on Mr Pope's Translation of Homer. With Two Letters Concerning Windsor Forest, and the Temple of Fame* (London, 1717).

Dennis, John, *Critical Works*, ed. Edward Niles Hooker, 2 vols (Baltimore, MD, 1939–43).

Digbeye, Glubech, *Robin's Pathetick Tale, an Heroic Poem* (London, 1727).

Dillon, Wentworth, Earl of Roscommon, *An Essay on Translated Verse* (London, 1684).

Dilworth, W. H., *The Life of Alexander Pope* (London, 1759).

Dowden, Edward, 'Wordsworth's Selections from Chaucer Modernised', in *Wordsworthiana: A Selection of Papers Read to the Wordsworth Society*, ed. William Knight (London, 1889), pp. 17–28.

Downame, George, *A Treatise Concerning Antichrist Divided into Two Bookes* (London, 1603).

Draxe, Thomas, *The Christian Armorie* (London, 1611).

Drayton, Michael, *The Battaile of Agincourt* (London, 1627).

Dryden, John, *Fables Ancient and Modern Translated into Verse, from Homer, Ovid, Boccace, & Chaucer; with Original Poems* (London, 1700).

Dryden, John, *The Fables … Ornamented with Engravings from the Pencil of the Right Hon. Lady Diana Beauclerk* (London, 1797).

Dryden, John, *Critical and Miscellaneous Prose Writings*, ed. Edmund Malone, 3 vols in 4 (London, 1800).

Dryden, John, *Fables from Boccacio [sic] and Chaucer*, ed. John Aikin (London, 1805, 1806).

Dryden, John, *Works of John Dryden: Now First Collected Illustrated with Notes, Historical, Critical, and Explanatory, and a Life of the Author*, ed. Walter Scott, 18 vols (London, 1808).

Dryden, John, *Poetical Works, Containing Original Poems, Tales and Translations*, with notes by Joseph Warton, John Warton et al., 4 vols (London, 1811).

Dryden, John, *Letters*, ed. Charles E. Ward (Durham, NC, 1942).

Dryden, John, *Works*, ed. H. T. Swedenberg et al., 20 vols (Berkeley, CA, 1956–2000).

Dryden, John, *Poems*, ed. Paul Hammond and David Hopkins, 5 vols (Harlow, 1995–2005).

Dunkin, William, 'The Character of a Good Parson. From Chaucer', in *Selected Poetical Works*, 2 vols (Dublin, 1769–70), pp. 480–1.

D'Urfey, Thomas, *Tales, Tragical and Comical* (London, 1707).

D'Urfey, Thomas, *Stories, Moral and Comical* (London, 1707).

Edgeworth, Maria, *The Modern Griselda* (London, 1805).

The Egg, or the Memoirs of Gregory Giddy (London, ?1772).

Eliot, John, *Poems, Consisting of Epistles and Epigrams, Satyrs, Epitaphs and Elogies, Songs and Sonnets* (London, 1658).

Eliot, T. S., *The Use of Poetry and the Use of Criticism* (London, 1933).

Ellis, George [as 'Sir Gregory Gander'], 'The Canterbury Tale', in *Poetical Tales* (Bath, 1778), pp. 16–26.

Ellis, George, ed., *Specimens of the Early English Poets*, 3 vols (London, 1801).

[Ellis, George], 'The Wife of Bath's Tale. From Chaucer' and 'The Death of Patient Grizel', in *The New Paradise of Dainty Devices* (London, 1777), pp. 15–26, 31–2.

Ellis, Steve, *Chaucer; An Oxford Guide* (Oxford, 2005).

Elstob, Elizabeth, *The Rudiments of Grammar for the English-Saxon Tongue* (London, 1715).

Espie, Jeff, 'Wordsworth's Chaucer: Mediation and Transformation in English Literary History', *PQ*, 94 (2015), 337–65.

Espie, Jeff, 'Literary Paternity and Narrative Revival: Chaucer's Soul(s) from Spenser to Dryden', *Modern Philology*, 114 (2016), 39–58.

Fairer, David, *English Poetry of the Eighteenth Century* (Harlow, 2003).

Fairer, David, 'Creating a National Poetry: The Tradition of Spenser and Milton', in *The Cambridge Companion to Eighteenth-Century Poetry*, ed. John Sitter (Cambridge, 2006), pp. 177–202.

Fayne, Gwendolyn D., 'Feminism in The Wife of Bath's Tale: Chaucer Versus Dryden', in *Papers from the Fifth Annual General Conference on Medievalism 1990*, ed. Ulrich Müller and Kathleen Verduin (Göppingen, 1996), pp. 73–82.

Felton, Henry, *A Dissertation on Reading the Classics and Forming a Just Style* (London, 1713).

Fenning, Daniel, *The Royal English Dictionary* (London, 1763).

Fenster, T. S. and Erler, M. C., eds, *Poems of Cupid, God of Love* (Leiden, 1990).

Fenton, Elijah, 'A Tale, Devised in the Plesaunt Manere of Gentil Maister Jeoffrey Chaucer', in *Poems on Several Occasions* (London, 1717).

Finley, William and Rosenblum, Joseph, eds, *Chaucer Illustrated: Five Hundred Years of The Canterbury Tales in Pictures* (Newcastle, DE and London, 2003).

Forni, Kathleen, *The Chaucerian Apocrypha, A Counterfeit Canon* (Gainesville, FL, 2001).

Foster, Gretchen M., *Pope Versus Dryden: A Controversy in Letters to 'The Gentleman's Magazine', 1789–1791* (Victoria, BC, 1989).

Fuller, Thomas, *The History of the Worthies of England* (London, 1662).

Garth, Samuel, *The Dispensary* (London, 1714).

Gay, John, *The Shepherd's Week. In Six Pastorals. By Mr. J. Gay* (London, 1714).

Gay, John, 'An Answer to the Sompner's Prologue of Chaucer in Imitation of Chaucer's Style', in *Poems on Several Occasions, By His Grace the Duke of Buckingham and Other Eminent Hands* (London, 1717), pp. 147–51.

Gay, John, *Dramatic Works*, ed. John Fuller, 2 vols (Oxford, 1983).

Gelineau, David, 'Following the Leaf through Part of Dryden's *Fables*', *Studies in English Literature, 1500–1900*, 50 (2010), 557–81.

Gerrard, Christine, ed., *A Companion to Eighteenth-Century Poetry* (Oxford, 2006).

Gildon, Charles, *The Post-Boy Rob'd of His Mail* (London, 1692).

Gildon, Charles, *Libertas Triumphans* (London, 1708).

Gildon, Charles, *The Complete Art of Poetry*, 2 vols (London, 1718).

Godfrey, Thomas, 'The Assembly of Birds; From Chaucer', in *Juvenile Poems, on Various Subjects* (Philadelphia, PA, 1765), pp. 83–90.

Godfrey, Thomas, 'The Court of Fancy', in *Juvenile Poems, on Various Subjects* (Philadelphia, PA, 1775), pp. 83–90.

Godwin, William, *The Life of Geoffrey Chaucer, The Early English Poet*, 2 vols (London, 1803).

Godwin, William, 'An Essay of History and Romance', in *Political and Philosophical Writings of William Godwin: Vol. 5: Educational and Literary Writings*, ed. Pamela Clemit (London, 1993), pp. 291–301.

Goldsmith, Netta Murray, *Alexander Pope: The Evolution of a Poet* (Aldershot, 2002).

Gostling, William, *A Walk in and About the City of Canterbury* (Canterbury, 1774).

Graver, Bruce, 'The Reception of Chaucer from Dryden to Wordsworth', in *Geoffrey Chaucer in Context*, ed. Ian Johnson (Cambridge, 2019), pp. 419–28.

Graver, Bruce, 'Why Chaucer's Prioress?', *The Wordsworth Circle*, 51 (2020), 92–103.

Gray, Douglas, ed., *The Oxford Companion to Chaucer* (Oxford, 2003).

Gray, Thomas, *Poems* (London, 1768).

Gray, Thomas, *The Poems ... To Which Are Prefixed Memoirs of His Life and Writings by W. Mason* (York, 1775).

Gray, Thomas, *Correspondence*, ed. Paget Toynbee and Leonard Whibley, 3 vols (Oxford, 1935, rpt. 1971).

Greene, Donald J., *Samuel Johnson's Library: An Annotated Guide* (Victoria, BC, 1975).

Greenwood, James, ed. *The Virgin Muse* (London, 1717).

Gregory, George, *Letters on Literature, Taste and Composition, Addressed to His Son*, 2 vols (London, 1808).

Grew, Nehemiah, *Musaeum Regalis Societatis* (London, 1685).

Grey, Zachary, *Critical, Historical, and Explanatory Notes on Shakespeare* (London, 1754).

Groom, Nick, ed., *Thomas Chatterton and Romantic Culture* (Basingstoke, 1999).

Grosvenor, Mr [= Eustace Budgell], *The Farmer and the Fryar: Or, The Sumner's Tale* (*London*, 1733)

Grosvenor, Robert, Marquis of Westminster, 'Annelida and Arcite. From Chaucer', in *Charlotte: An Elegy* (?London, ?1795), pp. 10–22.

Hammond, Eleanor Prescott, *Chaucer: A Bibliographical Manual* (New York, 1908; rpt. 1933).

Hammond, Paul, 'The Interplay of Past and Present in Dryden's "Palamon and Arcite"', *The Seventeenth Century*, 23 (2008), 142–59.

Hammond, Paul, 'Dryden and the Laurel', in *Literary Milieux: Essays in Text and Context Presented to Howard Erskine-Hill*, ed. David Womersley and Richard McCabe (Newark, DE, 2008), pp. 104–15.

Harrison, William, *Woodstock Park. A Poem* (London, 1706).

Harte, Walter, *Poems on Several Occasions* (London, 1727).

Haselkorn, Anne M. and Travitsky, Betty, eds, *The Renaissance Englishwoman in Print: Counterbalancing the Canon* (Amherst, MA, 1990).

Haslett, Moyra, *Pope to Burney, 1714–79: Scriblerians to Bluestockings* (London, 2003).

Hawkins, Sir John, *A General History of the Science and Practice of Music*, 5 vols (London, 1776).

Hawkins, Sir John, *The Life of Samuel Johnson*, ed. O. M. Brack (Athens, GA, 2009).

Hayley, William, *A Philosophical, Historical, and Moral Essay on Old Maids* (London, 1785).

Haywood, Eliza, *The Female Spectator*, 4 vols (London, 1745).

Haywood, Eliza, *Epistles for the Ladies*, 2 vols (London, 1749–50).

Hazlitt, William, *Lectures on the English Poets, Delivered at the Surrey Institution* (London, 1818).

Hazlitt, William, *Winterslow* (London, 1839).

Hopkins, David W., 'Introduction', in John Wilson ('Christopher North'), *Specimens of the British Critics* (Delmar, NY, 1978), pp. v–xiv.

Hopkins, David, *John Dryden* (Cambridge, 1986).

Hopkins, David, *Conversing with Antiquity: English Poetry and the Classics from Shakespeare to Pope* (Oxford, 2010).

Hopkins, David, 'A Translator's Annotation: Alexander Pope's Observations on His *Iliad*', in *Annotation in Eighteenth-Century Poetry*, ed. Michael Edson (Bethlehem, PA, 2017), pp. 105–28.

Hopkins, David and Mason, Tom, 'Two Uncollected Poems by Christopher Smart', *Notes and Queries*, 67 (2020), pp. 504–6.

Hopkins, John, *Milton's Paradise Lost Imitated in Rhyme, in the Fourth, Sixth, and Ninth Books* (London, 1699).

Howard, Edward, *Spenser Redivivus* (London, 1687).

Hughes, Jabez, *Verses Occasion'd by Reading Mr. Dryden's Fables* (London, 1721).

The Humble Petition of the Maior, Aldermen, and Common Councell, of the Citie of London (London, 1641).

The Humble Representation of Edmund Curll, Bookseller (London, 1725).

Hunt, Leigh, 'On Chaucer', in *The Round Table*, 2 vols. (London and Edinburgh, 1817), 1. 124–41.

Hunt, Leigh, 'The First Canto of the Squire's Tale of Chaucer, Modernized', *The Liberal*, 4 July 1823, 317–31.

Hunt, Leigh, 'Characteristic Specimens of the English Poets: Chaucer', *Leigh Hunt's London Journal* (London, 1835), pp. 180–1, 187–8, 195–6, 218–19, 228, 250–1.

Hunt, Leigh, *Wit and Humour: Selected from the English Poets* (London, 1846).

Hunt, Leigh, *Stories in Verse* (London, 1855).

Hunt, Leigh, *Autobiography* (London, 1860).

Hunter, Michael, 'Alexander Pope and Geoffrey Chaucer', in *The Warden's Meeting: A Tribute to John Sparrow*, ed. Anthony Davis (Oxford, 1977), pp. 9–32.

Hurd, Richard, *Letters on Chivalry and Romance* (2nd edn, London, 1762).

Jackson, Samuel, *Harvest-Home*, 3 vols (London, 1805).

Jacob, Giles, 'A Tale in Imitation of Mr. Prior's Earl Robert's Mice', in *A Miscellany of Poems* (London, 1718).

Jacob, Giles, *An Historical Account of the Lives and Writings of Our Most Considerable English Poets* (London, 1720).

Jevon, Thomas, *The Devil of a Wife* (London, 1686).

Jevon, Thomas, *The Conjurer; or Metamorphoses of Pride and Humility* (London, ?1770).

Johnson, Samuel, *Reflections on the History of Passive Obedience* (London, 1689).

Johnson, Samuel, *A Dictionary of the English Language*, 2 vols (London, 1755; rev. edn 1773).

Johnson, Samuel, *Prefaces, Biographical and Critical, to the Works of the English Poets*, 10 vols (London, 1779–81).

Johnson, Samuel, *The Yale Edition of the Works of Samuel Johnson*, ed. E. L. McAdam Jnr et al., 23 vols (New Haven, CT, 1958–).

Johnson, Samuel, *The Lives of the Most Eminent English Poets; with Critical Observations on Their Works*, ed. Roger Lonsdale, 4 vols (Oxford, 2006).

Johnson, Samuel and Steevens, George, eds, *The Plays of William Shakespeare in Ten Volumes* (London, 1778).

Johnson, Thomas, *Summer Productions; Or Progressive Miscellanies* (London, 1788).

Johnston, Arthur, *Enchanted Ground: The Study of Medieval Romance in the Eighteenth Century* (London, 1964).

Joliat, Eugène, 'Smollett, Editor of Voltaire', *Modern Language Notes*, 54 (1939), 429–36.

Jones, Claude, 'Christopher Smart, Robert Rolt, and *The Universal Visiter*', *The Library*, 4th series, 18 (1937), 212–14.

Junius, Franciscus [Francis Du Jon], *Etymologicum Anglicanum*, ed. Edward Lye (Oxford, 1743).

A Just Defence of the Royal Martyr, K. Charles I (London, 1699).

Kalter, Barrett, 'Chaucer Ancient and Modern', in *Modern Antiques: The Material Past in England, 1660–1780* (Lewisburg, PA, 2012), pp. 69–108.

Ken, Thomas, *Expostulatoria, or The Complaints of the Church of England* (London, 1711).

Kennett, White, *Wit against Wisdom, of a Panegyrick upon Folly. Penn'd in Latin by Desiderius Erasmus* (Oxford, 1683).

Keymer, Thomas and Mee, Jon, eds, *The Cambridge Companion to English Literature, 1740–1830* (Cambridge, 2004).

King, Richard G., 'John Christopher Smith's Pasticcio Oratorios', *Music and Letters*, 79 (1998), 190–218.

King, Robert, 'Poetic Imitation in the Ricardian and Georgian Periods', Unpublished PhD thesis, University of Bristol (1994).

King, William, *The Toast: An Heroick Poem in Four Books* (London, 1736).

Knight, G. Wilson, *The Poetry of Pope: Laureate of Peace* (London, 1965).

Koff, Leonard Michael, 'Wordsworth and the *Manciple's Tale*', *Chaucer Review*, 19 (1985), 338–51.

Korshin, Paul J., 'The Mythology of Johnson's Dictionary', in *Anniversary Essays on Johnson's Dictionary*, ed. Jack Lynch and Anne McDermott (Cambridge, 2005), pp. 10–23.

Kramnick, Jonathan Brody, *The Making of the English Canon* (Cambridge, 1998).

Kynaston, Sir Francis, *The Loves of Troilus and Creseid* (London, 1796).

La Fontaine, Jean de, *Fables, contes et nouvelles*, ed. René Groos and Jacques Shiffrin (Paris, 1954).

The Lamentation of Mary Magdalen, from Chaucer (Nottingham, 1775).

Langbaine, Gerard, *A Review of the Covenant* (Oxford, 1645).

Larson, Eric Duane, 'Telling New Tales: Modernizations of Chaucer in the Eighteenth Century', unpublished PhD dissertation (2016), University of Arkansas.

Lee, Nathaniel, *The Princess of Cleve* (London, 1689).

Leff, Amanda F., 'Johnson's Chaucer: Searching for the Medieval in "A Dictionary of the English Language"', *Age of Johnson*, 21 (2011), 1–20.

Lennox, Charlotte, 'The Story of Troilus and Cressida, from Chaucer', in *Shakespeare Illustrated*, 3 vols (London, 1754), 3. 55–87.

A Letter of Advice to a Young Clergy-Man, Entring upon a Cure of Souls (London, 1709).

Lewis, William Lillington, *The Thebaid of Statius, Translated into English Verse*, 2 vols. (Oxford, 1767).

The Liberal: Verse and Prose from the South (London, 1822).

Lobb, Richard, *The Contemplative Philosopher* (London, 1800).

Lounsbury, Thomas R., *Studies in Chaucer, His Life and Writings*, 3 vols (London, 1892).

Lowe, Robert W., *Thomas Betterton* (London, 1891).

Luctus Britannici, or The Tears of the British Muses for the Death of John Dryden (London, 1700).

Lupton, Donald, *The Glory of Their Times, or The Lives of the Primitive Fathers* (London, 1640).

Machan, Tim William, 'Speght's "Works" and the Invention of Chaucer', *Text*, 8 (1995), 145–70.

Mack, Maynard, *Collected in Himself: Essays Critical, Biographical, and Bibliographical on Pope and Some of His Contemporaries* (Newark, DE, 1982).

Mahony, Robert and Rizzo, Betty W., *Christopher Smart: An Annotated Bibliography, 1743–1983* (New York and London, 1984).

Maitland, Richard, Earl of Lauderdale, trans., *The Works of Virgil* (London, [1709]).

Manley, Delarivière, *The Power of Love: In Seven Novels* (London, 1720).

Mann, Jill, *Chaucer and Medieval Estates Satire: The Literature of Social Classes and the General Prologue to the 'Canterbury Tales'* (Cambridge, 1973).

Mant, Richard, 'Verses to the Memory of Joseph Warton', in *Harvest-Home*, ed. Samuel Jackson, 3 vols (London, 1805), 1. 63.

Mant, Richard, *Poems* (Oxford, 1806).

Markham, Gervase, *Cheape and Good Husbandry for the Well-Ordering of All Beasts and Fowles* (London, 1614).

Markland, John, 'The Shipman's Tale', in *Three New Poems* (London, 1721), pp. 1–26.

Martin, Benjamin, *Lingue Britannica Reformata: or, A New English Dictionary* (London, 1749).

Mason, Tom, 'Dryden's Version of *The Wife of Bath's Tale*', *Cambridge Quarterly*, 6 (1975), 240–56.

Mason, Tom, '"A Noble Poem of the Epique Kind"? Palamon and Arcite and Neoclassic Epic Theory', in *Dryden and the World of Neoclassicism*, ed. W. Görtschacher and H. Klein (Tubingen, 2001), 180–91.

Mason, Tom, 'Dryden's "The Cock and the Fox" and Chaucer's "Nun's Priest's Tale"', *Translation and Literature*, 16 (2007), 1–28.

Mason, Tom, 'Allusion and Quotation in Chaucerian Annotation, 1687–1798', in *Annotation in Eighteenth-Century Poetry*, ed. Michael Edson (Bethlehem, PA, 2017), pp. 129–50.

Mason, William, *Musaeus: A Monody to the Memory of Mr. Pope, in Imitation of Lycidas* (London, 1747).

Matthews, David, *The Making of Middle English, 1765–1910* (Minneapolis, MN, 1999).

Matthews, David, ed., *The Invention of Middle English: An Anthology of Sources* (University Park, PA, 2000).

Matthews, David, *Medievalism: A Critical History* (Martlesham, 2015).

Maynwaring, Arthur, trans., 'The Court of Love. A Tale from Chaucer', in *Ovid's Art of Love in Three Books* (London, 1709), pp. 351–68.

McGeough, Jared, '"Imperfect, Confused, Interrupted": Biography, Nationalism, and Generic Hybridity in William Godwin's Life of Chaucer', *European Romantic Review*, 30 (2019), 367–82.

McLaverty, James, *Pope, Print and Meaning* (Oxford, 2001).

Mennes, Sir John, *Musarum Deliciae* (London, 1656).

Middleton, Charles Theodore, *A New and Complete System of Geography*, 2 vols (London, 1777–78).

The Miller of Trompington, Being an Exercise upon Chaucer's Reeve's Tale (London, 1715).

Milns, William, *The Well-Bred Scholar* (London, 1794).

Milton, John, *Paradise Lost: A Poem*, ed. Thomas Newton, 2 vols (London, 1749).

Milton, John, *Paradise Regained*, ed. Thomas Newton, 2 vols (London, 1753).

Milton, John, *Paradise Regained, Samson Agonistes, and Poems on Several Occasions*, ed. Thomas Newton (London, 1760).

Milton, John, *Paradise Regained, With Notes of Various Authors*, ed. Charles Dunster (London, [1800]).

Mirth Diverts All Care, being Excellent New Songs (London, 1708).

Miscellaneous Poems, By Several Hands (London, 1726).

Miskimin, Alice, *The Renaissance Chaucer* (New Haven, CT, 1975).

Miskimin, Alice, 'The Illustrated Eighteenth-Century Chaucer', *Modern Philology*, 77 (1979), 26–55.

Minkova, Donka, 'The Forms of Verse', in *A Companion to Medieval English Literature and Culture, c.1350—c.1550*, ed. Peter Brown (Oxford, 2009), pp. 176–95.

Montaigne, Michael Seigneur de, *Essays*, trans. Charles Cotton, 3 vols (London, 1685–86).

Moore, Thomas, 'Lord Thurlow's Poems', *Edinburgh Review*, 23 (September 1814), 411–24.

Morell, Thomas, trans. and ed., *Poems on Divine Subjects, Original and Translated from the Latin of M. H. Vida and M. A. Flaminio* (London, 1732).

Morell, Thomas, trans. and ed., *The Epistles of Lucius Annaeus Seneca*, 2 vols (London, 1786).

Morley, John, ed., *Joe Miller's Jests* (9th edn, London, 1747).

Morse, Charlotte C. 'Popularizing Chaucer in the Nineteenth Century', *The Chaucer Review*, 38 (2003), 99–125.

Morse, Ruth and Windeatt, Barry, eds, *Chaucer Traditions, Studies in Honour of Derek Brewer* (Cambridge, 1990).

Musarum Deliciae (London, 1656).

Neve, Philip, *Cursory Remarks on Some of the Ancient English Poets, Particularly Milton* (London, 1789).

Nevile, Robert, *The Poor Scholar: A Comedy* (London, 1662).

A New Miscellany in Prose and Verse (London, 1742).

A New Voyage to the Island of Fools (London, 1713).

The Nine Muses, Or Poems Written by Several Ladies, Upon the Death of the Late Famous John Dryden, Esq. (London, 1700).

Nokes, David, *John Gay: A Profession of Friendship* (Oxford, 1995).

Ogle, George, *Gualtherus and Griselda: Or, The Clerk of Oxford's Tale. From Baccace, Petrarch and Chaucer* (London, 1739).

Oldmixon, John, *The Life and Posthumous Works of Arthur Maynwaring* (London, 1715).

Oldmixon, John, *An Essay on Criticism* (London, 1728).

Otway, Thomas, *Friendship in Fashion* (London, 1678).

Partridge, John, *Merlinus Liberatur: Being an Almanack for ... 1708* (London, [1708]).

Pask, Kevin, *The Emergence of the British Author* (Cambridge, 1996).

Pearsall, Derek A., ed., *The Floure and the Leafe and The Assembly of Ladies* (London, 1962).

Pearsall, Derek A., 'Chaucer's Meter: The Evidence of the Manuscripts', in *Medieval Literature: Texts and Interpretation*, ed. Tim Machan (Binghampton, NY, 1991), pp. 41–57.

Penn, John, *Critical and Poetical Works* (London, 1797).

Penn, John, *Poems, In Two Volumes* (London, 1801).

Pepys, Samuel, *Diary*, ed. Robert Latham and William Matthews, 11 vols (London, 1970–83).

Percy, Thomas, *Reliques of Ancient English Poetry*, 3 vols (London, 1765).

Perkins, David, *Is Literary History Possible?* (Baltimore, MD and London, 1992).

Philips, Captain, *The Romance of the Rose. Imitated from Chaucer* (London, 1709).

Phillips, Helen '"This Mystique Show"': Dryden and the Flower and the Leaf', *Reading Medieval Studies*, 27 (2003), 29–50.

Phoenix Britannicus ... Collected by J. Morgan (London, 1732).

Pittock, Joan, *The Ascendancy of Taste: The Achievement of Joseph and Thomas Warton* (London, 1973).

Plumptre, Anne, *The Rector's Son*, 3 vols (London, 1798).

The Poetical Works of Geoffrey Chaucer, 14 vols (Edinburgh, 1793).

Poets' Gallery... Painted for Mr. Macklin, by the Artists of Britain, Illustrative of the British Poets (London, 1789).

Pope, Alexander, *An Essay on Criticism* (London, 1711).

Pope, Alexander, *The Temple of Fame, A Vision* (London, 1715).

Pope, Alexander, *The Temple of Fame, A Vision*(2nd edn, London, 1715).

Pope, Alexander, *The Works of Mr. Alexander Pope* (London, 1717).

Pope, Alexander, *The Works of Alexander Pope, Esq.; with Explanatory Notes and Additions*, 6 vols (London, 1736).

Pope, Alexander, *The Works of Alexander Pope, Esq. with His Last Corrections, Additions, and Improvements*, ed. William Warburton, 9 vols (London, 1751).

Pope, Alexander, *The Works of Alexander Pope*, ed. Joseph Warton, 9 vols (London, 1797).

Pope, Alexander, *The Works of Alexander Pope Esq. in Verse and Prose*, ed. William Lisle Bowles. 10 vols (London, 1806).

Pope, Alexander, *The Works of Alexander Pope, Esq., with Notes and Illustrations of Himself and Others*, ed. William Roscoe, 10 vols (London, 1824).

Pope, Alexander, *Works*, ed. Whitwell Elwin and William John Courthope, 10 vols (London, 1886).

Pope, Alexander, *Prose Works*, ed. Norman Ault and Rosemary Cowler, 2 vols (Oxford, 1936–86).

Pope, Alexander, *The Twickenham Edition of the Poems of Alexander Pope*, ed. John Butt et al., 11 vols (London, 1939–69).

Pope, Alexander, *The Correspondence*, ed. George Sherburn, 5 vols (Oxford, 1956).

Pope, Alexander, *Poems, Vol. 1*, ed. Paul Baines and Julian Ferraro (London, 2019).

Potter, Robert, *The Art of Criticism; As Exemplified in Dr Johnson's Lives of the Most Eminent English Poets* (London, 1789).

Prendergast, Thomas A., *Chaucer's Dead Body: From Corpse to Corpus* (London, 2004).

Preston, Mr, *Aesop at the Bear Garden; a Vision in Imitation of the Temple of Fame* (London, 1715).

Prior, Matthew, *Two Imitations of Chaucer, 1. Susannah and the Two Elders, II. Earl Robert's Mice* (London, 1712).

Prior, Matthew, *Literary Works*, ed. H. Bunker Wright and Monroe K. Spears, 2 vols (2nd edn, Oxford, 1971).

Putter, Ad, 'In Appreciation of Metrical Abnormality: Headless Lines and Initial Inversion in Chaucer', in *Engaging with Chaucer: Practice, Authority, Reading*, ed. C. W. R. D. Moseley (New York and Oxford, 2021), pp. 55–75.

Rapin, René, *Reflections on Aristotle's Treatise of Poesie*, trans. Thomas Rymer (London, 1674).

Reddick, Allen, *The Making of Johnson's Dictionary, 1746–1773* (Cambridge, 1996).

Reeve, Clara, *The Progress of Romance through Times, Countries, and Manners*, 2 vols (Colchester, 1785).

Reynolds, Frances, Memoirs of Samuel Johnson, in *Johnsonian Miscellanies*, ed. George Birkbeck Hill, 2 vols (Oxford, 1897).

Richardson, Samuel, *Clarissa* (London, 1748).

Richetti, John, ed., *The Cambridge History of English Literature, 1660–1780* (Cambridge, 2005).

Rider, William, *A New Universal English Dictionary* (London, 1759).

Rogers, George, *The Horn Exalted. Or, Room for Cuckolds* (London, 1721).

Roscommon, Wentworth Dillon, Earl of, trans., *Horace's Art of Poetry* (London, 1680).

Ross, Trevor, *The Making of the English Literary Canon* (Montreal and London, 1998).

Rounce, Adam, ed., *Alexander Pope and His Critics*, 3 vols (London, 2003).

Rounce, Adam, 'Eighteenth-Century Responses to Dryden's *Fables*', *Translation and Literature*, 16 (2007), 29–52.

Ruffhead, Owen, *The Life of Alexander Pope* (London, 1769).

Ruggiers, Paul G., ed., *Editing Chaucer, The Great Tradition* (Norman, OK, 1984).

Rumbold, Valerie, 'Pope and the Gothic Past', unpublished PhD dissertation, University of Cambridge, 1983.

Saunders, John, *Cabinet Pictures of English Life* (London, 1845).

Scott, Walter, 'Godwin's *Life of Chaucer*', *Edinburgh Review*, January 1804, 445.

Seller, John, *The History of England* (London, 1703).

Seward, Anna *Letters*, 6 vols (Edinburgh, 1811).

Sewell, George, *The Proclamation of Cupid; or, a Defence of Women. A Poem from Chaucer* (London, 1718).

Sewell, George, 'The Song of Troilus', in *A New Collection of Original Poems* (London, 1720), pp. 82–5.

Shelley, Percy Bysshe, *The Major Works*, ed. Zachary Leader and Michael O'Neil (Oxford, 2009).

Sherbo, Arthur, 'Christopher Smart and *The Universal Visiter*', *The Library*, 5th series, 10 (1955), 203–5.

Singh, Devani, '"In His Old Dress": Packaging Thomas Speght's Chaucer for Renaissance Readers', *Chaucer Review*, 51 (2016), 478–502.

Sitter, John, *The Poetry of Pope's 'Dunciad'* (Minneapolis, MN, 1971).

Smallwood, Philip, 'Great Anna's Chaucer: Pope's *January and May* and the Logic of Settlement', in *Queen Anne and the Arts*, ed. Cedric D. Reverand II (Lewisburg, PA, 2015), pp. 99–117.

Smalridge, George, *Twelve Sermons Preach'd on Several Occasions* (Oxford, 1717).

Smart, Christopher ed., *The Universal Visiter and Monthly Memorialist* (London, 1756).

Smith, John, 'The Miller's Tale. From Geoffrey Chaucer', *in Poems upon Several Occasions* (London, 1713), pp. 307–57.

Smith, Ruth, 'Thomas Morell and His Letter about Handel', *Journal of the Royal Musical Association*, 127 (2002), 191–225.

South, Robert, *Twelve Sermons Preached upon Several Occasions* (London, 1694).

Spearing, A. C., 'Rewriting Romance: Chaucer's and Dryden's "Wife of Bath's Tale"', in *Chaucer Traditions*, ed. Ruth Morse and Barry Windeatt (Cambridge, 1990), pp. 234–48.

Spence, Joseph, *An Essay on Pope's Odyssey*, 2 vols (London, 1726–7).

Spence, Joseph, *Observations, Anecdotes and Characters of Books and Men*, ed. James M. Osborn, 2 vols (Oxford, 1966).

Spenser, Edmund, *The Works of Mr. Edmund Spenser*, ed. John Hughes (London, 1715).

Spenser, Edmund, *The Faerie Queene, A New Edition*, ed. John Upton, 2 vols (London, 1758).

Spenser, Edmund, *Shorter Poems*, ed. Richard A. McCabe (London, 1999).

Spurgeon, Caroline, *Five Hundred Years of Chaucer Criticism and Allusion, 1357–1900*, 3 vols (Cambridge, 1925).

Stanhope, George, trans., *Epictetus His Morals, with Simplicius His Comment, Made English from the Greek* (London, 1694).

Sterling, Joseph, *Cambuscan, or the Squire's Tale of Chaucer, Modernized by Mr Boyce; Continued from Spencer's Fairy Queen by Mr Ogle, and Concluded by Mr Sterling* (Dublin, 1785).

Stevenson, Kay Gilliland, *Milton to Pope: 1650–1720* (London, 2000).

Strutt, Joseph, *A Complete View of the Dress and Habits of the People of England*, 2 vols (London, 1796–99).

Stuart, Donald Clive, 'The Source of Two of Voltaire's "Contes en Vers"', *Modern Language Review*, 12 (1917), 177–81.

Stukeley, William, *Palæographia Britannica* (London, 1743).

Swete, Henry Barclay, *Church Services and Service-Books before the Reformation* (London, 1896).

Swift, Jonathan, *Miscellanies: The Last Volume* (London, 1728).

Swift, Jonathan, *A Tale of a Tub and Other Works*, ed. Marcus Walsh (Cambridge, 2010).

Taubman, Nathaniel, *Virtue in Distress, or The History of Mindana* (London, 1706).

Tenison, Thomas, *The Creed of Mr Hobbes Examined* (London, 1670).

Terry, Richard, *Poetry and the Making of the English Literary Past, 1660–1781* (Oxford, 2001).

Thomas, Elizabeth, *Miscellany Poems on Several Subjects* (London, 1722).

Thurlow, Edward Hovel, *Arcite and Palamon. After the Excellent Poet Geoffrey Chaucer* (London, 1822).

Thurlow, Edward Hovel, *The Knight's Tale and The Flower and the Leaf. After Geoffrey Chaucer* (2nd edn, London, 1822).

Todd, Henry J., *Illustrations of the Lives and Writings of Gower and Chaucer* (London, 1810).

Trapp, Joseph, *Lectures on Poetry* (London, 1742).

Travers, Henry, 'The Shipman's Tale, from Chaucer', in *Miscellaneous Poems and Translations* (London, 1731), pp. 104–30.

Travers, Henry, 'The Miller of Trompington, or The Reeve's Tale, from Chaucer', in *Miscellaneous Poems and Translations* (York, 1740), pp. 138–60.

Trigg, Stephanie, *Congenial Souls: Reading Chaucer from Medieval to Post Modern* (Minneapolis, MN, 2002).

Tyers, Thomas, *An Historical Rhapsody on Mr. Pope* (London, 1782).

Tyrwhitt, Thomas, ed., *Poems, Supposed to Have Been Written at Bristol, by Thomas Rowley* (London, 1778).

Tyrwhitt, Thomas, *A Vindication of the Appendix to Poems, called Rowley's* (London, 1782).

Valenza, Robin, *Literature, Language, and the Rise of the Intellectual Disciplines in Britain, 1680–1820* (Cambridge, 2009).

Vertue, George, *Twelve Celebrated English Poets* (London, 1730).

Voltaire [François-Marie Arouet], 'Ce qui plaît aux dames', in *Les Oeuvres Completes de Voltaire*, Vol. 57B, ed. Sylvain Menant, Christiane Mervaud, et al. (Oxford, 2014), pp. 23–62.

Voltaire [François-Marie Arouet], 'What Pleases the Ladies', in *The Works of M. de Voltaire*, vol. 25, trans. Tobias Smollett et al. (London 1765), pp. 11–24.

Wallis, Thomas, *The Farrier's and Horseman's Complete Dictionary* (London, 1759).

Wanley, Nathaniel, *The Wonders of the Little World* (London, 1673).

The Wanton Wife of Bath, in *A Collection of Old Ballads: Corrected from the Best and Most Ancient Copies Extant, with Introductions Historical, Critical, or Humorous. Illustrated with Copper Plates,* 2 vols (London, 1723), 2. 173–8.

Warton, Joseph, ed., *The Works of Virgil in Latin and English*, 4 vols (London, 1753).

Warton, Joseph, *An Essay on the Genius and Writings of Pope*, 2 vols (London, 1782).

Warton, Thomas, *Observations on the Fairy Queen of Spenser*, (London, 1754; 2nd edn, 2 vols., London, 1762).

Warton, Thomas, *The History of English Poetry*, 4 vols (London, 1774–81).

Weaver, Edmund, *The British Telescope; Being an Ephemeris of the Celestial Motions* (London [1743]).

The Weekly Museum, 2 vols (London, 1774).

Weinbrot, Howard D., *Britannia's Issue: The Rise of British Literature from Dryden to Ossian* (Cambridge, 1991).

Wesley, Samuel, *An Epistle to a Friend concerning Poetry* (London, 1700).

Wharton, Richard, 'Cambuscan, an Heroic Poem, in Six Books: Founded upon and Comprizing a Free Imitation of Chaucer's Fragment on That Subject', in *Fables: Consisting of Select Parts from Dante, Berni, Chaucer and Ariosto*, Vol. 2 (London, 1805).

Williams, Abigail, 'The Politics of Providence in Dryden's *Fables Ancient and Modern*', *Translation and Literature*, 17 (2008), 1–20.

Williams, Judith, 'Pope's Heroines', Unpublished PhD thesis, University of Bristol (1992).

Wilson, John ('Christopher North'), *Specimens of the British Critics* (Philadelphia, PA, 1846).

Woolf, Henry Bosley, 'Thomas Godfrey: Eighteenth-Century Chaucerian', *American Literature*, 12 (1941), 486–90.

Wooll, John, *Biographical Memoirs of the Late Joseph Warton* (London, 1806).

Wordsworth, William, *The River Duddon: A Series of Sonnets: Vaudracour and Julia: And Other Poems* (London, 1820).

Wordsworth, William, *Memorials of a Tour on the Continent, 1820* (London, 1822).

Wordsworth, William, *Prose Works*, ed. W. J. B. Owen and Jane Worthington Smyser, 3 vols (Oxford, 1974).

Wordsworth, William, *The Letters of William and Dorothy Wordsworth, Vol. 6: The Later Years*, ed. Ernest de Selincourt, rev. Alan G. Hill (Oxford, 1978–88).

Wordsworth, William, *Translations of Chaucer and Virgil*, ed. Bruce E. Graver (Ithaca, NY and London, 1998).

Wright, Herbert G., 'Robert Potter as a Critic of Dr Johnson', *Review of English Studies*, 12 (1936), 305–21.

Yadav, Alok, *Before the Empire of English* (New York, 2004).

Younge, Richard, *A Christian Library* (London, 1660).

Zwicker, Steven N., ed., *The Cambridge Companion to English Literature, 1650–1740* (Cambridge, 1998).

Index

[This Index focuses on the historic primary texts, poetic, critical and scholarly, that are the book's main subject. Modern scholarship, drawn on *passim* for support, illustration, or discussion, is listed in the Bibliography. The more important or detailed discussions are signaled in bold type.]